THE PAPERS OF
WILLIAM ALEXANDER GRAHAM

William Alexander Graham, 1804-1875. Photograph from the Brady-Handy Collection, Library of Congress.

The Papers of
William Alexander Graham

VOLUME VIII

1869-1875

Edited by

MAX R. WILLIAMS

and

MARY REYNOLDS PEACOCK

RALEIGH
NORTH CAROLINA DEPARTMENT OF CULTURAL RESOURCES
DIVISION OF ARCHIVES AND HISTORY
1992

ISBN 0-86526-245-4

CONTENTS

ILLUSTRATIONS

FOREWORD

The publication of the eighth volume of *The Papers of William Alexander Graham* brings to a close a distinguished documentary series. The first volume in the series was published under the editorship of J. G. de Roulhac Hamilton in 1957. At the midpoint in the series Max R. Williams assumed the editorship, and in this, the final volume, Mary Reynolds Peacock, formerly a historical publications editor who is now retired, joined him as coeditor. Mrs. Peacock had worked with Dr. Williams on earlier volumes in the series. Dr. Williams has devoted more than thirty years to the study of Graham and the Whig party in North Carolina. Without Dr. Williams's dedication and impeccable scholarship, this important series could not have reached a successful conclusion. The Division of Archives and History conveys its sincere gratitude to Dr. Williams for his hard work and perseverance.

William A. Graham ranks as one of the leading political figures of nineteenth-century North Carolina. Whereas his public career ended with the Civil War, his political influence remained as potent as ever throughout Reconstruction at both the state and regional levels. Behind the scenes Graham's advice and counsel were continuously sought as he lent his support and prestige to the Conservative cause that challenged the political, economic, and social reforms of Reconstruction. An antebellum Whig, Graham helped lead the Conservative opposition to the Republican party and newly enfranchised freedmen who tested their brittle rights in the turbulent politics of Reconstruction.

In guiding this volume through press Dr. Williams and Mrs. Peacock had the capable assistance of Kathleen B. Wyche and Lisa D. Bailey of the Historical Publications Section. Additionally, Robert Ferris prepared the index, which was edited by Ms. Bailey. Stephena K. Williams, formerly of the Historical Publications Section, entered the text and footnotes on a computer for typesetting. Likewise, Sandra T. Hall entered the index, front matter, and dust jacket copy on a computer. Appreciation is hereby expressed to each of those individuals who helped make this volume available to researchers and historians.

Jeffrey J. Crow
Historical Publications Administrator

July, 1992

ACKNOWLEDGMENTS

North Carolina has the most ambitious and successful public history program in the United States. While that program's most visible activities include historic sites, museums, and archives and records management, the Historical Publications Section of the Division of Archives and History is an invaluable asset to persons interested in the state's history. From the publication of popular pamphlets for public schoolchildren to county histories to the *North Carolina Historical Review* to voluminous documentaries, like the Graham Papers, the publications section stimulates interest in North Carolina history and thereby promotes its study and elaboration.

The Graham project illustrates the staying power and dedication of Archives and History administrators. With the publication of Volume VIII, a Graham volume will have been provided in each of five decades beginning with the 1950s and concluding with the 1990s. During that period there have been five agency directors and three publications section administrators—all committed to the expensive documentary series of which the Graham Papers are a part.

For the present editor, the publication of Graham Papers, Volume VIII, is the culmination of twenty-five years of work to make Graham more accessible. His hair has grayed and his children have become adults in the process. When the question arises as to why anyone would endure the tedium that attends editing historical documents, this editor ponders the query anew. The answer differs sometimes, ranging from interest in the subject to a stubborn determination to see the project completed. On reflection, though, the answer is fairly straightforward. Historians use sources as a natural aspect of their profession; historical editors take that process to a different level and make it easier for others to illuminate the past. This editor takes pride in seeing the Graham Papers quoted in various secondary works and in having received a letter from a British scholar indicating that the timely publication of one Graham volume saved him three months of research in the United States.

Many people have contributed to the publication of the Graham Papers, in addition to Governor Graham. Obviously Dr. Hamilton deserves recognition as the prime mover in this project. He set a high standard of scholarship that influenced his successors significantly. D. L. Corbitt, Memory F. Mitchell, and Jeffrey J. Crow, administrators of the Historical Publications Section, Division of Archives and History, have been uniformly supportive and professional in their direction of the Graham project. Among other contributions they provided excellent copy editors to improve the text and see the volumes through the press. In this capacity Mary Reynolds Peacock and Kathleen B. Wyche were primarily responsible for Volumes V and VI and Volumes VII and VIII respectively. They saved the present editor from more errors.

Upon her retirement from Archives and History Mrs. Peacock agreed to collaborate on the preparation of Volume VIII. A most agreeable colleague, she brought a keen eye and long experience to the project. Moreover, she had become enthralled with Graham, his family, and his associates. She was most helpful in verifying documentary texts and in the preparation of footnotes. Volume VIII is better for her involvement.

Historians are deeply indebted to those who collect, organize, and make available historical manuscripts. The documentary editor owes the existence of the craft to archivists and manuscript curators. Scholars of North Carolina and the South are especially fortunate to have superb manuscript collections in Chapel Hill, Durham, and Raleigh. Archivists at all three institutions mentioned above have been most helpful in making Graham materials available. Special mention is appropriate of Dr. Carolyn Wallace, former director of the Southern Historical Collection, and Dr. Thornton W. Mitchell, former state archivist, for allowing substantial portions of the Graham documents in their care to be microfilmed. One of two faculty research grants by Western Carolina University made this possible, thus rendering the distance from Cullowhee to pertinent manuscript depositories less consequential.

In the realization of this long project, the present editor has received encouragement and support from friends, colleagues, and family. Some deserve special recognition. Western Carolina graduate students Jesse R. (Dick) Lankford, Jr., and Edwin R. Andrews provided assistance in transcription and annotation. Jeanne L. Nienhuis and Joe Hamilton Ginn typed and proofed both documents and footnotes with admirable accuracy and good humor. Several professional colleagues, also friends, have been supportive in this project. They are John L. Bell, Jr., James A. Lewis, Clifford R. Lovin, and D. C. Sossomon of Cullowhee; and Gordon B. McKinney of Washington, D.C. Three mentors, now deceased, deserve grateful mention: Fletcher M. Green, Hugh T. Lefler, and Rosser H. Taylor.

It is altogether appropriate to acknowledge the role my family has had in the Graham project, Volumes V-VIII. My parents, Alexander Eugene and Hazel Trogdon Williams, have offered their unqualified love and concern, as have my parents-in-law, the late John William Johnson and Clyde Padgett Johnson. My children, Max Ray, Jr., John Alexander, and Elizabeth Leigh, have known Governor Graham most of their lives and seem no worse for the experience. Sarah Johnson Williams, my wife of thirty-six years, partner and helpmate in all things, has provided the loving support and tranquillity that allowed completion of the Graham Papers.

A heartfelt thanks to all!

Max R. Williams
Cullowhee, North Carolina

INTRODUCTION

William A. Graham died at Saratoga Springs, New York, on August 11, 1875. In lamenting his passing, Edward J. Hale, longtime editor of the *Fayetteville Observer* and at that time a New York book publisher, characterized Graham as "the representative man of the State in its better days, the type of all that was noble in her people." Hale noted that Graham's death "leaves no man approaching him in all good qualities." (E. J. Hale to Augustus W. Graham, August 20, 1875.) Samuel F. Phillips, an erstwhile Graham associate turned Republican, wrote: "I do not abandon some difference of opinion with Governor Graham or forget the names & careers of his great contemporaries, when I say that he was altogether the wisest man of our time in North Carolina. He possessed in full measure that royal faculty so rarely met—judgment." (Samuel F. Phillips to John W. Graham, August 13, 1875.) Long influenced by Graham, Josiah Turner, Jr., in reporting his death to the Constitutional Convention of 1875, declared: "Take him all in all, in person, manners, mind and morals, his like has not been seen." (Remarks of Josiah Turner, of Orange, in Announcing to the Convention the Death of the Late Hon. Wm. A. Graham.)

These sentiments were representative of those expressed at Graham's death. For over four decades, while active privately as a lawyer and planter, he had been at the center of public life in North Carolina. Sometimes he represented his state at the national level. He was successively an assemblyman (twice Speaker), a United States senator, governor, secretary of the navy, Whig vice-presidential nominee, North Carolina senator, member of the secession convention, and Confederate senator. Elected to the United States Senate in 1865 but denied his seat, Graham held no elective office after the Civil War. Not until 1873 was he pardoned for his Confederate service. Given his Unionist preferences prior to Lincoln's call for troops, Graham considered his disfranchisement particularly unfair. But he eschewed personal bitterness and continued to serve the public as his conscience required. His advice was widely sought and his views were influential in Conservative circles, more so because his sons John Washington and James A Graham were state legislators. Both were active in the 1870 legislature that impeached Governor William W. Holden. One of those whom historian C. Vann Woodward called "redeemers," Graham believed that southern civilization was at stake during Reconstruction. Conservative and cautious by nature, Graham, disturbed by the destruction of southern institutions, became a white supremacist after 1865. Near the end of his life, in advocating a convention to undo the North Carolina Constitution of 1868, he advised an old friend thusly: "We are yet engaged in a contest for self government by the native white race, and against the blacks, and their foreign allies. . . ." (William A. Graham to D. F. Caldwell, June 10, 1875.) It should be noted, however, that the same conservatism led Graham to oppose the lawlessness of the Ku Klux Klan.

The materials in this volume reflect Graham's perspective and that of his family, friends, and associates. Though hardly as dramatic as the Civil War and the early years of Reconstruction, the period from 1869 to 1875 was important as North Carolina sought to redefine the social, economic, and political fabric of the state. This volume is particularly enlightening regarding the following political events: Conservative attempts to wrest political control from the Republican party; the activities of the Ku Klux Klan; the Kirk-Holden War; the impeachment and removal of Governor Holden; and the movement that culminated in the Constitutional Convention of 1875. Graham's correspondence also includes his recollection of a crucial meeting with Jefferson Davis in March, 1865, when he and two fellow senators—Virginian Robert M. T. Hunter and South Carolinian James L. Orr—presented the concerns of the Confederate Senate about the fate of Richmond and proposed that peace negotiations be initiated. (William A. Graham to William P. Johnston, April 21, 1874.)

But politics was only part of Graham's public life in his last years. He continued his service as Peabody Fund trustee and as trustee of the North Carolina Railroad Company. He became a trustee of Columbian College (now George Washington University) and was instrumental in reopening the University of North Carolina. As members of the university's new board, he and Paul C. Cameron were apparently decisive in the decision to name Kemp P. Battle president of the revivified Chapel Hill institution. Graham's long-standing interest in history was manifested in various ways. He was founding member of the Historical Society of North Carolina, sought to recover the historical sources held by Mrs. David L. Swain, and wrote a detailed defense of the Mecklenburg Declaration of Independence as part of Charlotte's centennial celebration. He also prepared and delivered a memorial address honoring former chief justice Thomas Ruffin. At the time of his death William A. Graham was a member of a three-person committee to adjudicate the boundary dispute between Virginia and Maryland. All these matters are discussed in this volume.

Although many of Graham's friends, including Robert B. Gilliam, John Berry, and Thomas Ruffin, predeceased him in the years 1869 to 1875, he lived to see his offspring educated and established in life. Joseph and George were physicians; John, James, Robert, and Augustus either were or would become successful lawyers; William was a Lincoln County farmer who would later become North Carolina agriculture secretary; and Susan was married to Walter Clark, a man destined to have a distinguished career as lawyer and jurist. Graham lamented that his estate provided so modestly for his progeny; but his wife, Susannah Sarah (Susan) Washington Graham, reminded him and their children that his legacy to them transcended worldly things. They and North Carolina could take pride in the good name and distinguished public service of William Alexander Graham, 1804-1875.

EDITORIAL METHOD

Three essential tasks—selection, transcription, and annotation—confront the editor of historical documents. Each requires choices that test the editor's imagination and judgment. In this instance, the materials to be included in the Graham Papers were chosen from thousands of documents in various manuscript collections, from contemporary newspapers, and from pamphlets and broadsides. Letters make up approximately 95 percent of the published materials. The majority of Graham correspondence is located in the Southern Historical Collection, Wilson Library, University of North Carolina at Chapel Hill; but the North Carolina Division of Archives and History, Raleigh, and the Manuscript Department, Perkins Library, Duke University, Durham, hold important political and family papers respectively.

Dr. Joseph Gregoire de Roulhac Hamilton, founder of the Southern Historical Collection, chose the majority of items for publication in all eight volumes. His selections reflected his interest in politics and the University of North Carolina. He published four volumes before his death and left some three volumes transcribed and sparsely annotated materials for publication later. In the mid-1960s the present editor assumed responsibility for the project. All extant Graham materials that could be located were reread. The Hamilton transcriptions proved to be remarkably accurate; but hundreds of additional items related to social, economic, and family matters were added, some in the addendum to this volume. An effort was made to employ most of Hamilton's transcription practices. Readers who wish to know more of the methods used by Hamilton and Williams should see the introductions to Volumes I and VII. Both editors sought to make the materials as accessible to the reader as possible without distorting the intent of the authors.

As suggested above, the present editor included documents that give a broader view of Graham's activities; however, it should be noted that his legal and business papers were omitted. Samples of Graham's correspondence related to the North Carolina Railroad Company and the Peabody Fund were included. Although these additions to the materials selected by Hamilton are significant, perhaps the most obvious difference in the editorial practices of Hamilton and Williams lies in the annotations each provided. Hamilton's notes are, in general, brief and intermittent while Williams's are abundant, or excessive, depending on one's viewpoint. For example, in his volumes Williams has sought diligently to identify all persons mentioned and to explain events and circumstances discussed. There is ample precedent for both the Hamilton and Williams approaches to annotation.

Although the editors never met, the present editor observed the legendary Hamilton, then a vigorous octogenarian, in animated conversation with a colleague about North Carolina history. The collaboration in publishing the Graham Papers was not then anticipated; however, one suspects that there would have been fundamental agreement as to purpose. Both native Tar Heels, Hamilton and Williams would doubtless have concurred that their intent was to make the sources of North Carolina history more readily available to lay readers and scholars alike.

Gov. William Alexander Graham
1804-1875
m. 1836 Susannah Sarah Washington
1816-1890

Dr. Joseph Graham
1837-1907
m. 1859 Elizabeth Hill
1838-1912
5 children

Maj. William Alexander Graham
1839-1924
m. 1st. 1864 Julia Lane
1845-1909
11 children
m. 2nd. 1914 Sallie Hill Clark
1864-1936

Capt. Robert Davidson Graham
1843-1904

Judge Augustus William Graham
1849-1936
m. 1876 Lucy Anna Horner
1855-1936
4 children

Alfred Octavius Graham
1853-1854

Maj. John Washington Graham
1838-1928
m. 1st. 1867 Rebecca Bennehan Cameron
1840-1883
8 children
m. 2nd. 1887 Margaret Forrester Bailey
1861-1946
1 child

Capt. James Augustus Graham
1841-1909
m. 1869 Elizabeth Cheshire Webb
1845-1915
4 children

Dr. George Washington Graham
1847-1923
m. 1st. 1873 Sallie Shaver
1847-1887
4 children
m. 2nd. 1889 Alice Leonora Alexander
1842-1905
m. 3rd. 1910 Imogene Tunstall

Susan Washington Graham
1851-1909
m. 1874 Chief Justice Walter Clark
1946-1924
8 children

Eugene Berrien Graham
1858-1863

W. A. Graham Clark (comp), "Descendants of James Graham (1714-1763) of Ireland and Pennsylvania" (Washington, D.C., 1940), genealogical chart in the William A. Graham Papers, Southern Historical Collection, University of North Carolina Library at Chapel Hill.

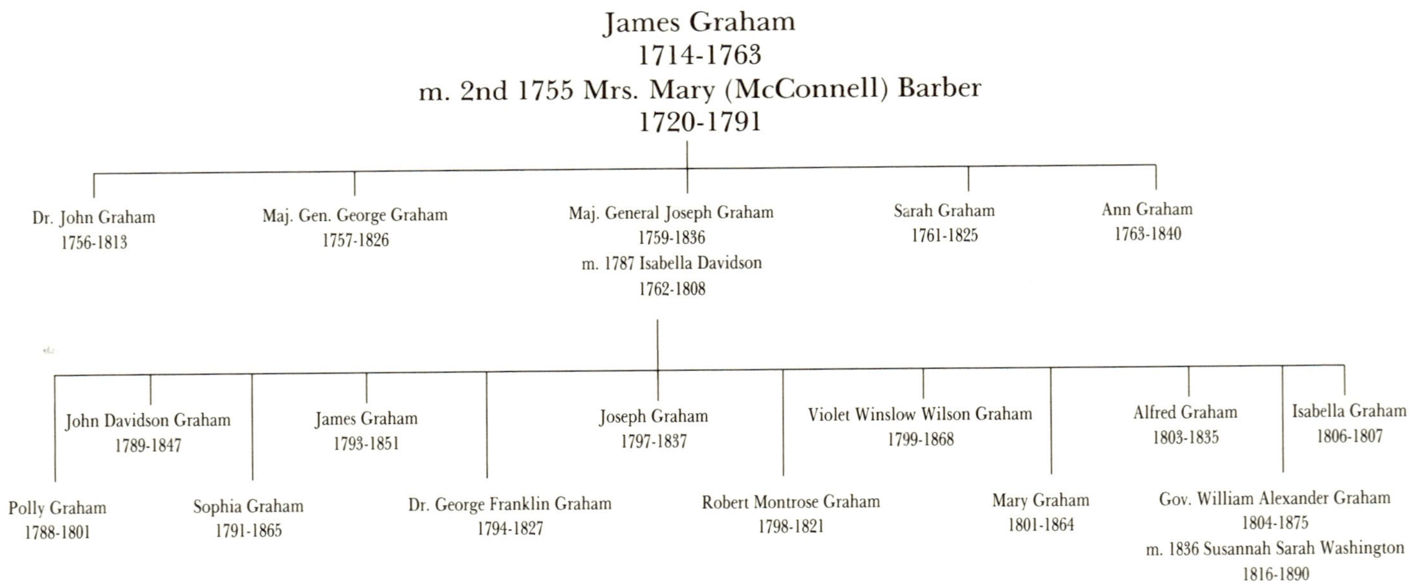

W. A. Graham Clark (comp), "Descendants of James Graham (1714-1763) of Ireland and Pennsylvania" (Washington, D.C., 1940), genealogical chart in the William A. Graham Papers, Southern Historical Collection, University of North Carolina Library at Chapel Hill.

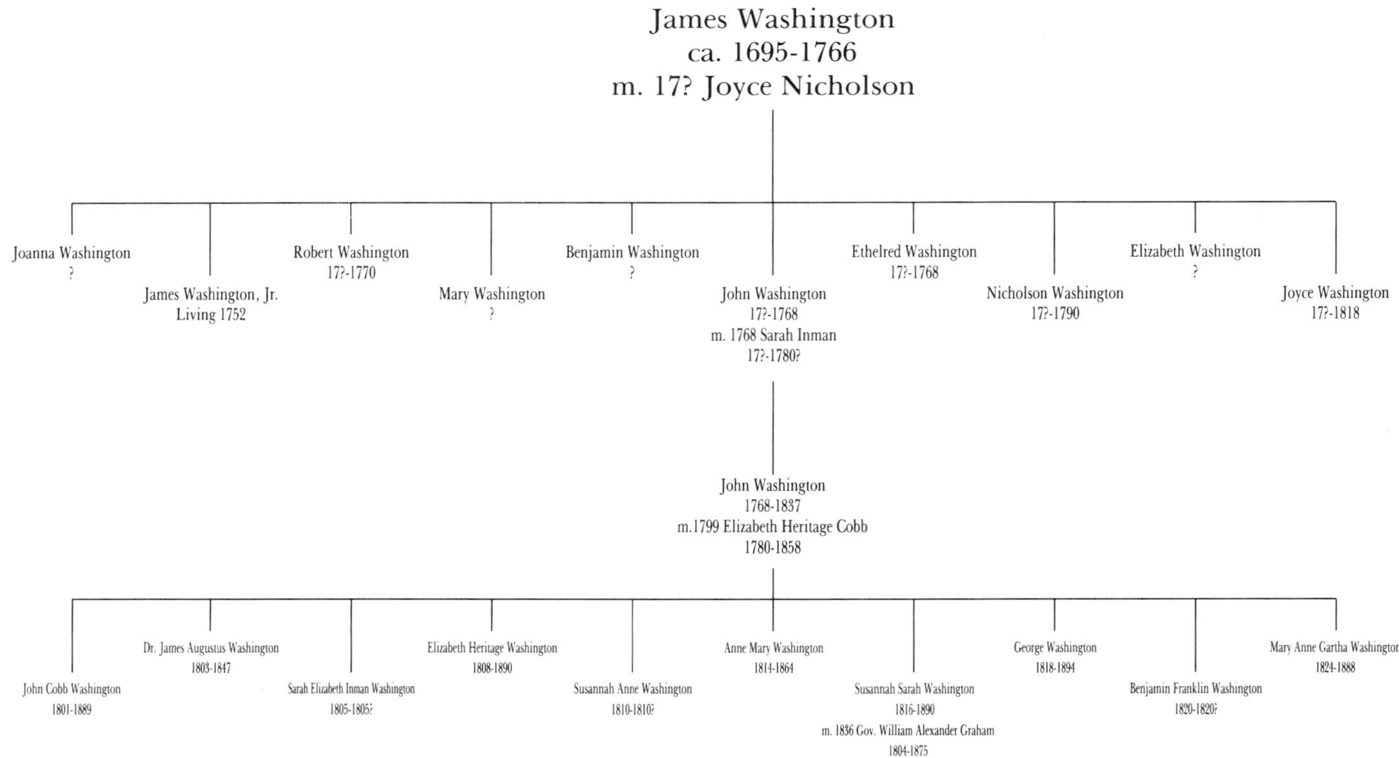

W. A. Graham Clark (comp), "Descendants of James Washington (d.1766) of Northampton County, N.C." (Washington, D.C., 1939), genealogical chart in the William A. Graham Papers, Southern Historical Collection, University of North Carolina Library at Chapel Hill.

CHRONOLOGICAL LIST OF THE PAPERS OF WILLIAM ALEXANDER GRAHAM 1869-1875 PRINTED IN THIS VOLUME

1869

Written by	Written to	Date
William A. Graham, Jr.	William A. Graham	January, 1869
Edward C. Cabell	William A. Graham	January, 1869
George W. Graham	William A. Graham	January 5, 1869
Jonathan Worth	William A. Graham	January 9, 1869
William A. Graham	William A. Smith	January 16, 1869
David F. Caldwell	William A. Graham	January 18, 1869
Augustus H. Garland	William A. Graham	January 20, 1869
Joseph G. Morrison	William A. Graham	January 21, 1869
William A. Graham	Susan Washington Graham	January 23, 186[9]
John H. Tillinghast	William A. Graham	January 25, 1869
James A. Graham	William A. Graham	February 5, 1869
Francis J. Murdoch	William A. Graham	February 8, 1869
Randolph A. Shotwell	William A. Graham	February 8, 1869
William A. Graham, Jr.	William A. Graham	February 10, 1869
William A. Graham	William A. Graham, Jr.	February 14, 1869
John W. Graham	William A. Graham	February 26, 1869
George W. Graham	William A. Graham	March 1, 1869
Francis E. Shober	William A. Graham	March 22, 1869
George Little	William A. Graham	March 24, 1869
William A. Graham	*Tax List*	April 1, 1869
M. A. Caldwell	William A. Graham	April 9, 1869
William A. Graham, Jr.	William A. Graham	April 22, 1869
George W. Graham	William A. Graham	April 24, 1869
E. J. Hale & Sons	William A. Graham	April 26, 1869
George W. Graham	Susan Washington Graham	May 6, 1869
Edward J. Hale	William A. Graham	May 8, 1869
George W. Graham	William A. Graham	May 17, 1869
H. C. Luce	William A. Graham	May 27, 1869
William A. Smith	William A. Graham	June 6, 1869
S. Finley Tomlinson	William A. Graham	June 8, 1869
M. A. Caldwell	William A. Graham	June 11, 1869
Robert C. Winthrop	William A. Graham	June 12, 1869
T. Apoleon Cheney	William A. Graham	July 12, 1869
M. C. C. Church	William A. Graham	July 15, 1869
Thomas B. Florence	William A. Graham	July 15, 1869
Kemp P. Battle	William A. Graham	July 20, 1869
Robert Ransom	William A. Graham	July 27, 1869
William A. Graham	William A. Graham, Jr.	August 9, 1869
Ann E. Young	William A. Graham	August 23, 1869
William Bingham, Jr.	William A. Graham	August 23, 1869
Augustus W. Graham	William A. Graham	September 1, 1869
William A. Graham	*Testimonial for William Hooper*	September 10, 1869

James A. Graham	William A. Graham	September 16, 1869
Joseph A. Engelhard	William A. Graham	September 21, 1869
John T. Mason	William A. Graham	September 22, 1869
John A. Cameron	William A. Graham	September 24, 1869
Leonidas Brown	William A. Graham	September 28, 1869
Charles Phillips	William A. Graham	October 4, 1869
Bartholomew F. Moore	William A. Graham	November 1, 1869
William A. Smith	William A. Graham	November 2, 1869
William Hooper	William A. Graham	November 2 [1869]
Charles D. Dickey	William A. Graham	November 10, 1869
William A. Smith	William A. Graham	November 25, 1869
Barnas Sears	William A. Graham	November 26, 1869
James A. Graham	William A. Graham	December 8, 1869
Robert C. Winthrop	William A. Graham	December 16, 1869
Augustus W. Graham	William A. Graham	December 23, 1869
Augustus W. Graham	William A. Graham	[December 25] 1869
Invitation to Peabody Funeral	William A. Graham	December 29, 1869

1870

WRITTEN BY	WRITTEN TO	DATE
Resolutions of Protest of Alamance County Citizens		[January, 1870]
Joseph Graham	William A. Graham	January 1, 1870
Robert C. Winthrop	William A. Graham	January 5, 1870
Joseph Graham	William A. Graham	January 12, 1870
William A. Graham	William H. Battle	January 15, 1870
William A. Graham	William A. Graham, Jr.	January 15, 1870
William H. Battle	William A. Graham	January 17, 1870
William A. Graham, Jr.	William A. Graham	January 22, 1870
George W. Graham	William A. Graham	January 23, 1870
William A. Graham	*Resolutions of Peabody Fund Board of Trustees*	February 15, 1870
William A. Graham	*Address to Peabody Fund Board of Trustees*	February 15, 1870
William A. Graham	Susan Washington Graham	February 17, 1870
Zebulon B. Vance	William A. Graham	February 19, 1870
William A. Graham	William A. Graham, Jr.	March 4, 1870
Charles Phillips	William A. Graham	March 9, 1870
James A. Graham	William A. Graham	March 16, 1870
William H. Battle	William A. Graham	March 25, 1870 [with enclosure]
Proposed Address to the Public		March, 1870 [enclosure]
William A. Graham	*Tax List*	April 1, 1870
William A. Graham	William A. Graham, Jr.	April 13, 1870
William A. Graham	William A. Graham, Jr.	April 16, 1870
Edward J. Hale	William A. Graham	April 18, 1870
Rufus Barringer	William A. Graham	April 22, 1870
Mike L. Woods	William A. Graham	April 23, 1870
Robert C. Winthrop	William A. Graham	April 28, 1870
Rockingham County Committee	William A. Graham	April 29, 1870

William A. Graham	Rockingham County Committee	May 2, 1870
George W. Graham	William A. Graham	May 11, 1870
James A. Graham	John W. Graham	May 13, 1870
Edward J. Hale	William A. Graham	May 15, 1870
Alexander H. Graham	William A. Graham	May 17, 1870
Kemp P. Battle	William A. Graham	June 3, 1870
Robert B. Gilliam	William A. Graham	June 21, 1870
Walter F. Leak	William A. Graham	June 24, 1870
Robert C. Winthrop	William A. Graham	June 24, 1870
Alexander H. Graham	William A. Graham	June 29, 1870
Mike L. Woods	William A. Graham	June 30, 1870
William A. Graham	William A. Graham, Jr.	July 1, 1870
Robert P. Waring	William A. Graham	July 5, 1870
Abial W. Fisher	*Special Military Order*	July 13, 1870
Josiah Turner, Jr.	William A. Graham	July 13, 1870 [telegram]
John L. Scott	William A. Graham	July 15, 1870 [telegram]
Edward S. Parker	William A. Graham	July 15, 1870 [telegram]
Edward S. Parker	William A. Graham	July 17, 1870 [telegram]
William H. Battle	William A. Graham	July 23, 1870
Thomas P. Atkinson	William A. Graham	July 26, 1870
Zebulon B. Vance	William A. Graham	July 28, 1870
William H. Battle	William A. Graham	July 28, 1870
E. Brock Holden	William A. Graham	July 28, 1870
William H. Battle	William A. Graham	July 30, 1870
James A. Graham	William A. Graham	August 2, 1870
Benjamin F. Mebane	William A. Graham	August 2, 18[70]
Thomas Bragg	William A. Graham	August 5, 1870 [telegram]
Zebulon B. Vance	William A. Graham	August 6, 1870
Edward S. Parker	William A. Graham	August 6, 1870 [telegram]
William H. Battle	William A. Graham	August 7, 1870 [telegram]
William H. Battle	William A. Graham	August 7, 1870
Lewis Hanes	William A. Graham	August 8, 1870
William H. Battle	William A. Graham	August 9, 1870
Josiah Turner, Jr.	William A. Graham	August 10, 1870 [telegram]
Leonidas C. Edwards	William A. Graham	August 10, 1870
William H. Battle	William A. Graham	August 11, 1870
W. H. Malone	William A. Graham	August 13, 1870
William H. Battle	William A. Graham	August 13, 1870
Robert B. Gilliam	William A. Graham	August 15, 1870
Junius I. Scales	William A. Graham	August 15, 1870
Reception Committee	William A. Graham	August 18, 1870 [with enclosure]
Invitation to Mass Reception		August 18, 1870 [enclosure]
William A. Graham	William A. Graham, Jr.	August 20, 1870
Hezekiah G. Spruill	William A. Graham	August 22, 1870
Deposition of John G. Albright		August 24, 1870
Thomas J. Womack	William A. Graham	September 1, 1870
William A. Coleman	William A. Graham	September 1, 1870
Edgecombe/Nash Committee	William A. Graham	September 7, 1870
Cornelia Phillips Spencer	William A. Graham	September 10, 1870
Virginia L. Farragut	William A. Graham	September 20, 1870

William H. Battle	William A. Graham	September 21, 1870
Invitation to Farragut Funeral	William A. Graham	September 24, 1870
William A. Graham	Edgecombe/Nash Committee	September 26, 1870
William A. Graham	Cornelia Phillips Spencer	September 29, 1870
William A. Graham	Windsor Committee	October 1, 1870
William A. Graham	Susan Washington Graham	October 6, 1870
William A. Graham	William A. Graham, Jr.	October 7, 1870
John McRae	William A. Graham	October 8, 1870
William A. Graham	George W. Mordecai	October 12, 1870
Thomas M. Moore	William A. Graham	October 13, 1870
William A. Graham	William A. Graham, Jr.	October 22, 1870
Martha Phoebe Ruffin	William A. Graham	[October 23, 1870]
William H. Battle	William A. Graham	October 24, 1870
Kemp P. Battle	William A. Graham	October 29, 1870
William H. Battle	William A. Graham	October 31, 1870
William H. Battle	William A. Graham	November 8, 1870
William C. Smith	William A. Graham	November 14, 1870
William A. Graham	William A. Graham, Jr.	November 18, 1870
James M. Leach	William A. Graham	November 20, 1870
William H. Battle	William A. Graham	November 22, 1870
John W. Graham	William A. Graham	November 24, 1870
Thomas P. Atkinson	William A. Graham	November 30, 1870
B. M. Jones	William A. Graham	December 1, 1870
Barnas Sears	William A. Graham	December 2, 1870
William A. Graham	William A. Graham, Jr.	December 10, 1870
Littleton Q. Washington	William A. Graham	December 10, 1870
Thomas Sparrow	William A. Graham	December 23, 1870
B. M. Jones	William A. Graham	December 26, 1870
B. M. Jones	William A. Graham	December 26, 1870

1871

WRITTEN BY	WRITTEN TO	DATE
William A. Graham	Thomas Sparrow	January 9, 1871
John W. Graham	William A. Graham	January 12, 1871
John Manning, Jr.	William A. Graham	January 27, 1871
John Kerr	William A. Graham	January 28, 1871
J. A. Petrie	William A. Graham	February 2, 1871
James G. Moore	William A. Graham	February 14, 1871
James G. Moore	William A. Graham	February 16, 1871
Green Andrews	William A. Graham	February 17, 1871
Charles Macalester	William A. Graham	February 18, 1871
T. Apoleon Cheney	William A. Graham	March 1, 1871
David F. Caldwell	William A. Graham	March 7, 1871
William A. Graham	*Notes for Impeachment Speech*	[1871]
Francis M. Carter	William A. Graham	March 16, 1871
Edward J. Hale	William A. Graham	March 28, 1871
William A. Graham	William A. Graham, Jr.	April 3, 1871
Robert C. Winthrop	William A. Graham	April 3, 1871

Columbian College Committee	William A. Graham	May 1, 1871
John Potts Brown	William A. Graham	May 1, 1871
Edward J. Hale	William A. Graham	May 5, 1871
William A. Graham	William A. Graham, Jr.	May 8, 1871
Kemp P. Battle	William A. Graham	May 17, 1871
J. H. Hubbell	William A. Graham	May 20, 1871
William A. Graham	Kemp P. Battle	May 22, 1871
Augustus S. Merrimon	William A. Graham	May 30, 1871
William A. Graham	Kemp P. Battle	June 2, 1871
A. C. Freeman	William A. Graham	June 8, 1871
George Little	William A. Graham	June 9, 1871
William A. Graham	A. C. Freeman	June 12, 1871 [copy]
Littleton Q. Washington	William A. Graham	June 28, 1871 [with enclosure]
Littleton Q. Washington	Philadelph Van Trump	June 28, 1871 [enclosure]
Joseph H. Wilson	William A. Graham	June 30, 1871
Archibald M. Aiken	William A. Graham	July 5, 1871
Thomas Ruffin, Jr.	William A. Graham	July 7, 1871
Edward S. Parker	William A. Graham	July 13, 1871
Jesse Turner	William A. Graham	July 19, 1871
Algernon S. Buford	William A. Graham	July 26, 1871
William A. Graham	William A. Graham, Jr.	August 4, 1871
Edward S. Parker	William A. Graham	August 11, 1871
James C. Welling	William A. Graham	August 16, 1871
Lease Agreement between William A. Graham and John Pickett		August 18, 1871
Robert C. Winthrop	William A. Graham	August 20, 1871
Algernon S. Buford	William A. Graham	August 23, 1871
Alfred J. Morrison	William A. Graham	September 9, 1871
William A. Graham	[Ralph Gorrell]	September 19, 1871 [with enclosure]
William A. Graham	*Appointment of Proxy*	September 19, 1871 [enclosure]
Benson J. Lossing	William A. Graham	September 22, 1871
Cornelia Phillips Spencer	William A. Graham	September 26, 1871
William Stickney	William A. Graham	September 28, 1871
James C. Welling	William A. Graham	September 29, 1871
William A. Hall	William A. Graham	October 7, 1871
William A. Graham	Cornelia Phillips Spencer	October 28, 1871
J. R. Cole	William A. Graham	November 7, 1871
James A. Graham	Susan Washington Graham	November 17, 1871
Edward J. Hale	William A. Graham	November 20, 1871
Lyman C. Draper	William A. Graham	November 22, 1871
E. S. Thompson	William A. Graham	November 24, 1871
William A. Graham	Susan Washington Graham	November 27, 1871
Cadwallader Jones	William A. Graham	December 8, 1871
William A. Graham	Susan Washington Graham	December 11, 1871
George F. Bason	William A. Graham	December 18, 1871
George F. Bason	William A. Graham	December 19, 1871
Stephen Moore	William A. Graham	December 21, 1871

1872

Written by	Written to	Date
E. J. Hale & Sons	William A. Graham	January 1, 1872
Frances A. Polk	William A. Graham	January 10, 1872
Daniel H. Hill	William A. Graham	February 10, 1872
Alexander McIver	William A. Graham	February 16, 1872
Algernon S. Buford	William A. Graham	February 19, 1872
Nicholas L. Williams	William A. Graham	February 19, 1872
Hardie H. Helper	William A. Graham	February 22, 1872
William Johnston	William A. Graham	February 29, 1872
William A. Graham	William A. Graham, Jr.	March 4, 1872
Benson J. Lossing	William A. Graham	March 18, 1872
James Grant	William A. Graham	March 27, 1872
William A. Graham	William A. Graham, Jr.	April 10, 1872
Nathan K. Hall	William A. Graham	April 10, 1872
James Grant	William A. Graham	April 15, 1872
Calvin E. Parish	William A. Graham	April 17, 1872
Charles G. Yates	William A. Graham	April 26, 1872
Daniel H. Hill	William A. Graham	April 27, 1872
Nathan K. Hall	William A. Graham	May 9, 1872
Alexander H. H. Stuart	William A. Graham	May 16, [18]72
Robert C. Winthrop	William A. Graham	May 16, 1872
Robert C. Winthrop	William A. Graham	May 25, 1872
Alexander H. H. Stuart	William A. Graham	May 29, 1872
Alexander H. H. Stuart	William A. Graham	June 6, 1872
Charles Phillips	William A. Graham	June 10, 1872
Robert C. Winthrop	William A. Graham	June 10, 1872
Alexander H. H. Stuart	William A. Graham	June 12, 1872
Nathan K. Hall	William A. Graham	June 21, 1872
Alfred J. Morrison	William A. Graham	July 7, 1872
James A. Graham	William A. Graham	July 12, 1872
Nathan K. Hall	William A. Graham	July 15, 1872
Benson J. Lossing	William A. Graham	July 19, 1872
William C. Rencher	William A. Graham	July 20, 1872
Charles Phillips	William A. Graham	July 20, 1872
Hardie H. Helper	William A. Graham	August 1, 1872
E. J. Hale & Sons	William A. Graham	August 8, 1872
Kenneth Rayner	William A. Graham	August 11, 1872
Augustus S. Merrimon	William A. Graham	August 14, 1872
James Farrow	William A. Graham	August 15, 1872
William A. Graham	Charles C. Jones, Jr.	August 30, 1872
Kenneth Rayner	William A. Graham	August 31, 1872
Sydenham B. Alexander	William A. Graham	September 5, 1872
Augustus S. Merrimon	William A. Graham	September 9, 1872
James M. Leach	William A. Graham	September 18, 1872
Alexander McIver	Bartholomew F. Moore, William H. Battle, and William A. Graham	September 18, 1872
Augustus Schell	William A. Graham	September 19, 1872
Daniel M. Barringer	William A. Graham	September 19, 1872 [with enclosure]

Augustus Schell	Daniel M. Barringer	September 19, 1872 [enclosure; telegram]
Augustus S. Merrimon	William A. Graham	September 19, 1872
William A. Graham	William A. Graham, Jr.	September 27, 1872
Lyman C. Draper	William A. Graham	October 1, 1872
Thomas D. McDowell	William A. Graham	October 8, 1872
Bartholomew F. Moore	William A. Graham	October 21, 1872
Augustus S. Merrimon	William A. Graham	November 16, 1872
Alfred J. Morrison	William A. Graham	November 18, 1872
Alfred J. Morrison	William A. Graham	November 20, 1872
Alfred J. Morrison	William A. Graham	November 22, 1872
James L. Alcorn	William A. Graham	December 3, 1872
John W. Norwood	William A. Graham	December 9, 1872
James L. Alcorn	William A. Graham	December 13, 1872
Robert D. Graham	William A. Graham	December 14, 1872 [with enclosure]
Robert D. Graham	Hamilton Fish	December 3, 1872 [enclosure; telegram]
Hamilton Fish	Robert D. Graham	December 3, 1872 [enclosure; telegram]

1873

WRITTEN BY	WRITTEN TO	DATE
William A. Graham	[Daniel H. Hill?]	[January] 1873
Lyman C. Draper	William A. Graham	January 7, 1873
William A. Graham	William A. Smith	January 7, 1873
William A. Smith	William A. Graham	January 11, 1873
William Johnston	William A. Graham	January 16, 1873 [with enclosure]
Lyman C. Draper	William Johnston	January 7, 1873 [enclosure]
Washington M. Wingate	William A. Graham	January 17, 1873
Nathan K. Hall	William A. Graham	January 18, 1873
William A. Graham	Susan Washington Graham	January 22, 1873
William W. Corcoran	William A. Graham	January 23, 1873
William A. Smith	William A. Graham	January 31, 1873
William A. Graham	Susan Washington Graham	February 1, 1873
Robert C. Winthrop	William A. Graham	February 6, 1873
Salmon P. Chase	William A. Graham	February 10, 1873
David A. Barnes	William A. Graham	February 19, 1873
Bartholomew F. Moore	William A. Graham	March 17, 1873
Bartholomew F. Moore	William A. Graham	March 21, 1873
Bartholomew F. Moore	William A. Graham	March 31, 1873
James Grant	William A. Graham	April 6, 1873
Maurice Q. Waddell	William A. Graham	May 16, 1873
Wilson G. Richardson	William A. Graham	June 6, 1873
T. H. Selby	William A. Graham	June 7, 1873 [with enclosure]
Convention Circular		June 9, 1873 [enclosure]
Alexander H. H. Stuart	William A. Graham	June 16, 1873
Frederick A. P. Barnard	William A. Graham	June 17, 1873
Hamilton Fish	William A. Graham	June 18, 1873
Wilson G. Richardson	William A. Graham	June 19, 1873
Robert C. Winthrop	William A. Graham	July 1, 1873

Wilson G. Richardson	William A. Graham	July 4, 1873
William A. Graham	Susan Washington Graham	July 18, 1873
William A. Graham	Susan Washington Graham	July 22, 1873
Lewis Ashmead	William A. Graham	July 22, 1873
William A. Graham	Susan Washington Graham	July 26, 1873
Seaton Gales	William A. Graham	August 23, 1873
William A. Graham	William A. Graham, Jr.	August 28, 1873
Joseph Graham	William A. Graham	August 28, 1873
Frances A. Polk	William A. Graham	September 6, 1873
Joseph Graham	William A. Graham	September 10, 1873
Alexander McIver	William A. Graham	September 10, 1873
Alexander McIver	William A. Graham	September 17, 1873
Henry B. Chapin	William A. Graham	September 22, 1873
Robert H. Morrison	William A. Graham	September 24, 1873
Daniel H. Hill	William A. Graham	October 15, 1873 [with enclosure]
Randolph A. Shotwell	Southern Home *Circular*	1873 [enclosure]
Eugene Grissom	William A. Graham	October 20, 1873
William A. Richardson	William A. Graham	November 8, 1873
Edward J. Hale	William A. Graham	November 14, 1873
Robert C. Winthrop	William A. Graham	November 14, 1873
Edward J. Hale	William A. Graham	November 21, 1873
James C. Welling	William A. Graham	December 18, 1873
Robert C. Winthrop	William A. Graham	December 24, 1873
William A. Graham	James C. Welling	December 31, 1873
Susan W. Graham	Augustus W. Graham	December 31, 1873

1874

Written by	Written to	Date
James C. Welling	William A. Graham	January 5, 1874
Stephen D. Pool	William A. Graham	January 9, 1874
William P. Johnston	William A. Graham	January 20, 1874
Charles Phillips	Eleanor H. Swain	January 26, 1874
Lyman C. Draper	William A. Graham	February 7, 1874
William A. Graham	William P. Johnston	February 12, 1874
William A. Graham	Robert M. T. Hunter	February 12, 1874
Joseph Graham	William A. Graham	February 12, 1874
William P. Johnston	William A. Graham	February 14, 1874 [telegram]
William A. Graham	Kemp P. Battle	February 14, 1874
William Eaton	William A. Graham	February 23, 1874
Nathan K. Hall	William A. Graham	February 27, 1874
William A. Graham	William A. Graham, Jr.	March 2, 1874
A. B. Shankland	William A. Graham	March 9, 1874
D. G. Stinson	William A. Graham	March 9, 1874
William P. Johnston	William A. Graham	March 25, 1874
Robert C. Winthrop	William A. Graham	March 26, 1874
D. G. Stinson	William A. Graham	March 26, 1874
William A. Graham	*Tax List*	April 1, 1874
James C. Welling	William A. Graham	April 7, 1874
Walter J. Budd	William A. Graham	April 8, 1874
William A. Graham	William P. Johnston	April 21, 1874

William P. Johnston	William A. Graham	April 29, 1874
Joseph Graham	William A. Graham	May 22, 1874 [with enclosure]
Joseph Graham	Jacob M. Da Costa	May 22, 1874 [enclosure]
William A. Graham	Montford McGehee	May 23, 1874
James B. Groome	William A. Graham	May 28, 1874
William A. Graham	Augustus W. Graham	May 29, 1874
Frederick A. P. Barnard	William A. Graham	June 3, 1874
Jeremiah S. Black	William A. Graham	June 4, 1874
Joseph Graham	William A. Graham	June 4, 1874
Willie Graham	William A. Graham	June 5, 1874
William A. Graham	James L. Kemper	June 8, 1874
William A. Graham	Jeremiah S. Black	June 8, 1874
Joseph J. Davis	William A. Graham	June 13, 1874
Jeremiah S. Black	William A. Graham	June 15, 1874
William A. Graham	Jeremiah S. Black	June 18, 1874
William A. Graham	James L. Kemper	June 18, 1874
Isaac W. Hayne	William A. Graham	[June 19, 1874] [with enclosure]
Isaac W. Hayne	Richard T. Brumby	June 19, 1874 [enclosure]
J. M. Cameron	William A. Graham	June 20, 1874
Raleigh T. Daniel	William A. Graham	June 20, 1874
Jeremiah S. Black	William A. Graham	June 26, 1874
D. G. Stinson	William A. Graham	July 8, 1874 [with enclosure]
Excerpt from Adams Autobiography [enclosure]		
Jeremiah S. Black	William A. Graham	July 11, 1874
William A. Graham	William A. Graham, Jr.	July 11, 1874
William J. Robertson	William A. Graham	July 14, 1874
Charles J. Jenkins	William A. Graham	July 15, 1874 [telegram]
Isaac D. Jones	William A. Graham	July 18, 1874
Charles J. Jenkins	William A. Graham	July 18, 1874
James L. Robinson	William A. Graham	July 18, 1874
Joseph Graham	Willie Graham	July 22, 1874
Zebulon B. Vance	William A. Graham	July 24, 1874
Frederick A. P. Barnard	William A. Graham	August 5, 1874
Augustus W. Graham	Susan Washington Graham	August 7, 1874
Charles J. Jenkins	William A. Graham	August 12, 1874
Patrick H. Winston, Jr.	William A. Graham	August 17, 1874
William A. Graham	Richard B. Haywood	August 19, 1874
Joseph Graham	William A. Graham	August 19, 1874
William A. Graham	Augustus W. Graham	August 24, 1874
Jeremiah S. Black	William A. Graham	September 5, 1874
John Spelman	William A. Graham	September 7, 1874 [with enclosure]
Newspaper Editorial		[September 4, 1874] [enclosure]
Charles J. Jenkins	William A. Graham	September 19, 1874
Alexander H. H. Stuart	William A. Graham	September 27, 1874
John Spelman	William A. Graham	September 29, 1874
William L. Saunders	William A. Graham	September 29, 1874
Raleigh T. Daniel	William A. Graham	October 12, 1874
Joseph Graham	William A. Graham	October 25, 1874
Joseph A. Engelhard	William A. Graham	October 26, 1874

Joseph B. Cherry	William A. Graham	November 6, 1874
Charles M. Cooke	William A. Graham	November 10, 1874
Charles M. Cooke	William A. Graham	November 24, 1874
John N. Staples	William A. Graham	December 9, 1874
Robert P. Waring and Other Senators	William A. Graham	December 9, 1874
William A. Graham	Conservative Senators	December 15, 1874
Horace M. Polk	William A. Graham	December 21, 1874
William R. Cox	William A. Graham	December 28 [1874]
Walter Leak Steele	William A. Graham	December 30, 1874 [with enclosure]
Walter Leak Steele	*Newspaper Article*	December 20, 1874 [enclosure]

1875

Written by	Written to	Date
James R. Dodge	William A. Graham	January 11, 1875
James A. Graham	William A. Graham	January 25, 1875
Appleton Oaksmith	William A. Graham	February 3, 1875
James C. Welling	William A. Graham	February 13, 1875
Robert D. Graham	William A. Graham	February 24, 187[5]
Matthias E. Manly	William A. Graham	March 19, 1875
Zebulon B. Vance	William A. Graham	March 22, 1875
Jeremiah S. Black	William A. Graham	March 23, 1875
Nereus Mendenhall	William A. Graham	March 23, 1875
George T. Swann	William A. Graham	March 25, 1875
William A. Graham	Cornelia Phillips Spencer	March 25, 1875
John A. Young	William A. Graham	March 26, 1875 [with enclosures]
Centennial Celebration Program		March 25, 1875 [enclosure]
Joseph Graham	William A. Graham	March 29, 1875
Kemp P. Battle	William A. Graham	March 30, 1875
William A. Graham	*Tax List*	April 1, 1875
Ralph H. Graves	William A. Graham	April 7, 1875
William Johnston	William A. Graham	April 15, 1875
Joseph Graham	William A. Graham	April 15, 1875
E. J. Hale & Sons	William A. Graham	April 17, 1875
John Alexander	William A. Graham	April 19, 1875
William Johnston	William A. Graham	April 20, 1875
William J. Wilson	William A. Graham	April 20, 1875
Augustus S. Merrimon	William A. Graham	April 23, 1875
James G. Bennett	William A. Graham	April 23, 1875
James C. Welling	William A. Graham	April 26, 1875
William A. Graham	Cornelia Phillips Spencer	April 26, 1875
Daniel H. Hill	William A. Graham	April 28, 1875
Matthias E. Manly	William A. Graham	April 28, 1875
John R. Winston	William A. Graham	May 1, 1875
James C. Welling	William A. Graham	May 5, 1875
Horace M. Polk	William A. Graham	May 6, 1875
John S. McEwen	William A. Graham	May 6, 1875
William A. Graham	Cornelia Phillips Spencer	May 7, 1875

William A. Graham	Editor of *New York Herald*	May 7, 1875
James C. Welling	William A. Graham	May 10, 1875
Jeremiah S. Black and William A. Graham	*Authorization of Arbitrator*	May 11, 1875
Thomas W. Dewey	William A. Graham	May 18, 1875 [with enclosure]
Centennial Circular [enclosure]		
Eleanor H. Swain	Historical Society Committee	May 19, 1875
William H. Polk	William A. Graham	May 20, 1875
Lyman C. Draper	William A. Graham	May 20, 1875
Cyrus L. Hunter	William A. Graham	May 27, 1875
William A. Graham	William A. Graham, Jr.	May 31, 1875
Eugene Grissom	William A. Graham	May 31, 1875
Stephen D. Pool	William A. Graham	May 31, 1875
Montford McGehee	William A. Graham	June 1, 1875
William A. Graham	Montford McGehee	June 6, 1875
Barnas Sears	William A. Graham	June 7, 1875
William A. Graham	Cornelia Phillips Spencer	June 7, 1875
John Hill Wheeler	William A. Graham	June 9, 1875
William A. Graham	David F. Caldwell	June 10, 1875
Samuel M. Hughes	William A. Graham	June 10, 1875 [with enclosures]
Newspaper Editorial		May 20, 1875 [enclosure]
Samuel M. Hughes	Stokes County Citizens	May 5, 1875 [enclosure]
Samuel M. Hughes	Stokes County Citizens	May 23, 1875 [enclosure]
Samuel M. Hughes	Stokes County Citizens	May 30, 1875 [enclosure]
E. J. Hale & Sons	William A. Graham	June 14, 1875 [with enclosures]
"E. K."	Editors of *New York Evening Post*	May 3, 1875 [enclosure]
"L. McC."	Editors of *New York Evening Post*	[May, 1875] [enclosure]
"X."	Editors of *New York Evening Post*	May 18, 1875 [enclosure]
Alexander McIver	William A. Graham	June 14 [1875]
Joseph Graham	William A. Graham	June 14, 1875
Alexander McIver	William A. Graham	June 19 [1875]
Charles J. Jenkins	William A. Graham	June 22, 1875
William P. Whyte	William A. Graham	June 25 [1875]
William A. Graham	Samuel M. Hughes	June 25, 1875
Raleigh T. Daniel	William A. Graham	June 29, 1875
Cornelia Phillips Spencer	William A. Graham	June 29, 1875
William P. Whyte	William A. Graham	July 1, 1875
William A. Graham	Cornelia Phillips Spencer	July 1, 1875
William A. Graham	Kemp P. Battle	July 9, 1875
George Davis	William A. Graham	July 13, 1875
Robert D. Graham	William A. Graham	July 14, 1875
Augustus H. Garland	William A. Graham	July 15, 1875
Donald MacRae	William A. Graham	July 16, 1875
William R. Cox	William A. Graham	July 16, 1875
Frederick A. P. Barnard	William A. Graham	July 16, 1875

William A. Graham	Orange County Citizens	July 17, 1875
William Reynolds	William A. Graham	July 21, 1875
William A. Graham	William A. Graham, Jr.	July 23, 1875
Samuel F. Phillips	Susan Washington Graham	July 31, 1875
George W. Graham	Susan Washington Graham	August 5, 1875 [telegram]
Augustus W. Graham	George W. Graham or Walter Clark	August 10, 1875
Robert R. Bridgers	Susan Washington Graham	August 11, 1875
John Hill Wheeler	Susan Washington Graham	August 11, 1875
Kate B. Washington	Susan Washington Graham	August 12, 1875
Proceedings of North Carolina Bar		August, 12 1875
Proceedings in North Carolina Supreme Court		August 13, 1875
Samuel F. Phillips	John W. Graham	August 13, 1875
George Washington	Susan Washington Graham	August 13, 1875
Newspaper Articles on Death of William A. Graham		August 13, 14, 1875
Zebulon B. Vance	Susan Washington Graham	August 14 [1875]
William A. Graham, Jr.	Julia Lane Graham	August 14, 1875
John C. Washington	Susan Washington Graham	August 15, 1875
William P. Whyte	Augustus W. Graham	August 16, 1875
C. A. Lewis	Susan Washington Graham	August 18, 1875
E. J. Hale	Augustus W. Graham	August 20, 1875
Resolutions of University Board of Trustees		August 31, 1875
Excerpts from Constitutional Convention Journal		September, 1875
Mary Washington Graham	Susan Washington Graham	September 12, 1875
Barnas Sears	Susan Washington Graham	September 13, 1875
Susan Washington Graham	William A. Graham, Jr.	September 29, 1875
William A. Graham	*Will*	1871
Proceedings of Peabody Fund Board of Trustees		October 8, 1875
Montford McGehee	John W. Graham	November 16, 1875
Robert D. Graham	Susan Washington Graham	November 29, 1875

After 1875

WRITTEN BY	WRITTEN TO	DATE
Alexander H. H. Stuart	Susan Washington Graham	June 7, 1877
William A. Graham, Jr.	R. D. W. Connor	September 20, 1907

ABBREVIATIONS USED TO DESIGNATE REPOSITORIES OF GRAHAM PAPERS

A&H	Division of Archives and History, North Carolina Department of Cultural Resources, William Alexander Graham Papers
A&H: Bryan	Division of Archives and History, North Carolina Department of Cultural Resources, John Herritage Bryan Collection
A&H: Clark	Division of Archives and History, North Carolina Department of Cultural Resources, Walter Clark Papers
A&H: Hale	Division of Archives and History, North Carolina Department of Cultural Resources, Edward Jones Hale Papers
A&H: Little-Mordecai	Division of Archives and History, North Carolina Department of Cultural Resources, Little-Mordecai Collection
A&H: Spencer	Division of Archives and History, North Carolina Department of Cultural Resources, Cornelia Phillips Spencer Papers
A&H: Swain	Division of Archives and History, North Carolina Department of Cultural Resources, David L. Swain Papers
A&H: Wiley	Division of Archives and History, North Carolina Department of Cultural Resources, Calvin H. Wiley Papers
A&H: Worth	Division of Archives and History, North Carolina Department of Cultural Resources, Jonathan Worth Papers
Duke	Duke University Library, Manuscript Department, William Alexander Graham Papers

Duke: Jones	Duke University Library, Manuscript Department, Charles Colcock Jones, Jr., Papers
LC: American Colonization Society	Library of Congress, American Colonization Society Collection
UNC	University of North Carolina Library at Chapel Hill, Southern Historical Collection, William Alexander Graham Papers
UNC: Barringer	University of North Carolina Library at Chapel Hill, Southern Historical Collection, Daniel Moreau Barringer Papers
UNC: Battle	University of North Carolina Library at Chapel Hill, Southern Historical Collection, Battle Family Papers
UNC: Gorrell	University of North Carolina Library at Chapel Hill, Southern Historical Collection, Ralph Gorrell Papers
UNC: Mordecai	University of North Carolina Library at Chapel Hill, Southern Historical Collection, George W. Mordecai Papers
UNC: Polk, Badger, McGehee	University of North Carolina Library at Chapel Hill, Southern Historical Collection, Polk, Badger, and McGehee Family Papers
UNC: Ruffin	University of North Carolina Library at Chapel Hill, Southern Historical Collection, Thomas Ruffin Papers
UNC: Sparrow	University of North Carolina Library at Chapel Hill, Southern Historical Collection, Thomas Sparrow Papers
UVA: Hunter	University of Virginia Library, Manuscript Department, Robert M. T. Hunter Papers

1869

William A. Graham, Jr.,[1] *to William A. Graham* DUKE

January, 1869

. . . .

I am going ahead with my coaling[2] and think I shall realize something from it. Barnett[3] has commenced to clear the piece of woods next [to] the Duncan field on the other side of the creek. I give him $3.37 ½ pr load and I get $6. I have to haul the coal. Wilkes[4] has paid me up very well so far. . . . My cotton press has been doing very well but takes too many hands to get the bales down.

---

[1]William Alexander Graham, Jr. (1839-1923), was born in Hillsborough and educated at the University of North Carolina (1856-1859) and Princeton College (A.B., 1860). Like his father, he opposed secession initially, but he served during the Civil War as a captain of North Carolina cavalry. Wounded in the Gettysburg campaign, he subsequently became a major and assistant adjutant general of North Carolina troops. His wife was Julia Lane (1848-1909) of Virginia, whom he married in 1864. After the war William Graham became a successful farmer in Lincoln County. He represented his county in the state Senate for two terms and in the state House for one term. From 1899 until 1908 he was a member of the state board of agriculture; and from 1908 until his death in 1923 he was commissioner of agriculture. During his tenure as commissioner North Carolina's national ranking in total value of crops produced rose from twenty-third to fifth. Cornelia Phillips Spencer Alumni Directory Project, University of North Carolina at Chapel Hill, hereinafter cited as Spencer Alumni Project; William S. Powell (ed.), *Dictionary of North Carolina Biography* (Chapel Hill: University of North Carolina Press, projected multivolume series, 1979—), II, 339-340, hereinafter cited as Powell, *DNCB*.

[2]Earlier correspondence indicated that the process of producing charcoal from wood was being tried at the Lincoln County plantation. The charcoal was used on the Graham farm and was sold to others, as well.

[3]The Lincoln County farms had a supervisor named Barnett, who has not been further identified.

[4]Charles Wilkes (1798-1877), a native of New York, was a naval officer, explorer, and writer who entered the navy in 1818. His interests were largely scientific. He was prominent in the depot of charts and instruments, out of which grew the naval observatory and hydrographic office. Beginning in 1838 and continuing for several years, Wilkes commanded a six-ship squadron of scientific explorers to Antarctica. Early in the Civil War he became a national hero when, while commanding the *San Jacinto*, he stopped the British steamer *Trent* and removed the Confederate commissioners Mason and Slidell. In 1862 he was promoted to commodore and in 1866 named admiral on the retired list. For a few years after the Civil War Wilkes owned and operated the High Shoals Ironworks, located on a tract of some 14,250 acres lying in Lincoln and Gaston counties. Mark Mayo Boatner III, *The Civil War Dictionary* (New York: David McKay Company, 1959), 925, hereinafter cited as Boatner, *Civil War Dictionary*; William L. Sherrill, *Annals of Lincoln County, North Carolina* (Charlotte, 1937; Baltimore: Regional Publishing Company, 1967), 65, hereinafter cited as Sherrill, *Annals of Lincoln County.*

Edward C. Cabell[1] *to William A. Graham* UNC

Southern Land Agency
New York,
Jan 1869

With a view to the practice of my profession, as well as for the more efficient prosecution of the Southern Land Agency in which I have been for some months engaged, I have formed a partnership with Judge Orlando Dorsey,[2] one of the soundest lawyers I know, & in all respects a very intelligent business man; and I can now confidently assure the most prompt & efficient attention to any kind of business entrusted to us.

In preparing a circular we wish to refer to some one prominent gentleman from each State, and I have taken the liberty to refer to you from Nor. Carolina.

I trust that you will not, in view of the kindly relations for a long time existing between us, consider that I have taken too great a liberty.

I am now keeping house in New York, near Mrs. Crittenden's,[3] and should be very happy to see you at my house, as would be my wife.

---

[1]Edward Carrington Cabell (1816-1896), a native of Virginia, graduated from the state university at Charlottesville in 1836. He settled in Florida and was a delegate to the territorial convention to draft a state constitution. He was admitted to the bar in 1840. When Florida became a state, Cabell served briefly in Congress in the winter of 1845-1846. Later he returned to the House of Representatives for three terms as a Whig, only to be defeated in the election of 1852. In 1859 he relocated his legal practice in St. Louis, Missouri. During the Civil War, Cabell served the Confederacy as a lieutenant colonel. After practicing law in New York (1868-1872), he returned to Missouri, where he was a member of the state Senate for four years (1878-1882). *Biographical Directory of the American Congress, 1774-1971 . . .* (Washington: United States Government Printing Office, 1971), 644, hereinafter cited as *Biographical Directory of Congress.*

[2]Judge Orlando Dorsey has not been further identified.

[3]Mrs. Crittenden has not been identified definitively. It seems logical that she was Mrs. John Jordan Crittenden of Kentucky, who might then have been living in New York with a daughter. For a biographical sketch of John Jordan Crittenden see T. Apoleon Cheney to William A. Graham, March 1, 1871, note 1, in this volume.

George W. Graham[1] *to William A. Graham* UNC

Univ of Va
Jan 5th 1869

My dear father

Your much esteemed letter, containing the money ($80.00) for which I am very much obliged, came to hand today. I wrote to Gus[2] a few days since and told him to ask you to send me a hundred dollars as I found after writing to you that eighty would not be enough. So if convenient please send me twenty dollars about the first of next month. The expenses here are much higher than represented in the catalogue. The Faculty charge us $12.00 a ton for coal and on each ton make about four dollars. Coal is selling in Richmond at retail for six or seven dollars and I should think could be much cheaper at wholesale the way it is bought for the University.

One of the students shot a bar room keeper through the leg last night and has run away as the sheriff was going to arrest him.

It is a flesh wound through the thigh & I believe not considered dangerous.

There has been a great deal of drinking here this session but as the college laws are so very lenient nothing has been done to stop it, in fact the Faculty dont seem to wish to find it out, and a man can drink as much as he desires just so he commits no other misdemeanor and misses no lectures. Chapel Hill was very much abused because it was said that the students did not study there and as compared with this Institution I think I think [*sic*] that the students studied as well in proportion to the number at the U.N.C. as those here.

I am sorry to hear that Roberts[3] transaction with Sinclair[4] turned out so badly. The Sentinel[5] began to come last week, for which I am very much obliged.

Love to all.

Your affectionate son

---

[1]George Washington Graham (1847-1923) received the A.B. degree from the University of North Carolina in 1868, attended the University of Virginia, and graduated with honors in medicine from the University of New York in 1870. He practiced in Atlanta and Raleigh before settling in Charlotte in 1880, where he became a foremost member of his profession. Spencer Alumni Project.

[2]Augustus Washington Graham (1849-1936) was the youngest Graham son to attain his maturity. He graduated from the University of North Carolina in 1868; obtained his law license in 1872; was a Hillsborough commissioner, 1875-1885; state senator, 1885-1887; member of the state House in 1901, 1903, 1905, 1909 (Speaker), and the extra session of 1913; secretary to the Virginia-Maryland Boundary Commission, 1874-1877; superior court judge, 1895-1897; and president of the American cotton exchange, 1919-1922. He was a Democrat and, after 1888, resided in Oxford. Upon Graham's death the *Oxford Public Ledger* commented: "He was a man of probity and industry and his keen intellect and interest in things and people made him one of the most popular men in the state during the active years of his life." Spencer Alumni Project; *Oxford Public Ledger*, October 16, 1936; Powell, *DNCB*, II, 330.

[3]Robert Davidson Graham (1842-1905), the fifth son of William A. Graham, farmed in Mecklenburg County before the Civil War. He attained the rank of captain in the Fifty-sixth North Carolina Regiment and was wounded in 1865. Besides being a lawyer and farmer, Robert Graham held various government appointments, 1884-1890. He never married. Spencer Alumni Project; W. A. Graham Clark (comp.), "Descendants of James Graham (1714-1763) of Ireland and Pennsylvania" (Washington, D.C., 1940), genealogical chart in the William A. Graham Papers, Southern Historical Collection, University of North Carolina Library at Chapel Hill, hereinafter cited as Clark, "Graham Descendants"; Walter Clark (ed.), *Histories of the Several Regiments and Battalions from North Carolina in the Great War, 1861-'65* (Raleigh and Goldsboro: State of North Carolina, 5 volumes, 1901), III, 314, 323, 331, 372, hereinafter cited as Clark, *Histories of the North Carolina Regiments*; Powell, *DNCB*, II, 337.

[4]Sinclair evidently was involved in the farming transactions of Robert Graham, who operated one of the family plantations.

[5]This is the Raleigh *Sentinel*, various editors of which included Seaton Gales, William E. Pell, Josiah W. Turner, and Theodore Kingsbury. It is especially enlightening to read the *Sentinel* for 1869-1871 for a Conservative version of the events of those years.

Jonathan Worth[1] *to William A. Graham* A&H

Raleigh
Jan. 9th 1969

Frank Wheeler,[2] a son of Jesse Wheeler,[3] the father well and favorably known to you I presume, desires to be appointed assessor of Int. Rev. in the Greensboro District to fill vacancy soon to occur by the resignation of his father. I know him well and have recommended his appointment to Prest. Johnson,[4] as a young man well qualified—of exemplary moral character and more acceptable to the respectable people of this district than any person I know who can take the teste oath and be confirmed by the Senate. He belongs to a class of men in Guilford who voted for Grant,[5] but who detest Holden,[6] Deweese,[7] Tourgée[8] & Co. and who do not approve of the reconstruction measures. His competitor, as I understand, hopes to be preferred on the ground of superior loyalty. Mr. Wheeler thinks anything you can say for him, based on my recomendation or other source of information (he says you do not personally know him) would be likely to benefit him.

If you think proper to say anything, and I suppose any Guilford gentleman will confirm my representation, I will forward what you may say to him.

---

[1]This letter also appears in J. G. de Roulhac Hamilton (ed.), The *Correspondence of Jonathan Worth* (Raleigh: North Carolina Historical Commission, 2 volumes, 1909), II, 1268.

Worth (1802-1869), a Quaker, had studied law under Archibald De Bow Murphey and was married to Martita Daniel, Murphey's niece. He had a distinguished political career climaxed by his election as governor in 1865. He was reelected in 1866. During his tenure of office Congress passed the reconstruction acts setting up five military districts in the South. Civil governments were declared provisional. Worth was adroit in reconciling hostile state factions, allaying suspicions of the Johnson administration, and coping with adverse northern opinion. He favored ratification of the Constitution of 1866 but did not approve of the Fourteenth Amendment. Allen Johnson, Dumas Malone, and others (eds.), *Dictionary of American Biography* (New York: Charles Scribner's Sons, 20 volumes, 1928; index and updating supplements), XX, 536, hereinafter cited as *DAB*.

[2]Except for the information in this letter, Frank Wheeler has not been identified.

[3]Jesse Wheeler, a native of Guilford County, was one of the founding stockholders in the Randolph Manufacturing Company, which established a cotton mill at Franklinville, Randolph County, in 1840. A friend of Jonathan Worth from those days, he was superintendent of the company at one time. In 1861 he fled North Carolina after being tried for helping the Reverend Daniel Worth distribute copies of Hinton Rowan Helper's *The Impending Crisis of the South.* A staunch Unionist, he remained in Indiana during the Civil War. Richard L. Zuber, *Jonathan Worth: A Biography of a Southern Unionist* (Chapel Hill: University of North Carolina Press, 1965), 33, hereinafter cited as Zuber, *Jonathan Worth*; *Randolph County, 1779-1979* (Winston-Salem: Hunter Publishing Company, 1980), 76-78, hereinafter cited as *Randolph County*; William T. Auman and David D. Scarboro, "The Heroes of America in Civil War North Carolina," *North Carolina Historical Review*, LVII (October, 1981), 337-338, hereinafter cited as Auman and Scarboro, "Heroes of America."

[4]President Andrew Johnson was in the position of a "lame duck," awaiting the inauguration of General Ulysses S. Grant, who had been elected president in November, 1868.

[5]Ulysses Simpson Grant (1822-1885), of Ohio, emerged from the Civil War as the principal northern military hero. He was drawn into the maelstrom of Reconstruction

politics and his reputation was tarnished by two undistinguished terms as president. Grant, although honest and well meaning, was simply out of his element. For two years after retiring as president, he enjoyed a triumphal world tour. Impoverished by the failure of an ill-considered business venture, Grant spend the last months of his life writing the two-volume *Personal Memoirs of U. S. Grant,* one of the greatest autobiographies in the English language. *DAB,* VII, 492-501; Boatner, *Civil War Dictionary,* 352-353.

[6]William Woods Holden (1818-1892), a native of Orange County, had been since 1843 editor of the partisan *North Carolina Standard* (Raleigh), the outstanding Democratic organ in the state. Holden had been a powerful force in the revitalization of the Democratic party but was denied the party's support for the high public offices that he coveted, as when Thomas Bragg was elected to the United States Senate. Never one to be trammeled by political philosophies, Holden was successively a Whig, a secession Democrat, a Unionist during the Civil War, and a Republican. He was appointed provisional governor by Andrew Johnson, was defeated for the governorship by Jonathan Worth late in 1865, and was elected to that position in 1868 after the franchise had been broadened and the freedmen galvanized to the Republican party. Holden was impeached in 1870 and in 1871 was convicted and removed from office. Holden, clearly a man of energy and ability, was one of the most controversial figures in North Carolina history. *DAB,* X, 138-140; Samuel A. Ashe and others (eds.), *Biographical History of North Carolina: From Colonial Times to the Present* (Greensboro: Charles L. Van Noppen, 8 volumes, 1905-1917), III, 184-206, hereinafter cited as Ashe, *Biographical History;* John Gilchrist McCormick, *Personnel of the Convention of 1861* (Chapel Hill: University of North Carolina Press, 1900), 45-46, hereinafter cited as McCormick, *Convention Personnel.*

[7]John Thomas Deweese (1835-1906) was born in Arkansas and was taught in his early years by his mother. He studied law and began his practice in Henderson, Kentucky. During the Civil War Deweese served in the Union forces and rose to the rank of colonel, although he never served in that capacity. After the war he moved to North Carolina and was elected to Congress in 1867, an office he resigned in 1870 pending the investigation of questionable appointments to the United States military and naval academies. Along with the other men mentioned in this letter, he was involved in the railroad frauds that occurred in North Carolina. *Biographical Directory of Congress,* 805; Joseph G. de Roulhac Hamilton, *Reconstruction in North Carolina* (1914; Gloucester, Mass.: Peter Smith, 1964), 430, 633, hereinafter cited as Hamilton, *Reconstruction in North Carolina;* Powell, *DNCB,* II, 61-62.

[8]Albion Winegar Tourgée (1838-1905), one of the best-known carpetbaggers to settle in North Carolina, had been twice wounded while serving as an enlistee in the Twenty-seventh New York Regiment. A native of Ohio temporarily in New York to attend the University of Rochester, Tourgée was admitted to the Ohio bar in 1864. He moved to Greensboro in the fall of 1865; there he opened a legal practice and organized an unsuccessful nursery company. In 1866 he entered politics, speaking at the Southern Loyalist Convention (Philadelphia) and publishing the *Union Register,* a new Greensboro weekly, from January to June, 1867. His purpose was to promote Radical Republican policies for the "poor, misguided, and mismanaged South." He was instrumental in securing the inclusion of a proviso in the Constitution of 1868 calling for the codification of state law. Later he participated in the codification process. From 1868 to 1874 he was a superior court judge. An excellent judge in nonpolitical cases, Tourgée tried unsuccessfully to use the bench as a stepping-stone to Congress. Eventually he left the state and settled in Maysville, New York, where he was a journalist, novelist, and lecturer. He described his perception of the reconstruction process in several novels, the best known of which is *A Fool's Errand* (1879). *DAB,* XVIII, 603-605.

William A. Graham to William A. Smith[1] UNC

Hillsboro
January 16th 1869

In compliance with the provision of Article 7th of the Mortgage Deed executed to me by the North Carolina Railroad Company, I have received into the sinking fund and cancelled as of the first day of January 1869, the following bonds and their coupons, issued and secured by the terms of said deed:

Namely, seventy Bonds of said company for Five Hundred dollars each, dated November 1st 1867, and running till November 1st 1877, and numbered from 330 to 389, inclusive; grand total of the principal of said Bonds being sixty five thousand dollars, and all having coupons attached payable from 1st of May 1869 till the maturity of said Bonds respectively: Which said cancelled Bonds and coupons I hold ready for the inspection of the committee of Finance of the company.

The Bonds of the company also issued under said Mortgage deed, and running twenty years from the said 1st of November 1867, having been but recently put forth, & their coupons commencing to be payable the 1st of May 1869, I deferred until the 1st of January 1870, and inactive on account of them.

All which is certified as required by the directive of the article aforesaid.

I am very Respectfully
Your Obdt Srvt
W. A. Graham
Trustee

P.S. Cancellation performed by cutting the seal, the signatures of the President and Trustee, and across the coupons.

---

[1]William Alexander Smith (1828-1888), a native of Warren County, attended the common schools and engaged in agricultural pursuits. He was a delegate to the Constitutional Convention of 1865, a state senator in 1870, president of the North Carolina Railroad and the Yadkin River Railroad, and a Republican congressman (1873-1875). *Biographical Directory of Congress*, 1625.

While no attempt has been made to include all of Graham's correspondence regarding his trusteeship of the North Carolina Railroad, this letter is typical.

David F. Caldwell[1] *to William A. Graham* UNC

Greensboro, N.C.,
January 18th., 1869.

I am satisfied that the thieves in and about Raleigh, have resolved to sell, or mortgage, all the State's interest in our Rail Roads to Holden, Littlefield,[2] Swepson,[3] Laflin,[4] & Co. Indeed, I may say I know this fact. I am largely interested in the stock of the road (the N.C.), and paid par for it, and more in hard labor, to say nothing of the risk I hazzarded in becoming a contractor. Consequently, I do not wish to be swindled out of my hard earnings by a set of unprincipled Scalawags & Carpet bagers. But I am satisfied they will succeed, if vigorous efforts are not taken to defeat their unholy combinations and purposes. I am in favor of calling a convention of all the individual stockholders, the holders of the 2 millions of bonds issued to pay the State's subscription to the road, & those interested in the mortgage now upon the road, to meet in convention at some central point, and agree to act together in adopting and carrying out some plan or system that will be calculated to secure and protect our respective interests.

You are doubtless aware that both in the charter of the N.C. Rail Road, as is also the case on the face of the two millions of bonds first issued to meet the State's subscription to the capital stock of the road, that the income of the road, over and above runing expenses, is pledged for the payment of the interest arising upon the said bonds, as well as the bonds themselves, in the event the State should fail to do so. Next came the preferred million. Then the 8 percent loan, & subsequently the mortgage. Then a pledge of the stock for the payment of the bonds to extend the road West from Salisbury. And the other day, the revenue, or income of the road, as well as the road itself, to raise money to pay Swepson's cuponds at par, which he bought at 60 cts. on the dollar, etc., etc. Now, my dear Sir, we can, or rather, you can, if you will but go to work and have a convention called of the parties interested in the 2 millions of bonds, the individual stockholders and all the other roads, but especially the individual stockholders in the N.C.R.R., and those who hold the 8 percent bonds, or those who are interested in the mortgage, the road can be saved, and made [to] pay handsomely. I know, I feel certain, that these great ends can be attained. Besides, such a convention would have a moral weight that would tell with great effect and *power upon the masses*, that would enable and encourage them to throw off the party shackles that have bound them to the rotten and corrupt central Holden clique. Will you, for one time in your life, act upon a suggestion made by one so humble as myself. I feel if you and such other gentlemen of the State as you may choose to associate with you, will make a call for a convention to meet early in the Spring, and to be composed of the parties named, but the call to be made more prominently for the individual stockholders in all, or in the N.C. Rail Road, as you may think best. We can, by so doing, organize a party, force, or power, I care not what you may choose to call it, that will be able to dethrone Holden, and his thieving, efemoral, Scalawag & Carpet bag host. I do not conceive it possible to originate any other movement that is likely to prove so efficient, to effect the great and constant desire of so many patriotic hearts within our borders.

The individual stockholders, backed by the capitalists in building the N.C.R.R., (the cheapest Road, all things considered, I have been frequently told, that has ever been built in America) are a *peculiar*, a *patriotic, deserving and* influential people, and if you, backed by others, will but make a call that will bring them all together in one place, we can organize, or rather, originate, a force in connection with the road as it extends West, that may be made to tell, with Herculean power, upon the future destinies of the State. The Road is a sicker man than Turckey, and will sooner fall into the hands of the Ring at Raleigh than Constantinople into the hands of

Zaar of Rusia, if we do not manage in the way I have managed, to prevent it. The stockholders, bondholders, & mortgagees can prevent this by making a joint effort to do so.

And mark the prediction, by no other means, or in no other way. I do hope, as you and I were at the inseption of this truly noble work, you will concent to call a convention, at as early a day as you may think practicable, to consider all such matters as may be calculated to promote or further the cause of Internal Improvements in N.C.

. . . .

---

[1]David Franklin Caldwell (1814-1898), of Guilford County, was active as a merchant, lawyer, and financier at various times in his career. An ardent Union Whig, he served five terms in the House of Commons in the antebellum period (1848-1859), and again in 1864. His loyalty to the Confederate cause was suspect; he was denied a commission in the army but served two years as a common soldier. Caldwell was a delegate to the Constitutional Convention of 1865 and a member of the state Senate in 1879. He was particularly interested in railroad building and was a prime mover in the North Carolina Railroad, the Greensboro and Cheraw, and the Cape Fear and Yadkin Valley. R. D. W. Connor (comp. and ed.), *A Manual of North Carolina . . . 1913* (Raleigh: North Carolina Historical Commission, 1913), 634-635, 882, hereinafter cited as Connor, *North Carolina Manual, 1913*; *Greensboro Patriot*, January 4, 1819; John L. Cheney, Jr. (ed.), *North Carolina Government, 1585-1977: A Narrative and Statistical History* . . . (Raleigh: North Carolina Department of the Secretary of State, second, updated edition, 1981), 317-318, 321, 323, 326, 331, 458, hereinafter cited as Cheney, *North Carolina Government*; Powell, *DNCB*, I, 302-303.

[2]Milton Smith Littlefield (1830-1899), Union general and "Prince of Carpetbaggers," was a native of New York who lived in Michigan and Illinois before the Civil War period. He rose from captain to brevet brigadier general, gaining citations for his actions at Shiloh. A business promoter with close ties to leading Republicans and northern financiers, Littlefield moved to North Carolina in 1867, where he became state chairman of the Union League and Republican lobbyist for all party projects during the Holden administration, 1868-1870. Allegedly he paid $240,000 in bribes to state legislators and received a five percent fee for securing a multimillion-dollar state bond issue for several North Carolina railroads. In 1869 he and George Swepson, a leading Democratic banker and railroad promoter, joined in a scheme to gain control of three Florida railroads, using the bonds of the Western North Carolina Railroad as security. Neither man was convicted of fraud, but their actions revealed much about the reconstruction process in the South. David C. Roller and Robert W. Twyman (eds.), *The Encyclopedia of Southern History* (Baton Rouge: Louisiana State University Press, 1979), 728-729, hereinafter cited as Roller and Twyman, *Encyclopedia of Southern History*.

[3]In 1868 George Swepson, a native of North Carolina, and Milton S. Littlefield, of New York, gained control of the Western Division of the Western North Carolina Railroad Company. As president from October of that year until October, 1869, Swepson misappropriated a large sum of money derived from the sale of special tax bonds by the state of North Carolina. He invested heavily in the Florida Railroad Company. Swepson's gross mishandling of finances evolved into a tangled web of legal problems that eventually involved not only the states of North Carolina and Florida but also European countries and individuals, particularly bondholders in Holland. Some of the most important men in North Carolina were duped by Swepson, an error in judgment that cost the state millions. C. K. Brown, "The Florida Investments of George W. Swepson," *North Carolina Historical Review*, V (July, 1928), 275-298.

[4]Byron Laflin (1821-1901) of New York, a native of Massachusetts and a brother of New York congressman Addison Henry Laflin, was brevetted brigadier general for his excellent Civil War service in the Thirty-fourth New York Regiment. After being mustered out of service in June, 1863, he settled in Pitt County, North Carolina, as soon as practicable for a northern man to do so. He was one of the first carpetbaggers to enter politics, calling for

and attending the Southern Unionists' Convention in Philadelphia. He represented Pitt County in the Constitutional Convention of 1868 and in the state legislature (1868-1870). In the latter position he was chairman of the Committee on Internal Improvements and the floor leader of the Littlefield-Swepson ring. Utterly corrupt, he was involved in every sort of dishonesty. When asked, upon leaving Raleigh at the end of the 1870 legislative session, whether or not he was coming back, Laflin replied, "Is there anything left to come back for?" Boatner, *Civil War Dictionary*, 469; *Biographical Directory of Congress*, 1183; Hamilton, *Reconstruction in North Carolina*, 179; Jonathan Daniels, *Prince of Carpetbaggers* (New York: J. B. Lippincott, 1958), 177-178, 230, hereinafter cited as Daniels, *Prince of Carpetbaggers*.

Augustus H. Garland[1] *to William A. Graham* A&H

Little Rock, Arkansas,
January 20th., 1869.

Your kind favor of the 11th. inst. came to hand, in due time, and I hasten to make a short reply.

Mr. Stephens[2] wrote me a long letter in answer to the one I sent you & him, but he did not approve of the plan, as he thought Grant knew all about affairs in our States,—as much as our leading men could tell him—and he seems to place great confidence in Grant's sense and patriotism, much more I believe, than either you or myself would. I did not answer Mr. S's letter, but left the matter there. The main point with me was for our representative men to assure Grant they would give him a cordial & generous support in the Southern States, and to make this impression on him before he was moulded, or manipulated by the fierce &, I fear, unrelenting spirit of the party whose candidate he was in the late presidential contest. Now, I greatly fear his trip East, to which you allude, has subjected him to influences which it will be difficult, if not, in truth, impossible, for our friends to remove, or in any way to counteract. I am of the opinion now, that he will be still, and permit his rulers to do as they please, and will take no stand positively. I believe, as you intimate, he has no ideas of his own, about the great questions that are to come before him as President. And in truth, the terrible outrages from which we are suffering in this State, (the one tenth of which you know nothing) will be upheld and sustained by him. I feel pretty satisfied that those in power here have a direct assurance of this. In this event our country is hopelessly gone.

I will not attend the Supreme Court this winter. I have some few cases there, but will submit them on briefs. I would be glad indeed to see you, & to talk freely with you. Be kind enough to write me after your trip to Baltimore, I would take it as an especial favor. I have pretty much lost all hope. I see nothing but trouble and suffering ahead for our people, but I am always glad to read or hear your views, for I know they are always considered. And I hope you will have a full and frank conversation with Grant, & try to "pump" one idea out of him.

I am hard at work, making a living—nothing more. I hope to hear from you before long.

---

[1]Augustus Hill Garland (1832-1899), a lawyer and politician, was a native of Tennessee,

but his family had settled in Arkansas while Garland was still an infant. A graduate of St. Joseph's College, he supported the Bell-Everett ticket in 1860 and opposed secession until the shelling of Fort Sumter. He served in the Confederate Congress as a representative (1861-1864) and as a senator (1864-1865). Having received a pardon from Andrew Johnson, Garland set about to reconstruct his state and class. He was elected to the United States Senate in 1866 and 1867 but was denied his seat by the Republican majority. Moreover, in the case *Ex parte Garland* he held that Congress had acted illegally in barring from practice before the United States Supreme Court those who could not take the ironclad oath required by Congress. The Court appparently agreed with his contention that Congress had violated the Constitution by passing an *ex post facto* law. A leader of the Arkansas Redeemers, he was governor (1874-1876) and United States senator (1877-1885). As United States attorney general in the first Cleveland administration (1885-1889), Garland held the most prominent post in the federal government of any southern Democrat since the Civil War. Roller and Twyman, *Encyclopedia of Southern History*, 509; Ezra J. Warner and W. Buck Yearns, *Biographical Register of the Confederate Congress* (Baton Rouge: Louisiana State University Press, 1975), 95-96, hereinafter cited as Warner and Yearns, *Biographical Register of the Confederate Congress*.

[2]Alexander Hamilton Stephens (1812-1883), of Georgia, was one of the most influential men in the South. After long service in the Georgia legislature, he began his national career as a states' rights Whig congressman, 1843-1859; but his concern for southern rights took him into the Democratic party about 1856. He was a bitter opponent of the Wilmot Proviso but counseled acceptance of the Compromise of 1850 and was largely responsible for the Georgia Platform. By the late 1850s he had begun to defend slavery as a positive good. He mistakenly believed that the South's place in the Union was safe at the time of his retirement from Congress in 1859. Following the election of Lincoln, Stephens succeeded in preventing Georgia's early rush to secession by a powerful speech delivered November 14, 1860; he advocated deliberation, with extreme action to be taken only after the infringement of southern rights. His speech attracted national attention and opened the way for a significant exchange of letters between Lincoln and Stephens. Lincoln was conciliatory but declined to give specific assurances. When the Georgia secession convention met in January, Stephens spoke only briefly, recommending that a southern convention be called.

He was elected vice-president of the Confederacy but exercised little influence as he became increasingly disgruntled with the Davis administration for what he considered encroachments upon the rights of the Confederate states. His plans for gaining independence by negotiation proved futile at the Hampton Roads Conference. A supporter of presidential reconstruction, Stephens was elected to the United States Senate in 1865 but was barred. Although he opposed congressional reconstruction, he advised acceptance. Stephens returned to the House of Representatives for ten years and was elected governor of Georgia a few months before his death. His *Constitutional View of the Late War between the States* (published 1868, 1870) is a valuable statement of the states' rights philosophy. *DAB*, XVII, 569-575.

Joseph G. Morrison[1] *to William A. Graham* UNC

San Joaquin Valley,
California
Jan 21st 69

My dear Uncle,

When I left North Carolina I promised to write you as soon as I became settled in business. I remained in San Francisco four or five months hoping to get into some suitable employment, but was disappointed, and at the suggestion of Dr. R. P. Ashe[2]—formerly of N.C.—I came to this valley with a view of farming. This move was very fortunate for me. I have located in a fertile section of country—have purchased 640 acres of good land & am now hard at work putting in a crop of wheat. Owing to the peculiar climate of California it is particularly adapted to wheat raising and for several years past this has been a most profitable occupation. There are a good many fears expressed about the business being over done, but I think unless some combination is made by shipping speculators that the price will always keep up, as California wheat enters the markets of Europe & the Eastern States—& the price will be regulated by them. We sow wheat here as late as March, and frequently 'tis the 1st of Jan before the ground is wet enough to commence ploughing. I have fifty acres now down & am getting in about 15 acres a week. I use a gang of three ploughs—four horses—and I have a seed-sower that sows eight feet—with a harrow attached. It sows much more evenly than by hand & is scarcely no labor.

Cousin Tom Witherspoon[3] & his brother-in-law, Hatch,[4] & three other young men from Ala. have rented land for two years within six miles of me. Cousin Tom expects his wife out in a few weeks. Thos Roulhac[5] is farming 10 miles from me. I see him occasionally—also Thos Devereaux[6] of Raleigh—who is near. They were both classmates with me at Dr. Wilson's[7]

A good many Southerners are coming to this section of California—principally from Ala & Miss. & the country is rapidly improving. For many years wealthy stockraisers have had control of the entire valley—(Gov'm't land). and have used every exertion to keep out settlers. But within the last two years there has been a change—and as last year was principally a test of the land for wheat & barley this year will bring many permanent residents.

My health has improved greatly since coming to this state—I thought at one time my lungs were affected, but they now have every appearance of being sound. I think the pure atmosphere here is fine for consumptives & hope it will prove a cure to Cousin Tom Witherspoon. He looks very thin & is not strong.

Remember me very kindly to Aunt Susan[8] & any other members of the family who may be at home.

---

[1]Joseph Graham Morrison (1842-1904), nephew of William A. Graham, was the son of Mary Graham and Robert Hall Morrison. During the Civil War he served as adjutant of the Fifty-seventh North Carolina Regiment and aide to General Stonewall Jackson, his brother-in-law, and later to Robert F. Hoke. He lost a foot in the engagement at Petersburg. Clark, "Graham Descendants"; Clark, *Histories of the North Carolina Regiments*, III, 427.

[2]Dr. R. P. Ashe has not been identified.

[3]Thomas Franklin Witherspoon (1825-1909), Graham's nephew, lived for a time in California and Kentucky before settling finally in Gallatin, Tennessee. He was the son of Graham's sister Sophia Graham Witherspoon (1791-1865) and her husband, Dr. John Ramsay Witherspoon (1774-1852), a native of Charleston, South Carolina. The Witherspoons settled at Brookland near Greensboro, Alabama. Clark, "Graham Descendants."

[4]Witherspoon's brother-in-law Hatch has not been further identified.

[5]Thomas Ruffin Roulhac (1846-1907), of Hillsborough, attended the Wilson school and the Hillsborough Military Academy, but the day after North Carolina seceded he ran away from school to become a soldier. Before he attained the age of fourteen, he was a Confederate drillmaster. Later he was a private and, after Gettysburg, a lieutenant in the Forty-ninth North Carolina Regiment. Captured at Five Forks, April 1, 1865, he was imprisoned briefly at Johnson's Island. Roulhac studied law with his eminent grandfather Thomas Ruffin, practiced in California, and married and settled in Alabama in 1870. He

practiced at Mobile, Greensboro, and Sheffield. He was a circuit court judge and later United States district attorney. Joel C. DuBose (ed.), *Notable Men of Alabama, Personal and Genealogical with Portraits* (Atlanta: Southern Historical Association, 2 volumes, 1904), II, 78-79.

[6]Thomas Pollock Devereux, Jr., was the son of John and Margaret Mordecai Devereux and the grandson of Thomas Pollock Devereux (1793-1869). He attended the Virginia Military Academy prior to joining the Confederate forces in 1863. He was courier for Brigadier General Junius Daniel, assigned to the Fourteenth Regiment. This regiment fought in several major engagements, including Gettysburg, Malvern Hill, and the Wilderness campaign of 1864. Beth G. Crabtree and James W. Patton (eds.), *"Journal of a Secesh Lady": The Diary of Catherine Ann Devereux Edmondston, 1860-1866* (Raleigh: Division of Archives and History, Department of Cultural Resources, 1979), xii, xxvii, 7n, 496n, hereinafter cited as Crabtree and Patton, *"Journal of a Secesh Lady."*

[7]Dr. Alexander Wilson conducted an excellent classical school at Melville in east Alamance County. Several of Graham's sons attended it. Walter Whitaker, *Centennial History of Alamance County, 1849-1949* (Burlington: Alamance County Historical Association, [1949]), 193, hereinafter cited as Whitaker, *Centennial History of Alamance.*

[8]Susannah Sarah (Susan) Washington Graham (1816-1890), daughter of John Washington of New Bern, married William A. Graham in 1836 and was his congenial, devoted, well-loved companion through successes and tribulations. She bore ten children, nine sons and one daughter. Clark, "Graham Descendants."

William A. Graham to Susan Washington Graham A&H

Baltimore,
Saturday, January 23rd., 1869

My Dear Wife

I have not before had an opportunity to write. We arrived here on Wednesday morning, as expected, had a full meeting of the Board,[1] except the member from New Orleans,[2]—Gen'l Grant present, and the City full of demonstrations of respect, etc. Many ladies of the Board here,—Mrs. Fish inquired kindly of you, as usual. The others you have not met in person. Mrs. Grant not here. There has been a party each evening, which, with the sessions of the Board, & visits to manufacturies by them, has kept me much occupied. I have seen but few of my old acquaintances.

I shall leave here for Washington today, and hope to get home Tuesday or Wednesday, whether in the morning or afternoon, I can't tell.

Mr. Peabody[3] is reported to be in very poor health. Mr. Winthrop[4] is here in tolerable spirits, but has evidently had a stroke of paralysis.

Rob't has formed many acquaintances, and will remain 'till night, & overtake me at Washington.

Love to all.

Ever affectionately Yours

---

[1]This reference is to the trustees of the Peabody Education Fund. They were Robert Charles Winthrop, Massachusetts; Hamilton Fish, New York; Bishop Charles Pettit McIlvaine, Ohio; President Ulysses Simpson Grant; Admiral David Glasgow Farragut, United States Navy; William Cabell Rives, Virginia; John Henry Clifford, Massachusetts; William Aiken, South Carolina; William Maxwell Evarts, New York; William Alexander Graham, North Carolina; Charles McAlester, Pennsylvania; George Washington Riggs,

Washington, D.C.; Samuel Wetmore, New York; Edward A. Bradford, Louisiana; George N. Eaton, Maryland; and George Peabody Russell, Massachusetts. Franklin Parker, *George Peabody: A Biography* (Nashvile: Vanderbilt University Press, 1971), 161-162, hereinafter cited as Parker, *George Peabody*.

[2]Edward A. Bradford (1813-1872), of Louisiana, was a graduate of Yale and the Harvard Law School. He was the law partner of Judah P. Benjamin before the war; Benjamin characterized him as the "most finished lawyer" he had ever known. Bradford was nominated to a position on the United States Supreme Court by Millard Fillmore, but he was not confirmed. His health failed about this time and he left New Orleans for Paris, where he spent his last years. Robert D. Meade, *Judah P. Benjamin, Confederate Statesman* (New York: Oxford University Press, 1943), 84, 95, 381.

[3]George Peabody (1795-1869) was a phenomenally successful merchant, financier, and philanthropist. His career in the business world began when he was only eleven years old, when he became an apprentice to a Danvers, Massachusetts, grocer. After a meteoric rise in the industrial world, Peabody in 1835 negotiated a loan in England, without a fee, for the state of Maryland, which was verging on bankruptcy. Two years later Peabody moved his residency to London, where he had already established the prestigious firm of George Peabody Company, which specialized in handling foreign exchange and American securities. He used much of his enormous wealth in philanthropic enterprises in America—a $1,500,000 fund to found the Peabody Institute at Baltimore; $250,000 for the Peabody Institute in Peabody, Massachusetts; and various other gifts for educational purposes. At the time of this letter, William A. Graham was serving on the original board appointed to administer the Peabody Education Fund of $3,500,000 for the promotion of education in the South. Peabody died in England later in 1869 and his body was returned for burial in Danvers, Massachusetts. Joseph G. E. Hopkins and others (eds.), *Concise Dictionary of American Biography* (New York: Charles Scribner's Sons, 1964), 774-775, hereinafter cited as *CDAB*.

[4]Robert Charles Winthrop (1809-1894) was a Bostonian who became life chairman of the Peabody Fund. After graduation from Harvard in 1828, Winthrop studied law in the office of Daniel Webster. He served Massachusetts in the United States House of Representatives (1840-1850) and from 1847 to 1849 was Speaker. When Webster resigned from the Senate in 1850, Winthrop, a Whig, was appointed as his successor but was defeated for reelection by Charles Sumner in 1851. Reluctant to oppose slavery, Winthrop was much in demand as an orator and was president of the Massachusetts Historical Society for thirty years. *CDAB*, 1236.

John H. Tillinghast[1] *to William A. Graham* UNC

Salisbury N.C.
Jan 25th/69

Having understood that you were agent for the "Peabody Education Fund" for this State; I write to make application for such pecuniary help, as may enable me to sustain and enlarge a charity school, wh[ich] I have recently undertaken here for the benefit of the poor white children of this community. I am now employing one teacher, with a school of 15 or 20; but c'd get to-gether easily from 50 to 100. I w'd make the effort if I had means to employ another teacher. The lady now employed, is relieved from pressing want for herself & 5 children by the small allowance wh[ich] so far I have been able to give her—I have no means to go on, save the monthly offering of my church, and such other assistance as comes from unsolicited donations. The undertaking so far, is a *double* charity as it gives employment to an unfortunate (cultivated) lady, and instruction to the poor children, who but for some such effort must grow up in ignorance & vice—There is no other effort or any prospect of any, looking to the same object. If you can process an appropriation therefore, I think I can safely promise that it shall be made available for the very purpose wh[ich] I conceive the Liberal Donor designed. I do not propose that it shall be *sectarian*, except in so far, as that I will be solely responsible, and will assume the entire control.

---

[1]John Huske Tillinghast (b. 1835) was a native of Hillsborough who attended the University of North Carolina in the 1850s. He taught school and in 1861 was ordained an Episcopalian deacon. After brief service as a minister in Rutherfordton, he was chaplain of the Forty-fourth North Carolina Regiment, 1862-1864. At the time of this letter he was rector in Salisbury. Later he served churches in Charleston and St. Johns, South Carolina. Daniel Lindsey Grant (ed.), *Alumni History of the University of North Carolina* (Durham: Christian and King Publishing Company, second edition, 1924), 623, hereinafter cited as Grant, *Alumni History*.

James A. Graham[1] *to William Graham* UNC

Graham N.C.
Feb 5th 1869

My dear Father

. . . .

Some persons pretending to belong to the Ku Klux organization, whipped an old negro man very severely one night last week, about 4 miles from here. He says they charged him with stealing wheat & chickens. One or two persons were arrested and tried before Squire Hardin[2] yesterday, but there was no evidence on which to commit any one, as they were all disguised and the only one whom the negro thought he recognised, proved that he was at home near the Shops at the time it happened. I saw a copy of the Hillsboro Recorder this morning and am glad to find it so much improved in appearance as well as the amount of news it contains. I see announced in it the deaths of old Mrs. Jenny McCauley[3] and Mrs. George Laws.[4]

I have been quite busy lately, have gotten some of Col Ruffin's[5] clients since he left and my business bids fair to increase this year 100 pr. ct over that of last year. Badham[6] has been away so much lately that the people are getting a good deal out with him and are commencing to say that he does not attend to his business.

I got a very good case week before last from which he had been discharged on account of his continued absence. Your old client Mrs. Delilah Allen[7] comes to see him quite often. She has quit coming to see me since I talked of charging her for advice, and I am truly glad of the riddance for she used to worry me a good deal. Please write me some time during the next week advising me concerning the cases I mentioned in the first part of letter. Love to all. Please say to Mother I will write to her soon.

Affectionately Your Son

---

[1]James Augustus Graham (1841-1909) graduated from the University of North Carolina in 1860. An officer in the Twenty-seventh North Carolina Regiment, Graham was wounded in action twice before his service to the Confederacy ended. He was a lawyer, state

senator, and university trustee after the war. Spencer Alumni Project; William A. Graham, Jr., *General Joseph Graham and His Papers on North Carolina Revolutionary History* (Raleigh: Edwards and Broughton, 1904), 183, hereinafter cited as Graham, *General Joseph Graham*; Connor, *North Carolina Manual, 1913.*

[2]Peter Hardin was a Republican magistrate in Alamance County. The episode to which this letter refers involved a black man named Caswell Holt. Allen W. Trelease, *White Terror: The Ku Klux Klan Conspiracy and Southern Reconstruction* (New York: Harper and Row, Publishers, Harper Torchbooks, 1972), 193-194, hereinafter cited as Trelease, *White Terror.*

[3]Mrs. Jenny McCauley has not been further identified.

[4]Mrs. Laws's husband, George (1808-1881), with Graham and others, had condemned the Ku Klux Klan and had recommended that Governor Holden commission Pride Jones to suppress the movement. Laws was a clerk of superior court for more than thirty years. Hugh Talmage Lefler and Paul Wager (eds.), *Orange County, 1752-1952* (Chapel Hill: Orange Printshop, 1953), 119, 193, 357, hereinafter cited as Lefler and Wager, *Orange County.*

[5]Thomas Ruffin, Jr. (1824-1889), of Orange County, was a graduate of the University of North Carolina (1844) who became a lawyer. A member of the Commons from Rockingham County, 1850-1852, he was a superior court judge, 1861-1862, and rose to the rank of colonel in Confederate service. Following in the steps of his illustrious father, he was an associate justice of the state supreme court, 1881-1883. Grant, *Alumni History*, 541; Cheney, *North Carolina Government,* 319, 362, 571.

[6]Henry Badham was a Graham lawyer who represented Caswell Holt in his attempts to secure legal redress against the Ku Klux Klan. Trelease, *White Terror*, 194.

[7]Mrs. Delilah Allen has not been identified.

F. J. Murdoch[1] to William A. Graham UNC

High Shoals Gaston Co
Feb 8th 69

It is now some four months since I came to take charge of a church in this county. I find that the people are living in most heathenish ignorance. The only schools near this place are most miserable. As a general thing the teachers are mere boys, being in most cases under twenty years of age.

We are now making an effort to build a school house here in which there is every prospect of being successful. The people here are poor and ought to have every encouragement to help themselves. The number of children who would attend the school is about seventy five. We have about that number connected with our Sunday School now.

Can we obtain any assistance from the Peabody fund to build a school house? Or if the rules of the Regents require that assistance shall be given only to educate but not to build, can we obtain assistance to educate some of the children here.

We are ready to agree with any requirements, and we are confident that we shall be able to educate on more liberal terms than any other institution in Carolina. The instruction will be thorough, and the school will be conducted on the Public School System.

Knowing no place where the people need assistance more than these do, and knowing that they are tired of the miserable system of school teaching they have had and are desiring better things. I write to find out whether any assistance can be obtained in any way for the people of this county.

[1]Francis J. Murdoch, born in Buncombe County in 1846, was a son of William and Margaret Nixon Murdoch, who had emigrated from Ireland to Pennsylvania. William was an excellent and progressive farmer, much interested in breeding fine cattle. Francis J. was educated at Colonel Stephen Lee's school in Asheville and later at the military academy of South Carolina. He entered the ministry in 1868 and was named pastor of St. John's Episcopal Church in Gaston County. From 1870 to 1872 he did missionary work in Asheville and in 1872 became rector of St. Luke's Episcopal Church in Salisbury, where he remained until his death. In 1890 the degree of doctor of sacred theology was conferred on him by the Episcopal University of the South at Sewanee, Tennessee. *Cyclopedia of Eminent and Representative Men of the Carolinas of the Nineteenth Century* (Madison, Wis.: Brant and Fuller, 2 volumes, 1892; Spartanburg: Reprint Company, 1973), II, 394-395, hereinafter cited as *Cyclopedia of Eminent Men.*

Randolph A. Shotwell[1] *to William A. Graham* UNC

Rutherfordton, N.C.,
February 8th., 1869.

Esteemed Sir:

Urged by strong personal considerations, and emboldened by public report of your generous courtesy, I take the liberty, which my acquaintance with you would by no means justify, to ask your endeavors, and influence in my behalf. And that you may the better recall who the writer is, permit me to mention a casual introduction by your son, James, at the cars in '67—during which year I was Editor of the New Bern Journal of Commerce—and, subsequently, our meeting at Rutherfordton at the time of your address to our people in '68.

My object in writing you may be briefly stated, as follows: In December last, on my twenty-fifth birthday, I gave up my newspaper, "The Western Vindicator," with the intention of studying law. Two months of study have convinced me that, before I can hope to rise in the profession, I must acquire a much better English and Classical education. But, as I have no means whatever, the idea of a collegiate course must be abandoned, unless I can secure some temporary accommodation. My father is a Presbyterian minister,[2] with a beggarly stipend, and there are no other avenues through which I could expect aid.

Under these circumstances, it has occurred to me that possibly, through yourself, as Trustee for the State of the Peabody Educational fund, I might *at least submit* the following proposition. If the committee will appropriate a sufficient sum to sustain an economical student for three years, at Davidson, Princeton, Virginia University, Yale, Washington College, or indeed, any college of character, I would gladly give bond for its reimbursement at the end of certain time, or give notes with sequrity for the same purpose.

This, I am aware, is a novel proposition; but it is an honest one, and a *dernier resort.*

I am aware also, that it will receive *no sort of consideration* from the Committee, *unless you feel sufficiently interested* to somewhat earnestly *advocate* it. And, in asking you to do this, I *have no appeal other than to your kindness, and known philanthropy,* in the cause of education.

It may be proper to add a few facts concerning myself, that you may understand the nature of the application.

And *first,* I would on *no account* ask it as an act of charity, but simply as an accomodation by which one of the many uneducated young men of the South may acquire means to benefit the State; *Second,* That the Committee may be assured the *funds are not misapplied,* let the *President* of the College, or *yourself,* direct their expenditure; *lastly,* of myself I may say that my character is at least untainted by crime or misdemeanor, that I left school in Pennsylvania in 1861 to cast my lot with the South; that I was promoted to a Captaincy, at 19 years of age, by order of Mr. Seddon,[3] Sec. of War, (I still have his commission, signed by President Davis); that I have been everything from a clerk to Editor of a Daily newspaper, and, subsequently, of a weekly; that I was considered worthy of the conservative nomination in Rutherford and Polk counties, for the convention to frame the new Constitution; that I was elected a delegate to the State Conservative Convention; of which I was a Secretary; and that it is my ambition to benefit my State, and species hereafter.

Please to overlook the prolixity of this communication, Dear Sir, and give it your *favorable* consideration. I should be pleased to have your views on its practicability, or otherwise, at as early a day as will be convenient.

If you will also consider this letter as entirely confidential, I shall be obliged.

With much regard, I remain, Sir.
Your ob't serv't
And friend

---

[1]Randolph A. Shotwell (1844-1885) became one of the most volatile and controversial figures of the Reconstruction era. He founded the *Western Vindicator* in 1868 and sold it to L. P. Erwin. The *Vindicator* was published 1868-1873. In 1869 Shotwell moved from Rutherfordton to Asheville, where he established the *Citizen,* a weekly newspaper. As a Ku Klux Klan leader, Shotwell was highly incensed in 1870 when Colonel V. S. Lusk, district attorney, sent bills of indictment to the Buncombe County grand jury against certain white men for "Ku-Kluxing some Negroes." Shotwell was not named but he harshly criticized Lusk in the *Citizen.* Shortly afterward the two men had a vicious quarrel on Pack Square. The quarrel developed into a fight that resulted in Lusk's drawing a pistol and shooting Shotwell in both legs. Shotwell gave Lusk a Masonic sign, effectively ending the fight; evidently Lusk was a fellow member of the Masonic Order. In 1872 Shotwell was convicted of "Ku-Kluxing" activities and was sentenced to a prison term to be served in Albany, New York. Ironically, it was Lusk, then the district attorney of the United States, who interceded for his old adversary and secured a pardon from President Grant. Shotwell returned to North Carolina, where he resumed his activities as a newspaperman and politician. He presumably bought the *Asheville News and Farmer,* a name he changed to the *Asheville Citizen.* From 1876 to 1877 he served as state representative from Mecklenburg County. Thad Stem, Jr., *The Tar Heel Press* (Charlotte: Heritage Printers, 1973), 51-52, 96-97, hereinafter cited as Stem, *Tar Heel Press*; Hamilton, *Reconstruction in North Carolina,* 462, 577-579; Cheney, *North Carolina Government,* 457; J. G. de Roulhac Hamilton (ed.), *The Papers of Randolph Abbott Shotwell* (Raleigh: North Carolina Historical Commission, 3 volumes, 1929-1936), I, xvii-xxv, hereinafter cited as Hamilton, *Shotwell Papers.*

[2]The Reverend Nathan Shotwell, a native Virginian, was a Presbyterian minister serving

in Rutherfordton at the time of this letter. Clarence W. Griffin, *History of Old Tryon and Rutherford Counties, North Carolina, 1730-1936* (Asheville: Miller Printing Company, 1937), 343, hereinafter cited as Griffin, *History of Old Tryon and Rutherford Counties.*

[3]James Alexander Seddon (1815-1880), of Virginia, graduated from the University of Virginia Law School in 1835 and established a successful Richmond practice. An ardent follower of Calhoun, Seddon was a Democratic congressman, 1845-1847 and 1849-1851, before retiring to the life of a country gentleman and plantation master. He was a delegate to the abortive Washington Peace Conference of 1861, where he voted against the compromise proposals and filed a minority report promoting the right of peaceful secession. After serving in the First Confederate Congress, in November, 1862, he assumed the important but difficult post of secretary of war. On the whole Davis's choice of Seddon was a good one, and the new secretary had considerable influence with the president, at least until the summer of 1863. Seddon was considerate of Lee and the two worked in close harmony. Early in 1865 Seddon resigned when the Virginia delegation to the Confederate Congress asked for reorganization of the cabinet. Crushed by the Confederate defeat, he considered his life wasted. After a brief imprisonment he retired to Sabot Hill, his beloved plantation, to resume his agricultural pursuits. *DAB*, XVI, 545-546.

William A. Graham, Jr., to William A. Graham DUKE

Iron Station, N.C.
Feby 10th, 1869

. . . .

I dont think you will lose anything by the delay for from all accounts cotton will reach 35 or 36 in N.Y. and 33 or 4 in Charlotte. The weights in Charlotte are light and there was a difference of near 30 lbs on my 3 bales as weighed by R.R. and by the weigher in C. but as it had gotten soaking wet on Tuesday I could not judge of the matter strictly.

I wrote you that Wooten[1] as agent for a Balt. firm would ship & guarantee 2 cts. per lb to cover all expenses including storage for 30 days. If you wish to ship to Balt. you can write Brother Joe[2] in regard to the matter. Wooten was formerly Book Keeper for Stenhouse & McCauley.

. . . .

I hope when you come up in March we can come to some conclusion about the disposition of the iron ore on this place. Although the iron business is a very disagreeable one, yet I believe we can make more by working than by selling the mine. It is on the Witherspoon tract and as Brevard[3] is now running his forge (has it leased) I expect we will hear from him as to his interest. This is a very annoying affair and I wish it could be settled. I shall write to Jo Graham[4] (Ark.) in a few days to learn if he recognized any such right in his day or if Brevard ever accounted to him for any interest in his land. Probably it would be best for you to do this yourself as he might go further into details & you could give the facts more correctly than I can. The "seed" ore (i.e. on ground) is very good and abundant. It is on a high hill immediately on the first branch you cross in travelling the road Uncle James[5] made from here toward Dr. Morrisons[6] and about 2 or 300 yrds up the branch fr. bridge.

As to our trip to Va we will postpone it until summer unless Julia's[7] mothers health becomes very bad. We are however much obliged to you for the offer of the money. . . .

[1]Wooten has not been further identified.

[2]Joseph Graham (1837-1907) was the eldest child and the first of nine sons born to William A. and Susan Washington Graham. After graduation from the University of North Carolina in 1857, he decided on a medical career. He studied briefly with the eminent Dr. Edmund Strudwick of Hillsborough before enrolling in Philadelphia's Jefferson Medical College, where he graduated in 1859. In 1860 he established his practice at Charlotte. When war came, Joseph Graham rushed to the Confederate colors, serving first as captain of artillery but after February 1, 1864, as a surgeon in the Sixty-seventh North Carolina Regiment. After the Civil War, he built a very successful Charlotte practice and was at one time president of the North Carolina Medical Association. Spencer Alumni Project; Louis H. Manarin and Weymouth T. Jordan, Jr. (eds.), *North Carolina Troops, 1861-1865: A Roster* (Raleigh: Division of Archives and History, Department of Cultural Resources, projected multivolume series, 1966—), I, 62, hereinafter cited as Manarin and Jordan, *North Carolina Troops.*

[3]Robert A. Brevard (1799-1879) was the son of Lincoln County pioneer ironmonger Alexander Brevard and his wife, Julia Davidson Brevard. He was a cousin of William A. Graham, Alexander Brevard and Graham's father, Joseph Graham, both having married daughters of John Davidson. Sherrill, *Annals of Lincoln County*, 100, 227-228; Powell, *DNCB*, I, 218-219.

[4]Joseph Montrose Graham (1823-1871), son of William A. Graham's brother John Davidson Graham (1789-1847), graduated from the University of North Carolina in 1844, lived for a time in Catawba County, and eventually settled in Arkansas. Family ties were even closer because the nephew married a younger sister of Susan Washington Graham. Clark, "Graham Descendants"; Spencer Alumni Project.

[5]James Graham (1793-1851) was the older brother of William A. Graham. He was a graduate of the University of North Carolina (1814) who practiced law, held several public offices, and engaged in agricultural pursuits. During the 1820s he was a member in five state legislatures. He also served in the United States House of Representatives, 1833-1835, 1836-1843, and 1845-1847. James Graham, who was his younger brother's political mentor, was a Whig. Earhart and Leeper plantations were inherited by William A. Graham upon the unexpected death of James Graham in 1851. *Biographical Directory of Congress*, 964; Powell, *DNCB*, 333.

[6]Robert Hall Morrison (1798-1889) was the husband of William A. Graham's sister Mary. Of Scottish descent and a native of Cabarrus County, he tied James K. Polk for first honors in the University of North Carolina's 1818 graduating class. Morrison was a devout Presbyterian minister and the first president of Davidson College, which he helped found in 1838. He resigned in 1840 at the height of his promise, broken in health and spirit, and took up residence at Cottage Home in Lincoln County. Although visitors were welcomed, he seldom left his home for the next fifty years except to preach at the local Unity, Castamea, and Machpelah Presbyterian churches. Three of his sons-in-law—Stonewall Jackson, Daniel H. Hill, and Rufus Barringer—were Confederate generals. Spencer Alumni Project; Charles L. Van Noppen Papers, Manuscript Department, Duke University Library, Durham, hereinafter cited as Van Noppen Papers.

[7]During the war William had met and married Julia Lane (1848-1909) of Virginia. Clark, "Graham Descendants."

William A. Graham to William A. Graham, Jr. A&H

Hillsboro
Feb. 14th, 1869

I returned last night at 9 o'clock from the 1st week of Granville Court, spending two days at the Supreme Court in Ral., and go back to Granville at 3 tomorrow morning. [I] find many letters to answer & cares and anxieties of one kind or other. Find your two letters of Feb. 5th & 10th. Joseph's little boy is so ill that, I fear, he cannot attend to sale of cotton. But for the promise to be at Oxford, I would go to Charlotte myself. I wrote Sydhm Alexr[1] from Raleigh, if neither you nor Joseph were there, to sell at the market price. I see that cotton has fallen since. I wld not take less than 28 cts. . . . I could go to Charlotte by the 23rd. But if it brings above 28, I would let it go upon arrival. Kerr[2] is so little suited to business that I don't think he could have it weighed accurately, or disposed of to advantage. I wish you could go down by the time it arrives if Joseph is not there. Ten bales have already arrived & been stored . . . by Kerr, and he has gone for the rest. There should be some 75000 lbs. in the 18 bales. You can take a piano at not more than $200 & pay for it out of proceeds of cotton, if sold; if not, I will send a check for the amount as soon as informed it is required.

I have so many affairs on my mind that I can't write more. I was in the Supreme Court yesterday when Pearson[3] had the Auditor Adams[4] brought in & ordered him to be sent to jail. The marshal carried him into Holden's office, who left him there. The Legislature had a fierce discussion over the matter & left it unsettled. In the evening I was told Adams was again before Court; meanwhile his papers & furniture had been hustled out. . . . Holden, it was said, had been sent for by the Court and refused to go, and threatened to rescue Adams. Coleman[5] was in the Supreme Court with his face banged up from the fight with young Holden[6] on Friday & said to be again drunk on Saturday.

Love to Julia & the children.

---

[1]Sydenham Benoni Alexander (1840-1921), of Mecklenburg County, was Graham's nephew, the son of Dr. Moses Winslow Alexander and Violet Graham Alexander. He was an 1860 graduate of the University of North Carolina who rose from private to captain in the Forty-second North Carolina Regiment. A farmer after the war, he was influential in the founding of North Carolina Agricultural and Mechanical College. He was a state senator, 1879-1881, 1883-1889, and 1901-1903; president of the North Carolina Railroad; and a Democratic congressman, 1891-1895. *Biographical Directory of Congress*, 467; Clark, "Graham Descendants."

[2]Kerr was the overseer for one of the Graham farms.

[3]Richmond Mumford Pearson (1805-1878) of Surry County, a native of Rowan, was chief justice of the North Carolina Supreme Court. He graduated from the University of North Carolina in 1823 and practiced law in Salisbury, where he gained a reputation as a thorough student of the law. He was a member of the Commons, 1829-1833; superior court judge, 1836-1848, where he proved to be an unusually able trial judge; and state supreme court judge, 1848 to 1868, chief justice after 1858. A truly great teacher, he operated a famous law school, where he trained more than one thousand attorneys. Pearson opposed secession on moral and legal grounds, had no love for the Confederacy, and incurred considerable unpopularity by his decisions in *habeas corpus* proceedings growing out of the Confederate conscription laws, which he believed to be illegal. Despite his opposition to certain policies of the Davis administration, no taint of disloyalty blemished his reputation. His conduct during Reconstruction was more controversial. Ignoring the traditional aloofness of the judiciary in political matters, Pearson publicly and covertly supported the Republican party. Although he issued writs of *habeas corpus* during the Kirk-Holden war, he declined to seek their enforcement, thus aiding Holden. He presided fairly at Holden's impeachment but was sympathetic to the governor, even to the extent of advising his counsel privately. Pearson feared impeachment proceedings himself but was spared that ordeal probably by his former students. *DAB*, XIV, 360-361.

[4]Henderson Adams, whom historian J. G. de Roulhac Hamilton characterized as a "nonentity," was state auditor. He became party to a dispute over allocation of office space in the State Capitol. It was this dispute to which Graham referred. A legislative committee

had assigned superintendent of public instruction S. S. Ashley and auditor Adams space normally used by the state supreme court. Early in 1869, when the court assembled in Raleigh, Richmond M. Pearson ordered that Ashley and Adams vacate their offices. Ashley complied but Adams refused, whereupon the chief justice ordered Adams's arrest. As Adams was being removed by a court marshal, Governor Holden intervened, saying: "Supreme Court or no Supreme Court, chief justice or no chief justice, d——d if my officials shall go to jail. If they do, it shall be over the dead bodies of my militia." Eventually a compromise was arranged, and the court resumed its former quarters. Hamilton, *Reconstruction in North Carolina*, 382-383, 414.

[5]William M. Coleman was a Republican elected attorney general in 1868. After his clash with "young Holden," Governor Holden exerted his influence to secure for him appointment as consul abroad. Coleman accepted a post in Stettin, Kingdom of Prussia, and left the state. Hamilton, *Reconstruction in North Carolina*, 397.

[6]Joseph William Holden was, at the time of this incident, Speaker of the state House of Representatives. Like his father, Governor William Woods Holden, he was an ardent Republican. Elected to two sessions, 1868-1869 and 1869-1870, he resigned his seat March 18, 1870, in order to assume active control of the *North Carolina Standard* (Raleigh). That paper was, of course, the organ of his father's administration and had been edited by the governor for decades. Cheney, *North Carolina Government*, 448, 449, 450, 554n; Stem, *Tar Heel Press*, 63-64; Hamilton, *Reconstruction in North Carolina*, 397.

John W. Graham[1] *to William A. Graham* UNC

Raleigh
Feb 26th 1869

My Dear Father

. . . .

We are having pretty warm discussion over Ashley School Bill.[2] There are 130 sections we have only finished 41 on 2d reading. The Revenue Bill has come over from the House and is now being read. It will be printed and made Special order for some day next week. The Committee from Vermont returned yesterday afternoon. Purefoy[3] has the bonds in the Smith debt[4] as I returned them after proving; I would much prefer that Purefoy should prove, and I will withdraw the Proof by Attorney. I think that Becca[5] and the Baby will come up with me next week. I do not think the Legislature will adjourn until the last of March. All pretty well at Mr. Mordecai's.[6] Robbins[7] has begun to take an Active part again and wants to make 4 or 5 speeches on almost every occasion. I do not know when we will get through with the School Bill which is now up again. I hope Mother will soon be well again. Love to all.

---

[1]John Washington Graham (1838-1928), the second of ten children born to William A. and Susan Washington Graham, was an 1857 graduate of the University of North Carolina. Later he was a tutor at his alma mater and read law with Samuel Field Phillips and William Horn Battle. He served the Confederacy with distinction, achieving the rank of major in the Fifty-sixth North Carolina Regiment. After the Civil War Graham was an opponent of Negro suffrage and a leading Conservative. He served as a delegate to the Constitutional Convention of 1868; a state senator from Orange County in the 1868, 1870, 1872, 1876, 1901, and 1911 sessions; trustee of the sinking fund of the North Carolina Railroad, 1877-1879; and a University of North Carolina trustee, 1877-1928. *News and Observer* (Raleigh), March 25, 1928; Spencer Alumni Project; Powell, *DNCB*, II, 334-335.

[2]Samuel Stanford Ashley (1819-1887) was a minister, educator, and missionary. The

eldest of eleven children, Ashley was reared in Ashford, Conecticut, and Providence, Rhode Island. He was educated at Oberlin College, graduating from the theological department. A Congregational minister in Ohio and Massachusetts, Ashley demonstrated his strong antislavery sentiments through support of the American Missionary Association. He was active in evangelical service with the Union troops during the Civil War and at the close of the war was employed by the Freedmen's Bureau to help in educating the freedmen. In September, 1865, he became assistant superintendent of education for the Wilmington, North Carolina, district. Working aggressively, he established ten schools that provided education for some 1,800 freedmen. Convinced that political equality for blacks was essential to secure their rights in the face of native white hostility, Ashley entered state politics and was a member of the Constitutional Convention of 1868. As chairman of the committee on education, he helped draft the article that provided for public education for blacks. Although the Republicans did not include plans for integrating the schools, Ashley's bill was bitterly attacked by Conservatives because it did not provide for segregated schools. From 1868 to 1871 Ashley was superintendent of public instruction and resuscitated the state system. When Conservatives gained control of the legislature in 1870 and began to reduce expenditures for education, he resigned lest his presence be a detriment to the education process. Ashley served the American Missionary Association in New Orleans (1871-1873) and in Atlanta (1874-1878) before retiring to Northborough, Massachusetts. Powell, *DNCB*, I, 58-59.

[3]J. S. Purefoy was a white Baptist minister who encouraged the work of Henry M. Tupper in his establishment of a small theological school in Raleigh in 1865. The school evolved into Shaw University. John L. Bell, Jr., "Baptists and the Negro in North Carolina during Reconstruction," *North Carolina Historical Review*, XLII (October, 1965), 405.

[4]No information has been found regarding the "Smith debt."

[5]John W. Graham's wife, Rebecca Cameron Graham, was the daughter of Paul Carrington and Anne Ruffin Cameron. Her first husband, Robert Walker Anderson, had been killed in the Battle of the Wilderness. Powell, *DNCB*, II, 334-335; Clark, "Graham Descendants."

[6]George W. Mordecai (1801-1871), a native of Warrenton, was educated at the local classical school of Marcus George and read law with his distinguished brother Moses Mordecai (1784-1824). Admitted to the bar in 1822, George Mordecai settled in Raleigh and built an excellent practice. He was a public-spirited citizen who was at one time president of the Raleigh and Gaston Railroad. In 1845 he was elected president of the Bank of North Carolina. He was a friend of the Grahams, who often visited in his home, sometimes as overnight guests. *The National Cyclopedia of American Biography* (New York: James T. White and Company, 57 volumes, 1898-1977), X, 442-443, hereinafter cited as *Cyclopedia of American Biography*.

[7]William McKendree Robbins (1828-1905), a native of Randolph County, attended Trinity College and was graduated by Randolph-Macon College about 1850. He studied law and was admitted to the Alabama bar in 1854. During the Civil War, he served as major in the Fourth Alabama Regiment. After returning to Rowan County, North Carolina, he was a Conservative member of the state Senate in the 1868, 1869, and 1870 sessions. Elected as a Democrat, he served three terms as a United States congressman, 1873-1879. He was appointed by President Grover Cleveland to the Gettysburg Battle Field Commission. *Biographical Directory of Congress*, 1526; Cheney, *North Carolina Government*, 447, 449, 451, 697, 698.

George W. Graham to William A. Graham UNC

Univ of Va
March 1st 1869

My dear father

Your favor of a late date reached me a few days since. I am very much obliged for your consent to my standing such examinations as I see fit. I am glad to hear that little Joe[1] is better and hope that he will soon recover.

We can never tell, here, whether we have answered the questions properly or not on examination until near the end of the session. . . . the Professors will not tell you until near the close of the session and then if you have not done well enough to graduate they will send you a note telling you [it is] useless to stand any more examinations as it is impossible for you to get a Certificate or Diploma. Most of my class will attend lectures in N.Y. next year, some few will return here. The theory is very well taught here but we have no practice at all. And it is utterly impossible to remember a great many points in Medicine unless we have them exemplified by practice. I have received several catalogues from N.Y. and I find that the opportunities for practice are far better there than here. Taking everything into consideration the expense is no [more] than at this school if as much. I wrote to Dr. Johnston[2] on the subject and he advised me to come on there immediately after leaving here, in June but there would be but little gained by it as there is very little done during the summer session. And besides I could not get there until it had been going on a month or so. As I have not seen any of my reports for this session I will be much obliged if you will send the one of last month. Dr. Maupin[3] allowed me the privilage of having my report sent to me but I thought it best for it to go home. A great many students who are over twenty one have their reports sent to them instead of their parents. Please send me $20.00 in your next as I have several small bills which I wish to settle.

Love to all.

---

[1]Joseph Graham (1862-1869), the son of Dr. and Mrs. Joseph Graham, did not survive the year. Clark, "Graham Descendants."

[2]Possibly this was William Henry Johnston (b. 1839), a native of Lincoln County who attended the University of North Carolina, 1858-1859. Later, he was a physician in Alabama. Grant, *Alumni History*, 325.

[3]Socrates Maupin (1809-1871), a native of Virginia, was on the faculty of the University of Virginia from 1853 until his death. He held the chair in chemistry and also served ably as chairman of the faculty from 1854 to 1870. *Cyclopedia of American Biography*, XIII, 134.

Francis E. Shober[1] to William A. Graham UNC

House of Representatives.
Washington,
March 22nd., 1869.

The chances for the removal of my disabilities are favorable, and I am procuring some very strong endorsements from some friends here among the Republicans. My name is regularly on the roll of members, but I have not been qualified, of course, because of my inability to take the 'test oath.'

Now my object in writing you is to request a letter to your friend, the Secretary of State,[2] requesting from him a recommendation to Congress to remove my disabilities, and to admit me to my seat.

Should you see proper to comply with my request, you will place me under a very great obligation.

A letter addressed to me in the House of Representatives will reach me.

[1]Francis Edwin Shober (1831-1896) was born in Salem and attended the common schools there and the Moravian school in Bethlehem, Pennsylvania. In 1851 he was graduated from the University of North Carolina, after which he studied law and was admitted to the bar in 1853. He established his practice in Salisbury and had a long and distinguished career, during which he was elected to political office numerous times and held important posts on both the state and national levels: member of the state House of Representatives, 1862, 1864; state Senate, 1865, 1887; Democratic member of the Forty-first and Forty-second congresses (March 4, 1869-March 3, 1873); chief clerk of the United States Senate in the Forty-fifth Congress; and acting secretary of the Senate, October 24, 1881-March 3, 1883. *Biographical Directory of Congress*, 1596.

[2]Hamilton Fish (1808-1893), a New York statesman, was educated at Columbia, graduating in 1827. He then read law and was admitted to the bar in 1830. He was a Whig congressman (1843-1845), governor of New York (1849-1851), and United States senator (1851-1857). His gubernatorial career was particularly noteworthy. As governor he established statewide free public schools and extended New York's canal system. He opposed slavery extension and eventually joined the Republican party, though he manifested no great enthusiasm for his new political affiliation. During the Civil War he served as Federal commissioner for the relief of prisoners. From 1869 to 1877 Fish served as United States secretary of state. It was in this capacity that he gained distinction. His administration was characterized by efficiency, caution, and patience. The most notable accomplishment achieved by Fish was settlement of the so-called *Alabama* claims against Great Britain. *DAB*, VI, 397.

George Little[1] to William A. Graham UNC

North Carolina Land Company,
Raleigh,
March 24th 1869

The North Carolina Land Company is now preparing a Gazetteer, for distribution, giving the Statistics of the State, Showing its resources etc. in order that Emigrants may be induced to Visit and Settle in our State. Several gentlemen have contributed articles to be published in the book, amongst them Gov. Holden, Gen. Barringer,[2] Gen Clingman,[3] Judge Rodman,[4] Prof. Kerr[5] and others.

Knowing the interest you feel in the prosperity of the State, we are induced to ask the favor of you, to contribute an article for publication, on such subject as you may select, and forward the same to the undersigned at your earliest convenience, as the book is now being printed, and we desire that your communication shall be inserted in it.

[1]George Little was a lawyer, former Whig, and friend of Graham and Zebulon B. Vance. Frequently a member of the Whig Central Committee, he was an avid supporter of the Bell-Everett ticket in 1860. During the Civil War he served as an aide to Governor Vance. After 1865 Little was active in attempting to bring foreign immigrants to North Carolina and in the sale of real estate. Frontis W. Johnston (ed.), *The Papers of Zebulon Baird Vance* (Raleigh: State Department of Archives and History, projected multivolume series, 1963—), I, 359n, hereinafter cited as Johnston, *Vance Papers*.

[2]Rufus Barringer (1821-1895), of Cabarrus County, was a lawyer, politician, Confederate general, farmer, and historian. After graduating in 1842 from the University of North Carolina, he studied law with his elder brother Daniel M. Barringer and at Judge Richmond M. Pearson's law school at Richmond Hill, Yadkin County. In politics he was a Whig who favored progressive policies. As a member of the Commons in the 1848-1849

session, he was influential in the establishment of the North Carolina Railroad Company. Barringer, a Bell-Everett elector in 1860, opposed secession but supported the Confederate effort. He rose in rank from captain to brigadier general, fought in seventy-six engagements, was wounded three times, and was captured on the retreat to Appomattox. He was married to William A. Graham's niece Eugenia Morrison (1833-1858), daughter of Robert Hall and Mary Graham Morrison. At one time he was the brother-in-law of Thomas J. (Stonewall) Jackson and Daniel H. Hill. After the Civil War Barringer favored conciliation and espoused Republican policies. Ashe, *Biographical History*, I, 116-125; Clark, "Graham Descendants"; Boatner, *Civil War Dictionary*, 46-47.

[3]Thomas Lanier Clingman (1812-1897), of Surry (now Yadkin) County, was a University of North Carolina graduate, read law with William A. Graham, and practiced his profession for sixty years in Asheville. Clingman served in the House of Commons (1835) and the state Senate (1840) before his election to the United States House of Representatives. He sat in the House from 1843 to 1845 and from 1847 to 1858. Initially, he was a dedicated Whig; but, as he became increasingly fearful of northern encroachments upon southern rights, Clingman wavered. He abandoned the Whigs for the Democratic party about 1852, recognizing that the Democracy was rapidly becoming the bastion of slavery. In 1858 he was elected to replace Asa Biggs in the United States Senate, where he sat until March 28, 1861. Clingman favored secession and quickly rushed to the Confederate colors, serving first as colonel of the Twenty-fifth North Carolina Regiment and later as a brigadier general. A participant in numerous engagements, Clingman was severely wounded during the defense of the Weldon Railroad in 1864. After the war he sought unsuccessfully to resume his place in the United States Senate. Although he remained influential in the Democratic party, his only official public service was as a delegate to the Constitutional Convention of 1875. Clingman was an avid mountain explorer and developer of Great Smoky mineral resources. *DAB*, IV, 220-221; *Biographical Directory of Congress*, 708; Boatner, *Civil War Dictionary*, 159.

[4]William Blount Rodman, Sr. (1817-1893), was born in Washington, North Carolina, and reared from age eight by his maternal grandfather, John Gray Blount. He graduated from the University of North Carolina in 1837 with first distinction. After reading law in the New Bern office of William Gaston, he was admitted to the bar in 1838. A thorough and learned attorney, he established a highly successful practice in his native city. He also was a planter with substantial holdings. In 1854 he joined B. F. Moore and Asa Biggs in revising the North Carolina code. In politics Rodman was a states' rights Democrat and a secessionist. He was a Breckinridge elector in 1860, and he raised a company of heavy artillery after North Carolina seceded. He served in Virginia as captain and major before being promoted colonel and appointed judge of a military court attached to the Army of Northern Virginia. Rodman was disappointed by the collapse of the Confederacy but with characteristic fortitude sought to rebuild his personal fortunes. He was a Republican delegate to the Constitutional Convention of 1868, where he exerted a conservative influence. From 1868 to 1878 he sat on the state supreme court as an associate justice, proving himself to be an able and conscientious jurist. Following his tenure as judge, Rodman resumed his private practice in Washington. Ashe, *Biographical History*, III, 344-354.

[5]Washington Caruthers Kerr (1827-1885) was a native North Carolinian, born in Guilford County, and a resident of the state until his death in Asheville. He was the state geologist, c. 1865-1882, and produced a state survey map in 1882. *CDAB*, 524.

Tax List of William A. Graham

W. A. Graham Tax List 1 April 1869

Lands—Homestead 56 acres—Meadow 5 acres—also pasture all enclosed
Ray tract 525 do—meadow 2 acres—about 150 enclosed
Difft district
Leased to two freedmen—Wm. Latta & Alfred Bright[1]
Estes tract 833, do Meadow 7 acres about 200 enclosed Leased to Whitaker & M. Conley
½ of Cole tract 92 do,
leased to Wm. Browning

Personal Property	
1 Mare 1 Colt $160—2 Mules 150. 2 do 80	$390.00
17 Head of cattle, cows, steers, yearlings, calves	136.
1 Carriage & Harness	200.
2 Old wagons 75 cart 20. 4 sets of gears 30	125.
Farming utensils & Wheat Fan & Corn sheller	45.
Library & paintings, prints—	1000.
Household & kitchen furniture	800.
Piano	200.
Silver plate	350.
2 Gold watches	150.
Deduct Household & kitchen furniture	3396.
p. 22	200.
500 lbs. Bacon	3196.
	90.
	3286.
Stocks & Bonds of N.C. Railroad Co all paid for by the Company—	
Solvent credits equalled by debits in state—	
Income from Property outside of the State otherwise than from Profession . . .	1000.40
Do from Profession as a Lawyer	2068.20
	3068.60
Deduct under act to provide for collection p. 21 $500.	500.
" Travelling expenses of profession, p. 21	100.
" Taxes other than income tax due State	207.98
" Expenses of supporting family—6 white persons	1000.
Paper Ink, Postage Books	1926.58
net income	1142.02

State Tax List
1869

Profession,	2.50	10
	18.75	50
	10.	10
	4.25	100
	3.	160
	5	63
	5	500
	19.20	40
	15	15
	4	40
	18.40	50
	9.	65
	4	60
	39.35	20
	6.25	65
	4.75	26.60
	7.75	5
	13.25	100
	189.45	129
		30
		20
		40
		29
		21.11
Exp of travelling 100.		100
Support of family 6 whites—		100
		50
		64
		25
		10
		65
		10
		40
		15
		129.50
		2257.65
		189.45
		2068.20

[1]None of the lessees mentioned in this tax list have been further identified.

M. A. Caldwell,[1] *Rufus Barringer, and Henderson Adams to William A. Graham* UNC

Office N.C. R.R. Co.
Company Shops,
April 9th 1869

The undersigned Committee of Finance in Compliance with an order of the Board of Directors, have this day recancelled and returned to The Honorable Wm A. Graham, Trustee of the Company ($65,000) Sixty five Thousand Dollars of the first mortgage Coupon Bonds of the Company: to wit, 70 Bonds of the Company of five Hundred dollars each, dated 1 Nov 1867 & runing till 1 Nov 1872 Numbered from No 694 to 719 and 907 to 950 both inclusive, and Sixty Bonds of said Company of like amount and date runing till 1 Nov 1877, and numbered from 330 to 389 inclusive.

Bonds runing 5 years	$35,000
" " 10 "	$30,000
	$65,000

[1]M. A. Caldwell was treasurer of the North Carolina Railroad, 1868-1869. *Proceedings of the Nineteenth Annual Meeting of the Stockholders of the North Carolina Rail Road Company Held at Raleigh, July 9th and 10th, 1868* (Company Shops: North Carolina Rail Road Print, 1868), 35. This letter is included because it is typical of several related to Graham's trusteeship of the North Carolina Railroad Company.

William A. Graham, Jr., to William A. Graham UNC

Forest Home
April 22, 1869

Reel & Randleman[1] are endeavoring to make a trade with Ballinger[2] for the lease of his forge and wish to know if we would sell them ore in the event of the trade. I did not like to give consent without first hearing from you. They wish to take the ore in the ground and are willing to pay customary price (which I do not at this time know). I see no objection to it myself. I did not take Ballinger's forge as he wanted $300. pr year and me to fit it up which would be almost half cost of building one and would allow no right to timber for coal.

In looking over the deeds &c of this place I find in the one given by the other heirs to J. R. Witherspoon[3] & wife (your name appearing on the face but not among the signers) the following inserted in brackets just before close: (Except the Reserved claim by the other parties of the old firm of Graham & Co in the Furnace & Forge in that part of the land which belonged to what is termed bounty land, which reservation consists in an equal part of the minerals belonging thereto.) R. A. Brevard is a witness to the Deed made in '37 registered in '38. I found Grand Pa's[4] deed to Brevard[5] registered in 1820; it is worded same [as] ours.

Reinhart bought of Mosteller[6] who warrants his tittle in "fee simple." I did not find B's deed to Mosteller. I have written to three parties in

Baltimore but all have "other arrangements." I have this week written to Lobdell Car Wheel Co. of Wilmington, Del., but I fear I could not make a trade if they would come out, as Smith & Reinhart are offering their property very low. Reinhart offers all the "works" & half the land for $12,500. Smith offers the forge at the Morrison ore bank, the Stonewall furnace (which will be within four miles of the branch R.R. fr Catawba Sta which passed legislature) and 9000 acres of land including an abundance of iron ore for $15000.00. I consider this the greatest bargain that I know of.

I sent Brother Joe some specimens from the gold mine which the Yankee to whom he showed [them] pronounced very good and said he would come up to look at the mine. I shall ask him $20,000 but sell at 15 if cant get any higher.

Julia & children have been sick for past week but are better now, but Julia is looking thinner than at any time since our marriage. The concord Presbytery meets with Castamea Church[7] on Thursday next and they expect us to entertain some of the delegates. I received information today that I had been appointed assessor for this township. I am much inclined to decline but as they first appointed two scallawags who could not write their names & a Yankee (I dont know who of them declined) I am afraid to do so. I finished all my cotton except a small patch today. We are using our new room as a dining room, as I have no stove. The carriage house will be done in a day or two more. Have finished my wagon shed, and if I can get my cotton room built at the mill & my stables covered, hope I will be thro' with building. By the help of my coal I have nearly squared up with everybody including my purchases of Brother Joe, but I am at this time without a collier and as the Furnace will hardly blow more than another month, I am afraid I will not do much more than get out of debt. It is doubtful whether Wilkes Co & Smith will agree for another year and if they do not I will be caught with upwards of 150 crds of wood on hand, but as it is all paid for I do not care much for that as there is not much probability that it will long remain still.

Julia joins me in love to you, Mother and all the family. I hope when you come up in May you & Mother will make us a visit of some length.

---

[1]Spaight N. Reel was Graham's overseer at Earhart Plantation. Randleman was also a foreman.

[2]Ballinger has not been identified.

[3]Dr. John Ramsay Witherspoon.

[4]Joseph Graham (1759-1836), Revolutionary soldier, politician, and Lincoln County iron entrepreneur, was William A. Graham's well-loved and venerated father. Educated at Charlotte's Queen's Museum (later Liberty Hall Academy), he was on hand when Mecklenburg patriots are alleged to have adopted a Declaration of Independence on May 20, 1775. Within the years 1778 to 1781 young Graham served periodically as a volunteer in the war against Great Britain. While rising from private to major, he participated in fifteen minor engagements in the Carolinas. He commanded William R. Davie's rear guard in the retreat from Charlotte. In checking Tarleton's cavalry in the ensuing fighting, he sustained nine wounds and was left on the field for dead, but he survived to fight another day.

After the Revolution Joseph Graham farmed near the Catawba River and participated in public affairs. He was sheriff of Mecklenburg County, 1784-1785, a delegate to the two

North Carolina conventions that met to consider ratification of the Constitution of 1787, and state senator, 1788-1793. In the early 1790s Graham, in partnership with in-laws John Davidson and Alexander Brevard, established an iron manufacturing company in east Lincoln County. Graham was to remain a planter and ironmonger until his retirement. He commanded North Carolina troops during the War of 1812, as brigadier general of volunteers.

After 1820 he assisted Archibald De Bow Murphey, who planned to write a state history, by writing remarkably accurate accounts of military actions against the British in the Carolinas. His vivid account of the events of May 20, 1775, based on memory became the principal authority for the disputed Mecklenburg Declaration of Independence. It is notable that in February, 1875, William A. Graham, in one of his last major public efforts, was the principal speaker at Charlotte's centennial celebration of the declaration. Powell, *DNCB*, II, 335-336. See also Graham, *General Joseph Graham.*

[5]Alexander Brevard (1755-1829) was a native of Iredell County. One of eight brothers who were Whigs, Brevard served in both the North Carolina militia and the Continental line. He was a militia captain during Cornwallis's southern campaign and underwent the fiercest fire at the Battle of Eutah Springs in South Carolina. Brevard married a daughter of Mecklenburger John Davidson and joined him and Joseph Graham, another Davidson son-in-law, in the manufacture of iron in Lincoln County. Like other Lincoln ironmongers he also engaged in agricultural pursuits.

In 1814 the partnership of Graham and Brevard was dissolved. Subsequently Brevard operated Mount Tirza Forge and Rehoboth Furnace very successfully. He marketed iron products in South Carolina with the assistance of his brother, Judge Joseph Brevard of Camden. Powell, *DNCB*, I, 218-219.

[6]Mosteller, Reinhart, and Smith mentioned in this paragraph have not been definitely identified, but the men are probably George Mosteller, Franklin M. Reinhardt, and David Smith. See various references in Sherrill, *Annals of Lincoln County.*

[7]Castamea Presbyterian Church was located in east Lincoln County and was long served by the Reverend Robert Hall Morrison. Van Noppen Papers.

George W. Graham to William A. Graham UNC

Univ of Va
April 24th/69

Yours of the 21st containing the money for which I am very much obliged, came to hand yesterday. We are now in the midst of examinations and will have them from now til the end of the session at intervals of two weeks. About half of the class are standing them and a much smaller number will graduate.

Mr. Oleonnon[1] of N.Y. who was expected to deliver an address before the two Literary Societies in July declined a few days since and now it is thought that the Committee will be unable to get another Orator as it is so late in the session. Mr. Oleonnon accepted the invitation three or four months ago but declined it not long since, (I think) without stating his reason.

Spring has at last set in tho' it was right much retarded by the snow which we had about ten days or two weeks since. The wheat around here looks very fine, corn is just beginning to be planted.

I must close to be in time for the mail, am thankful for the pants and vest, love to all. Write soon to your

aff son

[1]Mr. Oleonnon has not been further identified.

E. J. Hale[1] *& Sons to William A. Graham* UNC

New York,
April 26th.,
1869.

. . . .

We are not disappointed in President Grant. Have had no hope of him since his declaration that "the will of the people was the supreme law of the land." His selection of a free trade Secretary of the Treasury,[2] and the immediate substitution of a high tariff man in his place, shows that he has no settled policy or principles. Has your association with him on the Peabody Committee given you a better opinion of him? The public men of the country are of so very low a grade that perhaps we have no right to look for anything better in a President. But it is a sad state of things.

---

[1]Edward Jones Hale (1802-1883), of Fayetteville, a native of Chatham County, was the editor of the influential *Fayetteville Observer*. He had learned his journalism with Joseph Gales, editor of the *Raleigh Register*, and Gales and William W. Seaton of the *National Intelligencer* (Washington, D.C.). While in Washington learning his trade, he met the great men of the day and established an enduring friendship with Henry Clay. Not suprisingly he was a Clay Whig in politics. Hale lived at Haymount plantation near Fayetteville, enjoyed a large income, and traveled extensively. In the 1850s he declined two important New York offers, including one to become editor of the *New York World*. A Unionist who supported the Bell-Everett ticket in 1860, Hale opposed secession but, as a southern man and North Carolinian, went with his state. He supported Zebulon B. Vance for governor, remained loyal to the Confederate cause, and denounced Holden's peace movement in vitriolic terms editorially and privately. Federal troops destroyed Hale's presses and offices in 1865, and his association with the *Observer* ended after forty years as editor. In 1866 he established the New York publishing house of E. J. Hale and Sons. Hale has been eulogized as the ablest southern editor of his day. Ashe, *Biographical History*, VIII, 179-184.

[2]President Grant nominated for secretary of the treasury Alexander T. Stewart (1803-1876), a native of England who became a millionaire New York merchant. His nomination was refused because of a statute providing that no person engaged in importing could be treasury secretary. George S. Boutwell, a high protectionist, assumed the treasury portfolio. James G. Randall and David Donald, *The Civil War and Reconstruction* (Lexington, Mass.: D. C. Heath and Company, second revised edition, 1969), 654, hereinafter cited as Randall and Donald, *Civil War and Reconstruction*.

George W. Graham to Susan W. Graham UNC

Univ of Va
May 6th 1869

My dear mother

. . . .

Received a letter from cousin Julia Graham[1] a few days since. She inquired after you all. She is living at Lexington about sixty miles above here. Her lady friend who she requested me to call on left a few days since much to my joy. Called on her only once, (on the 14th of April) but did not go again as as [*sic*] the walk (2 miles) was more than I cared to take.

Gen Lee[2] passed here about ten days or two weeks since but I did not see him. He has passed several times this session but I never happened at the depot on those days and consequently have not seen him yet. Students are leaving very rapidly now as the session is getting near its end. I will be glad when my time comes to leave these "Classic Shades" as a nine months session is most too long, although thus far it has passed away very rapidly. We are now over the most important part of our course and consequently will not be worked so hard i.e. those of us (which is ¾ of the class) who are not applying for M.D.

We will not have much else but the practice of medicine from now til the end of the session, nor will we learn a great deal as the professor of that is rather inferior.

Love to all, write soon to

Your affectionate son

Hope to be home on the first of July—

---

[1]Julia Adelaide Graham (1833-1876) was the daughter of the John Davidson Grahams. Clark, "Graham Descendants."

[2]General Robert E. Lee (1807-1870) had assumed the presidency of Washington College in Lexington, Virginia, in September, 1865. *CDAB*, 556-557.

Edward J. Hale to William A. Graham UNC

New York
May 8, 1869

Your favor of the 6th is at hand, & we enclose receipt, & balance in postage stamps.

We are not only grieved but surprised to hear of the pecuniary distress existing in our State. We have supposed that the good crop of last year, & the high prices obtained from it, had made money comparatively abundant, especially as there are no slaves in which to invest, & few people care to invest in banks, or even in lands. We think that the generality of Southern merchants who have been in N.Y. this Spring bought their stocks of goods with reference to such an impression of the ease in the money market. They will of course be disappointed. As to the finances of the country, we should think, but for the amazing capacity of endurance heretofore displayed, that everything was plunging to the bottom with accelerated speed. We are importing so much more than we export, sending so many hundreds of millions in bonds to Europe, that it is not easy to see how we can stand it. The taxes here are of course very high, but we fear that in N.C. they are dreadfully in excess of the ability of many to pay. We wish we could hope for the speedy displacement of the corrupt & irresponsible legislators who have inflicted these & other evils upon the good old State.

George W. Graham to William A. Graham UNC

Univ of Va
May 17th 1869

Your highly appreciated letter came to hand several days since but the clothes have not yet arrived suppose they will be here tomorrow (Tuesday). Am sorry that they were not sent via Raleigh as they would have reached here 24 hours earlier by that rout [*sic*]. Suppose they must be delayed at Greensboro or Richmond more probable the former place. The package should have been here last Saturday if it had come directly thru. If they dont come within the next three or four days I will write to the agents at the above mentioned places and inquire about the package. All of my lectures except the practice of medicine will be completed about the 20th of June and that will be finished a few days later. So if you have no objection I will leave here about that time as I wish to make a visit to Amelia Co. and also to spend a few days with one of my college friends before going home. It will not be worth the while for me to stay until the Practice of Medicine is completed as we will be over the most important part before the middle of June. The Chair in that department is not filled as well as it might be, and the cause given is that we have not learned a great deal about it during the session. The professor prescribes General blood letting and Saline purgative for nearly every disease he takes up. While on the other hand the other professors advise us to resort to every thing else before blood letting.

Was glad to hear that Robert had recovered his money from Sinclair. I was afraid that he would not get it as I heard that Sinclair had gone in to Bankruptcy. Please send me as early as convenient $55. as need another suit of clothes and also have several bills which I wish to settle. Noo [*sic*] news. Love to *all*, your aff' son.

In haste

H. C. Luce[1] *to William A. Graham* UNC

Office of the Lincoln Iron Co.
New York
May 27, 1869

I have not the pleasure of your acquaintance (tho. I had the pleasure of voting for You for Vice President once) but you know my partner Ed. Wilkes[2] (Wilkes Luce & Co.) & Your son knows us both. After many trials & difficulties safely passed through we are at last finding the proper conditions for successfully operating the Lincoln Co. furnaces & am confident of being able to ship north by July 15th at the outside from Rehoboth & Stonewall furnaces at least 14 tons a day 6 days in the week. Our development of the mineral resources of your State will have cost us $100000. in cash. The old firm now sells to the incorporated firm all its rights & property for $150,000 stock & its debts, about $25000. in other words we have merged the firm into an incorporation under the laws of N.Y. State with a Capital Stock of $150,000, owned by the partners in the old firm C. Goddard, E. Wilkes & H.

C. Luce. Mr G is Prest. Mr. Wilkes Manager of the Works myself Sec'y Treasr. & Agent, Capt Geo L. Luce depy Tr at Iron Station, Lincoln Co.

Our new Company is named for the County the "Lincoln Iron Co."

We are said to be the first exporter of pig iron from Your State. We would have taken a charter from the State of North Carolina but we failed to get a Charter last winter for building & operating a tram road in Lincoln Co. & doubted our Success in getting a Charter for any other business, besides which our stock is mostly owned in N.Y. & we prefer to control our own property.

We are preparing a mortgage of $50000. upon our property leases improvements etc with an issue of bonds secured by said mortge [*sic*] the bonds $500 ea with coupons bearing 77 interest in gold payable in New York City.

We expect to raise money in this manner to extend our operations. Before we make any purchases of property in fee simple we would like a reliable abstract of title. Mr. Wilkes thought You would give it to us.

Can you do so? We would like an abstract of the transfer of the properties originally granted to Mrs. Graham Forny[3] & Brevard down to the present time with any record or copy of agreement by which the "Big Ore Bank" is held in common by several parties owning furnaces & forges in Lincoln Co.

We would like to know to whom the Big Ore Bank belongs & what proceedings would be necessary to get a partition of it.

Can you at once attend to this abstract & give it to us say by June 10th prox?

And will you have any objections to acting as Trustee of our mortgage?

---

[1]Except for internal identification provided by this letter, no positive identification has been made of H. C. Luce, C. Goddard, and George L. Luce.

[2]Ed. Wilkes was probably Edmund Wilkes, a son of Charles Wilkes who went bankrupt and moved west.

[3]Mrs. Graham Forney, as indicated in this letter, was a landowner in Lincoln County. Peter and Abram Forney were among the pioneers in the Lincoln County iron industry. At one time they owned the Big Ore Bank and operated furnaces nearby. In 1791 Peter Forney sold his interests to Major John Davidson and his sons-in-law, General Joseph Graham and Alexander Brevard. Sherrill, *Annals of Lincoln County*, 57, 100.

W. A. Smith to William A. Graham UNC

President's Office,
North Carolina Rail Road Company
Company Shops, N.C.
June 6th 1869

Enclosed please find complimentary pass to Norfolk & Return. We anticipate a pleasant trip and would feel highly honored by your company. On our arrival at Portsmouth a Steamer will be in waiting to take us to Old Point and other places of interest. We will return same evening to Norfolk and next morning start for home.

S. Finley Tomlinson[1] *to William A. Graham* UNC

Sylvan Academy Alamance Co
June 8/69

In addressing you this letter, my object is to call your attention to the subject of education in the Counties of Randolph, Alamance, Chatham, etc. There are but few schools in these counties now in operation & but little money to support them. The spirit of education is at a very low ebb. It appears to me that, the only way in which this spirit may be resuscitated, is, by sustaining the schools now in operation & by establishing, as far as practicable, others.

Four long years of war & four years since, without schools, have witnessed the rearing of a numerous progeny in ignorance & intellectual darkness.

If, as has been said, "The wealth of a nation is in the breasts of its sons," then North Carolina is poor—miserably poor! This wealth can only be developed by education. For this purpose, I (in behalf of this section of country), call upon you, as one of the Trustees of the "Peabody Fund", for some assistance in sustaining this institution (Sylvan Academy, in Alamance Co) of which I have charge. It has been successfully carried on for three years past by the aid of the "Baltimore Association of Friends"; but its fund is nearly exhausted & the schools must look to the people of N.C. to sustain them. There are a few young men now in school who served in the confederate army, during the late war, were wounded &, consequently, are unable for manual labor. They are desirous of preparing themselves for teachers.

Necessity forces them to leave school, unless they may receive aid from other sources. There are a few others very desirous of entering school but means prevent them. The cases alluded to are worthy of help—they are moral, high-toned, young men, & would go out as teachers to scatter good seed in other sections of the state. I ask no help for any of the Friends (Quakers), but for those of other denominations or of no denomination. This institution merits assistance, probably more than many others, from the fact that, it is preparing & has prepared several for teachers under the most improved methods of teaching.

The leading object of our school are to prepare—
1st Qualified Teachers
2nd Efficient Business Men
3rd To make good useful citizens

If you think our claims are worthy to be complied with, you can appoint a committee on admission. If the cases above alluded to, can only receive enough to pay for Books & Tuition it will enable the most of them to return.

You will please inform me at an early day, what our chances of receiving help may be.

---

[1]Samuel Finley Tomlinson (b. 1840) was a native of Bush Hill (now Archdale) in Randolph County. He was the scion of a prominent Quaker family that had settled in Randolph in 1786. After preparing for further study at the Trinity Institute, he was graduated by Haverford College; subsequently, he was associated for several years with his

brother Allen Josiah Tomlinson in the operation of the Sylvan Academy at Cone Creek, Alamance County. A representative of Randolph County in the 1870 legislature, S. F. Tomlinson was for a time superintendent of the North Carolina Institute for the Deaf, Dumb, and Blind. Later he was engaged in the manufacture of furniture. He was the first president of the Tomlinson Chair Manufacturing Company of High Point, a concern of great prominence in the furniture industry. *Trinity Alumni Register*, I (April, 1915), 85; Cheney, *North Carolina Government*, 453; Max R. Williams, biographical sketch of Sidney Halstead Tomlinson, Sr., prepared for forthcoming volume of Powell, *DNCB*.

M. A. Caldwell to William A. Graham UNC

Company Shops, N.C.
June 11th 1869

The Committee of Finance will be in Session to day and to morrow & if not convenient for you to meet with the Committee on either day, we would be pleased for you to designate as early a day as you can conveniently meet & receive $76,500 Dollars of the Bonds of The Co. runing 20 yrs from 1 Nov 1868 or Such portions Thereof as you may deem proper, or to make some Suggestion as to the residue of Said Bond. That in closeing the Books for the fiscal year, the entries may be consistant with any future action contemplated in the premises.

Robert C. Winthrop to William A. Graham UNC

Brookline,
near Boston,
June 12th., 1869.

You will have observed the sudden return of our noble friend, Mr. Peabody. He reached Boston yesterday, in better health than I had anticipated, but quite feeble. His first interest is in our Southern Commission, & he is quite disposed to aid us further in the execution of his Trust. With this view, he desires to meet at least a Quorum of the Trustees as soon as he is sufficiently recovered from the fatigues of his voyage & journey. Dr. Sears[1] is fortunately, here, & after consultation with him & Gov. Clifford[2] & myself, Mr. Peabody has decided on *July 1st.*, as the day, & Newport, (R.I.) as the place, for meeting us.

We had better keep all this to *ourselves* for the present, & I have told Mr. Russell[3] that he need not send any formal notices.

Please give me assurance, at your earliest convenience, whether we can rely on *You* as one of a Quorum. I hope you will be able to join us.

---

[1]Barnas Sears (1802-1880), of Massachusetts, was a Baptist clergyman and educator. After graduating from Brown University in 1825, he studied theology at Newton Theological Institution and was ordained in 1827. He served briefly as a pastor in Hartford, Connecticut, before becoming a teacher at Hamilton (New York) Literary and Theological Institution, 1829-1833 and 1835. Sears studied language, literature, and theology in Germany from 1833 to 1835. He was professor of theology at Newton, 1836-1848, and president there, 1839-1848. In 1848 he succeeded Horace Mann as secretary of the Massachusetts Board of Education. He left that position in 1855 to become president of

Brown University. For twelve years, despite the Civil War, Sears contributed significantly to the development of Brown. In 1867 he responded to a unique challenge—he became general secretary to the Peabody Education Fund and until his death worked diligently in planning and executing the uses of that fund in the South. *DAB*, XVI, 537-538; Jabez Lamar Monroe Curry, *A Brief Sketch of George Peabody and a History of the Peabody Education Fund through Thirty Years* (Cambridge: John Wilson and Son, 1898), 68-71.

[2]John Henry Clifford (1809-1876), a native of Rhode Island, was a lawyer, politician, and railroad president. An 1827 Brown University graduate, he read law and established a practice in New Bedford, Massachusetts. He entered politics in 1835 as a delegate to the General Court. Later he served as Massachusetts attorney general and governor. In 1862 Clifford was elected to the state Senate (serving as president), where he vigorously supported Lincoln's war policies. He became president of the Boston and Providence Railroad Company in 1867—a position he held until his death. Frequently an overseer of Harvard College, Clifford, an intimate friend of George Peabody, was a trustee of the Peabody Education Fund. *DAB*, IV, 215.

[3]George Peabody Russell of Salem, Massachusetts, the nephew of George Peabody, was one of the Peabody Education Fund trustees. Parker, *George Peabody*, 162, 174.

T. Apoleon Cheney[1] *to William A. Graham* UNC

Georgic Library,
Watkins,
Schuyler Co., N. York,
July 12th, 1869.

I will beg your indulgence in thus assuming liberty of writing you, 'though I may only plead as some apology, that I have long noticed with especial interest, not less than with sentiments of profound admiration, your very able and eminent public career, whilst you had occupied distinguished positions as Senator in Congress, as Gov. of N.C., or as Sec'y of the Navy; and I can but express the anticipation that you may continue to gather the ampliest awards of honorable and pre-eminent fame.

I will presume in mentioning here, that I have been arranging a very choice, select Album, for which the greater number of the pre-eminent Statesmen, Jurists, Divines, Artists, Authors, Generals, etc., of our time, have already contributed their photographs. I would be extremely gratified if you may find it at your convenience to honor me with enclosure of your photograph, with *your* autograph written *beneath* the picture, and which I may be allowed pleasure of placing in this Album, where it would indeed form a treasure of priceless value. I will indulge earnest anticipation that you can favor me with *your photograph.*

The Library includes a rare and valuable Souvenir, now containing the Autographs of large numbers of the most eminent illustrious men of present Century; there remains, however, several whose autographs have not yet been added to our collection, but which I have been very anxious to obtain, from the intrinsic value they would possess, as well as worth in completing this Souvenir. It has occurred to my mind, from the intimate association you have held with the illustrious Statesmen of our country, that *you* might have it in your power to render the exceeding favor of contributing to this Souvenir some of the Autographs so particularly desired, *and,* if it may be at your convenience to enclose an Autograph—some letter with date, or even the signature—of *any* of the Statesmen below named: Pres't *Zachary Taylor*,[2] Hon. *Willie P. Mangum*,[3] Hon. Thomas Corwin,[4] Hon. John Bell,[5] Hon. Samuel L. Southard,[6] Hon. William C. Preston,[7] Hon. *Nathaniel Macon*,[8] Hon. Hugh S. Legare,[9] Hon. Peter Y. Daniel[10] (Asso. Justice, S.C.), and, as they would be of inestimable value in this *Souvenir*, rendering it *nearly* complete as originally designed, be assured I should gratefully appreciate your *especial* kindness in conferring such a priceless, exceeding favor. I suppose that you may have no *spare* autograph-*signature* of Hon. *John Marshall*[11] (Chief Justice), or, of Pres't *William H. Harrison*,[12] (which our Asso. Just. Swayne[13] had vainly endeavored to procure for me), or of Pres't *John Tyler*,[14] that would also be in your power to contribute to the Souvenir.

I will venture to mention that I have been engaged in researches relating to History of Central N.Y., the preliminary part of this work, the M.S. of my "Historical Sketch of Chemung Valley, Etc.," read before "Buffalo Hist. Soc.," was issued last season, and if you may think the work would interest you, I shall take pleasure in mailing you a copy?

I shall be extremely gratified in your allowing the great favor of writing me at your *early* convenience; will anticipate pleasure of hearing from you *soon*.

---

[1]Theseus Apoleon Cheney, LL.D., of New York state, was a librarian and historian. Head of the Georgic Library later located in Leon, Cattaraugus County, he was author of "Historical Sketch of the Chemung Valley. . . ." (See T. Apoleon Cheney to William A. Graham, March 1, 1871, in this volume.) Cheney had written Graham a similar "collecting" letter on August 3, 1867.

[2]Zachary Taylor (1784-1850) achieved a status of popular military hero by virtue of his daring achievements as an Indian fighter and later against the Mexicans over the annexation of Texas, 1846-1847. He was the successful Whig candidate for president in 1848 but expressed a dislike for both northern and southern extremists on the question of slavery. His two years in office were marked by his involvment with extraordinarily controversial domestic problems and a lack of success in foreign relations. He died before the passage of the bills that evolved as the Compromise of 1850. Millard Fillmore then became president, and Graham joined the cabinet as secretary of the navy.

Although he lacked political skill and experience, Taylor was a man of practical wisdom, common sense, and unwavering convictions. *CDAB*, 1049-1050.

[3]Willie Person Mangum (1792-1861) was a native of Orange County who received three degrees from the University of North Carolina: A.B., 1815; A.M., 1818; and LL.D., 1845. Mangum held various important political offices, including these: representative of Orange County in the state House of Representatives, 1818-1819; state senator, 1840; judge of the superior court, 1819-1823, 1828; United States representative, 1823-1827; and United States senator, 1831-1837, 1841-1853, president of the Senate, 1842-1845. Before his break with Andrew Jackson over the bank issue, Mangum had been a leading Democrat. Subsequently he became a founder of the Whig party. Grant, *Alumni History*, 410; *CDAB*, 634.

[4]Thomas Corwin (1794-1865), a native of Kentucky, enjoyed a long political career in Ohio, where he grew up. A lawyer by profession, Corwin was a Whig congressman (1831-1840), governor of Ohio (1840-1842), a United States senator (1845-1850), secretary of the treasury (1850-1853), and United States minister to Mexico (1861-1864). He and Graham were colleagues in the Fillmore cabinet. *CDAB*, 194; *Biographical Directory of Congress*, 740.

[5]John Bell (1797-1869), Tennessee lawyer and statesman, was a graduate of Cumberland College. He was a Democratic congressman until he broke with Jackson and became a leading Whig. He served in the House of Representatives from 1827 to 1841. Called by

William Henry Harrison to be secretary of war, he resigned because of differences with President John Tyler. A moderate southerner with a national perspective, Bell was a United States senator, 1847-1859. He was a slave owner but never became an apostle of slavery. He joined John Quincy Adams in defending the right of petition, agreed that Congress could legally prohibit slavery in the territories, and opposed the Kansas-Nebraska Act because it reopened the bitter sectional controversy over slavery. In 1860 Bell was the presidential candidate of the Constitutional Union party, formed by a group of moderate former Whigs. Pleading for preservation of the Union, Bell carried Tennessee, Virginia, and Kentucky but could not stem the Lincoln tide. His career finished, he endured the war years in sad lamentations for the Union and the South. *DAB*, II, 157-159.

[6]Samuel Lewis Southard (1787-1842), of New Jersey, had an active career as jurist and statesman. The principal offices he held were as follows: associate justice, New Jersey Supreme Court, 1815-1820; United States senator, 1821-1823 and 1833-1842; secretary of the navy, 1823-1829; and governor of New Jersey, 1832-1833. Originally a Democrat, he became a Whig in the 1830s and strongly opposed Jacksonian policies. *CDAB*, 984.

[7]William Campbell Preston (1794-1860), of South Carolina, was a lawyer, legislator, and educator. He was an intense states' rightist and advocate of slavery. Elected in 1833 as United States senator, he served until 1842, first as a Democrat and then as a Whig. From 1846 to 1851 Preston was president of South Carolina College. *CDAB*, 823.

[8]Nathaniel Macon (1758-1837), of Warren County, was a patriot in the American Revolution; but he subscribed to the views of Willie Jones in opposing the federal convention and the ratification of the United States Constitution. He represented North Carolina as a (Democrat) Republican member of Congress, 1791-1815 (Speaker, 1801-1807). From 1815 to 1828 he was a member of the United States Senate. Macon opposed the protective tariff in any form, policies of internal improvement, and the rechartering of the United States Bank in 1811 and 1816. He staunchly defended slavery and voted against the Missouri Compromise. *CDAB*, 625.

[9]Hugh Swinton Legaré (1797-1843) was a South Carolina lawyer, legislator, and diplomat. A graduate of South Carolina College (1814), he also studied in Edinburgh and Paris. He was coeditor of the *Southern Review*, 1828-1832; United States chargé d'affaires in Belgium, 1832-1836; Union Democratic congressman, 1837-1839; and United States attorney general from 1841 until his death. He opposed John C. Calhoun during the nullification controversy. *CDAB*, 559; *Biographical Directory of Congress*, 1209.

[10]Apparently this reference was to Peter Vivian Daniel (1784-1860), of Virginia, who was associate justice, United States Supreme Court, 1841-1860. *CDAB*, 214.

[11]John Marshall (1755-1835), the eldest of fifteen children, was the son of Thomas Marshall and was born and reared in Germantown, Virginia. Possessed of a superior intellect and an innate feeling of responsibility, Marshall acquired an amazing command of law through self-education, having access to the first American edition of Blackstone's *Commentaries* through his father's subscription in 1772. For a brief time in 1780 when he was between military assignments in the American Revolution, he studied law under George Wythe at the College of William and Mary—his only formal training. After the war Marshall launched his meteoric career in law at Richmond, Virginia. He saw the need for a strong central government and became an avid advocate of constitutional reform. He supported President Washington and the financial views of Alexander Hamilton. Recognized as the Federalist leader in Virginia, he became secretary of state under John Adams in 1800 and chief justice of the United States in 1801. For thirty-five years thereafter Marshall availed himself of the opportunity to mold the Supreme Court into a powerful, cohesive instrument. His leadership was firm and uncompromising. His opinions on constitutional doctrine and his love of the Union were made indelibly clear in decisions of the Court. *CDAB*, 642-645.

[12]William Henry Harrison (1773-1841) was a son of Benjamin Harrison of Charles City, Virginia. He attended Hampden-Sydney College and studied medicine for a short time with Benjamin Rush. He served in the army during the conflict with the Indians in the Northwest Territory and remained on garrison duty at North Bend and Fort Washington. In 1795 he married Anna Symmes and in 1798 resigned from the army to accept an appointment as secretary of the Northwest Territory. After his election as governor of Indiana in 1800, Harrison tried sincerely to deal fairly with the Indians but to obtain from

them by sale as much land as possible for the United States. The Indians, unwilling to continue selling their land, could not be appeased and became increasingly hostile. Harrison in his capacity as regular brigadier general of the army and supreme commander of the Army of the Northwest led the United States military forces against the Indians, acquiring in the process the status of national hero. After he resigned from the army in 1814, Harrison undertook several unprofitable business enterprises but managed to have a fairly successful political career. In 1836 he was the unsuccessful anti-Van Buren candidate for president but in 1840 was selected over Henry Clay as the Whig candidate. With John Tyler as his running mate and the appealing slogan "Tippecanoe and Tyler too," Harrison was elected ninth president of the United States. He died of pneumonia a month after his inauguration. *CDAB*, 407-408.

[13]Noah Haynes Swayne (1804-1884) was born and reared in Frederick County, Virginia. He became a highly successful lawyer in Ohio and in 1862 was appointed a justice of the United States Supreme Court. Swayne earned a reputation as the most nationalistic-minded jurist of the Court. *CDAB*, 1036-1037.

[14]John Tyler (1790-1862), like his predecessor in the White House, William Henry Harrison, was born in Charles City, Virginia. Educated at William and Mary and tutored in law by his father, Tyler began his political career in 1811 as a member of the House of Delegates. He was a man of great ability and personal charm as well as a man with strong convictions, evinced during his many terms of public office, especially as governor of Virginia and in the United States Senate. In 1840 he ran as vice-president on the ticket with Harrison and succeeded to the presidency upon Harrison's death in April, 1841. Despite his rift with the national wing of the Whig party, Tyler proved to be an excellent administrator and negotiator. He achieved reform and much-needed reorganization of the navy, encouraged and opened trade with China, negotiated the Webster-Ashburton Treaty, and effected the annexation of Texas. Tyler declined renomination in 1844 but served in the Provisional Congress of the Confederacy. *CDAB*, 1091-1092.

M. C. C. Church[1] *to William A. Graham* UNC

Parkersburg, W. Va.
July 15/69

Herewith inclose you a "Proposed Preamble and Constitution for the United States," which I wish you to examine & criticise; also, to give me your views in regard to the inauguration of a Movement having for its object the ends therein proposed. Whatever you have to say, will be considered entirely confidential, unless you give permission to publish your letter in case that may be deemed necessary.

This Constitution is now being read & criticised by eminent gentlemen both North & South. If the movement is not premature, it is my purpose in connection with a number of others to commence operations as soon as this Constitution can be perfected; probably by Autumn. Papers will be started simultaneously in Washington, Chicago, & Nashville, for the purpose of advocating the adoption of the Constitution inclosed.

I have endeavored to guard the rights of *all* classes & think your sagacity will discern the necessity at this time of the proposed changes. Please consider this entire matter as *confidential.*

---

[1]M. C. C. Church has not been identified nor has the proposed constitution been located.

Thomas B. Florence[1] *to William A. Graham* UNC

Washington, D.C.,
July 15th., 1869.

In view of the present condition of affairs in your section of the country, and the effort which is being made by nearly all of the Southern States to invite emigrants thither, it has occurred to me that a necessity exists for the organization of an association, to enable such landholders as may wish to dispose of any portion of their property, to find a market for the same, and to promote and encourage such a class of emigration as will be most acceptable to the white population of the South, and thereby establish, in a corresponding degree, a feeling of harmony and friendship between them and the new settlers.

Impressed with this idea I have, in conjunction with a number of gentlemen of conservative political views, made arrangements for the establishment in this city of an association to be known as the "Southern Land and Emigration Company," with objects as already stated.

It is our intention in the accomplishment of this purpose, to rely, in a great measure, upon the assistance of the democratic press at the North and at the South, making the "Constitutional Union," of which I am Publisher and Editor, the principal organ of the movement.

Estimating the approval of prominent public men throughout the country, whose political views are in accord with our own, as of great importance to the success of the movement contemplated, I have the honor to request permission to use your name on our list of references, assuring you that in all things the organization will be so conducted as to place its affairs beyond criticism.

Hoping for an early and favorable response.

I am, truly, your friend

Ex-President Fillmore,[2] Gov. Hoffman,[3] of N.Y., Gov. Bowie,[4] of Md., Ex-Gov. Smith,[5] of Va., and many other distinguished gentlemen have signified their approval of the enterprise.

---

[1]Thomas Birch Florence (1812-1875) was a native of Pennsylvania who edited the *Constitutional Union* (Washington, D.C.). He had represented Pennsylvania in Congress as a Democrat, 1851-1861. A champion of temperance, he was known among workingmen as "the widow's friend." *CDAB*, 300.

[2]Millard Fillmore (1800-1874), born the son of a farmer in Locke, New York, was admitted to the bar in 1823 and established a practice in Buffalo in 1830. As a Whig, he served in Congress 1833-1835 and 1837-1843, acting as chairman of the Ways and Means Committee at the time the tariff of 1842 was devised. He was nominated for vice-president in 1848, inaugurated in 1849, and became president when Zachary Taylor died in office in July, 1850. Graham was appointed by Fillmore to his cabinet as secretary of the navy. *CDAB*, 292.

[3]John Thompson Hoffman (1828-1888) was by profession a lawyer. A Tammany politician, he was governor of New York, 1869-1873, after a term as mayor of New York City, 1865-1868. A popular leader, Hoffman was used as a screen by the Tweed Ring, which he ultimately repudiated. *CDAB*, 442-443.

[4]Oden Bowie (1826-1894), of Maryland, was a businessman and politician. He was the

Democratic governor of Maryland, 1867-1872. Aside from his public duties, he was president of the Baltimore and Potomac Railroad, 1860-1894. *CDAB*, 96.

[5]William "Extra Billy" Smith (1769-1887) was one of Virginia's remarkable men of the nineteenth century. A lawyer and a Democrat, he was a state senator, 1836-1841; successful mail contractor; United States congressman, 1841-1843 and 1853-1861; Virginia governor, 1846-1849 and 1864-1865; Confederate congressman; and Confederate brigadier general. After the war he farmed his estate, Monterosa, in Fauquier County. Smith's retirement from public life was interrupted when, at the age of eighty, he was elected to the Virginia House of Delegates, where he served from 1877 to 1879. *DAB*, XVII, 361.

Kemp P. Battle[1] to William A. Graham A&H

Raleigh,
July 20th., 1869.

I have just come into possession of a little piece of gossip which may amuse you this hot day.

Judge Pearson tells me that at a late meeting of the Trustees of the Univ'y it was moved to send for Mr. Att'y Ed. Haywood,[2] to advise in regard to the land scrip. Lewis paid $125,000. into the B'k of Republic, and that sum has been there on deposite for 12 mos.[3]

Mr. H. advised that the Trustees are responsible for the present price of the scrip in market. Said he, "Sue Gov. Graham, Gov. Manly,[4] Judge Ruffin, Mr. Kemp Battle for the whole, they will draw the $125,000. for their own indemnity as far as it goes, and the new Trustees will recover of them 85 cts. per acre." Says Judge P., "Do you mean to give it as your professional opinion that such gentlemen as those named and Gov. Worth, Judge Battle,[5] etc., who served *without reward*, can be made liable for *gross neglect* in this case?" "Certainly, sir, that is my advice." "Then, sir," said Pearson, "I give it as *my* opinion that they *cannot*." "It is admitted they served without reward, and got no part of the fund. A bird in the hand is worth two in the bush. I move we draw the money and invest in U.S. bonds, and give Lewis a release, if necessary." This was carried with only two dissenting voices—Jim Taylor[6] or Cbe Harris[7] being one.

I think Judge Pearson took some pleasure in tripping Mr. Haywood up, on ac't of his signing the protest.[8] To do him justice, he certainly uses his influence to stop vindictive proceedings against "men of the old school."

---

[1]Kemp Plummer Battle (1831-1919), of Franklin County and Chapel Hill, was the son of William Horn and Lucy Plummer Battle. He was graduated in 1848 with honors by the University of North Carolina, where he was subsequently tutor, chairman of the board of trustees, president (1876-1891), and professor of history (1891-1907). His best-known literary work was his *History of the University of North Carolina* in two volumes. In politics Battle was a Union Whig who, as a delegate to the Constitutional Convention of 1861, opposed secession. Once war came, he supported the state and was influential in the election of Zebulon B. Vance as governor. A genial, humorous, humane man, Battle was greatly respected and loved by the people of North Carolina. *DAB*, II, 57-58; McCormick, *Convention Personnel*, 17-18; Powell, *DNCB*, I, 114-115.

[2]Edward Graham Haywood (d. 1891) was a native of Raleigh and the son of William H. Haywood, a former Democratic United States senator. Both men were eminent lawyers. The younger Haywood was particularly active in the hotly contested election of 1860. At

that time he was described by a Whig adversary as "the finest orator in the Democratic party." After the Civil War he participated in several highly controversial cases, and his popularity declined apace. He lived in Washington during the last years of his life. Moses N. Amis, *Historical Raleigh, from Its Foundation in 1792* (Raleigh: Edwards and Broughton, 1902), 101, hereinafter cited as Amis, *Historical Raleigh*; Kemp Plummer Battle, *Memories of an Old-Time Tar Heel* (Chapel Hill: University of North Carolina Press, 1945), 163; *News and Observer* (Raleigh), June 2, 1891.

[3]The background to the episode described here was rather complex. At the end of the Civil War the position of the university was desperate. Loss of its endowment, indebtedness, physical depredations, declining enrollments, and hostility toward President David L. Swain combined to threaten the very existence of the institution. Nevertheless, Swain worked unceasingly to gain financial support for the university. In 1866 he was able to secure a state appropriation of $7,000—the first direct assistance ever approved by the North Carolina legislature. This one-year appropriation was clearly just a stopgap measure.

Early in February, 1867, Swain was able to persuade the legislature to transfer to the institution the state's right to western lands under provisions of the Morrill Land Grant Act of 1862. The purpose of that legislation was to promote agricultural and mechanical education; therefore, Swain had to agree to changes in the university as follow: (1) agricultural and mechanical programs would be established as required by the congressional act; (2) at least two professors were to be employed "in order to promote the liberal and practical education of the industrial classes in the several pursuits and professions of life"; (3) each county would be allowed to send one indigent student to the university annually with free tuition; and (4) students would be admitted to the programs in agricultural and mechanical arts without having acquired the educational background required for regular college courses.

Swain promptly proceeded to Washington, D.C., where he was successful in securing land scrip for 170,000 acres of western land, largely through his personal influence with President Andrew Johnson. Although Congress had suspended the allocation of lands going to the former Confederate states, the scrip itself was valuable and transferable. In August, 1867, the university trustees authorized the sale of the land scrip to G. F. Lewis and his associates Fisher, Booth, and Company, Detroit, Michigan, for fifty cents an acre. Trustee William A. Graham then moved that $13,500 of the first installment be paid to the university; he reasoned that this was sanctioned by a provision in the Morrill Land Grant Act that authorized that ten percent of the proceeds realized from land sales might be invested in college sites and experimental farms. In the case of the university no such purchases were necesary, so Graham proposed that the sum of $13,500 be applied to general expenses. He also suggested that the trustees act in this matter without prior assent from the General Assembly, since that body was prohibited from meeting by military order. In the advocacy of his proposals, Graham said that sometimes circumstances required that public servants take responsibilities that went beyond their instructions. The trustees gave their approval, anticipating that the next General Assembly would assent retroactively.

Meanwhile, Congress decided that no western lands would be allotted to the former Confederate states until all provisions of the 1867 Military Reconstruction Acts had been met. After North Carolina returned to the Union, Governor Holden, then chairman of the trustees, and his colleagues sought unsuccessfully to break the contract with Lewis and his associates. Kemp P. Battle, *History of the University of North Carolina from Its Beginning to the Death of President Swain, 1789-1868*, Volume I; *From 1868 to 1912*, Volume II (Raleigh: Edwards and Broughton, 2 volumes, 1907, 1912), I, 756-759, hereinafter cited as Battle, *History of the University*.

[4]Charles Manly (1795-1871), a native of Chatham County, was the brother of Judge Matthias E. Manly and the Reverend Basil Manly, president of the University of Alabama. He graduated from the University of North Carolina in 1814 and was a lawyer by profession. Politically Manly aligned himself with the Whig party, serving for many years as a member of its central committee. As governor of North Carolina (1849-1851) he was an advocate of education and internal improvements. He was secretary and treasurer of the University of North Carolina trustees from 1821 to 1869, except when he was governor. Ashe, *Biographical History*, VI, 357-366.

[5]William Horn Battle (1802-1879), a native of Edgecombe County, graduated from the University of North Carolina and read law with Judge Leonard Henderson. A Whig in politics, he devoted his talents to the law, serving as the state supreme court reporter, a superior court judge, and an associate justice of the state supreme court, 1852-1868. He was professor of law at the University of North Carolina from 1845 to 1868. Twice he contributed to a revision of the statutes of North Carolina. After the Civil War he was for a time president of the Raleigh National Bank. *DAB*, II, 58.

[6]James Fauntleroy Taylor (1821-1903), a Raleigh attorney, was graduated by the University of North Carolina in 1841. A Republican after the war, he was a university trustee, 1869-1870. Grant, *Alumni History*, 611, 949.

[7]Ceburn L. H. Harris (1822-1908), of Rutherford County, was a large landholder who became interested in public service during the Civil War. He was a lieutenant colonel of militia; delegate to the conventions of 1865 and 1868; state senator, 1865-1867; and superintendent of public works, 1868-1872, when the legislature reduced his salary, forcing his resignation. In his capacity as superintendent of public works, Harris was an *ex officio* member of the University of North Carolina Board of Trustees under the state constitution of 1868. Personally honest but a partisan Republican, Harris broke with Holden and other Republican leaders as a consequence of proposed frauds. After Recostruction he held minor federal appointments and was mayor of Rutherfordton. Griffin, *History of Old Tryon and Rutherford Counties*, 319-320; Battle, *History of the University*, II, 8, 785.

[8]Prompted by concern over the extent to which state jurists were politically active during Reconstruction, Bartholomew F. Moore, then the "father of the bar," drew up a powerfully written document entitled "A Solemn Protest of the Bar of North Carolina against Judicial Interference in Political Affairs." One hundred and eight lawyers signed it, and on April 19, 1869, it appeared in the *Sentinel* (Raleigh) and other newspapers. No one expected what followed.

When the supreme court met in June, Chief Justice Richmond M. Pearson stated that the protest constituted contempt of court. He directed that a rule be served on twenty-five of the petitioners who practiced before the supreme court calling upon them to show cause why they should not be silenced. By arrangement the rule was served on three men only: B. F. Moore, Edward G. Haywood, and Thomas Bragg. Moore, in reply, admitted his role in the affair but defended himself ably. He denied the jurisdiction of the court, claimed that the publication was not libelous, and, while admitting that the protest was intended to express disapproval, disavowed any intention of committing a contempt. Moore contended that his sole purpose was to preserve the purity that had always characterized the administration of justice by the courts of the state. On June 19 Pearson read the decision of the court. While brushing aside the contentions of the signers and their counsel, he accepted the disavowal of contemptuous intent. Nevertheless, the chief justice scolded Moore personally. Bent on revenge, the court had taken an indefensible position and suffered a severe blow in reputation and public respect.

For an account of this affair see Hamilton, *Reconstruction in North Carolina*, 390-395, or the sketch on Moore in Ashe, *Biographical History*, V, 284-285.

Robert Ransom[1] to William A. Graham UNC

Wilmington N.C.
July 27th, 1869

The citizens of this place are trying to have built a large Seminary for young ladies.[2] They propose to buy a suitable lot & have proper buildings placed on it. The very reduced circumstances of those most interested requires all the assistance that can be obtained; & at the request of some of the directors in the matter I wish to see if they can through you get any aid from the Peabody Fund. They would give for a loan personal security or a mortgage upon the property. Knowing only that you are one of the Trustees of that Fund they through me communicate their request, & hopingly trust that you may be able to render some aid in an enterprise intended for the benefit of the women of the next & succeeding generations. If a gift can be obtained, it will of course be most acceptable, but they leave to you the arrangement, & will be glad to get in firm reply any suggestion which may further the accomplishment of our purpose.

---

[1]Robert Ransom, Jr. (1828-1892), a native of Warren County and a resident of Wilmington, was a graduate of West Point. In 1861 he resigned from the United States Army and became colonel of the First North Carolina Cavalry. He was promoted to brigadier general in 1862 and major general in 1863. Immediately after the Civil War he was chief of police in Wilmington. At one time Ransom had about 100 policemen, a force of Confederate veterans used to control the numerous freedmen in the town. Later he was a farmer and engineer. Boatner, *Civil War Dictionary*, 679; William McKee Evans, *Ballots and Fence Rails: Reconstruction on the Lower Cape Fear* (Chapel Hill: University of North Carolina Press, 1967), 80, 84, 101-103, 137, hereinafter cited as Evans, *Ballots and Fence Rails.*

[2]Mrs. Ransom operated a female seminary at one time. Evans, *Ballots and Fence Rails*, 237.

William A. Graham to William A. Graham, Jr. A&H

Hillsboro',
August 9th. 1869.

. . . The election in this Township resulted in the choice of one negro Magistrate and 3 incompetent whites, one or two negroes on school committee, said to be result of colonizing negroes from other districts; have heard nothing from Lincoln, but the report is, that the conservatives have done well in the West. We witnessed the total eclipse of the sun on Friday afternoon, with no clouds to interrupt. On Saturday night Ku Klux invaded the town, took keys of jail from Sheriff,[1] took out two negroes, charged with burning three Barns on Cove Creek, shot one slightly,[2] frightened the other, and turned them loose. The negroes came back and were put in jail. The Sheriff summoned a party after daylight, saw traces of company estimated at 75 men, on road towards Cove Creek, but made no discovery of persons.

The drought continues with great severity—slight rains occasionally, but not sufficient to do any good.

Love to Julia and the children from us all.

Rob't wrote after arriving at Mr. Lawson's[3]—all well.

Affectionately yours,

J. M. Graham left here for Camp meeting last Wednesday evening.

---

[1]John Turner was Orange County sheriff from August 15, 1868, to September 5, 1870. Lefler and Wager, *Orange County*, 355.

[2]The Negro who was shot died of his wounds. For more information about the events described in this letter, see Lefler and Wager, *Orange County*, 118, or Trelease, *White Terror*, 195.

[3]Mr. Lawson has not been identified.

Ann E. Young[1] *to William A. Graham* UNC

Washington City
August 23/69

I hardly know how to commence, but it has come to *this.* I must do something to support my family, Annie my oldest daughter educated herself—and a very good education she has. Her sisters not having the energy she had, Annie obtained an office to send them to school in Baltimore. She and I depending on Jim, about 3 months since [she] was dismiss'd. The only reason given was appointed by a democrat. Col Moore[2] private Sec to President Johnson—he was my first boarder—knew all about us—was very much interested in all the children. Annie has made every effort to get back in office. Told her last week it was no use trying as she was appointed by Col M it was a great piece of impudence, etc. So then ends that. As you are one of the Trustees of the Peabody fund, and must have some influence with Genrl. Grant, or Mr. Corcoran,[3] thought if we could get a letter from you it might be some use. Mr. C. lives very near us. When Annie lost her office, we had no money to pay house rent and did not know what to do. Jim was at sea. Dr. Edwards[4] offer'd his house rent free till Oct. Then I dont know what we will do, as the children must return to Baltimore. That will take all Jim allows me. Annie and I must do something. God only know what. I was in hopes when working so hard to keep them together I would rest when they were grown, but it grows darker.

My object is to have Helie graduate, she and Annie open a school in our own House which I hope to get in by that time, an [injunc]tion is laid on it now—which will be settled by a law suit in Oct. but this cant be done for two years. I hope the South will be settled, with me it has been hope on hope always. I have almost given up that. I heard from you and family, by Mrs. Chesney (Kate Murphy) I can hardly believe those little boys married men and Susan[5] a young lady. My love to Mrs. Graham and all the rest. I wonder if they have forgotten. Jim has just returned after a cruise of 25 months—looking very badly—but hope he will soon be well. I am in hopes he will be stationed near home. I am determined he shall send his sisters to Baltimore (and Annie and I do for ourselves), if he does that it is as much as I can expect.

Hoping to see you and yours some day. When we will be better off.

---

[1]Several people mentioned in this letter, as well as the writer, Ann E. Young, have not been identified.

[2]Colonel William G. Moore had served as a Union officer during the Civil War. At one time Edwin M. Stanton's confidential secretary, he served as President Andrew Johnson's executive secretary through most of the Tennessean's term in office. He was Johnson's confidant, and no man had closer daily contact with the president. Moore left shorthand diaries in which he candidly speculated about Johnson's character, meditations, and beliefs. Transcriptions of the Moore diaries may be found in the Andrew Johnson Papers, Library of Congress, Washington, D.C. Lately Thomas, *The First President Johnson: The Three Lives of the Seventeenth President of the United States of America* (New York: William Morrow and Company, 1968), 539, 637; R. N. Scott and others (eds.), *The War of the Rebellion: A Compilation of the Official Records of the Union and Confederate*

Armies (Washington: Government Printing Office, 70 volumes, 1880-1901), Series I, I, 46.

[3]William Wilson Corcoran (1798-1888), a lifetime resident of Washington, D.C., was a banker and philanthropist. He began his banking career after a brief venture into business as a merchant. The firm of Corcoran and Riggs, bankers, was very successful, and Corcoran was able to inaugurate the Corcoran Gallery of Art in 1872 in Washington, D.C.; it had been begun in 1859, but Corcoran used his own collection as a nucleus and endowed the gallery. He also made many substantial gifts to universities, churches, and religious institutions. *CDAB*, 193.

[4]Dr. Edwards has not been identified.

[5]Susan Washington Graham (1851-1909), sometimes referred to as "Sissy," "Sister," and "Sudie," was the only daughter among the ten children born to the William A. Grahams. A favorite of her father, who carefully supervised her education, she attended the Nash-Kollock Female School in Hillsborough and briefly, after the Civil War, Madame Roustan's French School in New York City. In 1874 she married Judge Walter Clark, later chief justice of the North Carolina Supreme Court. Clark, "Graham Descendants"; Ann Strudwick Nash, *Ladies in the Making* (Durham: Seeman Printery, 1964), 28-30; Aubrey Lee Brooks, *Walter Clark: Fighting Judge* (Chapel Hill: University of North Carolina Press, 1944), 48-49, 66, hereinafter cited as Brooks, *Walter Clark*.

William Bingham, Jr.,[1] *to William A. Graham* UNC

Hillsborough, N.C.
Aug. 23rd 1869

It has been suggested to me that perhaps high schools might receive some assistance from the Peabody fund; and concluding that the mention of the subject will at least do no harm, I take the liberty of proposing that in case it shall not be inconsistent with the plan upon which the fund is administered to assist us with a loan, I would secure the payment of the money with interest at six per cent, and in consideration of the accommodation thus granted would farther agree to teach a certain number of poor boys free of charge for tuition, during so long a time as I should have the use of such funds.

The disaster to the cotton interest in 1867 not only inflicted on us a heavy pecuniary loss, but so reduced our resources that our improvements here have come to a standstill. The school is decidedly looking up at present, and our prospect for next year is good; but still, we shall not have means, unless we seek for them abroad, to finish the improvements in the way of school buildings, etc., of which we stand in need. The foregoing plan has suggested itself to my mind, as one by which the poor can be assisted without actual diminution of the fund, while the advantage to ourselves of a moderate rate of interest would compensate us for the additional labor of instruction. Permit me to add that I have had twice as much money offered me as I need, but at the ruinous market rate of 18% per year, compounded every ninety days.

If you think my proposal a proper one to entertain, please favor me with a reply at y'r earliest convenience.

---

[1]William Bingham, Jr. (1835-1873), of Orange County, was the son of William J. Bingham and was the third Bingham to head the famous classical school of that name. He graduated from the University of North Carolina in 1856 with the highest honors in a class of seventy. The author of several notable textbooks, Bingham has been characterized as being "in the front rank of educators, excelled by none, equaled by few." Ashe, *Biographical History*, VI, 74-83; Powell, *DNCB*, I, 160-161.

Augustus W. Graham to William A. Graham UNC

Charlotte, N.C.
Sept. 1st 1869

I came down yesterday evening to have a check cashed. I got the money ($50.00) and sent twenty five dollars of it to Willie last night by express. I found a letter from you to Kerr enclosed in one to Brother Joe. We tried to find some one going to that neighborhood but did not succeed. This morning I hired a horse from the driving stable and went to the plantation. Kerr was not there, he had gone over to Mr. Wm McLean's[1] or somewhere else, so I did not see him. He sold enough wheat to pay the taxes. The taxes were $185.00/100. Kerr paid it the 10th of Aug. and got a receipt. They have cut the meadows and made three small stacks of hay. The straw that he put up behind the barn is nearly all rotten. The children chickens or hogs have made holes on top of it by crawling over it and the rains settle in it is decaying fast. The cowpen has not been commenced. He made two of the boys cut briars one day. They have had several rains within the last ten days, but it was very dry before.

The hands were all pulling fodder; they have finished nearly all of the uplands. They have cut part of the timber for the screw. Kerr has engaged no one as yet to fix the screw.

They have been feeding on tops and fodder but are wasting both, for want of cutting knives. The corn on the bottoms is very good, but on the upland it is rather trifling. The cotton is small but seems to be pretty well filled with bolls. Some of it has commenced to open. Told Chambers,[2] as he was fartherest on with his fodder, to fix a turnip patch this evening, in the corners of the lot, just beyond the orchard on the road, and left direction for Kerr to sow the seed the first thing in the morning, and to make another patch some where else on the plantation.

I will return to Lincoln tomorrow. Julia Johnston[3] is to be married tonight but I am not invited to the wedding so I do not expect to go.

Tell Willie, Wilkes Luce & Co. owe him about one hundred and seventy five ($175.) dollars, including the check I received from them on yesterday.

Sister Bettie[4] sends love to all.

---

[1]This reference was probably to Dr. William B. McLean of the Beattie's Ford section. He was the son of William and Mary Davidson McLean and was William A. Graham's first cousin. Sherrill, *Annals of Lincoln County*, 59.

[2]Chambers was possibly one of Graham's tenants.

[3]Julia Martha Johnston (1846-1915) married Colonel A. B. Andrews (1841-1915) in 1869. A daughter of the William Johnstons, she was William A. Graham's grandniece. Clark, "Graham Descendants."

[4]Elizabeth Hill (1838-1912) had married Joseph Graham in 1859. Clark, "Graham Descendants."

Testimonial of William A. Graham on Behalf of William Hooper[1] A&H

From Hon. Wm. A. Graham, Ex-Governor of N.C. and Ex-Secretary of the Navy.

Hillsboro' N.C.
Sept. 10th., 1869.

To All Whom It May Concern.

My friend the Rev. Wm. Hooper, L.L.D., to whom this is delivered informs me that he contemplates establishing himself as teacher of Young Ladies, at Norfolk Virginia. It affords me very sincere pleasure to declare that in the whole range of my acquaintance I can call to mind no individual better fitted for such employment; by his tastes, his acquirements and habits of study, as well as by the purity of his morals and the elevation of his character. Having filled with acceptance, the Professorships of ancient Languages, and Belles Lettres in the University of N.C., and of the former also in S.C. College, as well as like positions in other Institutions of learning, he is so well known in these States as a Scholar, instructor and writer of pure and undefiled English, that no testimonials of his merits are required in them. And I shall esteem any community fortunate, whose youth, especially of the gentler sex, may enjoy the benefit of his instructions in the pursuit of liberal studies, and in the formation of their tastes, morals and manners.

(Signed,) WM. A. GRAHAM.

From a private letter accompanying the above Certificate.

. . . If the Citizens of Norfolk can be induced to send to you, Young Ladies who have finished a course in the Seminaries to complete their education in the higher branches of learning, I have no doubt you will be eminently serviceable to them and will realize profit and reputation yourself.

W. A. GRAHAM.

---

[1]The testimonial, intended for use as a published endorsement, was accompanied by a letter to Hooper; the final paragraph of that letter was also published.

William Hooper (1792-1876), a grandson of the signer of the Declaration of Independence who bore the same name, was born in Hillsborough. While he was still a boy, his mother became the second wife of University of North Carolina president Joseph Caldwell. Hooper was a scholar who held the following degrees: A.B., 1809, A.M., 1812, honorary LL.D., 1837, and honorary D.D., 1857, University of North Carolina; and A.M., Princeton, 1818. An ordained priest of the Protestant Episcopal church (1822), he became a Baptist in 1831, having left the Episcopal church because of its doctrines of regeneration and infant baptism.

Hooper taught at the university from 1810 to 1822 and from 1825 to 1837; he held the chair of ancient languages, 1828-1837. Subsequently he was professor of theology at Furman Institute (1838-1840), professor of Roman literature at the College of South Carolina (1840-1846), president at Wake Forest College (1846-1849), teacher of a classical school for boys near Littleton (1849-1851), president of Chowan Female Collegiate Institute (1855-1861), teacher in the Female Seminary, Fayetteville (1861-1865), and associate principal of the Wilson Collegiate Seminary for Young Ladies (1866-1875). He served briefly as a pastoral minister during his long career. Hooper died shortly after attending centennial ceremonies in Philadelphia commemorating the signing of the Declaration of Independence. Battle, *History of the University*, I, 436-437; Grant, *Alumni History*, 296.

James A. Graham to William A. Graham UNC

Law Office of Jas. A. Graham
Graham, N.C.
Sept 16th 1869

. . . .

Negroes are becoming quite scarce about here. About the time of the election our streets were filled with them, but I have been unable to hire one for the past 3 or 4 days to do a little work. They have gone to the R.R.s in western North Carolina and some to Tennessee with Mr. Hunter[1] who has been here on a visit. Will you go to Caswell Court in October? I think I shall come down to Hillsboro and go from there, as it will be cheaper than hiring a horse here. Our sheriff has been unable to collect more than one fourth of his taxes so far. The people have not the money to pay. I doubt very much if he will get more than one half except by sale.

Lizzie[2] joins me in love to all.

Affectionately Your Son

---

[1]Mr. Hunter has not been identified.

[2]Earlier in the year James A. Graham had married Elizabeth Cheshire Webb (1845-1915). She was a daughter of James and Sarah Elizabeth Cheshire Webb of Orange County. Clark, "Graham Descendants."

Joseph A. Engelhard[1] *to William A. Graham* UNC

Office of The Journal,
Wilmington, N.C.,
September 21st., 1869.

I am very anxious to publish a proper obituary notice of the late Gov. Worth. There is no man who has figured in public life in North Carolina, since the war, who deserved more from his fellow-citizens, or whose memory should be held in higher estimation. In reflecting over his compeers and friends, it struck me that you would be better able to do justice [to] the subject, and I write to you, hoping you may find it convenient to comply with my request.[2] I am authorized to say that Maj. Bagley[3] would permit you to see his papers and letters, and render you any assistance you may need.

Hoping to hear from you, with the assurance that a favorable reply will be gratefully appreciated.

---

[1]Joseph Adolphus Engelhard (1832-1879) of Edgecombe County, a native of Mississippi,

was a graduate of the University of North Carolina, a Confederate major, an editor in Raleigh and Wilmington, and North Carolina secretary of state, 1877-1879. A Conservative in politics, he was clerk of the Senate in the sessions of 1865-1866 and 1866-1867. Spencer Alumni Project; Powell, *DNCB*, II, 157-158; Connor, *North Carolina Manual, 1913*, 474-475; Hamilton, *Reconstruction in North Carolina*, 362n.

[2]There is no indication that Graham complied with this request for a tribute to Worth, a trusted friend. Worth had died on September 5, 1869. For an account of Worth's last months, a period of declining health, and death, see Zuber, *Jonathan Worth*, 294-299.

[3]William H. Bagley was Worth's son-in-law, having married Adelaide "Addie" Worth in March, 1866. Zuber, *Jonathan Worth*, 289.

John T. Mason[1] to William A. Graham UNC

Baltimore
Sep 22nd 1869

At a former period, when we were in Congress together, I had the honor of your acquaintance. I still remember you with pleasure, though possibly you may have forgotten me. Availing myself of your probable recollection, I beg herewith to enclose a communication from my kinsman and law partner, Maj. Rowland,[2] formerly on Gen'l. Ransom's staff, and to ask for it your attentive consideration, and expecially to commend Miss Stewart[3] to your kindness.

This application is made to you as one of the Trustees of the Peabody fund, with out knowing precisely how far it may fall within your power or duties in connection with that important trust.

With my sincere regards, and best wishes, I am very truly and respectfully yours.

---

[1]John Thomson Mason (1815-1873), of Maryland, graduated from Princeton in 1836. A lawyer, he was a state legislator in 1838 and 1839, a Democratic congressman (1841-1843), judge of the court of appeals (1851-1857), and collector of customs at Baltimore (1857-1861). Subsequently, he engaged in the practice of law. Mason was a member of the House of Representatives when Graham was a United States senator. *Biographical Directory of Congress*, 1273.

[2]Thomas W. Rowland, assistant adjutant on Robert Ransom's staff, was characterized as "an educated, accomplished soldier, of uncommon intelligence in all lines of his duty." Rowland died a few years after 1865 from tuberculosis contracted while he was a soldier. Clark, *Histories of the North Carolina Regiments*, IV, 577.

[3]Miss Stewart has not been identified.

John A. Cameron[1] to William A. Graham UNC

Summerville, Harnett Co., N.C.
September 24th 1869

I have been informed that you are the proper source to apply to for information in order to secure the benefit of a part of the Peabody fund for my school at this place.

I wrote to you on this subject five or six weeks ago, but as I have heard nothing from you I fear my letter was lost.

There are within four miles of the academy one hundred and twenty nine white children, between the ages of six and twenty-one, not more than thirty of whom are in school.

If you will be so kind as to send me the necessary directions, you will greatly oblige me. I was introduced to you at Chapel Hill, while I was a student at the Univ., and am brother-in-law of Prof. Martin,[2] formerly one of the Professors at that place.

I trust that my object will be a sufficient apology for my troubling you.

---

[1]John Atkins Cameron (1840-1891), of Harnett County, received the A.B. and A.M. degrees from the University of North Carolina in 1862 and 1866 respectively. He was a sergeant in the Confederate army. Grant, *Alumni History*, 95.

[2]William Joseph Martin (1830-1896) of Virginia, who attended that state's university, held the chair of natural sciences at Washington (now Washington and Jefferson) College before being elected, in 1858, to the chair of chemistry at the University of North Carolina. When the Civil War began, Martin abandoned his academic pursuits to become an ideal Confederate officer. After Gettysburg, where he was wounded for the first of six times, Martin was colonel of the Eleventh North Carolina Regiment, Army of Northern Virginia. He founded Columbia High School, Columbia, Tennessee, before accepting the chair of chemistry at Davidson College in 1870. He was widely respected as a Christian scholar and challenging teacher. Van Noppen Papers.

Leonidas Brown[1] *to William A. Graham* UNC

Salisbury
Rowan County, N.C.
Sept 28th 1869

Having been informed that you were the "Trustee" of "The Peabody School Fund for this State," and advised by mutual friends to communicate with you, I beg leave respectfully to submit the following facts: viz: Salisbury has attempted a Free School.

The town of Salisbury levied this year a School Tax, amounting to about Three Hundred and Fifty Dollars. In July last I was appointed teacher of the "Male Department," and the Rev. Mr. Plyler[2] of the "Female." The corporation funds are now exhausted, and with this week my school must close, unless, I can obtain assistance to continue it. Sixty Five Pupils' names are on my list, and but few of the whole number can pay *anything* for tuition. Shall such a field be abandoned? My salary has not paid my expenses: but rather than see this school stop, I would cheerfully continue to make sacrifices. Can you my Dear Sir, render me any aid in this matter? Whatever is to be done, should be done immediately. If the school closes for any time, it may be difficult to reorganize. My boys are now well classed, are learning rapidly, and should be encouraged. Close it, and God only knows where these boys may turn. But it is worse than useless to argue this palpable question. The question is, can any aid be hoped for?

P.S.

I can suggest a scheme by which I can *establish* a permanent Male School, with ($3000) Three Thousand Dollars. It is this. I can rent here, at reasonable rates, a secure and commodious house—for a "Joint Book and Grocery

Store." The Books to be sold to pupils *at cost.* The Groceries to their parents at cost. Outsiders would more than repay the original investment. I have a son and hireling to conduct the business, without charge, and will give a lien on the whole stock, both Books and Groceries, for the return of the original sum loaned. The school to be maintained from the Joint Stock. It can be done, and I can do it. With ($3000) Three Thousand Dollars, I can conduct the School and Store, with a firm belief in the permanency of the School and a certainty as to the investment being a paying one. The Rent of the House will be my only expense. The profit is certain.

Would you be so kind as to suggest the above Scheme to Mr. Peabody?

---

[1]Leonidas Brown (1830-1905), of Salisbury, attended the University of North Carolina in the 1840s. He was a teacher, lawyer, and journalist during a long career. Grant, *Alumni History*, 78.

[2]The Reverend Calvin Plyler, a Methodist minister, was a native of Rowan County. Jethro Rumple, *A History of Rowan County, North Carolina, Containing Sketches of Prominent Families and Distinguished Men* (Salisbury: J. J. Bruner, 1881; Raleigh: Edwards and Broughton, 1929), 294, hereinafter cited as Rumple, *Rowan County*.

Charles Phillips[1] *to William A. Graham* UNC

Davidson College, N.C.,
Monday, October 4th., 1869.

Hon. & dear Sir,

Unexpectedly, I find it necessary to ask for your opinion of Col. Martin, (W. J.) lately one of our Professors at the Univ. of N.C. *as it was.* I am authorized to present Col. M's name as that of a candidate for the vacant Chair of Chemistry, Geology, etc., in this Institution, at the meeting of our Trustees in Charlotte tomorrow week. (12th.) I hope to have by that time testimonials in favour of my former colleague, from former members of our Faculty at C. Hill. I shall thank you to add the weight of your name to the movement in favour of my friend.

The Trustees here have just bought the Cabinet of Prof. Brumby,[2] formerly of Tuscaloosa, Ala., for $1745. It is, I suppose, without a rival in matters Mineralogical, Geological, & Conchological in the South. Now, if we can secure Col. M's energy & knowledge to teach by it, we shall have here another claim on the public for patronage. There are 111 students here now, a number greater by 25 than ever known here before at this time in the session. This is in spite of deficient crops, and of a 20 mile ride in a hack. I hope one day to see the affairs of D. Coll. so managed, that men of all parties in Politics, and of various creeds in Religion, will unite in it's support.

Wishing for you all health and happiness, and presenting my respects to Mrs. Graham,

I am, very respectfully,

The Mail for Davidson College leaves Charlotte on Tuesdays—Thursdays—and Saturdays at 1 P. M.

If Gov'r Graham can do me the favour asked, I shall be glad to receive it by next Saturday's Mail.

---

[1]Charles Phillips (1822-1889), educator, was the son of James Phillips and the brother of Samuel F. Phillips and Cornelia Phillips Spencer. Over time he received four academic degrees: A.B., A.M., and D.D. from the University of North Carolina in 1841, 1844, and 1868 respectively; and LL.D. from Davidson College in 1876. He taught at the University of North Carolina as tutor or professor of engineering or math from 1844 to 1868 and from 1875 to 1879. While his alma mater was closed, 1869-1875, he taught at Davidson College. Grant, *Alumni History*, 492.

[2]Professor Richard T. Brumby of Tuscaloosa, Alabama, was interested in a number of sciences. At one time he was Alabama's state geologist and later was appointed to the chair of chemistry in the University of Alabama. James F. Sulzby, Jr., *Historical Alabama Hotels and Resorts* (Montgomery: University of Alabama Press, 1960), 52, 64.

Bartholomew F. Moore[1] *to William A. Graham* UNC

Raleigh,
November 1st., 1869.

I would be pleased to have your views upon the proposed lease of the N.C.R.R. I own no stock in it, I am a large lender to it. And a large stockholder in the R.&G.R.R.[2]

When the matter was mentioned to me, which was after the terms had been agreed, I doubted very much, and still do doubt, whether the lease would not sink my stock in value. I have considered the matter very gravely, and I have at length consented. As a stockholder of the R&G. Railroad Co. I expect to gain little, if anything. Were I a stockholder in N.C. RR Co. I should be exceedingly anxious for it. If the stock of that Compy will go up as alleged by some it will do, which, under its present condition, it will not do. There is an open avowal as I learn, by Littlefield, Dewese Wilkes[3] & others of that kind that the road must be sold. Their object will be to allow the proceeds of sale to be paid with State bonds, and the unprincipled men will again be feeding on the vitals of the State. If, for a considerable space of time its status were fixed, & placed beyond the reach of the ring, and it could afford to the stockholders a fair dividend, even of 3 or 4 percent, it would be very valuable stock. If then the State chose to sell, the sale would be at a high rate.

I think that some decided action should be taken to thwart the intended swindle by sale. What can be done so sure, as to lease?

It has been said that the W.&W.R.R. Co.[4] will advance the bid. I feel satisfied, though I am a considerable stockholder in that road, that it cannot give the satisfactory security.

I shall be at Halifax Court for a fortnight from date.

I am very truly
Yours,

---

[1]Bartholomew Figures Moore (1801-1878) was a native of Halifax County, a graduate of the University of North Carolina, a learned and profound lawyer, and a courageous and

devoted public servant. He began his political life as a Crawford Republican but eventually became a staunch Henry Clay Whig. He sat in the 1836, 1840, 1842, and 1844 sessions of the House of Commons, where he championed the North Carolina Whig program of reforms and internal improvements. He was North Carolina attorney general, 1848-1851. Moore's successful brief in *State* v. *Will* signaled the end of the harsher features of the state's slave codes. Although he felt that the South was aggrieved, Moore denied the right of secession and never changed that opinion. He refused to swear an oath of allegiance to the Confederacy and was thus barred from practicing in Confederate courts. He did not join the peace movement in North Carolina but made no secret of his Union sentiments. Moore opposed the Johnson plan of reconstruction, favoring continuation of existing southern legislatures. When he was made privy to Johnson's plans and asked to recommend a provisional governor, Moore declined. Moore was a leader in the Constitutional Convention of 1865. He drafted the repeal of the secession ordinance but, predictably, was bitterly opposed to repudiation of Confederate debts. He had little sympathy with the Conservatives in the troubled years 1866-1868, but even less with the Radical Republicans. Moore had a large and successful practice in United States Supreme Court cases until his death. *DAB*, XIII, 114-115.

[2]In 1869 the Raleigh and Gaston Railroad sought to lease the North Carolina Railroad for $240,000 annually. The directors of the North Carolina Railroad Company rejected the offer. John F. Stover, *The Railroads of the South, 1865-1900* (Chapel Hill: University of North Carolina Press, 1955), 110, hereinafter cited as Stover, *Railroads of the South.*

[3]John Wilkes (1827-c. 1900), a Charlotte businessman, was born in New York City, the son of the Charles Wilkeses. After a stint at sea as a boy, he was graduated by the United States Naval Academy, first in the class of 1847. Assigned to the cruiser *Mississippi*, he saw action in the Mexican War. In 1853 he resigned his commission. He moved to Charlotte, where he purchased mining and milling properties. By 1858 he was the owner of the Mecklenburg Flour Mills, and one year later he acquired the Mecklenburg Iron Works. Unlike his illustrious father, John Wilkes sided with the Confederate States of America. He gave one flour mill and his ironworks to the Confederacy to promote the "lost cause." He also built the railroad from Greensboro to Danville. Having lost his fortune during the Civil War, Wilkes received a Federal pardon and worked energetically to recoup his losses. He was president of the First National Bank of Charlotte (1865-1869) and engaged in iron manufacturing. Jon L. Wakelyn, *Biographical Dictionary of the Confederacy* (Westport, Conn.: Greenwood Press, 1977), 439, hereinafter cited as Wakelyn, *Biographical Dictionary of the Confederacy.*

[4]Wilmington and Weldon Railroad Company.

William A. Smith to William A. Graham UNC

Company Shops, N.C.
Nov 2nd 1869

I enclose you a communication which will explain itself. I wish to say one wourd [*sic*] to you upon the subject farther. Our income is mostly derived from the Fall & Winter months, as we carry freight both ways in those months while in the spring we only carry one way, the cotton or the most of it haveing been shiped by the spring months. During Spring and Summer we spend the most of our money as we cannot put iron down in the winter to any advantage. Sills are also put down in Spring and Summer months. The point I am after is this. I think we will have on hand first day January at least two hundred thousand dollars in cash—with the amt & Lease money added it is clear we can pay all the debt of the company in two years. Or we can retire to the sinking fund what is necessary until the debt is extinguished and pay five per cent per annum to the stockholders and the company will not be embarrassed. I am satisfied, Gov., this lease is the best thing possible to do. You cannot imagine how hard it is to keep this road out of debt, and it needs a great many things on it now which it has not. I have worked it close I think with as little expense as possible. We must have next year at least four first class engines and new Passengers coaches besides bridges & other works must be built. Then again the road has allways been controled by party and as long as it is, it will be impossible for it to pay the Stockholders long at a time. I am in hopes if you think this lease the best that can be done you would give it your great influance. If not, I am willing to submit to your better Judgement.

William Hooper to William A. Graham A&H

Hertford,
November 2nd. [1869]

I cannot satisfy myself without thanking you by letter for the very special and laudatory certificate which you sent me, and which you will see with others of like kind spread on this sheet. But all would not do. Si Pergama dextr Defendi possent, etiam hac defensa fuissent.[1]

If any testimonials would have given me success, I might have hoped it from these. But schools have so multiplied, and teachers are now obliged to use so many arts and so much electioneering to obtain a share of patronage, that those who come into the *arena* late, are sure to be foiled. I joined with a lady holding the first credentials, having taught with acceptance in Gen. Lee's family, & other places, and I had reason to think that my character as attested on this sheet and corroberated by the reputation I had from my old pupils at Portsmouth (on that side of the line) would bring, in addition to Mrs. G's school, the very *elite* kind of girls which your letter suggested. But all was forestalled, & *not one* was offered in addition on account of my name. I had countenance, however, in my disappointment. An Episcopal gentleman, before liberally patronized, opened with so small a number that he closed his doors. Another, Rev. Mr. Geer,[2] formerly at Wilmington and Washington, had the same fate. The truth is, that the larger share of patronage in such a city as Norfolk, is from the illiterate, who are no judges of qualifications, and are often most grossly imposed on by pretenders. The richer and more intelligent send to schools of high reputation abroad, where large endowments enable them to furnish the school with all those facilities and showy attractions which are sure to decide the choice of parent and child. Since "giving up the ship" at Norfolk, I have been circulating among my old pupils in this section of the State. They are numerous, and all affectionate and hospitable, so that my time is spent very agreeably, and I suppose, as it is admitted I preach better than I ever did, if I were younger I might be settled down as a pastor somewhere in the region, were it not that my age forbids that activity and endurance which such a position demands. Our school at Wilson, though moderately prosperous, is struggling, like others, from the "hard times." In all this country, I understand, except Hyde and Tyrell, where they have made large corn crops, the drought has been severe.

[1]"If Troy had been able to guard its right side, even now it would be defended."
[2]The Reverend Mr. Geer has not been further identified, although it is likely that he was Edwin Geer, who was an Episcopal minister.

Charles D. Dickey[1] *to William A. Graham* UNC

London England
10 Nov/69

One of my Partners here, Mr. Hamilton, being very desirous of obtaining reliable information in respect to the prospects of the Securities of No. Carolina, I have volunteered to ask of you the favor of an expression of your opinion thereof, knowing no one more likely to be so well informed upon such points.

I have before me quotations of 29 Oct. at New York in which North Carolina
6%s are placed at abt 47
New bonds " " 38
00 special tax " 39½

I have also before me a copy of a private letter written by Hon. T L Clingman to Henry Cl[ews] & Co. N. York under date of 6 Oct last going very fully into the matter of N.C. State bonds and especially in regard to the "Special tax bonds" as being *unquestionably good.* Perhaps you may have seen the letter I allude to. If so would be glad to know what weight may fairly be attached to an opinion emanating from Mr. C. who I only know as a representative man from your State.

The apparently low price of these Special tax bonds leads me to suppose they must carry a reduced rate of interest. If you can inform me upon this point, also whether at about Current prices you would regard these bonds as a safe permanent investment, and if so, which particular Class of Bonds are to be preferred in. . . . I will appreciate the favor.

I am over here with Mary and the family for recreation for the Winter and as we expect shortly to leave for the South of Europe, I would feel obliged by your addressing your reply to my Partner
"F. A. Hamilton
Brown Shipley & Co.
London"
who will feel obliged therefor and will treat your views as confidential.

Mary is very well and enjoying her rest from Home Cares vastly. She sends much Love to you & your family, to which I beg to add my kind regards. . . .

[1]Mary Sophia Witherspoon (1829-1880), Graham's niece, had married Charles Denslow Dickey (b. 1820) in 1856. They were residents of New York City. Clark, "Graham Descendants."

William A. Smith to William A. Graham UNC

President's Office,
North Carolina Rail Road Company,
Company Shops, N.C.,
November 25th, 1869.

I was at Raleigh yesterday, and from what I learned, the Legislature will certainly take some action in relation to the N.C.R. Road. Many projects are talked of by the members and others. Some, for selling the entire State's interest for the bonds of the State. Some, for endowing the University with a portion of the stock. Others, for consolidation with the A&NC RRoad.[1] Others for allowing R&D RR Co[2] to build a track of their gauge from Greensboro to Charlotte. The Legislature will refuse to give the private stockholders the scale they desire, so as to give the management to the private stockholders, as it is too big a political machine for that. But, if the State is determined to sell, which I believe is the case, would it not be the best policy to sell only one million and a half, or two millions, and reserve the ballance for the purpose of holding the ballance of power should a portion of the stockholders wish by their action to destroy the road as a public convenience, the State could vote with the opposition, and control the matter.

The State is compelled to raise money to pay interest without making the taxes higher. This stock is all they have, it is a struggle for party ascendancy. If necessary for success, they will not hesitate. You have great influence with all conservative members of both parties. I think you could control enough votes to carry out the plan I suggest, if they are determined to take action upon the matter, which I have not the least doubt.

I am not wedded to any particular plan, and would be guided by your better Judgement upon any plan that would protect the private stockholders. I feel, in any event, (unless the private stockholders can control the road) that my chances are slim for re-election, as my party friends are somewhat against me.

Yours with Great Respect,

[1]The Atlantic and North Carolina Railroad ran from Morehead City to Goldsboro, where it connected with the North Carolina Railroad. In 1854 the state bought two thirds of the company's stock. Stover, *Railroads of the South*, 31.

[2]The Richmond and Danville Railroad Company opened its service between the two cities in 1856. During the war the line was extended from Danville to Greensboro, a distance of forty-eight miles. Stover, *Railroads of the South*, 107.

Barnas Sears to William A. Graham UNC

Staunton, Virginia.,
November 26th., 1869

I submit herewith a check for $500, & blank receipts to be signed and returned.

So our noble friend, the great philanthropist, has passed away.[1] On arriving at Liverpool, he went the same day to London. His friend, Mr. Curtis Lampson[2] & family were in Scotland, not expecting him. He was taken with a chill, (as he had been once or twice at White Sulphur Springs last summer) soon after reaching London. Mr. Lampson was telegraphed, and got there immediately. He so far rallied as [to] dine down stairs several times. Then he was seized with a nervous chill, & was insensible after it. He continued some day or two, though the physician thought he could live but a few hours. When it was announced that the Queen and the Prince of Wales had telegraphed to know how he was, he appeared unconscious. A clergyman, who was a passenger with Mr. P. was announced. Mr. P. said, "he is a good man," and said he would like to see him. The clergyman made a short prayer, & Mr. P. "seemed very grateful." That was all the consciousness he showed. These particulars, etc., Bp. McIlvaine[3] learned from his daughter.

How fortunate it was that he came to this Country as he did! How well his work is done!

I have just returned from Tennessee and Georgia, where there were important meetings of the State Teachers Associations, and next week I set out for Texas, according to Mr. Peabody's request. I expect to return just in time for the annual meeting.

I send kind remembrances to Mrs. Graham, & your sons.

Yours faithfully,

---

[1]George Peabody died on November 4, 1869, in London at the age of seventy-four. For an account of his death, Westminster Abbey services, and burial in the Harmony Grove Cemetery, which lay on the boundary between Peabody and Salem, Massachusetts, see Parker, *George Peabody*, 180-187.

[2]Sir Curtis Miranda Lampson (1806-1885), a native of Vermont, had settled in London in 1830, married an English woman, and become a naturalized British subject in 1849. He made a fortune in the fur trade and was a senior partner in the merchandising firm of C. M. Lampson and Company of London. For his outstanding work as a director of the Atlantic Telegraph Company, he was made a baronet. He and George Peabody were close friends. Parker, *George Peabody*, 66-67.

[3]Charles Pettit McIlvaine (1799-1873), noted theologian and educator, was a native of New Jersey and a graduate of the College of New Jersey (now Princeton University). In the early 1820s he was pastor of Christ Church in Georgetown, D.C., and was chaplain of the United States Senate. Later he was chaplain at West Point, where he taught geography, history, and ethics. In addition, he held intensely emotional revivals that provoked controversy. After serving briefly as rector of St. Ann's Church in Brooklyn, New York, he became, in 1832, the Protestant Episcopal bishop of Ohio. A very active bishop and famous preacher, he traveled widely while retaining an affiliation with Kenyon College's divinity school. On one occasion his travels took on national significance. After the potentially disastrous *Trent* affair, McIlvaine, at the request of President Lincoln, sought to enlist the English clergy on the United States's side. His efforts were influential and largely effective. In 1873 he died in Florence, Italy, and, after a funeral service in London's Westminster Abbey, was interred in Clifton, Ohio. His most important theological study was entitled *Oxford Divinity Compared with That of Romanish and Anglican Churches. DAB*, XII, 64-65.

James A. Graham to William A. Graham UNC

Graham, N.C.,
Dec 8th 1869.

I received on Saturday morning your letter and the books sent by Mr. Webb,[1] and am much obliged for them. I did not return from Randolph Court before that time.

There was a good deal of business done there on the Civil Docket, but very little on the State Docket. I get some little practice there and hope to get more after awhile. They are a great people for employing a number of lawyers in their cases. They very seldom have less than two lawyers on each side and generally three or four.

I have been quite busy all this week drawing answers & complaints for our Court, and preparing for the capital case in which I appear. I fear it will be quite a difficult matter to clear the poor fellow, as nearly all the evidence that can be had is the dying declaration of / of the deceased; there being no other persons present when the deed was done. I have not, however, yet learned all the minute particulars of the shooting, but expect to get them from the Sheriff today. There is a trial going on today at the Shops before W. D. Faucett[2] J. P. of some men charged with being Ku Klux and whipping a man by the name of Cauliss[3] who teaches a negro school at the Shops. I have not heard what is the evidence against them. I heard yesterday that the lot adjoining mine, belonging to Providence Church, would be sold during Court week. If so I think I shall buy it unless it goes too high. Please bring me, when you come up, $96. of the money I asked you to take care of for me, last spring. I want to pay for the bonds I bought some two or three weeks ago. There is no news. Lizzie joins me in love to all.

Affectionately Your Son

[1]This is almost certainly a reference to James Webb, whose daughter, Elizabeth Cheshire Webb, had recently married James A. Graham.

[2]William Dollison Faucett was an Alamance County justice of the peace.

[3]Alonzo B. Corliss was a partially crippled Quaker from the North. He taught a school for Negroes at Company Shops in Alamance County. In November, 1869, he was visited by the Alamance Ku Klux Klan. After calling him from his house, the Klansmen took him to a nearby wood, where he was beaten with a rawhide and hickory sticks. Thirty lashes were administered. Then one side of his head was shaved and painted black, and he was encouraged to leave the county. Corliss tried to carry on with the assistance of a small squad of soldiers provided by Governor Holden. He was forced to leave Alamance when his landlord evicted him for fear his house would be damaged. Four men were arrested at Corliss's direction. Three admitted their guilt privately, but no one was prosecuted. Trelease, *White Terror*, 202.

Robert C. Winthrop to William A. Graham A&H

Brookline, Mass.,
December 16th., 1869.

As Mr. Russell is absent, I write informally to remind you of the Meeting of the Trustees at Washington on the 19th. of January. The remains of our lamented friend are expected at Portland soon after the 1st., and the funeral will take place four or five days afterwards at Danvers. If there be no detention, this will give time for us who must attend the funeral to reach Washington seasonably. Should there be any greater delay, so that a postponement of the meeting should be necessary, I will telegraph the members; but I do not anticipate it.

Some of our members, Macalister,[1] Wetmore,[2] and others, are coming on to attend the ceremonies. If you and Aiken could find it convenient, it would be gratifying to us all; but it is almost too long a journey at this Season. Meantime, I trust that you will prepare a draft of some appropriate resolutions to go upon our records at Washington. They should come from the South, and nobody could prepare them more fitly than yourself & Gov. Aiken. Nothing is necessary to add to his fame, but it is due to ourselves to take appropriate notice of his death.

Let me hear from you, and believe me always,

With great regard,
Yours sincerely,

---

[1]Charles Macalester (1798-1873) of Pennsylvania was a banker. He was the Philadelphia agent and correspondent for George Peabody. He donated land for the site of Macalester College in Minneapolis, Minnesota, in 1873. *CDAB*, 598.

[2]Samuel Wetmore, a retired New York businessman, was seventy-three years of age when he died in 1885. A native of Connecticut, he went to China as a young man; there he represented the New York import firm of Wetmore, Cryden and Company. After his return from China, Wetmore accumulated a fortune in business. He was a charter member of the Union League Club of New York City. An original Peabody Eduation Fund trustee, he was treasurer of the fund at the time of his death. *New York Times*, March 28, 1885; Parker, *George Peabody*, 161.

Augustus W. Graham to William A. Graham[1] UNC

Amazonia S.C.
Dec. 23rd 1869

My Dear father,

I received your letter of the 18th inst. today and will reply immediately as I have an opportunity of sending my letter to Charlotte by George, who is going tomorrow or the next day if he can cross the river. It rained very hard here on night before last and part of yesterday in consequence of which the river is very much swollen. I expected to have killed three of the hogs this evening and carried them to Charlotte in the morning to Brother Joe, but Mr. Craige[2] says that we cannot possibly cross the river tomorrow and maybe not on the next day as it was still rising to-day. The river has backed over half of the creek bottoms below the spring lot.

I went up to Willie's on Saturday and remained until Tuesday. Florrie[3] was a great deal better when I left although she had been quite ill the week before. I met Mr. Carruthers at Willie's on Tuesday morning. He agreed to take charge of affairs next year, but wanted enough land to work one horse. He said that he would be here to-night but I suppose the high waters prevented him. He seems to be a very respectable man and, I think, will do as well as anyone we could get. I saw Cousin John McLean[4] to-day and he said a man named Lee Hand had asked him to reccomend him for the situation, which he (Cousin John) said he would most Cheerfully do as he thought that Hand would suit the place better than any man he knows. But as we have already engaged Mr. Carruthers I do not think it worth while to make any propositions to Mr. Hand.

I have had six bales of cotton ginned and packed and think there will be about four more coming to us. The screw works very well. *Three* hands can run a bale of 400 lbs almost down without the help of a horse. The gin worked very well until yesterday when it commenced to *nap* the cotton so badly that I stopped until it could be fixed and will not gin any more until after Christmas.

I bought a book in Charlotte and have taken an inventory of almost every thing on the plantation, as you directed. I hope to complete the inventory in the morning. All the hands had their tools in right good order and in their places except Paul who had his scattered over the plantation. He is a right good hand but has a very trifling family.

Jim raised 4045 lbs of cotton in the seed, Chambers & Sam 4018 ditto, Ned 6573 ditto, & Paul 911 ditto = 15,547 lbs. Joe paid 260 lbs seed cotton for rent. Tobe has paid one bale I have not weighed it yet, Thompson says it weighs 400 lbs. He had 270 lbs lint cotton besides his rent.

I paid Millan $50 last Saturday. He says you can pay the rest when it is convenient to you. I bought a saddle in Charlotte for nine dollars ($9).

I have had a good shelter for the young calves, of which there are five, made on the south east side of the cow pen next to the cotton patch. I, also reduced the cowpen to about one third the size of the first one and filled it and the stalls with leaves. I made a pen and shelter for the dry cattle by the shuck house in the spring lot and will have them put up every night. There is about one bushel and a half of wheat in the lumber house that has been soaked, but the ground has been too wet to sow it since I have been here and I am afraid it will spoil. Kerr sent a bushel and a half to the mill for our use on Monday and there is still about a bushel or perhaps more in the lumber house. There are twenty five bushels of oats (so Kerr says) in the lumber house and four bushels of rye.

Paul will not have near enough cotton to pay his debts. He owes Wright about $35., Craige 6 or 7 and the plantation nearly $20. He wishes you to stand his security with Wright for $25. for another year and says he will have enough corn & cotton to pay his bill at Craige's and the plantation and, also, $10 to Wright. It will take all of Chambers cotton to pay his bill at Wrights and for the cow that he killed.

---

[1]This letter and the one following, dated Christmas, 1869, were included for the information given about agricultural affairs, despite the fact that most of the people mentioned cannot be identified definitively.

[2]Newton Craige, apparently a South Carolina merchant, is mentioned in the following letter, but the Craige of this letter does not appear to be the same man.

[3]Florence Lane Graham (1866-1900) was the eldest child of William A., Jr., and Julia Lane Graham. Clark, "Graham Descendants."

[4]John Davidson McLean (1779-1870), a physician and planter who lived in the Point section of south Gaston County, was the son of Dr. William and Mary Davidson McLean of Lincoln County. He was William A. Graham's first cousin. Prior to the Civil War "Cousin John" apparently exercised a general supervisory authority over Graham's western plantations. After Graham's sons were involved in the management of the plantations, he still gave advice about local folk. Robert F. Cope and Manly Wade Wellman, *The County of Gaston: Two Centuries of a North Carolina Region* (Charlotte: Gaston County Historical Society, 1961), 59, hereinafter cited as Cope and Wellman, *County of Gaston*; Chalmers Gaston Davidson, *Major John Davidson of "Rural Hill," Mecklenburg County, N.C.: Pioneer, Industrialist, Planter* (Charlotte: Lassiter Press, 1943), 72-73, hereinafter cited as Davidson, *Major John Davidson*; Sherrill, *Annals of Lincoln County*, 59, 99-100.

Augustus W. Graham to William A. Graham UNC

Amazonia, S.C.
Christmas, 1869

Dear Father,

George could not get across the river yesterday but will try to do so to-day. Please send me ten or fifteen dollars by next Thursday or Friday as I will have to pay Kerr, Wright, Craige & others nearly all I have. I went to see Newton Craige yesterday, but lost the road and did not get there until quite late and did not have time to get a copy of the whole account against you. He says that you and himself have never had a settlement, and he has an account against the plantation running back to Uncle James time. He says Uncle James made the last settlement a year or two before his death and he has one or two articles charged during the last year of his life. He has you credited up to 1862 with $77.17 and in debt to him $114.17 leaving a balance due him of $37.00 up to that time. He said that he and Wallis agreed to trade leather for produce at old prices during the war; and he has a good many things charged at Confederate prices and I did not have time to calculate what it would amount to in "*ante bellum*" currency so I told him that I would possibly come back or that the better plan would be for him to come down and see you when you came here: he said he would if you would send one of the negroes to let him know when you were here.

It has been raining steadily since daybreak and I am afraid that I will not reach Charlotte before the last of next week.

Mr. Carruthers has just arrived and I must close as George is waiting for the letter. Love to all.

Your affectionate son

Notice of George Peabody Funeral UNC

The funeral of the late
Mr. George Peabody

Will take place in this, his native town, soon after the arrival of his remains in this country.

The services will be held at the South Congregational Church, upon a day and at an hour whch will be herefter and seasonably announced, in the public prints.

You are respectfully invited to be present on the occasion, and to unite with us in solemnizing the funeral obsequies of one, who was not only our especial benefactor and friend, but who was the friend of humanity,—whose death two continents deplore, and whose memory will be always and everywhere revered.

A Committee will be in attendance at the Institute upon the day of the funeral, to furnish tickets of admission to the Church to invited guests, and to give all desired information.

In behalf of the Trustees of the Peabody Institute, and of the Committee of the town of Peabody, we are,

With respect,
Yours,

Lewis Allen
E. W. Upton
Francis Baker
George F. Osborne
Thos E. Proctor
Wm Sutton
Henry Poor.
Committee of Invitation.

Peabody, Mass., Dec. 29, 1869.

1870

Protest from Alamance County[1] A&H

[January, 1870]

The people of Alamance County, having assembled in public meeting, to make known their sentiments on measures of the highest interest to the Country, do resolve:

That we have seen with alarm and indignation a Copy of a Bill,[2] introduced into the Senate by one of the members from this County, with the deceptive title of "an act to secure the better protection of life and property;" by which it is proposed:

1st. To establish at the discretion of the Governor, military authority in any County of the State.

2nd. To request the President of the United States to be guilty of an usurpation, and suspend the writ of *Habeas Corpus* in any County that the Governor may declare to be in a state of insurrection.

3rd. To allow the solicitor for any district to remove the trial of any person indicted for certain offenses to any other County that he, the solicitor, may designate, and all this in the face of a State Constitution, which declares that "the military shall be kept under strict subordination to, and governed by, the civil power;" "that the priviledge of the writ of *Habeas Corpus* shall not be suspended;" and in the face of the Constitution of the United States, which denies any power to suspend this great writ of right, to the President, and forbids it also to Congress "unless where in cases of *rebellion or invasion* the public safety may require it;" in the face of the declaration of independence of the United States, which points out, as one of the particular acts of tyranny complained of, in the British King, that he caused men to be arrested at their homes, and sent them to a distant country to be tried.

Resolved, that the introduction and entertainment of such a bill shews an ignorance of the first principles of free Government, and a malignant desire to promote controversy, by exciting strife among the people, and to shed the blood of war in a time of peace.

Resolved, that it is utterly false, that there is, or has been, any insurrection or resistence to the lawful authority of the State in this County, or, so far as our information goes, in any other County in the State; it is true that some violations of the law, which we regret, have been committed in secret, by persons who appear to have suddenly assembled, and as suddenly dispersed, but to hold the orderly and innocent people of the country responsible for these proceedings, and to punish them without conviction of any crime, by quartering armed militia among them, and laying upon them the hand of military tyranny, would be an oppression against which we earnestly protest.

Resolved, that we have seen with surprise the pretension set up by a portion of the members of the present General Assembly, that they are entitled to hold their places for four years instead of two; and to rob the people of their right to elect representatives of their choice, on the first Thursday of August, 1870, as is expressly provided in the Constitution; the Constitution, for the sake of convenience, did allow them to hold from April, 1868, an irregular time of election, 'till August in that year, and then for the regular period, two years; but to pervert this into a tenure for four years would be an act of usurpation, which should subject those who may perpetrate it, to the penalties of treason, which the Grand Juries should enforce by Indictment.

Resolved, that the attempt to obtain from the Supreme Court an opinion on this question, out of the course of its Judicial duty, when the same question will have to be considered, if this construction be persisted in, in a much more solemn form, we hope will receive no countenance from that Court; the Legislative and Judicial departments of the Government are made separate and distinct, and no power is given to the Court to determine in advance, who shall compose the General Assembly.

Resolved, that where constitutional elections end, tyranny begins, and that this is not an occasion where a true friend of constitutional liberty would seek the exercise of power by inquiring of a lawyer what he *may* do, but would consult with honor and justice, what he *ought* to do. All know that the people elected the present members but for two years after August, 1868, and provided expressly for the election of successors in August, 1870; and to attempt to hold over and longer, would be an open outrage upon the popular will, which no ingenuity can successfully defend.

Resolved, that the people of the State have no cause to desire a continuance in power of the present General Assembly. When we have seen the public credit sink, since the commencement [of] its first session, from seventy five cents in the dollar for State Bonds to 40 cents, the present rate, for the same Bonds; and for the other class of bonds 29 cents in the dollar; (but little more than the premium commanded by our old bonds when first put in market); the rise in the same time of the public taxes; the increase of the Legislative and other expenses; the reckless issues of State obligations; the indisposition to correct the error by calling in a portion, at least, of these Bonds, or to make inquiry as to their present state, and what disposition has [been] made of them, and what has been received as their equivalent; and other abuses which can be readily specified; there is abundant reason to desire, that their labors may be speedily closed; and that new representatives may be chosen to arrest, if possible, the downward progress in our affairs.

---

[1]While there is no conclusive evidence that Graham authored this protest, the document bears strong resemblance to his political views and literary style. Among his papers is a copy in his handwriting.

[2]Prepared by United States Senator John Pool in hopes of keeping the state Republican, the bill in question was introduced in the North Carolina legislature by Alamance County Senator T. M. Shoffner in December, 1869, and thereafter bore his name. It gave the governor, beginning with the incumbent William W. Holden, the power to declare a county in a state of insurrection and authorized the use of the militia to quell such disturbances. The governor could not suspend the writ of *habeas corpus* himself, but he could call upon the president of the United States to do so. The Shoffner bill passed the

Senate on the day it was introduced but was blocked in the House of Representatives by irate Conservatives in the absence of many Republicans, who would have constituted a majority if present. Vehemently opposed by Conservatives as unnecessary and unconstitutional, the measure was taken up again after the Christmas recess and passed in January. Some Republicans opposed it, arguing that it did not go far enough and should have given the governor the power to suspend *habeas corpus*.

This unpopular law, which presaged the Kirk-Holden War and Governor Holden's impeachment and removal from office, was repealed early in the 1870 legislative session. The vote for repeal was as follows: Senate, 32-7; House, 79-23. Hamilton, *Reconstruction in North Carolina*, 402-403, 559.

Joseph Graham to William A. Graham UNC

Charlotte
Jan 1st/70

My dear Father,

Yours containing coupons, also the one to Gus received. I have collected the five coupons $87.50 - $4.37(Int. Rev. Tax) = $83.13. I enclose the check of Mssrs T. R. Tate[1] & T. W. Dewey[2] on Ral. Nat Bank of N.C. for the $83.13 Eighty three dollars & thirteen cents. I conferred with Dewey relative to "deposits on time and interest thereon". He says they will give you 10 pr. ct. same as Mr. P. C. Cameron[3] draws. But that is not their regular rate, as they only pay at home here 8 pr. ct. I presume he does not care to have you inform others that he allows you that amount. The Banking firm goes under the name and Style of Thos. R. Tate & T. W. Dewey, Bankers. I have rented five rooms in Mrs. Steeles[4] house, and half of the garden, and the stables . . . for $300. and hope to move next week. Her house is the next beyond J. Y. Boyce,[5] toward the Lincolnton depot. I had to pay $350. here.

Sinclair and McDougald[6] inform me they will pay $1000. Jan 10th and cannot pay the remainder of first note till expiration of ninety days thereafter. I told them I would accept that but I must have a good note for balance at 8 pr cent interest, and no deception about pay when the time arrives. To this they have agreed. I think, if this is all done the plantation will bring the balance at any time of failure to pay, and I will be perfectly safe. Please say to Mr. Cameron I will send his certificates and money by Gus.

I met Mr. Turner[7] on the street this morning. I hope the murderers of Blalock[8] will be detected.

On Monday next I expect to be at Davidson College to assist Ephraim Brevard[9] in an operation for removal of ovarian tumor. The same as performed upon Mrs. Ryan of Raleigh by Dr. Atlee[10] of Philadelphia. Our case however is not one very favourable to success, but a derriér resort.

I think Dr. Draper's[11] proposition a very good one for George. I don't know that he will acquire much information professionally, but the general information will be worth something.

The receipts from my profession have not near paid me out this year. It is an expensive place to live in.

Bettie joins me in love to all. Hattie Jones[12] left for Lincolnton this morning.

Your Affect Son

---

[1]Thomas Randolph Tate was the son-in-law of Henry Humphreys, who owned the profitable Mount Hecla Steam Cotton Mill at Greensboro. About 1846 Tate built a mill for manufacturing cotton and woolen cloth at a site near Mountain Island on the Catawba River in Gaston County. Machinery from Humphreys's mill was incorporated into Tate's new mill, which he called the Mountain Island Mill. Tate's mill proved to be a very successful enterprise and continued in operation through the Civil War, although with a skeleton crew. By 1884 it was again in full production with 150 looms, 6,000 spindles, and a work force of seventy-five. Cope and Wellman, *County of Gaston*, 6, 66-67, 104, 119.

[2]Thomas Weber Dewey (1827-1875) was at this time a banker in Charlotte. A native of Raleigh, Dewey graduated from the University of North Carolina in 1847. Grant, *Alumni History*, 163.

[3]Paul Carrington Cameron (1808-1891), son of Duncan and Rebecca Bennehan Cameron and father-in-law of John W. Graham, was born at Stagville, home of his grandfather Richard Bennehan. After graduation from Washington (now Trinity) College at Hartford, Connecticut, Cameron read law in his father's office but never pursued that profession. At one time Cameron was perhaps the wealthiest man in the state, having amassed much property and 1,900 slaves, according to his own account. He was much interested in building railroads, was a banker and industrialist, and was interested in politics, although he seldom ran for office himself. Ashe, *Biographical History*, III, 48-56; Grant, *Alumni History*, 939; Powell, *DNCB*, I, 312-313; Clark, "Graham Descendants."

[4]Mrs. Steele has not been further identified.

[5]J. Y. Boyce has not been further identified.

[6]Evidently McDougald, like Sinclair, was a Graham tenant.

[7]Josiah Turner, Jr. (1820-1901), of Hillsborough, was a lawyer, political journalist extraordinary, and politician. He was always an admirer of William A. Graham, whose advice he frequently sought and followed. He was a Whig member of Commons in 1852, 1854, 1858, and 1860 and was elected as a Conservative to the state Senate in 1868 but did not take his seat. He opposed secession but became a Confederate captain of cavalry. Wounded and disabled in the New Bern campaign, Turner resigned. In 1863 he was elected to the Confederate Congress as a peace candidate. He was actively hostile to the Davis administration and urgently desired peace.

After the war Turner became a Conservative and was an enthusiastic enemy of William W. Holden. In 1868 he purchased the Raleigh *Sentinel* and edited it as an anti-Holden organ. Bitterly opposed to congressional reconstruction, Turner soon displayed a genius for political polemic as he held the carpetbag government up to ridicule and abuse. He was probably the one man most responsible for overturning congressional reconstruction in North Carolina. During the Kirk-Holden War, Turner was imprisoned after issuing a public dare to Governor Holden. Later, Turner's arrest was one of the charges brought against Holden in impeachment proceedings.

In later life Turner was a pathetic figure who seemed to lose his balance. He went bankrupt, lost the *Sentinel,* and never got the political preferment he desired. The Democrats distrusted his instability and erratic behavior, and he died a Republican. *DAB*, XIX, 68-69; Ashe, *Biographical History*, III, 415-426.

[8]This refers to the brutal murder of Reuben Blaylock, a crippled Confederate veteran whose body was found in his Hillsborough residence on the previous Christmas Day. His mouth had been stuffed with rags, his throat cut, and his head smashed. Robbery had been the motive. Shortly thereafter three Negroes named Gunn, Young, and Lutterloh were arrested. Bob Gunn, who seems to have been the leader of the group, was located and arrested in Greensboro with the assistance of Hillsborough blacks. Later, Joseph Lutterloh was found innocent. The case created quite a sensation at the time. *Hillsborough Recorder*, January 26, February 16, 1870; *Daily Sentinel* (Raleigh), December 29, 1869, January 4, 1870.

[9]Dr. Ephraim A. Brevard was the son of Judge and Mrs. Theodorus W. Brevard and the grandson of Alexander and Rebecca Davidson Brevard. Young Brevard and Joseph Graham were second cousins. In 1871, at age thirty-two, Dr. Brevard was thrown from a horse and killed. Sherrill, *Annals of Lincoln County*, 100, 225.

[10]Washington Lemuel Atlee (1808-1878), surgeon, and his older brother, John Light Atlee (1799-1885), an expert in obstetrical surgery, were both early proponents of ovariotomy. *CDAB*, 33.

[11]Probably this was John William Draper (1811-1882), son of John Christopher Draper, famous British scientist. After his father died, John William Draper, with other members of his family, emigrated to the United States around 1830. With the financial assistance of his sister Dorothy, Draper pursued a career in medicine; he was particularly interested in the action of oxygen and carbon dioxide in the bloodstream and made significant contributions through his experiments and research. Draper was professor of chemistry and natural philosophy at Hampden-Sydney College, Virginia, 1836-1838; in 1838 he was named professor of chemistry at the University of the City of New York. Very quickly he became actively involved in organizing a school of medicine at the university. In 1865 Dr. Draper lost his valuable library, research materials, apparatus, and notes in a catastropic fire that destroyed the school of medicine building. His most significant scientific contribution was his work on radiant energy. He was also a pioneer in photography. A versatile man, Draper wrote a three-volume *History of the American Civil War* (1867-1870). Henry Draper (1837-1882), son of John William Draper, succeeded his father in the chair of chemistry at the University of the City of New York but died himself eleven months later. *DAB*, V, 438-441.

[12]Hattie Jones has not been identified.

Robert C. Winthrop to William A. Graham A&H

Brookline, Mass.,
January 5th., 1870

Your two favors of the 24th. & 29th. have reached me duly. In reply to the latter, I can say, that I think there is not the slightest probability of our being able to conform to the date fixed for our meeting. I have been afraid positively to postpone it, because it is impossible to say exactly *when* it can be held. We must wait 'till the Fleet arrives at Portland, which may not be before the 20th., and is not likely to be before the 17th. Possibly, it may be as late as the 1st. of Feb'y.

When it is fairly at Portland, the day of the Funeral will be announced; probably the best part of a week after the arrival; and then it will take three or four days after the funeral for us to get to Washington. I have written to Gov. Fish that he, as our Vice Chairman, must adjourn the meeting, on the 20th., if we are not there, 'till such day as I may name, after the day of the Funeral is fixed. We will have it all announced by the Associated Press Telegraph.

Gov. Aiken's[1] cough, I regret to learn, will not allow him to come, even to Washington. So we must rely on you to offer the Resolutions. The good Bishop will consult with you about them, and I will make a little Introductory announcement.

Dr. Sears will, doubtless, bear his testimony.

With the best wishes of the Season,

[1]William Aiken (1806-1887) was governor of South Carolina, 1844-1866. As a member of the House of Representatives, 1851-1857, he served on important committees and was influential in his office. He was defeated as Speaker after 133 ballots during the Thirty-fourth Congress. In 1867 he was elected again to represent his state but was not permitted to qualify and resumed his vocation as a planter near Charleston. *Biographical Directory of Congress*, 462; *CDAB*, 11.

Joseph Graham to William A. Graham UNC

Charlotte,
Jan 12th/70

My dear Father,

Your bonds recd and Mr. Johnston[1] says they are not paying any of these bonds, but exchanging the bonds of the Charlotte Columbia & Augusta R. for them. That is the consolidated road. They only pay the interest due, when you present the bonds for exchange. I will hold them for further instructions. Rankin[2] accepted your offer $250. 5 bush wheat & oats over today. Our little Willie[3] is quite sick today with high fever. We would move were he well enough. In haste. I will pay John's note tomorrow. Say to Robt I have paid Kearns[4] $100.

Love to all.

Your affect Son

[1]William Johnston (1817-1896), of Charlotte, a native of Lincoln (now Gaston) County, was of Scotch-Irish parentage. He graduated from the University of North Carolina in 1840 and read law with Richmond M. Pearson. He practiced law in Charlotte and was associated with the building and administration of plank roads and railroads. Johnston represented Mecklenburg County in the convention of 1861. The Democrats vainly supported him against Vance in the gubernatorial election of 1862. After the Civil War he was instrumental in securing a railroad linking Charlotte, Columbia, and Augusta. Johnston was married to Ann Eliza Graham (1826-1881), William A. Graham's niece. Ashe, *Biographical History*, I, 341-349; Clark, "Graham Descendants."

[2]This was A. M. Rankin, with whom Graham was negotiating and who served as overseer at Amazonia, one of the farms. See William A. Graham to William A. Graham, Jr., January 15, 1870, in this volume.

[3]William A. Graham (1865-1930), "little Willie," attended the University of North Carolina and the University of Virginia and was graduated by the College of Physicians and Surgeons in 1888. He practiced his profession in Charlotte for many years. Clark, "Graham Descendants"; Grant, *Alumni History*, 229.

[4]Kearns has not been identified.

William A. Graham to William H. Battle UNC

Hillsboro',
January 15th., 1870

The Funeral services of Judge Ruffin[1] will take place at the Episcopal church in this place, Monday next, at 11 o'clock A.M.

If you, or others of our friends of the profession at Raleigh, would be pleased to attend, I will be glad to have you come to my house, on the arrival of the train at 10 o'clock, whence you can go to the obsequies, and after dining, leave for Raleigh, if you wish, at 5 P.M.

The Judge expired at 2 o'clock this morning, Saturday 15th.

Please mention to your sons, & bring them with you to my house in town.

---

[1]Thomas Ruffin (1787-1870), a native of Virginia, graduated from the College of New Jersey (Princeton) in 1805. He studied law in Petersburg, Virginia, and with Archibald De Bow Murphey in North Carolina. He established his practice in Hillsborough in 1808. After holding various minor court positions, he served on the North Carolina Supreme Court from 1829 to 1852, presiding as chief justice from 1833 until his retirement. He returned to the court for one year in 1858. Judge Ruffin was widely respected for his knowledge in common law and equity; in constitutional law he is ranked with John Marshall and Lemuel Shaw. Unlike his Virginia cousin, Edmund Ruffin, Thomas Ruffin was an ardent Unionist who denied that secession was legal. When all attempts at compromise failed, he voted for secession in the Constitutional Convention of 1861 and supported the Confederate war effort. McCormick, *Convention Personnel*, 70-71; *DAB*, XVI, 216-217.

William A. Graham to William A. Graham, Jr. A&H

Hillsboro',
January 15th., 1870

Dear Wm—

This has been a sad week to our Community. Judge Ruffin died this morning of pneumonia. His interment will take place on Monday at 11 o'clock. Capt. Berry[1] died last Tuesday, & was buried on Thursday. Old Mrs. Thomas Anderson,[2] and Miss Fanny Thompson[3] are both said to be at the point of death.

Augus[tus] got home at 11 o'clock last night, having installed an overseer named Rankin from Mecklenburg, who is very highly recommended, a single man,—at $250. wages, and the common findings. No other hands employed but those we had last year. Henry is in the neighborhood, and may be hired, and George is here, but going back. I doubt whether to take the latter at all.

It is supposed there is sufficient evidence to convict all three of the negroes who murdered Blalock, and now in jail here. While they sat up with the corpse of Capt. Berry, Dr. Montgomery[4] walked up the public road from the house in the night, and was attacked violently by a negro with a knife, who cut his clothing in several places, but, after a severe scuffle, broke loose & ran off. The villain has not been apprehended yet, though there are suspicions of a fellow on the premises.

. . . .

Affectionately Yours

---

[1]Captain John Berry (1798-1870), of Hillsborough, was a skilled brickmason, builder, and architect. Unusually intelligent, this self-educated man was widely respected. He

represented Orange County in the state Senate (1848, 1850, 1852, 1864, and 1866) and in the Secession Convention of 1861. A Democrat in politics, Berry joined Graham in opposing secession. Lefler and Wager, *Orange County*, 324; McCormick, *Convention Personnel*, 19.

[2]Mrs. Thomas Anderson has not been identified.

[3]Miss Fanny Thompson has not been identified.

[4]Dr. D. A. Montgomery of Alamance County was the son-in-law of John Berry. This attack occurred on a main public road about two miles east of Hillsborough. *Daily Sentinel* (Raleigh), January 17, 1870.

William Horn Battle to William A. Graham UNC

Raleigh,
January 17th, 1870

I received your kind invitation to go to Hillsborough for the purpose of attending the funeral of C[hief]. J[ustice]. Ruffin to-day, and made some arrangements to do so, but I had, last night, one of the nervous attacks to which I have of late been subject, and I thought it would be imprudent to turn out so early in the morning, especially as it was raining at the time I ought to have started.

I regret that I could not be present to assist in paying the last sad tribute of respect to one of the greatest of our Judges, and the most useful of our citizens.

William A. Graham, Jr., to William A. Graham UNC

Charlotte
Jan 22nd/70

My dear Father

Mr. Rankin has just come to tell me that he will have to back out from staying at "Amazonia", that he could make nothing for you there with that set of negroes. They would all leave if he undertook to govern them. He has had no riot with them; but Ned among others has told him that "you allowed them to do their own way pretty much, and if they cannot continue pretty much as formerly they can easily get new homes."

He says he regrets very much having to leave, but that he could not earn his wages with them, that he might just stay there and carry the keys, but only make such crop as the hands chose. (This is all the paper I have in the house.)

I think Gus had better return immediately, and if you could be there yourself, it would be of service. I told him to go back and try and get Hand to go over & stay *at least* till Gus could get back, probably about Wednesday. If it were in Dec. I would advise clearing the plantation & making a new start for hands, but it would hardly be advisable. . . .

George W. Graham to William A. Graham UNC

426 E. 26th St.
[New York]
Jan 23rd 1870

My dear father

I will need about $60 more to carry me through this session provided I dont buy any instruments. And will be much obliged, if you will send me that amount by the 8th or 10th of next month. If I succeed in getting the appointment on the imigrant vessel, I will purchase what instruments I need in Europe, as they can be bought there much cheaper, and of better quality than in this country. Will not be able to tell much about the appointment before the last of next month or the first of March. Heard yesterday of the death of Judge Ruffin. Suppose his death was rather looked for than otherwise as he had been so very feeble for such a long time. I received the copy of the Recorder, with an account of the murder of Blalock, for which I am very much obliged. The Sentinel has been coming very regularly of late and I was very glad to learn thru it of the election of Mr. Whitesides[1] to the Legislature. Mr. Turner[2] gives quite an amusing account of his trip thru western N.C. just before the election. There are a great many cases of Small Pox in the city just now or rather they are at Charity Hospital as they are sent there as soon as they are attacked. I think it is one of the laws of the city that every Physician shall report each case that he is called to, in order that it may be sent over to Blackwells Island and thereby prevent the disease from spreading. My examination will take place about the middle of next month as I am among the first to stand. The Commencement will take place during the first week in March. Expect we will have between eighty and a hundred graduates. Hope Mother has recovered from her spell of sickness by this time. Love to all.

---

[1]This is a reference to George M. Whiteside, elected as a state senator to succeed J. B. Eaves from Rutherford County. Cheney, *North Carolina Government*, 449, 451, 554n.

[2]Josiah Turner, Jr.

Resolutions of Peabody Fund Trustees[1] UNC

Feb. 15, 1870

1. *Resolved*, That this Board, having been honored by our lamented and beloved friend, the late George Peabody, with the trust of the greatest of his great gifts in America, do hereby record our profound veneration for his character and his eminent philanthropy, with our painful sense of the bereavement to his friends, and the loss to his country, occasioned by his death. Participating to the utmost in that appreciation of his worth and works, which has united two great countries of kindred blood in such tributes to his memory as were never before paid to individual merit, it is the priviledge of those who knew him in the confidential relations of this great Trust, to speak with special testimony of that shining purity of motive, and

of that careful consideration of duty to God and man, which gave birth, form and direction to all his bountiful gifts. We take a mournful pleasure in recording our loving homage to a beneficence as admirable in heart as in deed; so wise and comprehensive in the choice of its objects; too thoughtful to be profuse, too maturely planned to be impulsive. Enlarged beyond all sectional and national boundaries, it has created a bond of peace between the North and South of his own land, and between them both, as one nation, and their venerated mother-land, which we pray may never be broken. His native country, which he so dearly loved, will fondly remember the son that so adorned her history; whose institutions of learning and of general education he so enriched, and, after having given her children an example how inflexible integrity and unselfish enterprise may accumulate wealth, added the more-needed lesson, how, in their own lifetime, and by their own hands, it may be wisely and nobly dispensed; who, by riches so obtained and used, became the benefactor of nations in both hemispheres, and taught the poor in each to call him blessed; whose most enduring monuments will be found in countless schools for the poor and ignorant, and in cheerful, comfortable homes for the destitute and wretched; who, amidst all the flattering homage of the great, and the applause of the multitude, preserved unblemished, to the end of a long career, the modest simplicity of life and manners inherited in his youth. It was fit that the mortal remains of such a man, having been attended by dignitaries of the Church, and ministers of the Crown of England, to a temporary resting-place assigned them among the sepulchres of the wise and great, should be carried by the joined hands of Great Britain and America, and with their united honors, to the burial he desired, in his own native village, and near the graves of his father and mother.

2. *Resolved,* That for his well-ordered philanthropy and princely munificence he deserves to be ranked among heroes and sages, the inventors of useful arts, and the founders of States, the admitted benefactors of preceding ages, whose labors or contributions have marked eras in the amelioration and progress of mankind; and that his name and memory should be cherished among those of the great Americans who have given renown to their country, and done good for its people.

3. *Resolved,* That, in the unexampled tributes which have been paid to the life and character of George Peabody, we rejoice to recognize an emphatic testimony of nations and governments to the greatness of simple virtue and beneficent philanthropy,—especially in the faithful stewardship of riches,—which eminently redounds to their honor, and gives additional weight to a lesson of wisdom and duty for all generations.

4. *Resolved,* That this Board, deprived, by the afflicting dispensation of Divine Providence, of the advice and countenance of our departed friend and Founder, will ever remember our gratification on the last occasion of his presence with us, and especially in his satisfaction then expressed with our administration of his trust, not only in assuring words, but by the large addition then made thereto; teaching us to feel more than ever our responsibility to God for the talents committed to our care, while we look for

guidance and blessing to Him from whom all good counsels and just works proceed.

The Resolutions having been read, and their adoption moved by Bishop McIlvaine, Governor Graham seconded the motion, and addressed the Board.

---

[1]From "Proceedings of the Peabody Education Fund," February 15, 1870. Although Bishop McIlvaine chaired the committee that prepared these resolutions, they were written by Graham and therefore are included here. See Robert C. Winthrop to William A. Graham, January 5, 1870, in this volume.

Address of Graham to Peabody Fund Trustees UNC

Feb. 15, 1870

Mr. Chairman,—Although funeral honors with all the ceremonies at the command of two great nations, and with the cordial approbation of the people of both, have been already paid to the Founder of this charity; and although by yourself and others the language of eulogy and panegyric upon his great acts of beneficence has been exhausted,—yet I beg leave to detain you a moment in seconding the Resolutions of the Committee, reported by its venerable Chairman.

As the sole member of this Board who happens to be present from the vast region between this capital and the Rio Grande frontier,—a region for the relief and assistance of whose inhabitants his last and greatest donation was made,—I feel that silence would be an injustice approaching somewhat in criminality to a betrayal of my trust; and that the thousands of parents, and tens of thousands of children,—not a few of them orphans,—in this territory, who are the objects of his bounty, and their sympathizing friends everywhere, would feel that their voice had been suppressed in the general tribute of praise to his memory, and that they had no proper representation in the Board of Trustees.

In their name, and in their behalf, regretting the absence of our colleagues, Governor Aiken of South Carolina, and Judge Bradford of Louisiana,—both, as I regret to learn, from illhealth,—I give my hearty assent to the declaration, that, for his well ordered philanthropy and princely munificence, George Peabody deserves to be ranked with heroes and sages, the inventors of useful arts, and the founders of States, those benefactors of our species whose labors or contributions have signalized eras in the amelioration and progress of mankind; and that his name and memory should be cherished among those of the great Americans who have given renown to their country, and done good for its people.

Assuming further to speak in their name, I render thanks to the Governments of Great Britain and the United States, representing the sincere and generous feeling of the people of both countries, and the State and Municipal authorities of Maine, in which his remains first reached the American shore, and of his native Commonwealth of Massachusetts, in which, by his patriotic direction they were destined to final repose; as well as to you, sir, and to the other members of this Board, who attended his final obsequies, for the very imposing and appropriate tributes of respect to his character which were paid in the long progress from Westminster Abbey to his native town, which furnishes his mausoleum, and shall perpetuate his name. Such offerings do honor to the living as well as to the dead; they but manifest the public and universal sense of his noble charities, and encourage others to like good works.

They tend, moreover, to curb the worse elements of our nature, and to the promotion of peace and good-will among men. And as in his death two great powers of common language and kindred blood have found a common subject of mourning, and, as it were, voyaged abreast and marched hand in hand to his tomb; so let us trust that, in the dispensations of Providence, the lately warring sections of our own country will be chastened of angry passions and jealousies, and be joined in new bonds of peace and union by common admiration of his example, and gratitude for his beneficence in all future time. If the North shall indulge a commendable pride in the reflection that he was their countryman, the South will venerate him as their neighbor, benefactor, and friend, who poured oil into the wounds of desolating war, and provided for the moral and intellectual wants of their children in the day of impoverishment and affliction.

William A. Graham to Susan Washington Graham A&H

Arlington House,
Washington City,
Feb. 17th., 1870.

My Dear Wife

Your letter enclosing one from Joseph has just been received, a previous one came from Robert, enclosing that of Hand. A telegram came last night from George, asking if he could come to Washington on Friday morning. The Board having agreed to adjourn today, except for a visit to Baltimore tomorrow, and the accounts of expenses being made out, I replied, informing of the adjournment, and advising that he could stop a day or two here on his return home; which would be early in March; and that he could return after a brief visit home, to see the hospital practice in New York for a few months. I suppose his trip to Europe is not at all probable now.

There have been two dinings of our party in the Hotel. This evening at seven we are to dine with the Secretary of State[1], and tomorrow evening at the same hour with the President—invited tomorrow also to a reception of Mrs. Fish, and a party at Mr. Carliles;[2] but shall hardly get to these; at least to both; as I must leave on Saturday for the South.

Augustus has been out a good deal; went to a reception at Gen'l Sherman's[3] one night after the dinner here, and Miss Kennedy[4] (census) has shewn him to some places of curiosity and taken him out to visit.

We go tomorrow morning to Baltimore, to hear a eulogy on Mr. Peabody from S. Teakle Wallace,[5] and return in the evening in time to dine with the President. He came to the meeting of the Board the second day, heard the report of the Gen'l Agent; and invited us all to dine with him on Friday evening. I had called with Augus on Monday, about 3, but he, being out, I left cards, and have not as yet seen Mrs. Grant.[6]

I called yesterday on the Secretary of the Navy,[7] found him a short, jolly man in spectacles, who appeared very cordial and obliging; met there old Commodore Smith,[8] and Admiral Porter.[9] Went afterwards to call on Admiral and Mrs. Shubrick,[10] and Mrs. Clymer,[11] and on Mrs. Riggs,[12] whom I found receiving company. Her husband afterwards called to ask me to take a family dinner, but I had engaged to dine here.

Our Board has had harmonious session, and will meet next winter in Phila. with, probably, a previous meeting in Memphis.

We have walked by our old house, now the residence of Admiral Porter, and found additions on top and west side, with ornamentations very profuse, but not, I think, in the best taste.

Commander Shubrick feels sore under the aversion of his S.C. friends for his part in the war. He was 80 years of age, quite infirm, and with impaired vision.

I have gotten your articles of clothing and [illegible]. I am struck with the quantity of hair worn by the ladies on the back of the head. The season is very gay, and a good deal of beauty in the society. The city shows considerable improvement, and prosperity. But the despotism of radicals seems not to abate. The negro[13] and Gen'l Ames[14] are probably admitted today as Senators from Miss.

Love to Sudie, Rob't &
Rebecca.
Ever Affectionately Yours

---

[1]Hamilton Fish.

[2]John Snyder Carlile (1817-1878), born in Winchester, Virginia, suffered serious financial difficulties during his earliest business ventures but rallied to become a successful lawyer in the Kanawha section after he moved to Beverly, and later to Clarksburg, West Virginia. Carlile rose to prominence quickly in the field of politics, first in Virginia and then in West Virginia. An extreme Unionist, he attended the Secession Convention of 1861 and incurred the hostility of the *Richmond Enquirer*, whereupon he began to work for the creation of a new state of West Virginia. His ideas were embodied in a "Declaration of the People of Virginia," adopted by the second Wheeling convention, June 17, 1861. He effectively engineered the creation of a new state government and served as a United States senator from Virginia, 1861-1863, and from West Virginia, 1863-1865. Appointed to be ambassador to Sweden by President Grant, he was not confirmed in this appointment by the Senate. *DAB*, III, 493-495.

[3]At this time William T. Sherman was commanding general of the army. *CDAB*, 951.

[4]Miss Kennedy has not been identified.

[5]Severn Teackle Wallis (1816-1894), a native of Baltimore, Maryland, was graduated from St. Mary's College in 1832, after which he studied law with William Wirt and Judge John Glenn. He was also an avid historian and a prolific writer of addresses, verses, and literary criticisms. Four volumes of his work were collected as *Writings of Severn Teackle Wallis*, memorial edition (1896). At first a Whig in his political philosphy, he became a Democrat—but one who retained his independence of opinion. In 1858 Wallis was part of the reform movement in Baltimore, and in 1861 his sympathy was with the Confederacy, although he did not advocate secession. His protests against the doctrine of military necessity led to his arrest and subsequent imprisonment for fourteen months. He was an

eloquent speaker and the acknowledged leader of the Maryland bar for fifty years. One of the original trustees of the Peabody Fund, Wallis was president of the board in 1894. One of his most prestigious positions was the presidency of the Maryland Historical Society (1892-1894). *DAB*, XIX, 385-386.

[6]Mrs. Ulysses S. Grant.

[7]George Maxwell Robeson (1829-1897), of New Jersey, was an honor graduate of the College of New Jersey (Princeton) and a lawyer by profession. He was successively prosecutor of Camden County; brigadier general of New Jersey troops during the Civil War; secretary of the navy, 1869-1877; and a Republican member of the United States House of Representatives, 1879-1883. While serving as navy secretary, he was severely criticized in Congress for extravagance and favoritism. *CDAB*, 872; *Biographical Directory of Congress*, 1529.

[8]Joseph Smith (1790-1877) had served as chief of the Bureau of Navy Yards and Docks, 1846-1869 (*CDAB*, 974). He and Graham had been acquainted since the early 1850s, when Graham was secretary of the navy.

[9]David Dixon Porter (1813-1891) had a distinguished career in the United States Navy during the Civil War and was commended for his part in the surrender of Arkansas Post and Vicksburg and the attack on Fort Fisher, 1864-1865. After the war he was superintendent of the United States Naval Academy, 1865-1869; "advisor" to the secretary of the navy, 1869-1870; and successor to Farragut with the rank of full admiral, 1870. *CDAB*, 813.

[10]Admiral William Branford Shubrick (1790-1874), a native of South Carolina, was accorded particular honor for his command of the expedition sent to settle difficulties with Paraguay in 1861 and was designated rear admiral (retired) in 1862. *CDAB*, 955-956.

[11]Mrs. Clymer has not been identified.

[12]Mrs. Riggs was the wife of George Washington Riggs (1813-1881), a native of Georgetown, D.C., and a merchant, banker, railroad builder, and philanthropist. He attended the Round Hill School in Northampton, Massachusetts, and Yale, leaving the latter institution at the end of his junior year. He worked in his father's mercantile house in New York City and later engaged in a highly successful banking venture with William N. Corcoran. Upon his return to the District of Columbia Riggs served on the board of aldermen and was instrumental in the change from territorial status to the present governmental form. He built the Riggs House (a famous hotel), was an organizer of the Washington and Georgetown Railroad Company, and served as a trustee of the Peabody Education Fund and the Corcoran Gallery of Art. As treasurer of the Mount Vernon Ladies' Association of the Union, he advanced the money necessary to preserve Mount Vernon as a historic site. *DAB*, XV, 603-604.

[13]Hiram Rhoades Revels (1822-1901), black clergyman, educator, and United States senator, was born in Fayetteville, the son of free parents. For a time he was a barber in Lincolnton, but in 1844 he moved to Indiana. There and in Ohio he received a secondary and college education. Ordained a minister in the African Methodist church, he worked among Negroes in Ohio, Illinois, Indiana, Missouri, Kansas, Kentucky, and Tennessee before settling in Baltimore, Maryland. During the Civil War he helped organize two Negro regiments in Maryland, established a school for freedmen in St. Louis, and served as chaplain in a Mississippi regiment. After about two years of church work in Kentucky and Kansas, he settled in Natchez, Mississippi, in 1866. Upon the encouragement of blacks and whites, Revels entered politics, suppressing his fears that a political career might interfere with his religious work as a Methodist Episcopal minister. He was successively town alderman, state senator, and United States senator, January, 1870, to March, 1871. A Republican in politics, he eschewed radicalism and conducted himself with dignity. Revels was president of Alcorn University and continued his religious efforts as time and circumstances permitted. His only other significant venture into politics came in 1875, when he helped Mississippi Democrats end Republican rule in that state. *DAB*, XV, 513; *Biographical Directory of Congress*, 1510.

[14]Adelbert Ames (1835-1933) was a native of Maine. During his youth Ames lived the life of a sailor for a few years before he received an appointment to the United States Military Academy, from which he graduated in 1861. During the Civil War he was a Union officer and participated in the important battles of First Manassas, Yorktown, Gaines's Mill, Malvern Hill, Antietam, Fredericksburg, Chancellorsville, and Gettysburg. His direction

of the attack on Fort Fisher was an important factor in the capture of that fort in January, 1865. In 1868 Ames was appointed by President Grant as provisional governor of Mississippi. From 1870 to 1874 he served in the United States Senate and then was elected to serve again as governor of Mississippi (January 4, 1874-March 29, 1876). From the outset his tenure in office was marked by serious troubles within the state, culminating in the Vicksburg riot of December 7, 1874. Faced with impeachment proceedings, Ames resigned and moved to New York. Later he moved again to Tewksbury, Massachusetts. A close friend of John D. Rockefeller during his later years, Ames lived to the age of ninety-eight. His wife was Blanche Butler, daughter of Benjamin F. Butler. *DAB*, XXI (Supplement One), 27-28.

Zebulon B. Vance[1] *to William A. Graham* UNC

Charlotte, N.C.
Feb 19, 1870

My Dear Sir,

Have you ever considered the question that is engaging the attention of the profession here to some extent, whether or not the 14th Amendment bars us from a seat in the Legislature? H. W. Guion[2] has written a very ingenious argument to prove that we are not barred, based mainly on the fact that a legislator does not hold an *office* within the meaning of the 14th Amendment. To this effect also is Worthy v. Barrett & others 2 Phillips 199. Please look into it and give me your opinion. Should you concur, we desire to publish an argument & endeavor to get our friends generally to take this position. And also if deemed advisable I shall stand for the legislature from this county & desire to see you go from Orange. In fact if the position is thought tenable we ought to put out our most experienced men all over the State.

Regard this last as confidential for the present.

---

[1]Zebulon Baird Vance (1830-1894), of Buncombe County, was one of nineteenth-century North Carolina's most popular men. After attending Buncombe County schools, Washington College (Tennessee), and the University of North Carolina, Vance studied law and was admitted to the bar in 1852. Not a close student of the law, he soon found that politics was his abiding interest. Vance began his political life as a Henry Clay Whig. Upon the disruption of the Whig party he spurned Democratic overtures and united with the American party. After one term in the House of Commons, Vance was elected to the United States House of Representatives, where he served from 1858 to 1861. A Unionist, he supported the Constitutional Union ticket of Bell and Everett in 1860.

After opposing secession vigorously until Lincoln's call for troops, Vance raised a company of Buncombe volunteers and was elected colonel of the Twenty-sixth North Carolina Regiment, which contingent he led ably until his election to the governorship in 1862. Vance was a tremendously popular war governor who quarreled with Confederate authorities and Holden's peace faction with equal enthusiasm. Following a brief imprisonment in 1865, he practiced law until his political disabilities were finally removed in 1872.

In 1876 Vance, always a powerful stump speaker, was elected governor in a hotly contested confrontation with the native Republican Thomas Settle. His second administration marked a new era in North Carolina history as "home rule" was restored. From 1879 to 1891 Zeb Vance served his state as a United States senator. His Senate career was characterized by his constructive and conciliatory attitude. *DAB*, XIX, 158-161.

[2]Haywood Williams Guion (1814-1876) was a native of New Bern who earned an A.B. degree from the University of North Carolina in 1835 and an A.M. in 1846. He established his law practice in Charlotte. Grant, *Alumni History*, 241.

William A. Graham to William A. Graham, Jr. A&H

Hillsboro',
March 4th., 1870.

. . . .

Augustus & I had a pleasant visit to Washington—dined with the President, and with the Sec'y of State, attended an evening reception also at Gov. Fish's, & Mr. Carlile's; (the latter having married the widow of Gen'l Anderson,[1] of this State.)

We also went with the board of Trustees to Baltimore, to hear a eulogy on Mr. Peabody from S. Teakle Wallace, & returned to Washington same day. Augus. also went with Bishop McIlvaine's party to a reception at Gen'l Sherman's, and saw all the sights to be seen while there. I met many old friends. But the spirit of the Congress which rules the Pres't is proscriptive & hostile in the highest degree, and the (so called) Southern members are but tools of Sumner,[2] Butler,[3] & Co., and despised by them as much as by us, though they use them for their selfish ends. Deweese[4] and a fellow named Whittemore[5] from S.C. you see have been expelled for selling Cadets places. I didn't see the negro Revels, but was told by Garret Davis[6] that he and Ames (a belted General, who had elected himself) would both be admitted. Revels is so common a free negroe's name, that he is said to be from various places, Fayetteville, Granville, and—as you say—Catawba.

Negroes are still leaving this section. At Granville I found an acquaintance from New Orleans, who with a friend were to take off 100 last Monday. It is estimated that 500 have left that County—some 300 this—4 or 500 Person, etc. Swepson & Littlefield, Tate,[7] Clingman, etc., were in Raleigh, and the examination was going on before the Commission[8] of Bragg,[9] Phillips[10] & Scott,[11] & Walker's Com'tee[12] of the Legislature. If the matter is properly exposed, there will [be] some damaging disclosures to the ring, and to Holden.

. . . .

F. Strudwick,[13] who has been opposed to John, told me on coming up from Raleigh the other night, that he wielded more power than any man in the Senate, and was conceded to be the ablest lawyer in the body, and was prominently spoken of as a candidate for Congress. You heard of the hanging of the negro, Wyatt Outlaw,[14] in Graham last Saturday night. There is to be a public meeting there tomorrow to disapprove it.

I write in haste to get the letter in mail tonight.

I regret to hear that Florie still has chills.

Love to Julia & the children.

Affectionately Yours

---

[1]George Burgwyn Anderson (1831-1862), son of Colonel William E. and Eliza Burgwyn (Burgwin) Anderson, was born in Orange County. After attending the university for the year 1847-1848, Anderson was appointed to the United States Military Academy at West Point. After graduation in 1852 he was assigned to military posts in the western states. He was involved in the problems of Kansas and Utah, serving in Utah under Colonel Albert Sydney Johnston. When the Civil War erupted, Lieutenant Anderson resigned his commis-

sion with the United States Army and accepted a commission as colonel of the Fourth Regiment of North Carolina in May, 1861. His troops participated in the skirmishing at Yorktown and in the Battle of Seven Pines, in which his heroism was noted by President Jefferson Davis, who commissioned him brigadier general. During the battle at Malvern Hill Anderson was slightly wounded and on September 17, 1862, during the battle of Antietam, he received a wound that proved to be fatal. Anderson was a brother of Captain Walker Anderson and Colonel William E. Anderson. His wife was Mildred Ewing, of Louisville, Kentucky. Ashe, *Biographical History*, IV, 28-31.

[2]Charles Sumner and Benjamin F. Butler were, of course, leading Republicans. Sumner (1811-1874), of Massachusetts, was a prominent leader in the struggle against slavery and for racial equality. Educated at Harvard College and the Harvard Law School, Sumner moved in the best Boston social circles and traveled extensively in Europe. He was a founder of the Free-Soil party and was elected to the United States Senate in 1851 by a coalition of Free-Soilers and Democrats. Subsequently, Sumner was reelected as a Republican in 1857, 1863, and 1871. *DAB*, XVIII, 208-214.

[3]Benjamin Franklin Butler (1818-1893) had been the first major general of volunteers to be appointed by Lincoln. He demonstrated no great military ability during the Civil War but contributed greatly because of his status as a popular and colorful Democrat. After the war he aligned himself with the Radical Republicans, sat in the national House of Representatives from 1867 to 1875, and was one of the House managers in impeachment proceedings against Andrew Johnson. He returned to Congress for one term, 1877-1879, as a Greenbacker. In 1882, by the combined efforts of the Greenback and Democratic parties, Butler was elected governor of Massachusetts. He was the unsuccessful presidential candidate of the National (Greenback) party in 1884. *DAB*, III, 357-359; Ezra J. Warner, *Generals in Blue: Lives of the Union Commanders* (Baton Rouge: Louisiana State University Press, 1964), 60-61.

[4]John Thomas Deweese.

[5]Benjamin Franklin Whittemore (1824-1894) was born in Massachusetts, educated at Amherst, and during the Civil War was a chaplain in the Fifty-third Regiment, Massachusetts Volunteers (and later with the Thirtieth Regiment, Veteran Volunteers). After the war he settled in Darlington, South Carolina, where he became active in state politics as a Republican. Whittemore served at various times in both the House and the Senate, resigning from the Senate in 1877 to return to Massachusetts, where he settled in Montvale, a suburb of Woburn. *Biographical Directory of Congress*, 1916-1917.

[6]Garret Davis (1801-1872), a Kentuckian, Whig, and great friend of Henry Clay, was a lawyer, state legislator, congressman, 1839-1847, and United States senator, 1861-1872. He declined the presidential nomination of the American party in 1856, supported the Bell-Everett ticket in 1860, and was influential in keeping Kentucky in the Union. By 1864 and subsequently, he was astonishingly critical of the Lincoln administration and the Radical Republicans. *DAB*, V, 113-114; *Biographical Directory of Congress*, 782.

[7]Samuel McDowell Tate (1830-1897), a Morganton Democrat, had served in the Sixth North Carolina Regiment during the Civil War, attaining the rank of lieutenant colonel and participating in several major engagements. After the war Tate became president of the Western North Carolina Railroad. He advocated division of the railroad and establishment of a new corporation, the Western Division of the Western North Carolina Railroad, which came under the control of George W. Swepson. Although Holden removed him as president in 1868, Tate continued as financial agent of the stockholders and trustee for the payment of debts already incurred. He later sat in the General Assembly, served as a federal bank examiner, and was appointed state treasurer in 1892. Ashe, *Biographical History*, IV, 430-439; Cheney, *North Carolina Government*, 425, 435n.

[8]This commission was established by the legislature in January, 1870, to investigate fraud, especially in the matter of railroad bonds. While the investigation was an embarrassment to Republicans, no action resulted. Hamilton, *Reconstruction in North Carolina*, 404-405.

[9]Thomas Bragg (1810-1872), a brother of Confederate General Braxton Bragg, was born in Warrenton. He was educated in a local academy and had three years at the famous Partridge Military School in Middleton, Connecticut. He was admitted to the bar in 1833 and established a successful legal practice in Northampton County. In politics Bragg was a

Democrat in a Whig stronghold; nevertheless, he won a seat in the Commons in 1842, was North Carolina governor, 1855-1859, and sat in the United States Senate, 1859-1861. He and Holden were rivals for the leadership of the Democratic party, with Bragg usually having a dominant position. *DAB*, II, 588-589.

[10]Samuel Field Phillips (1824-1903), a native of Harlem, New York, was the son of James Phillips, University of North Carolina professor of math, 1826-1867. He was the brother of Charles Phillips and Cornelia Phillips Spencer. In 1841 he graduated from the university with the highest honors in his class and read law with both David L. Swain and William Horn Battle prior to opening a Chapel Hill practice. He was a state legislator, delegate to the Constitutional Convention of 1865, reporter of the North Carolina Supreme Court, commissioner of war claims, assistant district attorney in the justice department, and United States solicitor general. In politics he was a firm Union Whig, but he opposed the excesses of the Democratic party during Reconstruction. By 1870 he was a Republican and was that party's unsuccessful candidate for state attorney general. As a federal official Phillips prosecuted many Ku Klux Klan cases. He aspired to a seat on the United States Supreme Court but was frustrated in this ambition. Van Noppen Papers; Spencer Alumni Project.

[11]William Lafayette Scott (1828-1872), of Greensboro, was a graduate of the university, a lawyer, lieutenant colonel of the Twenty-first North Carolina Regiment in the Civil War, and a member of the fraud commission of 1870. Spencer Alumni Project.

[12]The editors have found no reference to a Welker or Walker committee; however, George W. Welker, senator from Guilford County, was a prominent legislator in this session. This reference is almost certainly to him.

Welker had come to North Carolina in 1841 and had served since as a pastor of the German Reformed Church. A consistent Unionist, he was very unpopular during the Civil War. Afterward his Union predilections led him to cooperate with carpetbaggers and native scalawags. He became a Republican and was active in the Constitutional Convention of 1868 and in the legislatures of 1868-1869 and 1869-1870. In time he was repelled by fraud and corruption, especially where state railroads were concerned, and in February, 1870, introduced resolutions calling for fiscal honesty and punishment of wrongdoers. He further denounced the vitriolic tone of public addresses and newspaper editorials. He pledged moderation and conciliation and called on others to join him. After Milton Littlefield succeeded in frustrating legislative investigation of his conduct as railroad magnate, Welker began to vote with the Conservatives.

For contemporary accounts of Welker's resolutions see the *Daily Sentinel* (Raleigh), February 19, 1870, and the *Daily North Carolina Standard* (Raleigh) of the same date. On February 21 the *Standard* denounced these resolutions as unworthy of Republican support. See also Otto H. Olsen, *Carpetbagger's Crusade*: *The Life of Albion Winegar Tourgée* (Baltimore: John Hopkins University Press, 1965), 161, hereinafter cited as Olsen, *Carpetbagger's Crusade.*

[13]Frederick N. Strudwick (d. 1890), of Hillsborough, had attended the University of North Carolina and was a lawyer. An ardent Conservative, he was at one time head of the White Brotherhood in Orange County and was also active in Klan activities. On one occasion early in 1870 he led a band of sixty Orange and Chatham County men in an abortive attempt to assassinate T. M. Shoffner of Alamance County. Shortly thereafter he was sent to the legislature to replace John J. Allison, who had resigned. He was reelected to the legislature that assembled in November, 1870. Subsequently he was active in Democratic politics, serving as solicitor of the Fifth Judicial District and as a presidential elector (1888). Grant, *Alumni History*, 599; Trelease, *White Terror*, 203; Lefler and Wager, *Orange County*, 113, 116; Cheney, *North Carolina Government*, 450, 453, 558n.

[14]Wyatt Outlaw, the most prominent Negro in Alamance County, was hanged by seventy-five Klansmen on February 26, 1870, within thirty feet of the county courthouse in Graham. He was a member of the Graham town council and founder and president of the local Union League. Outlaw was murdered for political and racial reasons upon the flimsy justification that he had fired on mounted Klansmen a year earlier. Trelease, *White Terror*, 205; Richard L. Zuber, *North Carolina during Reconstruction* (Raleigh: Division of Archives and History, Department of Cultural Resources, 1975), 29, hereinafter cited as Zuber, *North Carolina during Reconstruction.*

Otto Olsen, a close scholar of this era, has described Outlaw as a man whose reputation and character were "exceptionally good" and whose "real sins were his ability and leadership." Olsen, *Carpetbagger's Crusade*, 161.

Charles Phillips to William A. Graham UNC

Davidson College, N.C.,
Wednesday, March 9th., 1870.

The members of the late Faculty at the University of N.C. are already indebted to you for many acts of kindness. Nevertheless, I must ask you for another. Will you send to the Rev. Dr. McGill,[1] at Princeton, N. Jersey, your opinion of Prof. Hepburn[2] as a man, and as a Professor? Prof. Hepburn, (Andrew D.) is a candidate for the vacancy in the chair of English Belles Lettres, Logic, etc., that now exists, (or will shortly be) at Nassau Hall, and his father-in-law, Dr. McGuffey,[3] of the University of Virginia asks me to procure from those who knew Prof. Hepburn while in N.C. some testimonials of his fitness for that place, and to lose no time in doing so. I have been hoping that Prof. Hepburn, now at Miami College, Oxford, Ohio, might be again a colleague of mine here at Davidson College. But there is no prospect of that hope being realized shortly. At Nassau Hall, Prof. Hepburn can do us more good than he can at Miami, and I would have a man of his abilities and attainments where his voice and example will be most powerful.

Dr. Joseph Graham has paid our community here several visits of late. I can tell you what I might not tell him, that he has made many friends by his courtesy as a gentleman, and his skill as a physician. His principal patient, our President, Dr. McPhail,[4] is—as I am—slowly getting able to go to work again. Dr. Graham came to see me while I was in bed with the Rheumatism, and his visit was said to do me as much good as Dr. Holt's Calomel and Colchicum.

With my wife's love to Mrs. Graham, and her expression of hope that she will one day see Mrs. Graham and Miss Susan here, in our own home, and with my own sincere wishes for the continuance of your own health and prosperity, I am,

Very respectfully,

---

[1]Alexander Taggart McGill (1807-1889), born in Canonsburg, Pennsylvania, was graduated from Jefferson College in 1826. Within a brief time he moved to Georgia, where he studied law and was admitted to the bar in 1830. However, McGill elected to pursue his interest in ministerial work, returned to Canonsburg, and began to study for the ministry in the Associate Presbyterian Seminary. After his ordination in 1835 he began pastoral work in three small churches in Carlisle, Pennsylvania, where he remained until 1842, when he became a member of the faculty at Western Theological Seminary, Allegheny, Pennsylvania. In later years he taught at the Presbyterian seminaries at Columbia, South Carolina (1842-1852), and at Princeton, New Jersey (1853-1883). Throughout the years he was a prominent member of the general assembly of the Presbyterian church, serving at various times in the posts of moderator, permanent clerk, and stated clerk. He was awarded the D.D. degree by Marshall College in 1842 and the LL.D. by Princeton in 1868. *Cyclopedia of American Biography*, XII, 364.

[2]Andrew Dousa Hepburn (1830-1921) joined the faculty of the University of North

Carolina in 1859 as professor of logic and rhetoric. He felt strongly that the university needed to raise its standards of scholarship and to make fundamental changes in its curriculum. He expressed his opinions freely and was supported by colleagues Charles Phillips and William Joseph Martin as well as by such respected educators as William Bingham, principal of the renowned Bingham Academy. Hepburn, a graduate of Jefferson College in Pennsylvania, had also studied at the University of Virginia and the Princeton Theological Seminary. Disappointed at what he perceived to be a failure of the trustees to understand the necessity for reform, Hepburn resigned in June, 1867, to join the faculty of Davidson College, which he later served as president, 1877-1885. During his late years of teaching, he was a professor of language at Miami University in Ohio. Cornelia Rebekah Shaw, *Davidson College* (New York: Fleming H. Revell Company, 1923), 145-158 passim, hereinafter cited as Shaw, *Davidson College*; Robin Brabham, "Defining the American University: The University of North Carolina, 1865-1875," *North Carolina Historical Review*, XVII (October, 1980), 436, 436n, 440, 442-443, 445.

[3]William Holmes McGuffie (1800-1873), Presbyterian minister and noted educator, was at this time professor of moral philosophy at the University of Virginia. A native of Pennsylvania and a graduate of Washington College (now Washington and Jefferson), he was successively professor of languages, Miami University, 1826-1836; president, Cincinnati College, 1836-1839; and president, Ohio College, 1839-1843, before his appointment to the faculty in Charlottesville in 1843. He was an earnest advocate of public education and is best known for his remarkable series of *Eclectic Readers*, which eventually sold more than 120 million copies. Through these "McGuffie Readers," he exerted a major influence on the nineteenth-century mind. *CDAB*, 613-614.

[4]George Wilson McPhail (1816-1871) has been described as "a profound scholar, an able preacher, and a warm-hearted Christian gentleman." Born in Norfolk, Virginia, he studied for two years at Hampden-Sydney College before transferring to Yale, from which he was graduated in 1835. McPhail then studied theology at Hampden-Sydney. After serving as pastor of a church in Cumberland County, Virginia, he moved to Fredericksburg, where he conducted a seminary for girls in addition to serving as a church pastor. From 1854 until 1857 he was pastor of the Brainard Church in Easton, Pennsylvania. In 1857 he became president of Lafayette College and served in this position until 1863, when he resigned to assume a seminary position in Philadelphia. Soon after the Civil War was over, he became president of Davidson College, a position he held until his death. In 1857 Jefferson College conferred upon him an honorary D.D. degree. *Cyclopedia of American Biography*, XI, 242.

James A. Graham to William A. Graham UNC

Graham, N.C.,
March 16th, 1870.

My dear Father

. . . .

The company of troops stationed here are quartered in Patterson's old store near the Court House.[1] They keep a sentinel walking across the street all the time. The Lieut. in command told me that this was to keep his men away from the groceries, which are near there. In spite of that, though, they get drunk pretty often and have beaten several negroes. They do not interfere with any one else, and behave very well while they are sober. They all pretend to be good democrats. I have become acquainted with Lieut. McTaggart,[2] who is in command, and he seems to be a very clever man. There is another officer also, Lt. Fenno,[3] but I have not met him yet.

One of Holden's detectives[4] has been here most of the time for two or three weeks past. At least that is what is supposed by every body to be his business, as he is from Raleigh, and apparently has no other business here. I learned a day or so ago that Holden had also appointed one of our own citizens a detective. It is Boyd,[5] the tailor, who has a shop in the same house with my office. He is a very worthless kind of a fellow, and would about suit such business.

I heard last week that the Ku Klux had whipped two or three negroes in different parts of the County, and the Standard says that one had been hung. This is false so far as I can learn. An old crazy negro[6] was taken from his home by some disguised men, so his wife says, and has not been seen since. Most persons whom I have heard speak of it think he has run away, as he had stolen some geese a short while before and was afraid of being arrested.

. . . .

Affectionately your son

---

[1]Alarmed by the murder of Wyatt Outlaw and the continuing violence in Alamance County, Governor Holden declared on March 7, 1870, that a state of insurrection existed there. Upon his call forty federal troops were stationed there, with some located in Graham and others at Company Shops. Their presence restricted Klan activities to the countryside, but they were ineffectual in arresting Klansmen. Eventually they were withdrawn, and Holden turned to more vigorous measures. Trelease, *White Terror*, 210.

[2]Calvin P. McTaggard (d. 1872), a native of Canada, served in the Michigan volunteers during the Civil War. He was recognized for gallant and meritorious conduct at Fair Oaks. At the time of this letter he was a second lieutenant in the regular army, Seventeenth Infantry Regiment. Francis B. Heitman, *Historical Register and Dictionary of the United States Army, from Its Organization, September 29, 1789, to March 2, 1903* (Washington: Government Printing Office, 2 volumes, 1903), I, 682, hereinafter cited as Heitman, *Historical Register and Dictionary of the Army*.

[3]Darwin G. Fenno, of Wisconsin, had served in that state's volunteers until he was mustered out honorably in March, 1866. He reentered service in the regular army on September 30, 1867, as a second lieutenant in the Seventeenth Infantry. Heitman, *Historical Register and Dictionary of the Army*, 416.

[4]Among Holden's detectives was Joseph G. Hester, later a deputy United States marshal. Born in Granville County, he had served on the *Sumter* and had been captain of a blockade runner. For several years after the war he was in the real estate business in North Carolina. Hester was active in opposition to the Klan throughout the state. Hamilton, *Reconstruction in North Carolina*, 577; Trelease, *White Terror*, 386, 404, 408-409, 415-417; *Testimony Taken by the Joint Committee to Inquire into the Condition of Affairs in the Late Insurrectionary States* (Washington: Government Printing Office, 13 volumes, 1872), II, 13, hereinafter cited as *Ku Klux Klan Conspiracy Papers*.

[5]No definitive indentification of Boyd has been made. He was not, however, James Edmund Boyd, the Graham lawyer who broke with the Klan because of its excesses. See Trelease, *White Terror*, 199, 203, 204.

[6]About two weeks after Outlaw's murder by Klansmen, a Negro named William Puryear disappeared from his home by night. Intermittently insane or semi-idiotic (or both), he had recently claimed that he saw and recognized two of the raiders returning to their homes. Two months later Puryear's weighted body was found in a millpond. While he was probably a victim of the Ku Klux Klan, rumors circulated to the effect that he was abducted and murdered by Negroes at the behest of his wife. Trelease, *White Terror*, 205.

William H. Battle to William A. Graham A&H
[with enclosure]

Raleigh,
March 25th., 1870

As it seems to be agreed that there is to be no general Convention of those people of the State who are opposed to the party which has now the control of its government, it has been suggested, and somewhat discussed here, whether a short address to the public, such a one as I now send, or something like it, might not be a proper move.[1]

All good citizens must necessarily be dissatisfied with the present condition of affairs, and must desire a change. What will be the most effectual means for bringing about a change for the better is, therefore, a momentous question. I have, for thirty years, been so little of a politician, that I have no confidence in my own judgment about matters connected with politics, and am willing to be guided by the opinion of those of greater experience.

If such an address as I speak of be proper, by how many persons ought it to be signed, and where ought it to be issued? I hear that some men of note, who have heretofore been classed with the Radical party, would be willing to sign such a paper,—ought they to be permitted to do it?

If your time will permit, please let me hear from you, and if you desire it, your answer shall be strictly confidential.

There is another matter about which I should like to have a word from you. A member of the bar (Mr. Dowd,[2] the partner of Gov. Vance) came to me and told me that he heard a wish expressed among some members of our profession that I would write sketches of the lives of the Chief Justices, and of some of the other Judges, of the State. They referred, as I supposed, to those who are dead. Some time before that, Judge Merrison[3] suggested to me that I should write sketches of the Bench and Bar of the State. I fear that I have neither competency nor time for the task, and I shall very certainly not undertake it, unless encouraged to do so by some of my friends in whom I have confidence. I have spoken to only one or two about it; Mr. Mordecai rather encouraged it. What think you of it? I can assure you that I shall take it in good part, if you advise against it.

---

[1]The Conservative members of the legislature had prepared an address to the people urging calm in the face of Republican efforts to extend the term of the present legislature for another two years. This plan, though frustrated by the state supreme court, had outraged a large segment of the public. Signed by forty-six Conservative legislators, the address was a plea for unity without reference to past differences, coupled with a declaration that the issue was now one of honesty, economy, and the preservation of personal rights. It condemned Holden's declaring Alamance in insurrection as part of a deliberated plan to carry the state election by force. For the text of this Conservative address see the *Daily Sentinel* (Raleigh), March 28, 1870.

[2]Clement Dowd (1832-1898), of Charlotte, was a native of Moore County. He graduated from the state university in 1856 in preparation for a long career as lawyer, banker, and author. During the Civil War he was a major in the state quartermaster's department. After the war he was mayor of Charlotte, 1869-1871; president of the Merchants and Farmers National Bank, 1871-1874; Democratic congressman, 1881-1885; state bank examiner, 1885-1886; and collector of internal revenue, 1886-1887. He and Vance were Charlotte law

partners for a time, and Dowd wrote *Life of Zebulon B. Vance* (1897). *Biographical Directory of Congress*, 826; Spencer Alumni Project.

[3]Battle may refer to Augustus Summerfield Merrimon (1830-1892) of Buncombe County, a lawyer and highly regarded judge. He was a Union Whig commoner in 1860; briefly a Confederate soldier in 1861; solicitor, 1861-1865; and superior court judge, 1865-1867. In 1867 he moved to Raleigh, where he became one of the chief opponents of congressional reconstruction, serving on the panel that presented the case against Holden in impeachment proceedings. He declined the nomination for governor in 1868 but accepted in 1872 and was defeated. Merrimon was a Democratic United States senator, 1873-1879; associate justice of the state supreme court, 1883-1889; and chief justice, 1889-1892. *DAB*, XII, 569.

[Enclosure]
Proposed Address to the Public

The present condition of North Carolina, both financially and politically, is one of great disorganization and discouragement. This is due, in part, to the excitement, violence, intolerance, and acerbity which have characterized party movements in the State. To correct this evil the best citizens ought to unite in a common effort to restore our prosperity. The obstacle to this does not so much arise from a want of patriotism, as from pride of opinion and party prejudice.

A proper ground, we think, can be found, upon which all good men may be united for the promotion of the prosperity of the State—There is an event in the history of North Carolina which may avail us in the selection of a name under which all her citizens may act in concert, for the advancement of her welfare. On the 20th. of May, 1775, the Mecklenburg Declaration of Independence was made, which dissolved the political bonds that 'till then had fettered the State. In the year following, on the 4th. July, 1776, thirteen States endorsed this action, and by their unanimous declaration of Independence, laid the foundation of this mighty Republic.

Accepting this illustrious example as our guide, let us now proclaim independence of all party bonds, and restrictions. As to all past issues, party trammels, and prejudices, we would say, "let the dead bury their dead." A deluge has swept over the land, and a new world lies before us. Freed from all past entanglements, let us move forward with vigor, with public spirit, and with hope, into the great and bright future which invites us onward.

Let us resolve, too, that the civil and political rights of every citizens, whether colored or white, shall be maintained in all their length and breadth, and that the person and property of every resident of our State shall have the most ample and complete protection. To effect these great results, and to restore the prosperity of North Carolina, and make her place among the first in the Union, we now commend that independent candidates come forward in every part of the State for public position. Let those thus elected consult together, and co-operate for the advancement of our State, and the welfare of her people. Such an independent organization as we proposed may soon be extended throughout the United States.

Raleigh,
March, 1870.

Tax List of William A. Graham UNC

W. A. Graham Tax List 1st April 1870

No Taxable Poll—

Lands- Lot in Hillsboro' 2 ½ acres, formerly E. A. Turrentine
" Estes tract 833 acres
" Old Homestead near Hillsboro 56 acres
" Half of Cole tract leased to Wm. Browning 92 acres

Personal 1. Mare $150— 2 Mules $150		$300.00
Property 15 Head Cattle, grown, yearlings & calves		120.00
1 Carriage harness		175.00
Farming utensils 40, two old wagons 70[,] cart 20[,] [guns], 20		150.00
Library Paintings & Prints		~~1000.00~~
Household & Kitchen Furniture		~~750.00~~
Piano		200.00
Silver plate & plated ware		350.00
2 Gold watches 1020		150.00
		3195.00
Provisions $100, wearing apparel 300,		400.00
Money on hand		10.00
		3605.00
Deduct exemption of wearing apparel &c		300.00
		3305.00
Stock & Bonds of N.C.R. Co all paid by the Company		
Same of stock in [Lit. Mi.] R. Co.		
Solvent credits in excess of debts in state		700.00
Income from Profession		4401.
Do outside of state & profession		1499
		5900
Deduct from income	500	
Expense family	1000	
State Tax	137.	
Repairs	101.32	1738
		4162

William A. Graham to William A. Graham, Jr. A&H

Hillsboro',
April 13th., 1870

. . . .

. . . I regretted to learn from your letter of the probable failure of Wilkes, and that you were in danger of losing some five or six hundred dollars by him. Such disappointments are very annoying; but we may expect to meet them now and then in the business of life. I think by June or July, I can spare you $100 or 200; and for absolute necessity will at any time raise what you need. The rate of interest is so high at Bank that I dislike to borrow, though, I now owe one of them some $550. My receipts so far this year from my profession have not been at all equal to the last one, but I hope to make some collections in the next few months.

. . . .

John, you see in the papers, declines to be a candidate for reelection. F. Strudwick, who was formerly very much disposed to set himself in opposition to him, told me, he was much gratified to see the stand he had taken in the Legislature; that he was the best lawyer, and most influential member of the Senate. I did not read his speech on the Finances 'till yesterday. He has certainly given the best exposition of the debt, taxes and folly of the Legislature that has come out as yet. Mr. Cameron[1] urges him to go to Norfolk, and practice his profession there, but I think he and Rebecca are not much inclined to go.

I don't think I can afford to buy concentrated manures even on credit. The demands on me for money are so great that I find a constant pressure to meet them.

. . . .

I have just seen in the Sentinel the letter of A. H. Jones[2] exposing Swepson, Littlefield, Clingman & Co., the pamphlet of the last is a wretched piece of vanity, malignity, & effrontery.[3] Jones' paper and the Bragg report shew that the whole concern ought to be in the Penitentiary.

I am urged to be a candidate for the Senate, but will not consent. I have no relish for such employment now, and my time is necessary to realize a competent income for my family.

Some villain stole our only Turkey from the yard yesterday morning about daylight, have made no discovery as yet.

. . . .

---

[1]Paul Carrington Cameron.

[2]The *Sentinel* (Raleigh), April 12, 1870, published a letter by Alexander Hamilton Jones that described the ways in which Swepson and Littlefield evaded making a report of their transactions with state bonds. Jones (1822-1901), of Henderson County, became a merchant after attending Emory and Henry College. He joined the Union army in 1863 and subsequently was captured and imprisoned. He escaped and returned to the army. A delegate to the Constitutional Convention of 1865, Jones was elected to Congress later in the year but was not seated. He was elected again and served as a Republican congressman from 1868 to 1871. He lived in Washington, D.C., and Maryland until 1884, when he

moved to Asheville, then to Oklahoma, and finally to California. *Biographical Directory of Congress*, 1134.

[3]Thomas L. Clingman's pamphlet, *Address to the Citizens of North Carolina*, was published in Raleigh on March 10, 1870. First denounced by the *Daily Sentinel* (Raleigh) eight days later, the pamphlet was, among other things, a veiled attack on Graham and his political associates. Clingman praised the Constitution of 1868 and defended carpetbaggers in general. In a manner reminiscent of his antebellum attacks on the Whig "central clique," Clingman charged that Graham and his ilk had opposed the Constitution of 1865 because it provided for new elections and in doing so threatened the old power structure.

William A. Graham to William A. Graham, Jr. A&H

Hillsboro',
April 16th., 1870.

Dear Wm

. . . .

The persons from a distance whom I met in Raleigh seem sanguine as to a conservative triumph in the election in the State, but the Raleigh Com'tee, with few exceptions, is not disposed to be active, unless stirred up. They complain of a want of money, and it will be necessary to raise some in the Counties for them. The bar at Raleigh has been so entangled in the Legislature and Railroad frauds, that they are embarrassed, and shorn of influence. John and I go to Person on Monday morning. After that comes the Court in Orange. I can't go to the plantation 'till that is over, say second or third week in May. Your Mother's health is still delicate. Give our congratulations to Julia in the recurrence of her birthday.

Affectionately yours,

Edward J. Hale to William A. Graham UNC

New York,
April 18th, 1870.

The great want of the South, in School Books, has been a School History of the U.S. which a Southern man can put into his child's hands without indignation or mortification. We have been endeavoring for a year or two past to get some author to write one.

Professor Holmes[1] of the Va. University has promised one so long that people have dispaired of seeing it. Suddenly we are surprised by the issue of a very unattractive one at Baltimore, & by the ascertainment that Mr. Alex. H. Stephens of Geo. is preparing another, & that Professor Venable[2] is to make still another. This will be rather too much of a good thing. We have become jointly interested in publishing Mr. Stephens', and are anxious that it should be all that can be desired. As a help to this, we wish North Carolina to have a fair showing in it. Of course you know Mr. S., and we hope well enough to give him material facts in regard to our State—facts of which we fear he is, like most of the outside world, but indifferently informed.

In the Baltimore book, no allusion is made to the Mecklenburg Declaration, which is perhaps not very surprising, nor to the Battle of Bethel, which *is* surprising.

May we ask the favor of you to furnish him with the documents relative to the Mecklenburg Declaration, and such other things as you may have at command? There is no time to spare, as our amanuensis is to commence writing out Mr. S's illegible MS. this week, & we have written to have a copy sent to us as fast as possible. We wish to get it out in advance of Venable's.

For some reason Mr. S. has not allowed his purpose to be announced, and perhaps that is well for us, if it shall enable us to anticipate the issue of Venable's.

Your son, the Doctor,[3] was in two days ago, looking very well.

Yours truly

---

[1]George Frederick Holmes (1820-1897), a native of British Guiana, was educated in England before settling in America in 1837. An educator and scholar, he was contributor to the *Southern Literary Messenger* and in 1848 became the first president of the University of Mississippi. He was a professor at Richmond College, 1845-1847, and the College of William and Mary, 1849-1857; and from 1857 to 1897 he was professor of history and political economy at the University of Virginia. He was probably best known for his series of readers that were widely used in the South. A contemporary characterized him as "a free trader, a believer in slavery, and an advocate of states' rights." *DAB*, V, 164-165.

[2]Charles Scott Venable (1827-1900), a Virginia native, was an educator and a soldier. An 1842 graduate of Hampden-Sydney College, he also studied at the University of Virginia. He was professor of mathematics at Hampden-Sydney and the College of South Carolina prior to service on General R. E. Lee's staff during the Civil War. From 1865 to 1896 he was professor of mathematics at the University of Virginia. There he was "largely responsible for the development . . . of schools of applied chemistry and engineering, astronomy, biology, and agriculture." *CDAB*, 1113.

[3]George Washington Graham.

Rufus Barringer[1] *to William A. Graham* UNC

Charlotte
April 22, 1870

Our committee of Finance will meet at the Shops on the 9th and 10th of May. One or two matters connected with the Bond may render it desirable to have you present & I asked Mr. Stagg[2] to notify you.

It struck me that at the same time we might agree upon & make to the Stockholders in July, some kind of Report, that would bring before the people at the August Election, the question of separating, as far as possible, the management of our Rail Road, from the political control & influence of the State. Mr. Wilkes[3] will agree with us; & I think the time favorable for a movement in that direction. Of course Holden & Smith will oppose it; but they are both virtually committed, by their action on the "lease," to the conclusion that the present system is a bad one.[4]

Please try to meet us & in the mean time prepare an outline of your views.

---

[1]A moving force in the building of the North Carolina Railroad, Barringer was at the time of this letter a proponent of state divestiture of the railroad so that the company could

be removed from politics. Although he had advocated acceptance of congressional reconstruction, his views on the railroad were similar to those of his erstwhile Conservative friends. Powell, *DNCB*, I, 102; Allen W. Trelease, "The Passive Voice: The State and the North Carolina Railroad, 1849-1871," *North Carolina Historical Review*, LXI (April, 1984), 192, hereinafter cited as Trelease, "The State and the North Carolina Railroad."

[2]John A. Stagg served for many years as secretary of the North Carolina Railroad Company. His service spanned the late 1850s, the Civil War, and most of the Reconstruction era. *Proceedings of the Twentieth Annual Meeting of the Stockholders of the North Carolina Rail Road Company Held at Salisbury July 8th, 1869* (Company Shops: North Carolina Rail Road Print, 1869), 51, hereinafter cited as *North Carolina Rail Road Proceedings, 1869.*

[3]John Wilkes was at this time a major stockholder in the North Carolina Railroad.

[4]It was with good reason that Rufus Barringer wished to see the North Carolina Railroad detached from politics. State involvement in the enterprise had become a source of great controversy during Reconstruction. After W. W. Holden was elected Republican governor in 1868, he replaced Josiah Turner, Jr., with William A. Smith as company president and reconstituted the board of directors by exercising his legal right to appoint eight of the twelve directors. In 1869 the directors declined to lease the North Carolina Railroad to the Raleigh and Gaston company. Instead, Holden and Smith envisioned expansion of the North Carolina by promoting the purchase of the road to the south, the Charlotte, Columbia, and Augusta. This venture was blocked by the directors.

Meanwhile, the Richmond and Danville Railroad Company, which already controlled the link from Danville to Greensboro, cast covetous eyes on the North Carolina Railroad line from Greensboro to Charlotte. Faced with the prospect that the Richmond and Danville might build along a parallel route, the directors of the North Carolina Railroad Company in September, 1871, approved a thirty-year lease to the Richmond and Danville for $260,000 annually. Trelease, "The State and the North Carolina Railroad," 192-204 passim; Stover, *Railroads of the South*, 110.

Mike L. Woods[1] to William A. Graham UNC

Law Offices, 317 Broadway,
New York
April 23d 1870.

Dear Sir

Mr. Thos. D. Carter[2] of your State is here and proposes to prosecute George W. Swepson and others for their conduct in regard to the Rail Road Bonds issued by the State to aid their road. He requests me to write you, stating what I consider to be necessary etc, as evidence to procure and sustain an indictment.

We have a statute which provides that "every person, who with intent to cheat or defraud another, shall designedly, by color of any false token, or writing or by any other false pretence, obtain from any person, any money, personal property or valuable thing: upon conviction thereof, shall be punished by imprisonment in a State prison not exceeding three years, or in a county jail not exceeding one year, or by a fine not exceeding three times the value of the money, property, or thing so obtained, or by both, such fine and imprisonment."

We also have another Statute which provides: "If two or more persons shall conspire to cheat any person of any property, by any means which, if executed, would amount to a cheat, or to obtaining [paper cut] shall be deemed guilty of a misdemeanor."

The act incorporating the Western N.C.R.R. Company, I am informed, provides that before the Treasurer shall subscribe for Stock on the part of the State, as provided by the act, the President of the Company shall certify that 5 per cent of the subscriptions on the part of individuals has been actually paid into the Treasury of the Company.

Also that the act amendatory of that act provides that the President of the road shall certify the solvency of all such subscriptions by individuals, before the Treasurer shall subscribe for stock on the part of the State.

Also that the act provides that the whole of the road should be placed under contract for building, before the Treasurer should subscribe for stock on the part of the State, but how this fact was to be shown I am not informed, but I suppose by certificate of the President.

I learn that Mr. Swepson made an affidavit or certificate that 5 per cent of the subscription had been paid, when in point of fact, none or if any, very little thereof, had been paid; and that he certified the solvency of the subscriptions when it was notorious that one or more of the largest subscribers were totally insolvent.

That the Road has never been put under contract even up to this time; but what the President did in regard to this condition, I am not advised.

That upon the making of the affidavit and certificate the Treasurer made the subscription on the part of the State and issued bonds therefor.

These bonds were brought to this market and sold to different parties; [paper cut] issued having been brought to light together with the subsequent conduct of Mr. Swepson has so reduced their value in the market that the purchasers feel that they have been swindled and are anxious to prosecute all the parties.

There is probably no doubt that George W. Swepson, Robert R. Swepson,[3] General Littlefield and others (perhaps the Governor) inaugurated the whole movement for the purposes which were accomplished, for Mr. George W. Swepson, I learn, openly states that he paid $240,000 to members of the Legislature and others to secure the passage of the act; nor has he, as I am informed, ever made any report of his stewardship.

I am clearly of the opinion therefore that these facts being the case within either of the Statutes quoted. Mr. Carter will want properly certified copies of the Certificates made by Mr. Swepson, and such evidence as is necessary to show their falsity. The proof of the obtaining of the money can be had here.

The District Attorney will afford such facilities as are necessary to bring the matter before the grand jury, and if an indictment is found there will in my opinion be no difficulty in getting a requisition from the Governor.

---

[1]Mike L. Woods has not been identified.

[2]Thomas Deweese Carter (1834-1894), a native of Yancey County, owned a large interest in the Cranberry iron mine in Mitchell (now Avery) County. During the Civil War, tools and supplies for the Confederate government were manufactured there. In 1870 Carter's articles pertaining to the political situation were published in the *Sentinel* (Raleigh) and the *Asheville Citizen.* These began Carter's experience as a newspaper editor. He was deeply involved in the Swepson and Littlefield frauds. John Preston Arthur, *Western North Carolina: A History from 1730 to 1913* (Raleigh: Edwards and Broughton, 1914), 456, hereinafter cited as Arthur, *Western North Carolina.*

[3]Robert R. Swepson was the brother of George W. Swepson. Apparently he disapproved of George's machinations regarding the Western North Carolina Railroad stock. A month earlier, Robert Swepson characterized his brother, with whom he had quarreled, as a "self-willed, money-loving man" and avowed his intention to "deal firmly with him." Daniels, *Prince of Carpetbaggers*, 246-247.

Robert C. Winthrop to William A. Graham A&H

Brookline, Mass.,
April 28th., 1870.

I trust the 50 copies of our Proceedings at Washington reached you duly. I sent them by Express. We are having 3000 copies printed. Most of them will go to Dr. Sears, for his use at the South. But you can have more, if you wish, and will write me *early* to that effect.

You should send them to your Newspapers, and to all Collegiate and other public libraries. It seems to me an excellent pamphlet, and I trust you find no errors in your speech, which was too good to be marred by misprints.

Mr. Russell sailed for Europe yesterday, but promises to return in August.

Invitation from Rockingham County Committee UNC

Wentworth, N.C.,
April 29th, 1870.

At a meeting of the Bar, and Citizens of Rockingham County, among other appropriate resolutions, it was unanimously resolved that a Committee should be appointed to select some gentleman of the Bar in North Carolina, to deliver, at such time and place as he might select, an address upon the life & character of the late Chief Justice Ruffin. After the Conference, the undersigned who were appointed members of the Committee, have unanimously agreed to place this high and sacred duty in your hands, to be discharged at such time & place as you may select.

Allow us to express the hope that you will not feel at liberty to decline our request, & that at your convenience you will inform us as to the time and place.

With high respect, we are your obed't Servt's

E. T. Brodnax[1]
D. S. Reid[2]
A. L. Boyce[3] Committee.
Geo. L. Aiken[4]
A. M. Scales[5]

Address us at Wentworth.

---

[1]Edward Travis Brodnax (1796-1874), a native of Virginia, was a soldier in the War of 1812. He was educated at the University of Pennsylvania, where he earned a medical degree. Brodnax settled on a plantation in Rockingham County and became one of the

most influential men in the area. He was a member of the House of Commons, 1822-1823, and of the state Senate, 1827-1828; he was also a delegate to the conventions of 1835 and 1861. Brodnax married Janet Hamilton Chalmers. Having no children of their own, the couple adopted Mrs. Brodnax's nephew, Chalmers Lanier Glenn, and his wife, and later the three sons of the Glenns, including Robert B. Glenn, who became governor of North Carolina. Powell, *DNCB*, 232-233.

[2]David Settle Reid (1813-1891), of Rockingham County, was a successful lawyer and Democratic political leader. A conservative, pro-southern man, he served as a state legislator, United States congressman (1843-1847), North Carolina governor (1851-1854), and United States senator (1854-1859). Reid was generally considered to be the wisest and most resourceful Democratic leader between the day of Nathaniel Macon and the Civil War. *CDAB*, 852-853.

[3]A. L. Boyce has not been identified.

[4]George L. Aiken has not been identified.

[5]Alfred Moore Scales (1827-1892), a native of Reidsville, was educated at Caldwell Institute before his entrance into the University of North Carolina at Chapel Hill. After graduation at the university Scales studied law at Chapel Hill with Judge William H. Battle, after which he was admitted to the bar and established a law practice in Madison. Actively interested in politics, he became a solicitor and then was elected for four sessions in the House of Commons (1852, 1853, 1856, and 1857) and for two years as a Democratic representative in Congress (1857-1859). During the Civil War, Scales saw active duty in the Thirteenth Regiment, North Carolina Volunteers, rising to the rank of brigadier general. He was wounded at Chancellorsville and at Gettysburg. After the war Scales resumed his law practice and established an office in Greensboro. In 1875 he was elected to Congress and held that position until he was elected governor of North Carolina in 1884. During his tenure as governor he worked for better schools and more diversified activity by the State Department of Agriculture. *Biographical Directory of Congress*, 1566; Beth G. Crabtree, *North Carolina Governors, 1585-1974: Brief Sketches* (Raleigh: Division of Archives and History, Department of Cultural Resources, revised edition, 1974), 104-105, hereinafter cited as Crabtree, *North Carolina Governors*.

Reply to Rockingham County Committee UNC

Hillsboro',
May 2nd, 1870.

Gentlemen

I have had the honor to receive your letter of the 29th. ult. desiring that I should at such time and place as may be convenient, deliver an address on the Life and Character of the late Chief Justice Ruffin; such a tribute to his memory having been voted in a public meeting of the Bar and the Citizens of Rockingham County, and you being its committee to select a speaker for the occasion.

I concur warmly in the sentiments which prompted this tribute, and feel flattered that your choice has been directed to me for its fulfilment, and although I could have wished that it had fallen on some one of more leisure and greater competency for the task, I do not feel at liberty to withhold any service of mine, in an attempt to do justice to a character so eminent in the jurisprudence and history of the State, and so cherished in the recollection of his neighbors, admirers, and troops of friends. My engagements at present are such that I must defer the arrangement of time and place for future correspondence.

I am, Gentlemen,
With the highest respect,
Your obed't Serv't.,
W. A. Graham.

George W. Graham to William A. Graham UNC

116 East 23rd St
[New York]
May 11, 1870

My dear father,

Your letter, containing the money for which I am very much obliged, has just been received. I will get the check cashed and dispose of the coupon when I go down town tomorrow. My expenses for board, washing etc. are about $2.50 per week more than last winter but I get much better fare and live in a more pleasant part of the city. The house I boarded at last session for $8.50 was not as agreeable as I would wish to have, but I had to be near the college and was as good as I could get for that price. My application has been made out and will be handed in tomorrow or next day. I will be very much obliged for the letters to Mssrs Wetmore and Everts.[1] I dont know that they will have any direct bearing on my application unless through them I may get a letter to Mr. Tweed[2] (who is the Democratic king of New York City) and get him [to] recommend me to the Board of Health. Then I would be certain of the position, for these Democrats will do anything that he says. For instance, a young man who stood for his license to practice law, last week failed, and then obtained a letter from Mr. Tweed to the examining committee requesting them to pass him and they did it after a pretended examination. My application has been endorsed and highly recommended by Admiral Farragut[3] and several of my professors. Dr. Loomis[4] says the more political influence I can bring to bear upon it the better for that will go farther than one's knowledge of Medicine. Admiral Farragut is still sick and is not able to leave his room.

I attended the "Womans Rights Convention"[5] yesterday but had to leave before it adjourned as I was quite unwell and have been for several days past. The speakers (all women) seemed to put themselves on the same footing with the slaves of the South and said now that the negroes had been emancipated and allowed to vote it was time they were getting from under mans controll and asserting their right to the ballot box. The prayer at the opening of the convention was also offered by a woman and it was of the most peculi[ar] strain that I ever listened to. She prayed "the Lord to assist them in obtaining their suffrage from man for without his help they could do nothing with the stronger sex." They reported such success in the North, East and West, but said nothing about their progress at the South. They have appointed a committee to edit a paper here called "The Revolution". I sent a copy to Evans[6] and probably you may see extracts from it in the "Recorder". The Convention met again to day, but it is to wet for me to attend. Among other things, they said (I suppose they refered to the examination of some of the witnesses in the McFarland trial)[7] "female witnesses should be examined by women and all the crimes they committed should be tried by them, and not allowed to be insulted by lawyers as some had lately been." Love to all

Your affectionate son
Geo. W. Graham

P.S.

Please send the letters of introduction as soon as convenient.

---

[1]Almost certainly this was William Maxwell Evarts (1818-1901), a leading New York lawyer who had entered public life as assistant United States attorney for the southern district of New York, 1849-1853. In 1863-1864 he went to England in an effort to stop British aid to the Confederacy in building and equipping navy vessels. After the war Evarts was attorney general in President Johnson's cabinet. From 1870 to 1880 he was president of the New York Bar Association, an office he used to fight the corruption of the "Tweed Ring" in the state. *CDAB*, 278-279.

[2]William Marcy Tweed (1823-1878) rose from being a saddler and bookkeeper to become the political boss of New York City, with influence beyond. He acquired unprecedented power through graft and corruption. In dictating the nomination of John T. Hoffman as governor of New York in 1868, he assured his political hold on the entire state. Finally halted in his ignominious career, Tweed was arrested and sentenced to jail. An amount estimated at between $30 million and $200 million was stolen from the city by the "Tweed Ring." *CDAB*, 1090-1091.

[3]David Glasgow Farragut (1801-1870), of Virginia, was a native of Tennessee. Virtually adopted by David Porter, he entered the navy in 1810, served on the *Essex*, and was taken prisoner by the British in 1814. Although his studious nature made him unpopular in the conservative antebellum navy, he rose about as rapidly as was usual in his day. He was stationed in Norfolk most of the time between 1823 and 1855, though he saw active service in the Mexican War and established the Mare Island navy yard. Farragut remained loyal to the Union and won great fame as a bold naval warrior during the Civil War. He captured New Orleans, cleared the Mississippi, and won the Battle of Mobile Bay. Farragut became a vice admiral in 1864 and the navy's first full admiral in 1866. *DAB*, 286-291.

[4]Possibly Mahlon Loomis (1826-1886), a native of New York, who practiced dentistry and, after 1865, experimented with the transmission of electricity in the Virginia mountains. These experiments suggest the possibility that George W. Graham may have known him. *CDAB*, 584.

[5]This refers to a meeting of the National Women's Suffrage Association. About 300 women, joined by a sprinkling of male supporters, attended the sessions. The principal speaker on the first day was the redoubtable Susan B. Anthony, who presented a litany of reasons women should be enfranchised. Among other things, she announced that Clement L. Vallandigham was prepared to introduce resolutions calling for the vote for women at the next Ohio Democratic party convention. For a full account of the meeting see the *New York Times*, May 11, 12, 1870.

[6]At the time of this letter Charles Napoleon Bonaparte Evans and Thomas Clancy Evans were listed as editors and publishers of the *Hillsborough Recorder*.

[7]This reference is to the lurid trial of Daniel McFarland, who had assassinated journalist Albert D. Richardson, alleging alienation of affection by the victim. The trial, which lasted several weeks, had great dramatic appeal: a theatrical setting, free love, adultery, drugs, drunkenness, expert witnesses, etc. The murder occurred in the editorial offices of the *New York Tribune*; Horace Greeley testified. The prosecution alleged that McFarland had abused and neglected his wife of twenty years and that she had left him for a better

man (Richardson), who later married her. The defense claimed that Richardson had disrupted a happy home and had alienated a wife and children from the cuckolded McFarland. Subsequent events produced an emotional collapse that led McFarland to heavy drinking and, allegedly, temporary insanity at the time of the murder. The jury found McFarland not guilty by reason of insanity, much to the chagrin of nineteenth-century feminists. For a full account of the McFarland trial see the *New York Times* of April and May, 1870.

James A. Graham to John W. Graham UNC

Graham,
May 13th, 1870.

Dear Johnny

. . . .

I learn this morning that Phillips has been nominated by the radicals for Atto. Gen'l,[1] and that Dick Badger[2] made a speech at their Convention. I suppose from that, that they have both gone fully over. We are having plenty of politics here, lots of candidates, none of whom give general satisfaction. I believe if I was to start now, I could get the nomination for the House easily, but I would not have it at present.

Our radicals are jubilant over their Convention in Raleigh, but seem to take no interest in County politics. I hope the split in Orange will be healed before the next meeting.

Lizzie joins me in love to all.

Affectionately your Brother

---

[1]No greater shock came to political North Carolina in this era than that caused by the defection of Samuel F. Phillips. His letters prior to this time had indicated his dissatisfaction with the opinions of many people with whom he was closely associated. However, it was unfortunate for his reputation that he announced the change of political affiliation at the same time that he accepted the nomination for office from a party that had reached, in the expressive phrase of William A. Dunning, "the nadir of disgrace." An analysis of Phillips's actions may be found in Robert D. Miller, "Samuel Field Phillips: The Odyssey of a Southern Dissenter," *North Carolina Historical Review*, LVIII (July, 1981), 263-280.

[2]Richard Cogdell Badger (1839-1882), son of Delia Haywood Williams and George Edmund Badger, became a much-respected statesman and was a friend of William A. Graham. After graduating from the University of North Carolina in 1859, he was briefly a Wake County attorney before serving in the Confederate forces as a major. His postwar career included these positions: member of the North Carolina General Assembly, 1872; United States district attorney, 1873-1877; and delegate to the Constitutional Convention of 1875. Grant, *Alumni History*, 26; Powell, *DNCB*, I, 79-80.

Edward J. Hale to William A. Graham UNC

New York,
May 15th, 1870.

Yours of the 11th. is just at hand. I regret that you feel obliged in this instance to act out the characteristic reticence of our people. But I have written to Duffie and Chapman, his Publishers, with whom we are to be associated, asking them to draw Mr. Stephens' attention to the Mecklenburg Declaration, and to tell him that I think you may probably be able to loan him a copy of the "Rev. Hist. of N.C."[1] if he should not already have one. I trust you will be able to do so, if he should apply. *I* have no copy, or would send it. I had it, of course, but it is either boxed up with my books in N.C. or borrowed by some one and never returned, as I am inclined to think is the case.

We would be very glad to publish another Ed'n of the Rev. Hist. but our means are too limited to justify the publication of anything which would have a slow sale. When reprinted, your Greensboro' paper of 1858[2] should be attached, and some of the latter might be printed alone, separately, for those who already have the former volume. I wish we could hope for such a demand as would justify a republication. But our people buy few books, and too often, I regret to say, prefer Northern to Southern books.

Will you not be able to beat Harris[3] for Congress? I hope so.

---

[1]See Jo[seph] Seawell Jones, *A Defense of the Revolutionary History of North Carolina from the Aspersions of Mr. Jefferson* (Boston: Charles Bowen; Raleigh: Turner and Hughes, 1834).

[2]This refers to an address by Graham entitled "The Life and Character of General Nathanael Greene," delivered on January 20, 1859, to the Greene Monument Association. See J. G. de Roulhac Hamilton and Max R. Williams (eds.), *The Papers of William Alexander Graham* (Raleigh: Division of Archives and History, Department of Cultural Resources, projected 8 volumes, 1957—), V, 64-85, hereinafter cited as Hamilton and Williams, *Graham Papers.*

[3]In 1870 James H. Harris, a noted black orator and Republican politician, was a candidate for Congress from the Fourth District. He was defeated by Conservative Sion H. Rogers. Hamilton, *Reconstruction in North Carolina,* 493; *Biographical Directory of Congress,* 1537.

Alexander H. Graham[1] to William A. Graham UNC

Bagdad, Williamson Co,
Texas
May 17th 1870

My Dear Uncle,

I am requested by the Trustees of the Bagdad Institute at Bagdad Williamson Co Texas, to enquire of you as a Trustee of the Peabody fund in regard to the fund appropriated by Mr. Geo. Peabody to the Southern states for school purposes,—whether the fund is designed to aid in the building of Houses for schools, as well as supporting schools where the buildings are already finished, and what course wuld be necessary to pursue to obtain aid from the fund, if it can be had. Our building is already roofed, but we are too hard pressed to push it forward at once. Our House is chiefly under the control of the Masonic fraternity, but is a public school so far as regards the white population, and uncontroled by politics or sectarianism. Our population though large enough to sustain a fine school consists mostly of men of but little means, and consequently this enquiry is made for the purpose of aid in the completion of the building and putting under headway such a school as our neighborhood demands. Our village is 24 miles N.W. from Austin on the Mail Road from Austin to Burnett and Lampasas Springs, and 15 miles west from Georgetown the county seat of this county. Our population is mostly white—very few freedmen living in this section of the country—about 80 families live within a radius of five miles of our village. The majority of them are farmers and stockraisers. Our village contains 3 Dry Goods Stores, 1 Bl'k smith Shop 1 Wood or Wagon shop, 1 Cotton Gin, 1 Steam Saw mill, 1 Drug Store, 1 Hotel, 1 Church & one school House *unfinished.* Our crops of corn wheat & cotton are promising.

Hoping to hear from you soon. I remain truly

Your nephew

---

[1]Dr. Alexander Hamilton Graham (b. 1835), William A. Graham's nephew, the son of John Davidson Graham (1789-1847) of Lincoln County, had settled in Leander, Williamson County, Texas, about 1857. He served as a Confederate surgeon. Clark, "Graham Descendants"; Graham, *General Joseph Graham*, 174.

Kemp P. Battle to William A. Graham UNC

Raleigh, N.C.,
June 3, 1870

At a meeting of the Executive Committee of the N.C. Agricultural Society,[1] held this afternoon, I was instructed in behalf of the Society, to request you to deliver an Address before the Society during the week of the next Fair, on the Life and Character of it's late President, Judge Thomas Ruffin.

We earnestly hope you will comply with our request.

---

[1]By agreement the Rockingham County bar and the Agricultural Society joined as sponsors for the address.

Robert B. Gilliam[1] *to William A. Graham* UNC

Oxford,
June 21st., 1870.

I have been so long out of political training that I feel a good deal in want of help. Having, as you know, great confidence in your judgment, I will be glad to have your views upon two or three subjects, if it is not taxing your time too much to give them.

To what subjects of State and Federal politicks ought chief prominence to be given?

Supposing the public debt of the State to be under discussion, how ought it to be treated?

And, if the subject of taxing United States Bonds is under discussion, how ought that to be treated? The rule that the Government should comply with her contract with her creditors, of course cannot be disputed, and it follows that where the contract exempts the bonds of the U. States from taxation, it must be carried out in good faith; but a distinction is taken between taxing the bonds themselves, and taxing the income derived from them. What do you think of it?

What do you think is the proper Conservative platform, in regard to the Tariff? No ground upon that subject has been taken by our friends in this State, so far as I know, nor indeed, anywhere in the South. At the North, the Democratic party, whether old Democrats or old Whigs, seem to be exceedingly hostile to the present Tariff system.

My first inquiry embraces any other subjects which you may feel inclined to call to my attention.

There is another subject about which I feel some embarrassment, partly on public, and partly on private accounts. And that is, what ought Rogers[2] and myself to do in regard to the opposing candidates in the Canvass?

Ought we to request a mixed or free discussion, and, if not, ought we to accept the proposition if it is made on the other side? Rogers seems to be very much opposed to it, & I confess I am not very favorable to it myself, on several accounts.

I will be glad to know when you will be in Raleigh, and, if it is not too soon for me, I shall be glad to meet you there, but in the meantime, let me hear from you, if you can spare the time.

Some of our friends are very sanguine as to the result of the elections in this County, and think we will carry our ticket. I am not so sanguine, tho' I think we will gain considerably on the last vote for Congress. We are, I fear, in some danger of trouble in forming our County ticket, both for legislative and local appointments, which indicates, by the way, the expectation of a successful result on the part of some of our friends, for if they did not count upon success, there would be no rivalry for the nominations.

---

[1]Robert B. Gilliam (1805-1870), of Oxford, was a graduate of the University of North Carolina, a prominent attorney, and an interested Whig politician. He was a delegate to the Constitutional Convention of 1835, several times a member of the General Assembly (Speaker of the Commons in 1848 and 1862), and a superior court judge. He was elected to the United States House of Representatives in 1870 but died before taking office. For thirty years Gilliam was a trustee of the university. Graham and Gilliam often corresponded regarding political affairs. Spencer Alumni Project; Connor, *North Carolina Manual, 1913*, 449, 472-473, 880.

[2]Sion Hart Rogers (1825-1874), of Wake County, was graduated by the University of North Carolina in 1846, became a lawyer, and served as lieutenant and colonel in the Fourteenth and Forty-seventh North Carolina regiments respectively. He resigned his colonelcy in January, 1863, to become state attorney general. In the congressional elections of 1870, Rogers, running as a Democrat, was elected over James H. Harris. *Biographical Directory of Congress*, 1537; Hamilton, *Reconstruction in North Carolina*, 492.

Walter F. Leak[1] *to William A. Graham* UNC

Rockingham,
June 24th., 1870.

I have this day understood that O. H. Dockery[2] had written home from Washington, (on yesterday) to his Father, Gen'l Dockery,[3] that Pool[4] & Abbot[5] were both in Washington, & that they had come on for the purpose of having some official steps taken to protect their party from the *alleged* outrages of the "Ku Klux" organization in N.C.

He further stated, that it was proposed to take yourself & some other prominent citizens of this State, as "Hostages," to protect their party from the abuses of the organization aforesaid.

I give you this information for what it is worth, but of one thing there is *no doubt*, and that is, that Gen'l Dockery rec'd the letter aforesaid, from his son.

Instead of our condition getting better, I really fear it is really getting worse, & I begin seriously to fear that it must end in *Bloodshed.*

I should be pleased to have your views, upon matters and things in general.

---

[1]Walter F. Leak (1799-1897), of Richmond County, was a planter and lawyer of note. He was a member of the Commons in the 1821 and 1831 sessions and a state senator in 1832. A strong secessionist, he was a member of the Constitutional Convention of 1861-1862. McCormick, *Convention Personnel*, 53; Cheney, *North Carolina Government*, 279, 297, 298, 387; Grant, *Alumni History*, 357.

[2]Oliver Hart Dockery (1830-1906), a farmer and the son of Alfred Dockery of Richmond County, attended Wake Forest College and was graduated from the University of North Carolina in 1848. After serving briefly in the Confederate army, Dockery resigned and advocated restoration of the Union. After the war he was a Republican. Elected to the Fortieth Congress, he was reelected to the Forty-first and served from 1868 to 1871. After failing to win election as governor in 1888, in 1889 he was appointed United States consul general at Rio de Janeiro, a post he held until 1893. *Biographical Directory of Congress*, 818.

[3]Alfred Dockery (1797-1875), a Richmond County planter, was a member of the House of Commons, 1822, state Senate, 1836-1844, and United States House of Representatives, 1845-1847 and 1851-1853; he was an unsuccessful Whig candidate for governor in 1854. *Biographical Directory of Congress,* 817.

[4]John Pool (1826-1884), of Pasquotank County, was a graduate of the University of North Carolina, a lawyer, and a politician. He was state senator, 1856-1860 and 1864-1865, unsuccessful Whig candidate for governor in 1860, delegate to the Constitutional Convention of 1865, and United States senator, 1868-1873. After retiring from the Senate, he practiced law in Washington, D.C. A strong Unionist, Pool took no part in the secession movement and opposed the war, gaining election to the state Senate as a peace candidate. After the Civil War Pool was associated with the Radical Republicans but was never so partisan as others. He was very influential in getting national anti-Ku Klux Klan legislation passed. *DAB*, XV, 64-65.

[5]Joseph Carter Abbott (1825-1881), a native of New Hampshire—lawyer, editor, Union general, manufacturer, political lobbyist, and United States senator—took part in the final attack on Fort Fisher; and, seeing the promise of economic and political preferment in southeastern North Carolina, he settled in Wilmington. An influential delegate to the Constitutional Convention of 1868, he was elected as a Republican to the United States Senate (1868-1871). He worked diligently to promote the completion of the Wilmington, Charlotte, and Rutherfordton Railroad and to secure federal aid to improve the harbor at

Wilmington. After the political reversal occasioned by his unsuccessful bid for another term in the Senate, Abbott encountered economic problems that ended in his bankruptcy. It would be easy to brand Abbott as an opportunistic carpetbagger, as contemporary editors and later historians have done, but it should be noted that he joined his fortunes with those of the Cape Fear region. There were few complaints from Democrats or Republicans, whether native-born or not, so long as Abbott was successful in contributing to the growth and prosperity of southeastern North Carolina. Powell, *DNCB*, I, 2-3.

Robert C. Winthrop to William A. Graham A&H

Brookline, Mass.,
June 24th., 1870

I believe you were the mover of the Resolution that our Board hold a special Meeting in Memphis next Oct'r, to be notified by the Chairman or Secretary, *unless* otherwise determined in the mean time. I have thought it best to inform you, without further delay, that there seems to be a general disposition to abandon the meeting for this year. Mr. Russell, our Sec'y, is in England, and his return is uncertain. Bishop McIlvaine is on the other side, also, & will only return in season for the Evangelical Alliance, which will engross him this autumn. Bradford is so ill as to tender his resignation, which I will keep until we meet in Phila. Gov. Aiken writes against going to Memphis, & will not promise to be there. Mr. Wetmore is strongly opposed to it. We cannot rely on Gen'l Grant, and Gov. Fish, as their public business may detain them, even should they be disposed to go so far. Mr. Evarts has an Oration to deliver at the Cambridge Law School at the very time proposed.

On the whole, it seems to Dr. Sears & myself that it is best to postpone the visit to Memphis until a more convenient Season. Whenever we go there, we ought to have a full Board, with all our notabilities. As there is no special business requiring our attention, and as the expense of such a meeting would be very considerable, we hardly ought to undertake it, unless it can be carried through in a manner to interest and gratify that part of the Country. A meagre, pro forma meeting would disappoint every body.

I feel sure you will acquiesce in this view.

Alexander H. Graham to William A. Graham UNC

Bagdad, Williamson Co.,
Texas
June 29th 1870

My Dear Uncle,

Your favor of May 30th was recd. some three weeks ago. I have delayed answering hoping to receive the pamphlet before writing again. It has not yet reached me. Will you be so good as to forward me another pamphlet containing proceedings of Peabody Trustees. Our Trustees would prefer seeing the pamphlet before making application for aid from Rev. B. Sears, agent Peabody fund.

Our section is settling up rapidly and with a very good class of people altho they as a general thing have but little means. Our crops of wheat corn and cotton are looking well. We have had an abundance of rain & with more regularity than any season since I came to this state. Our prospects for good crops of cotton & good sales for our stock are better now than at any time since 59.

I am living on the main road from Austin to Lampasas Spring's distance 60 miles 20 from Austin & 40 from Lampasas, with no intervening village. Our's is a high dry rolling prairie county with 10 miles width of post oak timber 4 miles off to our East (the *crop* timbers) and immense cedar brakes within three miles of us to the west, extending ten miles to the Colorado River. . . . This place Bagdad is in the centre of a beautiful rolling prarie valley 6 miles wide by seven long, surrounded by post oak & cedar timber. Within two miles of us is a the [*sic*] finest marble quarry in the State. Several of our houses are built of this material. I live in the centre of the village, have 8 ½ acres (live oak grove) in my lot. I am practising my profession as well as carrying on a Dry Goods Grocery & Drug Store combined.

Our location is such that in a few years I think we will have a new county, with this place for the county seat. I have four children, Chas Joseph, Minnie May, John Davidson Jr. and Mary Louise. The two eldest are now going to school at this place. Two of my wifes brothers live on each side of this place within ½ mile, & one in the village. I was considerably worsted by the war having lost most of my means through Bishop Gregg[1] in S.C. and by money loaned here during the war. I have got a start again & am now doing very well. I have been trying to induce Brother Charles[2] & Col Sloan[3] to come to Austin. This section of the state is said to be progressing faster than any portion of the south. In the course of 9 or 12 months we will have a Rail Road running from Galveston to Austin direct. I think those of your sons in the Legal Profession could do well in either Austin, Georgetown or Lampasas. The county is too healthy for doctors, altho Lampasas is a good opening for a physician, attending to the invalids who resort there during the summer. Lampasas is a growing place situated in a beautiful valley. The sulphur springs there are the largest I ever saw, & the strongest in sulphur. For chronic diseases of various kinds they are very beneficial. As many as two thousand persons from the lower county resort there every summer.

I have not heard from Chas or Jas[4] or our N.C. relatives for some time. Our Trustees will in a short time apply to Dr. Sears for what aid if any he may choose to bestow upon us. We think of applying to him in behalf of all our people including the Negro & allotting to the Negroes there proportionate share of the fund. They, the Negroes, are now erecting a building within 1 mile of us, the whites aiding them. We also think of getting the Gov. Davis & other prominent men to endorse our petition. Present my kind regards to Aunt Sue & family. Will be pleased to hear from you at any time & glad to receive any information on the above.

Truly your nephew

---

[1]Alexander Gregg (1819-1893), a native of South Carolina and a lawyer who turned to religion, was elected the first Protestant Episcopal bishop of Texas in 1859. In 1874, when

the Texas church was divided, he became bishop of the southern district. Galveston then became his home. In addition to his various contributions to church literature, Gregg also wrote a *History of Old Cheraw* (1867), concerning Indian and white settlements in the Peedee River valley and the Revolutionary history of the region. *Cyclopedia of American Biography*, XII, 315.

[2]Charles Connor Graham (1819-1886), the son of the John Davidson Grahams of Lincoln County, lived in Memphis, Tennessee. Clark, "Graham Descendants."

[3]This was John Alexander Sloan (1839-1886) of Guilford County, who had been colonel of the Twenty-seventh North Carolina Regiment. Clark, *Histories of the North Carolina Regiments*, II, 425-427.

[4]This probably refers to Charles Connor Graham or his son James Franklin Graham (1850-1915). Clark, "Graham Descendants."

Mike L. Woods to William A. Graham UNC

317 Broadway New York
June 30th 1870

Mr. Thomas D. Carter leaves here tonight to visit you to solicit your attendance here in his matters pertaining to "Cranberry".[1]

I had the pleasure of writing you some time ago upon the question of a criminal proceeding against George W. Swepson and others on account of their conduct in the procuring and selling of North Carolina Special Tax bonds; and at that time gave . . . extracts from our Statutes. I have had occasion since then to further investigate, both the law and the facts, and I am confirmed in the opinion which I then gave, that they are liable to indictment.

I have also the opinion of one or two of our best lawyers upon the question and they are firmly of the same opinion. I fully concur with Mr. Carter in the views which he entertains as to the importance of your coming here. It will in my judgment result in an immediate settlement of his whole difficulties; or if not, then, in the proper punishment of a set of swindlers who have for a long while been preying upon the public and private interests of your state. Mr. Carter is so thoroughly and accurately informed as to his rights and situation, and as to my views that I deem it unnecessary to say more than I have. There is in my judgment an absolute certainty that the Messrs. Russell have committed perjury in their answer, punishable here.

---

[1]This concerns a court case that involved Graham. Thomas Deweese Carter had named Graham as his counsel in *Thomas D. Carter* v. *Robert F. Hoke and others*, 64 N.C. 348 (1870), which evolved over the Cranberry Mine Works. Cranberry Ore Bank in Mitchell (now Avery) County was declared by geologist W. C. Kerr to be "one of the most remarkable iron deposits in America." Located on the western slope of Iron Mountain, it derived its name from Cranberry Creek, which flows near the outcrop at the foot of the mountain. The history of litigation over the Cranberry mine goes back to around 1850, when John Hardin or his son Councill Hardin sold the property to General R. F. Hoke for $10,000. Thomas D. Carter had an equitable contract for the sale of a part of the interest held under bond for title by John Hardin and two others. This led to the litigation that culminated in the *Carter* v. *Hoke* case.

In May, 1867, Carter agreed to convey his interest in the mine to General Hoke and others for $44,000. Carter tendered the deed and "was given a sight draft on a New York bank for the amount of the purchase money, which draft was protested and never paid," apparently because parties involved had understood that, although it was a sight draft, the funds required were to have come from proceeds of a sale of the property by Hoke and his associates to a second purchaser. Carter defeated the anticipated sale.

A receiver was appointed and the sale of the property was enjoined. At the spring term, 1869, of the superior court of Madison County, Hoke moved to dissolve the injunction and end the receivership. At this point it became apparent that Hoke had effected a sale of the property for $50,000 to Charles W. Russell and Francis B. Russell, referred to in this letter, who claimed to be innocent purchasers. Hoke's motion was granted by Judge James L. Henry, but the case was appealed to the North Carolina Supreme Court. The injunction was declared in effect until Carter was paid and the innocence of the Russells as purchasers was decided in court. Hoke and his associates compromised with Carter, however, effectively settling title to the property as far as Carter was concerned. Arthur, *Western North Carolina*, 415-417, 557.

William A. Graham to William A. Graham, Jr. A&H

Hillsboro',
July 1st., 1870.

I wrote you a note by the mail of yesterday, but receiving yours today, in which you desire I shall suggest my views as to the course you should take in regard to the candidacy in your district, I write again.

I had heard nothing in respect to movements there, except that Bynum[1] had said to two or three persons in Raleigh, before the Convention met, that you would be nominated for the Senate; and John Hoke[2] was asked by Turner, in my presence, whether they had nominated candidates, and he gave the account I mentioned in my letter yesterday, and said there was much dissatisfaction with the nominations. I was aware of very strong political prejudices on the part of some of the population of the district, arising from a feeling, I thought, of envy, but I supposed it had died out in a good measure with the war; and, as the older Schencks were Whigs, I didn't know that it pervaded them. The present one,[3] I suppose, apprehends that you may be in *his* way, in the competitions of the district.

Those Conventions are very much nurseries of intrigue and fraud, and do not often reflect the wishes of the people. Having gone into one, however, the reasons ought to be cogent to cause one to oppose it's nominee. I cannot advise upon it decisively, without realizing all the circumstances, and the conditions of things in the district. Of course you would not undertake the canvass without strong assurances of success, & nor be provoked into it by mere personal feeling. Your state of health, your family and business interests are all against it, besides the charge of personal ambition, and disregard of the success of party; on the other is the betrayal of their trusts by the members of the Convention, and especially that the Gaston delegates should abandon any agency, but agree to submit to the men of Lincoln, etc., and the avowal of a determination to withdraw confidence from men because they are Whigs.

On the whole, there are so many reasons against it, that unless you feel yourself committed, or owe it to your self-respect to become a candidate, I think I should decline. Your health would probably give way in an active canvass, and if you go into it, you should carry it on, with vigor. I do not know anything else I can suggest, except that I would have Mr. S. & all like him to know, that if they expect to proscribe men thus early for being Whigs, it will be some time before they are installed in power. They should know that, but for the cooperation they have had from the Whigs, they could do but little in organizing a party in 9 Counties in 10, of the State.

We have nothing new—the weather very hot. John wrote from Norfolk, but I have not heard the contents of the letter.

Affectionately

---

[1]William Preston Bynum (1820-1909) was born and reared in Stokes County. He was valedictorian of his class at Davidson College in 1842 and after graduation studied law with Richmond M. Pearson. He practiced law in Rutherfordton and Lincolnton prior to the Civil War. He served in the war with distinction as lieutenant and then colonel in the Second North Carolina Regiment until March 21, 1863, when he resigned from the army to become solicitor of the Seventh Judicial District. A Whig before the war, Bynum was a member of the Constitutional Convention of 1865 and a state senator in 1866. Although he was elected through the support of both Republicans and Democrats, Bynum in the 1868 election embraced the Republican party, supporting Holden and Grant. From 1873 until 1879 he served ably as an associate justice of the North Carolina Supreme Court. Powell, *DNCB*, I, 294-295; *DAB*, II, 382-383.

[2]John Franklin Hoke (1820-1888) of Lincoln County, a brother of Michael Hoke, graduated from the University of North Carolina and read law with David L. Swain and Richmond M. Pearson. He served as a regular army officer in Mexico with Winfield Scott. A lifelong Democrat, he was a state senator in 1850, 1852, and 1854 and a commoner in 1860. After brief service as North Carolina's adjutant general, Hoke was made colonel of the Thirteenth North Carolina Regiment (later the Twenty-third). He resigned in the spring of 1862 because of poor health and became a colonel of senior reserves. Late in the war he was given charge of the Salisbury prison, a thankless task. Hoke held no public office after the war. Van Noppen Papers.

[3]David L. Schenck (1835-1902), son of Dr. David Warlick Schenck and grandson of prosperous Lincolnton millowner Michael Schenck, was descended from Englishmen who had been exiled to Switzerland because of their religious convictions. David Schenck was educated at the South Carolina Lindsley School, studied law under Haywood W. Guion, and was graduated from the law school of Chief Justice Richmond Pearson. He established a law practice in Gaston County but in 1860 returned to Lincoln County. In 1861 he was a delegate to the Secession Convention. Schenck in 1874 became superior court judge for the Ninth Judicial District. A man of many interests and endowed with a great sense of civic responsibility, he was awarded an LL.D. degree by the University of North Carolina in 1880. In 1881 he resigned as judge to assume the position of general counsel for the Richmond and Danville Railroad and moved to Greensboro. In 1883 he was appointed by Governor Jarvis to be associate justice of the North Carolina Supreme Court, an honor he declined. For the rest of his life Schenck was important in many facets of community life in Greensboro. He was a town commissioner and was especially interested in the schools. Always interested in historical matters, he was instrumental in reclaiming and developing the Guilford Memorial Battleground. His law and historical library was extensive, and at his death the *News and Observer* (Raleigh) published an editorial tribute to him entitled "Greatest Man in the State." Betty D. Caldwell, *Founders and Builders of Greensboro* (Greensboro: Jos. J. Stone and Company, 1925), 273-285, hereinafter cited as Caldwell, *Founders and Builders of Greensboro.*

Robert P. Waring[1] *to William A. Graham* UNC

Charlotte
July 5 1870

Dear Sir

Regarding you as the recognized leader and oracle of our party I take the liberty to write asking your opinion. Whether in a legal point of view the 3rd Section of the Howard Amendment[2] disables those who were in office before the War from taking seats in the State Legislature. In other words whether you concur with Mr. H. W. Guion's published opinion of the subject.[3] I am a candidate for the House and as a convention meets here on Saturday next to nominate a Candidate for the Senate in place of Gov Vance believed I would be highly gratified to have your opinion before that time.

---

[1]Robert Payne Waring (b. 1827) of Charlotte was a native of Virginia and a graduate of the University of Virginia. After serving as commonwealth attorney, Waring was appointed consul to St. Thomas. When he returned to the United States in 1861, he was arrested for saluting the Confederate flag but soon was released. During the Civil War he held the rank of captain in the Confederate army; he was captured and imprisoned by Union forces. At one point Waring was tried by a military commission for alleged criticism of the military government of the South and was acquitted. After the war Waring became an editor in Charlotte. He was a member of the state House of Representatives, 1870-1872 and 1885, and of the state Senate, 1872-1875. His later years were devoted to farming in his native Virginia. Daniel A. Tompkins, *History of Mecklenburg County and the City of Charlotte from 1740 to 1903* (Charlotte: Observer Printing House, 2 volumes, 1903-1904), II, 82, hereinafter cited as Tompkins, *History of Mecklenburg*; Cheney, *North Carolina Government*, 453, 455, 465.

[2]The Fourteenth Amendment, section 3, provided that any person who had sworn to uphold the United States Constitution in the capacity of state or federal officer and then "shall have engaged in insurrection or rebellion . . ." was barred from holding public office prior to having his disabilities removed by a two-thirds vote of each house of Congress.

[3]Haywood W. Guion's opinion is discussed in Zebulon B. Vance to William A. Graham, February 19, 1870, in this volume.

Special Military Order[1] UNC

State of North Carolina
Adjutant General's Office
Raleigh, July 13, 1870

Special Orders
No 11.

Col. G. W. Kirk,[2] Comdg 2d Regt North Carolina State Troops will at once procure the necessary transportation for his camp equipage and proceed to Yanceyville and assume command of Alamance and Caswell counties. He will take the necessary steps to preserve order and to give the fullest protection to life and property. He will take charge of the public buildings and arrest and hold for examination persons accused of felonies—especially those charged with or of being accessory to the murder of J. W. Stephens and Wyatt Outlaw.

By command of Gov. Holden, Commander-in-chief

A. W. Fisher, Adjt Gen'l[3]

[Note on back]

Office Private Secretary,
Raleigh, N.C. June 14, 1871

The Adjutant General of the State being absent I, John B. Neathery,[4] Private Secretary to His Excellency the Governor do hereby certify that I have examined the records in the Office of the Adjutant General and find Special Orders N. 11, of which the foregoing is a true copy.

Given under my hand, this 14th June 1871

J. B. Neathery
Private Secretary

---

[1]This special military order signaled the beginning of the Kirk-Holden War, a period of intense excitement that eventually ended in the impeachment and removal from office of Governor William W. Holden. The social and political climate in Reconstruction North Carolina was explosive, as the Union League sought to include blacks in the political process and the Ku Klux Klan sought to promote white supremacy in general. Klan activities in the state had resulted in numerous acts of violence and murder. Two murders, those of Wyatt Outlaw and John W. "Chicken" Stephens, were particularly noteworthy. Outlaw was, as noted previously, a moderate black leader of the Union League in Alamance County. He was hanged within a few feet of the county courthouse. Stephens, one of the most controversial figures of this era, was a successful businessman and politician who was close to the freedmen of Caswell County. He was especially hostile toward the former slaveholding class. Anathema to the Conservatives, Stephens was considered to be a most unsavory scalawag and was blamed by the Conservatives for black lawlessness in Caswell. On May 21, 1870, while a Conservative party convention was being held in the Caswell County courthouse, Stephens was murdered in a room below the main floor. Years later it became known that prominent men had been involved in this assassination.

Having gained no active support from federal authorities, Governor Holden decided to use military force to quell the lawlessness in Alamance and Caswell counties. His critics contend that he merely wished to control the state elections to be held in August. Whatever his motives, Holden acted by appointing George W. Kirk colonel of state troops and ordering him to occupy and assume command of Alamance and Caswell. The result was the arrest of scores of North Carolina citizens and a bitter confrontation over whether those arrested were to be released under a writ of *habeas corpus*. Chief Justice Richmond M. Pearson of the state supreme court believed that the prisoners held by Kirk and Holden should be the beneficiaries of *habeas corpus* but equivocated when Holden defied him. Finally, federal judge George W. Brooks, a North Carolinian, issued writs on behalf of the prisoners; and, upon the advice of President Ulysses S. Grant that he should obey the federal court order, Holden reluctantly complied. It was out of these circumstances that the impeachment of Governor Holden arose. Graham was at the heart of Consevative efforts to free those arrested and "get Holden," as his correspondence reveals.

Historians have viewed these events in very different ways. Several older studies, of which J. G. de Roulhac Hamilton's *Reconstruction in North Carolina* (1914) is typical, were vitriolic in their treatment of the Union League, carpetbaggers, and scalawags—and especially Holden. At the same time, the Conservative faction and the Ku Klux Klan were characterized as the defenders of southern civilization. Several recent works have proposed revisions of the older Hamilton interpretation. Of particular interest are the following: Otto H. Olsen, *Carpetbagger's Crusade: The Life of Albion Winegar Tourgée* (Baltimore:

Johns Hopkins University Press, 1965), and Allen W. Trelease, *White Terror: The Ku Klux Klan Conspiracy and Southern Reconstruction* (New York: Harper and Row, Publishers, 1972). In their biographies of Holden, Edgar W. Folk and Bynum Shaw, Horace Raper, and William C. Harris have sought to explain the governor's actions and, by implication, have suggested significant revisions in North Carolina Reconstruction history.

[2]George W. Kirk (b. 1833), a native of Tennessee, had been a colonel of the Third North Carolina United States Volunteers during the Civil War. He had acquired the reputation of being notoriously brutal. At the end of the war he was mentioned as a possible candidate for provisional governor of North Carolina, although, of course, it was Holden who was actually appointed by President Johnson when the delegation from North Carolina, headed by Holden, met with the president on May 18, 1865. Holden decided that Kirk could be of use to him in 1870, when he thought the courts in Alamance and Caswell were being derelict in handling the Ku Klux Klan in those counties. Despite the fact that General Edward R. S. Canby was in charge of military affairs in North Carolina, Kirk was put in command of forces ordered to special duty in the two counties involved. Kirk had numerous local citizens jailed under military arrest, and both Holden and Kirk refused to recognize writs of *habeas corpus* for their release issued by state judges, even though William A. Graham, Judge Augustus S. Merrimon, and others had Chief Justice Pearson to order the writs for Adolphus G. Moore and other prominent persons. Only the intervention of President Grant and the Conservative victory at the polls in 1870 brought an end to the so-called Kirk-Holden War. Kirk's troops were mustered out in September, 1870. Kirk was allowed to escape into Virginia and make his way to Washington, D.C., where he became an officer of the police force for government buildings there. Hamilton, *Reconstruction in North Carolina*, 107n, 499-572 passim.

[3]Abial W. Fisher served in the Union forces and after the war became a carpetbagger and settled in Bladen County. He attended the convention called by General Canby on January 14, 1868, and was appointed adjutant general by Governor Holden shortly after the latter assumed office. To suppress the Ku Klux Klan, Fisher was empowered by Holden to appoint more than twenty detectives, including himself, to assist Colonel Kirk. The detectives were expensive and ineffective. Hamilton, *Reconstruction in North Carolina*, 254n, 346, 483-537 passim.

[4]John B. Neathery (1835-1894), of Raleigh, was private secretary to Governors Holden, Caldwell, and Brogden. Also, he was employed in the North Carolina adjutant general's office at various times. When a controversy over payment for Kirk's troops developed, Neathery was appointed paymaster and paid the troops, despite legal efforts to prevent this expenditure of state funds. Clark, *Histories of the North Carolina Regiments*, I, 51, V, 678; Hamilton, *Reconstruction in North Carolina*, 531-532.

Josiah Turner, Jr., to William A. Graham UNC
[Telegram]

Raleigh, NC
July 13 1870.

Judge Battle,[1] Bragg[2] and Moore[3] join with me in asking you to come here tonight with a view of going to Washington.

---

[1]William H. Battle.

[2]Thomas Bragg.

[3]Bartholomew Figures Moore.

John L. Scott[1] *to William A. Graham* UNC
[Telegram]

Co. Shops
July 15 1870.

Come to Company Shops by this evenings freight train. My brother[2] and James E. Boyd[3] are held by the Military be sure to come on the frieght this evening. Answer.

---

[1]John L. Scott was a well-known citizen of Alamance County. He was a state senator in the 1885 legislature. Cheney, *North Carolina Government*, 464.

[2]On July 15, 1870, James S. Scott, a Graham merchant, was arrested by George B. Bergen on orders issued by Kirk. Hamilton, *Reconstruction in North Carolina*, 507; Whitaker, *Centennial History of Alamance*, 130.

[3]James Edmund Boyd (1845-1935) was born in the part of Orange County that later became Alamance, attended Graham Academy and Davidson College (1862-1864), and joined the Confederate forces at the age of sixteen. As a member of the First North Carolina Cavalry he fought with Lee and Jackson in Virginia and was a courier at Appomattox. After the war Boyd read law with Judge Thomas Ruffin and established a law practice in Graham in 1868. He was a member of the General Assembly, 1874-1875; United States attorney for the western district of North Carolina, 1880-1885; and federal court judge in the western district of North Carolina, 1901-1924. At the time of this letter Boyd was the Conservative candidate for the House of Representatives in his district. Powell, *DNCB*, I, 202; Hamilton, *Reconstruction in North Carolina*, 507, 517-518, 552-553.

Edward S. Parker[1] *to William A. Graham* UNC
[Telegram]

Company Shops,
July 15th.,
1870.

Bring the Military Bill, as it is called, with you this evening. Be certain to come on the freight this evening, as Mr. J. L. Scott requested. Answer immediately.

---

[1]Edward S. Parker, of Alamance County, a native of Cumberland, had been captain and commissary of the Fiftieth North Carolina Regiment and was at this time a Graham attorney. In 1875 he established the *Alamance Gleaner*. He was a state senator, 1897-1899. Parker was something of a local folk hero. Captured during the Civil War, he assisted in the take-over of a vessel carrying prisoners north and escaped. Clark, *Histories of the North Carolina Regiments*, III, 161, 202; Whitaker, *Centennial History of Alamance*, 275; Cheney, *North Carolina Government*, 475.

Edward S. Parker to William A. Graham UNC
[Telegram]

Shops N.C.
July 17th 1870

Writs served.[1] Not obeyed. I go down tonight.

[1]This refers to the writs of *habeas corpus* issued by Chief Justice Pearson and ignored by Holden and Kirk. Holden's answer to Pearson of July 19 appears in Hamilton, *Reconstruction in North Carolina*, 508-509.

William H. Battle to William A. Graham UNC

Raleigh,
July 23rd., 1870.

Chief Justice Pearson having announced yesterday that he would pronounce his opinion at 9 o'clock this morning, it was awaited with much anxiety by us all. You will see the opinion in full in the Sentinel of today.[1] He decides:

1. That the writ of *habeas corpus* is not suspended in the State.
2. That sufficient cause has been shown for the non-return to the writ, and he must therefore decline to issue a writ of attachment against Col. Kirk.
3. But that the petitioners are entitled to a precept to have their bodies brought before him.

That, being satisfied that this precept cannot be executed by the sheriff, or any other officer in the county of Alamance, and that an attempt to have it executed by any such officer would result in bloodshed, he therefore will direct it to the Marshall of the Court, and that it shall be served on the Governor by the Marshall.

Gov. Bragg and myself agree in the opinion that we get substantially, (though you will see in an ungracious way) all we could have expected, though not all which we thought we had a right to expect. We agree further, that you ought to go on to see the President, and, (at least) the Attorney General, in relation to the condition of the State at this time. Your expenses will be provided for.

. . . .

I write this in the midst of much interruption and excitement.

The Marshall has served the precept upon the Governor, & he says he will take until Tuesday to decide upon his return. I think he wants to hear from the President.

Col. Brown[2] is here, has been to Washington, but I have not heard what news he brings. I think you had better hold yourself in readiness to go to see the Pres't.

It is late and I must close.

[In pencil in the margin]

The C. J. has granted writs of habeas corpus for 18 Caswell prisoners.

[1]Pearson, a conservative Republican elected with bipartisan support, was in a difficult position. While warning Holden that he had no alternative but to issue writs of *habeas corpus* for those arrested, he agreed to declare the power of the judiciary exhausted if the writs were not obeyed. He cited as precedent the impasse between President Lincoln and Chief Justice Roger B. Taney in *Ex parte Merryman*. For accounts of Pearson's role in the imbroglio see Hamilton, *Reconstruction in North Carolina*, 507-515, and Trelease, *White Terror*, 220-222.

[2]Bedford Brown (1795-1870), of Caswell County, was an active North Carolina political figure for many years. He was a member of Commons, 1815-1818; state senator, 1828-1829 and 1858-1863; and United States senator, 1829-1840. He was wholehearted in his support of the Jackson-Van Buren administration and became so disgruntled that he left the state for six years when the Calhoun wing of the Democratic party refused to return him to the Senate in 1842. He was an advocate of states' rights within the Union and opposed secession in the convention of 1861, but he urged vigorous prosecution of the war. By 1863 this militant mood had passed. Subsequently, his old Unionist posture caused both Governors Holden and Worth to use him as a mediator in Washington. Although Brown's intellectual equipment was mediocre and he was an unusually poor speaker, he exerted considerable influence in the Jacksonian era. Jackson was his great friend and model. Brown owned a large plantation, Locust Hill, in Caswell County. *DAB*, III, 104-105; McCormick, *Convention Personnel*, 22; *Biographical Directory of Congress*, 606.

Thomas P. Atkinson[1] *to William A. Graham* UNC

Danville, Virginia,
July 26th., 1870.

Your favor of 23rd. inst. was received yesterday, and today I was so fortunate as to meet with Col. George Williamson,[2] who is just from Raleigh, with the process to serve on Kirk and others, and who goes to Yanceyville this afternoon, for that purpose.

He says that he will execute the process immediately on reaching there. I have entrusted your letter to him, and he assures me that he will deliver it to Judge Kerr[3] before he sleeps.

He informs me that the Chief Justice had a summons served on the arch fiend, Holden, yesterday, who says that he will take time to determine what he will do. The Colonel is waiting here until this afternoon, with the expectation of receiving a telegram from Gov'r Bragg, at 2 o'clock, informing him of Holden's determination.

Our friends in your State have our sincere sympathy in their present humiliating position, and if it were deemed prudent, we would go promptly to the release of the prisoners at Yanceyville. Kirk arrested Capt. Wm. P. Graves,[4] of this place, on Sunday last, who went over to Yanceyville to see his friends.

He was released, after some hours confinement. Our Gov'r has been informed of this high-handed measure. It is a singular coincidence that Holden's Lieutenant, *Kirk*, should have the same name of the infamous tool of the infamous *Jeffreys*,[5] of Star Chamber notoriety.

His *Lambs*, I presume, are as wolfish and as cruel as were those of his prototype of old, who were designated, (as you doubtless remember) as "Kirke's Lambs."[6]

Is it possible, (as we hear) that Holden is sustained by President Grant?

If so, we are a nation of slaves. Is there any hope of relief for the oppressed people of the South?

Command me at any time, in this, or any other service.

---

[1]Dr. Thomas P. Atkinson of Danville, Virginia, probably wrote this letter. He died on August 30, 1874, at the age of nearly eighty. *People's Press* (Salem), September 3, 1874.

[2]George Williamson (b. 1826), of Caswell County, attempted to serve a writ of *habeas corpus* on Kirk. The latter would not see him and had an armed squad order Williamson to leave or be shot. Williamson was a stable citizen who owned a flour mill. In 1888 he was elected president of the Caswell County Farmers' Alliance Number 756. He was a stockholder in the Bank of Yanceyville, 1852, and in the Farmer's Bank at Milton, 1869. Interested in all kinds of civic matters, he was instrumental in founding the Dan River Institute in Yanceyville, 1847, and in the development of railroads in the area. He served as a state senator from Caswell County, 1850-1851, 1874-1875, and 1879-1880. Cheney, *North Carolina Government*, 318, 455, 458; William S. Powell, *When the Past Refused to Die: A History of Caswell County, North Carolina, 1777-1977* (Durham: Moore Publishing Company, 1977), 118, 269, 334, 345, 369, 383, 477, 502, 507, hereinafter cited as Powell, *History of Caswell County*.

[3]John Kerr (1811-1879), of Caswell County, read law with Richmond M. Pearson. Defeated as the Whig gubernatorial candidate in 1852, he served one term in the United States House of Representatives, 1853-1855, where he was deeply influenced by the Kansas-Nebraska debates. Having entered Congress as a Union Whig, he returned a Democrat and southern rights man. Kerr was a member of the Commons in 1858 and 1860 and a superior court judge, 1862-1863 and 1874-1879. *Biographical Directory of Congress*, 1159; Van Noppen Papers; Cheney, *North Carolina Government*, 326, 327, 362, 574, 587.

[4]William P. Graves, of Danville, Virginia, was a native of Caswell County and a member of a large family.

[5]George Jeffreys, first baron Jeffreys of Wem (1648-1689), British lord chief justice and lord chancellor, was notorious for his brutality. In 1685 he conducted the Bloody Assizes, in which he ordered the execution of a large number of rebels against King James II. Leslie Stephen and Sidney Lee (eds.), *Dictionary of National Biography* (New York: Macmillan and Company, 63 volumes, 1885-1900, index and supplements), XXIX, 277-283, hereinafter cited as *DNB*.

[6]Kirke's Lambs were troops commanded by Percy Kirke (1646?-1691), lieutenant general with a reputation for cruelty who, according to tradition, served as Jeffreys's escort during the Bloody Assizes. *DNB*, XXXI, 214-216.

Zebulon B. Vance to William A. Graham A&H

Charlotte, N.C.
July 28, 1870

Dear Govr-

I can not refrain from asking yr opinion as to what is best for us to do in these extraordinary times. There is some confusion in the public mind here & I fear some timidity. I regard Pearson's conduct as more infamous than Holden's and have so denounced him on the stump, & charged that he was in full accord with Holden in the whole matter.

West of this [place] our prospects are good except that in many counties our friends are much confused about their local candidates. I fear we will lose a member in this county & one in Lincoln on this account. But Harper[1] & Shober will be elected by larger majorities & Shipp[2] will run with them. I hear of great changes in the quaker sections of Guilford Randolph & Davidson. Is this true? Do you think we stand any chance to carry the Legislature, or even the Commons? I have been speaking diligently for the past two weeks & think we will carry all the counties west of Salisbury but 4 or 5.

Can not a writ of Habeas Corpus be obtained from C. J. Chase?[3] I have not examined the question but Mr. Guion said this morning it could be done. If so it ought to be done immediately.

Please write me.

[1]James C. Harper was elected and served in the United States House of Representatives, 1871-1873. Earlier, he had been elected to serve in the state House, 1868-1869, but Governor Holden by proclamation declared him ineligible to hold office and a new election was ordered. Cheney, *North Carolina Government*, 448, 553n, 695.

[2]William Marcus Shipp (1819-1890) was elected attorney general in the August 4 contest. A native of Charlotte and a graduate of the University of North Carolina in 1840, he served the state in several capacities: member of the House of Commons, 1854; delegate to the convention of 1861; state senator, 1862; superior court judge, 1868, 1881-1890; attorney general, 1871-1872; and reporter for the supreme court. Grant, *Alumni History*, 561; Sherrill, *Annals of Lincoln County*, 254-255.

[3]Salmon Portland Chase (1808-1873), of Ohio, was a native of New Hampshire and a graduate of Dartmouth College. After a long career as United States senator and Ohio governor, Chase, a presidential aspirant himself, joined the Lincoln cabinet as secretary of the treasury. Long active in the antislavery movement, he criticized Lincoln for what he believed to be indecisiveness and took part in movements to force the president to reorganize his cabinet and to withdraw from the 1864 presidential race. Lincoln overlooked Chase's activities because he believed the treasury secretary to be an effective administrator. In 1864 Lincoln finally accepted Chase's third offer to resign. In the same year Lincoln appointed Chase chief justice of the United States Supreme Court. Although he favored Negro suffrage and radical reconstruction, Chase became disillusioned at the corruption and excesses of the postwar years. *DAB*, IV, 27-34.

William H. Battle to William A. Graham UNC

Raleigh,
July 28th., 1870.

Your letter of yesterday came to hand this morning, and I have shown it to Messrs. Bragg and Merrimon. Mr. Moore lost his only grand child a few days ago, and I have not seen him today.

Yesterday morning Messrs. Bragg, Merrimon and myself made the motion, a copy of which I send you. The C. J. directed a copy to be served immediately on Mr. Badger,[1] and appointed 4 o'clock P.M. as the time when he would hear us. I opened the argument, Badger opposed the motion in a short, moderate, speech, and was followed by Judge Merrimon. The C. J. then said he would announce his decision at 9 o'clock this morning. Accordingly, at the time appointed, he read a short paper refusing the motion for either mode of redress. He said, as to the third, that it was useless to send the Marshal on so fruitless an errand, but that if we wished to apply to C. J. Chase for a writ of *habeas corpus* we might take it as a fact, stated by him, that the Marshall had gone to Kirk's Camp, and that he had refused to deliver up the prisoners. This was said upon our having suggested to him that, having invoked in vain the State Judiciary for redress, we thought we had a right, under the 1st. Sec. of 14th. amd. [amendment] to the Con., to apply to a U.S. Judge for a writ of *hab. cor.*

Gen'l Ransom is here, & says he will start to night to see Judge Brooks[2], & Gov. Bragg is drawing up the necessary papers.

The writs we prepared in behalf of all the Caswell prisoners, was attempted to be served, but the bearer of them was ordered off and threatened to be shot. He will probably be here tonight to make an affidavit of the fact, and then we shall apply for an attachment against Kirk, and we shall leave to the C. J. no excuse for bringing in the Governor to take Kirk's place.

Boyd[3] and many others have made confessions acknowledging Ku Klux organizations, etc. These will appear in the Standard of Saturday, & others in the papers of Monday.

---

[1]Richard Cogdell Badger.

[2]George Washington Brooks (1821-1882) of Elizabeth City, a former Unionist, was federal district judge of North Carolina, a position he held from 1865 to 1882. Brooks attended Henry Riddick's school and Belvedere Academy, a school operated by the Society of Friends in Perquimans County. He was not able financially to attend college but studied law with Charles R. Kinney and later with John C. B. Ehringhaus of Elizabeth City. By 1860 he had become a respected, successful lawyer. Although he owned slaves himself, Brooks became convinced that the practice was wrong. He opposed secession and took no part in the Civil War. Appointed the sole district judge in North Carolina by Andrew Johnson in 1865, Brooks was influential in terminating the so-called Kirk-Holden War. As the Graham papers reveal, Brooks ordered the prisoners arrested by Kirk to be brought before him at the federal court in Salisbury. Upon their presentation by Kirk, the prisoners were dismissed by Brooks, an act that brought the judge into large esteem in the eyes of his fellow townsmen at Elizabeth City and moderates throughout the state.

[3]James E. Boyd shocked his Conservative friends by confessing membership in the Klan and by persuading others to do likewise. His motives were to gain immunity for himself and to end Klan violence. For breaking his Klan oath of secrecy, Boyd was ostracized socially and his legal practice ruined. Hamilton believes Boyd's actions were thoroughly self-serving and reprehensible. See Trelease, *White Terror*, 219-220; Hamilton, *Reconstruction in North Carolina*, 517-518.

The *Daily Standard* (Raleigh), July 30, 1870, published the confession and listed the signers as Clement C. Curtis, James E. Boyd, Robert Hanner, John R. Stockard, Jacob Michael, J. H. N. [*sic*] Clendenin, Henry Albright, James W. Foust, D. P. Teague, A. J. Patterson, J. A. J. Patterson, John G. Albright, Carist. C. Curtis, S. A. Curtis, W. S. Bradshaw, and Jasper N. Wood.

E. Brock Holden[1] *to William A. Graham* UNC

Pea Ridge,
Caswell County.
July 28th., 1870.

I was in Yanceyville on day before yesterday, and my wife saw Mr. F. A. Wiley[2] and he wishes to procure your services before the Court-martial, that is to assemble in Yanceyville soon, probably next Monday.

All of the prisoners want you to appear for them. Please make your arrangements so that you can come at any time.

---

[1]Brock Holden was Governor Holden's brother and the brother-in-law of Sheriff F. A. Wiley. *Daily Sentinel* (Raleigh), July 22, 1870.

[2]Frank A. Wiley, an ex-sheriff of Caswell County, was a Democrat whom John W. Stephens had offered to support for reelection. Stephens evidently did not realize that Wiley was in sympathy with the Klan, if not an actual member. In the plot to murder Stephens, Wiley's alleged part was to persuade Stephens to go with him to a back room of the courthouse, where several men lay in wait for the victim. The perpetrators made an effort to blame Negroes for the murder. The *Sentinel* (Raleigh) carried a letter from Wiley declaring that he had last seen Stephens with an unknown Negro. Later, John G. Lea, a

witness to the murder, pointed to Wiley as a key figure in the affair. (For Lea's statement, see Zuber, *North Carolina during Reconstruction*, 80-82.) Wiley was working in his fields when he was arrested; he was bound over, released on bond, and his case quietly buried by local authorities. Trelease, *White Terror*, 213-214, 217, 222.

William H. Battle to William A. Graham UNC

Raleigh,
July 30th., 1870.

Your telegram was received to day. The Governor's return to the Chief Justice, avowing his refusal to surrender the Alamance prisoners, and all the papers relating thereto, are in the possession of the Clerk of the Supreme Court. No demand has, as yet, been made on the Governor for the Caswell prisoners. We obtained from the C. J. writs of hab. cor. for them, and the writs were attempted to be served by Mr. George Williamson, but upon his affidavit of what he had done being read before the C. J. he decided that there had been no service, and then ordered that the writs should be served by Mr. Wicker[1], the Marshall of the Supreme Court, who is now on his way to Yanceyville for the purpose of serving them upon Col. Kirk. You will no doubt see what occurred in relation to the matter in the Sentinel of today. I thought the C. J. displayed a little more spirit today than he did on a former occasion, but the prevailing opinion here is, that he will not direct force enough to be employed, to accomplish the release of the prisoners.

It is said that a Military Court has been ordered to try the prisoners, but I can hardly believe it will be held. It is certainly threatened, but I cannot yet think that Holden will commit as rash, and to him, terribly dangerous, act.

I am sorry to say that the Court has decided your case against us. They had all the argument I could make, in addition to the written one of your son John which I filed.

It is said that the next issue of the N. Y. Herald will contain an article written by its correspondent, who has been at Yanceyville & is now here, which will charge that the persons were murdered by negroes, & not by Ku Klux.

---

[1]David Wicker was marshal of the North Carolina Supreme Court. *Daily Standard* (Raleigh), August 3, 1870.

James A. Graham to William A. Graham UNC

Graham, N. C.,
August 2nd., 1870.

I received your note by Gus at the depot yesterday afternoon. I cannot find any one who knows of the hanging of Patton;[1] of his own knowledge; except Dr. Clendinin,[2] a radical, and I suppose he would not make affidavit to it. I hear that Lt. Col. Bergen[3] says he did it, but can find no man who heard him say so. I will get the evidence, if possible. Syd Scott[4] & Shff. Murray[5] are here, having been released on parole. I have had but little opportunity of talking with them yet. Jno. G. Albright,[6] who was arrested last week and released yesterday, told me to-day that he wanted to sue whoever was liable, and that he would spend everything he was worth, in the attempt to make them pay for it.

Shff. Murray tells me it is a mistake as to Judge Kerr's being deranged, though he is very much depressed.

We had a large crowd in town today. The negroes all hurrahed for Smith,[7] Welker[8] and White,[9] but few others spoke favorably of them. Col. Gilmer's[10] speech was very much complimented. If we can get our people to vote, we will yet carry the County, but very many of them are very badly frightened. The arrests still continue, and a squad of Kirk's men passed through town just before the speaking commenced to-day. I think it was as much for intimidation as for anything else, but they did not scare the crowd very much.

Smith, in his speech to-day, said that every man who signed the conservative legislative address, was a member of the Ku Klux Klan, except Melcher[11] and Hodnett.[12] I immediately pronounced it false, as far as John was concerned, and when Smith was done speaking, called him off to one side to ask him about it. When I told him then that it was false as to John, he said he would correct it in his speech tomorrow at Greensboro', and immediately afterwards told me that he did not believe John was one, though his informant, (Boyd) had told him Dr. Moore[13] told him some time ago, that all the conservative members of the legislature were Ku Klux, except the two above mentioned, but Boyd told him he did not think John was.

The only fear is that our people will not come out. Our friends who are not cowed are using every exertion to get everybody out, and we have great hopes of Gilmer's election, and possibly Patterson[14] may also come in.

As there were speakers enough, I did not make any speech to-day, but talked to everybody I could see.

I have just learned that Dr. B. F. Mebane[15] and Col. Bingham[16] were arrested, and passed through on their way to the Shops this afternoon. I will write tomorrow, and send the writs and prosecution bonds you wished.

Love to all

I have written in great haste, as it is very late,

Affectionately Your Son

P.S. Mr. Cook[17] & Jas. Anderson[18] at Haw River were arrested yesterday afternoon, & Mr. Jim Holt[19] notified to appear at Camp this morning. Mr. Holt was not detained. I don't know whether the others were kept or not.

Green Andrews[20] and all his sons were arrested Saturday evening, or Sunday morning, but they have all been released, I understand.

---

[1]The Kirk-Holden War resulted in numerous allegations of brutality to those arrested. Three men, including William Patton of Alamance County, were allegedly hanged by Holden's men in attempts to extract confessions of Klan activities. Patton was subjected to the noose, drawn up until he fainted, and called a "God damned liar." He was then tied up for the night. When Governor Holden received reports of this episode, he ordered such methods to be abandoned and noted: "Evidence obtained in this way is worthless. All

prisoners, no matter how guilty they may supposed to be, should be treated humanely." *Daily Sentinel* (Raleigh), August 2, 1870; Hamilton, *Reconstruction in North Carolina*, 518-519; Horace W. Raper, *William W. Holden: North Carolina's Political Enigma* (Chapel Hill: University of North Carolina Press, 1985), 185-186, hereinafter cited as Raper, *Holden*.

[2]Dr. Clendinin has not been definitively identified. However, one Clendenin was among the signers of James E. Boyd's confession. See William H. Battle to Graham, July 28, 1870, note 3, in this volume.

[3]George B. Bergen, of New Jersey, was lieutenant colonel of Holden's state troops. On July 15, Bergen arrested James S. Scott, James E. Boyd, and Adolphus G. Moore. Without giving them a reason for their arrest, Bergen placed them in jail. Evidence indicates that, at Company Shops, he partially hanged three prisoners and threatened death in order to get information about Wyatt Outlaw's murderers. Bergen was later indicted and accused of accepting bribes, but Judge Hugh L. Bond released him and he escaped punishment. His appointment as consul to Pernambuco, Brazil, was withdrawn at Holden's request. Trelease, *White Terror*, 217, 219; Hamilton, *Reconstruction in North Carolina*, 499-501, 504-505, 515-516; Whitaker, *Centennial History of Alamance*, 138; Raper, *Holden*, 198.

[4]James S. Scott.

[5]Albert Murray was sheriff of Alamance County and a member of the Ku Klux Klan; he was chief of one of the ten camps in the county. He did not aid soldiers sent by Holden in March, 1870, to make arrests and later was arrested himself. Trelease, *White Terror*, 198, 201, 205, 210; Hamilton, *Reconstruction in North Carolina*, 462n.

[6]John G. Albright was one of the early property owners in Graham. Whitaker, *Centennial History of Alamance*, 94.

[7]William A. Smith, at this time living in Alamance County, was a Republican candidate for the state Senate from the Twenty-sixth District. He was elected, seated, and promptly unseated because of the contention that military rule in the area had made a free election impossible. James A. Graham, the Conservative candidate, was elected in a special poll and joined his brother, John W. Graham, in the Senate. Although William A. Graham was not himself a member, his views were well represented. Raper, *Holden*, 202; Hamilton, *Reconstruction in North Carolina*, 534-535; Cheney, *North Carolina Government*, 451, 558.

[8]George W. Welker.

[9]Probably this was Republican John White, who was elected to represent Alamance County in the state House but was denied his seat because of the presence of the military on election day. Raper, *Holden*, 202.

[10]John A. Gilmer (1838-1892), of Guilford County, son of a distinguished father of the same name, was a Conservative candidate for the state Senate in this election. He attacked the Holden administration for its extravagance and gross mismanagement and accused the governor of seeking to frustrate the popular will by means of a "foreign militia." Gilmer was elected, and he was allowed to take his seat despite alleged irregularities in Alamance County because his majority in Guilford was sufficient to elect him exclusive of the Alamance vote. Raper, *Holden*, 202.

[11]Christopher Melchor, of Cabarrus County, was a state senator, 1868-1870. Cheney, *North Carolina Government*, 447, 449.

[12]Philip Hodnett, of Caswell County, was a member of the House of Commons, 1865-1867, and of the House of Representatives, 1868-1870. Cheney, *North Carolina Government*, 333, 335, 448, 449.

[13]Dr. John A. Moore, who represented Alamance County in three legislatures (1865, 1868, and 1869), was a Klansman who believed that the order had become too violent. In early 1870 he had prevented the assassination of T. M. Shoffner by telling some sixty armed Orange and Chatham County Klansmen that their intended victim had gone to Greensboro. Trelease, *White Terror*, 200-204; Cheney, *North Carolina Government*, 333, 448, 449.

[14]Patterson aparently was a former sheriff or deputy sheriff of Alamance County and was a Conservative legislative candidate.

[15]Benjamin Franklin Mebane (1832-1884) was a native of Orange County. After receiving his A.B. degree from the University of North Carolina in 1847, he studied medicine at the

University of Pennsylvania and was awarded a medical degree in 1850. Mebane was a member of the General Assembly, 1879-1881. Grant, *Alumni History*, 422.

[16]William Bingham (1835-1873) operated the famous Bingham School in Mebane as a military academy during the Civil War. He was granted the ex officio rank of colonel in the state militia. Powell, *DNCB*, I, 160.

[17]Mr. Cook has not been identified.

[18]James Anderson was superintendent of the company shops, North Carolina Railroad, until his removal in 1868. He moved to Hendersonville in 1886. Durward T. Stokes, *Company Shops: The Town Built by a Railroad* (Winston-Salem: John F. Blair Publisher, 1981), 57, 122, hereinafter cited as Stokes, *Company Shops*.

[19]Jim Holt may have been J. C. Holt of Company Shops.

[20]Green Andrews has not been identified.

Benjamin F. Mebane to William A. Graham UNC

Mebanesville, N.C.,
August 2nd., 18[70]

I have been arrested by a squad of Kirk's men this morning about daylight, they have also gone down to arrest Col. Bingham, in Orange. I know not concerning the guilt of any one, but I am as innocent of anything against the Laws of N.C., & as regards any association, as a new born babe. Some men, they have carried with them all night, through the rain. How long is this to continue? I would be pleased to have your advice, if you think proper you can write to me at this place, and my wife will send your letter to me.

I saw the list the officer had, and he is ordered to arrest almost everyone. I expect to endure it all with Christian patience, but it is hard at times to prevent giving way to the evil spirit. Ah, just to think of it, my dear Sir, a free American citizen, to be called up from his family in the dead hours of night, in time of peace, and draged away, and no redress in law.

Thomas Bragg to William A. Graham UNC
[Telegram]

Raleigh,
August 5th., 1870.

Have no resistance to Turner arrest.[1] Shall surely get speedy relief from new quarters. Will write by mail.

---

[1]Josiah Turner, Jr., editor of the *Sentinel* (Raleigh) and a bitter opponent of the Holden administration, had been arrested that morning in Orange County—a county that had not been declared in insurrection. The arrest followed a vitriolic challenge to the governor, which read:

> Gov. Holden:
> You say you will handle me in due time. You white-livered miscreant, do it now. You dare me to resist you, I dare you to arrest me. I am here to protect my family; the jacobins of your club after shooting powder in the face of Mrs. Turner, threw a five pound rock in her window which struck near one of my children. Your ignorant jacobins are incited to this by your lying charges against me, that I am

> King of the Ku Klux. You villain, come and arrest a man, and order your secret clubs not to molest women and children. Yours with contempt and defiance—*habeas corpus* or no *habeas corpus*. (*Daily Sentinel* [Raleigh], August 3, 1870.)

Although the provocation of Turner's challenge was great, Holden overplayed his hand in sanctioning the arrest.

Zebulon B. Vance to William A. Graham A&H

Charlotte
Aug 6th 70

Dear Sir,

Yours recd. this morning.

I have little or no doubt now but that we have carried the State & the Legislature. Much depends on our using our victory wisely. I will start all the papers in this section after Holden on account of Turner's arrest.

I agree with you in relation to the best means of stopping these illegal arrests. *It must be done*, and I am willing to join a posse to execute any fiat of any Judge or magistrate. Mr. Guion asks me to call your attention to the 27th Section of the Habeas Corpus act Chapter 110, 1868-9—and to suggest that bench warrants should be issued vs Holden & Kirk for a violation thereof. On reading that Section I am much impressed with the conviction that this would be the proper course to pursue with these malefactors.

The news west of this is good as far as recd. Lincoln & Gaston about 250 majority for us, each; Catawba 900, Cleveland very large, precise figures not given, & Rutherford reported for us. Same way up Western Road.

In good heart & great haste.

Edward S. Parker to William A. Graham UNC
[Telegram]

Goldsboro',
August 6th., 1870.

Write me by tonight's mail if party should go to Raleigh Monday to make affidavit for Alamance prisoners, and all the particulars that should be done in their behalf. Write fully, their friends wants all don [*sic*] that can be for them.

William H. Battle to William A. Graham UNC
[Telegram]

Raleigh, N.C.,
August 7th., 1870.

Letter received. Writs issued, returnable to Salisbury this week. Brooks all right. Gov. Bragg and I will go up. So must you. Send names of other Alamance prisoners.

William H. Battle to William A. Graham UNC

Raleigh,
August 7th., 1870.
Near 7 O'Clock, P.M.

Upon receiving your telegram about 5 O'Clock, I went to Gov. Bragg's, and found that he had gone to see Judge Brooks. I followed him, and found him and Merrimon with the Judge. The latter was signing the writs for the purpose of writing them, when I left. Gov. B. & myself think that you had better get some person to go up to Salisbury who can make the necessary affidavit to the petition in favor of all the Alamance prisoners, not already embraced in the petition now before the Judge. These are only Moore, and one or two of those first arrested. We do not know enough of the facts to make the affidavit for those whose names you have just sent. The Judge is as firm as a rock in the matter. Thinks the arrest and continued detention of the prisoners a great outrage, and is determined to give relief, if possible. Holden called to see him today, and intimated that there might be blood-shed, etc. It will not be necessary for us to go up until we learn that the prisoners will be taken up. We will arrange with the person who goes to serve the writ, to send us a telegram, and we will let you know in the same way. Holden will probably call upon the President to sustain him, & I think he will back down at once if that aid cannot be obtained. He is now a desperate man, and, in my opinion, a ruined one.

I write in great haste—excuse errors, etc.

Very truly yours,

We think we have carried every thing in the election. Judge Brooks is glad of it.

William H. Battle to William A. Graham UNC

Raleigh,
August 9th., 1870.

You know already that the writs of *habeas corpus*, in favor of the Caswell and several of the Alamance prisoners, were issued on Sunday by Judge Brooks, and delivered to a Deputy Marshall, who went off with them on the night of that day. The writs were served on Col. Kirk at Yanceyville yesterday, and the Colonel informed the Judge (whether verbally or in writing I do not know) that he would make returns as soon as he got orders from Gov. Holden. This we learn by a telegram from Salisbury, received to-day. The law of Congress under which we are proceeding allows a few days for the return, so that we are not surprised at the delay. Indeed we think Kirk could not well have acted otherwise, under the circumstances in which he is placed. It is believed here now that Holden will instruct Kirk to take the bodies of the prisoners before the Judge, as commanded by the writs. It is said that Dick Badger has so advised him.

Gov. Bragg and myself will not go up to Salisbury until we learn that the prisoners have been carried up, unless, in the mean time, Judge Merrimon shall summon us to go up. In that event we will let you know.

A Mr. Scott[1] came down from Graham yesterday for the purpose of taking out writs for the other Alamance prisoners. I prepared a petition for them, and Mr. Scott was to go up to Salisbury last night to make the necessary affidavit before the Judge. Judge Merrimon went up with him, and will attend to the business of issuing the writs, so that I hope we shall have all the prisoners from both Counties before the judge in due season.

You will see in the Sentinel of to-day (9th.) an article under the editorial head, entitled *Judge Brooks and Governor Holden*, which I prepared for the purpose of letting the people know why Judge Brooks is interposing in this matter. Hereabouts they had very vague ideas about it. Gen'l Hunt[2] has ordered ten copies of the paper which he will send North.

I sincerely hope that our friends Kerr, Turner, and others, will soon be able once more to breathe the sweet air of liberty.

---

[1]Most probably John L. Scott; see Scott to Graham, July 15, 1870, in this volume.

[2]In July, 1870, upon the request of Governor Holden, President Grant sent additional federal troops to troubled North Carolina. Colonel Henry Jackson Hunt (1819-1889) was ordered to their command and was directed to establish a temporary military district. Raper, *Holden*, 179.

Josiah Turner, Jr., to William A. Graham UNC
[Telegram]

Yanceyville,
North Carolina.
August 10th., 1870.

I forbid most positively any writ of Habeas Corpus issued for me. I defy Holden, Kirk, chains, and Court Martial.

Leonidas C. Edwards[1] *to William A. Graham* A&H

Oxford, N.C.
Aug. 10th 1870

. . . .

Do all that you can to strengthen the courage and patriotism of Brooks. He has, now, such an opportunity to make for himself a name in history as will never be offered him again. Surely he is neither so shortsighted nor fainthearted as Pearson has shown himself to be.

For your kind sympathy, in regard to my defeat in the late election, I thank you. My friends insist upon our contesting the right of our opponents to the seats; asserting that, at least, two hundred fradulent votes were polled in Granville alone.

I will scruitinize the polls carefully, and if I find I have been cheated in the election . . . I will most assuredly contest the election.

[1]Leonidas Compton Edwards (1825-1908), a native of Person County who settled in Oxford, graduated from the University of North Carolina in 1844 and read law with Judge Richmond M. Pearson. As a lawyer he was thorough, logical, and eloquent. Prior to the Civil War his political convictions were those of a Clay Whig. He was the assistant secretary of the Constitutional Convention of 1861 and a state senator, 1870-1872. Edwards was an unsuccessful candidate for Congress. McCormick, *Convention Personnel*, 92-93; *Oxford Public Ledger*, September 19, 1908.

William H. Battle to William A. Graham UNC

Raleigh,
August 11th., 1870.

Know you will like to hear as often as possible how the case of our imprisoned clients is progressing. I write to give you the latest intelligence we have here. It is said, (and the news reaches me in such a way that I am bound to believe it) that Grant will not interfere to prevent the service of any writ or precept that Judge Brooks may feel it to be his duty to issue.[1] I have just been told that Dick Badger will go to Salisbury to-night, and it is supposed that Holden wishes to obtain some terms of compromise, but of what kind I do not know. Judge Merrimon will be apprised by telegram of the movement, and the counsel here are for insisting upon the strictest terms of the law.

I prepared a short article for the Sentinel this morning, to show that Kirk will not be allowed more than ten days for his return. Holden and his counsel, Badger, are claiming twenty.

I had a very interesting interview with Mr. Ireland,[2] (one of the prisoners, just from Yanceyville) today. He told me he saw you last night, and that you had advised him to surrender himself into the custody of Col. Kirk, when the prisoners were taken before Judge Brooks. I told him that I fully concurred with you, and that he ought by all means to follow the advice, which he promised to do.

Copies of the article I prepared for the Sentinel the other day, headed "Judge Brooks and Gov. Holden," were sent on by Gen'l Hunt as part of his despatches to his superior officer. The General said he thought the article showed clearly that Judge Brooks had jurisdiction in the cases, and he did not see how the President could interfere in behalf of Holden, and he did not believe he would do so.

A letter on business from Judge Heath,[3] just rec'd, closes by congratulating us in this State on our great political victory. He says we ought to call a convention at once, and get clear of all radical officers, etc. He stated that there is not a radical Judge, Justice, or peace officer in Tenn.

[1]On August 6, 1870, United States District Court judge George W. Brooks, who, ironically, had been appointed to the bench in 1865 upon the recommendation of Holden, issued a writ of *habeas corpus* for all the prisoners arrested in the Kirk-Holden War. Holden sought advice in Washington; but to his chagrin President Grant, upon the advice of Attorney General Amos T. Akerman, suggested that "the state authorities yield to the United States judiciary." Holden had little choice but to comply. William C. Harris,

William Woods Holden: Firebrand of North Carolina Politics (Baton Rouge: Louisiana State University Press, 1987), 295-296, hereinafter cited as Harris, *Holden*.

[2]A leader of the Ku Klux Klan in Alamance County, Deputy Sheriff John R. Ireland was arrested in July and held at Kirk's headquarters at Yanceyville. Later he was a miller and sawyer and a member of the Grange. Raper, *Holden*, 175; Stokes, *Company Shops*, 67, 85, 114.

On his notes involving those implicated in the civil troubles in Alamance County, William A. Graham inscribed the following: "John R. Ireland did not whip Garrison."

[3]Robert R. Heath had served briefly as a superior court judge (1858) before relocating in Tennessee. He returned to North Carolina in 1867 to serve as an attorney in defense of the disputed will of James C. Johnston. Cheney, *North Carolina Government*, 362.

W. H. Malone[1] *to William A. Graham* UNC

Washington City D.C.
Aug 13th 1870

My Dear Sir

Our friend and client Mr. Thos. D. Carter and myself have been making a vigorous effort (within the last few days) to settle the "Cranberry Controversy". And I regret to say that every effort has proven a failure. Over ten days ago, Genl Hoke[2] then in (Jersey City NJ) expressed to me a desire to have a friendly meeting of the parties in Jersey City with a view to settle the matter. I suggested the proposition to our client and Col. Woodfin[3] being also present. We consented to the proposition, and in the meantime Mr. Carter caused a written proposition through Col. Woodfin to be submitted to each of the parties, by which he proposed to take the *amount of the Draft with interest and costs*, and also give assurances that on a compliance with these terms all suits pending in regard to "Cranberry" should be forthwith dismissed. This appears to me to have been a fair and liberal proposition when we take into consideration the magnitude of the conspiracy and fraudulent combination against our client. The parties all met, but very strange to say, the defendants manifested no disposition to accept the proposition, but submitted 1. a proposition *to rescind*. 2. a proposition to form a *joint stock company*.

The *first proposition* contained no *allegation of fraud* on the part of our client so as to justify a recision. The second was a mere subterfuge in (my opinion).

Mr. Carter has felt it his duty acting as he considers upon the most indubitable evidence to discharge Col. Woodfin as counsel on the ground of *unfaithfulness* to his cause.

I regret this, very much, for we would ordinarily hesitate very long, before giving credence to the idea of treachery on the part of a Lawyer to his client.

But since our Savior was betrayed for the paltry sum of thirty pieces of silver; and since human nature is proned to corruption, our surprise is lessened.

And It does seem that Geo. W. Swepson has had unusual success in corrupting men, and directing events favorable to his own monstrous schemes of fraud and villainy. I am *reluctantly* compelled to believe that Mr. Carter has been made the dupe of an unparalleled combination against him.

Mr. Carter will visit you and fully explain the dilemma in which he is placed in regard to Col. Woodfin, and the entire case.

The conduct of Swepson Littlefield & Co is involved in some mystery to me. But I think it apparent that their ulterior object is to defraud the States of N. C. & Florida of the millions now under their control. The contracts made with the "Commissioners" of the Western Division of the W. N. C. R. R. are entirely worthless.

Mr. Carter will take your advice in regard to the propriety of instuting *other* proceedings in the State of North Carolina.

I have the honor to remain yours truly

---

[1]W. H. Malone, born in Wythe County, Virginia, was the son of Martha Holden and Theophilus Malone. His family lived for some time in Tennessee, where Malone was educated and began a career as teacher before he began the study of law. After admittance to the bar, he established a practice in eastern Tennessee. During the Civil War he served in the Confederate forces, and when the war was over he bought the *Western Expositor* from T. D. Carter, although Carter retained control of the editorials until after the campaign of 1876, when Democrats regained control of political affairs in North Carolina. In 1886 Malone was defeated in a bid for Congress and thereafter he declined to enter himself as a candidate for public office. A very successful lawyer in Asheville, Malone was twice married—first to Elizabeth Easley (1852) and second to Mrs. Mary E. Murray. Arthur, *Western North Carolina*, 456; *Cyclopedia of Eminent Men*, II, 173-175.

[2]Robert Frederick Hoke (1837-1912), of Lincoln County, after attending the Kentucky Military Academy went into the family manufacturing business. Entering the Confederate army as a lieutenant in the Bethel Regiment, he became major and lieutenant colonel of the Thirty-third Regiment and colonel of the Twenty-first. He distinguished himself at New Bern, the Seven Days, Second Manassas, Sharpsburg, and Fredericksburg. Promoted to brigadier general, he again distinguished himself at Chancellorsville and in eastern North Carolina. When his forces captured Plymouth, Hoke was promoted to major general on the field. He served well at Drewry's Bluff, Cold Harbor, Petersburg, and Bentonville. The end of the war marked the end of his military service; he rarely mentioned military matters thereafter, preferring to devote himself to constructive work in mining and refusing to take any public part in politics. *DAB*, IX, 126-127; Boatner, *Civil War Dictionary*, 404-405.

[3]Nicholas Washington Woodfin (1810-1876), born in Buncombe County, was the son of Mary Grady and John Woodfin. He was educated at an early age in local schools and then was tutored informally by a highly educated lawyer, Colonel Michael Frances. Although he did not attend college, Woodfin was a superior student, read law with David L. Swain, and was admitted to the bar in 1831. Married in 1840 to Eliza Grace McDowell, Woodfin became a successful lawyer. He served in the state Senate, 1844-1854. He managed his extensive farmland in a progressive style, promoted the building of the North Carolina Railroad, and maintained an avid interest in cultural and educational affairs. In 1870 he was a member of the commission appointed to investigate the suspected fraud involved in the activities of George Swepson and Milton S. Littlefield in their selling of bonds to build the railroad. Woodfin was superintendent of the North Carolina Salt Works during the Civil War. Ashe, *Biographical History*, II, 481-486; Arthur, *Western North Carolina*, 146, 147, 200, 362, 365, 392, 462.

William H. Battle to William A. Graham UNC

Raleigh, N.C.,
August 13th., 1870

Your letter of yesterday came to hand this morning, and Messrs. Moore, Bragg, Merrimon and myself had what I believe the Scotch call a "sederunt" upon it. We learn that an order has been sent to Col. Kirk to bring all the prisoners from Yanceyville to the Company Shops, and have them there on Monday. A proposition was made to us by R. Badger on behalf of the Governor, to have the prisoners brought to this City, agreeing to have the writs altered so as to make them returnable here, instead of at Salisbury, and agreeing further, to take no advantage of the change of place. We were, at first, inclined to agree to it, but as we had some reason to believe that an attempt would be made to get the C. J.[1] here, and make a return of the prisoners for whom he had issued writs, before him, and then make a return of that fact before Judge Brooks, we concluded to decline any arrangement different from that prescribed by law.

You and I both, have been under a mistake as to the day of the return of the writs. They were served last Monday, and, excluding that day, the 10th. will fall on next Thursday. Judge Merrimon says that is the day Judge Brooks expects the writs to be returned before him.

Judge Merrimon will go to Morganton on Monday, and he and Judge Brooks will be in Salisbury on Thursday. Gov. Bragg and myself, and perhaps Mr. Moore, will leave here at 1 O'clock, A.M. of that day, and hope to get to Salisbury to breakfast. You had better join us on the cars that morning.

We learn that Holden and Kirk are both alarmed. The quarrel between Holden and Pool is said to be bitter, and will bring about some ugly disclosures.

We agree to the propriety of most of the suggestions you make as to our course of action against the guilty parties, after the trial of the prisoners is over. Merrimon suggests some changes in your plan, which we think you will agree to adopt. We can talk more fully about the whole matter when we meet.

---

[1]Richmond M. Pearson.

Robert B. Gilliam to William A. Graham UNC

Oxford,
August 15th., 1870.

. . . .

I have strong hopes that your efforts to sustain the laws, and the great principles of Civil liberty before Judge Brooks will be successful. It is stated in the Sentinel that Holden has determined to have the prisoners before the Judge on Thursday, which looks as if he was preparing to back down. I thought he was becoming uneasy when I saw he had sent his professional henchman[1] to Yanceyville on a special errand.

[1]The reference evidently is to Richard C. Badger, Holden's counsel in all these proceedings.

Junius I. Scales[1] *to William A. Graham* UNC

Greensboro', N.C.,
August 15th., 1870.

The members of the Bar, residing here, held a meeting today, to take into consideration Judge Tourgee's letter to Gen'l Abbott, of May 24th. 1870, published in the N.Y. Tribune of 3rd. Inst., and his subsequent letter to the Tribune, published in the Sentinel of last week.[2] It was the unanimous conclusion of the meeting, that these letters are infamous libels upon this Judicial District, and upon the State at large; and a Committee, with Mr. Gorrell[3] at it's head, was appointed to address Judge Tourgee a note, requesting him to avow, or disavow, their authorship. We think it degrading to the profession to rest quietly, any longer, under the misrepresentations and falsehoods of this partisan Judge, and that these letters, of and by themselves, show him totally unfit to hold the scales of Justice. In short, it is presumed that no member of the profession has the slightest confidence in him, either as a man or a Judge.

It was in view of all this further considered, that we owed it to ourselves and the Country, to take some action in the matter.

As Secr'ty of the meeting, I was therefore instructed to address a note to yourself, and others of our non-resident brethren, who are in the habit of attending this Bar, notifying you of an adjourned meeting to be held on Friday night next, and requesting your presence, and your counsel, on that occasion.

Should [it] be inconvenient to attend, we would be glad to have your views by letter.

[1]Junius Irving Scales (1832-1880) was a native of Rockingham County and an alumnus of the University of North Carolina, having been awarded an A.B. degree in 1853. He served as colonel in the Thirtieth Mississippi Regiment during the Civil War. A lawyer by profession, he served in the North Carolina House of Commons, 1858, and in the state Senate, 1876-1879. Grant, *Alumni History*, 548.

[2]The letter in question was addressed to Senator Joseph C. Abbott and described the situation in North Carolina with a fair degree of accuracy. Tourgée gave Governor Holden a copy of the letter, and the governor subsequently presented it to a northern reporter. Tourgée was very angry about Holden's action and was dismayed when the letter was published in garbled form. He subsequently wrote a piece for the *Tribune* correcting errors in the letter originally given to Holden. The second letter also appeared in the *Sentinel* (Raleigh) on August 13, 1870. Olsen, *Carpetbagger's Crusade*, 167-168.

[3]Ralph Gorrell (1803-1875) of Guilford County, a Scotch-Irish Presbyterian, graduated from the university in 1825. A lawyer and a Whig, he was a member of the Commons in 1834, 1835, and 1854; of the state Senate in 1856 and 1858; and of the Constitutional Convention of 1861. Gorrell at first opposed secession but later changed his views. At the

time of this letter he was a Democrat. McCormick, *Convention Personnel,* 38; Connor, *North Carolina Manual, 1913,* 633-634; Spencer Alumni Project; Caldwell, *Founders and Builders of Greensboro,* 87-92.

John P. Leach,[1] *A. L. Adams,*[2] *and Benjamin F. Cheatham*[3] *to William A. Graham* [with enclosure] UNC

Raleigh, N.C.,
August 18th., 1870.

We have taken the liberty of using your name as an Honorary Marshal for the Grand Mass Reception to be given Hon. Josiah Turner, Jr., the fearless champion of civil rights and liberty, and his fellow prisoners, as soon as they are released and reach this city.

We trust it may meet with your approval, and that you will honor us with your presence on the occasion.

---

[1]John Pelopidas Leach, of Halifax County, a Democratic planter from River township, served as a senator from Warren County, 1893. Cheney, *North Carolina Government,* 471, 557n, 561n; Manly Wade Wellman, *The County of Warren, 1586-1917* (Chapel Hill: University of North Carolina Press, 1959), 198.

[2]A. L. Adams has not been identified.

[3]Prior to the Civil War, Benjamin F. Cheatham (b. 1834) resided in Warren County, where he was a merchant. It is not known when he established his residence in Raleigh, but in 1871 he was on the Raleigh Board of Trade. Murray, *Wake,* 500, 574.

Invitation to Mass Reception [Enclosure] UNC

You are respectfully invited to attend
A Grand Mass Reception

to be given in this City, by the Citizens of Wake County to Hons. Josiah Turner, Jr., Samuel P. Hill, Judge Kerr, and other prisoners now in custody of Col. George W. Kirk, by order of Gov. W. W. Holden, as soon as they are released, due notice of which will be given through the public press.

J. P. Leach,
A. L. Adams
B. F. Cheatham,
Committee.

Marshals:[1]

Capt. J. G. DeCarteret,
" J. G. Hester,
Dr. James McKee,
" C. F. Dowd,
Capt. W. Hal. Harrison,
Major A. G. Lee,
" B. C. Manly,

Celedon Hutchings, Esq.,
A. N. McKimmon, Esq.,
N. J. Whitaker, Esq.,
N. A. Steadman, Jr., Esq.,
C. R. Harris, Esq.,
J. G. Bagwell, Esq.,
C. E. McCullers, Esq.,

Col. L. D. Stevenson,
J. P. Leach, Esq.,
B. F. Cheatham, Esq.,
L. H. Adams, Esq.,
J. H. Kirkham, Esq.,
Geo. W. Wynne, Esq.,
P. J. Brown, Jr., Esq.,
William Mills, Esq.,
Thomas Waring, Esq.,
Jno. C. Syme, Esq.,
A. L. Adams, Esq.,
Jno. C. Askew, Esq.,
Thomas Badger, Esq.,
W. G. Upchurch, Esq.,
David Lewis, Esq.,
J. R. H. Carmer, Esq.,
C. D. Heartt, Esq.,
Z. J. Lemay, Esq.,

Honorary Marshals.

Hon. A. S. Merrimon,
" W. A. Graham,
" Will. H. Battle,
" J. M. Leach,
" B. F. Moore,
" Jos. J. Davis,
" J. T. Leach,
" Daniel G. Fowle,
" K. P. Battle,
" Abram Rencher,
Hon. Sion H. Rogers,
" Q R. B. Gilliam,
" A. M. Waddell,
Maj. Seaton Gales,
Hon. W. M. Shipp,
" Wm. T. Dortch,
" Plato Durham,
" A. H. Arrington,
" F. E. Shober,
" J. C. Harper,

Raleigh, August 18, 1870.

[1]No attempt has been made to identify all those serving as marshals, although the list includes many familiar names.

William A. Graham to William A. Graham, Jr. A&H

Hillsboro',
August 20th., 1870.

. . . I returned from Salisbury last night, all the prisoners carried there were discharged, to the credit of Judge Brooks, who has acted nobly.

Kirk carried about 20 to Raleigh before Pearson, whom Holden prevailed on to go to Raleigh, & try to revive his dead proceedings in their cases. This we frustrated by withdrawing every Petition from before him. He had to assent to it, and was left without cases before him. To countervail this, an affidavit was made before him by Burgin [Bergen], Kirk's Lieut. Col., charging ex-Sheriff Wiley[1] with the murder of Stevens,[2] & Pearson issued a warrant, to arrest him in Kirk's custody, and has appointed Monday next for the investigation—and we hear that he has also issued warrants for Judge Kerr, Dr. Roan,[3] & all the other prisoners. Judge Brooks, not recognizing Pearson's right to interfere again, after Kirk had been served with his writs, issued a rule on Kirk to shew cause on Tuesday next, why he should not be attached for not bringing all the prisoners to Salisbury. This will be returned before Brooks at Raleigh on Tuesday next, he having an extra Court there next week.

Turner was the first man discharged, and had an ovation from that time forward, bouquets, fruits, etc., were sent to him at Salisbury, at Lexington, Thomasville, Greensboro', he was met at the depot with illuminations, etc., and at Hillsboro' there was a general turnout, with torches, at 11 o'clock at night, cannon firing, etc., and he was drawn by men, in a carriage into town, etc., etc. Today the cannon is fired again, and another speech.[4]

I go to Raleigh tomorrow night to attend to the Caswell prisoners. . . . The victory in the State is complete. There will be a reception of Turner, and a grand celebration next Thursday, at Raleigh.

. . . .

---

[1]Frank A. Wiley.

[2]John W. Stephens.

[3]This is evidently a reference to Felix R. Roan (1837-1891) of Yanceyville. Roan received an A.B. degree from the University of North Carolina in 1857 and served in the Confederate forces with the rank of captain. He was register of deeds in Caswell County. On August 18, Attorney General Lewis P. Olds applied for a bench warrant against seven men, including Felix Roan, for complicity in the Stephens murder and conspiracy in Klan activities. A ruling was delayed by the chief justice until August 22. Roan was one of three people not discharged immediately, although he was released later because of a lack of evidence. Grant, *Alumni History*, 526; Hamilton, *Reconstruction in North Carolina*, 516; Raper, *Holden*, 194.

[4]This was undoubtedly the high point in Turner's career.

Hezekiah G. Spruill[1] *to William A. Graham* UNC

Elizabeth City, N.C.
Aug 22nd 1870

I wish to obtain the appointment of Principal Clerk of the Senate, at the next meeting of the General Assembly.

I ask this office, with the full assurance of my ability to discharge the duties; and, also because it will be agreeable to me in a pecuniary point of view.

I shall receive the warm support of all the senators, in the extreme East, (we have elected conservatives, in the four first districts), and Capt Jarvis,[2] reelected from Tyrrel, is interesting himself in my behalf.

Will you allow me to refer to you? May I ask of you, to speak of me, to such of the newly elected Conservative Senators as you may meet?

We are all filled with joy at result of our elections. And we are happy to know that we have one Judge, who is too just & pure to be governed by the baneful influences about Raleigh—Judge Brooks, has done & will do his duty.

---

[1]Hezekiah G. Spruill, of Tyrrell County, served in the Constitutional Convention of 1835 and in six legislatures between 1831 and 1845. He and Graham were old Whig allies. Cheney, *North Carolina Government*, 297, 305, 308, 309, 311, 313, 818.

[2]Thomas Jordan Jarvis (1836-1915) was a descendant of Thomas Jarvis, deputy governor of Albemarle in 1691. In 1860 Jarvis, a native of Currituck County, was awarded an A.B. degree from Randolph-Macon College and in 1861 received a master's degree from the

same school. During the war he served in the Eighth and Seventeenth North Carolina regiments and rose to the rank of captain before he was injured at Drewry's Bluff. After the war, Jarvis studied law and became interested in politics. A Democrat, he entered the state House in 1868 and was elected Speaker in 1870. As lieutenant governor, he was Zebulon Vance's successor as state chief executive when Vance was elected to the United States Senate in 1879. Reelected in 1880, Jarvis worked for education and mental health facilities and against governmental extravagance and corruption. Crabtree, *North Carolina Governors*, 103-104; *DAB*, IX, 623-624; Powell, *DNCB*, III, 273.

Deposition of John G. Albright UNC

August 24, 1870
United States of America
District of North Carolina

John G. Albright being sworn, deposeth and saith, that he is a citizen of the United States, and of the state of North Carolina, of the age of Fifty three years, now residing and has always resided in the county of Alamance North Carolina, that he met, on last Sunday afternoon, 21st instant, in the Town of Graham, G. B. Bergen claiming to be Lieutenant Colonel under G. W. Kirke of an armed force called N.C. State Troops. He accosted this affiant, who had been a prisoner under the arrests of him & Kirk for several weeks, & still subject to their penal, saying "See here, I understand Rogers[1] & Murray[2] say that I hung them." It is a damned lie, and I intend to shoot them on sight, and if you tell it I will shoot you." This affiant replied, that he had not spoken of his (Bergen's) hanging of Rogers & Murray, that he had spoken of his hanging Patten;[3] but that he, Bergen, & his officers had told it first. To the threat of shooting, this affiant replied, that "if his hands were untied he could shoot back," and walked off and left him.

This affiant further states, that he resides in the Town of Graham, was arrested by said Bergen's order, on or about the 26th or 27th of July last, and was placed at night in a tent with Lucian H. Murray, George Rogers, William Patten & James W. Faust;[4] that he, the affiant, saw said Bergen, a lieutenant Hunycut[5] and Henry Wiggins,[6] called a sergeant, take said Patten from said tent, into said Bergen's tent; they tied the door pieces of this affiant's tent, so as endeavours to prevent being seen in Bergen's tent. But the cloth being scant, there was a space not closed, through which, this affiant saw into said Bergen's tent, and observed that a rope was placed around the neck of said Patten, heard Bergen say, he was going to hang him, and he & his men aforesaid & others, went off with him toward the woods; and after being absent some time, probably an hour, they brought him back, and placed him under a tree not allowing him to communicate with other prisoners, said Bergen returned in advance of the party, and said, they had hung Patten & made him tell of the murder of Outlaw, and addressing George S. Rogers, said, I have hung Patten and made him tell, "and now damn you I intend to hang you and make you tell all about it." The same party as before then took said Rogers off toward the woods, and in about an hour brought him back. This affiant heard Bergen tell him not to tell any thing of what had been done.

This affiant was asleep, he supposes, when the said Murray was taken off & returned as stated in his affidavit; but the next morning, the said Murray, being apparently afraid to speak, as he was closely watched by the guards, pointed this affiant's attention to his neck, on which this affiant saw distinctly the mark of a rope, as if he had been hanged. This affiant further states, that there is a company of United States regular troops, under the command of Brevet Colonel Andrews, who have been stationed in the said Town of Graham, and still continue there. That this, and a preceding company have kept up a regular garrison in said Town, since a few days after the murder of Wyatt Outlaw in the month of February last, with an interval of only a few days, that said company was & is all sufficient for the preservation of order, if any military force should be deemed necessary; and the introduction of the troops of said Kirke into the county, seems designed to arrest and imprison the inhabitants without any legal precept or process; that since the 15th of July last, they have siezed and imprisoned more than one Hundred citizens, as this affiant believes, without legal warrant in a single instance, treating them generally with great harshness, & in many cases with extreme brutality; in the cases of some discharging by military order, in others taking paroles to report to the said Kirke, and in others confining the persons, defying and continuing writs Habeas Corpus, issued by the Chief Justice of the State, until like writs were issued by the district Judge of the United States, and ten days allowed for the returned, had nearly expired. And after more than Forty of said citizens had been compelled to be brought before the said district judge, not a particle of evidence was offered against any one of them, and they have all been discharged.

This affiant states, that the conduct of the said Kirke & Bergen and the armed men under their command in thus arresting and annoying the people of the said county and the adjoining county of Caswell is a great grievance and oppression; that notwithstanding the discharges on Habeas Corpus, of so many citizens as aforesaid, this affiant has been informed & believes, that arrests have been made by said troops, in the county of Caswell within a week past, in the illegal manner aforesaid; and he fears that the like arrests are still to be continued in the County of Alamance, and that himself and his neighbors are in danger of being deprived of their liberties by this lawless violence. That, he himself, has been held as a prisoner for twenty six days, a part of the time, on parole, and has been discharged by His Honor Judge Brooks, on the 23rd instant, without any charge being preferred against him.

He states of his own knowledge, that no insurrection has existed or now exists in the said county of Alamance; that the courts of justice in the county have been constantly open, the regular terms [of] the superior court have been held, at the times appointed by law; that at the last term, in June of the present year, one colored man was convicted & sentenced to death, for a rape committed some time before; others were sentenced to imprisonment in the penitentiary, and the business usual in such tribunals was all disposed of in the customary manner, and in the most perfect quiet and good order. And this affiant avers, that any process of law could at any time have been executed on any citizen of the said county of Alamance before the arrival of the troops of the aforesaid Kirk in the same; and can now be executed by the peace officers of the said county, if the said Kirk & his officers shall not interfere to prevent it.

He further states, that he has heard read the affidavits of the aforesaid Lucien H. Murray & George A. Rogers in relation to the maltreatment of themselves, by the said Bergen, and he believes their statements therein made, to be true; that he is well acquainted with them, and knows their general characters, and that the character of each is good as a person of truthfulness and good morals.

Sworn & subscribed before me this 24th of August 1870.

John G. Albright

Sworn and subscribed before me this 24th Augt. 1870.

J. N. Bunting,[7] Clerk of the Superior Court Wake

Sworn and subscribed before me.

N. P. Reddick,[8] Clerk of the U.S. Circuit Court

---

[1]George S. Rogers, a twenty-year-old farmer who lived in Alamance County, had been arrested at Graham in July; threatened and questioned about the murder of Wyatt Outlaw; and detained until August 19, when Judge George Brooks released him. *Impeachment Trial of William W. Holden* (Raleigh: State of North Carolina, 3 volumes, 1871), I, 701-704, hereinafter cited as *Holden Trial.*

[2]Lucien H. Murray, a native of Guilford County and a Confederate veteran, was among those arrested in Alamance County in July, 1870. Manarin and Jordan, *North Carolina Troops*, III, 229.

[3]William Patton.

[4]James W. Faust, of Alamance County, had served as a private in the Army of Northern Virginia. He was arrested during the Kirk-Holden War. Manarin and Jordan, *North Carolina Troops*, V, 578.

[5]Lieutenant John Hunnicutt was an officer serving under Kirk's command. It was Hunnicutt, acting upon orders from Bergen, who arrested Josiah Turner, Jr. Horace Raper, a Holden biographer, says that Bergen acted without the governor's formal approval, believing that Holden wished to arrest Turner but lacked the nerve. Raper, *Holden*, 188-189.

[6]Henry Wiggins has not been further identified.

[7]J. N. Bunting represented Wake County in the state House in 1881. Cheney, *North Carolina Government*, 461.

[8]N. P. Reddick has not been further identified.

Thomas J. Womack[1] *to William A. Graham* UNC

Yanceyville, N.C.,
September 1st., 1870.

I was held as prisoner by Kirk, through Gov. Holden's orders, for five weeks, was released by the Gov. under the pretext of "*a mistake* in arresting me," after I went to Raleigh with the other prisoners, went before Judge Pearson, & was discharged by him, as the other men were,—now I wish to know if I can't recover damages from Holden for false imprisonment. I wish you to reply immediately, & if you think I can recover damages, I will get a writ, have it filled out & send to you as soon as possible. My brother-in-law, Hon. Giles Mebane,[2] advises me to sue, & selected you as my attorney, he says he will stand on the bond for the maintenance of suit, etc., he says I ought to bring suit for twenty thousand dollars. I leave the amount claimed discretionary with you & am willing to give you half of what I recover, after deducting all expenses of suit.

---

[1]Thomas J. Womack has not been identified further.

[2]Giles Mebane (1809-1899), a native of Orange County, was graduated by the University of North Carolina in 1831. A lawyer by profession, he was a Whig in politics. He served Orange County in the House of Commons in the 1844, 1846, and 1848 sessions and Alamance in the 1854 and 1860 sessions. Representing Alamance County, he was Speaker of the state Senate in the 1862 and 1864 sessions. In 1879 he represented Caswell County in the state Senate. Mebane was also a delegate to the constitutional conventions of 1861-1862 and 1865-1866. Grant, *Alumni History*, 423; Cheney, *North Carolina Government*, 314, 315, 317, 322, 327, 328, 329, 330, 331, 458, 824, 832.

William A. Coleman[1] *to William A. Graham* UNC

Kinston, N.C.,
September 1st., 1870.

The Conservatives of Lenoir County will celebrate their triumph over the Radicals in this State by a grand Barbecue and Dinner, to be given in this place on Thursday, 8th. of Sept., and have authorized me to invite you to be present with us on that occasion.

Always justly proud of their great men and Statesmen, North Carolinians will rejoice ever more at your bold and manly course in opposition to the late illegal arrests, false imprisonment, tyranny, & usurpation in their State.

Hoping you will find it convenient to be with us at that time.

---

[1]William Augustus Coleman (b. 1839) was the son of Colonel William Blount Coleman, one of the incorporators of Kinston. In 1868 he married Elizabeth Peebles, offspring of an old Kinston family. Talmage C. Johnson and Charles R. Holloman, *The Story of Kinston and Lenoir County* (Raleigh: Edwards and Broughton Company, 1954), 214-215.

Benjamin H. Bunn,[1] *John J. Battle,*[2] *and Samuel T. Williams*[3] *to William A. Graham* UNC

Rocky Mount, N.C.,
September 7th., 1870.

Permit us the honor to request you to address the citizens of this vicinity, at our grand celebration to be held at this place for the counties of Edgecombe and Nash, on the 29th. Inst., in honor of our recent political victory.

---

[1]Benjamin Hickman Bunn (1844-1907), of Nash County, was a lawyer by profession. During the Civil War he served in the Confederate forces, rising to the rank of captain. After the war he was active in politics and served in several offices. In 1875 he was a

convention delegate; he was a member of the state House of Representatives, 1883-1885; and from 1889 through 1895 he was a Democratic member of Congress. Powell, *DNCB*, I, 270.

[2]John Joseph Battle (1831-1889) was a planter in Edgecombe County. In 1877 he was elected an associate justice of the inferior court of Edgecombe County. Joseph Kelly Turner and John L. Bridgers, Jr., *History of Edgecombe County* (Raleigh: Edwards and Broughton, 1920), 281.

[3]Samuel T. Williams, a lawyer in Rocky Mount, was at one time a partner of Benjamin Hickman Bunn. He was also a delegate to the constitutional conventions of 1861-1862 and 1865-1866.

Cornelia Phillips Spencer[1] *to William A. Graham* A&H

Chapel Hill,
September 10th., 1870.

I received not long since, a letter from Mrs. Swain,[2] which is the occasion of my writing to you. And I trust that, since no selfish motive prompts me, you will excuse the intrusion on your valuable time, and allow me to consult you on a matter which is, or ought to be, dear to every educated N. Carolinian.

Mrs. Swain mentioned having seen you & Judge Battle lately, & regretted to tell me that, in speaking of the University, you had *both* expressed the opinion that there was no hope of its restoration shortly; that the Legislature would not be able to effect any changes; that, the Institution being bankrupt, the Land-scrip lost, & the property there undergoing constant deterioration, there seemed nothing in prospect but further and entire ruin.

My dear Gov. Graham, you are still, as you have been for many years, the foremost citizen of this State, & when 9/10 of your fellow-citizens hear you quoted as having said such & such a thing, they set it down as certain to be just as you say.

If the members of the Legislature understand that you, and such men as you and Judge Battle think they cannot move upon Chapel Hill, & there is no use in attempting to do anything for it, they will assuredly leave it to its fate. If, on the contrary, you are known to have expressed a decided opinion that something *ought* to be done, & *must* be done, & *will* be done, & that it is the solemn duty of the General Assembly to take hold of it—if necessary by a *coup d'etat* & reform & restore it, & make it once more worthy of the State, & worthy of its former reputation, I believe it will be done. Does the State really mean to let Chapel Hill die? Every month that it is let to languish in its present condition sinks it lower, and farther from aid.

That the State property here is undergoing constant deterioration is very true, and is at the same time the strongest argument in favor of speedy reformation. These persons now in charge have but one motive of action; their own interests & how to make the most of their position.

The last detachment of Gov. Holden's troops broke into the Phi. Library & defaced and carried off, I am told, valuable books. ("Picture-books" it is to be presumed, as they had not the appearance of literary characters.) I mention this as one of the latest outrages. You have no doubt heard of one of Mr. Pool's[3] students kicking out the doors of the Di. & Phi. Archive rooms, & scattering the papers. A few more years of negro & white soldiery, & carpet-bag & scalawag faculty rule, & the property will indeed be past all necessity for oversight.

The people of Chapel Hill & the neighboring country will assuredly fix their eyes on the Legislature with the expectation of receiving some relief at its hands. Can you tell me who are likely to be the leaders in either House? Gov. Vance writes me that there will be many very young men in the Commons—'mere boys.' There will certainly be some Alumni of the Uni. among them. The younger & the less unhackneyed, & the less reputation to hazard, the more likely they will be to do some generous, uncalculating act. Would it avail anything, dear Sir, if I were to write to your son, Mr. Jno. Graham, & ask him to go to Raleigh determined to do something for the University, either with the Law—or without it?

Two years ago it was the opinion of some of our best men, that in the then desperate and bankrupt condition of the Institution, it w'd be best to lease the property to a company of Teachers, whose reputation would attract students, & let them do what they could to keep it alive & going for a term of years. Would that plan be feasible now?

Is it quite true that the Legis. will not be able to touch the present incumbents? Can nothing be done except by a Convention? With the present Board of Trustees I presume nothing can be done. The Legis. may refuse, as formerly, to grant supplies, but while Mr. Ashley[4] has the Common S. Fund at his disposal, they will be independent, & will go on as long as money is supplied. These "Professors" say openly it makes no difference to them whether any students come here or not. There are now some 15 boys from abroad, all from the lower classes of society—all beneficiaries, & most of them boarding with negroes.

Chapel Hill is in a peculiar sense the child of the State. The whole place—every inch of private property in it—is dependent on the State as no other place can be. Our merchants, mechanics, & day laborers are all closely connected with the State, look to it for their means of living, & are ruined if it casts them off.

All this you know, dear Governor Graham, as well as I do. I know you love the place & have grieved over its fate as a son should do for his foster-mother. But if you had lived here this past two years, & had your righteous soul vexed from day to day by the ungodly deeds of the men in power, you would kindle such a flame of indignation in N. Carolina as would burn out the last vestige of its oppression and degradation.

May I beg you to write to me to say if there is any *chance* of reform and relief for Chapel Hill this winter. In the midst of our late triumph, my first thought was: Now something will be done for Chapel Hill. I cannot write of it, or think of it, without emotion. Hallowed & most affecting are all my associations with it, & there is nothing that a woman can do that I would not undertake for its redemption. This is my only apology for intruding on your time—& I feel sure it will avail.

Believe me, dear Sir,

With high regard & affection

[1]Cornelia Ann Phillips Spencer (1825-1908), author and educational reformer, the youngest child and only daughter of Professor and Mrs. James Phillips, was long a Chapel Hill fixture. A woman of unusual force of character, she was schooled in classical languages and widely read. She bemoaned the social custom that allowed her only the "crumbs from the college table," but her devotion to the University of North Carolina never flagged. The South's defeat in the Civil War led her to analyze North Carolina's weaknesses and to urge her fellow citizens to improve its image and institutions. Particularly interested in education, Cornelia Spencer was influential in sustaining the university through the troubled Reconstruction era.

She began her literary career by writing for the *Watchman*, a New York magazine, articles on conditions in North Carolina during the final weeks of the Civil War. For this purpose she corresponded with a wide circle of knowledgeable friends and public men, including Graham. The accounts she gathered were published as *The Last Ninety Days of the War in North Carolina* (1866). Friend and advisor to three university presidents—David L. Swain, Kemp P. Battle, and George T. Winston—Mrs. Spencer was awarded the LL.D. degree from the university in 1895. She was the first person so honored. Edward T. James and others, *Notable American Women, 1607-1950: A Biographical Dictionary* (Cambridge: Belknap Press, 3 volumes, 1971), III, 333.

[2]Eleanor Swain, the widow of David L. Swain.

[3]Solomon Pool (1832-1901), of Pasquotank County, a brother of John Pool, was a product of the planter class. In 1853 he graduated from the University of North Carolina. In the same year he began two decades of service to his alma mater. He was a tutor, 1853-1860; adjunct professor, 1860-1867; and president, 1869-1874, although the university was closed for several years during that time. *Cyclopedia of Eminent Men*, II, 401-402; Hamilton, *Reconstruction in North Carolina*, 625-628.

[4]Samuel Stanford Ashley, the New England carpetbagger who was state superintendent of public instruction, was, under provisions of the Constitution of 1868, secretary of the newly created board of education, whose members were ex officio members of the university board of trustees.

Ashley was a controversial figure whose extraordinary career warrants closer examination. Writing in 1914, J. G. de Roulhac Hamilton characterized Ashley as "corrupt" and with apparent reluctance concluded:

> He was not lacking in ability, but only in character and in a suitable temperament for his position. He was full of prejudices which made him narrow and regardless of the wishes of the people among whom he had elected to live. This was clearly apparent from his course in the convention. He favored mixed schools, and, like all of his kind, was far more interested in the welfare of the negroes than in anything else except himself. If the charge that he was of negro descent be true, this feeling was not at all unnatural. There is no convincing evidence of his having been as corrupt as some of his colleagues, but he was hand in glove with them, supporting their every act, and he was regarded as one of the most unpleasant carpetbaggers in the State. (Hamilton, *Reconstruction in North Carolina*, 611.)

Professor Hamilton's description of Ashley reflected the view of the Dunning school of Reconstruction historiography in branding all carpetbaggers self-serving and corrupt. With the advantage of a longer perspective, historians in recent years have granted that humanitarian motives, especially concern for the freedmen, were of primary importance to many northern men who came to the South after the Civil War. One suspects that Ashley was among their number. A review of his career in the South, which spanned over twenty years, would suggest that his intentions were to benefit blacks and, in his view, all southerners. There is little indication that his purpose was to capitalize on the socio-economic distress of post-1865 southerners.

Virginia L. Farragut[1] *to William A. Graham* UNC

113 East 36th, N.Y.,
Sept. 20th, 1870

Your kind words were most grateful in my bereavement for it is a comforting thought to find those who have had opportunities of knowing my beloved and honored husband appreciate like yourself his true character

I have received many assurances of this fact but not one has been more valued than your own—for I knew he ever held your opinions in high esteem from the time he first approached you as his Chief in the Navy Dept. I cannot but feel that the least ray of light now given me in this bleak and dreary world is not unknown to him in that higher and better world to which I trust he has gone and that his spirit is helping me to keep the moans of my heart from bursting into *weariness* which might rob me of the hope I now indulge of an union eternal with him in Heaven where we are promised there will be no more of these dreadful partings!

I came here a few days ago with my son to make arrangements to have my dear husband very tenderly, but quietly consigned to his last earthly resting place but I have been compelled to acquiesce to the entreaties of his warm friends to permit some public demonstration and now the arrangements are in the hands of the Mayor of N York but this causes a delay of the day, and prolongs the sorrowful agitations necessarily, but I cannot hesitate to sacrifice my personal feelings, when I perceive the earnest desire of his friends to honor his *memory—particularly* when those upon whom he had the best claims failed him in the dark hour but this neglect has been so publicly rebuked that nothing is left the wife of the Admiral but to cover herself with his beautiful *garment* of silence and Charity for he put his faith in God! not in the Princes of this world.

With my kind regards to Mrs. Graham and your son

Very sincerely yours

[1]Virginia Loyall Farragut was the widow of Admiral David G. Farragut.

William H. Battle to William A. Graham UNC

Raleigh,
September 21st., 1870

You will see in the Sentinel of to day that I have undertaken to report the proceedings in the late habeas corpus cases. I shall be glad to be able to give the arguments of counsel, if I can procure them. Can you furnish me with yours, particularly your argument before C. J. Pearson upon the four questions proposed by him after he had received Gov. Holden's letter.

I have written to Judge Brooks, and requested him to write out opinions upon the questions argued before, and decided by him, and to send me copies for my report. I hope to get, also, an opinion from Judge Bond[1] of the Circuit Court, which, I feel confident, will sustain Judge Brooks.

[1]Hugh L. Bond (1828-1893) was born in Baltimore but moved to New York in his childhood. After graduation from the University of the City of New York, he established a law practice in Baltimore in 1851. Vitally interested in the welfare of blacks, he was a fearless advocate of justice. In 1870 he became judge of the Fourth United States Circuit Court, comprised of Maryland, Virginia, West Virginia, North Carolina, and South Carolina. President Grant appointed him because he was thought to be a suitable judge to hear Ku Klux Klan cases. On August 29 he came to Raleigh to hear the cases against Bergen and Kirk. After hearing the Bergen case, Bond reserved his opinion for several days and on October 24 secretly dismissed Bergen. Later, he handed down his decision overruling Judge Brooks. Bond also released Kirk a week after Bergen's release. *DAB*, II, 431-432; *Cyclopedia of American Biography*, XI, 408; Hamilton, *Reconstruction in North Carolina*, 532-533.

Invitation to Admiral Farragut's Funeral[1] UNC

Committee Room—Chamber Board of Supervisors.
Court House.

New York,
September 24th., 1870.

Sir

The Committee of Arrangements of the Common Council respectfully tender to you an invitation to take part in the funeral obsequies of our lamented fellow citizen, the late Admiral David G. Farragut.

It is earnestly hoped that you may be present and participate in this tribute of respect to the honored remains of our country's great naval hero, to take place at this City on the 30th. day of September inst.

The Committee will meet those who may be invited to participate in the funeral obsequies in the Governor's Room, City Hall, at 10 o'clock on the morning of the 30th. inst.

Ald. Jerome	Asst. Ald. Littlefield
" Hart	" " Odell
" Cuddy	" " Durnin
" Welch	" " O'Brien
" Irvinh	" " Robinson
John Hardy, Clerk.	Committee.[2]

[1]After David Glasgow Farragut's death in August, 1870, the citizens of New York requested that his body be conveyed to that city. This was done, and on September 30 a procession including President Grant, members of his cabinet, officers of the army and navy, and 10,000 soldiers escorted Farragut's body to a Forty-seventh Street train, which conveyed it to Woodlawn Cemetery. *DAB*, VI, 286-291.

[2]No effort has been made to identify the members of this committee.

William A. Graham to Benjamin H. Bunn, John J. Battle, and Samuel T. Williams[1] UNC

Hillsboro' N.C.,
Sept. 26th. 1870

Gentlemen,

I regret that it is not in my power to accept your invitation to be present and address the people at your grand celebration by the citizens of Edgecombe and Nash, at Rocky Mount, of the recent political victory in the State. It is an event worthy to be commemorated by all good citizens and patriots; and with none would I more gladly unite in the exchange of congratulations and kind greetings, than those of your community.

The result of no election was ever more creditable to the deliberation and intelligence of the people, or inspired a more hopeful confidence in their capacity and zeal to take care of their great interests, public and individual.

"It was no common party race
Jostling by dark intrigue for place;"

but the expression of the calm judgment of the grand inquest of electors, without the excitements of an active canvass, in vindication and rebuke of confidence abused, public credit ruined, public and private interests sacrificed, and the dearest and most sacred rights of individuals, and of society violated. There was quite sufficient cause for the overthrow of our adversaries, in what was done and tolerated by the Legislature, and Executive, months ago; but when to these were added a military invasion, by an armed force, in great part from East Tennessee, its seizure and incarceration of many of our best citizens, the very pillars of society, in their several neighborhoods, and the announcement was made that the judiciary was impotent for any relief, their defeat became a rout. The opportune moment having arrived in this crisis, for the people to speak through the ballot box, they resolved to provide remedies for these evils, if none could now be found, by entrusting power to other hands, and demanding new guards for their future security. In no uncertain tones, they proclaimed that "the military is subordinate to, and must be governed by, the civil power;" and that the privilege of the writ of Habeas [corpus], is not a mere paper declaration, but a substantial right, which shall not be suspended, by state authority, in peace, or in war; and that the mere issuing of the writ is a mockery, unless its execution be enforced, and the aggrieved and innocent prisoner restored to his liberty. I trust, the lesson it inculcates will not be lost to us; that it will teach us patience in future trials, if any are to fall to our lot; and, above all, that there is in this Country something "more terrible than an army with banners;" and that is the decrees of a free and brave people at the polls.

It would be a great mistake to suppose that our triumph implied any disposition to abridge the present rights of the colored race, or a contravention of the policy of the United States in conferring these rights. The people of the State are wearied of agitation, and long for repose. Many reforms will doubtless claim the attention of those invested with authority, but no change, I feel assured, is meditated in these particulars.

---

[1]Copy in Graham's handwriting.

William A. Graham
to Cornelia Phillips Spencer A&H: SPENCER

Hillsboro',
Sept. 29th, 1870.

. . . .

In regard to the University, in which I am pleased to find your interest has suffered no abatement, Mrs. Swain perhaps slightly misunderstood the remark to which you allude. I probably mentioned to her that I thought, considering the experience of the last two years, there was no hope of the revival of the University under the management of the present Board of Trustees, and that a Convention to change the Constitution would be necessary to effect this, and that measure would require time.

I concur with you heartily in the necessity of re-establishing the Institution as soon as is practicable, and think I see already the want of the annual crop of educated young men we were wont to send forth from our Commencements.

What will be the most effective means to this end when authority shall permit action, will require more information and thought, than I can now command. With a sparse population and general poverty, as is our case, I very much incline to the system of educating downwards; and that more good may be accomplished with limited means, by endowing the University, or at least sustaining it, than expending a like amount in Common Schools. Whether or not this be so, I am clearly of opinion that the magnificent grounds, groves, buildings, libraries, etc. of our University should not be allowed to lie in disuse or go to waste, any longer than want of power for restoration shall paralyze our energies.

I am gratified to perceive in the columns of "the Presbyterian" that your pen is not idle.

With sentiments of great respect

William A. Graham to the Windsor Committee[1]

Hillsboro', N.C.,
October 1, 1870.

Gentlemen:

I have had the honor to receive your kind invitation to a public dinner of the Conservative party of Bertie, at Windsor, on the 4th. inst., in honor of the recent victory achieved in the late election, and regret, that business engagements deny me the pleasure of attending.

I beg you, however, and those you represent, to be assured of my cordial good wishes and sincere congratulations on the event which brings you together. The grand result of the election, attained as it was, by the calm and spontaneous determination of the people, not only without any undue means to sway them in that direction, but in the face of patronage and power, and the appliance of a military force, actually distributed and stationed at the precincts in sundry counties; and after arresting and holding in prison many of our most respected and influential men, to drive them to the contrary, affords abundant cause for rejoicing, and thanksgiving, by all good and patriotic citizens. It demonstrates that the people are fully alive to the magnitude of the interests involved in the contest, and that the power to control the government is again in the hands of those who expect permanently to live under it, to pay its costs, and to feel, in their persons and interests, the consequence of good or evil counsels and policy. It is thus that it revives hope in the breasts of those who may have been doubtful or despondent; and induces them to thank God and take courage, to rebuild their waste places, and make lasting homes in their native land. It opens up for the future a new vista. Faith must be kept with the Federal Government, by a full observance of the rights and a proper care of the interests of the colored race; (which no one among us would now disturb if he could), but all else in our system of internal government and police, is in the hands of the people of the State. It is for them that this Government exists; by them it is paid for and maintained, and it should conform to their interests, wants and tastes. It is manifest that much of the existing system is of foreign importation and not the offspring of the deliberate judgment of the people. These parts were copied from the institutions of States differently circumstanced as to wealth, density of population, and the habits and industrial pursuits of the inhabitants. They do not suit us, and will require careful revision. There is nothing in this task at all calculated to induce any collision with Congress, the members of which would be as far from interfering in our domestic and municipal affairs, as they would be jealous of our interference with theirs; save only, as they are affected by the recent amendments of the Constitution of the United States. Nothing should be done rashly, or in a spirit of factious hostility. But we need a cheaper system, one more responsible, and less novel and strange to the people.

At best, our path is beset with difficulties. In the paucity of our resources, the wild legislation and maladministration of the last two years have done as much to damage our finances and public credit, as was done by the war. But the downward tendency in this respect, it is to be hoped, has been arrested by the changes to be effected by the election, and we may look again for the prudence, integrity, and economy of former times. I trust also, that we have arrived at the dawn, at least, of a day of better feeling between the people of the late hostile sections of our common country; and that the people of the North will see, in the exercise of power by the Conservative people of the State, only a faithful observance of the obligations imposed by a common Constitution, and that all predictions to the contrary have been the offspring of misrepresentation and injustice.

Believe me, gentlemen,
With great respect,
Your obedient servant,
W. A. GRAHAM.

To Messrs. J. B. Cherry,[2] P. H. Winston,[3] etc., Committee.

[1]From the *Daily Sentinel* (Raleigh), October 13, 1870.

[2]Joseph Blount Cherry (ca. 1816-1882), a Bertie County planter and lawyer, was a son of Solomon Cherry. He was a student at the university for one year, 1836-1837; although he did not graduate, Cherry was throughout his life extremely interested in public education. As a representative (1848, 1850, 1852) and a state senator (1856-1860), he introduced important bills promoting better schools and educators. A Unionist prior to the Civil War, Cherry supported the Confederacy when war began. After the war he was an energetic leader in the Democratic party and actively worked for improvement in transportation, especially through the construction of canals and railroads. Powell, *DNCB*, I, 361.

[3]Patrick Henry Winston (1820-1886), of Bertie County, farmed and practiced law after graduating from Columbian University. He was a member of the state Commons in 1850 and 1854; financial agent between North Carolina and the Confederacy; president of the Council of State in 1864; a member of the Constitutional Convention of 1865, representing Franklin County; and a university trustee, 1874-1883. Ashe, *Biographical History*, II, 441-449; Connor, *North Carolina Manual, 1913*, 379, 439, 503; Spencer Alumni Project.

William A. Graham to Susan Washington Graham A&H

Raleigh,
Oct. 6th, 1870

My Dear Wife,

. . . .

It is arranged, that my address be delivered on friday of the Fair. I must go to Person on monday, & return on wednesday night to Hillsboro', & thence down on Thursday morning.

Tell Wm. we sent him 20 bushels seed wheat—very fine quality on monday, freight paid to Charlotte. . . . He should sow his wheat as early as practicable, preparing the ground well. We were greatly relieved by Julia's letter to Robt. saying little Sudie[1] was convalescent. . . . The Synod is in session here, but in the two days I have been in town, I have not been able to see its session, which commenced last night. . . .

There is much talk of sickness among the persons I have met, and several deaths of valuable men, Genl. Stubbs of Martin,[2] Mr. Speed and Mr. Watkins[3] of Granville & others. New buildings are going up on Fayville. & Wilmington streets, and quite a lively appearance of things in Raleigh.

Mr. Turner is in the East attending political meetings. There are great preparations making for the Fair. The Yarborough House under Dr Blacknall[4] is quite an improvement in Hotels.

We shall miss you much at home, & hope your visit will soon be out.

Love to the children & little ones.

Ever Affectionately Yours

[1]Susan Washington Graham (1868-1897) was the daughter of Julia Lane and William A. Graham, Jr. Clark, "Graham Descendants."

[2]This was probably Jesse R. Stubbs, a state senator from Martin County in 1860-1861 and 1864-1865. He also served in the state House of Commons from Beaufort County, 1850-1851, 1852, 1854-1855, and 1856-1857; was a member of the Council of State, 1863-1864; was elected to serve in Congress in 1865; and sat in the Constitutional Convention of 1865-1866. Cheney, *North Carolina Government*, 179, 193n, 318, 321, 322, 324, 327, 330, 691, 832.

[3]Mr. Speed and Mr. Watkins have not been identified.

[4]In 1870 the proprietor of the hotel was George S. Blacknall, who changed the spelling from Yarbrough to Yarborough. Murray, *Wake*, 373.

William A. Graham to William A. Graham, Jr. A&H

Hillsboro',
October 7th., 1870.

. . . .

I returned from Raleigh last night. French Strange[1] came with me, from there, on his way to Georgia, to look out for a home. If George were here, it would be a good opportunity to go with him, and prospect together. He goes on, on Monday.

The Sup'r Court was sitting at Raleigh, trying negroes, as usual. Ransom[2] was there, very busy electioneering for the Senate, thinks his chances good, I am told. Merrimon also spoke to me of it, says if the Legislature is disposed to elect without regard to disabilities, he does not expect to be in, but if those of that class are excluded, his chances are good. He thinks Ransom's idea is to appeal to the democrats as such, and rally the whole of them, and then combine with any party that promises success.

Rob't and James have been to Caswell Court this week. Tourgee turned out in a new character, charged the G'd Jury that Kirk's arrests were all illegal, and indictable, and several Bills of Indictment were found against Kirk, and his officers. Bulla,[3] solicitor, rose in open Court, and declared there was no evidence on which to found an Indictment against Wiley, Roan, etc., bound over by Pearson, and they were discharged.

The negro, Graves, who testified against Roan, was convicted of stealing money, and sent to the Penitentiary for 18 months.

. . . .

Affectionately Yours,

---

[1]French Strange, of Cumberland County, had served in the First and Fifth North Carolina regiments during the Civil War. He was appointed adjutant with the rank of lieutenant and was paroled at Appomattox. Manarin and Jordan, *North Carolina Troops*, II, 382, III, 45, 142.

[2]Matt Whitaker Ransom (1826-1904), of Warren County, graduated from the University of North Carolina in 1847 and, having studied law his senior year, was immediately admitted to the bar. A magnetic public speaker, he enjoyed considerable success as a jury lawyer. He was a Whig in politics originally and gained an excellent reputation as an active elector on the Scott-Graham ticket in 1852. Elected by a Democratic legislature, Ransom served three years as state attorney general. With the disruption of the Whig party in the 1850s, he became a Democrat and represented Northampton County in the House of Commons from 1858 to 1861. He opposed disunion until Lincoln called for troops but soon afterward volunteered as a private in the Confederate army. Almost immediately commissioned lieutenant colonel of the First North Carolina Regiment, he became colonel of the Thirty-fifth and in June, 1863, was promoted to brigadier general, succeeding his brother Robert in command of a brigade of which his old regiment was a part. He fought in numerous battles, including Seven Pines, Malvern Hill, Antietam, Plymouth, Drewry's Bluff, Fort Stedman, and Five Forks, and surrendered his brigade at Appomattox. Although not a trained tactician, he proved to be an effective leader and was beloved by his subordinates.

Ransom took no part in public affairs until 1870, when he became alarmed at Governor Holden's suspension of *habeas corpus*. He persuaded United States District Court judge George W. Brooks to issue the writ. When the federal government upheld Ransom's position, Holden's attempt to overawe the state collapsed. In 1872 Ransom, a Democrat, was elected a United States senator, and he was returned to the Senate until 1895, when a fusion of Populists and Republicans in North Carolina resulted in his defeat. President Grover Cleveland immediately appointed him minister to Mexico, a post he held for two years. Thereafter he retired permanently to private life. *DAB*, XV, 379.

[3]James R. Bulla, a strong Randolph County Unionist and Republican, was the solicitor in Judge Tourgée's judicial district. Hamilton described him as "a very timid man" and "of no assistance to the judge in obtaining evidence." Hamilton, *Reconstruction in North Carolina*, 484; Raper, *Holden*, 192-193.

John McRae[1] *to William A. Graham* UNC

Fayetteville No Car
Oct 8, 1870

Gov Graham

I believe you are one of a Committee appointed by the stock-holders of the North Carolina Rail R Co. to procure the passage of an act to divest the State of the Control of the Road. Such an act ought to be *general* & to include all the Public Works. Where the State is a stockholder the experience of the last few years has demonstrated the evil of State Control. No argument on that point will be necessary. Cannot a *general Bill* or plan be found that will be just to the State, while it will not be ruinous to the companies. Doubtless such an one can be found. Will you not give your mind to it & after such consultation as may be necessary, put it in shape. I have had some correspondence with H. W. Guion & K. P. Battle Eqr & find them fully agreeing to the plan. For our Road, we shall first have to get up a *special bill* to get us possession. Our annual meeting is not till *Apl* next, we want it *now* or it will be *ruined*, & lost to us stockholders, that is if we do not use legal means to prevent. I am a $11,000 stockholder & do not like to lose my money. That *Special Bill* we have already drawn. It merely places us where the *Holden* administration found us. The stock-holders electing 5 Directors & the Bank & the State 4. We thought we would only ask that in the *Special Bill* & rely upon the *general Bill* for the entire control after next annual meeting. I have been the Secy & Treas. of our Road from its organization, until this *Holden dynasty* removed me.

I am thinking of a Bill with something like the following provisions: 1st the State to surrender the management of all the Public Works to the private stockholders.
2nd to Provide some responsibility or guarantee for mismanagement by reason of corruption, negligence, etc.
3rd to Provide for an examination into the affairs of any Company by any commission or agency appointed by the state at any time.
4 The Cos., to report under oath as to all its actions to the state.

Can you not put this or a better plan in Shape & let us all have a Consultation in Raleigh when the Legislature meets & procure its passage at once.

Of our management I can only say, the *world never saw such.* Neither *Prest* or *Directors* (with one exception) were *stockholders,* or residents of this *town* or *County,* had *no interest* in either *Road town* or *County* except what they expected to *plunder* from them, all of which has doubtless been successfully done. We must get clear of them & that *at once.*

Hope you are well, & that advancing years bear lightly on you. I am myself Considerably *frosted* am now 55.

[1]Other than the information given in this letter, John McRae has not been identified.

William A. Graham to George W. Mordecai UNC: MORDECAI

Hillsboro',
October 12th., 1870.

I accept with much pleasure your kind invitation to your house during the Fair.

Having first to attend Person Court, in that week, I shall not arrive earlier than Thursday morning.

With best compliments to the ladies of your household,

Thomas M. Moore[1] *to William A. Graham* UNC

Asheboro',
North Carolina,
October 13th., 1870.

At the request of a portion of the prominent Citizens of Randolph County, I have been authorized to address you, and to solicit you to come among them, and give them your views in a public address, on the various subjects that now occupy and adgitate the public mind. This feeling and partiality for you, and confidence in your counsels, is universal with all classes of our citizens. They desire to hear you on the condition of the country generally, and what are your views in relation to a limited Convention. Without further remark, should this request meet with your approval, you will please designate the time it will suit your convenience to comply, and at what time you will be at High Point, when and where a conveyance will be in attendance to bring you to Asheboro', and convey you back to the Rail Road, at such time as it may be your pleasure to depart.

Very Respectfully,

Should this request meet with your inclination and convenience, we would like to know it at your earliest opportunity, so as to make your comeing among us generally known through the County, and that all our people may have an opportunity to hear you.

[1]Thomas M. Moore, evidently a Conservative, was a retired Asheboro merchant. Charlesanna Fox, Carolyn Neely Hager, and Dwight M. Holland (eds.), *Randolph County, 1779-1979* (Winston-Salem: Hunter Publishing Company, 1980), 47.

William A. Graham to William A. Graham, Jr. A&H

Hillsboro',
October 22nd., 1870.

Your Mother reached home on Tuesday morning. John, Rob't & I went to Person Court on Monday morning, & returned Wednesday night, and went next morning to the Fair at Raleigh, where I delivered my address,[1] as you will see from the papers, on Friday. Mr. C. Phillips made his on Thursday,[2] just after my arrival on the Fair ground. The attendance was large—especially of young people, not many prosperous Farmers. Many Horses, but too much prominence given to racing in sulkies—a good deal of poultry, cattle & hogs not much, and the sheep so inferior, that no premium was allowed on that stock. I will send you a copy of my address, when printed. Laws[3] tells me the Standard praises it—a somewhat bad sign.

I have a letter from Charlotte, requesting that I shall speak at the Mecklenburg Fair, 1st. Dec'r, but shall not be able to comply.

. . . .

The death of Judge Gilliam,[4] I very deeply regret. He was one of my truest and best friends. Jos. J. Davis[5] ought to be his successor in Congress, and I hope will be, unless the men who have disabilities removed make the test on that, exclude him.

George & Rob't came from Raleigh this afternoon—I have been so much from home, that I have made no disposition yet of the Estes place for next year—

[torn]

---

[1]Graham's address on Thomas Ruffin, delivered on October 21, 1870, was printed in various newspapers at the time and in a large pamphlet edition later. It can be found in J. G. de Roulhac Hamilton (ed.), *The Papers of Thomas Ruffin* (Raleigh: North Carolina Historical Commission, 4 volumes, 1918-1920), I, 18-35, hereinafter cited as Hamilton, *Ruffin Papers*.

[2]The address of Charles Phillips was delivered before the North Carolina Agricultural Society on October 20, 1870. It contained a tribute to David L. Swain, and its general subject was the necessary relationship between the arm and the brain.

[3]George Laws.

[4]Robert B. Gilliam.

[5]Joseph Jonathan Davis (1828-1892), of Franklin County, attended Wake Forest and William and Mary colleges and graduated from the University of North Carolina in 1850, having studied law under Judge William Horn Battle. He practiced law in Oxford before settling permanently at Louisburg. During the Civil War Davis was a captain in the Forty-seventh North Carolina Regiment. Captured at Gettysburg, he was imprisoned at Fort Delaware and Johnson's Island. At the latter place he established a law school among the prisoners so their time might pass profitably. He was a state legislator, 1868-1870; a Democratic congressman, 1875-1881; and a respected associate justice of the North Carolina Supreme Court, 1887-1892. *Biographical Directory of Congress*, 786; *Cyclopedia of American Biography*, VII, 484-485; Grant, *Alumni History*, 155.

Martha Phoebe Ruffin[1] *to William A. Graham* UNC

At home
[Oct. 23, 1870]

My dear Gov. Graham!

At Mama's wish, I write to express her grateful acknowledgements for the beautiful tribute you paid to my dear Father's memory in your address of last Friday, and to ask if you are quite willing to part with it, that you would send her the manuscript copy of the address, after it is returned to you from the publisher's hands. It will be valued and preserved by us. Of all my Father's friends, I think Mama would have preferred that this act of friendship should have come from you, for you knew and understood him well. And you were a friend that he valued and cherished, as long as his life lasted.

In remembrance of that friendship, I am sure you will allow me to say, that I shall ever look up to you with the most respectful and affectionate feelings.

Mama desires her best wishes and kindest regards.

---

[1]Martha Phoebe (Patty) Ruffin (1831-1896) was the seventh daughter and twelfth child of Thomas and Anne Kirkland Ruffin of Hillsborough. She never married. Ashe, *Biographical History*, XVI, 216.

William H. Battle to William A. Graham UNC

Raleigh,
October 24th., 1870.

I am sorry that I omitted, while you were in Raleigh last week, to enquire when you could furnish me with your first argument in the *habeas corpus* cases. I am very desirous to commence the printing of my pamphlet, the first of next week, and I shall be very much obliged to you to send the argument by that time.

I have been much gratified to learn that your Memoir of C. J. Ruffin has met with a very favorable reception. I knew that the Profession would be pleased with it, and I have heard many others express their approbation of it.

Kemp P. Battle to William A. Graham UNC

Office of North Carolina Agricultural Society.

Raleigh, N.C.,
October 29th., 1870.

This Society has passed a resolution of thanks for your most interesting, valuable address *in memoriam* of the late Judge Ruffin, and instructs me to request a copy for publication.

I sincerely hope you will comply with this request.

William H. Battle to William A. Graham UNC

Raleigh,
October 31st., 1870.

Yours of the 29th. is before me. I deem your argument as of so much importance to my proposed publication,[1] that I do not know that I shall commence the work unless I can get it. Please let me know when you can furnish it.

I have not yet received Judge Brook's opinion, though I hope I shall hear from him in two or three days. Both he and Judge Bond have promised to furnish me their opinions. I look upon both as essential to the publication, and hope I shall get them in time to get the pamphlets out by the meeting of the General Assembly.

I am sorry to say that our friend Mr. Mordecai continues very ill. Though the Doctors say that there is no immediate danger of his death, yet I cannot help fearing that the disease, attended as it is with frequent very great pain, will eventually break down his vital powers, and terminate fatally. His death would be a greater loss to this community than that of almost any other man.

[1]This refers to the publication of William Horn Battle's *A Report of the Proceedings in the Habeas Corpus Cases on the Petitions of Adolphus G. Moore, and Others, and of John Kerr and Others, before the Chief Justice of the Supreme Court* ([Raleigh]: Nichols and Gorman, Printers, 1870). A copy of this pamphlet can be found in the North Carolina Collection, University of North Carolina Library, Chapel Hill.

William H. Battle to William A. Graham UNC

Raleigh,
Nov. 8th, 1870.

I hope you will not consider that I trouble you too much about the same matter. I have received a copy of Judge Brook's opinion in the habeas *corpus cases,* which insures the publication of my pamphlet, and I shall commence the printing as soon as I can learn that I can get your argument before Judge Pearson in a few days. As soon as it is ready, please send it by Express at my expense.

Judge Brook's opinion is given upon the motion made to him to attach Kirk for a contempt in not having produced the body of A. G. Moore[1] before him at Salisbury; but in it he discusses the question of his jurisdiction to issue the writ of *habeas corpus* on Moore's petition. If you can prepare the argument you made before Judge Brooks on the motion for the attachment in the course of the next two weeks, I shall be very much obliged to you for it.

I have written another letter to Judge Bond, and hope to get his opinion in Bergen's case in time to insert it in my pamphlet.

[1]Adolphus G. Moore had been arrested at Graham on July 15. On November 22, Moore

presented a memorial to the General Assembly, which had convened on November 21, asking for the impeachment of Governor Holden and Chief Justice Pearson. Hamilton, *Reconstruction in North Carolina*, 507, 512, 540, 545.

William C. Smith[1] *to William A. Graham* UNC

Hillsboro',
November 14th., 1870.

Hon. & Dear Sir,

I have desired for some time past to have an interview with you on the subject of personal religion, but I have been at a loss to know how to intimate such a thing, or in any way to broach the subject, but I feel, venerable and dear Sir, that you will not repel me, or deem me presumptuous for penning these few lines, which I feel moved to address you this evening.

As we walked together yesterday afternoon, my heart burned within me, and I longed to say something, but I knew not what to say.

As I mentioned that I had been called on since my residence in Hillsboro' to conduct nine funeral services, I felt like asking with tenderest and most earnest solicitude, if you felt prepared, Governor, for that change which it is appointed unto us once to undergo, and the judgment which is after, and which awaits us all. Will you now allow me to ask the question which I then failed to ask, and entreat your most earnest consideration of the same.

If it meets with your pleasure, and is consistent with your pressing and imperative duties, it will be gratifying to me to receive some expression of your views, and feelings, in any way you may deem best to communicate them.

I am, dear Governor, with sincerest regards, most truly, and the desire of being yours most *faithfully*, has prompted this note, with the prayer that He, who has all power in heaven and in earth will bless it to your eternal good and our mutual joy.

---

[1]William Cuttino Smith (1837-1932), a native of South Carolina, was pastor of the Hillsborough Presbyterian Church, 1869-1872. He attended the University of Virginia, 1857-1860, and was a chaplain in the Confederate army. Pauline O. Lloyd and Allen A. Lloyd, *History of the Churches of Hillsborough, N.C.* (N.p., [1962]), 127, 130.

William A. Graham to William A. Graham, Jr. A&H

Hillsboro'
Nov 18th 1870

I regret to inform you, that Augustus, having been out shooting partridges all day on yesterday: just before sunset, while loading a barrel of his gun, the other being loaded discharged from some cause, while his hand was on the muzzle, and the shot cut of [*sic*] the end of his little finger, and the nails of three fingers of the right hand, besides wounding severely the thumb. He got home after dark in this condition suffering great pain & the wounds bleeding freely. Dr. Strudwick[1] & George dressed the wounds, but they bled considerably, and the pain continued through the night in spite of opiates. He slept but little, 2 or 3 hours, and the pain is still severe in the small finger. It cannot yet be determined whether the hand will be permanently disabled. The little finger probably down to the first joint will probably be lost. He seems better this afternoon, but the pain is yet severe. . . . George was to have set off for Atlanta tonight, but in consequence of this accident, will remain till Monday night. His instruments were locked up, & his mother had the keys, last night, but he showed great readiness in dealing with Aug's wounds.

John & Rebecca are well. He will go to the Legislature on Monday; and Rebecca will go with him. Maj. G. Collins[2] has gone to Missipi.

I have succeeded in getting judgments at Columbia against the Chas. & S.C. R. Co. They have paid the interest on the bonds sued on, till 15th inst. and are to pay the principal 1st Feb.

George met Sissy at the Weldon Fair, and they brought home with them, young Mr & Miss Hobson of Davie, who stayed till she went to Morganton.

I have cribbed my corn in the shock and am sowing wheat, interrupted by hauling wood. Your mother & Aunt think well of James' place & that he is succeeding well in business. If a new election is ordered, he will be urged to go to the Legislature, but I hope he will refuse. Mr. Hill[3] hears today, that Joseph's children have measles. Mrs. Hill there, and improving. Robt. has gone this week to Chatham Court, over insurance business & not returned.

Jo. Holden[4] spoke here yesterday to a small company of negroes & whites. Manning[5] has not been out, and the people know, but little of him. If he can bring out the people, I think, he can be elected.

Our love to Julia & the children. I wished Augus. to go to the Catawba & have the Pork butchered, etc, the first of next month, but I fear, he will not [be] recovered sufficiently.

Affectionately Yours

---

[1]Edmund Charles Fox Strudwick (1802-1879), of Hillsborough, began his medical studies under the eminent townsman Dr. James Webb, received his M.D. from the University of Pennsylvania in 1824, and, after two years of service to a Philadelphia almshouse, established his practice in Hillsborough. He was a general practitioner and also a talented surgeon. Strudwick was a concerned citizen, active in public affairs, and a Whig. He opposed secession until 1860, when a trip to Alabama convinced him that North Carolina must inevitably join the lower South. On April 14, 1861, he presided over the first war meeting held in Hillsborough. His ardent support of the Confederacy resulted in financial ruin. Refusing to take advantage of bankruptcy proceedings, Strudwick surrendered all to his creditors and took up residence in a two-room cottage. He was the first president of the North Carolina Medical Society. *DAB*, XVIII, 158.

[2]George Pumpelly Collins (1835-1903), a son of Josiah Collins III of Somerset Place, Washington County, served as quartermaster of General James Johnston Pettigrew's brigade during the Civil War. He married Anne Ruffin Cameron, daughter of Paul C. Cameron, and after the war went to Mississippi to manage one of the Cameron plantations. Collins later returned to North Carolina and lived near Hillsborough. Jerry L. Cross, "The Collins Family: Brief Sketches of Four Members" (unpublished report, Research Branch, Division of Archives and History, Raleigh, 1987), 4-5, 7-8; Clark, *Histories of the North Carolina Regiments*, II, 407, IV, 556.

[3]Thomas Blount Hill was Joseph Graham's father-in-law. Clark, "Graham Descendants."

[4]Joseph William Holden.

[5]John Manning, Jr. (1830-1899), a native of Edenton and later a resident of Chatham County, received an A.B. degree from the university in 1850 and A.M. and LL.D. degrees in 1883. He achieved the rank of captain in the Thirteenth North Carolina Regiment during the war. He was a member of the state House, 1871-1873. From 1881 until 1889 he was a professor of law at the University of North Carolina. Grant, *Alumni History*, 412.

James M. Leach[1] *to William A. Graham* UNC

Lexington,
November 20th., 1870.

. . . .

I reached home this morning (Sunday) from Forsyth, & among many letters, I find yours of the 16th., to which I hasten to make reply.

I intended, as I intimated, to have written a Communication to the Sentinel, urging your nomination, but Communications poured in so thick and fast, & controversies between the claims of the *banned* & *unbanned*, having waxed pretty warm, I determined to say nothing through the Sentinel, as I thought it would be more likely to *defeat* than promote, my object, as the *weight*, or rather *number*, of the squibs suggesting almost every body's name, seemed to favor some one who labors under *no disabilities*.

I have therefore written to some members, & saw others, urging them to discriminate in *favor of*, & not against, the *banned*, on the ground that for Congress to refuse to remove disabilities of a Senator elect would go far to secure the election of the Conservative and Democratic candidate for the next Presidency, & the election in Missouri, West Virginia, etc., *proves this*. Such men as the 2 Robbins,[2] who I fear will not support you, for I have urged them to do so without full success, & Jno. A. Gilmer & Turner Morehead[3] & 'Esquire' Spencer Adams,[4] from Stokes & Dr. Worth,[5] will all include the Robbins, oppose making this a test, but will go for leaving this an open question, & not allowing it to affect the claims of any gentleman, one way or the other. So I think you are mistaken in supposing this difficulty will be in the way.

The main force and moral power of the election in Mo. & W. Va. mean that *men* shall not be longer banned in the South, that universal amnesty, the removal of all disabilities, & an end of re-construction, & an intermeddling Executive, whether by letter, telegrams, proscription in office, or the Military, whether in *South* or in N. York, *has been* and *will be rebuked*, & the only hope of Republicanism is in pursuing a generous, manly course to the South.

This being out of the way, I think the Contest is between yourself and Vance. Vance said, only a few days ago, (I have it but second hand) that Merrimon and Ransom were "nowhere in the race," that *you* would be elected, that he wanted it greatly, but you would beat all, tho' saying this I am quite sure he thinks he will succeed, & I know he is working for it.

Confidentially, as you know, he got up the Lee demonstration,[6] & fixed the time—next Wednesday to make headway for himself on the next

Tuesday, rousing & exciting, as well as directing and concentrating members on himself by his great praises of Gen. Lee. I told him at Raleigh I was for you against all the world—& himself next, but that you were entitled, & could do the State much & great good, & that as a *true* & *loving* North Carolinian influenced me above all other things, etc.

John Gilmer is for you as strong as myself, & I think Dr. Worth—Adams—Morehead—Ham Jones[7] *on fence* (a little out with Vance) though afraid possibly, to oppose him. You ought to go right down and see *Gilmer*, Worth, Morehead, etc. I *know* how Gilmer is, & first *secure* certainly a *majority* (as I think will be anyway) against dropping banned gentlemen, & then through safe & true friends, let them go to work to urge *you*, thus electing a man that all the other rivals will be satisfied with, who in age & experience, talents & influence, stands out, and above them all, & this will best satisfy them & put an end to heart burnings & personal rivalries.

Both the Robbins pledge me they will oppose making this test, but leave the field open & if [MackR.][8] makes a speech for *this*, as he promises faithfully he will, he has much influence, & it will carry. Gilmer will do the same, & Worth *must* be got to do it. He has a great deal of hard sense, and a word from him would tell.

He, after a long talk with me, was with me, for you first & Vance next, I think if Vance was out of the way you would win in the second or 3rd. ballot, even if no nomination were made, & in a Caucus, as Vance & Merrimon will be to some extent rivals, I think you will get a plurality at first, or very soon. Vance talked freely with me at Fair, & I told him I should go for you, but did not propose to be active; he seemed to hate it a little, but did not complain, & of course said no word prejudicial to you as a man, or to the propriety of running you—only that *he* wanted it. Of course you will never speak of this, to him or any one, though the conversation was not confidential, but I should regret for him to know I had been a little more active than perhaps he thought I *would be*. Serious[ly] we are living under a new regime, & dynasty, & all of us partake perhaps to much of the manners of the times, by electioneering, etc., but I think you should go and be in communication with friends, go anyway by Wednesday & stay the week out, if you are not there on day of election. I think you should go to-morrow night, as about Thursday night, I reckon, or Friday night, the Caucus will be held for Tuesday.

Wishing and hoping you may be brought forward & elected, & am as ever.

Truly your friend,

Excuse haste, as I have many letters to answer & other things to do, & to leave home at 10 tonight.

P.S. I would think that Senator Waddell[9] of Johnson, out of old friendship, locality, & associations, would go for you.

---

[1]James Madison Leach (1815-1891), a native of Randolph County, graduated from West Point in 1838 but soon abandoned the army for a career as lawyer and politician. He settled in Lexington about 1842 and began a legal practice there. He was a member of the House

of Commons, 1848-1858; American party elector, 1856; state senator in the 1865, 1866, and 1879 sessions, where he promoted education and internal improvements; Whig party member of the United States House of Representatives, 1859-1861, and Democratic member, 1871-1875; lieutenant colonel of the Twenty-first North Carolina Regiment; and a peace delegate in the Confederate Congress, 1864-1865. Leach was a Conservative in the era of Reconstruction. *Biographical Directory of Congress*, 1202; Cheney, *North Carolina Government*, 317, 318, 321, 323, 324, 332, 334, 458; Hamilton, *Reconstruction in North Carolina*, 492n, 587n.

[2]William McKendree Robbins has been identified earlier in this volume. Franklin Childs Robbins, senator from Davidson County, was a lawyer who was attorney for the railway company Winston-Salem Southbound. During the Civil War he attained the rank of captain in the Forty-eighth Infantry Regiment. He was a delegate to the Constitutional Convention of 1875 and was a state senator, 1870-1872. President of the Female Seminary, Robbins was honored by having a local school named for him. M. Jewell Sink and Mary Green Matthews, *Pathfinders Past and Present: A History of Davidson County, North Carolina* (High Point: Hall Printing Company, 1972), 65, 89, 96, 179, 184, 190, 319, 401, 407, 421.

[3]James Turner Morehead, Jr. (1835-1919), of Greensboro, was a graduate of the university and a lawyer. He was a colonel in the Forty-third North Carolina Regiment during the war and after the war was a member of the state legislature in 1866, 1872, 1874, and 1883. His father, James Turner, Sr. (1799-1875), had been a member of the state Senate from 1835 to 1844 and of the United States House of Representatives, 1851-1853. Spencer Alumni Project; Clark, *Histories of the North Carolina Regiments*, III, 36; *Biographical Directory of Congress*, 1354.

[4]No Spencer Adams could be identified. Sterling Adams was a member of the legislature from Stokes County.

[5]John Milton Worth (1811-1900) was a son of David and Eunice Gardner Worth. He studied medicine at the Medical College, Lexington, Kentucky, but became interested in gold mining and farming, as well. His wife was Sarah Dicks; the couple settled in Montgomery County and later moved to Randolph. Worth was a Clay Whig and avidly interested in politics, although he was not a talented orator. In 1842 he was elected state senator from Moore and Montgomery counties and was reelected in 1844 and 1848. In 1870 he was again elected senator, from Randolph and Moore counties. He served as state treasurer, 1876-1884, and was president of the Bank of Randolph as well as owner of Worth Manufacturing Company. Ashe, *Biographical History*, III, 454-460; Cheney, *North Carolina Government*, 425, 435n.

[6]The death of Robert E. Lee on October 12, 1870, touched southerners deeply and occasioned memorials across the states of the old Confederacy. The *Daily Sentinel* (Raleigh) of October 19, 1870, reported that Zeb Vance had memorialized Lee in a "most touching and powerful speech" at an October 14 meeting of the stockholders of the Western North Carolina Railroad in Morganton. The former governor was also instrumental as an organizer of and participant in an official memorial to Lee that took place in Raleigh on November 23. On November 25 the *Sentinel* noted that Vance spoke for an hour on that occasion. Comments in this letter suggest that some of his contemporaries considered his actions and words politically self-serving.

[7]Hamilton Chamberlain Jones, Jr. (1837-1904), was a native of Rowan County and a graduate of the University of North Carolina. During the Civil War he served in the Fifth and Fifty-seventh North Carolina regiments, reaching the rank of colonel. He practiced law in Charlotte and edited the *Charlotte News* for a time. Jones sat in the state Senate from 1869 to 1872 and was United States district attorney, 1885-1889. He was an active Democrat in Mecklenburg County. Powell, *DNCB*, III, 319.

[8]This probably refers to Duncan Granger MacRae (1808-1895) of Fayetteville, son of Duncan and Rhoda Young MacRae. A Wilmington steamboat agent for his father's company and president of the Fayetteville and Western Railroad Company, he served as a justice of the peace and as clerk of the Cumberland County court. When, as a civil court judge while Sherman's troops held Fayetteville, MacRae rendered a decision that displeased Federal military authorities, he was arrested and held at Fort Macon for several months as

a prisoner of war. Lawrence MacRae (comp.), *Descendants of Duncan and Ann (Cameron) MacRae of Scotland and North Carolina* (N.p., n.d.).

[9]Leigh Richmond Waddell (1831-1892), of Smithfield, was a native of Chatham County and a graduate of the University of North Carolina. Among public offices he held were those of superior court clerk and state senator, 1870-1872, 1874-1875, 1876-1877, and 1879-1880. Cheney, *North Carolina Government*, 451, 455, 457, 458; Grant, *Alumni History*, 639.

William H. Battle to William A. Graham UNC

Raleigh,
November 22nd., 1870.

I regret very much your inability to furnish me this week with a copy of your argument in the *habeas corpus* cases before C. J. Pearson, & I regret still more one of the causes which has produced the result. I have a high regard for all your sons, and am very much pained to learn that one of them has received so serious an injury. I hope the wound may not prove so bad as you fear, and that he may soon recover from the effects of it.

If you can still furnish me with a brief of your argument by Tuesday of next week, I can wait for it. I shall probably place in the hands of the printer on Friday next, matter which will make one, or perhaps two forms of sixteen pages each, and which will not be struck off before the time I mention.

Unless I hear from you again, I shall act upon the supposition that you will either bring, or send me your brief by Tuesday of next week.

Gov. Vance and Gen'l Ransom are both in the City, and it is understood that they and Judge Merrimon are canvassing for the seat in the Senate of the United States.

John W. Graham to William A. Graham UNC

Raleigh, N.C.,
November 24th., 1870.

My Dear Father,

I write a short note to inform you of the progress of events here.[1] We had a joint caucus of both Houses last night on the Senatorial Question. Resolutions were introduced to limit the selection to men not banned and a substitute to open the whole field. Both were discussed at some length, but no final action was taken. The majority, I think, is very decidedly against limiting, and several expressed themselves as under no obligation to regard any such action. There was a very bold attempt, in the interest of Vance, to force the selection last night, but the resolution to take a ballot was laid on the table by a decided vote. Jones of Caldwell[2] was put forward by Waring[3] to make the motion, which he did in a very injudicious and insulting speech, charging corrupt combination, which he was compelled to retract. Jones of Mecklenburg[4] made a speech for Vance, though he is a very warm friend of yours, and thinks you are the choice of the people, but thinks he ought to act in deference to his immediate Constituents. Dr. Worth is working hard for you, and is very sanguine.

Dr. Speed[5] made a speech, urging that we select no one banned. He asked me afterwards if you would consent to be a Candidate, and said he had understood that you had advised that no one who was banned should be selected. Upon my telling him that he was mistaken, he said if the selection was not limited, he should nominate you. I told him that Dr. Worth had written to you on the subject, and could also give him your views. Dr. S. asked me if I would not write to you asking you to come down. I told him you would be down on Monday, and I did not think would like to come before, merely to electioneer. He said he thought that you ought to be selected, if there was any hope of your admission. I think it might [be] as well for you to write to him, or to me, that I might show it to him. I think there are a good many like Dr. S., and if they vote their choice, will go for you. I believe this to be Cowles[6] position, though I do not know positively. I judge Ransom's and Warren's[7] friends are urging proscription. Merrimon, I do not think, is, as he expresses himself to me as very favorable to you. McAfee[8] came out for Vance. I think all the Candidates and their friends are anxious for you, in case they, themselves, should fail, and the feeling toward each other among the *small fry*, is so bitter, that they cannot effect combinations. This is Fred Strudwick's opinion, and he thinks there is no doubt of your selection, unless proscription is made the rule. I think he is working judiciously. Vance made a very good speech on Gen'l Lee, and the effort was to force him through, under the Confederate zeal. I think he will be weaker every day, and if the election can be postponed until Monday night, you will be safe.

Welch[9] is very bitter on the subject of Western Grievances, since Jarvis beat him for Speaker.

P.S. I shall not be up on Friday night, as I think it more important to vote here than for Manning.

---

[1]William A. Graham was apparently a receptive candidate for election to the United States Senate at this time.

[2]Edmund Jones (1848-1920) of Caldwell County was a member of the state House in the sessions of 1870-1872, 1879-1880, and 1893. Educated at the University of North Carolina and the University of Virginia, he served in the Confederate army. In 1881 he opened a law practice at Lenoir. Jones served as chief of the Customs Division, United States Treasury Department, from 1885 until 1889. He was a captain of infantry during the Spanish-American War. Powell, *DNCB*, III, 316-317.

[3]Robert P. Waring.

[4]Hamilton C. Jones.

[5]Rufus K. Speed of Chowan County was a member of the state Senate at this time. Cheney, *North Carolina Government*, 450.

[6]Andrew C. Cowles of Yadkin County was a member of the state Senate at this time. Cheney, *North Carolina Government*, 451.

[7]Edward Jenner Warren (1826-1876), a native of Vermont and a graduate of Dartmouth College, settled in Washington, North Carolina, in 1846, where he taught school and studied law. Admitted to the bar in 1848, he soon established a successful practice in competition with a distinguished group of attorneys including David M. Carter (later his

partner), Thomas Sparrow, Fenner Bryan Satterthwaite, and Richard Spaight Donnell. In his youth Warren had been influenced by Daniel Webster and turned naturally to the Whig party. A Union Whig, he opposed secession while a delegate to the convention of 1861. As a state senator from Beaufort County, 1862-1865, he sought consistently to point up the importance of eastern North Carolina and sought state and Confederate action to rid the area of northerners. An intimate of Graham and Vance, Warren was a member of Governor Vance's council and spokesman for the administration in the legislature. He was a delegate to the Constitutional Convention of 1865. After the war he considered himself a Conservative and was reluctant to affiliate with either the Democratic or Republican factions. He was again in the state Senate in 1870, when he voted to impeach Holden. He died on December 10, 1876, after supporting Vance for the United States Senate. Lindsay C. Warren, *Beaufort County's Contribution to a Notable Era of North Carolina History* (Washington, D.C.: Government Printing Office, 1930), 1-32 passim, hereinafter cited as Warren, *Beaufort County's Contribution.*

[8]Lee M. McAfee, of Cleveland County, had served ably as colonel of the Forty-ninth North Carolina Regiment during the Civil War. After the war he was an active member of the Ku Klux Klan in the western part of the state. In 1870 he was serving as a representative in the legislature. Grant, *Alumni History*, 381.

[9]William Pinckney Welch (1838-1896), scion of two pioneer Haywood County families, was educated privately in Asheville and was enrolled in Emory and Henry College when the Civil War began. He returned home and volunteered for service in the Twenty-fifth North Carolina Regiment. As first lieutenant of Company C, he was assigned to duty in eastern North Carolina before the regiment was sent to Virginia to join the Army of Northern Virginia. He fought in a number of battles with considerable gallantry. Late in 1864 he transferred to the engineer corps, where he rose to captain. He was wounded in the defense of Petersburg. After the war he read law and became a very successful Waynesville attorney. A Democrat in politics, he served in three state legislatures, including the 1870-1872 session, when he took an "active and aggressive" part in Holden's impeachment. In 1876 Welch moved to Georgia, where he became associated with the Georgia Manufacturing Company. He remained there until his death and is buried in Athens. W. C. Allen, *The Annals of Haywood County, North Carolina* (Waynesville: The author, 1935; Spartanburg, S.C.: Reprint Company, 1982), 133-136, hereinafter cited as Allen, *Annals of Haywood County.*

Thomas P. Atkinson to William A. Graham UNC

Danville, Va.,
November 30th., 1870.

I write to introduce my son in law, Col. B. M. Jones,[1] a Civil Engineer of much experience and of high reputation in our State, who is now the Chief Engineer, as he is the originator of the Norfolk and Great Western Rail Road, as well as the first to suggest the building of the Richmond and Danville Rail Road, of which last named improvement, he was, during the whole time of its construction, the Principal Assistant Engineer.

He has some original views on the subject of the proper inducements to persons living on the line of any proposed Rail Road, to take stock in the same, which I know are highly approved by judicious individuals in different portions of the South. These, I understand, he desires to communicate to you. I ask that you will give them a consideration, and that you will give him a hearing on a proposition of a direct communication, by Rail Road, between Hillsboro' and Richmond.

I congratulate you, most heartily, on the favorable turn which political matters have recently taken in your misgoverned State; and I hope that the majesty of the Law may be triumphantly vindicated by the awarding of an adequate punishment to those who have so ruthlessly trampled it under their feet.

It may interest you to know that the notorious *Bergen* was arrested in this place, this afternoon, and is now before the Mayor of the Town for examination.

[1]Jones has not been further identified.

B. M. Jones to William A. Graham UNC

Norfolk and Great Western Railroad Co.

Danville, Virginia,
December 1st., 1870.

With the accompanying letters of introduction, I take the liberty of troubling you with a subject in which I hope you may feel some interest.

My conversation with Dr. Roan was principally in regard to a road through Caswell, for which he wishes to procure a charter, and about which he wished to confer with me. I advised him to apply for a charter, from some point on the State line, by Yanceyville, to such point on the North Carolina road as may be deemed most advisable, not specyfying it in the charter, and told him that I thought that Hillsboro' should be the point. I informed him that I had suggested to Mr. Evans[1] the expediency of applying for a charter from Egypt, by Hillsboro', to the State line, not naming the point. My suggestion to Mr. Evans contemplated allowing the friends of a road from Hillsboro', to connect with the Virginia roads, the widest range. I understood from Mr. Evans that there was some anxiety on the part of your people for a rail road to Virginia; and told him that I would write to, and advise with him. I inferred that the wish was to connect with the R. & Danville road. Even if that is the wish, I am sorry to say that I think you could make much better terms with that Co. by not placing yourselves in its power. If the object was to reach Richmond, by means of the R. & D. road, the connection ought, in view of the interest of your people, to be at South Boston; but the R. & D. road would not be willing to lend much aid to a branch that would give about as short a line, from Richmond to Greensboro', as it now has by its own line.

A short time before seeing Mr. Evans I had occasion to look into the subject of rail road communication between Clarksville, Va., and Richmond; and I have advised some of my friends, who are deeply interested in that subject, to aim for an independent line from Clarksville, by Blacks & Whites, (on the South Side) to Richmond, rather than to try to get the connection with the R. & D. road at Keysville, and in examining into the subject, I had decided that the independent line, by Clarksville to the State line, to connect with a line from that point to Hillsboro forming a connection with the N.C. road. (This plan I have not as yet informed Mr. Evans of, but intend doing so. I am ascertaining whether the prospects in favour of the Virginia part of the line are sufficiently encouraging to satisfy me that it can be built, and shall know in a short time whether it will be advisable to try it. I think that it will be.)

My reasons for making Hillsboro' the point are as follows. Such a line would open up a new trade to Richmond, and consequently, be highly advantageous to the Virginia part of the line. It would also afford as short a line from Richmond to Greensboro', (via Clarksville, Hillsboro', and the North Carolina road) as there is at present via the R. & D., and the Piedmont roads. Such a line would enable the North Carolina road to retain the trade and travel between Charlotte and Richmond upon its road, all the way to Hillsboro', instead of parting with it at Greensboro', which, counted both ways, would probably be worth $75,000 or $100,000 per annum to the North Carolina road; and if the new independent line should adopt the gage of the North Carolina road, it would be still more in its favour. In that view of the case it occurs to me that the North Carolina road could afford to lend some aid to the line from Hillsboro' to the State line, by endorsing bonds.

I would have you to bear in mind that my advice in regard to having the point on the State line not specified, would give you the option of connecting with the R. & D., the N. & G. W., or this proposed line from Richmond to the Roanoke. The line suggested by me should pass through a part of a Person & a part of Granville, and the Co. should have the right, when it deemed it advisable to do so, to make branches to Oxford and to Roxboro'. The line from Egypt, by Pittsboro', & Chapel Hill, would be of great advantage to your plan, enabling you to procure Coal on most favourable terms; bring you a good local trade, and affording your farmers a very direct communication with Wilmington; and they could select between the Market of Wilmington, & Richmond. The direct line to Richmond would afford a material saving in the freights on Wheat & other Produce, and on the travel to the North.

The Counties of Chatham, Orange, Granville, & Person, would be greatly benefited by the proposed line, in the saving on freights, in the enhanced value of the lands, and in the increase in population which would follow upon having speedy and cheap transportation to market.

I have very little doubt of my being able to get up this proposed line, if it should meet the approval of you gentlemen in and around Hillsboro'; and the active cooperation of, and *material aid from, the N. C. road.*

I flatter myself that I could lay before you a plan which would convince you of the practicability of carrying out my views in regard to this road, but that plan applies to other roads as well, and is a policy which I am not prepared as yet to make public, and will only say at this time it meets the cordial approval of some of the most intelligent gentlemen of my acquaintance, one of them—a prominent rail road man—saying, that "it has all the elements of success."

I will say that the plan referred to not only applies to proposed lines, but will have a very great effect on the *value of the stock of existing lines*, and with discreet and energetic management, would open up an abundant field for perfectly legitimate and safe speculation in rail road stocks, and will result in placing the control of the great and rapidly increasing rail road interest in the only safe hands, for such an immense plan, that of the farmers and tax payers along the respective lines.

If entirely agreeable to you to do so, I will request that you will give me your views on the plan now submited for your consideration, and especially as to whether the North Carolina road will probably take any interest in this enterprise. If your opinion should be favourable, a charter should be applied for without delay, and I think that I might be able to make some suggestions that would be of service before the charter is presented to the Legislature.

I think it desirable, for the present, that the intention of aiming at an entirely new connection with Richmond should not be made public, and it is particularly important that my instrumentality in the premises should not be known as yet, and I must therefore request that you will consider this as confidential.

It is important that I shall hear from you at your earliest convenience.

---

[1]It has not been determined whether Jones was alluding to C. N. B. Evans or T. C. Evans, both of whom edited the *Milton Chronicle* and the *Hillsborough Recorder*.

Barnas Sears to William A. Graham UNC

Staunton, Va.
Dec. 2. 1870.

My dear Sir,

By an oversight I omitted to recommend $500 for Hillsboro' at the proper time, but since receiving your letter I have forwarded it to the Committee. I regret that the payment will be delayed until the 1st of Jan., as Mr. Wetmore will not make another deposit till that time.

My regards to your wife and family.

William A. Graham to William A. Graham, Jr. A&H

Hillsboro'
Dec. 10th 1870

Yours of the 7th is received on my return from Raleigh last night, where the Fall Court is sitting. I think you may venture to take $1,000. stock in the proposed Railroad, to be paid as you suggest, whether it runs by the one route, to wit plank road or by Keevers and Lowe place. I will raise the money as it may be required. It wont do to have a narrow guage, unless it runs all the way to Charlotte, as that would involve reloading at the junction with Lincoln road, at the river. Mr. Smith[1] for the interest in his Iron works, might afford a larger subscription. I suppose, it would by either route, run, within a mile & half of the furnace.

I received this morning from Hand a letter & by the cars over 2500 lbs of pork after leaving one hog for Joseph. There are some 4 or 5 more to kill, not yet in good order. Hand wrote me, some week or two ago, saying he did not wish to remain at the plantation next year. I must therefore look out for some one else. He has no skills, but has kept me informed of the state of things at the place, and obeyed orders pretty well. If you can recommend any one, I will be glad to be informed. Robt. has engaged a man in Caswell & has gone now to hurry him off; I do not contemplate raising Tobacco. I have paid off Ruffin for James' house, and must devote this crop of Cotton to reducing at least the Rankin debt—and am inclined to sell as it may be ready for market. I go next week to Alamance Court, & thence back to the Fall Court by Thursday, when I expect to try Olcott's case. I hope . . . immediately after Christmas to arrange plantation affairs.

I saw not much of the Legislature, when in Raleigh—was told that a resolution to impeach Holden was introduced yesterday,[2] and referred to a Committee; some Conservatives in Caucus refusing to sustain it, but, I suppose, they calculate on a majority. Rebecca is with John at Mr. Mordecai's—he, Mr. M,—is in very poor health, and I fear, will never be well again. I am afraid there is not much practical talent in the Legislature, and that the State will be disappointed in its action.

Lizzie came down to the wedding of Miss Curtis, and will return to Graham on Monday. James is quite busy, she says, in preparing for court, and did not come. He is much pressed to be a candidate for the Legislature at the election of the 24th; but I advised him against it. If elected, as I presume he could be, it would greatly interfere with his business & business prospects. George has written twice from Atlanta, but has seen too little of the town to know much of it. Augus. hand improves slowly. He goes about walking & occasionally riding, but his fingers dont heal a great deal.

I have finished sowing wheat—some 16 or 18 bushels, expect to sell the Pork today, butcher the remaining steer next week; and get the turnips taken up and put under lock next week also, and then haul the winter wood. There is now a passable way on the Academy Hill for a wagon.

Hand says nothing of disease among Hogs, and I hope mine have escaped. I shall advise him to use precautions however. Love to Julia & the children.

Affectionately yours,

Miss Mary Bynum came with Sissy from Charlotte & stayed with her till after the wedding. Your mother having all the parties here the evening before they were married. I was absent at Raleigh after Tuesday. Clingman was confined to his room, from the beating Turner gave him. Turner has a small patch on his forehead, and his right hand is somewhat hurt, but has not been laid up, and came home the day after the encounter.

---

[1]Although Mr. Smith and some local persons mentioned in this letter could not be further identified, the letter was included because of its importance to social historians in particular.

[2]Frederick N. Strudwick introduced the impeachment resolution on December 9, 1870 (Raper, *Holden*, 205-206). Some Conservatives were afraid that, because of Strudwick's Klan activities, the impeachment movement might seem to emanate from the Klan. The resolution was referred, reported favorably, and passed by a vote of sixty to forty-six. Hamilton, *Reconstruction in North Carolina*, 541-543.

Littleton Q. Washington[1] *to William A. Graham* UNC

Washington, D.C.,
December 10th., 1870.

I am desirous of obtaining a list of the members of the North Carolina Legislature, now in session, but do not know whether any of my acquaintances are at Raleigh, or not. May I ask the favor of you to forward this, or write yourself, to some one of the members, & ask him to send a list to me at this City?

I am pretty closely at work here, on various Conservative papers, but I have kept watch over the struggle in your State with the deepest sympathy & interest for your people. I am profoundly grateful at the turn things have taken.

A very wholesome reaction is going on all over the Country. The public are thoroughly imbued with the idea that the Administration is weak and corrupt. But of even more value than the great popular change, I count the rapid disintegration & bitter feuds in the Republican party. So I think the end cannot be far off. I wish your disabilities were removed, as we greatly need such men as yourself in public life. You ought, at any rate, to be in the next National Dem. Convention, for, with prudence, the victory is certain.

---

[1]Littleton Quinter Washington (d. 1902), scion of a distinguished Virginia family, was a widely known journalist. He lived in Washington, D.C., all his life except for the Civil War years, when he served the Confederacy as chief clerk in the Department of State. At one time on the staff of the *National Intelligencer,* he was after 1865 a foreign correspondent of the *London Telegram. New York Times,* November 5, 1902.

Thomas Sparrow[1] *to William A. Graham* UNC

Raleigh, N.C.,
December 23rd., 1870.

I am directed by the board of Impeachment Managers, of which I am Chairman, to secure your services in the prosecution of the Governor before the Senate, if possible.[2]

The House Resolution, & the Rules of the Senate, both, authorise the employment of counsel. We have already secured the services of Gov. Bragg, & Judge Merrimon, the latter with especial reference to making up the case during the recess. We are especially anxious to add to these the weight of your name & learning, & known familiarity with questions of constitutional law; having as vindicators of a violated constitution, in the interest of the people, a representative man from each of the old parties. The Governor is to file his answer by the 23rd. proximo., replication is to be made in six days thereafter, and the trial is set for the 30th. I trust that this time may so suit your convenience as to enable you to consent to an appearance.

The question of fees has not been discussed, and will be arranged to suit your views, & the wishes of your associates, should you appear.

I leave for Washington in the morning, where I shall be pleased to hear from you at your earliest convenience.

[1]Thomas Sparrow (1819-1884) of Beaufort County, a native of New Bern, graduated at Princeton in 1842, read law with William Gaston, and practiced law in Washington, North Carolina. He was a member of the state Commons in 1858, then he moved to Illinois but returned the following year. A captain of the Washington Grays in the Seventeenth North Carolina Regiment, Sparrow was captured at Hatteras and imprisoned for about six months. After his exchange he was a major in the Tenth North Carolina Regiment and saw considerable active service. He served in the state House of Representatives, 1870-1872, and as chairman of the board of managers in the impeachment of Governor Holden. Warren, *Beaufort County's Contribution*, 5, 7-9, 26; Connor, *North Carolina Manual, 1913*, 498-499; Clark, *Histories of the North Carolina Regiments*, V, 35-54, 680.

[2]Graham was the leading counsel for the managers in the impeachment trial, both in the examination of witnesses and in the presentation of the case against Holden. Graham's speech was one of the most important ones made for the prosecution. Edward Conigland, a temperamental Irishman from Halifax, was one of the counsels for Holden. In a letter to his daughter, Conigland wrote the following tart comment on Graham:

> Next to Sparrow sits Graham—a fine looking man, very dignified; he is a fine specimen of the North Carolina gentleman. Sometimes, however, his dignity mounts so high that he appears like a man upon stilts, and one cannot help wishing that he would not open his mouth as if he had not studied the most becoming way to do so. He has more to say in the case than any of his associates. (Edward Conigland to Frances [Fannie] Conigland, February 28, 1871, Edward Conigland Papers, Southern Historical Collection, University of North Carolina Library, Chapel Hill.)

Conigland and all of Holden's counsels had many reasons to wish that Graham "would not open his mouth."

B. M. Jones to William A. Graham UNC

Danville, Virginia,
December 26th., 1870.

As I can not have a personal interview with you, I will lay before you the plan of which I wrote in a former letter. You will readily perceive the importance to me of not making it public at present; and that the least thing said about it might effectually prevent me from accomplishing one object that I have [in] view. That is, to make it compensate me and my advisors, among whom I would be very much pleased to have you, provided you fully and cordially approve of the policy which [I] propose. If you should not concur with me, or from any cause should prefer not to be connected with it, you will oblige me by returning the paper, with your objections, and not mentioning that any such plan is in contemplation. I believe that it will be adopted very generally, and that it will greatly enhance the value of the stock of most roads,—the roads in North Carolina, generally, being included. You see that it would open up a wide field for legitimate speculation, and I see no reason why it should not be made to pay. If I had the funds to purchase largely of the stock of any one line, the increased value would amply compensate me, but as I have not, there is no reason why others, who have, should not pay me a good percentage on any profits they may make by information furnished by me.

Among the gentlemen who fully approve the plan are the Hon'b'l John W. Johnston,[1] (U.S. Senate) Gen'l Joseph R. Anderson,[2] of Richmond, Mr. John Wickham,[3] of St. Louis, Mr. R. P. Atkinson,[4] of the N. W. R. R., and

Mr. Sam'l G. Jones,[5] of Alabama, the last two being Engineers of high standing, and strong practical sense.

If you should decide to have any connection with it, I will be very glad to receive any suggestions that you may make, and the names of any prominent men, in your State, with whom you would be willing to co-operate. There may be even such in Raleigh, and in Wilmington.

I believe that if Charters could be obtained for a road from Egypt by Hillsboro' to the Virginia line, at such point as I would decide upon, with the view of reaching Richmond; and for one from Hillsboro' by Yancyville, to the State line, with the view of reaching Danville; that I could, by this plan, get a sufficient subscription to insure the construction of the roads. The first named road is much the more important to your people, as it would soon be connected with the South Carolina roads at Cheraw; and at Richmond I would expect to connect with a new, and more direct line to Baltimore. So it would be an important through line, besides the facilities it would afford the farmers of Alamance & Orange, in sending off wheat, and receiving fertilizers. If you concur with me, you will greatly oblige me by giving the necessary attention to procuring suitable Charters from your present Legislature, and I would like to make some suggestions about the Charters.

I am persuaded that both in a pecuniary and practical point of view, my plan will be of incalculable advantage to the country, and I do not doubt that you will excuse me for trespassing so much upon your time.

---

[1]John Warfield Johnston (1818-1889) was born in Panicello, near Abingdon, Virginia, and attended Abingdon Academy, South Carolina College at Columbia, and the law department of the University of Virginia. Admitted to the bar in 1839, he established a law practice in Tazewell, Virginia. Johnston was commonwealth attorney for Tazewell County, 1844-1846; state senator, 1846-1848; judge of the circuit court of Virginia, 1866-1870; and United States senator, 1870-1883. *Biographical Directory of Congress*, 1199.

[2]Joseph Reid Anderson (1813-1892), of Virginia, was a graduate of West Point. He resigned from the army in 1837 and became assistant state engineer of Virginia, chief engineer of the Valley Turnpike Company, and, from 1841, head of the Tredegar Iron Works in Richmond. A secessionist, he entered the Confederate army as a brigadier general and saw active service until he was wounded at Frayser's Farm in 1862. Thereafter, he masterfully managed the Tredegar works and thereby performed invaluable service for the Confederacy. *DAB*, I, 268-269.

[3]John Wickham, a native of Virginia, was a judge in St. Louis.

[4]R. P. Atkinson has not been further identified.

[5]Samuel Goode Jones (1816-1878), of Alabama, was a graduate of Williams College. He became an engineer of prominence, serving as chief engineer of the Alabama and Cincinnati Railroad. He held the military position of captain in the Home Guard. Jones was elected to office as a state legislator. The town of Jonesboro, Georgia, was named for him. *Cyclopedia of American Biography*, X, 437.

B. M. Jones to William A. Graham UNC

Engineer's Office, N. & G. W. R. R.,
Danville, Virginia,
December 26, 1870.

I respectfully invite your consideration of the following views upon the ownership, and control of the great rail road interest of the country.

The business of common carriers has, in all ages, been very profitable, and nations, cities, companies, and individuals have amassed great wealth by embarking in it. The rail roads of the country have become the great highways to, and from, market, and should afford cheap transportation to the sections through which they pass. This cannot be the case when they are owned and controlled by capitalists, generally non-residents, who produce nothing to send, and who may seldom travel over them, who will always charge moderate freights for the through business, (for which there is strong competition) and high freights for local business. (Of which they have a monopoly). Farmers and planters are beginning to comprehend the fact that it is very bad economy to permit stock gamblers, and non-residents, to fix the rates at which produce shall be sent to market, and they and their families allowed to travel, and their only remedy for that evil, is for them to become the owners of the road which they use. As a class, farmers are very cautious about investing in stocks, and can only be induced to do so by being satisfied, beyond all peradventure, that they would, in some way, receive an equally good, and certain, return upon the amount, as they would by lending it out at the usual rate of interest, or by purchasing government bonds. This could very readily be done, in the case of a proposed road, or of one already in operation, by allowing the subscriber to, or the purchaser of the stock, any member of his family, any person in his employment, *or* any tenant, the right to haul over the road, a stated number of miles per annum, for each share of stock held by him, at the commencement of the fiscal year, free of all charge, or at a rate not exceeding one cent per mile; and to have carried one ton of fertilizer, or one half ton of coal per annum, for each share of stock, free of all charge, or at a rate not exceeding one cent per ton per mile, the fertilizer or coal to be in bags, or barrels, and carried at the convenience of the company, but the company to be required to carry either, at least six months in the year. This right should extend with the charter, and be transferable, with the stock on the books of the company. The details of the plan can be readily arranged, but it is unnecessary to give them, as they would vary on different roads, but the distance which the stockholder should be allowed to travel free, should be such as to make the difference between paying for it, at the regular local rates, and having a free pass, fully equal to the prevailing rate of interest on the par value of the stock, so that the amount saved on the freights on fertilizers, or coal, would be that much more than the interest, and thus afford an additional inducement to the party to own the stock.

It can not be objected to this policy that the free tickets would occasion such a reduction of the net income as to endanger the road, and cars being kept in good repair. The stock would be held principally by the *local patrons* of the line, and on most of the roads, the total amount received from *Local Travel* might be deducted from the net income, and there would be a balance left for the contingent fund. But it would not be right to deduct the total amount received from that source, as there would always be a large proportion of the local patrons of the line, (probably one third), who would never become stockholders. There would doubtless be a large increase of local passengers, but on most of our roads that would scarcely produce any effect upon the *net income* of the company, as it would cost very little more to carry the cars entirely full, instead of only half full of passengers. The gross income of the company would not be reduced as much as might at first be supposed, parties holding free tickets generally use them freely, and, in many cases, the free ticket would be exhausted before the end of the year, and the holder would have to purchase some tickets at the regular local rates. The right to carry fertilizer free (at the convenience of the company), would cost scarcely anything, as the cars frequently run empty one way to carry freight the other; and for every ton of fertilizer carried for nothing, the company would probably carry two tons of produce at the regular rates, and that policy would, in a few years, become a source of greatly increased income. Under this policy the company would have to rely chiefly upon the through business for its net income, and would consequently keep the road, and cars, in good condition in order to attract the travel.

The amount saved by the stockholders in free tickets would not be the only advantage which they would derive from this policy, as they would, by it, have the right to fix the local freights, which would, on many roads, be worth as much as the interest on the par value of the stock, but the greatest benefit would be in the increased production of the farms, which would follow upon a liberal use of lime and plaster, the best and cheapest fertilizers that can be used, provided the freight on them will admit of their being used. I am fully persuaded that the productions of the farm along the line of the road which adopts this proposed policy, would be more than doubled in a few years, and the increased production would, in most cases, be worth at least fifty per cent per annum upon the cost of the road.

It is scarcely necessary to trouble you with an example to show the amount that would be saved by a stockholder, as you can readily suppose a case for yourself.

This policy would not work oppressively in any case. Parties living along a road in which they are stockholders, would retain an amount of stock that would enable them to derive the full benefit from the free tickets, and could sell the balance to their neighbors, who would gladly purchase at par. Parties who have purchased stock at a reduced price, on speculation, would have an opportunity of selling at a much higher profit than they could possibly have anticipated.

In companies in which the State is a large stockholder this policy would enable the State to sell, to its own citizens along the line, *at par*, or parties who have full faith in the plan, would gladly purchase the State's interest at a higher rate than the stock is now selling, knowing that they would be enabled to sell in a short time at par.

It may be supposed that there are not men enough along our roads to purchase up the stock, or if there are a sufficient number that they are not able to purchase. By a fair estimate of the area of country which uses any road, (one hundred miles long), and of the white men, over twenty years [old] in it, you will find that there is a sufficient number. It can not be disputed that our people have not *cash* enough to pay for the stock, but they have land enough, which they cannot cultivate, to form a basis of credit for that purpose, and this proposed policy would enable them to sell it much more rapidly than they can at present, but apart from the land, a system of credit can be presented which would effectual[ly] protect the seller of the stock, and would induce any tolerably intelligent farmer, who sends his produce over the road, (and who lives in the country through which it passes), to purchase *at par* a sufficient number of shares to enable him to derive the full benefit which this plan would afford him. It is not necessary to explain that branch of the subject at present, as it would occupy too much of your time, perhaps uselessly.

The greatest danger, in a pecuniary point of view, with which our farmers and planters are now threatened, is in permitting their *highway to market* to pass into the hands of, comparatively, a few capitalists, who are purchasing and leasing long lines of road. The farmers of Orange and Chatham doubtless think that they are taxed enormously high, and most of their acquaintances would fully concur with them, and yet an income of 5 cents per bushel on the freight on wheat, and a correspondent increase in the freight on every thing that is sent from, or brought to their farms, would probably double the amount of tax which they now pay; and a saving to that extent on their present freights would save them the entire present tax. A very moderate increase of the freight on the wheat and tobacco crop of Virginia, and North Carolina would pay the entire State taxes. And when the farmers shall loose all control of the roads which they use, can they doubt that the purchasers, who look to dividends, will tax them, (in the way of freights), to the last dollar that they can force them to pay.

Formerly the *practical men,* (so called), of our country, taught the farmers to look with some distrust upon the *visionary enthusiasts* who advised them to invest in the stock of a road which they would necessarily have to use, and persuaded them that land and negroes were the only safe investments for farmers. Recent events have shown that rail road stocks can stand the heaviest shock better than any other stocks, or bonds; and, under this proposed policy the farmers would now prefer such stock to any investment that could be presented to them.

The indignation against the discrimination against local, in favor of through rates, is alrady ver great, and is rapidly becoming very formidable to the interest of some very prominent roads. This proposed plan would effectually put a stop to that feeling, as it would place the roads in the hands of the local patrons.

Some of the leading journals of the country are sounding the alarm at the dangers to be apprehended in a political point of view, from allowing the great rail road combinations to buy up Congress, & such men as Jim Fiske, Jr.,[1] to purchase up the State Legislatures. This proposed policy would be a sovereign remedy for that evil, as it would place the enormous income of the rail roads in the only hands to which it can safely be entrusted by any government. The great body of tax payers, who have the deepest interest in procuring and preserving a good and stable government.

You will confer a favor by giving me your opinion upon this subject at your earliest convenience.

If I have omited any branch of the subject which you think impotant, or if I have failed to make plain any portion of it, you will be kind enough to call my attention to it.

---

[1]James Fisk, Jr. (1834-1872), a wealthy businessman and financier, was notorious for unethical conduct. He lived extravagantly and flamboyantly. Fisk died from a gunshot wound inflicted by a jealous rival for the affections of the actress Josie Mansfield. *Cyclopedia of American Biography*, XXII, 170-171; *DAB*, III, 414-415; *New York Times*, January 7, 1872.

1871

William A. Graham to Thomas Sparrow UNC: SPARROW

Hillsboro'
Jan'y 9th. 1871.

Dear Sir

Having been absent from home, for near a fortnight, I did not receive your letter of the 23rd. ult. until very recently, and take an early opportunity to reply.

I feel honored by the invitation of the Board of Managers, to appear for the Prosecution against the Governor of the State before the Court of Impeachment, and do not deem myself at liberty to decline it. I expect to be in Raleigh next week, and will have the pleasure to meet you, and other gentlemen of the Board, and will endeavour to cooperate in such preparatory steps as may be necessary—

With assurances of high regard

I am very truly Yours

John W. Graham to William A. Graham UNC

State of North Carolina
Senate Chamber, Raleigh
Jany 12th 1871

My dear Father

. . . .

I have mentioned the subject of your letter to a good many and we have a caucus on the subject to-night. Gilmer, Worth, and myself have had a good deal of talk on the subject and the matter has been mentioned in caucus and that it would be offered for consideration at our next meeting.

Paul[1] is somewhat better but he has been quite sick and has suffered a great deal from rising in his ears. One has broken and is constantly running and the other one still pains him very much.

I have succeeded in passing the Revenue Bill on the 3rd Reading this morning. It levies a tax of 35 cents on the $100.00—a reduction from 52 last year. The Legislature may levy a further tax of 6 2/3 on the $100.00 for Education but this is doubtful. It would then leave 25 cents on the $100.00 for county purposes.

Gus, Jimmie, and Alfred Morrison[2] will go up to dine with me to-day. With best love to all. I hope Mother is improved from her trip and enjoyed it very much.

Your afft. Son

[1]Paul Cameron Graham (1869-1932), son of John W. and Rebecca Cameron Graham, was graduated from the University of North Carolina with a Ph.B. degree in 1891. He was mayor of Durham, 1905-1909; alderman in 1910; and county attorney after 1899. Grant, *Alumni History*, 228; Clark, "Graham Descendants."

[2]Graham's nephew Alfred James Morrison (1849-1876) became a Presbyterian minister and lived in Lincoln County and Selma, Alabama. He is buried at Machpelah Church in Lincoln County. Clark, "Graham Descendants"; Graham, *General Joseph Graham*, 181.

John Manning, Jr., to William A. Graham UNC

House of Representatives.

Washington, D.C.
Jan. 27, 1871

I have been unable to obtain but two copies of Rep & Docs on Southern outrages, and I sent one of these to Gov. Bragg,[1] thinking that he would have an opportunity of consulting with prominent gentlemen throughout the State. I desire that these Docs should be read, and let each member of the Legislature from the counties in which these outrages occurred, furnish me as soon as possible a detailed statement of the facts connected with the outrages named.

I am preparing some remarks on this subject which I hope to deliver in the next ten days, and I would be exceedingly obliged to you for any suggestions, connected with the condition of affairs in our State. Will you give me the names of some gentlemen who can give the facts as to the outrages said to have taken place in Orange? I wish to give their names to Senator Bayard,[2] that he may have them summoned.

This is a matter of great importance to us, for I think that the Radicals intend to make these *outrages* in N.C. the cause of a new departure from our Constitution, and for further hostile proceedings against our people.

Mr. Shober and myself have to fight the whole band gathered here, and we have hard work, but, by the blessing of God, I hope to foil them yet. I hope that there will be no more Ku Kluxing by whites, at least. It would be most injurious to us.

If at any time you should want any Documents, do oblige me by writing for them.

[1]Former governor Thomas Bragg.

[2]Thomas Francis Bayard (1828-1898), lawyer and statesman, was a native of Wilmington, Delaware, and a staunch Democrat. In 1869 he succeeded his father, James A. Bayard (1799-1880), as United States senator from Delaware. In 1871 Bayard served on a joint committee to investigate activities of the Ku Klux Klan and similar organizations in the South. He remained in the Senate until 1885, when Grover Cleveland appointed him secretary of state. He persistently contended that only necessary laws should be enacted and that government should be honest and frugal above all else. Bayard was a member of the electoral commission in 1877 and ambassador to Great Britain, 1893-1897. *CDAB*, 57; *Biographical Directory of Congress*, 528.

John Kerr to William A. Graham UNC

Yanceyville
Jan 28th 1871

I was Summoned yesterday to be in Raleigh on the 30th inst. The weather is excedingly unpropitious, it is now raining and promises to continue for the whole day and probably tomorrow. I am very much indisposed with an attack of influenza, and my children—two of them—are also not well. I do not feel that I can safely venture an exposure of myself to the present inclemency of weather in my State of health. I therefore have determined not to leave home before Monday. If my health improves—as I hope with proper care, it may—I shall leave home on Monday afternoon & hope to reach Raleigh on Tuesday morning. This will probably be in good time, as I do not anticipate that you will reach the charges founded on the invasion of Caswell, before Tuesday, probably not so soon as that day. The Alamance charges come first in the articles of Impeachment, according to my recollections.

At no time could a call to leave home have been more inconvenient to me. My own health & the health of my family and many other considerations make it very desirable on my part to be at home, but I am disposed to do whatever duty in the premises may demand of me.

I will try to reach Raleigh by the time I have above indicated.

J. A. Petrie[1] *to William A. Graham* UNC

Elizabeth, N.J.,
Feb. 2nd., 1871.

Being referred to you by the Hon. M. Fillmore, my friend, I write to ask favors of you. Can you, and will you, let me have, from among your old papers and letter files, *one* Autograph letter, from any of the old members of the Cabinet to which you had the honor to belong, and any of the members of other Cabinets which you may chance to have.

Mr. Fillmore would give me anything I might want, but he has parted with most that I wished.

Will you also please give me the present Post Office addresses so far as you can, of the following named persons of prominence of your State: Geo. E. Badger,[2] John Branch,[3] each an old Cabinet officer. Also the following, prominent in Confederate History. George Davis[4] & Wm. S. Dortch,[5] Senators, Gov. Z. B. Vance, Generals Theo. N. Holmes,[6] W. W. Goring,[7] Dan'l H. Hill,[8] R. C. Gatlin,[9] R. Ransom, and any and all others of rank of General in the Confederate Army.

If you can send me *one* Autograph letter from any of these, all will be thankfully received.

I wish to communicate with each of those whose P. O. address I have asked for, to obtain Historic information for a work which I have in preparation.

[1]J. A. Petrie has not been identified.

[2]Apparently Petrie had not heard of George Edmund Badger's death in 1866. Badger (b. 1795) was reared and educated a Federalist, joined the Jacksonians about 1828, and was a Whig by 1836. He was briefly secretary of the navy prior to the dissolution of the Harrison cabinet. He served as a United States senator from 1846 to 1855. In the Senate Badger supported southern rights while maintaining a nationalist posture. He opposed Polk's war policies and the Wilmot Proviso, although he upheld the constitutionality of the right of Congress to limit slavery in the territories. He favored all the 1850 compromise measures except the one abolishing the slave trade in Washington. Badger refused to accept the doctrine of popular sovereignty but voted for the Kansas-Nebraska bill—a vote he lamented as the biggest mistake of his political life. A firm Unionist, Badger was a party founder and an elector on the Constitutional Union ticket. As a delegate to the North Carolina Secession Convention, he opposed secession and proposed a declaration of southern independence as the proper expedient. Badger supported the war without enthusiasm until his health failed in 1863. By profession Badger was a lawyer with a wide and successful practice. He frequently argued cases before the United States Supreme Court and ranked with Webster, Crittenden, Berrien, and Cushing as one of the ablest advocates of his day. *DAB*, I, 485-486.

[3]John Branch had died in 1863. Born in Halifax in 1782, he was a wealthy man who became a liberal in his political philosophy, serving as president of the American Colonization Society and working for better education, internal improvements, less severe penal laws, and the abolition of imprisonment for debt. Branch was for three years governor of North Carolina, 1817-1820; served six years in the United States Senate; and was secretary of the navy in Andrew Jackson's cabinet. Generally admired for his wit, charm, and hospitality, Branch eventually moved to the territory of Florida, where he acquired large tracts of land and was in 1843 appointed governor by President Tyler. Crabtree, *North Carolina Governors*, 67-68; Powell, *DNCB*, I, 210-211.

[4]George Davis (1820-1896), of New Hanover County, was graduated with highest honors by the University of North Carolina in 1838. By profession a learned lawyer and eloquent advocate, Davis was a Union Whig and the "mentor of his party" in southeastern North Carolina. As a delegate to the Washington Peace Conference in 1861, he sought to promote compromise until secession became a reality. After North Carolina left the Union, he supported the state, serving as a Confederate senator, 1861-1864, and as Confederate attorney general, 1864-1865. Ashe, *Biographical History*, II, 71-81.

[5]William Theophilus Dortch (1824-1889) was born on a Nash County plantation, studied at the Bingham school, read law with Bartholomew F. Moore, and became one of the most successful lawyers in eastern North Carolina. He was a member of the state House of Commons from 1852 to 1861 (Speaker in 1860); a Confederate senator, 1861-1865; and a state senator, 1876-1885 (Speaker in 1881). An original secessionist who greatly admired Jefferson Davis, Dortch was conservative during Reconstruction and was an ardent Democrat. Van Noppen Papers.

[6]Theophilus Hunter Holmes (1804-1880), of Sampson County, graduated from West Point in 1829 third from the bottom of his class of forty-six. Jefferson Davis was his classmate and friend. Holmes saw duty in the Seminole and Mexican wars and served on garrison duty before resigning (with the rank of major) in 1861 to return to North Carolina. Successively Confederate brigadier, major, and lieutenant general, he may have been promoted beyond his capacity. Holmes served effectively but not brilliantly in North Carolina, Virginia, west of the Mississippi, and again in North Carolina. After the war, he farmed a small tract in Cumberland County. Boatner, *Civil War Dictionary*, 406; *DAB*, IX, 176.

[7]William Wing Loring (1818-1886) settled in Florida but was a native of North Carolina. At the age of fourteen Loring enlisted in the army but later resigned and studied at Georgetown College. After graduation he practiced law in Florida, where he was a state legislator, before returning to the army to serve as a major in the Seminole War. He was brevetted a colonel in the Mexican War. He sustained the loss of an arm and afterward held several military posts. As a Confederate major general in the Civil War, Loring was an effective officer despite his handicap. However, at one point while in command of the

Army of the Northwest he defied General Thomas J. Jackson's orders, resulting in his transfer from Jackson's command. In 1869 Loring offered his services to the Egyptian army, in which he commanded a division in the Abyssinian War; he was made pasha. He returned to the United States in 1879. *CDAB*, 586; Boatner, *Civil War Dictionary*, 492-493.

[8]Daniel Harvey Hill (1821-1889), who in 1848 married Graham's niece Isabella Sophia Morrison (1825-1904), was born in the York District of South Carolina, the son of an ironmaster and Revolutionary War soldier. He was reared and educated by his widowed mother, a devout Presbyterian. He graduated from West Point in 1842, in a class that furnished twelve Civil War generals, including Hill. He served with distinction in the Mexican War but resigned his commission to teach, first at Washington College (now Washington and Lee) and then at Davidson College, 1854-1859. In 1859 he became superintendent of the North Carolina Military Institute in Charlotte. During the Civil War he was appointed first colonel, then brigadier general, then major general, and finally lieutenant general, only to have the last promotion blocked by President Davis. He fought well at Bethel, Seven Pines, Seven Days, and South Mountain, but his service as Braxton Bragg's subordinate in the western campaigns of 1863 was controversial. After Chickamauga he signed, and possibly wrote, the petition seeking Bragg's removal for incompetence. Davis, sympathetic to his old friend Bragg, relieved Hill of command and blocked his promotion, leaving him in a military limbo until Bentonville. After the war Hill edited the *Land We Love* and the *Southern Home* to vindicate the southern way of life; was president of the University of Arkansas, 1877-1884; and headed Middle Georgia Military and Agricultural College (later Georgia Military College), 1885-1889. *DAB*, IX, 27-28; Clark, "Graham Descendants."

[9]Richard Caswell Gatlin (1809-1896), of Lenoir County, who was a veteran of the Black Hawk, Seminole, and Mexican wars, graduated from West Point in 1832. He resigned from the United States Army in May, 1861, and was named adjutant general of North Carolina troops. In early July, 1861, he was promoted to Confederate brigadier general and placed in command of coastal defenses in the southern department. He was seriously ill during the New Bern campaign and resigned in September, 1862, under a shadow. Gatlin subsequently served as state adjutant and inspector general. Boatner, *Civil War Dictionary*, 327.

James G. Moore[1] *to William A. Graham* UNC

Company Shops,
Feb. 14, 1871.

Gov. Graham:

There is summoned from this county the following witnesses for Def.

Dan'l Whitesell[2]

Alphonzo Geringer[3]

Both of the above parties voted the Conservative Ticket. If Gerringer says he was *mistreated, ask him by whom and what for,* he has *invariably* stated here that it was done by Dan'l Whitsell & one other person. Cause assigned is this, vulgar abuse of a Lady & a threat of personal violence by Gerringer, the said Lady being a sister to the other party, not named.

Peter Hughes[4] has testified heretofore, that he was not a *sworn* member of the K.K., he is also a Conservative.

---

[1]James G. Moore (b. 1831) was a merchant of Alamance County who was arrested by Kirk. Stokes, *Company Shops*, 71, 74-75, 84, 86, 89, 93, 102, 125.

[2]Daniel Whitsell was a member of a large family in Alamance County living in Gibsonville. He joined the White Brotherhood in 1869 at the behest of Peter Hughes. He was initiated at night by men in white caps and gowns and was told that troublesome

blacks not subject to the law would be punished. Whitsell took part in whipping a black named Daniel Jordan for thievery but denied any knowledge of the Outlaw and Puryear murders. *Holden Trial*, II, 1555-1567.

[3]Alphonoso Gerringer, of Guilford County, and his cousin, William Gerringer, approached an Alamance County schoolhouse, where they planned to attend a debate. After hearing an unnatural "haloo," they were stopped on the road by two robed men adorned with large horns. Abandoned by his cousin, Alphonoso was taken into the woods and threatened with hanging. He was not hurt but, upon being released, was ordered to run. Later he said, "Then you had better seen me running—I told my legs to save my body if they could. . . ." Apparently Gerringer was treated in this manner because it was alleged that he had insulted an elderly woman. *Holden Trial*, II, 1466-1469.

[4]Peter Hughes, a farmer who lived near Company Shops in Alamance County, was a member of the White Brotherhood, one of the secret organizations that operated in North Carolina and were known collectively as the Ku Klux Klan. For information regarding the ideas to which Hughes subscribed, see his testimony in the impeachment proceedings against Holden. *Holden Trial*, II, 1247-1297; Ninth Census of the United States, 1870: Alamance County, North Carolina, Population Schedule, microfilm of National Archives manuscript copy, Archives, Division of Archives and History, Raleigh, hereinafer cited as Ninth Census, 1870, with appropriate county and schedule.

James G. Moore to William A. Graham[1] UNC

Company Shops
Feby 16th 1871

Below you will find a list of parties summoned by deft. John Curtice[2] will contradict Robt Mebanes daughters, Alfred Trolinger[3] ought to say that he was at Graham to watch the voters for the Rads & can tell about discharging on act politicks. Leonard Rippy was whiped for sleeping with Negro woman was taken out of bed from her.[4] So I learn.

Sam Garrison[5] was whiped for rascality.

Joe Harvy[6] was whiped for Stealing and for insolence to his old mistress.

Wife of Puryear,[7]

George Anthony Son of Daniel Anthony,[8]

G. D. Boon.[9] Postmaster at Shops he knows about discharging for voting if you can get him to tell it.

---

[1]Presumably all of the people in this letter were involved in the Kirk-Holden trouble. The ten "chiefs," leaders of the ten camps of the White Brotherhood in Alamance County, were Jacob A. Long, Jasper N. Wood, John T. Trolinger, Albert Murray, George Anthony, David Mebane, William Stockard, John Durham, James Bradsher, and Job Faucette. Hamilton, *Reconstruction in North Carolina*, 462n.

[2]As this letter indicates, John Curtis was called as a witness for the defense in the impeachment trial. *Holden Trial*, II, 1873-1875.

[3]Alfred Trolinger was a black man called by the defense in the impeachment proceedings against Holden. He was questioned about the whipping of Alonzo Corliss, a white who conducted a school for blacks. Corliss headed the Union League, an organization to which Trolinger belonged. Trolinger was threatened by the Klan. *Holden Trial*, II, 1700-1703; Raper, *Holden*, 161.

[4]William A. Graham made mention of this testimony in his notes on the arrests.

[5]Sam Garrison, a former Alamance County slave, was whipped by five men in white robes in November, 1869, for reasons that were never made clear to him. He was afraid to seek legal remedy but did report his abuse to federal troops in March, 1870. David Allred, who lived near Company Shops, testified that Garrison had worked for him two years and

that he had a reputation as good as "any black man's." Allred believed the beating severe. *Holden Trial*, II, 1220-1227, 1238-1241. In 1870 Garrison was a domestic servant, age 50, living in Morton's Township. Ninth Census, 1870, Alamance County, Population Schedule.

[6]Joseph Harvey (Harvie), a black member of the Union League, was given 150 lashes and his baby was clubbed to death in March, 1869, in Alamance County. According to Graham's notes on the trial, Harvey and his wife both were taken from their house. Harvey was accused of insulting a white woman and knocking down a white man. Harvey testified that he was taken from his house by twelve robed men, stripped of his night clothes, beaten, and pulled from the ground by a rope around his neck. One man intervened on his behalf or he probably would have been killed. Harvey did not learn that his wife and child had been clubbed until he returned home. *Holden Trial*, II, 1427-1441; Trelease, *White Terror*, 194.

[7]As noted earlier in this volume, William Puryear apparently recognized two Klansmen who were returning home after the murder of Wyatt Outlaw. Puryear was taken from his home at night by persons unknown, and several weeks later his body was found in a pond. The murder was never resolved. Some blamed the Klan, but others claimed that he was murdered at the behest of his wife. Whitaker, *Centennial History of Alamance*, 129; Trelease, *White Terror*, 205. During the Holden trial the wife, Matilda Puryear, gave testimony describing her husband's abduction. *Holden Trial*, II, 1301-1311.

[8]George Anthony and his father, Daniel Anthony, were mentioned briefly in Graham's notes on the trial as having been examined before Peter Hardin. George was chief of camp 5 of the White Brotherhood in Alamance County and also, apparently, was at one time head of klan 5 of the Constitutional Union Guard. Hamilton, *Reconstruction in North Carolina*, 462n.

[9]George D. Boone was postmaster at Company Shops and also worked for the railroad. A Republican in politics, he saw several Klansmen coming from Graham in November, 1869. In March, 1870, when federal troops came to Graham, Boone was warned not to tell what he had observed. A paper threat to Boone was posted near the post office and showed three coffins; his name was on one. Boone gave the warning to the federal commander in Graham. *Holden Trial*, II, 1695-1699.

Green Andrews to William A. Graham UNC

Company Shops, N.C.,
February 17th., 1871.

If Red Eye Albright[1] is before the Court of Impeachment, or is to be before it, I think you would do well to have Wm. Fogleman, Ruffin Fogleman,[2] A. A. Andrews, and myself, summoned.

We can prove that he tried to intimidate voters. We also can prove that he acted as Brig. General, ordered us into Camp, signed furloughs, etc. We know a great deal about him. W. A. Smith[3] was surety for us, and Red Eye took Bonds, etc.

---

[1]William R. Albright (b. 1829), of Alamance County, was commonly known as "Red Eye Bill." He was mayor of Graham in 1869; in 1870 Holden appointed him a brigadier general of state troops and a member of the military commission to try Graham and other leading Conservatives. At a Union League meeting in March, 1869, he and Wyatt Outlaw opposed a policy of retaliation "in kind" by blacks; instead, they proposed a reliance on law and sent for a company of militia from Raleigh. When seventy-five Klansmen rode into Graham on the night of February 26, 1870, they left a note on Mayor Albright's gate threatening him with hanging. Trelease, *White Terror*, 194, 199, 200, 204, 205, 216, 219. See *Holden Trial*, II, 1881-1926, for Albright's testimony as to Klan activities in Alamance County.

[2]One member of the Fogleman family, John T. Fogleman, was one of the five klan leaders of the Constitutional Union Guard in Alamance County. Hamilton, *Reconstruction in North Carolina,* 462n.

[3]William Alexander Smith.

Charles Macalester to William A. Graham UNC

Philadelphia,
February 18th., 1871.

I duly received your note of 10th., which I submitted to the Trustees, & which is now on their files. We were all disappointed that you were not present. We, however, had a quorum, the absentees being Mr. Bradford, Gov'r Aiken, yourself, Mr. Eaton,[1] Gen'l Grant, & Secretary Fish. The board adjourned yesterday, after a pleasant session;—and I hope, and believe, they found Philad'a an agreeable City to visit. Mr. Bradford resigned, & Mr. A. Stuart[2] of Virginia, formerly Secretary of the Interior, and General Richard Taylor,[3] of Louisiana, were elected to fill the two vacancies.

The Board was disposed to accord great consideration to your nominations, but it was considered of great importance, for various reasons, that Virginia should have one representative, and the Gulf States one. General Taylor, (with others) was strongly recommended by Mr. Bradford.

---

[1]George N. Eaton, of Baltimore, Maryland, was an original member of the Peabody Education Fund trustees. Parker, *George Peabody,* 162.

[2]Alexander Hugh Holmes Stuart (1807-1891), of Virginia, a graduate of the University of Virginia, was a lawyer and legislator. A Henry Clay Whig, Stuart served in the United States Congress (1841-1843) and as secretary of the interior (1850-1853). Stuart's national service coincided with that of William A. Graham, who was first a senator and then secretary of the navy in the Fillmore cabinet. Unlike Graham, Stuart became a Know-Nothing in the 1850s. Stuart opposed secession so long as a Unionist stance was feasible but supported his state when war came. After the war he played a large part in the restoration of "home rule" to Virginia. *CDAB,* 1026.

[3]Richard Taylor (1820-1879), a planter in Louisiana, was a native of Kentucky and a son of Zachary Taylor. Taylor was a graduate of Yale and served as a state legislator and a delegate to the Secession Convention. During the Civil War he rose to the rank of lieutenant general in the Confederate army and commander of the District of Louisiana. He earned a reputation as a talented organizer. After the war he was active in his opposition to the Radicals during Reconstruction and was the author of *Destruction and Reconstruction. CDAB,* 1048.

T. Apoleon Cheney to William A. Graham UNC

Georgic Library
Leon, Cattaraugus Co, NY
March 1st, 1871

I had the honor of receiving your very kind favor of some eighteen months since in which you had (if I remember correctly, cannot *here* turn to papers) generously assured me of contributing toward the objects of our Library soon as you might have more leisure, could examine your papers, &c. Such, in response to the complimentary segment you had given for copy of my "Historical Sketch of the Chemung Valley, Etc.", I had taken pleasure of mailing to you copy of 1st edition of this humble work, which I trust, though I have not since heard from you, reached its destination. I too have indulged hope to have had the 2d & enlarged edition ready for pub. ere present time, but ill health has thus far prevented.

I may mention that I have been very successful in the objects *before* referred to, in former letters.

I will still be exceedingly gratified if you may now find it at your convenience to allow honor of enclosing to me *your* carte-de-visite, *with your autograph written below* picture—and which I may avail myself of pleasure of placing in [panel] which I had *reserved* for it in Album, and where amid illustrious group of Statesmen, Etc., *it* would form a treasure of inestimable worth.

I too have been very successful in making valuable & extensive coll. of autographs—A.L.S.—for Library Souvenir; have doubtless obtained several which I requested from you, but I yet want, and will be especially obliged if you may, ere long, find it at your convenience to confer invaluable favor of enclosing to me the Autograph (letter or note if practicable to send, over signature) of Prest Wm H. Harrison—H. Clay—(signature of J. J. Crittenden[1]—Nath. Macon[2]—Charlotte Bronte[3]—Wm C. Preston—Hugh S. Legaré—Henry Laurens[4]—Wm C. Pinckney—or Charles Pinckney[5]—S. S. Prentiss[6] of La.,—Asso. Justices John McLean[7]—Philip P. Barbour[8]—Gabriel Duvall[9]—P. Y. Daniels[10]—H. W. Hilliard[11]—J. C. Campbell[12] (Ala.)—J. M. Morehead.[13]

I can only anticipate that you may favor me with such of these autos as you may find it at your convenience to spare from your papers, that you will take *no* trouble to search elsewhere for them—as I assure you, for *any* of those named which you may be able to send, for the "Souvenier", I should feel exceedingly indebted.

It will again afford me extreme pleasure in your allowing honor of writing me at your early convenience. Be glad to learn if the "Histl Sketch" duly reached you? Let me hear from you soon.

I remain, with great respect, Truly Yrs.

Excuse this- am *not* well.

[In margin]

I beg do *not* fail to *favor* me with *your* card—photograph, & autograph attached.

---

[1]John Jordan Crittenden (1787-1863), Kentucky lawyer and statesman, was a moving spirit in efforts to compromise sectional disputes so that the Union might be preserved. He was an important national figure from the time of his election to the United States Senate in 1835 until his death. For twenty-five years he was a close personal friend and political ally of Henry Clay. Crittenden and William A. Graham were friends and political colleagues. Their association began when Graham was a young senator (1840-1843) and grew closer when both men were members of the Fillmore cabinet. *DAB*, IV, 546-549.

[2]Nathaniel Macon.

[3]Charlotte Brontë (1816-1855), the English novelist, authored *Jane Eyre, Wuthering Heights, Agnes Grey*, and *Villette*.

[4]Henry Laurens (1724-1792) was probably the most successful merchant of Charleston before the American Revolution and was a leader of the revolutionary movement in the South. Captured by the British in 1780 when he was en route to negotiate a treaty with the Dutch, Laurens was exchanged for Lord Cornwallis. Cheney must have thought that Laurens might have corresponded with Joseph Graham, father of William A. Graham. *CDAB*, 549.

[5]William Pinckney and Charles Pinckney were members of a prominent South Carolina family. One Charles (1699-1758) was married to Eliza Lucas, renowned for her experimentations with indigo and other plants. Their two sons, Charles Cotesworth Pinckney (1746-1825) and Thomas Pinckney (1750-1828), were both influential statesmen. William Pinckney was a brother of the elder Charles Pinckney. Possibly Cheney erred in the name William C. Pinckney; he may have been thinking of Charles Cotesworth Pinckney or of William Pinkney (1764-1822), the Maryland diplomat, who was not related to the South Carolina Pinckneys. Elise Pinckney (ed.), *The Letterbook of Eliza Lucas Pinckney, 1739-1762* (Chapel Hill: University of North Carolina Press, 1972), xv-xxix; *CDAB*, 801-802.

[6]Sergeant Smith Prentiss (1808-1850) was born in Maine; graduated from Bowdoin College in 1826; studied law in Gorham, Maine, and Cincinnati, Ohio; and then moved to Mississippi and practiced law in Vicksburg. He was elected to the state House of Representatives in 1835 and to the Twenty-fifth Congress in 1838. In 1845 he moved to New Orleans and died five years later at his home near Natchez, Mississippi. *Biographical Directory of Congress*, 1480; *CDAB*, 822.

[7]John McLean (1785-1861) was born in New Jersey but lived most of his life in Ohio and served as a congressman from that state, 1813-1816. From 1816 until 1822 he was an associate judge of the Ohio State Supreme Court. From 1829 until his death McLean was an associate justice of the Supreme Court of the United States. *Biographical Directory of Congress*, 1310; *CDAB*, 621.

[8]Phillip Pendleton Barbour (1783-1841), of Virginia, served his state in a number of important offices before he was appointed associate justice of the United States Supreme Court in 1836, an office he maintained until his death. *Biographical Directory of Congress*, 514; *CDAB*, 47.

[9]Gabriel Duvall (1752-1844) had a long and distinguished political career in Maryland before his appointment by President James Madison in 1811 as an associate justice of the Supreme Court, a position from which he resigned in 1835 because of deafness. *Biographical Directory of Congress*, 839-840; *CDAB*, 256.

[10]Peter Vivian Daniel.

[11]Henry Washington Hilliard (1808-1892), born in Fayetteville, was a graduate of South Carolina College, studied law, and practiced his profession first in Georgia and then in Alabama. Active in the Whig party, he served in the United States House of Representatives, 1845-1851, and was presidential elector on the national ticket of Fillmore and Donelson in 1856. *Biographical Directory of Congress*, 1057; *CDAB*, 437.

[12]Possibly Cheney erred in this name and was thinking of John Archibald Campbell (1811-1898), a native of Georgia who established a law practice in Alabama and became a distinguished jurist. He was appointed to the United States Supreme Court in 1853. His opinions in the Dred Scott case brought him criticism from abolitionists. Campbell was a man of convictions who believed in a strict interpretation of the Constitution. When the Civil War came, he resigned from the Supreme Court and became assistant secretary of war in the Confederate government. *CDAB*, 140.

[13]John Motley Morehead (1796-1866), scion of a substantial Virginia family that moved to North Carolina, attended the "log college" of David Caldwell and graduated from the University of North Carolina in 1817. He read law with Archibald De Bow Murphey. Until 1835 Morehead was a Jacksonian Democrat, but as a delegate to the Constitutional Convention of 1835 he associated himself with the western group favoring constitutional revision, internal improvements, and public education. As North Carolina's second Whig governor (1841-1845), he actively sought the goals suggested above while fostering significant humanitarian reforms such as a state school for the blind and deaf. Morehead opposed the dissolution of the Union and was a delegate to the abortive Washington Peace

Conference in February, 1861. He was briefly a delegate to the Provisional Confederate Congress. In addition to his many political connections, Morehead was very influential in state business circles. He was involved in railroad building, textile manufacturing, and commercial and mercantile enterprises. At one time president of the North Carolina Railroad Company, he advocated development of a complete transportation system. *DAB*, XIII, 159.

David F. Caldwell to William A. Graham UNC

Washington Street,
Greensboro', N.C.,
March 7, 1871.

I have not attempted to practice law since the new Yanke code went into opperation, nor do I intend to do so while it remains in opperation. Consequently I rented my office to a Radical magistrate, but I keep my [board] and library in it, and I have seen much that has transpired in his Court. And never before have I seen such proceedings in the way of taking bail. I have seen negroes who were caught while in the store thay had broken into, others for highway Robbery, and for other high offences, bailed out on bonds for $50., with negrow securities that are notoriously insolvent &c. Of course scoundrulls all failed to appear—and that was the last of the matter, and even when Revenue officers become bail and the parties failed to appear, not a cent of the bond was ever collected, or will be. I have been the cause of having letters written to Caswell, Alamance, etc., requesting the clerks to send you a certified coppy of all the criminal cases on those dockets, of what race, what charged, and how disposed off. This record, if fairly gotten up, will speak louder than seven peals of tundur, and louder still if the politics of these criminals was made known.

Pardon me, will you, for the interest I take in this matter, for venturing to suggest to you to examine closely as you possibly can J. R. Bulla, as to the amount of compromises, nonsuits, nolprossing, he has entered, and the number of convictions he has made, etc., and Judge Tourgee as to the new Trials, and how and what has been the only sentence he can inflict on rogues. You may think me very presumptious, and no doubt will, for venturing to call these things in this hurrid manner to your attention, but, my dear Sir, much as you may have seen and know of the workings of radicalism, I feel confident you have seen, heard, or know but little of the extent of this partial rascality and fraud that has and is still practiced on the part of the Radical Judges, Solicitors, Magistrates, and other officers in this State. They have and are in my humble opinion doing more to corrupt the people and encourage *Thieves and rogurey* than did the notorious Jonathan Wild. And I hope that the prosecutors of Holden will spare neither time or expence to ventilate as much of the proceedings of Tourgee and Bulla as possible; it is due to truth, justice, and the people of this section of N. Carolina, and may God help you to do those notorious disturbers of the peace & leaders of faction *Justice*. If this could be done, then they would be comparatively harmless, and gradually die an infamous death. I wish to call your especal attention to the perils that are at the present moment threatening the existance of the N.C. Rail Road. So sure as you live, the Baltimore and

Ohio Rail Road will proceed at once to organize and build the Danville and Coal Field Rail Road from Danville to Statesville. This will give a rout some 50 miles shorter, from Charlotte to Lynchburg, Alexandria, Washington, Philadelphia or New York than any and all other routs passing through N.C. without any break of bulk or change of guage or bagage to any point North of Statesville. This will, under existing arangements, on the N.C. Rail Road, simply destroy it—and that to a moral certainty. Of course I cannot enter into a lengthened argument to prove this assertion in a letter. Yet I assert once for all, such will be the fact, and the only way to prevent this result will be to give the P. C. R. Road a fair chance to compeat with the B. & O. Road. If the proper steps are taken, they can be strained up to give a liberal price for the N.C. Road, in part, or the whole of it. And pardon me for again presuming to say that I think you ought to look to this matter carefully. I have long had about $5,000., most of which cost me dollar for dollar, and I can't now afford to be swindled out of it by narrow minded and bigoted legislation.

Graham's Notes for a Speech during Holden Impeachment A&H
[1871]

Exerdium - Congratulation on approach to conclusion. First time in over a century, that it has been found necessary to resort to the remedy of Impeachment against the first officer of the state.

Before proceeding to discuss the case it may be necessary in reply to observations of the counsel who opened the defence, to say a word in justification of the appearance of counsel in behalf of the managers. The subject is [illegible], the principles involved of Parlimentary law not familiar to our practice & the evidence voluminous. It would have been difficult, if not impossible for a member of the House of Representatives within the limits of the usual sessions of the Legislature, to give attention to this trial, & due diligence to his his [*sic*] Legislative duties; and the House would feel seriously the withdrawal from their labors there of seven gentlemen who are among its most effective & useful members. The practice in other states where impeachments have been more frequent than here.

The proceeding is an important one. The citizens of two populous counties, have complained to the House of Representatives in the Genl. Assembly, that they have been greatly injured and maltreated, and that the chief magistrate of the state is the author of this injustice. Our Constitution is a law to rulers, as to the people, & in view of the abuses that may be practised in the exercise of power has ordained, that the malfeasanses of public offices shall be remedied by impeachment. As in offences against social rights punishments are demanded so in official negligences or trespasses remedies are full and complete. As in the former case, if the citizen be guilty of heinous crimes he shall be cut off as too dangerous to live. So if he shall pervert the powers placed in his hands for the promotion of the public weal to the oppression & injury of the people, he shall be deposed from his high position & the official powers committed him, shall be transferred to other hands.

The House of Representatives have hearkened to the complaints of the people of these counties & pronounced them to be well founded; and have cited the Respondent to leave his official position & office at the bar of this tribunal, to make answer & proof as to the high crimes & misdemeanors imputed to him, and be adjudged in the premises.

These articles are 8 in number. They charge, that that [*sic*] the respondent &c

1. Falsely proclaimed Insurection in Alamance & imprisoned & detained citizens committing a high crime & misdemeanor.

2. Proclaimed do in Caswell & imprisoned & detained citizens &c.

3. Imprisoned Josiah Turner.

4. Without warrant of law, did incite procure Kirk, Bergen & other evil disposed persons to assault & imprison Hill,[1] Bowes,[2] Roan[3] & other citizens of Caswell.

5. Arrest of Moore[4] & refusal & obstruction of the service of the writ of Habeas Corpus.

6. Arrest of John Kerr & others & like refusal & obstruction.

7. That in contravention and subversion of the Constitution of the state & *United States*, recruited a large body of desperate & lawless men, did seize imprison a large number of desperate & lawless men, [*sic*] seized and imprisoned a large number of citizens, and thrust some of them into a dungeon &c and drew money from the Treasury for their support.

8. That without warrant of law he drew his warrants on the Treasury for large sums of money for support of these unlawful troops, & having placed it in the hands of A. D. Jenkins paymaster.[5] R. M. Allison[6] obtained an Enjunction against the disbursements of these monies for such object against said Jenkins, when the s[ai]d Holden prevailed on him to turn over the monies to J. B. Neathery another Agent appointed by himself, and caused the said Injunction to be contravened & defeated.

1. The answer admits at page 23 that the persons named in the 1st Article were arrested, with his approval; but charges, that each of them were suspected persons & arrested on probable cause, for crimes alleged to have been committed by them and each of them. Now what probable cause on the return of Hab. Cor. has been shown, against any of them? No evidence was adduced against a single one on Habeas Corpus, or now.

2. Similar admission as to persons named in Article 2, at page 26. What evidence has been adduced against any of them? Not a particle. He adds to the injury of imprisonment and the infliction of personal punishment, the foul imputation of high crimes, either as "accessories or principals."

3. What right has he to arrest? That power is a judicial function, as has been already demonstrated in an earlier stage of this proceeding. The legal principles in such case are these: 1. When the courts of justice are open there is a state of peace in judgment of law. 2. Even the King of England cannot order the arrest of a subject; it can only be effected by warrant of a magistrate in a proper affidavit, in time of peace. *The courts were open here, and there was peace.* The Governor therefore had no authority to make arrests. The proof is overwhelming, that the courts were open; that there was no resistance to the execution of the law; and no insurrection.

4. If Military aid had been wanting there were U.S. troops in Alamance from an early day in March, and in Caswell from the 9th July 1871. These facts are carefully suppressed, throughout his answer. A perusal of that would inspire the belief that there was not a Federal soldier in the state.

I therefore objected on an early day of this trial, to the reception of evidence of secret societies in these counties on the commission of secret crimes therein. Because if true, they constituted no insurrection, and could furnish no justification for arrests upon the orders of the Governor, by means of a military force raised by his directive.

5. But it has been contended, that the act of 1869-70 p. 64 justifies the act of the Governor in declaring the county in a state of insurrection, and making arrests of the citizens of these two counties. It is has been [*sic*] heretofore suggested, that a declaration of insurrection, could not make an insurrection, unless it existed in fact; that such declaration according to the rule of construing penal statutes, was but a caution & a warning, which could not deprive the citizens of their rights as such, unless this denunciation had been contained in the statute. But conceding that it did have this effect, for the time being, and subjected them to arrest: the Governor is liable to impeachment for the abuse of this power, if he proclaimed it unnecessarily & corruptly, as we allege that he did. Just as he may be impeached for the perversion of any other power of his office, the power of pardon for example. A pardon granted by him, no matter from what motive must operate to remit punishment; but if granted corruptly and mischievously, he should be made to atone for it by impeachment. In the same manner a judge is impeachable for the corrupt exercise of any discretionary power, and the claim set up in the respondent's answer at page 25 is wholly inadmissable. A Court of Impeachment has power, upon prosecution by the representatives of the people, to "question any action or officers of the Executive or Judicial branches of the Govt. and to impute the abuse of such powers as high crimes & misdemeanors. The power of Impeachment has so seldom been brought into action in this state, that the respondent even in his solemn answer has fallen into an error which claims for him privileges & immunities savoring of the prerogatives of royalty.

Now the allegations in his answer, as to a state of insurrection in these counties has been proven to be false. He alleges ps. 24-5, 1st, that a secret society existed for the perpetration of crime, & protection of the perpetrators, to the numbering a majority of the adult men in Alamance. It is proved that this organization to which this power is imported never amounted to more than 200 in Alamance, and had been disbanded as early as May or June 1869, and is not proved to have existed at all in the county of Caswell. "2nd that the grand juries had refused to find Bills of Indictment, against members of these organizations, or if per chance any were found against such members public juries refused to convict; magistrates failed to act, and the judges & solicitors attended courts as a matter of form, a reign of terror existed, and the administration of justice was wholly impeded . . . murder stalked abroad in the land, and those whose hands were red with the blood of their victims remained, unnoticed & unpunished." This is the grossest exaggeration—contradicted by all the evidence.

Morbid partisanship
6. The respondent seems to have been actuated by a morbid partisanship from the beginning of his administration, which prompted him to look upon every crime as the offspring of political feeling & hostility to the Govt. The ungracious reference to the protests of Govr Worth, the frequency of his proclamations, the character of the Proclamations, looking only in one direction, the protection of the political rights of the freedmen &c.
7. Instead of devoting himself to the noble studies by which states are made prosperous & their people happy, his mind was occupied in questions of new party.

There could in his estimation be no offenses against the peace & good order of society except from political causes. Hence the counties of Alamance & Caswell have reked from end to end—the harlots, & publicans, adulterers & thieves, have been summoned here, and the unlawful infliction of punishments on them have been are [*sic*] brought forward as evidence of the insurrectionary character of the people. Much "foul crime has been brought forward to be resolved in public." Even self condemned offenders who acknowledge that they got no more than they deserved are brought forward in the lists of martyrs. And his answer he charges that corruption had reached such a stage, that justice could not be administered.
8. If this were so, the law had provided, that causes might be moved out of the county, to be tried elsewhere by the civil courts. No law had pretended to authorize any military court to try offenders.
Motives
9. His aim from the beginning was to supersede the civil courts, and to substitute military courts. This was an unlawful & unconstitutional intent, for which there can be no excuse. His Letters of the N.C. members of Congress, March 14th 1870, report of trial p. 166, calling for suspension of Habeas Corpus. Letter to Senator Abbott[7] of March 17th to same effect. Although he knew, that the Legislature had stricken out of the Bill of Jany. 1870, the section in relation to such suspension.

See also letter to Kirk July 17th 1870, declaring that court will be held on 25 July & look after Plato Durhams[8] [illegible], p. 233. Also Aug. 3rd gives the names of the officers who were to constitute the court—p. 1147. Brutal conduct to to [*sic*] prisoners. This letter [illegible] then approves it.
10. 1. He had been asked to embody Militia & appoint Ray[9] commander. See Letter of Albright, Hardin & others Feb 28 p. 1134. This not heeded.
2. Pride Jones[10] asks, that his commission may extend to Alamance, and to operate in the Leagues as well. This not heeded.
3. Delay advertised for apprehension of murderers of Outlaw till 6th June in general proclamation.
4. Sending off for Kirk, & his East Tennessee troops to inspire terror. A slur upon all state officers which would have justified resignation.
5. The ferocious placard written by his own hand, which is a war cry, instead of a call for troops.
6. Court sat on 7th of June. No step to stimulate a judicial investigation. Military plans being all that were designed. Justice regularly administered. Yet Kirk is sent out, with liberty to seize imprison & try by military court.

7. The suppression of his correspondence only those communications on Letter Book.
8. Removal of Telegrams of orders.
9. Letters found in the court house in Graham, show, that the purpose was to control elections, &c.
10. 10th. The characters of the persons arrested, show that the object was not to ferret out crime, but to terrorize over the people. Henderson Scott,[11] J. S. Scott,[12] Bingham,[13] Mebane[14] Gent and indeed the whole. Some few of them are found to have been members of the white brotherhood; but the great body of them were peaceable citizens, who had been guilty of no crime or even impropriety.
11. The treatment of the prisoners shows a design to extract evidence by torture.
11. He can't disguise his motives, by arousing prejudice against assassins—stratagem of Persistratus. He charges innocent men as assassins. Even these assassins evinced their dread of the law, by disguise & concealment; he manifests his contempt for it, going in open day to commit outrages no less justifiable than theirs—seizing, charging with crimes, cursing, abusing, hanging, and committing to jail &c. He defies Habeas Corpus, and at the last moment, send for the Ch. J. to break his fall.
12. These apply for the writ—his introduction on the stage &c. Correspondence with the Ch. J. & with Kirk. Holding out to the former, that he may after a while surrender the prisoners. While he is preparing a military court for them. His subsequent correspondence with the Prest. U.S. and the Ch. J. professing to the Ch. J. that he had always contemplated the surrender of the prisoners to him; while to the President, he appeals for force to avoid this surrender at all, & begs that U.S. troops may not be used to coerce him.
13. Such was his unlawful conduct.

The means employed in it was equally unlawful, and dangerous. He was only authorized to employ militia by calling them into service. Great dread of standing armies. Militia provided for in Constitution. Hamilton in Fed[era]list 130, Act of 1868, Ch. 22, for organization. Do 27th Jany. 1870, for "calling into service. Col Clark proves that these were recruited men, no regard was had to their being of the Militia. He had the greatest contempt for this kind of force. If this army was of the Militia where is it now? No commisssions produced, Because they would show this force unlawful.
14. No inference to be drawn, that any favor is designed to be shown to secret & illegal combinations against law, or favor to assassins, from this prosecution. The counsels of Washington against party excess & combinations are the true doctrines of a Republic.
15. Arbitrary suspension of the privilege of Habeas Corpus, and terror over the Judiciary. Executive order not [illegible] by law does not justify an illegal act. Tracy v Swartwout 10 Peters 80. Duty of court to inquire on Habeas Corpus, whether insurrection exists. [Comtte] ex rel. Coggins v Frink, 4 Law Reg. U.S. 700.
16. Drawing money illegally from Treasury to pay this army illegal—if force was[15]

[1]Samuel P. Hill, a Confederate veteran and attorney who resided in Yanceyville, Caswell County, was among those arrested in the Kirk-Holden War. He was a Conservative in politics. Powell, *History of Caswell County*, 200, 238; *Holden Trial*, II, 789-815, III, 2540.

[2]William B. Bowe, a sixty-three-year-old Caswell County farmer, was among those arrested in Yanceyville by Kirk. An old-line Whig and then a Conservative, Bowe was repeatedly cursed and threatened with death. *Holden Trial*, II, 836-850, III, 2540.

[3]Felix Roan.

[4]Adolphus G. Moore.

[5]Aaron D. Jenkins, assistant clerk of the state treasury, was directed to act as paymaster to "state troops" and received $60,000 to finance the Kirk-Holden War. At about the same time, he was appointed teller in the treasury department. *Holden Trial*, II, 218, 228.

[6]Richard Monroe Allison (1821-1884), a lawyer and judge of Iredell County, attended the University of North Carolina and Davidson College. He was a first lieutenant in Company B, Nineteenth North Carolina Regiment during the Civil War. Grant, *Alumni History*, 10; Manarin and Jordan, *North Carolina Troops*, II, 114.

[7]Joseph C. Abbott.

[8]Plato Durham (1840-1875), of Cleveland County, was one of thirteen children of Micajah and Esther Durham. He had served the Confederacy as a courier and then captain in the Twelfth North Carolina Regiment. After the war Durham practiced law in Shelby and represented Cleveland County in the state legislature (1866, 1868, and 1869) and in the constitutional conventions in 1868 (where he led a small group of Conservatives in contesting the majority Radicals at every juncture) and 1875. He was grand chief of the Cleveland County Klan but sought to disband the secret organization when rowdy elements began to use it for lawless purposes. Among those in Rutherford and Cleveland counties arrested in 1871 for Klan activities, Durham was never brought to trial and subsequently worked to free other Klansmen who had been imprisoned. In the Constitutional Convention of 1875 he was a leader in dismantling radical reconstruction. *Our Heritage: A History of Cleveland County* (Shelby: Shelby Daily Star, 1976), 129-130; Cheney, *North Carolina Government*, 334, 448, 449, 845, 874; Powell, *DNCB*, II, 126-127.

[9]Henry Milton Ray, of Alamance County, was a delegate to the Constitutional Convention of 1868. Holden appointed him to the military commission in 1870 with the rank of colonel. Cheney, *North Carolina Government*, 845; Hamilton, *Reconstruction in North Carolina*, 505. Ray's testimony in Holden's impeachment may be found in *Holden Trial*, II, 1707-1728.

[10]Pride Jones (1815-1889), of Hillsborough, was a graduate of the University of North Carolina and a Confederate lieutenant colonel. He served in the state legislature in the 1858 and 1872 sessions. In 1870 Holden commissioned Jones, a Conservative, as captain in the Orange County militia, to work for the suppression of the Klan and the restoration of peace and order. Raper, *Holden*, 163; Spencer Alumni Project; Cheney, *North Carolina Government*, 326, 454.

[11]Henderson Scott, a Graham merchant, was one of the Klan leaders arrested and brought before Kirk by Colonel Bergen. Kirk refused to grant bail and ordered the prisoners sent to Yanceyville, where the Caswell County courthouse was used as his official headquarters and jail. Raper, *Holden*, 175, 317n.

[12]James S. Scott.

[13]William Bingham.

[14]Benjamin Franklin Mebane.

[15]Graham's notes end abruptly at this point. For his entire speech, delivered on the thirty-eighth day of the proceedings, see *Holden Trial*, III, 2271-2311.

William A. Graham's childhood home at Vesuvius Furnace in Lincoln County. Photograph from William A. Graham, Jr., *General Joseph Graham and His Papers on North Carolina Revolutionary History* (Raleigh: Edwards and Broughton, 1904), facing 159.

John Davidson Graham, 1789-1847, the brother of William A. Graham. Portrait from Graham, *General Joseph Graham*, facing 174.

James Graham, 1793-1851, the brother of William A. Graham. Portrait from Graham, *General Joseph Graham*, facing 176.

Dr. Joseph Graham. Photograph from *Cyclopedia of Eminent and Representative Men of the Carolinas of the Nineteenth Century* (Madison, Wis.: Brant and Fuller, 2 volumes, 1892; Spartanburg: Reprint Company, 1973), II, facing 251.

John Washington Graham. Photograph from Josephus Daniels, *Editor in Politics* (Chapel Hill: University of North Carolina Press, 1941), facing 419.

William Alexander Graham, Jr. Photograph from William A. Graham, Jr., *History of the South Fork Baptist Association* (1901).

Augustus Washington Graham. Photograph from Aubrey Lee Brooks and Hugh Talmage Lefler (eds.), *The Papers of Walter Clark* (Chapel Hill: University of North Carolina Press, 2 volumes, 1948-1950), II, facing 440.

Susan Washington Graham (1851-1909), Graham's only daughter, married Walter Clark in January, 1874. Photograph from Brooks and Lefler, *Clark Papers.*

Francis M. Carter[1] *to William A. Graham* UNC

Farmington,
Missouri.
March 16th., A.D. 1871.

Dear Sir, & esteemed friend,

I understand that in case Gov. Holden of North Carolina should be removed, the Legislature will renovate our old Alma Mater, (Chapel Hill), by the appointment of a president, and the reinstating of the old faculty. I sincerely hope that such a happy state of affairs may be brought about at that venerable institution of learning.

I, for one, am deeply interested in the selection of a gentleman for president, who will attract the first young men of the country to that institution, the mother of statesmen. I think no gentleman is more calculated to accomplish that design than Gen. D. H. Hill. He would attract students from all parts of the nation. I think the Legislature ought to use all their efforts to get him to accept that position, and to allow him a salary sufficient to remunerate him for his time and services. If they could not succeed in getting him to accept the position, they ought to get some one of the notable Southern leaders to accept the same. But I presume Gen. Hill would do so.

The Southern leaders are becoming popular rapidly in the North. They are not only viewed as men of great mind, but also as men of great integrity. I understand that you have a son who is in the N.C. Senate. I presume that he is a gentleman of influence. I know, of my own Knowledge, that you have almost unbounded influence in North Carolina. Every effort ought to be made to bring up Chapel Hill to a standard equal to, if not superior to, any other college in the Union. The president and professors ought to be allowed the same salaries as are allowed the president and professors of Harvard or Yale. Then, the Trustees of the institution can employ the best talent in the nation. North Carolina is able to patronize her State University to that amount.

I hope that affairs are getting better in North Carolina. We have today received the news of the glorious Democratic victory in New Hampshire.

---

[1]Francis Marion Carter of Carter County, Missouri, had earned an A.B. degree at the University of North Carolina in 1862. He had served in the Confederate army, where he may have known D. H. Hill. Grant, *Alumni History*, 103.

Edward J. Hale to William A. Graham UNC

E. J. Hale & Son
17 Murray Street,
New York,
March 28th., 1871.

. . . .

We have been deeply interested in the proceedings of the Court of Impeachment, & rejoiced greatly at the result. Especially were we gratified—as well as surprised—at the accession of several Radical Senators to the ranks of the majority. This is a degree of honesty that we did not look for. An uncharitable person here has remarked that they were preparing the way for a leap over the fence into the ranks of the majority.

It would be fortunate indeed for the State, if you could get rid of all the other bad men who have done their best,—or worst,—to ruin and disgrace her.

William A. Graham to William A. Graham, Jr. A&H

Hillsboro
April 3rd., 1871

James has gone this morning. He obtained leave of absence from the Legislature, they expect to adjourn on Thursday. John was here yesterday, went to Raleigh this morning. George is to leave tomorrow—will stop to see you. I hope he will meet with success in Atlanta; which is, I presume, very much of a frontier Town.

The conviction of Holden brought no reconstruction, as was predicted. Neither will the passage of the Convention Act. He seems to have fled to avoid being sued in the State; and will probably not return. I think this shews that he grew rich from the frauds practised on the State Finances.[1] What the commission appointed by the Legislature[2] will bring out I don't know. But fear it will not be thorough. . . .

I have some money of the N.C. R. Co. to redeem bonds 1st Nov. 1872. If you see an opportunity to use, say $1,000. at 8 percent interest; and can return it punctually at that time, you can take that amount.

Your mother prepares to go to Kinston on a visit of 8 or 10 days, next week. I write in haste before leaving for court. Love to Julia and the children.

Affectionately yours,

[1]There is no evidence that Holden ever shared in the fraud that discredited his administration. It should be noted, however, that he apparently did little or nothing to prevent the fraudulent actions of his political friends. Graham was wrong when he speculated that Holden had left North Carolina permanently.

[2]The legislature had appointed a commission composed of William M. Shipp, chairman, Joseph G. Batchelor, and James G. Martin to investigate the frauds. For their findings see *Report of the Commission to Investigate Charges of Fraud and Corruption, under Act of Assembly, Session 1871-72* (Raleigh: J. H. Moore, 1872). The report is 576 pages long.

Robert C. Winthrop to William A. Graham UNC

Boston,
April 3, 1871.

You will have rec'd, I trust, ere this, a parcel by Express, containing copies of our Proceedings at Philadelphia, with Dr. Sears's Report. I hope you will be able to distribute them among the Public Libraries & Journals, & among such leading individuals as ought to be informed as to our doings.

We were very sorry to lose your presence at our meeting. You will have seen how we filled the vacancies in our Board. Your suggestions as to Candidates were not unheeded; but after much deliberation we decided on Mr. Stuart & Gen'l Taylor. The latter was warmly recommended by Mr. Bradford.

You will have rec'd, also, the copy of our Memorial to the Legislature of Mississippi, which I sent you by mail. If you know any one at Jackson who could aid our Memorial, or if any way occurs to you for promoting its success, I hope you will do what you can. We have left it to take care of itself for the present, having transmitted copies for presentation to the two Houses & for distribution among the members. It may serve as an entering wedge, if nothing more; but I hope it will lead to action of some sort at no distant day.

. . . .

You can have more copies of the Proceedings & Report, if you can use them to advantage.

Believe me,
With great regard,
Yours sincerely,

Columbian College[1] Committee to William A. Graham UNC

Washington, D.C.,
May 1st., 1871.

We have the honor to inform you that at the Triennial Election for Trustees of the Columbian College held this day, you were elected a member of that body for the ensuing three years.

A meeting for the organization of said Board will be held at the Law Building on 5th. Street, on Friday, May 5th., at 4 o'clock P.M.

Respectfully yours,
A. Rothwell,[2]
Robert C. Fox.[3]
Committee on Election.

[1]The Columbian College, later Columbian University (1873) and now George Washington University (1904), was established in 1821 in the District of Columbia. The institution is tangibly linked to Washington. Ironically, it was he who promoted the idea, never fulfilled, of a nonsectarian national university in the federal city. See Elmer Louis

Kayser, *Bricks without Straw: The Evolution of George Washington University* (New York: Appleton-Century-Crofts, 1970), hereinafter cited as Kayser, *Bricks without Straw*.

[2]The Reverend Andrew Rothwell (d. 1883) was one of the trustees of Columbian College and University from 1835 to 1883. A respected Baptist minister, he gave "almost daily attention to the affairs of the College." Of Rothwell a historian of the institution says, "No other Trustee was as regular in attendance at meetings, as assiduous in auditing financial statements, heading committees, and preparing reports." Kayser, *Bricks without Straw*, 132.

[3]Robert Claybrook Fox (b. 1834) was a native of Virginia who attended the University of Virginia and served as a tutor at Columbian College before entering a business venture. Later he became secretary and treasurer of Columbian College. In addition, he was secretary of Columbian Institute for the Deaf and Dumb. *Cyclopedia of American Biography*, III, 251.

John Potts Brown[1] *to William A. Graham* A&H

Minneapolis, Minn.
May 1, 1871.

I hope you will pardon the liberty I take in sending by same mail with this a "Minneapolis Tribune" of yest'y,[2] cont'g a vile aspersion vs. No. Carolina as well as vs. Gov. Vance. I am unwilling to hear, much less believe, such foul reports & very often have rough words in combatting them.

If you know anything about the matter stated, would you drop me a line in explanation, with leave to publish what you say, if no objection? I have addressed a copy of same paper to Gov. Vance, care J. W. Osborne,[3] Charlotte—hoping to reach him—not knowing the Gov's whereabouts.

I trust you are well, prosperous, & happy—and with a vivid & delightful recollection of the *long ago*, I am, in perfect respect.

---

[1]John Potts Brown (b. 1811) was a native of Wilmington and an 1829 graduate of the University of North Carolina at Chapel Hill. Brown lived for some time in Minnesota before moving to New York. Grant, *Alumni History*, 77.

[2]This was not found.

[3]James Walker Osborne (1811-1869), born in Salisbury, was a lawyer, judge, and public servant. Graduated by the University of North Carolina in 1830, he read law with William A. Graham. In 1833 he was admitted to the bar and established a Charlotte practice. He was active in the movement for internal improvements, especially railroads. Osborne was superintendent of the Charlotte mint from 1849 to 1853 and a superior court judge from 1859 to 1866. He was a state senator, 1868-1869. Grant, *Alumni History*, 467; Tompkins, *History of Mecklenburg*, II, 78.

Edward J. Hale to William A. Graham UNC

17 Murray Street,
New York,
May 5, 1871.

I owe you very hearty thanks for the copy of your Memorial Oration.[1] It brings before me so vividly its venerable subject, & many cherished recollections of him, & of many others whom you had occasion to mention, that I seem to be back in North Carolina, contemplating him, & them, with the admiration & reverence of past, & happier days. To say nothing of his Judicial career, (& with that I was profoundly impressed whilst reprinting several vols. of the N.C. Reports). I have two special reminiscences of him on which I dwell with pleasure. In dining with him at Mr. Roulhac's, during one Episcopal Convention some years ago, I witnessed a little byplay between himself & Mrs. R., when he drank with her to the health of the absent wife & mother, which impressed me so deeply as to his domestic affections & happiness. I cannot describe the scene, but I can never forget it.

The other to which I allude was personal to myself. You know we had always been politically opposed till the War. In the course of that struggle he wrote me a long letter,[2] the first—not the last—I ever received from him, of which I was, & am, very proud. It was, in all respects, a remarkable letter, & in my gratification I took it to my good old friend Mr. Haigh.[3] He read it, and remarked that it was a letter to hand down to my children. And so I shall hand it down. Since that time he, & Mr. Badger, & Mr. Haigh, & Mr. Devereux,[4] & Gov. Morehead, & now Gov. Manly, are all gone, not to mention scores of others whom I esteemed.

---

[1]This refers to Graham's address memorializing Thomas Ruffin.

[2]The letter was dated August 17, 1863. It is in the North Carolina Archives but is so badly burned that it is impossible to transcribe a satisfactory copy.

[3]William Hooper Haigh was the head of a large and prominent Fayetteville family. The son of Major Charles Haigh and his wife, Alice Marsden Swann, William Hooper was a lawyer. John Alexander Oates, *The Story of Fayetteville and the Upper Cape Fear* (Fayetteville: Privately published, 1950), 104, 257, 810, hereinafter cited as Oates, *Story of Fayetteville.*

[4]Thomas Pollock Devereux (1793-1869), son of Frances Pollock and John Devereux, Sr., was graduated at Yale in 1813 and received an honorary master's degree from the University of North Carolina in 1818. He was a prominent lawyer and served as a United States district attorney and reporter for the state supreme court before he decided to abandon the practice of law and devote his full time to the management of the very large Devereux estate, part of which lay in Raleigh and part in the northeastern area of the state, in Bertie and Halifax counties. His first wife was Catherine Ann Johnson of Connecticut, with whom he had one son and six daughters; his second wife was Ann Mary Maitland of New York. The Civil War brought devastation and financial ruin to Devereux, so that he was forced to declare bankruptcy in 1868. Unable to recoup their prewar fortune, the family members eventually lost most of their property. In his early career, Devereux had been a Whig leader, a close friend of George Badger, and a supporter of William A. Graham in his bid for the office of governor. Crabtree and Patton, *"Journal of a Secesh Lady,"* xxi-xxiv.

William A. Graham to William A. Graham, Jr. A&H

Hillsboro
May 8th 1871

Dear Wm

I have been so much occupied, that I have not found leisure to reply to your inquiry for my opinion as to the expediency of erecting a Flouring mill with the means you have in hand. Such questions depend so much on local considerations, which you can judge of better than I can, that I am at a loss, to come to a conclusion. As to the extent of custom, that might be expected, I suppose, it might be considerable on the northern side; but with Rehoboth on the West, Brevards & Hunters on the South, the river mills on the East, I think, the neighborhood custom would not be very great. To make the adventure yield much profit therefore, it would be necessary to buy wheat & calculate on selling flour. This would involve the necessity [of] a wagon & team to send off 20 to 50 miles, as the neighboring country would have no great surplus; the same team might haul to Charlotte, or the depot; but wagonage is a great drawback in any business, besides, the liability to losses from negligent wagoneers, & wear & tear. I suppose, it would be necessary to build a new mill house, fit for storing grain, besides machinery & bolting apparatus. Insurance against fire & high water should also be taken into the calculation. Still the question recurs, what better use can one make of capital; and being already advanced to the extent of a corn mill, is a reason for such an establishment as may give full employment to a miller. I don't know what would be the cost of such a mill. The insurance against floods should be well estimated. Robt. Brevard considered his expenditure on his mill a poor investment; but his may not have been a favorable experiment.

I propose, to go to Charlotte next Saturday night & thence to the plantation; and will endeavor to go to see you in the course of the week, and may have other views to suggest upon more reflection. I suppose, I shall have to get a horse from the livery stable, to go to Amazonia, & may go up from there or return to Charlotte & go up by rail. If you wish any thing down there, & will write me, I will attend to it for you. I think, you should endeavor to raise more stock of all kinds. Mules, cattle, Hogs & sheep. Brevard Davidson[1] could give more information, as to the value of milling than any person of my acquaintance, but he has the advantage in Charlotte market of the East side of the river, & not more than half your distance; and I think he does not speak of it very favorably. But you should first have accurate estimates of the cost.

I think, I shall sell my cotton upon this visit. It has not improved but rather declined in 5 or more months, that I have held it. I am much inclined to do a good deal of breaking up and sow clover, and try stock next year instead of cotton, on any extended scale.

Orange Court is over. A Bill of Indictment was found against Holden for perjury. Turner was out of the way, when his suit was called for false imprisonment, and I had to continue it. He came in afterwards, & was much chagrined & disappointed but found the mishap his own fault, in not keeping an eye on the state of business. There was no occurence of any interest in the court.

James was returned to Alamance today. John went to Raleigh for his family—will remain till after the formal ceremonies of the 10th. Judge Shipp & Major Gales[2] who have been spending a day with Mr. Cameron went down with him.

I sent Theodore Brevard[3] a copy of my Address on Judge Ruffin, and will be glad to be able to go and see him, when I come up, as I hear his health is bad. Brown's[4] sale took place last Thursday. I bo't the Lot west of my stable, half acre at $125. John bo't the large store house, Mr. Cameron the

Carmichael corner, some New York creditors, the Hotel, others Brown's house. The Tobacco market here is giving animation to business, & four manufacturies are being started. Your mother has been speaking of going West with me, but has given it out.

Our love to Julia and the children.

Affectionately yours,

---

[1]Adam Brevard Davidson of Rural Hill plantation, Mecklenburg County, was a paternal cousin of William A. Graham. Davidson, *Major John Davidson*, 75-79.

[2]Seaton Gales (1828-1878), of Raleigh, was the son of Weston Gales and succeeded his father as editor of the *Raleigh Register*. Only twenty years old at the time of his father's death in July, 1848, Seaton Gales had graduated the previous month from the University of North Carolina, sharing top honors with a classmate. He became the first trained newspaper editor in North Carolina. Under young Gales's editorship the *Register* continued to be an organ of the Whig party. He took a moderate position on the question of sectional differences. Like many other Whigs he was perplexed at the declining fortunes of the party and by the mid-1850s had embraced Know-Nothingism. This defection, which rankled old-line Whigs, combined with financial difficulties to cause Seaton Gales to assign the *Register* and all its debts to Daniel G. Fowle. The paper was sold at public auction and thus passed from the Gales family to other hands.

For the next several years Gales was associated with the North Carolina Bank. When the Civil War came, he was appointed adjutant of the Fourth North Carolina Regiment. He rose to major while serving in the Army of Northern Virginia. Captured at Fisher's Hill in October, 1864, he was imprisoned at Johnson's Island. After the war Seaton Gales was briefly associate editor of the Raleigh *Sentinel* but soon accepted a position as secretary of the North Carolina Home Insurance Company of Raleigh, a position he held until 1877. Robert Neal Elliott, Jr., *The Raleigh Register, 1799-1863* (Chapel Hill: University of North Carolina Press, 1955), 89-90, 100-101.

[3]Theodore (Theodorus) W. Brevard (d. 1877) was brother to Robert Brevard and cousin to William A. Graham. He had been a lawyer and county court judge in Alabama and state comptroller in Florida but returned to Lincolnton after the Civil War and operated a boarding school there. Sherrill, *Annals of Lincoln County*, 225; Powell, *DNCB*, I, 218-219.

[4]Brown has not been further identified.

Kemp P. Battle to William A. Graham UNC

Raleigh
May 17/71

I have agreed to deliver an Address at Bingham's School on June 6th. In order to be accurate in some statements of a historical nature, I desire to make, I will thank you to enlighten me on a few points.

1. On what occasion did the Scotch-Irish from Pennsylvania remove to N.C., i.e., was there a *general* exodus, or did your grandmother[1] and others remove from Penn. alone? My impression is, that a colony of Scotch-Irish removed to the Yadkin, & Catawba, and Haw River Valley from Penn., & that their descendants give tone to Caldwell & other counties, which appear always to take manly & sensible views of public affairs.

2. What caused the removal of the Scotch-Irish to America? Was that from any political convulsion, or merely from private motives?

3. Was your family Scotch-Irish? I have assumed in Question 1. that it is, but then your name, Graham = Grahame = *Graeme*, (vide Fortunes of Nigel) smacks of Celtic or Highland origin.

4. When did the Scotch-Irish settle in Ulster? Ulster was settled both by English & Scotch on the conquests of Henry & [blank] But was there any one settlement of Scotch of a character so marked as to give the people of Ulster, who removed to the U.S. the honorable name of *Scotch*-Irish.

What I cannot understand is that the emigrants to America from Ulster should be called *Scotch*-Irish instead of *English*-Irish.

And then I desire to know whether the settlers in N.C. from Penn. kept together in bands or selected homes sporadically.

Pardon me, my dear Sir, for troubling you. I probably might find the points I wish by *studying history*, but I have not time to do so just now, & I presume on your kindness, which I have never found to fail when called on.

I have no idea of writing a historical address, but I want my allusions *to be accurate.*

---

[1]In volume I of *The Papers of William Alexander Graham*, pages 66-127, appears an address on Graham delivered by Frank Nash entitled *Address at the Unveiling of the Bust of William A. Graham, by the North Carolina Historical Commission, in the Rotunda of the State Capitol, Delivered in the Hall of the House of Representatives, January 12, 1910* (Raleigh: Edwards and Broughton Printing Company, 1910). In his address Nash says this about Graham's grandmother:

> Of this sturdy and virile race [Scotch-Irish] was James Graham, who at the age of nineteen years, in 1773 [*sic*; 1733], migrated from County Down, Ireland, to Berks County, Pennsylvania. He was twice married, his second wife being the widow Mary Barber, and died in 1763. By the last marriage there were five children. In 1768 Mrs. Graham, with her children, coming by sea to Charleston, S.C., thence across country, located in Mecklenburg County, N.C. In 1771 she purchased a tract of land containing two hundred acres within three miles of the then little hamlet of Charlotte. Most of these Scotch-Irish, and there were many of them, migrated from Pennsylvania south in search of fertile lands in a milder climate. It is probable that this was Mrs. Graham's motive, induced thereto also by the fact that many of her neighbors and friends had preceded her. She must have been a woman of remarkable courage and strength of character to undertake this long, tedious and dangerous journey with six young children, the youngest scarcely more than four years of age (p. 67).

Graham, in his letter of June 2, 1871, in this volume, indicates that his grandmother came from Pennsylvania in 1765, stayed in Mecklenburg County for two years, moved to South Carolina for a year, and then returned to Mecklenburg.

J. H. Hubbell[1] *to William A. Graham* UNC

New York,
May 20th 1871

I mail you today a Copy of my legal Directory for 1871 which please accept with my compliments. I have endeavored to improve on the "National Legal Directory" sent you last year and which you were kind enough to speak well of.

If not too much engaged I should be pleased to have you examine the list of Attorneys given for your state, and favor me with your opinion as to the standing of those with whom you may be acquainted, and also concerning the Collection Laws ETC as given.

You will note that I have inserted your name as attorney for your place which I trust will be satisfactory.

Trusting that I shall have the pleasure of hearing from you at your earliest convenience I am

Yours truly

---

[1]This letter indicates that Hubbell had compiled a legal directory. He has not been further identified.

William A. Graham to Kemp P. Battle UNC: BATTLE

Hillsboro'
May 22nd 1871.

My Dear Sir

I was absent last week in the Catawba and therefore the delay in replying to yours of 17th inst. You will find all your inquiries answered, I think, in "Foote's Sketches of N.C."—My copy is out of place, and I cannot lay my hand on it. You will find it, if not in the public library of the State, in that of Dr. Lacey[1] or Atkinson.[2]

1. The people of all original Ireland were Celtic; where not displaced by immigrants, they are so still. The Roman Catholics in the Southern & middle parts of the Island are all Celts. But you will see in Foote, and in "Carruthers Life of Caldwell," which is before me, p. 86, 87, that in the reign of James 1st, the great Earls of Tyrone & Tyrconnel, having conspired against the Government were obliged to flee, and their great estates comprising 500,000 acres of land were confiscated. The Scotch King of England found it an admirable mode of carrying civilization in to this territory, which had been thinly peopled by Roman Catholic Celts, & infested with robbers, by making grants to his countrymen, who would emigrate from Scotland. This was the beginning of the exodus: but it was stimulated, by the establishment of Prelacy in Scotland under Charles 1st. in 1637, & Char. 2nd. in 1661, so that the North Eastern Counties in time became settled with a population almost purely Scotch, though upon Irish soil. Hence the name of Scotch-Irish. They carried with them, the Presbyterian form of religion, which supplanted Catholicism, and the habits of thrift, economy, stern morals, & care for the education of children, which has characterized them everywhere.

2. I know of no special reason for the emigration of the Scotch Irish to America, Pennsylvania, except the usual one, that the swarm had become too large for the hive

3. My own family originally Scotch are said to have gone to Ireland in the reign of Charles 2nd. My grand father[3] arrived in Pennsylvania in 1733, being a native of the County of Down, in the part near Carlingford Bay, and then 18 years of age.

4. Their emigration to N.C. took place in 1767 or 8—going first to Tyger river in South Carolina, but returning & locating three miles North of

Charlotte within a year or two, because of danger from the vicinity of the Indians, and the want of schools for children. My grand mother, a widow, having a family of six.

5. The habits of the people were in a great degree pastoral at that time: they relied on beef cattle for exportation, and a means of livelihood: and the chief inducement for coming South was, the rich natural pastures, affording range for cattle. These were driven to Philadelphia, and it may be to Boston in some instances, to market. My Father who was born in 1759, could remember to have seen at his home in Chester Co. Penna friends of his family, arrive from the "Haw fields of Carolina," with one or more pack horses laden with peltries, who gave enchanting accounts of the fertility of the soil, & especially its pasturage.

6. The stream of emigration of the Scotch Irish from Pennsylvania is distinctly traced, through the valley of Virginia, North Carolina, South Carolina & Georgia before the Revolution. Where ever it went, it carried the lights of education & high morality. The preacher of the congregation being a classical scholar, and the teacher of its youth, if it had no other.

The M'Dowells, Prestons, Houstons (Texas Sam) being of it in Va. the Polks, Davidsons, Alexanders, Harrises &c in N.C., the Calhouns, Pickenses, Butlers &c in S.C. It was met by another current of emigrants direct from the old Country of Ireland, in the Witherspoons, Friersons, Bradleys, Wilsons, Crawfords, coming through Charleston to upper S.C. among whom was the family of Andrew Jackson, the second Jackson is, I believe of the same stock in Va. In Dr. Hawks' lecture,[4] bound up with those of Govr. Swain & myself, you will find a good description of these people & their characteristics.

7. At Queens College (after the declaration of Independence Liberty Hall) in Charlotte, the seminary of these people were educated Jackson, Adair of Chester, afterwards of Kentucky, the Polks, Davidsons, Brevards and Harrises, Wilsons & Robinsons of N.C.: and many of the most distinguished divines, lawyers & physicians of S.C. & Georgia at that early period

8. The emigration from Penna. was in considerable companies, i.e. several families as comrades.

The Dickeys of Orange, now Alamance, Lindseys of Guilford & others (stopping among their friends in these counties,) came with my ancestors, who went on with the Moores to S.C. at first, but returned to Mecklenburg as before stated, prior to the Regulation.

In the life of Genl. Davidson, in appendix to "Lee's Memoirs of the War in the South", you will see, that he was a native of Lancaster Penn. but educated at Charlotte.

If these hasty notes should be of any service to you, I will be gratified.

---

[1]The Reverend Drury Lacy (1802-1884), a native of Virginia and a graduate of Hampden-Sydney College, taught school prior to being converted to Christianity in 1828. Subsequently, he attended the Union Theological Seminary in Richmond. Ordained in 1833, he became minister of the New Bern Presbyterian Church on January 1, 1834; he held that appointment for three years before accepting the call of a Raleigh church. He was eminently successful in the Raleigh appointment and remained until 1855, when he began a six-year tenure as president of Davidson College. At the outbreak of war, Lacy became a

Confederate chaplain and ministered to thousands. After the Civil War ended, he resettled his family in Raleigh where, while he served as a supply pastor in the Orange Presbytery, his second wife, Mary Ritchie Rice, founded a girls' school that was incorporated as Peace Institute in 1872. L. C. Vass, *History of the Presbyterian Church in New Bern, N.C., with a Resumé of Early Ecclesiastical Affairs in Eastern North Carolina and a Sketch of the Early Days of New Bern, N.C.* (Richmond: Whittet and Shepperson, Printers, 1886), 148-158 passim; Shaw, *Davidson College*, 72, 81, 97, 111.

[2]Joseph Mayo Atkinson (1820-1891) was one of four brothers who became Presbyterian clergymen. After a successful career as pastor of churches in Virginia and Maryland, he was elected pastor of First Presbyterian Church in Raleigh. He succeeded Drury Lacy, who became president of Davidson College. Except for a period of two years when his health forced him to seek teaching as a means of livelihood, Atkinson was pastor of either First Presbyterian Church (1855-1875) or Second Presbyterian Church (1877-1890). Although he did not like the idea of slavery or of secession, Atkinson remained loyal to the South and did much to maintain the morale of his Confederate congregations. Powell, *DNCB*, I, 62.

[3]James Graham (ca. 1716-1763).

[4]The lecture to which Graham refers is entitled "The Mecklenburg Declaration of Independence" and was delivered before the Historical Society of New York, December 18, 1852. It was printed in the *University of North Carolina Magazine*, II (November, 1853). Francis Lister Hawks (1798-1866) of New Bern, a lawyer early in his career, became an Episcopal clergyman, a professor of divinity and ecclesiastical history, a prolific author, and a popular conversationalist and lecturer. He wrote a two-volume history of North Carolina. Powell, *DNCB*, III, 76-77.

Augustus S. Merrimon to William A. Graham A&H

Raleigh,
May 30th., 1871.

Our political friends in the Western part of the State are very anxious that you shall visit that section and address the people there in reference to the proposed Convention, between this time and that of the election. Letters of a recent date urge that you make such a visit, and that I join you.

Our Ex-Gov.[1] I am instructed to say, joins me in urging you to go, if you can make it at all convenient to do so.

I beg to suggest that I think you can accomplish much good in the West; the people there place a high estimate upon your opinions, and great worth, as a citizen and statesman, and scores of middle aged and old men who met you years ago, would be delighted to meet and renew their acquaintance with you. I trust you will go if you can. I think the trip would be pleasant to you, and let me suggest, that you ought to see that portion of the State once more, before you pass away.

If you find you cannot make the trip suggested, then I trust you will find it convenient to make public your views of the proposed Convention—its legality, propriety, etc., and the necessity for it. I suggest you might place there in the shape of a letter or a speech on some appropriate occasion. Suppose you deliver an address in this city some evening during the sitting of the Circuit Court?

Pardon the freedom with which I write. I trust a warm interest in a common cause of moment will serve for an apology.

Our information here from all quarters of the State in reference to the Convention, is encouraging indeed, and I feel the strongest confidence that we shall succeed.

---

[1]Zebulon B. Vance.

William A. Graham to Kemp P. Battle UNC: BATTLE

Hillsboro'
June 2nd, 1871.

My Dear Sir

Alamance is understood to be an original Indian name—C. H. Wiley[1] wrote a novel by this name, and gave it a wrong spelling from which it is not likely to escape. It should be "Allamance"—Mr. Hugh Waddell[2] informed me that he had seen an old French Map (it may be now at Moorefields F. N. Waddell's[3] residence 2½ miles west of Hillsboro') where it is called "Allemangue." It is a river discharging into Haw river a mile below Ruffin's Mills, & running within 200 yards of the Judge's old mansion. It has two branches "Little" & "Big" which are creeks of some size. It was fordable, on the public road passing South through Ruffin's plantation, but contained 5 times as much water as Eno at Hillsboro, & quite deep. It is now bridged at a point higher up, where fording would be very difficult. It is about such a river at the mouth as Contentnea at Snow Hill.

I have never been informed of the precise place of residence of Genl. Alexander Mebane,[4] the Father of James,[5] & grandfather of Giles. It was however in the Haw fields, and not far from Mebaneville. David Mebane lived about 5 miles South East of Mebaneville on the public Road from Hillsboro' to Ruffin's Mills or Butler's ford. That may have been the residence of his Father. It was a well known place as "Mebanes" when Lee & Pickens were maneuvering with Tarleton in that action in Feb. & March 1781—

I know nothing of the origin of the Ruffin Family beyond their settlement in Va. the Judge's grand father Robert is mentioned in an act of the Coll. legislature as a commissioner with others to lay out the Town of Petersburg. The name of Rufin is mentioned, if I recollect rightly among the Fathers who wrote after the Apostles, but I forget, if I ever knew, of what country he was.

Robert Mebane (I suppose a brother of Alexr.) was a Lt. Col. in the Continental Line from N.C. and served in Jersey, Penna. & Delaware while our troops were at the North in 77, 78, 79—He was killed by a tory whom he was endeavoring to capture in 80 or 81, in Alamance or Chatham.

I was mistaken in my last letter in a date, in respect to my own family—they emigrated from Penna. in 1765, stopped in Mecklenburg for two years, went to S.C. & stayed a year, & then returned to Mecklenburg. I believe I have noticed the several matters of your inquiry.

Very truly Yours

I expect to be at the Fedl. court on Monday next, and hope to see you.

---

[1]Calvin Henderson Wiley (1819-1887), of Guilford County, was educated by the Caldwell Institute and the University of North Carolina. He was a lawyer, editor, novelist, and educator. Early in life he became concerned about the backwardness of North Carolina social and economic conditions. As a Whig legislator, 1850-1852, he was a moving spirit in an effort to improve the state's common schools. In 1853 Wiley became the state's first

superintendent of common schools, a position he occupied until 1865. He wrote textbooks, edited an education journal, and propagandized the need for universal free education and better schools. In the process he earned recognition as one of the nation's foremost educators. Unlike many of his contemporaries, Wiley was a warm advocate of public education for the freedmen. In his later years he engaged in various religious and patriotic endeavors. *DAB*, XX, 213.

[2]Hugh Waddell (1799-1879) of Orange County, an 1818 graduate of the University of North Carolina, was a lawyer by profession. He served as a member of the House of Commons in 1828; state senator in 1836, 1844, and 1846; and lieutenant governor in 1836. Waddell was at one time a Whig and a close friend of Graham. Lefler and Wager, *Orange County*, 340; Spencer Alumni Project.

[3]Francis N. Waddell (1796-1881) was a native of Wilmington who later became a planter in Hillsborough. He attended the state university in 1818 and was a member of the North Carolina House of Commons, 1820-1821. Grant, *Alumni History*, 639.

[4]Alexander Mebane (1744-1795) was a delegate to the Provincial Congress of North Carolina, 1776; a member of the Hillsborough convention in 1788 and the Fayetteville convention in 1789; and a representative in the state House of Commons, 1787-1792. Mebane served in the United States Congress, 1793-1795. *Biographical Directory of Congress*, 1319.

[5]James Mebane (1774-1857) was born in Orange County and later became a planter in Caswell County. While a student at the university in 1795, he was elected the first president of the Diocletian Society. He served in the House of Commons in the sessions of 1798, 1803, 1818, 1820-1823 (Speaker, 1821), and 1831 and was a member of the state Senate in the sessions of 1808-1811 and 1828. Grant, *Alumni History*, 423; Cheney, *North Carolina Government*, 238, 247, 254, 256, 258, 260, 273, 277, 278, 279, 280, 282, 291, 297.

A. C. Freeman[1] *to William A. Graham* UNC

Albemarle NC
June 8th 1871

You will please pardon an old friend for troubling you with a request, one which I hope you will cheerfully comply with. I am requested by a great many of your friends here, (of whom I am proud to say you have many), to write to you & ask of you your views on the constitutionality of the Convention bill, now before the people. At the same time to assure you that your views will have more *influence* on the minds of the people than any other man in the State. As to myself, I am well aware of the views you have of it, I having heard your able address delivered in the Senate of N.C. in 1854, on your substitute for Mr. Boyd's[2] free Suffrage bill. (I then occupied a seat near you, as the representative of this, & Cabarrus County). I see it published in the last Sentinel. I suppose your views are the same as they were then. I consider the matter a very important one, & I think every person should do every thing in their power to accomplish the end desired. I think our County will go largely for Convention, if the matter is properly explained to them, however plain and simple the question may be to us, to others it is more difficult. Your views, given through the press, or otherwise, will do more to remove that difficulty in the minds of the people here than any other way I can think off. I hope, therefore, you will comply with so reasonable a request. . . .

---

[1]A. C. Freeman, of Stanly County, was a state senator, 1854-1858, and a member of the state House of Representatives, 1874-1876. Cheney, *North Carolina Government*, 322, 324, 456.

[2]George Dillard Boyd (1797-1886), born in Rockingham County, was a legislator, merchant, planter, and millowner. He maintained his various interests while serving as a member of the House of Commons, 1840-1842, and as a state senator, 1842-1859. An ardent Democrat, Boyd was defeated by the Whig candidate R. C. Puryear in his bid for Congress in 1853. Boyd was twice married, first to Minerva Hill and then to Eliza C. Webb. Powell, *DNCB*, I, 201.

George Little to William A. Graham UNC

Office
Commissioner of Immigration
For North Carolina.

Raleigh, N.C.,
June 9th., 1871.

I have received a number of letters from persons in the North, and in England, (besides those, herewith enclosed for your perusal,[1] from our Agent, Mr. Holmes,[2] in Birmingham) expressing grave apprehensions about coming to North Carolina to settle, for fear of the *Ku Klux.*

To dispel the apprehensions and fears of these persons, who do not understand the workings of our institutions, especially in England, and the causes which gave rise to these proceedings, which have damaged us so much, I will thank you to address me a letter on the subject, which others, as well as yourself, may sign, to be sent abroad for this purpose.

[1]Not found.

[2]Mr. Holmes has not been further identified.

William A. Graham to A. C. Freeman A&H

[Copy]

Hillsboro',
June 12th., 1871.

Yours of the 8th. inst. has been received, in which you state that it is the desire of many persons in your section of Country that I shall present my views on the question of the Constitutional power of the Legislature, to provide the means of ascertaining the sense of the people on the subject of amending the Constitution, and, if it be in the affirmative, to call a Convention for this purpose.

My time is much occupied at present. In the course of a week or two I may find leisure to present my opinion through the public press. But, in the mean time, I beg leave to say, that subsequent reflection and discussion have only tended to confirm the convictions I expressed and published, on this question in 1854, when I served with you as a member of the Legislature.

The right of the people of a State, by a vote of a majority, fairly ascertained by a mode appointed by the Legislature, and of course with its sanction, to call a Convention, and reform their Constitution in matters not regulated by the Constitution of the United States, is one of the essential rights of sovreignty which they have never surrendered. It was asserted in the declaration of rights in the old Constitution, in these words: "That the people of this State ought to have the sole and exclusive right of regulating the internal Government and police thereof."

In the present Constitution, the idea is amplified in these terms, "that the people of this State have the inherent, sole, and exclusive right of regulating the internal Government and police thereof; and of altering and abolishing their Constitution and form [of] Government, whenever it may be necessary for their safety and happiness; but every such right should be exercised in pursuance of law, and consistently with the Constitution of the United States."

Now the people are about to exercise this right, and in pursuance of a law passed upon mature deliberation, and by large majorities in both branches of the General Assembly. It is proposed that they shall "alter," not abolish, their Constitution and form of Government in a mode provided in pursuance of law. And an outcry is raised that this is revolution, and forbidden by the Constitution; because the Constitution declares that, "No Convention of the people shall be called by the *General Assembly*, unless by the concurrence of two thirds of all the members of each house of the *General Assembly*." And it is argued, as if this was in substance a declaration, that "No change shall ever be made in this Constitution except by a Convention, called by majorities of two thirds of the General Assembly in each House. Or that "No Convention shall ever be called except by the General Assembly, and then by a majority of two thirds in each House." The language of the Constitution cannot be tortured into such an interpretation. It is an interdict on the Legislature against calling a Convention, (as was done in May, 1861) except by the concurrence of two thirds of each House; and it is nothing more. It imposes no restriction upon the right of the people, nor upon the power of the Legislature, by an ordinary majority, to provide the means of enabling the people to exercise this right. The people unquestionably had this right, the means of its exercise, however, to be approved by the Legislature prior to the incorporation of this language in the Constitution. They had exercised it in calling the Convention of 1835, as well as in the notable Conventions of 1788 & 1789. And it is not to be taken away by any strained implication; otherwise the bold assertion in the Bill [of] rights of their power "of altering and abolishing their Constitution and form of Government whenever it may be necessary to their safety & happiness; but every such right should be exercised in pursuance of law," etc., dwindles almost to insignificance and is subject to the qualificaiton; that "if one third of each House of the General Assembly forbid, this right shall not be exercised."

It is fortunate for us that the Journals and Report of the debates of the Convention of 1835 have been preserved, as well as that some of its members survive. It is clearly proved by these, that the Convention of 1835 had no intention to abridge the right of the people, with the approbation of the existing Legislature, to call a Convention, and amend their Constitution. This is abundantly shewn in the recent able letter of the Hon. D. M.

Barringer,[1] himself a member from Cabarrus; who has recited the proceedings on the proposition of Mr. Meares,[2] that "No Convention shall be called, unless by the concurrence of two thirds, etc., of the General Assembly;" he shews that Mr. Giles[3] of Rowan interposed, and inquired with emphasis whether it was designed to prevent a Convention from being called by the people? That such a purpose was disclaimed; and in order to recognize and preserve this right, the words "by the General Assembly" were inserted after the word "called," so as to confine the provision to a restriction upon the authority of the General Assembly; and this accounts for the tautology of using the words "the General Assembly" twice in the same brief sentence.

It is still more fortunate that we have the precedents of 1787 & 1789. It has been asserted in a document communicated by the Executive [to] the General Assembly, that "calling a Convention is an act of Legislation, and it follows that no Convention can be called unless it be done by the General Assembly. This is a dogma which simply begs the question in dispute, is contradicted by history. If it be true, North Carolina is not to this day a member of the Federal Union. Both the Convention of 1787, and that of 1788 were assembled upon a *recommendation* in the form of a joint resolution: 1st. "Resolved, that it is the opinion of this House that a new Convention be *recommended* for the purposes of reconsidering the new Constitution . . . . for the Government of the United States.

2. "Resolved, that it be *recommended* to such of the inhabitants of this State as are entitled to vote for members of the Houses of Commons at the annual election to be held in each County on, etc., to vote for five persons in each County, and one person in each borough Town, to sit as a State Convention for the purpose of deliberating & determining on the proposed Federal Constitution," etc.

By other and separate resolutions it was recommended to these Conventions, in 1788 to select a place for a permanent seat of Government, and 1878 [*sic*] to consider the propriety of allowing the Town of Fayetteville a member in the House of Commons—

These [*sic*]

---

[1]Daniel Moreau Barringer (1806-1873), of Cabarrus County, a lawyer, politician, and diplomat, was a graduate of the University of North Carolina. He served in five sessions of the General Assembly; was a Whig member of the United States House of Representatives, 1843-1849; held the post of minister to Spain, 1849-1853; and was a delegate to the futile Washington Peace Conference of 1861. From 1858 until his death Barringer lived in Raleigh. In 1867 he publicly urged cooperation with congressional reconstruction but by 1868 was actively supporting the Conservative presidential campaign. In 1872 he was chairman of the state Democratic Conservative executive committee. *CDAB*, 50; Powell, *DNCB*, I, 99-100.

[2]William Belvidere Meares (1787-1840) was born in New Hanover County, educated at the Bingham School, and graduated from the University of North Carolina. He read law with William Gaston and had a distinguished legal career, although he devoted much time, especially during his final years, to agriculture, experimenting with progressive ideas and scientific methods. He was also very interested in the development of railroads and internal improvements; both interests were evident during his service in the state assembly. Meares was town representative for Wilmington during the assemblies of 1818, 1819, and

1820; served as a delegate to the Constitutional Convention of 1835; and was a state senator from New Hanover County, 1828-1833. *Cyclopedia of Eminent Men*, II, 100-102; Cheney, *North Carolina Government*, 274, 275, 291, 300, 351n, 818.

[3]John Giles was a native of Salisbury and clerk of the Rowan County Superior Court for many years. He was graduated from the University of North Carolina in 1808 and studied law, after which he established a law practice in Salisbury. Rumple, *Rowan County*, 228-229, 321.

Littleton Q. Washington to William A. Graham UNC
[with enclosure]

Washington, D.C.,
June 28th., 1871.

Mr. Strudwick[1] brought me your note of introduction. I have had a good deal of conversation with him, & have introduced him to Messrs. Beck[2] and Van Trump[3]—the two Democratic members of the Committee who are present. There is a probability that he will have questions put to him by the Radical members of the Committee, which he will be compelled to decline answering. They will doubtless report him to the two Houses next winter, as in contempt, but I doubt if any more will come of it. However, he will be able to explain this to you better when he sees you than I can possibly do in a note.

Mr. Beck tells me that the result of the testimony is very much in our favor, in all the States so far except North Carolina, & there, he says, he has had little or no help from the public men. What is needed is for public men to act in conjunction with our friends on the Committee, supply the names of proper witnesses to be summoned, in a word, prove up their case, as the Radicals from that State are now doing.

But it is not at all too late for practical action. The Committee here have appointed a sub-committee, composed of Messrs. Scott,[4] Stevenson,[5] & Van Trump, to go to North and South Carolina to take testimony.

Scott & Stevenson are intense Radical partisans, though measured in manner. Van Trump is a sensible, upright Dem. from Ohio, not so keen or well posted a man as we need for such a work; but then Beck must remain here, as he will be our only Representative at the general meetings of the Committee. The sub Com. leave on Friday for one of the two States. The place where they ought to begin testimony will be announced by telegraph, ere they reach there, in the press.

Now, it is immensely important that some of our best men in South Carolina should be there to meet them on their arrival, so as to post Van Trump, tell him what questions to ask Radical witnesses, to be a sort of Counsel to him, & also ready with a list of witnesses to be summoned from each County, especially those Counties which are the object of Radical attacks, say Rutherford, Alamance, Caswell, Cleveland, Orange, etc., etc.

I enclose you a note to Mr. Van Trump, & hope you will be able to meet him on his arrival, & to get others to do so. Your State is especially the object of assault. As to South Carolina, the proof of corruption & misgovernment is so notorious, that I think they will make very little out of it.

[1]Apparently Frederick N. Strudwick was questioned by members of the Joint Select Committee to Inquire into the Condition of Affairs in the Late Insurrectionary States. The committee consisted of seven United States senators—Thomas F. Bayard of Delaware, Francis P. Blair, Jr., of Missouri, Zachariah Chandler of Michigan, John Pool of North Carolina, Daniel D. Pratt of Indiana, Benjamin R. Rice of Arkansas, and John Scott of Pennsylvania—and fourteen representatives—James B. Beck of Kentucky, Benjamin F. Butler of Massachusetts, John Coburn of Indiana, Samuel S. Cox of New York, John F. Farnsworth of Illinois, James M. Hanks of Arkansas, William E. Lansing of New York, Horace Maynard of Tennessee, Luke P. Poland of Vermont, James C. Robinson of Illinois, Glenni W. Scofield of Pennsylvania, Job E. Stevenson of Ohio, Philadelph Van Trump of Ohio, and Alfred M. Waddell of North Carolina. This number included eight Democrats—Bayard, Beck, Blair, Cox, Hanks, Robinson, Van Trump, and Waddell.

The investigating body carried out a lengthy inquiry into the activities of the Ku Klux Klan and similar secret societies in the South. It questioned hundreds of witnesses and produced a thirteen-volume report. Formed in April, 1871, the joint committee functioned after a Senate committee of five—Chandler, James W. Nye of Nevada, Rice, Scott, and Henry Wilson of Massachusetts—sat during the first three months of 1871, examined fifty-three witnesses, and reported that the Klan was active in North Carolina. On April 20, 1871, Congress passed the last of three acts that outlawed terrorist activities by secret organizations; made interference in elections a federal offense and put national elections under federal control; and authorized the president to suspend *habeas corpus* and use federal forces to uphold the laws. Hamilton, *Reconstruction in North Carolina*, 572-575; Rembert W. Patrick, *The Reconstruction of the Nation* (New York: Oxford University Press, 1967), 155-156; *Biographical Directory of Congress*, 191, 193-194, 196-199, 532.

[2]James Burnie Beck (1822-1890) was a native of Scotland who immigrated to the United States in 1838. He settled for a few years in Wyoming County, New York, but after his graduation from Transylvania College Beck established a law practice in Lexington, Kentucky. From 1867 until 1875 he served as a Democratic member of the House of Representatives and from 1877 until 1890 was a United States senator. In 1876 he acted as a member of the commission to settle the Virginia-Maryland boundary question. *Biographical Directory of Congress*, 532.

[3]Philadelph Van Trump (1810-1874) was a lawyer and a state judge. After several unsuccessful attempts to secure political office, Van Trump in 1867 was elected as a representative to Congress from Ohio, an office he held until 1873. *Biographical Directory of Congress*, 1750.

[4]John Scott (1824-1896), a native of Huntingdon County, Pennsylvania, was a United States senator from 1869 to 1875. Active in Pennsylvania legal and political life before becoming senator, he later was general counsel of the Pennsylvania Railroad, 1875-1877, and general solicitor, 1877-1895. A Republican, Scott conducted the hearings into Klan activities in North Carolina and served as chairman of the joint committee investigating secret organizations in the South. *Biographical Directory of Congress*, 1573; Trelease, *White Terror*, 392.

[5]Job Evans Stevenson (1832-1922), an Ohio lawyer, agriculturalist, and politician, served as a Republican in the United States House of Representatives from 1869 to 1873 before resuming his legal practice in Cincinnati. Later he resided in Lexington and Corinth, Kentucky. *Biographical Directory of Congress*, 1655.

[Enclosure]
Littleton Q. Washington to Philadelph Van Trump

Washington, D.C.
June 28th., 1871.

My friend, Gov. Wm. A. Graham, of Hillsboro', North Carolina, will hand you this letter. He is doubtless already well known to you by reason of the many trusts he has had from the people of North Carolina, & by his prominent connection with Federal politics. He enjoys the confidence and respect of the people of his State, & is intimately acquainted with their affairs. I am sure his experience & good judgement will be very useful in facilitating your labors on the Committee.

Very truly yours,

Joseph H. Wilson[1] *to William A. Graham* UNC

Yarborough House

Raleigh, N.C.,
June 30th., 1871.

I have seen Dr. Smith[2] in regard to the imputation thrown upon the character of our mutual friend, the late Judge Osborne, by the testimony of Mr. Jupiter,[3] before the investigating Committee. He seems much surprised at the information, stated that he had no knowledge of the alledged matter, and had no recollection of having had any conversation with Mr. Jupiter on the subject. That he regarded Judge Osborne's character as above reproach. Expressed a willingness to appear before the Committee and testify in vindication of his character. I re[quested] Judge Shipp to have him summoned and examined, which he promised me he would do.

---

[1]Joseph H. Wilson of Mecklenburg County served as Speaker of the North Carolina Senate, 1866-1867. Cheney, *North Carolina Government*, 334.

[2]Dr. Smith has not been identified.

[3]The published report of William M. Shipp's legislative committee investigating railroad fraud makes no mention of Jupiter as a witness or otherwise, nor is the name of James W. Osborne mentioned.

Archibald M. Aiken[1] *to William A. Graham* UNC

Danville, Virginia,
July 5th., 1871.

Your kind letter reached me yesterday morning. I am glad you did not deprive yourself of your only copy of the oration, as it was not my intention that you should. If you will pardon me this annoyance, I would ask of you to inform me from whom I may probably secure one, in Raleigh or Chapel Hill? It will save you the inconvenience of inquiring. I am curious about this, because it has been my misfortune never to have seen any remembrance of my dead ancestor, save the kind tribute you have given him, and what I could learn from persons who had only an indistinct recollection of him. I have regretted frequently, my inability to show my respect to the memory of my Grandfather,[2] by erecting some mark or monument over his tomb. I am now very poor, but should I live, and am so blessed with prosperity as to enable me to raise a memorial of which I would not be ashamed, it is my determined intention to do it. I sincerely hope that all knowledge of the whereabouts of his grave will not be forgotten before I can mark it. It really grieves me that I am unable to do it at present. It is my desire to do it *myself*, without the pecuniary aid of any one.

Thanking you, my dear Sir, for the warm and heartfelt consideration you give to Judge Murphey's worth, and your kind reply to my letter, I remain.

---

[1]Archibald Murphey Aiken (1849-1913), of Danville, Virginia, was a grandson of Archibald D. Murphey. Aiken was a distinguished lawyer, judge, and corporation counsel. Lyon Gardiner Tyler (ed.), *Encyclopedia of Virginia Biography* (New York: Lewis Publishing Company, 5 volumes, 1915), V, 746.

[2]Archibald De Bow Murphey (ca. 1777-1832), born in Caswell County, was graduated with honors by the University of North Carolina in 1799. He settled in Hillsborough, where he practiced law. From 1812 to 1818 he represented Orange County in the North Carolina Senate. Murphey, whom state historians regard as the greatest statesman of his generation, was an idealist who envisioned several social and economic improvements that he hoped would promote state development. He advocated reform of the criminal code, abolition of imprisonment for debt, colonization of free Negroes, and public education. He sought to promote internal improvements to the extent that he was imprisoned for debt when a canal venture in which he had invested failed. Ironically, while he died in poverty before his dreams came to fruition, Murphey inspired his friends and admirers—William A. Graham among them—to adopt reform as a goal. Ruth Blackwelder, *The Age of Orange: Political and Intellectual Leadership in North Carolina, 1752-1861* (Charlotte: William Loftin, Publisher, 1961), 75-79, 143, hereinafter cited as Blackwelder, *Age of Orange*; *CDAB*, 716.

Thomas Ruffin, Jr., to William A. Graham UNC

Hillsboro',
July 7th., 1871.

I take the liberty of sending you this cane, & asking you to accept it of me.

As it belonged to my father, & was much prized by him, I believe you will value it.

The Stick was made for him by his oldest friend, Mr. Robert Brodnax,[1] with his own hands, out of a piece of mahogany taken from the old Spanish fort at St. Augustine; & the Headpiece is of Moss agate, sent him by another friend, from Mt. Vesuvius.

My Mother gave it to me some time since, & I resolved to ask you to accept it, so soon as I could get [it] repolished.

There is no one, of all his friends, to whom his children feel under more obligations than to yourself; & therefore it is that I am anxious that this token of him should pass into your hands.

I have the honor to be,
Sir,
With very great respect,
Your ob't serv't,

---

[1]Robert Brodnax, like Ruffin, came to North Carolina from Virginia. The two had known each other from childhood and were fellow students at the Warrenton Academy. Brodnax, a son of Edward and Sallie Brodnax, settled in Rockingham County, where he was a large planter with holdings located on the Dan River. He and a brother, Edward Travis Brodnax, had great influence on the social and economic life of Rockingham County. Powell, *DNCB*, I, 232-233; Hamilton, *Ruffin Papers*, I, 20, 37.

Edward S. Parker to William A. Graham UNC

Law Office of Parker & Long

Graham, N.C.,
July 13th., 1871.

Please indulge me in a request. The posters announcing that W. J. Murray,[1] our Convention candidate, the canvassers appointed for the County, & others, would address the people at the various times and places therein mentioned, have been out for a week. The opposition have no candidate, that I am aware of, but I hear, incidentally, that their speakers will be on hand at the time and places mentioned in our posters, for the purpose, of course, of addressing the people. I think, not without some reason, for so doing, that they propose inaugurating a boistrous campaign, wherein abuse and threats will seem more meet than in an orderly contest. I should not be surprised if they contemplated just attending the different townships, and, without asking a division of time, or other ceremony, to act as if the meeting had been called as much by themselves as by us.

I know the man who will doubtless shape their course in this county, and know him, in politics especially, capable of anything. Should they pursue this course, I apprehend some trouble, which I am inclined to think they desire. Boyd[2] is to canvass, so I hear, & in certain portions he may not be treated with a great deal of consideration.

Should they act as if the meetings were as much theirs as ours, what course should we pursue? Should we join in the discussions, thus accepting their assumption? Should they, after getting to the first township, ask a division of time, should we, think you, accede to it? Common courtesy would demand that we would have at least some time for the consideration of any proposition from them. By troubling yourself to give your opinion as to what course would be proper in the case supposed, you will very much oblige.

I am Chairman of the Co. Ex. Co., which fact may place me prominent in any controversy that may arise, and knowing that your opinion would mark the proper course to pursue, I have taken the liberty thus to ask.

---

[1]William J. Murray (b. 1803) was at various times a deputy sheriff and sheriff of Alamance County and from 1872 to 1874 was a state senator. Cheney, *North Carolina Government*, 453.

[2]James Edmund Boyd.

Jesse Turner[1] to William A. Graham UNC

Van Buren, Arkansas,
July 19th., 1871.

I am greatly obliged to you for a copy of your "Memorial Oration" on the Life and Character of the late Chief Justice Ruffin. I remember Judge Ruffin well. When a stripling, I used to hear him at the Hillsboro' Bar, and was much impressed with the force and vigor of his speeches. In oratory, he was surpassed by Hawks,[2] and perhaps by some others, but as a lawyer he seemed to me to be without a rival, unless Badger was entitled to that eminence. Judge Ruffin, although averse to embarking in politics extensively, was understood, I believe, to have had very decided political opinions. Indeed, (although I believe very uncommon with him) I heard him make a political speech in the old C. H. at Hillsboro', in 1824, on a subject then agitating the public mind in N.C., especially in the Western part of the State. It was the question of a State Convention, a number of speeches were made. Mebane,[3] Mangum,[4] and others spoke. A loud call was then made for Ruffin, and all eyes were fixed upon him. He rose with apparent reluctance, and even seemed to be embarrassed. Apologized for attempting to speak upon such a subject, and proceeded to deliver a thrilling speech, of marked ability and eloquence. Some of his allusions to revolutionary Whigs of Orange County, Gov. Burke[5] and others, were particularly happy, and deeply moved his audience, so I conclude that Judge Ruffin might have been as distinguished in politics, or rather, as a *Statesman*, as he was distinguished as a lawyer and Judge, if he had drawn that field for the execution of his great talents.

Again thanking you for your admirable Oration, and hoping to hear from you again.

---

[1]Jesse Turner (1805-1894), a native of Orange County and of Scotch-Irish descent, studied law in the 1820s prior to settling in Arkansas Territory in 1831. In 1838 he located permanently in Van Buren, Crawford County. A Whig in politics, he served in the state legislature; was a presidential elector in 1848; was federal district attorney for the western district of Arkansas, 1850-1853; opposed secession until after the firing on Fort Sumter; and, having become a Democrat after 1865, opposed congressional reconstruction while a state senator. In 1878 he was appointed associate justice of the Arkansas Supreme Court, a position he filled ably. He promoted internal improvements, serving as president of the Little Rock and Fort Smith Railroad from 1857 to 1868, and public education at state expense. John Hallum, *Biographical and Pictorial History of Arkansas* (Albany, Ark.: Weed, Parsons and Company, Printers, 1887), 244-252.

[2]Francis Lister Hawks.

[3]Alexander Mebane.

[4]Willie Person Mangum.

[5]Thomas Burke (1747-1783), a native of Ireland, came first to Virginia but settled in Orange County in 1771. He practiced both law and medicine at various times. He was one of the three framers of the North Carolina Constitution of 1776; an influential member of Congress; and governor, 1781-1782. *DAB*, III, 282-283.

Algernon S. Buford[1] to William A. Graham[2] UNC

Richmond and Danville Railroad Company,
President's Office,
Richmond, Va., July 26th 1871

Some months since I mentioned to you that in the event the interests of this Co. in your State, should, as I then thought likely, require professional advice or other representation, we would be disposed to have your services if agreeable to yourself, & understood from you that you were willing to represent the Co. in such event. Nothing having been since said on the subject between us, & the necessity for such services being more probable, indeed required, I deem it proper to inquire if it is still your pleasure to represent the Co. as occasion may require, & if so, to say if you will indicate such reasonable retaining fee as you require, it will be remitted to you. Only adding, that if compatible with your present engagements & views, I shall be pleased to have you as our retained counsel.

---

[1]Algernon Sidney Buford (b. 1826), a native of Rowan County, was builder of the Atlanta and Charlotte Railroad and president of the Richmond and Danville Railroad Company. He took over construction of the Western North Carolina Railroad in 1880 when W. J. Best's syndicate collapsed. A resident of Virginia, Buford in 1893 made an unsuccessful bid for the governorship of that state. Elgiva D. Watson, "The Election Campaign of Governor Jarvis, 1880: A Study of the Issues," *North Carolina Historical Review*, XLVIII (July, 1971), 298; Margaret W. Morris, "The Completion of the Western North Carolina Railroad: Politics of Concealment," *North Carolina Historical Review*, LII (July, 1975), 266, 272.

[2]Attached to this letter was an 1872 pass on the Richmond and Danville Railroad Company, North Carolina Division.

William A. Graham to William A. Graham, Jr. A&H

Hillsboro',
August 4th., 1871.

The election yesterday passed off quietly—but every negro in the land was at the polls, and voted the radical ticket. At this precinct the Conservative majority was 3, at Chapel [Hill] 6, at Cates' Store a tie. The returns are not required to be made 'till 12 tomorrow, but it is estimated that we have carried the election for Convention by about 500, and for delegates by a still greater majority.[1]

Last year Shipp's majority over Phillips, in Orange, was upwards of 700. Allison,[2] at Cedar Grove, played false, and we lost 100 votes there; on Flat River we sustained the next greatest loss, though there was a great negro vote there. Young Turrentine[3] is the only white man in Town who voted radical. Argo[4] & Duke[5] are far behind the anticonvention ticket. In Alamance, we hear, Convention prevailed, by 350 majority.

A gain in Ral. of 280. but Wake Co. lost. It is uncertain how the majority has gone in the State, though, unless the mountains deceive us, I think Convention has prevailed. James has canvassed Alamance for Murray. . . . We have heard nothing from Person or Granville. I closed my canvass by a speech at Gibsonville, Guilford last Saturday—

My wheat here yielded 55 to 19½ sown, at Leper's, so Rob't writes, 195 to 38. The drought here is very oppressive, and still continues. A pretty good season last Friday night, when Mr. Nash's house was struck by lightning—no injury to persons.

We are as well as usual

Love to Julia & children & Sudie

Affectionately

[1]The Conservatives were hopeful that this election would result in the call for a constitutional convention to undo the Constitution of 1868. The vote was 86,007 for the convention and 95,252 against. Delegates were chosen in the event that the convention was approved. The Conservatives elected sixty-one delegates and the Republicans fifty-nine. Graham and Pride Jones were chosen from Orange County. Hamilton, *Reconstruction in North Carolina*, 567-568; *Daily Sentinel* (Raleigh), August 8, 1871. Graham and his political allies were bitterly disappointed with the results of the convention vote.

[2]Presumably this was Joseph Allison.

[3]Possibly this was James A. Turrentine, who was Confederate tax assessor in 1864. He served Alamance County as state representative and state senator in the legislatures of 1881 and 1905 respectively. Lefler and Wager, *Orange County*, 190; Cheney, *North Carolina Government*, 460, 483.

[4]Thomas Munro Argo (1841-1909) spent his boyhood in Tennessee. He graduated from the University of North Carolina and studied law. During the Civil War he served in the Confederate forces as second lieutenant in Company D, First Battalion, North Carolina Heavy Artillery. Argo resided for some time in Chapel Hill but moved to Raleigh in 1872. He was a Conservative member of the House of Representatives in the 1868 and 1870 sessions. Reputed to be a brilliant jury lawyer, Argo served as solicitor of the Fourth Judicial District, 1887-1891. He became a Republican during his years in Raleigh. Powell, *DNCB*, I, 40; Grant, *Alumni History*, 17.

[5]Duke has not been identified definitively, but it may be that this refers to Washington Duke. This supposition is strengthened by the fact that Graham defeated Duke when Orange County delegates were elected to serve in the Constitutional Convention of 1875. Lefler and Wager, *Orange County*, 120.

Washington Duke and his sons were Republicans in politics. Duke would have opposed a call for a constitutional convention. For Washington Duke's political views see Robert F. Durden, *The Dukes of Durham, 1865-1929* (Durham: Duke University Press, 1975), 6-7, 100-104.

Edward S. Parker to William A. Graham UNC

Law Office of Parker & Long, Graham, N.C.
Aug. 11th 1871

I was employed by the N.C. R. R. Co in July 1869, to look after all matters of lost freights, Stock killed, overcharge of tariff on freights, claims against the C. and in favor of the C. as well as all law suits then pending, or that might afterwards be instituted wherein the Co. was a party. I was discharged in January 1871, leaving many of the suits against the Road just in the condition I found them, and a few yet pending that were instituted after my employment by the Co. I was never paid anything more nor less than regular wages, to look after the general interest of the Co coming under the above Statement of my duties being my business.

My services as just mentioned were dispensed with the first of last January. Of course I am retained in no manner by the Co. Could I now accept a fee to appear against the Co. in a case I found and left pending? Could I accept a fee in case instituted during my employment by the Co. wherein I filed either answer or complaint—I have been applied to in cases such as stated to appear provided I could with propriety do so. Will you pardon my asking your counsel. I don't wish to do anything improper but if I can appear against the Co. in suits, wherein it was my duty while employed so to do to appear for the Co. without any professional inpropriety,

I might secure some good fees which my situation in the world renders especially desirable.

I have mentioned the matter to several gentlemen, older in the profession than myself, who think my right to appear in all cases wherein the Co was concerned perfectly clear. My position is different from an attorney employed in a particular cause and afterwards discharged. I have taken the liberty to ask your advice, knowing your nice sense of propriety and large experience.

James C. Welling[1] *to William A. Graham* UNC

College of New Jersey,
Princeton, New Jersey.
[August 16, 1871]

Having been recently elected to the Presidency of the Columbian College, in Washington, D.C., and having already resigned my Professorship in this institution, with a view to it's acceptance, I trust you will pardon me if I venture to express the satisfaction with which I have learned that you are now one of the Trustees of the Columbian College.

My former residence in Washington, & my long connexion with the old National Intelligencer, (though that connexion dated from a few years after your retirement from Federal office) have, of course, made me familiar with your public life, though I have not had the honor of your private acquaintance.

As in the "old Whig days" it was our fortune to "think alike concerning the Republic," and as such community of thought among the Romans was held to be a bond of association, I hope that the new relations into which we are now brought, may secure for me the advantages of your advice and support in the new duties I am about to undertake. The city of Washington, I need not tell you, offers a rare combination of advantages as the seat of an institution for higher academic learning, while the cosmopolitan tone of its society makes it a most desirable place of residence.

The deplorable condition into which the Colleges of your State have been brought by the evils of the time, would seem to make it necessary for your people to rely, at least for the present, on institutions established without your borders.

It will be my aim to make the Columbian College as broad and catholic in its tone as the "Republic of Letters" itself, in which there is no place for sectional asperities. Washington is a neutral ground, on which all extremes of opinion meet, and practise towards each other a mutual toleration. And I can further engage that, while under my administration, the College will, I hope, maintain its character as an institution based on Christian principles, it shall be kept wholly free from *sectarianism*, in any proper sense of that word.

Again cordially inviting your co-operation under these auspices, I beg leave to add, Dear Sir,

how truly I am,
Your ob't serv't,

[1]James Clarke Welling (1825-1894), a native of New Jersey, was a graduate of Princeton. He began his career as a journalist with the *National Intelligencer*. For two years, 1848-1850, he served as literary editor of the *Intelligencer* and then assumed the editor's position. Although he was a liberal in his political philosophy, an antislavery proponent, and a close friend of Abraham Lincoln, Welling opposed Lincoln's exercise of the war power and did not approve of the Emancipation Proclamation. He was president of St. John's College, 1867-1870; professor at Princeton, 1870-1871; and president of Columbian College (now George Washington University), 1871-1894. *CDAB*, 1169.

Lease Agreement between William A. Graham and John Pickett[1]

UNC

August 18, 1871

Memorandum of agreement between W. A. Graham of the first part, and John Pickett of the second part, Witnesseth, that the said William A. Graham doth hereby lease, to the said John Pickett, the open land of his Estes plantation in Orange County on the waters of Eno river and Spirit branch, lying south of a line running East & West, of which the stone wall on said place is a part, for the year ending the 15th of November 1872, with the buildings standing thereon, with the privilege of firewood for the use of the family of said Pickett on said tract of land, and timber for rails & repairs on the same, but not for the sale of any wood.

The John Pickett agrees to cultivate the said plantation with industry & care, and in a husbandlike manner: to mow the meadows twice and to sprout them out; to save & stack all the Hay from the same; to pay to the said Graham for rent, one third of all the wheat, Oats, Corn, Tobacco or other crop raised on said place in that year, excepting the produce of one acre for a garden which shall be free of rent; and of the Hay he shall pay one half at each cutting, after it is stacked, the said Graham having the choice of stacks. The said Pickett shall also repair the fences on said place, putting on the same the new rails, he was to make by contract for the year 1871, and to make & put up Fifteen Hundred new rails for 1872. He is to keep his own stock, & all other off the meadow above the ford of the creek, and protect as well [as] he can the fruit trees, he to have one half of the fruit from the same, and the said Graham the other half.

The parties do also agree that the said Graham shall have a lien on all the crop on said plantation, for the payment of the rent aforesaid.

The said Graham reserves the free use of all the woodland, and may if he chooses cut off a space not exceeding six acres immediately south of the East & West line aforesaid on the West side of the plantation including the spring in the field for a new settlement; and may cause ditches to be dug so as better to water the meadow. He may also remove the materials of the cow stable which has fallen down.

Witness the bonds & seals of the parties this 18th of August 1871.

William A. Graham [seal]
John Pickett his mark [seal]

[1]John Pickett has not been further identified.

Robert C. Winthrop to William A. Graham A&H

Brookline, Mass.,
August 20th., 1871.

Your favor of the 10th. inst. was duly welcomed. I have great reason to hope that Governor Alcorn[1] will help our Claims next winter, though I have heard nothing from him directly. I doubt not that your appeal to him will be serviceable.

Your "Memorial Oration" was received many weeks ago, and I thank you sincerely for it. I ought to have acknowledged it sooner. I have read it with great pleasure. It is most creditable to both subject and author.

Judge Ruffin was a remarkable man, and worthy of your Eulogy.

---

[1]James Lusk Alcorn (1816-1894) was a native of Illinois who grew up in Kentucky and was educated at Cumberland College. After moving to Mississippi, Alcorn became an extensive planter and served in the state legislature for many years. A leader in the Whig party, Alcorn opposed secession. During the Civil War he served in the Confederate troops as a brigadier general. Alcorn participated in military actions in Kentucky and was very successful in raising troops. In 1865 he was elected United States senator but was not seated. He was governor of Mississippi, 1870-1871, and was a member of the United States Senate, 1871-1877. *Biographical Directory of Congress*, 464; *CDAB*, 12.

Algernon S. Buford to William A. Graham UNC

Richmond and Danville Railroad Company
President's Office
Richmond, Va., Aug. 23d 1871

Yours of the 1st was duly recd. Business engagements elsewhere have in part prevented an earlier acknowledgement. I am obliged to you for the frank and explicit Statement of your views in regard to the matters affecting the interests of this Co. in your State, & beg you to allow me to present some considerations that may not have been considered by you in their true aspect, as apparent to us. It is proper to say to you distinctly—though doubtless inferred by you from our previous conversations & correspondence—that the professional services desired from you, embraced your attention & aid in endeavoring fairly to procure a lease or other equivalent use of the N. Ca. Railroad, & when procured to maintain the same against all contestants. A retainer more restricted than this, would render your services much less valuable than we desire, & is therefore not what we want. The pending legal controversy as to the proper appointing power of Directors & proxy to represent the State, to which you refer, & to which you have been made a formal party, is a matter that we desire to avoid becoming in any manner party to, unless compelled to be, in the maintenance of any interests that this Co. may, as they shall be advised, legally & properly acquire in connection with the N. Ca. Rd. Should such interests be acquired, we desire your services in protecting them in all respects, as shall become necessary.

Of course we would neither desire or be content with any interests illegally acquired & therefore insecurely held. Hence I do not perceive any necessary conflict between your your [*sic*] present personal views & our future . . . interests in the matter. But I think it probable that some cloud has arisen between us by reason of some degree of misapprehension as to the views & purposes of this Co. in regard to their Ints. in N.C. You observe that if a lease of the N.C. Rd. by this Co. be desired, "it could not have your concurrence with the view of a change of guage" between Greensboro & Charlotte. We are willing to lease the whole Road & determine the question of guage upon development of what is necessary & best for its successful & useful operation, both to us & its patrons. Perhaps *no* change would be found necessary, or if any, of the whole line. Or, it is by no means an impossible contingency that a change of our guage may be made. What is essentially required for the interests of all, people patrons, Stockholders & States, connected with both Roads, is the *thorough* & *permanent Co-operation* of both, which we think can *only* be had by *identification*—and that too without great delay, which only hazards permanent antagonism & consequent unnecessary injury to both.

You will allow me to suggest therefore, that if you will be content to let the question of gauge rest & be determined by the future demands for one or the other in securing effective operation, we should not be likely to disagree I think, as to what the interests of Stockholders & patrons would require under the situation as at present. I am absolutely certain that *results* would satisfy & gratify you, as I am equally certain the interests you value & would protect, both personal & general, would not only be protected from injury—perhaps rescued from prostration—but be permanently & securely promoted & advanced. And I should be very much gratified, if on further consideration, your views could be so far modified as to be able to render us the services & cooperation as desired. Not knowing whether the explanation I have given would induce any change of your position, we have deemed it proper to engage the services of Gov. Bragg. Messers Bragg & Strong[1] of Raleigh, recently, whose unqualified efforts we are assured of. Still we desire to have you associated if on further consideration you consider it proper. If the guage is the only trouble in respect of our position, I do not see why we cannot satisfy what I understand to be your difficulties on that Score. And if necessary, will at your suggestion see you & exchange views more fully than is practicable in this mode. At any rate I beg that you will not consider me indelicately importunate in this matter. I think it is a very important interest to the people of both communities, & that it might be settled so to be very useful to both.

---

[1]George Vaughan Strong (1827-1897), of Wayne County, a native of Sampson, graduated from the University of North Carolina in 1845 with highest honors, read law with George W. Mordecai, and established a practice in Goldsboro in 1853. He was a member of the Constitutional Convention of 1861 and served the Confederacy as district attorney of North Carolina. In 1871 he moved to Raleigh, where he practiced law first as the partner of Thomas Bragg and later with William N. H. Smith. He represented Wake County in the state House in 1874 and was for a time judge of the Wake County criminal court. McCormick, *Convention Personnel*, 80-81; Spencer Alumni Project.

Alfred J. Morrison to William A. Graham UNC

Cottage Home, N.C.
Sept. 9th 1871

My dear Uncle:

A short time before I left college I wrote you asking advice in regard to a profession, and your kind reply to my letter prompts me to write again.

For more than two years I have been staying at home helping my father in the management of his farm, but if I am going to read Law, which I have long wished to do, I have not time to lose.

There are so many things to engage my attention on the farm that I have found it impossible to do much studying of any kind; and I am anxious to spend next year at some Law school, or other place where I can pursue my studies without interruption.

I have been thinking of going to the U'vty of Va., but the expenses there are so heavy, I fear I would be unable to get through without pecuniary difficulty. And, more than this, from what you said to me in a former letter, I doubt if going to the U'vty at this time would be the best plan for me to adopt. If Gus is reading with you, or if you have any other students, so that examining me occasionally would not add much to your trouble, I would be greatly gratified to begin a course of reading under you.

There is no man in N.C. whose character I have been taught to venerate as I have yours; and should you find it convenient to spend a portion of your leisure time, instructing me in the Law, the kindness would be warmly appreciated, and ever remembered with affectionate gratitude.

Of course, I would expect to pay you the regular tuition fees, and suppose I could get board, lodging, etc., at a reasonable price with some family near your office. I will esteem it a favor, if you inform me what my expenses in Hillsboro would probably be, beginning about the 15th of October and continuing to 15th of June 72.

If receiving me as a student would be too great a tax on your time, or in any way put you to inconvenience, I hope that you will not hesitate to so inform me; and in that event, please be kind enough to advise me where to go, and with whom to study. Living up here in Lincoln, I have had very poor facilities for learning anything of the different Law schools in the country, and would be at a loss to make selection.

My father's[1] health is much better than it was two years ago, and by getting an honest tenant to attend to his feeding in the morning, he will be able to get on comfortably without me, and has consented to my leaving home.

I saw Robt. and Cousin Sudie at Cousin Isabella Davidson's[2] wedding a few days since. Both were well, and I believe have gone to Burke. Cousin Willie and family were well when I last saw them.

With much love to Aunt Susan, I am,

Y'r affectionate nephew,

[1]Robert Hall Morrison.

[2]In 1787 Isabella Davidson (d. January 15, 1808), daughter of Major John Davidson, married the Revolutionary War hero Joseph Graham. William Alexander Graham was the eleventh child and youngest son of the couple. (For details about the antecedents of William A. Graham, see Hamilton and Williams, *Graham Papers*, I, 1-127, 460-468.) The Isabella Davidson mentioned in this letter was likely a namesake of Isabella Davidson Graham and a descendant of Major John Davidson; she has not been further identified.

William A. Graham to [Ralph Gorrell] UNC: GORRELL [with enclosure]

Hillsboro'
Sept. 19th 1871

My Dear Sir

I suppose, the parties who combined to prevent the general meeting of stockholders of the N.C. R. Co. in July, do not intend to allow a meeting on the 20th. But I think, the stockholders who intend to observe the charter, and not forfeit, or basely surrender any of their rights, should assemble, ascertain what stock is represented, and make a memorial of their proceedings—

The affair has been a pure *coup de etat*—A set of directors whose term had expired combine to prevent a meeting, to inquire into their administration—no reports made of President or any other officer—hold over by usurpation, and then alien away the whole property, for a term, which in England, in case of land is regarded as equal to the fee—

1. No Board of directors has any power "to farm out &c—Sec. 19—this is a right of "the Company" not of the directors whose powers are specified in various sections—

2. The Board of Directors of last year, were out of office—the latter clause of section 8, applied only to the state of the Company, prior to the State's becoming a subscriber—

3. The stockholders including the State, must ratify and confirm the lease before it can bind the Company: the delivery of possession was an usurpation by the directors, intended to forestall the action of the stockholders—

4. What has become of the material on hand, Fire wood, cross-ties, Iron, Coal workshops & tools, provisions for hands? of which the Company has been careful to have an account kept? Does the lessee get all this thrown in?

I have heard nothing of Judge Bonds decision on the application for Injunction—

If the stockholders are not permitted to hold a meeting to inquire into the disposition of their property, there remain two other modes of remedy—1st—To get a committee of the Gen'l Assembly to inquire into it. It is now an Executive proceeding, the Governor through his directors, originating & sanctioning it all—

2 For any one or more stockholders to apply to a court of Justice to rescind & restore the *status quo*—

It may be that a lease would be advantageous: the stockholders will doubtless be captivated with the idea of 6 ½ per cent on Five millions—But it is usual to let the proprietors have a chance to judge of the dispositions of their property, before selling it off.—the property aliened, cost 6 millions—and the supplies on hand now, are worth several hundred thousand dollars—What securities are taken for the fulfilment of the contract, we are wholly ignorant—

I am about going to the Catawba—the whole matter must be ventilated at the meeting of the Assembly, if no opportunity is allowed before—

Very truly Yours

[Enclosure]
Appointment of Proxy

Know all men by these presents, that I William A. Graham, a stockholder in the North Carolina Railroad Company, do hereby appoint Ralph Gorrell Esquire of Greensborough my proxy and substitute to represent me in the adjourned meeting of the stockholders of said Company, to be held at Greensborough N.C. on the 20th day of September 1871—hereby ratifying and confirming whatsoever my said proxy shall do in the premises—

Witness my hand and seal, this 19th day of September 1871—

W. A. Graham [seal]

Benson J. Lossing[1] *to William A. Graham* UNC

The Ridge
Dover Plains, N.Y.
Sept. 22, 1871

I beg leave to call your attention to the accompanying prospectus of a magazine about to be published in Philadelphia under my editorial management, and to solicit your cooperation, if the plan meets your approval, by contributions to its pages, of any historical facts concerning our country at any period.

I intend to use my best endeavors to make the work creditable to our historical literature, and useful in its field of labor.

I am, very truly,
Your friend & fellow citizen,

[1]Benson John Lossing (1813-1891) was a wood-carver and the author of popular books on American history, the most famous of which were *Pictorial Field Book of the Revolution* (1850-1852) and *Pictorial Field Book of the War of 1812* (1868). *CDAB*, 587.

Cornelia Phillips Spencer to William A. Graham A&H

Chapel Hill,
Sept. 26th., 1871.

Permit me to engross a half hour of your valuable time, on a subject, which I feel confident, is as interesting to you, as to any other citizen of North Carolina.

Mr. Lassiter[1] was in C. Hill yesterday, having come up to oversee the present condition of affairs—the college property, & requested permission to call on me, accompanied by Mr. McIver.[2] He had a good deal to say about this place & the Institution, without having, apparently, any definite ideas as to their future, and the object of his visit to me transpired at last, in formally requesting me to "suggest some plan that could be laid before the Board of Trustees at their approaching meeting in Nov."

I think anybody might be forgiven for smiling at this turn of affairs. Why Mr. Lassiter should have condescended to consult me, is indeed mysterious, unless it was due to Mr. McIver, who probably finding him unable to originate, & unwilling to adopt any ideas out of a certain track, thought that perhaps a lady might influence him. Unless I am mistaken in Mr. McIver, he is sincerely anxious to retrieve any false steps he may have taken in relation to the Uni., & is ready to assist in placing it in better hands. Have you, dear Sir, noticed a communication over the signature "Justice," which appeared lately in the N.C. Pres'n, and simultaneously in the Baptist and Methodist Church papers? This was written by Mr. McIver, & appeared to me to indicate the only way by which the Uni. can be revived.

I said to Mr. Lassiter that, though I had felt as deeply as any one, the ruin of this place, & would rejoice to be counted worthy to assist in its restoration, I had certainly formed no "plans," & did not feel fitted for such work. To which he replied—in substance—that after many consultations & much trouble, he had found no man in the ranks of the Rep. Party who had any thing to suggest, & was willing to undertake any work concerning the Uni., that the other "Party" was so bitter & impracticable he would not apply to them, & it had occurred to him that I might write something which would commend itself to the good sense of both sides, & might induce Conservatives & the Alumni to *co-operate* with the present directors. He pledged himself to print anything I would send him. I replied that the only plan which appeared to me likely to restore public confidence to the Uni. would be to withdraw it entirely from all Party relations, that the present Board of Trustees—or of Education—should formally resign their connection with it, and call upon the Alumni to assume the direction of affairs *unconditionally*—that I did not think the Alumni would be willing to *co-operate* at all, there must be an entire re-organization.

He objected that the Alumni were all Conservatives, & they w'd make it as much of a Party affair as it now was. He seems indeed very much bound to his "Party," & unwilling to relinquish their hold here, though he admitted their total failure. He seems *very tired* of his connection with Uni. affairs, & said they all were—yet Party pride makes them reluctant to forego their power. He said it was "neither honor nor profit to be a Trustee." I said, it might not be now, but it certainly used to be—the best men in the State were selected, & had felt it to be a compliment when so selected.

Mr. McIver seconded all I had to say, & declared that, if he had a million dollars, he would not give one to the Institution unless it was entirely reorganized, & placed in the hands of the Alumni, unrestricted by Party, or Church, or personal considerations.

Mr. Lassiter was very fond of a certain phrase concerning *"co-operation,"* which I was at some pains to convince him could not be hoped for. The present Administration is a strictly Party one. We must get rid of all suspicion of Party—the Alumni do embrace men of all parties and creeds—the Conservatives may be in the majority among them, but there are enough Rep's to give their own Party confidence. Besides, the word Party should not be used, or once though of. Let the best men be appointed.

It is an utterly wearisome thing to talk to a man of Mr. Lassiter's mental calibre. He kept reverting to his own phrases, saying the same thing over. Yet there was an evident and honest wish to have something done, or suggested, by which his "Party" may get rid of their elephant, handsomely & creditably.

I told him it would redound infinitely to their credit & would be their handsomest way out of the difficulty to come forward frankly, & say: "fellow-citizens, we have failed in this thing, let others try their hand—we resign."

Mr. L. admitted this—admitted pretty much all that I had to say—yet I do not think that when he left he was any wiser than when he came, or had *expanded* in the least.

However, it is something to hear that they are open to suggestion, and conviction may follow in time.

Does it appear likely to your judgment, my dear Sir, that the Alumni, as a body, will be willing to accept this responsibility—shoulder the Uni. and its debts, & carry it triumphantly through its present slough of Despond?

Will you take half an hour & write me a letter, & tell me what you think, or would advise? Has any plan ever been matured in your mind—have you any hopes for the future? This College is very dear to its old Students. I am convinced of that. But whether their affection reaches as far down as to their pursestrings, is another thing. I believe that my bro., Sam, has the intention of appealing to the Alumni at the approaching State Fair. Is there any chance that he will be heard? Mr. L. spoke of waiting the slow turn of events, by which all the present Board would be rotated out of office—by 1878, I think he said, they would all be gone. We cannot wait 'till 1878. Something must be done speedily.

May I beg you, dear Governor, to give my compliments to Mrs. Graham, and tell her that I received her kind and very satisfactory reply to my inquiries. That it plunged me at once in despair of ever trying to emulate anything so brilliant, in our present low estate. But that, even if we had found actors & material, we should have been compelled to abandon our design for want of a room. Mr. Brewer,[3] having charge of the College buildings refused the use of any one of them. I have just received a long and very handsome letter from Mrs. Swain.[4] I believe that Mrs. Graham also corresponds with her, or I should be tempted to enclose it, as giving a most graphic account of her surroundings & impressions in Illinois.

Hoping that you will let me hear from you, dear Sir, & that you will not refuse me the benefit of any suggestions that may occur to you, I am

With high regard,
Yours,

P.S. I forgot to say that on Mr. L's asking what the people of C. Hill would do in the event of the reorganization of the Uni., & whether they would "co-operate." Mr. McIver assured him he had grounds for saying they would cheerfully relinquish all debts due them from the College, on assurance that it would be resuscitated.

---

[1]Robert W. Lassiter, an attorney, represented Granville County in the state Senate from 1862 until 1872, except for the years 1866-1867. In July, 1868, the University of North Carolina trustees elected him secretary and treasurer. Battle, *History of the University*, II, 5; Cheney, *North Carolina Government*, 329, 331, 447, 449, 451; Hamilton, *Reconstruction in North Carolina*, 623-629 passim.

[2]Alexander McIver (1822-1902), of Moore County, became a farmer after he graduated from the University of North Carolina. However, in 1860 he joined the faculty of Davidson College and remained there until he became a professor at the University of North Carolina, 1869-1870. In 1871 the Democratic legislature decreased the salary of the state superintendent of public instruction and denied him funds for clerical help and travel. This action led to the resignation of Superintendent Samuel S. Ashley, who was succeeded by McIver. McIver was a moderate Republican who was sincerely interested in the welfare of the university and worked diligently for its rehabilitation. Hugh Talmage Lefler and Albert Ray Newsome, *North Carolina: The History of a Southern State* (Chapel Hill: University of North Carolina Press, third edition, 1973), 502, hereinafter cited as Lefler and Newsome, *North Carolina;* Hamilton, *Reconstruction in North Carolina*, 625-630; Grant, *Alumni History*, 392.

[3]It seems probable that this was Fisk P. Brewer, appointed professor of Greek at the university in 1869. Brewer had alienated some of his townsmen by accepting a Negro as a boarder in his home in Chapel Hill and by entertaining Negroes in his home while he was a teacher in a school for blacks in Raleigh. Fisk Brewer's father was Josiah Brewer, a missionary to Turkey. Battle, *History of the University*, II, 10, 25, 26, 43; Grant, *Alumni History*, 392; Hamilton, *Reconstruction in North Carolina*, 625.

[4]Eleanor Swain, the widow of David L. Swain.

William Stickney[1] *to William A. Graham* UNC

Copy of Resolutions adopted by the Board
of Trustees of Columbian College.
September 28, 1871.

Resolved. That a Committee of Five Trustees, with whom President Welling is requested to act, be chosen to wait upon W. W. Corcoran, Esq.,[2] President of this Board, and convey to him the assurance of our hearty good will and respect, our gratification that his health is greatly improved, and our hope that his contemplated voyage will fully establish his health and strength; to inform him that the Board have elected a Vice-President who will act as President whenever that officer is unable to be present at the meetings of the Board, and to inform him that we should be glad to confer with him in regard to such a plan as he may deem wise and expedient for converting the Columbian College into a National University, bearing his name, and offering to the people of the United States the fullest opportunity of instruction and culture in Science, literature, and art, and in this way crowning a long life of generous benevolence with the establishment of a seat of American learning worthy of universal approval and admiration.

The above is a true copy from the Record.

William Stickney,
Secretary and Treasurer.

The following gentlemen have been appointed the Committee contemplated in the foregoing Resolution, viz:

John A. Bolles.[3]
William Stickney
William A. Graham
C. H. Nichols[4]
William Gunton[5]
James C. Welling, President, etc.

With sincere respect of W. Stickney, Sec'y.
Sept. 28th., 1871.

---

[1]After Columbian College, a forerunner of George Washington University, was reorganized and renamed the Columbian University in 1873 in an attempt to make the institution a national university, William Stickney was elected secretary and treasurer of the newly instituted university corporation. Kayser, *Bricks without Straw*, 143.

[2]William W. Corcoran has been identified earlier in this volume.

[3]John A. Bolles (1809-1878) was a lawyer in Eastford, Connecticut. After graduation from Brown University in 1829, he studied law and was admitted to the bar in 1833. He began his law practice in Boston. From 1862 until 1865 he was judge advocate on the staff of General John A. Dix, his brother-in-law. James Grant Wilson and John Fiske (eds.), *Appleton's Cyclopaedia of American Biography* (New York: D. Appleton and Company, 7 volumes, 1887-1900), I, 308, hereinafter cited as *Appleton's Cyclopaedia.*

[4]Charles Henry Nichols (1820-1889) was a physician and the first superintendent of the Government Hospital for the Insane (now St. Elizabeth's Hospital) in Washington, D.C. He was appointed to the position by President Millard Fillmore in 1852. During the Civil War Nichols was volunteer surgeon at St. Elizabeth's General Army Hospital and was with General Irvin McDowell at the Battle of Bull Run. In 1877 he became medical superintendent of Bloomingdale Asylum in New York City. An eminent psychiatrist, Nichols's sympathy for the mentally ill possibly stemmed from his upbringing among Quakers, who made notable pioneering efforts in the field of psychiatry. His first wife was Ellen G. Maury; his second, Sallie Lathrop Garlic. *DAB*, XIII, 489.

[5]William Gunton has not been further identified.

James C. Welling to William A. Graham UNC

The Columbian College,
Washington.
September 29th., 1871.

You will be officially notified of your appointment on a Committee of the Board of Trustees of the Columbian College, who are instructed to confer with Mr. Corcoran, of this City, on the subject of endowing and "re-constructing" this institution under the name of the "Corcoran National University."

The subject matter of this communication has been already brought to the knowledge of Mr. Corcoran, and he is now holding it under advisement.

I do not suppose that he will request the Committee to give him a formal audience, but, if he should, it would indicate that he was disposed to consider the proposition favorably, and would "greatly refresh our souls!"

As we could hardly expect you to visit Washington for the purpose of being present at such audience, I beg leave to request that you will be good enough to signify to the Chairman of the Committee, the Hon. John A. Bolles, your concurrence or non-concurrence in the action of the Board.

A note to the Hon. Mr. Bolles, Navy Department, Washington, will be sufficient in the premises.

I have to thank you for your very kind letter in reply to my communication from Princeton.

William A. Hall[1] *to William A. Graham* UNC

Raleigh
Octr 7th 1871

Dear friend,

Please read the book containing this line with care. It may do you good. "Search the scriptures" is a divine command. "Believe on the Lord Jesus Christ & thou shalt be saved." is God's *great* command to us. "The blood of Jesus cleanseth from all sin;" on which we are to rest our hope for heaven, is a truth most precious. If you would know what it is to be a Christian, Christ says, "Ye are my friends if ye do whatsoever I command you." Again, "Hereby shall ye know, that ye have passed from death unto life, if ye love the *brethren*," meaning God's people. Suffer me to remind you, as a friend, that the "chief end of man is to glorify God & enjoy Him forever." May this blessed enjoyment be yours.

Affectionately yours,

---

[1]William Alexander Hall (1799-1877) was a Presbyterian minister who served a number of churches in North Carolina and Tennessee. Prepared for higher education by a celebrated teacher, the Reverend John Mushat of Statesville, Hall was graduated by the University of North Carolina in 1822. He was a contemporary of Graham at the Chapel Hill institution. Hall was licensed to preach by the Presbytery of Concord in August, 1827; he was ordained the following year and began to serve churches in Rowan County. After twenty-five years of faithful service to Joppa and Unity churches, a time when he founded the Franklin Presbyterian Church, Hall relocated in Tennessee, where he joined the Presbytery of the western district. He organized and pastored a number of Tennessee churches. He and his wife, Olivia C. Hall of Bethany, North Carolina, are buried at Mt. Carmel Church, Tipton County, Tennessee. Claude Fisher Thomason, *History of Franklin Presbyterian Church* (n.p., c. 1977), 28-29.

William A. Graham to
Cornelia Phillips Spencer A&H: SPENCER

Hillsboro'
Oct. 28th 1871

. . . .

I thank you for the freedom of your communication in relation to the University, and the inside view it presents of the ideas and plans, or the want of them, of the present Board of Trustees. Upon assuming their trust, the individuals, suddenly elevated to such duties, seemed exceedingly confident, aggressive, polemical. Their first step was to dismiss, in a most offensive manner, every member of the old faculty, by resolutions affecting to accept their resignations, when no resignations were before them. And to guard against any legal redress for such a wrong, a further resolve was adopted, declaring the offices of every member of the Faculty abolished, so that the whole structure should be dismantled and a University placed in their grasp without Professors or Professorships. This was done in the presence of Governor Swain,[1] who was invited to be present as Pres't of the Univ., and *ex officio* a member of the Board. He gave me the details of these proceedings on his bed of death. They have been carefully kept from the public.

The next step was to arraign the old Board of Trustees for a most unwise sale of the land scrip of the Agricultural fund; and this was considered so available a theme for electioneering and party capital, that a Pamphlet[2] was issued, drawn up by a Judge of the Supreme Court, but fathered by Judge Cantwell.[3] The purport of the charge was that the scrip had been sold at 50 cents per acre, and a year or two subsequently had risen to 90 cents. This was held up as a blunder and even a crime. The States in these donations were not allowed to locate the warrants or scrip, and hold the land, but were necessitated to sell, After that of North Carolina had by the Legislature been turned over to the University, by consummate address on the part of Gov. Swain, the Secretary of the Interior and Pres't Johnson were prevailed on to issue the warrants before issues had been made to any other Southern State. Careful inquiry was then made with a view to a sale on the most advantageous terms. Being in New York I procured inquiry to be made by one of the most famous houses in Wall Street, and 50 cents was found to be the highest price then current; and finally a sale was concluded by a full Board at Raleigh, at 50 cents per acre, to be paid for as delivered, in instalments; and unless the whole was paid for by a designated day, the contract to end. In process of time and for causes not necessary to be investigated, the price advanced; and our new Board of Trustees seemed delighted that a loss had been sustained and a failure to realize a higher price under the auspices of their predecessors. They published a pamphlet to proclaim it to the world, and seriously considered whether they would not refuse to take the money, sue the members of the old Board, and urge that the warrants should not be permitted to be located. The Secretary of the Interior by this time was Gov. Cox.[4] When the case was laid before him with a proposition to stop the issue of the warrants, he replied, that the price received was not inadequate—as Gov. of Ohio, he himself had sold his scrip of like kind at 55 cents per acre. This has not been given to the public, but it stopped the mouths of the Clamorers, who then took the money, $135,000. or thereabouts, and signalized their adeptness in finance by investing in special tax bonds, or Swepson bonds, now worth nothing, and were notoriously procured to be issued by fraud, and no reasonable man could expect them to be paid at par. Such was the result of the management of these critics in finance.

Having a carte blanche as to a Faculty, they proceeded, I suppose, to re-establish Professorships, and appoint the individuals of their choice, and at the end of three years have realized a failure, which all are forced to acknowledge.

And they themselves, Mr. Lassiter[5] being more than an average representative of their fitness for their office, are forced to the inquiry, "What next?"

It would have been far more easy to have shown how the wreck which has been made, might have been prevented. But in dealing with the matter as it stands, and with an earnest desire to see the University revived, I think it is Indispensable: 1st. that the present Board of Trustees, or a large part of it at least, should resign. The parents in the State who can educate sons, will not consent that they shall take diplomas with the signatures of many of them. But if these resign will the Board of Education appoint any that are more acceptable? It consists of the Gov. and the Executive Officers around him at the Capitol elected by the radicals and mainly by the negroes. Can they be expected, to shew so much respect or toleration for the men of character of the opposite party as to make appointments from among them?

The provision of the Constitution puts us under the dominion of this Board of Education, and there is hardly any ground on which the loss of the Convention question is more to be regretted than the necessity for a change in this particular.

Granting that this difficulty were surmounted, I think the Alumni might be relied on for a liberal contribution to the extent of their means. But this would not raise an endowment sufficient for the permanent support of the University. It would still be necessary to call on the Legislature for aid, temporarily at least, and if the other troubles were out of the way, I should not despair of this. With the ample provision of buildings, grounds, and appliances, a few thousand dollars per year would set it in motion, and with the number of students carried up to what it was at the beginning of the war, it would be self-supporting. If it can be brought once to this point, there is reason to hope, that people of fortune may in time add much to its resources. There is a wonderful ambition of that kind now prevailing in the Northern States at least. But we must "have" before "it shall be given" us. It may not be necessary to have fortune, but it must be demonstrated that we have capacity in every respect to carry on such an Institution with success.

It is to be hoped, that the litigation respecting the debt of the University will come to an end this winter. That incumbrance must be taken off before we can start in a new career. People will not give to pay the debts of others.

I have not been able to work out any plan, which would be effectual for relief, without a concurrence on the part of the radical party, which we have no reason to expect. I shall at all times, however, be pleased to confer with those who have the true interests of the University at heart, and to concur in any possible plan to restore its benefits to the people of the State.

. . . .

Regretting that I am unable to present more hopeful views as to the subject of your letter at present, I am,

---

[1]David L. Swain (1801-1868), a native of Buncombe County, and Graham had enjoyed a close friendship, shared a common interest in history and the university, and been political allies. Swain, after a brief stay at the University of North Carolina as a student, studied law and was admitted to the bar in 1822. He experienced immediate success and was a superior court judge before he reached the age of thirty. He represented Buncombe County in the North Carolina House of Commons for several terms before becoming the youngest governor in North Carolina history. During his tenure as governor, Swain proved to be a constructive figure of the first rank. He championed tax revision, internal improvements, public education, and constitutional reform. After influencing the calling of the Constitutional Convention of 1835, Swain led the western factions, which sought reform.

In 1835 Swain became president of the University of North Carolina. One disgruntled professor allegedly remarked that North Carolinians had elected Swain to every office in their power and were now sending him to the university to be educated. Fortunately, Swain proved to be a gifted teacher and skillful administrator. Under his leadership the university flourished. He was president until just prior to his death. *DAB*, XVIII, 230-231.

[2]A copy of this pamphlet has not been found.

[3]Edward P. Cantwell (1826-1891), an attorney and judge in New Hanover County, was a university trustee. A graduate of Harvard, he wrote and compiled law books and authored *Cantwell's Justice.* He served as clerk of the North Carolina House of Commons from 1856 to 1861. As state senator, 1874-1875, Cantwell voted to give the interest on the state's land grant fund to the university, which action by the General Assembly enabled the institution to reopen in 1875. Battle, *History of the University*, II, 785, 794; Crockette W. Hewlett and Leora H. McEachern, *Attorneys of New Hanover County, 1724-1978* (Wilmington, 1979), 29; Cheney, *North Carolina Government*, 324, 326, 327, 355n, 455; H. M. London (ed.), *Proceedings of the Twenty-seventh Annual Session of the North Carolina Bar Association* (Raleigh: Mitchell Printing Company, 1925), 69-71.

[4]Jacob Dolson Cox (1828-1900), of Ohio, a native of Canada, was an 1851 graduate of Oberlin College. He was an educator, politician, Union general, and author. Committed to an antislavery position, he supported Scott in 1852 and helped in the fusion of antislavery Whigs and Free-Soilers. He became a Republican senator in 1859, joining a radical antislavery faction that included Salmon P. Chase and James Garfield. A volunteer commissioned as brigadier general, he rose to major general. After commanding the forces that contested Braxton Bragg at Bentonville, he joined Sherman at Goldsboro. Elected Republican governor of Ohio (1866-1868), Cox lost the support of his party by proposing forcible segregation of Negroes, opposing Negro suffrage, and supporting the Johnson reconstruction policies. For a time he tried to mediate between Johnson and the radicals, but he later abandoned the embattled president. Cox favored civil service reform as secretary of the interior (1869-1870); he resigned that post because of differences with President Ulysses S. Grant. Cox became a liberal Republican and served one term as congressman, 1877-1879. Subsequently he was dean of the Cincinnati Law School and from 1885 to 1889 was president of the University of Cincinnati. He also authored several respected military histories. *DAB*, IV, 476-478.

[5]Robert W. Lassiter.

J. R. Cole[1] *to William A. Graham* UNC

House of Representatives, Austin, Texas
Nov. 7th 1871

I address through you the Agent of the Peabody fund. I would address him but am unacquainted with his address.

I received a communication from him while I was at home last Summer which stated that the rules adopted for the distribution of the fund in assisting institutions of learning only permitted about one third to be given any institution where two thirds were given from other sources, and that the Board were confining their assistance to schools which were under the control and assisted by the proper authorities where a system of public free schools existed. As I wish for assistance for the poor children in the vicinity of the school which I control I make the following statement: We have a house just built costing about $2000 with painting yet to be completed. This institution has been incorporated by the Legislature and I am Principal of the Institute. Its Corporate Name is Cedar Male and Female Institute.

In order to derive all the benefits from the Free School System just started in Texas, we have turned over to the Superintendent of Public Instruction the control of our building etc, and he has assigned me to the control of the school. The law requires all children between six and eighteen years of age to attend some school as long as four months in each year, and yet there will not be funds enough to pay their tuition for that term.

In the vicinity of Our Institute are about 200 children, of which number at least 75 are too poor to attend school unless their tuition be paid. I am compelled to have assistant teachers. I may receive from the note $800, or $1000 which will not support the school longer than four months. If our school can receive any amount from $400 to $1000 to assist the state fund, I am confident the school could continue ten months of every year—especially if the money furnished by the Peabody fund were distributed to pay for such of the more destitute as might be selected by the teacher, the trustees of the school or any one who might be selected. Any rules which would be satisfactory to those contributing the fund, would be satisfactory to me and those receiving. While I am doing all I can to educate the children around me, I cannot educate 75 children without *any* return. Any arrangement that you can make with the Superintendent or myself will be carried out according to your instructions. I hope you will forward this communication to Dr. Sears, and hope he will answer as soon as convenient and do what he can for my people.

Address me at Kentuckytown, Texas

---

[1]J. R. Cole, as this letter indicates, was a member of the House of Representatives in Texas. He has not been further identified.

James A. Graham to Susan Washington Graham UNC

Law Office of Jas. A. Graham, Graham, N.C.
Nov 17th 1871

My dear Mother

Your kind letter of 16th reached me this morning. I have thought a great deal of the temptations that will surround me this winter in Raleigh and to guard against that I have promised Lizzie not to touch a drop of intoxicating drink for a year and pray every day that God may enable me faithfully & firmly to keep it not only for that length of time, but during my whole life. Would that I had continued to abstain as I did for two years before I left Hillsboro. I would not then have caused you & father the sorrow & trouble that I have. No one can regret my course more than I do, now that I see it plainly. I received a very kind letter from father on Tuesday on the subject & I have been miserable ever since to think of the course I had pursued. Hardly an hour passes that I do not think of it and of the disgrace I may have brought on myself & the family by yielding to my appetite for drink which was growing upon me.

I expect it is fortunate for me that it was thus brought to my attention plainly this early in life as it will enable me to fight more strongly against such an appetite in the future. When I showed father's letter to Lizzie, poor darling, it seemed as if her heart would break. Ever since you first spoke to me on the subject—some little time ago—I have prayed that I might cease entirely or at least only touch it occasionally. The only excuse I can offer for myself if that is any excuse at all, is that my disposition is such that it is hard for me to say "no" and I have often yielded to temptation on that account. I feel that I have taken a drink too often, but am thankful I have seldom carried it to excess, even the least. I will, God helping me, by a better life wipe out any stain I have gotten so far and yet lead such a life as will cause you & father, as well as my own dear wife, to be proud of me instead of being a disgrace to the family as I might have been had I continued to let the habit of taking a drink grow upon me. I have endeavored, as you say, to hide it from myself and to think that I did not indulge too often, hoping that all my friends thought the same way, but now dear mother, thanks to you & father I see my sin in its true light. God grant that I may never again do anything to cause either you or him a moments pain & sorrow. I have not lived as a Christian should, but I am now determined with God's help to devote myself more faithfully to him and try to live nearer him than ever. Pray for me, dear mother, that I may succeed. With all my advantages in life, my education, position & family connections my sin is all the greater & my failings of this sort would be more noticed by every one.

I thank you, dear mother, that you have written me so plainly on the subject and hope I may profit by it. Morning & night my prayer shall be that I may never indulge in this sinful habit again and by the grace & help of God my life shall be a different one in many respects from what it has been. No one but God & myself can know how deeply I feel the sin of my course.

My last thought at night & first on waking is of it, and I hope that my repentance is true & sincere.

Affectionately your son

Edward J. Hale to William A. Graham UNC

17 Murray Street,
New York,
November 20th., 1871.

Mr. Stephens has consented, at our suggestion, to put the following, or anything like it that we may prefer, in his School History[1] now in press:

"North Carolina was ahead of all her sister colonies on the subject. On the 20th. of May, 1775, the day after news of the battle of Lexington was received, a Convention of Delegates from the various Captain's Districts in Mecklenburg Co., threw off all allegiance to the British cause, & declared North Carolina to be a sovereign and independent State."

Will this do? Please suggest any amendment.

Mr. S. requests us to send him a copy of the State Pamphlet. Ours was destroyed by Sherman. Can you *lend,* or give him one?

---

[1]Alexander Hamilton Stephens published *A Compendium of the History of the United States* in 1872. *DAB,* XVII, 574.

Lyman C. Draper[1] *to William A. Graham* UNC

State Historical Society of Wisconsin.
Madison, Wisconsin,
November 22nd., 1871.

I am collecting materials for a work on *Gen'l Th's Sumter,*[2] of So. Ca. It occurred to me that you may be possessed of facts or documents throwing light upon some of Sumter's operations—more especially relative to the affairs at Rocky Mount & Hanging Rock, where North Carolinians under *Col. Irwin,*[3] *Lt. Col. Heaggins,*[4] & Maj. *Davie*[5] served with him.

I wish to notice Col's *Irwin* & *Heaggins*—have you any unpublished facts about them? I am much puzzled about the latter, especially. I give the orthography of his name as recorded in Lee's Memoirs[6]—& yet his true name may have been *Hagins or Huggins.*

I think y'r father, Gen. Graham, left a Narrative of his recollections of Revolutionary events in the Mecklenburg region. Is it still preserved—& lengthy? If agreeable, I w'd be glad indeed to have a copy of it.

Gen. Sumter was so much in Mecklenburg, & had so much aid from the gallant men of that region, that I shall necessarily blend much of the border history of the two Carolinas, & especially so of the eventful year 1780. Hence, I seek all the light I can get.

I have a partial set of the N.C. University Magazine, & desire very much to complete it. I have a copy of the work containing your, Gov. Swain's, & Dr. Hawk's Addresses—have Wheeler's[7] & Dr. Carruther's[8] works.

I send you two parcels of pamphlets. Let me hope to hear from you, at y'r leisure.

---

[1]Lyman Copeland Draper (1815-1891) was a historian, librarian, and collector. He assiduously collected historical documents of all kinds and bequeathed his material to the

Wisconsin Historical Society. He was secretary to that organization, 1854-1886. He founded and edited the Wisconsin *Historical Collections. CDAB*, 246-247.

[2]Thomas Sumter (1734-1832) of South Carolina served as lieutenant colonel of the Sixth Continental Regiment and in 1780 became brigadier general of the South Carolina militia. Known as the "Gamecock of the Revolution," Sumter played an important role against British and loyalist forces in North and South Carolina, 1780-1782. After the war he was a congressman and a United States senator. *Who Was Who in America: Historical Volume, 1607-1896*, Volume I of *Who's Who in American History* (Chicago: Marquis Who's Who, revised edition, 1967), 587, hereinafter cited as *Who Was Who*; *CDAB*, 1034.

[3]Robert Irwin (1740-1800), a native of Pennsylvania, settled on Steele Creek, Mecklenburg County, in 1763. A son of William Irwin who reportedly signed the dubious Mecklenburg Declaration of Independence, he served in the expedition against the Cherokee in 1776 and was a delegate to the Fourth and Fifth provincial congresses. He commanded Mecklenburg militia at the Battle of Hanging Rock, having been positioned in the American center. Tompkins, *History of Mecklenburg*, II, 75; Blackwell P. Robinson, *William R. Davie* (Chapel Hill: University of North Carolina Press, 1957), 50-51, hereinafter cited as Robinson, *Davie*.

[4]William Heaggins commanded a body of Mecklenburg militia in the actions at Rocky Mount and Hanging Rock in 1780. The surname is spelled variously Hagins and Higgins. Robinson, *Davie*, 44, 416.

[5]William Richardson Davie (1756-1820), patriot hero active in the Carolina piedmont during the Revolution, came from England to South Carolina as a child. A staunch Federalist and framer of the Constitution, Davie introduced the bill that chartered the University of North Carolina. He served as governor of North Carolina, 1798-1799. Powell, *DNCB*, II, 28-29; see also Robinson, *Davie*.

[6]Robert E. Lee (ed.), *Memoirs of the War in the Southern Department of the United States by Henry Lee, Lieutenant-Colonel Commandant of the Partisan Legion during the American War. A New Edition, with Revisions, and a Biography of the Author* (New York: University Publishing Company, 1869).

[7]John Hill Wheeler (1806-1882), of Murfreesboro, was a graduate of Columbian College (now George Washington University). He was a lawyer, diplomat, journalist, and historical writer. One of his best-known works was *Historical Sketches of North Carolina*, published in 1851. His histories, however, are generally regarded as poorly organized and erroneous. He was a member of the Commons (1827-1830), superintendent of the Charlotte branch of the United States Mint (1837-1841), state treasurer (1843-1845), and minister to Nicaragua (1854-1857). *DAB*, XX, 50.

[8]Eli Washington Caruthers (1793-1865), son of James and Elizabeth Lawrence Caruthers, was born in Rowan County. Educated at the school of Joseph Kirkpatrick, a Presbyterian minister, Caruthers first attended Hampden-Sydney and then enrolled at Princeton, from which he was graduated in 1817. He prepared for the ministry at Princeton Theological Seminary. After serving other congregations in the area he settled as pastor at Alamance and remained until 1861. His sermons were "unusually didactic and . . . often elucidated by illustrations drawn from nature." He was avidly interested in education, was a fine Greek scholar, and is best known for his work as a historian. Caruthers's lack of sympathy for the cause of the South during the Civil War precipitated his resignation from the pastorate of the Alamance Presbyterian Church. Powell, *DNCB*, I, 337-338.

E. S. Thompson to William A. Graham[1] UNC

South Point, N.C.
Nov. 24/71

Sins my last the crop of corn has bin House we made in all about 1300 hundred bushels. To your part about 975. the crop of Cotton is something better than I thought for when you were here. we have gin Five Bags I think you will have elleven bags to your part. a part of the wheat that you sent me for seed had been heat and did not come up. I am havinge the grown sowed over with the wheat we raised here. I sold 6135 lbs of wheat coming to $184.15. we have some Twelve Hogs that be to kill about the middle of next month. I wood like for you to write me what disposition you wish made of them. ther will be some 15 yong hogs to kill about Christmas.

as regards my staying here for another year, I will stay for 300 Hundred and bord my self except bread. that is the best I can do.

we had [stiring] times here for the past three or fore weeks, they have arrested in all 135 of the best men of the county. it is said that some three Hundred have lift the county. the Scogginses[2] are in Gaston have made several arrest. I learn that a grate many are leaving for other parts.

Yours Respectfully,

---

[1]Obviously E. S. Thompson was tending farmland owned by Graham, probably at Leper plantation in Gaston County and York District, South Carolina. The editors inserted some periods in this letter to facilitate reading.

[2]The Scoggins referred to were part of a numerous Rutherford County family. After the Civil War some of the family were members of the Ku Klux Klan, Nathan among them. Nathan Scoggin (1827-1917), described after his defection to the Republican party as "a man of evil life and character," was appointed a United States commissioner and used that office against former Klansmen. His brother, William, was appointed a United States marshal and cooperated with Nathan in official activities. Needless to say, Conservatives in western North Carolina despised the brothers. Griffin, *History of Old Tryon and Rutherford Counties*, 320, 331; Hamilton, *Shotwell Papers*, II, 459-462, 469-470, 510, 537, 541, 552-553, 567.

William A. Graham to Susan Washington Graham A&H

Hillsboro
Nov 27th 1871

My dear Wife

I returned from Person Court on Saturday night. The judge having not opened the court till Wednesday morning. Transacted a good deal of business—among others got a judgment in the Insurance case for near $16,000. Judge French[1] attended, and we settled it without a trial.

I was glad to see your letter to Sudie on my return. I can scarcely give any account of home affairs. John & James came up on Saturday night, and with Rebecca & Lizzy were here yesterday evening. I had a very satisfactory letter from James in prompt reply to what I wrote him, and have no further anxiety on his account. He & John returned to Raleigh last night. I go today at 11 to the Federal Court—my stay will be uncertain, but will probably be back & forth for the ensuing two weeks. Judge Bond[2] will not attend, and there will [be] no K. K. trials. Neither circumstance affords me any regret. I have a very satisfactory letter from George this morning, indicating that he is taking rank among the physicians of Atlanta, and getting a share in the business of his profession. He describes the city as making wonderful advances in prosperity—Horses, mules, cattle & Hogs arriving in great numbers from the Western states, and new settlers in like proportion, to such an extent that they cannot get houses. The Legislature is sitting in Atlanta, and exciting times in relation to the resignation & flight of Gov.

Bullock.[3] The veto of a Bill providing for the election of a successor by the acting Governor, which has been passed over the veto—the dangers of collision with Grant etc. Says the common doctors annoy him a good deal, by borrowing his books, & keeping them, when he has occasion to consult them himself.

Thompson writes me from the plantation, crop of cotton rather better than expected. I shall get 11 bales. Offers to stay next year at $300. & house himself except bread. If Reel would go, I am not disposed to pay it. Have made him no reply as yet. Says, there have been many arrests in York & Gaston, and many people have fled. He does not speak, of any annoyance at my place, but if it becomes generally understood, that there is a suspension of law, there will be but little protection for property or persons.

Messrs Rev. Johnson[4] & Stanberry[5] former Atto. Genl. U.S. have passed Raleigh on way to Columbia to attend Judge Bonds court, this week, and defend the prisoners. We hear that Col. Cad. Jones[6] went to Washington [and] procured an order to parole his son,[7] out of jail in York.

I write in very great haste as I must be at the depot at 11 a.m. My love to Wm's family, supposing you will be with them, I direct this to their P.O.

Ever Affectionately yours.

---

[1]This may refer to Robert S. French of Robeson County, who had served as a superior court judge during the Civil War. Cheney, *North Carolina Government*, 362, 371n.

[2]Hugh L. Bond.

[3]Rufus Brown Bullock (1834-1907), born in New York, was a businessman and politician who served as Republican governor of Georgia, 1868-1871. He was charged with embezzling public funds, tried, and acquitted. *CDAB*, 123.

[4]Reverdy Johnson (1796-1876), a Marylander and graduate of St. John's College, Annapolis, studied law and was admitted to the bar in 1816. He enjoyed a long and distinguished career in law and politics and held the following positions: state senator, 1821-1829 and 1860-1861; United States senator (Whig) 1845-1849, (Democrat) 1863-1868; delegate to the Washington Peace Conference of 1861; and United States minister to Great Britain, 1868-1869.

Johnson deserted the Whig party in order to support Polk's Oregon and Mexican policies but opposed the annexation of Mexican Territory because he feared, correctly, that it would reopen the vexing question of slavery extensions. He urged compromise in 1850 and eventually favored allowing the Supreme Court to decide the fate of slavery in the territories. Renowned as one of the great constitutional lawyers of his day, Johnson represented the defense in *Dred Scott* v. *Sandford*.

Despite his sympathy for the South, Johnson considered secession treason and worked to preserve the Union. He upheld Lincoln's suspension of *habeas corpus* but supported McClellan in 1864 because he believed the Emancipation Proclamation to be unwise and resented the administration's interference in the Maryland elections. As a Democratic senator, he generally supported President Andrew Johnson's reconstruction plan. Although he opposed Negro suffrage, he did support the Fourteenth Amendment. *DAB*, X, 112-114.

[5]Henry Stanbery (1803-1881), a native of New York City whose family moved to Zanesville, Ohio, in 1814, graduated from Washington (later Washington and Jefferson) College at age sixteen. He read law and was admitted to the Ohio bar upon reaching his majority. Law partner of the distinguished Thomas Ewing, 1824-1831, he practiced in Lancaster, Columbus, and Cincinnati while gaining first rank among his Ohio colleagues. A Whig and later a Republican, he was Ohio attorney general; delegate to the Ohio Constitutional Convention of 1850; and United States attorney general, July, 1866, to March, 1868. Stanbery was a staunch supporter of Andrew Johnson's reconstruction plans;

and, when impeachment proceedings were brought against the president, he resigned his cabinet post to become Johnson's chief legal counsel. His skill as an advocate was important in securing an acquittal. Subsequently Stanbery was appointed attorney general and justice of the Supreme Court. Both appointments failed to be confirmed, and he returned to his Cincinnati practice. *DAB*, XVII, 498-499.

[6]Cadwallader Jones (1813-1899), from Hillsborough, graduated from the University of North Carolina, which he served as a trustee, 1840-1857. An attorney and cotton planter, he sat in the General Assembly, 1840-1843 and 1848-1851. Jones moved to South Carolina in 1857. After serving as an officer in the Confederate army, he was elected to the South Carolina legislature and the 1865 constitutional convention. Powell, *DNCB*, III, 315.

[7]Iredell Jones.

Cadwallader Jones to William A. Graham UNC

Rock Hill,
December 8th., 1871.

I was much gratified by the interest manifested for my son, in your letter of last month—not the less so, because I omitted to thank you. Your suggestions I laid before Col. Wilson,[1] Atto.; he was about to apply for the writ of habeas corpus, but delayed, hoping from day to day that the prisoners would be bound over to the Commissioner for examination, besides, Judge Bryan[2] was at Greenville. You have doubtless seen that Iredell, and many of the prisoners have been admitted to bail. Iredell was no K.K., but that made no difference, he was marked for a victim, a pretense for his arrest was got by a negro swearing that he was of the party that raided upon the malitia guns at our depot. The fellow will be prosecuted for perjury.

I was at Columbia last week, Mr. Reverdy Johnson was very confident that he can get a case before the Supreme Court, & that the act of Cong: will be declared unconstitutional. The Judges have already differed in opinion, upon a motion to quash.

You have seen a great deal about the outrages & "rebellion" in York. There had been, during last winter, very many outrages commited, in retaliation for Burnings, & as punishment for larceny, by the first of May all violence had ceased, and I assure you, at the time of the proclamation the County was perfectly quiet & peaceful—never more so; a good feeling was existing between the races. About this time A. S. Wallace;[3] M.C. returned home; he was received with contempt, & set vigorously to work to have his constituents punished, not for what they were doing, but for what they had done, his black friends were becoming too friendly with the whites, & martial law was procured, whatever may be the end of all this, he is *ruined.*

The negroes in my part of the County are not at all exultant, & are behaving remarkably well.

I think it quite probable that a party of moderate Republicans & Democrats will be formed, & will sweep the State.

You may look out for a terrible exposure of the Scott[4] Ring. The rogues are beginning to accuse each other, & their larcenies will come to the surface.

---

[1]William B. Wilson (b. 1827), a prominent attorney, attended South Carolina College,

graduating in 1846 as class valedictorian. He read law and opened a highly successful practice in York, South Carolina, in 1848. He was elected to the state legislature three times and was a delegate to the Secession Convention of 1860. During the Civil War Wilson rose from private to colonel in the service of the Confederacy. *Cyclopedia of Eminent Men*, I, 227-229.

[2]George S. Bryan (b. 1809), of South Carolina, read law with Thomas S. Grimke and practiced in Charleston, where his family was well connected and influential. A Henry Clay Whig and ardent Unionist, he was a leader of those who opposed secession. In 1866 he was appointed federal judge for the South Carolina district, a post he held until 1886. *Cyclopedia of Eminent Men*, I, 673-674.

[3]Alexander Stuart Wallace (1810-1893), of York, South Carolina, was a farmer who served first as a state legislator and then as a representative to Congress, 1870-1877, having been elected on the Republican ticket. *Biographical Directory of Congress*, 1767.

[4]Robert Kingston Scott (1826-1900), businessman, served as brevet major general in the Union army and head of the Freedmen's Bureau in South Carolina, 1865-1868. His administration as Republican governor of that state, 1868-1872, was marked by numerous financial scandals. *CDAB*, 925.

William A. Graham to Susan Washington Graham A&H

Graham
Dec 11th 1871

My Dear Wife

I have found little convenience for writing for a week or two past. After returning from Person, I went immediately to Raleigh, and have spent the last two weeks there, excepting Thanksgiving day and two Sundays. Sudie, Aug, & Alfred are taking care of things at home. Have gotten about half a supply of ice, among other things, during the cold seasons of last week. Melinda,[1] who you supposed would leave, is still there. . . . I came here last night with James. John was compelled to return to Raleigh. Lizzie did not come up. James wishes to return to his seat in the Legislature in a few days. I shall be detained here till Thursday or Friday, promised to be again in Raleigh next Monday, & have an engagement at home for Thursday of next week. So that I can hardly go west before Christmas. I shall be obliged to go before new year, to make plantation arrangements. We miss you much at home, but if you prefer could remain till I come, or return before; writing us what time to expect you.

Mr. Walter Clark[2] was at Hillsboro a week since and took Tea with us on Sunday evening. He also remained, Monday, when I returned to Raleigh.

I saw Misses Susan & Emma W.[3] They were both up and appeared pretty well. A large house is going up, on the the [*sic*] south lots they sold, designed for a boarding house, or second class hotel. Mrs. Swain will not return probably this winter. Sidham. Alexander[4] was at Raleigh on Saturday to endeavour to get his unfortunate sister in the Lun. Asylum, some recent regulation at Columbia requiring the patients from other states to be removed, to make room for residents. The session of the Legislature & court brings a great many persons to Raleigh, and there are appearances of considerable prosperity in the city. But it was a sad sight to see one or two hundred or more poor men from the Western part of the state, some the inmates of jails, and others in custody of officers thronging the court, as alleged Ku Klux. They were all, I believe, bailed out, and allowed to go home. No cases of the kind being tried at this time, by reason of the absence of Judge Bond. The cases from Charlotte were continued for the same reason. Joseph did not go to Raleigh.

I have not recd. letter from Cincinatti yet. I think the last one in September stated, that pay day was the 12th instead of 1st of the months of the quarter. Nor has Judge French written in respect to the Judgment against the Insurance Co. in Person.

Mr. Peyton[5] has sent me a third work of his, giving account of a journey he made in 1848, from Staunton to the North West. I have also a volume from Dr. Hammond[6] of New York on sleep &c, which may interest you.

I seize a few moments to write this, with bad ink & pen, before looking into my business here. James was notified by Mr. Olds,[7] that all the cases against Holden etc, will be moved out of this county.

Fearing you may need it, I enclose herein $20. My receipts have been very light at the courts I have been attending, but the earnings pretty fine.

My love to Wm. & Julia & the children, also Bettie & hers, if she is still with you.

Ever Affectionately yours,

Quite an effort was made at the Fedl. Court to fix charges on parties in Orange, but, I think, none have been sucessful. A Mr. Southgate[8] from Iredell is moving to Henry Brown's[9] house. He is agent for the Masons to collect money to build a Masonic Temple in Ral. A letter from George to Sudie last week. He needs more money. I much fear our supply of water has failed also Mrs. Roulhacs and the Gatte's well. I will have it thoroughly examined when I get home.

I wish Wm. would write me by next week or during it, what prospect there is, of getting an overseer instead of Thompson. I think he is disposed to insist on wages.

---

[1]Melinda has not been identified.

[2]Walter McKenzie Clark (1846-1924) became one of the state's most influential men. A native of Halifax County, Clark attended the schools of Vine Hill Academy, Ridgeway, and Belmont before he entered Colonel C. C. Tew's military academy in Hillsborough in 1860. At age fifteen he was selected drillmaster for North Carolina recruits and served the Confederacy in the Thirty-fifth North Carolina Regiment. He resigned his commission as first lieutenant in 1863 and resumed his education, studying at the University of North Carolina and graduating first in his class in 1864. After graduation he was elected major of the Sixth Battalion, North Carolina Junior Reserves, and rose to the rank of lieutenant colonel in the Seventieth Regiment.

After the war Clark studied law in New York and at Columbian Law School, Washington. His subsequent career as lawyer and jurist was a brilliant one culminating in thirty-five years of service on the North Carolina Supreme Court, after 1902 as chief justice. Clark actively participated in many of the most controversial questions of his day, always as a strong and determined leader for the causes he advocated. He was a dedicated historian who edited and compiled *The State Records of North Carolina* (16 volumes, 1895-1906) and *Histories of the Several Regiments and Battalions from North Carolina in the Great War, 1861-'65* (5 volumes, 1901). In January, 1874, Clark married Graham's daughter, Susan Washington Graham, by whom he fathered seven children. Powell, *DNCB*, I, 378-379. The *DNCB* erroneously gives the date of Clark's marriage as 1875.

[3]Susan and Emma W. have not been identified.

[4]Sydenham Benoni Alexander.

[5]John Lewis Peyton (1824-1896), of Virginia, graduated from the University of Virginia law school. He practiced law in Chicago before returning to his home state. He married Henrietta Elizabeth Clark Washington (1834-1907), Mrs. William A. Graham's niece. A Unionist who likened his political position to that of Graham, Peyton represented North Carolina in business in Europe until 1876. He was quite a prolific writer and was, for a while, a fellow of the Royal Geographical Society of Great Britain. Among his works was *The American Crisis; or, Pages from the Note-Book of a State Agent during the Civil War* (London: Saunders, Otley and Company, 2 volumes, 1867). *DAB*, XII, 520; W. A. Graham Clark (comp.), "Descendants of James Washington (d. 1766) of Northampton County, N.C." (Washington, D.C., 1939), genealogical chart in the William A. Graham Papers, Southern Historical Collection, University of North Carolina Library at Chapel Hill, hereinafter cited as Clark, "Washington Descendants."

[6]William Alexander Hammond (1828-1900), a native of Maryland, was a noted physician who pioneered in the field of neurology in the United States. Educated in Pennsylvania and New York City, he entered the United States Army as assistant surgeon in 1849. After serving at various frontier posts and at West Point, he resigned to become professor of anatomy and physiology at the University of Maryland, a post he held from 1859 to 1861. Early in the Civil War Hammond gained attention as a camp and hospital inspector and susequently, in 1862, was appointed surgeon general. In 1864 he clashed with Secretary of War Edwin M. Stanton and was court-martialed and dismissed from the army. (He was reinstated in 1878 and listed as a brigadier general on the retired roster.) Hammond then settled in New York, where he excelled as a physician and teacher in several medical colleges. A prolific writer, he was instrumental in founding four medical journals. Two—the *Maryland and Virginia Medical Journal* and the *Quarterly Journal of Psychological Medicine and Medical Jurisprudence*—he served as editor. In addition, Hammond established the Army Medical Museum and initiated a medical history of the Civil War. The book to which Graham refers in this letter was probably Hammond's *Treatise on Diseases of the Nervous System* (1871), described as the "first text-book on nervous diseases in English." *DAB*, VII, 210.

[7]Lewis P. Olds was North Carolina attorney general, 1869-1870, and represented Wake County in the state House of Representatives, 1870-1872. Cheney, *North Carolina Government*, 427, 451.

[8]James Southgate, a native of Virginia, attended that state's university and operated a military school in Norfolk. From 1862 to 1864 he served in the Norfolk Artillery Blues. Then he joined his wife in North Carolina, where she had opened the Louisburg Female College. Subsequently he was president of Olin College in north Iredell County. After a brief stay in New York City, where he sought funds to support Olin, Southgate settled in Hillsborough and engaged in a general commission business. In 1876 he moved to Durham, where he opened a successful firm offering life and fire insurance. Ashe, *Biographical History*, II, 410-411; Homer M. Keever, *Iredell, Piedmont County* (Statesville: Iredell County Bicentennial Commission, 1976), 212-214.

[9]While it was not possible to determine which Brown this was, it is tempting to conjecture that Graham referred to Henry N. Brown, who saw danger in the Ku Klux Klan movement and in March, 1870, joined with others, including Graham, in recommending to Governor Holden that Pride Jones be given a captain's commission to suppress it. Lefler and Wager, *Orange County*, 119.

George F. Bason[1] *to William A. Graham* UNC

Graham, N.C.,
December 18th., 1871.

Our worst fears are realized. Tourgee never left here at all, stayed at Hardin's[2] Saturday night, & all day Sunday. All the trouble arose out of a little personal difficulty between one Daniel Foust,[3] a deputy sheriff of the

County, & one Joe Bradshaw,[4] in consequence of which, Bradshaw gave some information implicating Foust, his two brothers, & some others, in some Ku Kluxing. Bench warrants were issued for the Foust boys, two of them were arrested, Dan the deputy escaped, his brothers were held to bail in the sum of $9,000.00 apiece, failing to give it, they were put in jail. This was soon after you left on Saturday night. Sunday morning warrants were placed in the hands of one Wilkins[5] for Dr. Lutterloh,[6] one Euliss,[7] & another. Wilkins summoned James Stockard,[8] (son of Mr. Gibbes Stockard, whom you perhaps know, & heretofore considered a staunch, determined, man), to aid him in making the arrests. Stockard went, and the arrests were made. On the return, two of the parties, Lutterloh & the other, were placed in the hands of Stockard alone. They, as soon as the officers were out of sight, made their escape. Stockard came on to town, & reported the escape to Wilkins. Tourgee thereupon took charge of Stockard, & by some means got out of him the information that he was present at the murder of Outlaw, & many other important facts, upon which warrants were sent all over the country, but by this time the news had spread, & nobody was found.

J. A. Long, Esq.,[9] was arrested on a charge of murder this morning, & held to bail in $10,000.00, which he gave, and is now at large.

No Court today. Court was called at 11 o'clock this morning, & adjourned to two. Nothing done at two, but adjournment until nine tomorrow morning. I will give you further news as it transpires.

---

[1]George Francis Bason (1840-1907), of Alamance County, was a member of the class of 1863 at the University of North Carolina. He served the Confederacy as a captain and ordnance officer in General Alfred M. Scales's brigade. After the war Bason practiced law before entering politics. He was a member of the state House of Representatives, 1884-1885, and was a federal district attorney, 1885-1889. Grant, *Alumni History*, 37; Cheney, *North Carolina Government*, 464, 556n; Battle, *History of the University*, I, 816-817.

[2]Probably this was Republican Peter R. Hardin, the Graham magistrate. His testimony in the impeachment proceedings against Holden can be found in *Holden Trial*, II, 1926-1930. But it may refer to John W. Hardin, a Graham merchant and Alamance County commissioner who also testified in the impeachment proceedings. See *Holden Trial*, II, 1855-1872.

[3]Daniel Foust has not been further identified.

[4]Joe Bradshaw has not been further identified.

[5]Wilkins has not been identified.

[6]Dr. Thomas Lutterloh, a physician, admitted to whipping a black man so severely that he later died. Trelease, *White Terror*, 202. See also *Holden Trial*, II, 1355-1362, for the testimony of Joseph Holt, which is germane.

[7]This may have been Eli S. Euliss, a leader of the Constitutional Union Guard in Alamance County. Hamilton, *Reconstruction in North Carolina*, 470. See also *Holden Trial*, II, 1984-1985.

[8]James Stockard may have been a brother of William Stockard, who headed a camp of the White Brotherhood in Alamance County. Hamilton, *Reconstruction in North Carolina*, 462n; *Holden Trial*, II, 2249.

[9]Jacob Alson Long (1846-1915), of Alamance, entered the Confederate army while he was just a schoolboy. A lawyer by training, Long became county chief of the Ku Klux Klan but abandoned the organization when he realized it could not be controlled. The case against him was dropped quickly for lack of evidence. Trelease, *White Terror*, 192-193, 201, 203, 217, 408. See also *Holden Trial*, II, 2227-2257.

George F. Bason to William A. Graham UNC

Graham, N.C.,
December 19th., 1871.

Court met at 11 o'clock today, & the Judge charged the grand jury, & adjourned until 2 o'clock. I do not suppose that the records of the world will furnish a paralell to that charge. I wished for you during the whole time it was being delivered. We have heard much, & have had a good deal of lawmaking upon the subject of intimidation of voters within the past few years. As yet, nothing has been said about the intimidation of grand jurors. I regret that this charge cannot be published, verbatim, so that we might have the freely expressed opinions of those skilled in the law upon it. First, the grand jury had minute and particular instructions as to the nature of the offences to be inquired into, next, their responsibility & accountability, next, a threat of dire vengeance upon them if all such duties were not fully & faithfully discharged. Next, a charge that certain unmentioned members of the body were Ku Klux themselves, and that they had personal knowledge of many crimes that had been committed, and that some of them were even participants in Ku Klux outrages. Next, the solicitor[1] who, by the way, does not seem to be a willing coadjutor of *his honor* in this work, was taken in hand, his duties & responsibilities set forth, & a threat administered that, upon a failure upon his part to do *all* of said duties, so set forth, "The Court would, without fear or favour do its duty." Now this charge may have been all proper and right, & strictly within the province of his Honor, but it was something entirely new to our people, and if not intimidation, something so nearly akin to it, that I am unable to draw the line of distinction. He charged Alamance with having been the "hot bed of crime" for several years, & that notwithstanding evidence of these crimes had been repeatedly brought before the grand jury, no action had been taken. A rather awkward thing for his Honor transpired this morning. Two men, Barbee[2] by name, had given information with regard to the whipping of Rippey,[3] in which J. N. H. Clendenin[4] was—according to Barbees so stated—a participant. Clendenin never saw Barbees in his life, & suggested that there must be some mistake in the name. They—the parties—were confronted in presence of his honor this morning, & the question asked of Barbees if they had not mistaken their man. Whereupon Barbees deny ever having mentioned Clendenin's name, until it was suggested by his honor and *Mr.* Albright[5] that he was there. This shows the animus with which this thing is being conducted. I understood this morning that one Faucett, familiarly known as "squirrel mouthed George Faucett,"[6] has been arrested, & made "important disclosures" as to the Outlaw affair, how true it is I cannot tell, as admittance to a witness of this character is out of the question. We are hoping still, that the important revelations boasted of as having been obtained, both from Stockard[7] & Faucett, have no existence in fact, & are only paraded for effect, in order to induce or intimidate others who really know something, into confession. I am induced to believe that many of our citizens have fled, for the reason that warrants for their apprehension were issued, & as yet the officers bearing them have not put in an appearance. Only one man, one Stafford,[8] a young man from your County, has been brought in today, he is held to bail in $1,000.00. I have not been able to learn the nature of the charges against him. The required bail of the Fousts, who are still in jail, has been increased to $30,000.00, no hope of their giving it. I do not know that you could assist us just now by your presence, although we would be glad to have you with us. I had to mail my letter last night on the train, I hope you received it. I intend letting you know from time to time what takes place, and I would be glad to receive any suggestion as to our course that you may deem appropriate. Since writing the above, the Court has met and adjourned without doing any further business. Pay us a visit soon, if you can. The Harveys[9] will be to see you in relation to their appeal bond today. I did not see them last night, or I would have saved you any trouble with them.

---

[1]James R. Bulla.

[2]The Barbees have not been identified.

[3]Leonard Rippy, a black man, was beaten by the Klan and died shortly thereafter. *Holden Trial*, II, 1355ff.

[4]J. N. H. Clendenin was among those who confessed to Klan activity along with James E. Boyd in July, 1870.

[5]William R. Albright.

[6]George Faucett has not been identified definitively.

[7]James Stockard.

[8]Stafford has not been identified.

[9]Presumably they were George Harvey of Alamance County, who was chief of camp number 4 of the Constitutional Union Guard, and a relative. *Holden Trial*, II, 2249.

Stephen Moore[1] *to William A. Graham* UNC

Washington,
Arkansas,
December 21st., 1871.

My dear friend,

Your esteemed favour of the 8th. Inst. was to hand a day or two since, somewhat comp[l]aining of not having been troubled with a letter from me in some time. I have written to you since I had the pleasure of receiving a similar favour from you until the present, but write with pleasure in reply to your last. I regret to hear of the continued outrages perpetrated on the people of your afflicted State. We have reason to fear the same, or worse here, the devil, I think, is turned loose at will, to try what improvements he can make in the destruction of all former ideas of honesty, from the highest to the meanest of inteligent creation. Within about a week there has been two cruel murders committed in our County, one of them in the town of Washington, two men, entire strangers, who had been looking about town all day, about dark, or a little after, got a negro man in the back lot of a negro hall, and murdered him, making their escape from town. As soon thereafter as the officer could get together a company of malitia they were found in an out house five or six miles from town. When ordered to open the door they commenced firing through the cracks and chinks of the house.

After quite a number of shots on bothe sides the attacking party succeeded in capturing one of the outlaws, withe several long k[n]ives, pistols, a shot gun, about a peck of keys, several small files with two or three screw drivers; up to the last account they had failed to capture the man who got away. The one caught acknowleges the killing, but says the other did it, he says they were hired to come and kill negroes, and that the one kil'd here makes the 12th. one they have murdered, in the last few weeks, there has been several heard of found dead in different neighbourhoods. Both the men were shot by the malitia, one through the mouth and the other lost a big toe. One of the attacking party shot through the leg, a flesh wound. The other was the most barbarous murder of a young lady who had gone on a visit of a few miles in the neighbourhood. She was found dead, with two bullet shots, and her throat cut. The brute that committed the outrage was soon arrested, and turned out to be a young man of the neighbourhood, who had been for some time courting her, and whom she had persistently refused to marry, it is supposed he violated her before the murder. Three of her fingers were nearly bitten off. The neighbours assembled forthwith, arrested him, soon he confest the crime, it was determined by those who had him in custody not to trouble the courts with him, and from what I learn, he was publickly hung yesterday in presence of a large crowd of his neighbors sanctioning the act. From the surroundings here we look for sights next summer. Our army of malitia are thoroughly organized, and at any time ready to obey orders.

There has been some cold weather with us much earlier than usual, heavy freezes, and more snow than I have seen here, at one time, from the commencement to the end of the storm about nine or ten inches. In November I kil'd a large lot of pork, and have had cool weather the most of the [ti]me since, enough so to make good bacon.

In reply to your request for any news from Texas I will copy a letter from our agents rec'v'd by me a few weeks ago.

Bonham,
Sept. 29th., 1871.

Mr. Stephen Moore
Dear Sir

Inclosed please find draft No. 1,793, dated Sherman, Texas, Sept. 26, 1871, pay'b'l to yourself or order for the sum of two hundred and forty five dollars, drawn on a Northrup & Heck of New York. Signed G. VanWinkle & Co. We had to sell your gold for 1.10 or else pay 5 pr. Ct. premium for exchange on New York. There are no sales of land in this section, money never so scarce, and prospects ahead gloomy. As we collect we shall forward.

We are very truly,
Your friends,
Roberts & Semple.

I am now hauling out my cotton, though our rivers are hardly beatable, as soon however as I can, will send you a draft for a part of the money received above, which I hope will be in a few weeks.

My general health is good, alough I am still crippled up by my chronic infirmities. My weight is about as much as it ever was, a little short of one hundred and ninety pounds. Please tender my kind remembrances to Miss Susan, and believe me, as ever,

Truly your friend,

N. B.
Will you do me the favour to order forthwith Turner's Paper, the Weekly Sentinel, Commencing with the opening of the Legislature, by so doing you will greatly ob'g me.

Very sincerely yrs,

---

[1]Stephen Moore was a former resident of Hillsborough. Lefler and Wager, *Orange County*, 180, 181.

1872

E. J. Hale & Sons to William A. Graham UNC

17 Murray Street,
New York,
January 1st., 1872.

We are much obliged for your favor of the 25th., & have concluded to send it at once to Mr. Stephens, with the expression of a hope that he will incorporate it in the History. We have some fears that he will regard it as entering more into particulars than is proper for a mere school History, & as anticipating events. But we shall urge it, as due to N.C.,—which has never had justice done her.

When you get it ready, please send to us, & we hope to be able to publish it.

Yours truly,

Allow us to wish you, very heartily, A Happy New Year

Frances A. Polk[1] *to William A. Graham* UNC

Nashville, Tenn.
Jan. 10th., 1872.

Many years ago, Gov. Swain procured from my husband, the late Bishop Polk,[2] many valuable papers which he had collected, bearing upon his Father's[3] life, & that of his Grandfather, Gen. Thos. Polk,[4] of Mecklenburg. Gov. Swain said he wished to use them in preparing a history of No. Ca. I am anxious that these papers, not having been used by the Governor, should not be lost to the family, & will be much obliged if you will obtain them for me, from his executors,—or, if this should be too troublesome, would like you to give me such information as will enable me to procure them.

---

[1]Frances Ann Devereux Polk (1807-1876), born in Raleigh, was the only daughter of John and Frances Pollock Devereux. She married Leonidas Polk, a childhood friend. After her husband's death in 1864 Frances Polk, a capable and well-educated woman, taught English literature at Columbia Institute and later established her own school in New Orleans. Crabtree and Patton, *"Journal of a Secesh Lady,"* xxv-xxvi, xxxiii.

[2]Leonidas Polk (1806-1864), a North Carolina kinsman of James K. Polk who came from the same sturdy Scotch-Irish stock, graduated from the United States Military Academy in 1827. Converted by the West Point chaplain, he resigned his commission, graduated from the Virginia Theological Seminary, and entered the Episcopal ministry. As missionary bishop of the Southwest Polk traveled 5,000 miles in his first six months of service. In 1841 he was named bishop of Louisiana. He tried to be both a successful bishop and a sugar planter, but his plantation was a financial failure. At one time Polk was the enlightened master of 400 slaves. He was instrumental in establishing the University of the South in Sewanee, Tennessee.

When the Civil War erupted, Polk believed that the South's cause was sacred, and he offered his services to President Jefferson Davis, a former West Point contemporary. His appointment as a general officer was made partly for its psychological and moral effect; but, although his service in the West was controversial, Polk was an effective corps commander, considering his limited experience. He was killed at Pine Mountain, near Marietta, Georgia, in June, 1864. *DAB*, XV, 39-40; Boatner, *Civil War Dictionary*, 657-658; Crabtree and Patton, *"Journal of a Secesh Lady,"* xxv-xxvi.

[3]Leonidas Polk was the second son of Colonel William Polk (1758-1834) and his second wife. Colonel Polk, a native of Mecklenburg County, served in the Revolutionary War; he was a major in the Ninth North Carolina Regiment, a lieutenant in the Fourth South Carolina Regiment, and then colonel of the Third South Carolina Regiment. In 1800 Polk moved to Raleigh and became vitally interested in state government and education. From 1792 until his death he was a trustee of the University of North Carolina. Crabtree and Patton, *"Journal of a Secesh Lady,"* 162n.

[4]Thomas Polk (ca. 1732-1793) was a native of Carlisle, Pennsylvania, who came to Mecklenburg County in 1750 and became a surveyor, planter, and miller. He quickly attained prominence in local affairs and was a member of the assembly in 1769 and of the provincial congress of 1775. As a colonel he saw service in the American Revolution in South Carolina and Pennsylvania as well as in North Carolina. Polk was promoted to brigadier general in 1781, but the legislature refused to confirm him. *CDAB*, 809; Ashe, *Biographical History*, V, 316-320.

Daniel H. Hill to William A. Graham UNC

Charlotte, N.C.,
February 10th., 1872.

Thanks for the Memoranda. We would be glad to publish all that you can send. I think that this section will feel great interest in it.[1]

. . . .

[1]General Hill was at this time editing a weekly paper, the *Southern Home*. The reference is almost certainly to "Mecklenburg in 1776—Extracts from the Memoranda of Doctor John Graham," which appeared in the February 12, 1872, issue of Hill's paper.

Alexander McIver to William A. Graham UNC

Office Superintendent of Public Instruction
Raleigh, N.C.,
February 16th., 1872.

Trustee of the University:

Dear Sir: On the 9th day of January last, a meeting of the Trustees of the University was held in the Executive Office, at which a resolution was adopted to appoint a Committee to confer with the Alumni of the University and ascertain upon what terms and to what extent they might be induced to come to the relief and support of the University. Hon. W. B. Rodman, Robert F. Lehman,[1] and Alexander McIver were appointed by his Excellency, Tod R. Caldwell,[2] upon said Committee.

A meeting of the Alumni was called to respond to this resolution, and on the first day of February, they met in the Senate Chamber, in the City of Raleigh, and re-organized the Alumni Association by electing the Hon. B. F. Moore, President, and Col. D. M. Carter,[3] Secretary. Upon the call of the successive years from 1820 to 1868, fifty-five names of Alumni were recorded as present.

On motion of Will. H. Battle, a committee of five were appointed to confer with the committee, and report an answer to the resolution of the Honorable Board of Trustees of the University.

The President appointed Hon's. Will. H. Battle, W. A. Graham, R. M. Pearson, R. P. Dick,[4] and D. M. Barringer upon this Committee. The Association then adjourned till the next day to allow the Committee time to report. The Association met on the next day and the Committee, through their Chairman, Hon. Will. H. Battle, submitted a report which had been unanimously agreed upon by the Committee. The substance of it was:

That party politics and sectarian influences should be totally and rigorously excluded from the organization and government of the University; and, for the purpose of securing popular favor and support, it was thought necessary by the Committee, that there should be an entire re-organization, both of the Trustees and Faculty of the University. The report further expressed a willingness on the part of the Alumni to aid in the re-organization of the University, if it should be desired, on the basis proposed, and afterwards give it their cordial continued and united support, and any financial assistance which they could render in relieving it of its present financial embarrassment.

This report was unanimously adopted by the Alumni Association, and afterwards entirely approved by the Committee of the Trustees and referred to the Honorable Board of Trustees at their meeting in the Executive office on the 8th instant, with the following resolution, which was unanimously adopted by the Trustees, to-wit:

"*Resolved*, That the Superintendent of Public Instruction communicate to each Trustee the substance of the proceedings of the Alumni, and request the approval or disapproval of each Trustee, and lay the information, thus received, before his Excellency, Tod R. Caldwell, Governor of North Carolina."

The intention of the resolution is to ascertain the opinion of each Trustee in regard to the propriety of a reorganization of the University. It is understood that each Trustee, who may *approve*, will tender his resignation as trustee.

The exercises of the University have been totally suspended for more than twelve months. The buildings, unoccupied, are going to waste. There are debts to the amount of seventy or eighty thousand dollars against it; all its buildings, lands, and other property are under mortgage; and a suit is now pending, asking for the sale of all the property to satisfy the debts secured by the mortgage.

In view of these facts, the Trustees who were present at the meeting on the 9th of January, appealed to the Alumni of the University to come to its relief. The appeal was responded to by the Alumni promptly, generously, and frankly. It was the wish of the Trustees who met on February the 8th, to submit the matter to each Trustee, so that each might act for himself. Several Trustees had resigned before the meeting of the 8th inst., and it was understood all who favored the scheme would resign.

The Educational interests of the State, which are the foundation of all its other interest, are liable at times to fall into the party contest of the day. But our wise men, who met in the Senate Chamber on the first of February, have virtually declared that party politics and sectarian influences should be totally and rigorously excluded from educational interests fostered by the State. This has been declared to be the basis upon which the University is proposed to be re-organized; and is readily accepted as the only true basis of all educational interests fostered by the State.

Very Respectfully,
ALEXANDER MCIVER,
Superintendent of Public Instruction.

[Handwritten note on same page]

Hon. W. A. Graham:

Dear Sir: The above indicates the present status of the movement in regard to the University. It occurred to me that it would be of interest to you.

Very respectfully,
A. McIver.

---

[1]Robert F. Lehman (d. 1876) went to New Bern from the North during or just after the Civil War. An active Republican, he and his family enjoyed the acceptance and respect of their neighbors. Lehman voted to convict Governor Holden on articles 5 and 6 during the impeachment trial. Hamilton, *Reconstruction in North Carolina*, 436-437, 556.

[2]Tod Robinson Caldwell (1818-1874), son of an Irish immigrant who resided in Morganton, was educated at the Bingham school in Hillsborough and was graduated with honors by the university in 1840. After reading law under David L. Swain, Caldwell established his practice in Burke County and embarked on a successful legal and political career. He was a staunch Whig, loyal to the Union even during the Civil War, although he took no active part in the conflict. His only son fought in Lee's army and died at Gettysburg. After the war Caldwell became a Republican and was elected lieutenant governor on the Holden-Caldwell ticket. He assumed gubernatorial duties in December, 1870, when Holden was impeached, and became governor on March 22, 1871, when Holden was convicted and removed from office. Although Caldwell was conscientious and moderate and worked diligently to restore some semblance of harmony between Conservatives and Republicans, he met with only moderate success. In 1872 he defeated Augustus S. Merrimon in the race for governor but died quite suddenly in Hillsborough before his term was completed. Powell, *DNCB*, I, 305-306.

[3]David Miller Carter (1830-1877), a graduate of the University of North Carolina, was a Beaufort County lawyer and planter. He was captain and later lieutenant colonel of the Fourth North Carolina Regiment, but he sustained a disabling wound at Seven Pines and was subsequently assigned to duty as judge of a military court with the rank of colonel. Carter was elected to represent Beaufort County in the North Carolina legislatures of 1862 and 1864. Clark, *Histories of the North Carolina Regiments*, I, 231, 244, 267, V, 8; Cheney, *North Carolina Government*, 329, 331.

[4]Robert Paine Dick (1823-1898), a native of Greensboro, was a graduate of Caldwell Institute and the University of North Carolina (1843). Dick, a Democrat, was a lawyer and served as federal district attorney from 1852 to 1861. He opposed secession as long as feasible, served on the Council of State, and in 1864 was elected to the state Senate as a peace candidate.

At the close of the war Dick declined President Andrew Johnson's appointment to the federal bench. Subsequently, he advocated acceptance of the Fourteenth Amendment, supported congressional reconstruction, and became an influential force in the Republican party. In 1868 he was elected an associate justice of the North Carolina Supreme Court, serving until 1872, when he was appointed federal district judge. Dick was a distinguished jurist who excelled in civil law. *DAB*, V, 287-288.

Algernon S. Buford to William A. Graham UNC

R & D R.R. Co
Richmond Feby 19th 1872

A prominent & intelligent citizen of N.C. in making some inquiry by letter as to our views in regard to the revocation & re-issue of free paper on the N. Ca. Rd., advises me of what I was not before informed of, that as Trustee for the N. Ca. Co. in respect of its funded Debt & Sinking Fund, & in that capacity charged with important trusts for the Co, you had received heretofore the courtesy of a free pass on the Road; & that under the application of our general orders to take up such papers as were not endorsed or issued by the present management, yours had been recalled. Also intimating the reported Statement of some rudeness in the *Conductor* in making the demand.

Recognizing readily the reasonableness of the courtesy heretofore extended to you by the Co., I with pleasure replace the ticket, which I enclose herewith, & beg you to state to me frankly the fact of any discourtesy shown you by the Conductor, if any, & his name that the proper discipline may be enforced. I hardly need inform you I suppose, that prior to the commencement of my administration of the Rd., a most irregular, & to some extent, pernicious system of *free tickets* had been allowed. To correct this reasonably was a necessary duty to all; and while I think the general interests of the people interested in the road will be best consulted by such reasonable modification of the regular fares & freights as a just regard to our obligations to the N Ca. Co. will allow, as I have been endeavoring to do & hope to do still further, instead of by a diffuse *free pass* policy, benifitting only a limited number of individuals, yet I desire to do in respect of the caller what is proper & liberal. In the transition from one system however to the other, from lack of timely information I may omit, as in your case, to do sometimes what I am ready to accord in this behalf. If other cases are personally known to you, I would feel obliged to have you mention them in reply.

P.S. My long & severe confinement has prevented me from giving such personal attention to these matters as I desired. Am not yet out, though improved I trust.

Nicholas L. Williams[1] *to William A. Graham* UNC

Panther Creek,
February 19th., 1872

I see from the Sentinel that the Conservative party will hold a Convention in Greensboro on the [blank] April. My pecuniary situation is such that an office would be very acceptable. I was in Raleigh about a year ago, where Govr. Manly suggested that if we could get a Convention that I should try and get the nomination of Secretary of State. I mentioned what the Govr said to me to W. H. Jones[2] of Raleigh—he seemed very much in favour of my getting the nomination. A day or two since I recd a letter from Mr. Jones saying that *he* would like to get the nomination himself, and that he thought I could get that of Comptroller. The office of Comptroller would suit Mr. Jones better than it would suit me.[3] Your influence in behalf of me would go a great way in getting the nomination of Secretary of State, and it will place me under lasting obligations to you.

---

[1]Nicholas Lanier Williams (1799-1886) was a student at the University of North Carolina in 1816. He became a planter in Yadkin County. Williams had been a member of the Council of State in 1864. Grant, *Alumni History*, 676; Cheney, *North Carolina Government*, 180.

[2]Probably this was William Hogan Jones of Wake County.

[3]Neither man was nominated.

Hardie H. Helper[1] *to William A. Graham* UNC

The Liberal Republican Movement.
To the Liberal Republicans of North Carolina.

[February 22, 1872]

This grand movement was wanted to be inaugurated in this State, as you well remember, early in 1868, by Hon. Daniel R. Goodloe,[2] Prof. B. S. Hedrick,[3] myself, and a few others. It failed for want of co-operation of the then apathetic old Whigs as well as the inflexible and apprehensive Democrats. That that failure brought untold misery, corruption, thievery of millions of money, and bankruptcy to the State, no one will now deny.

This movement as organized by the honest Republicans of Missouri, two years later, who, like a few of us in this State, have refused to bow down and worship the one-man power, represented in the person of General Grant, and accompanied as it is, by gross corruption, centralization and despotism, at once took vivid form, and resulted in complete success through the hearty co-operation of the Democratic party of that State.

It has long been apparent, especially here in North Carolina, that Grant and his majority in Congress prefer the meanest secessionists of the south—those who were loud-tonged dead weights to the Confederacy—who now for the sake of office are ready to bow down and worship them, to an honest life-long Republican or any Union man who loves his country more than his party, and his party more than the fortunes of one man and his mercenary followers.

The Radical-Grant party is rapidly disintegrating. It has ceased to be the party of liberty, of law and of rational progress; and has become the creature of a tyrant and his minions, who have attempted to overthrow the Constitution, trample on the reserved rights of the States, and on the liberty of the citizen, in order that they may revel in gifts, bribes and peculations with impunity. *A party which proscribes and subordinates intelligence, property and character, and enfranchises ignorance for political power, is not Republican.* Its leaders have become tyrants by virtue of demagogism; they are rioting in the possession of ill-gotton power; and like tyrants in all ages, they are slow to read the hand-writing on the wall, which proclaims their speedy overthrow.

The Liberal Republican movement of to-day in behalf of the life of the Nation, will crystalize *all* the elements of opposition to Radicalism. It will be sustained by the whole Democratic party of the country, as well as by the best, if not the most numerous portion of the Republican party. It will stand by the rights of all classes, native and foreign, white and black. It will "take no step backward," but will go forward. It will insist that all white men *shall* be enfranchised, as well as all colored men. It will defend the rights of the States against Federal encroachments, and the rights of the people against military domination.

Then, men and brethren, by all means, let us send delegates to the Liberal Republican Convention, which is to meet in Cincinnati on the 6th. day of May next. I have reason to believe, and indeed, I know, that there is a schism in the Radical party in this State. The most intelligent and respectable portion of that party are disgusted with the corruptions and excesses which are perpetrated in its name, and for which they, as well as the guilty actors are held responsible.

We should extend a cordial invitation to such men to join us, and there can be no doubt that thousands will unite with us in the efforts to throw off the degrading despotism which now runs riot in corruption.

The signs of the times are auspicious. All the leading Democratic newspapers of the country, North and South, have expressed a readiness, not merely to co-operate with Liberal Republicans for the purpose of defeating the malignants who follow the lead of Morton,[4] Conklin,[5] Chandler,[6] Edmonds,[7] Nye,[8] Howe,[9] and the treacherous little John Pool, with Grant as their nominal chief; but these Democratic journals, schooled by the misfortunes of the past several years, are now convinced of the expediency of voting for an honest Republican for President, of the type of Horace Greely,[10] Lyman Trumbull,[11] Gratz Brown,[12] David Davis,[13] James F. Wilson[14] of Iowa, or Jesse D. Cox,[15] of Ohio. Not only the leading newspapers and public men of the Democratic party have taken this rational and patriotic ground, but State Conventions of the party have done likewise. The distinguished gentlemen named are known to be in favor of universal—not general—Amnesty, they are opposed to centralization, and insist that the States have reserved the rights of local self-government, which the General Government must not invade. They are also in favor of Civil Service Reform, a retrenchment of the national expenditures, a reduction of taxes, and the subordination of the military to the civil power.

Every day seems to consolidate the coalition between Liberal Republicans, the Democrats, and the old Whigs, or Conservatives.

It must be manifest to all thinking men of the State, that another four years of Grant and his relatives (taking no heed of one of Moses' most sacred ordinances "thou shalt take no gift; for the gift blindeth the wise, and perverteth the words of the righteous,") will bring our common country down to infamy and disgrace, as Holden and his thieves brought our own beloved State in 1868-'9. But my friends, Grant and his minions are already on the wane, thanks to an overruling Providence. Arise! fellow countrymen, and aid us in the gracious work of overthrowing the Grant-Radical thieving and mercenary party. Do not delay for another hour. Go to work, call public meetings in the several Congressional Districts, and choose Delegates to the Cincinnati Convention for the 6th. of May next, where and when the next President and vice President of the United States will be named.

Respectfully,
HARDIE HOGAN HELPER.

Salisbury, N.C.
Feb. 22d, 1872.

P.S. The Labor Reform Convention held at Columbus, Ohio, bearing even date with the above letter, nominated David Davis of Illinois, now Associate Justice of the U. States Supreme Court, for President, and Joel Parker[16] of New Jersey, (now Governor of that State,) for Vice President. Judge Davis had always been a Henry Clay Whig up to 1854, when he became a Republican, and was, from early life, a close and confidential friend of Abraham Lincoln. Gov. Parker has always been a lifelong liberal Democrat.

H. H. H.

---

[1]Hardie Hogan Helper (b. 1822) of Rowan (now Davie) County, a liberal Republican, was a brother of Hinton Rowan Helper. He had lived in Illinois and had been a Union soldier. Like his brother, he was violently opposed to Holden and the Radicals and in 1868 published *The Holden Record*, which emphasized Holden's political shifts and inconsistencies and charged him with political dishonesty. Hamilton, *Reconstruction in North Carolina*, 90, 283, 418, 592.

[2]Daniel Reaves Goodloe (1814-1902) was born in Louisburg. After an indifferent education, he failed as a lawyer and journalist in North Carolina. He was, however, destined to have a substantial career as a political and social dissident. As early as 1832 he became a critic of slavery. In 1841 he began publishing anonymous antislavery tracts, and in 1844 he resettled in Washington, D.C., where he expressed his views in a number of influential pamphlets and books. In 1896 he returned to Raleigh.

His most significant work, *Inquiry into the Causes Which Have Retarded the Accumulation of Wealth and Increase of Population in the Southern States* (1846), attacked the peculiar institution of slavery on the grounds that it was impractical and detrimental to the South. This argument anticipated Hinton Rowan Helper by a decade. Goodloe advocated compensated emancipation, adequate protection of the freedmen, and suffrage for qualified blacks. Unlike Helper, he never advocated the removal of blacks. He served Presidents Lincoln and Johnson, the latter as a federal marshal in North Carolina. A conservative Republican who opposed W. W. Holden, he was generally respected by most

North Carolinians. Roller and Twyman, *Encyclopedia of Southern History*, 548; John Spencer Bassett, *Anti-Slavery Leaders of North Carolina* (Baltimore: Johns Hopkins Press, 1898; Spartanburg: Reprint Company, 1971), 456.

[3]Benjamin Sherwood Hedrick (1827-1886) was born near Salisbury of sturdy German stock. He was educated in local schools before attending the Lexington academy of the Reverend Jesse Rankin. In 1851 Hedrick graduated from the University of North Carolina with highest honors. Upon David L. Swain's recommendation William A. Graham, then secretary of the navy, appointed Hedrick clerk in the office of the *Nautical-Almanac*. He eventually settled in Cambridge, Massachusetts, and continued his studies of chemistry and mathematics at Harvard College. In 1854 Hedrick was appointed to the chair of analytical and agricultural chemistry at his alma mater.

By 1856 he had become convinced that slavery was detrimental to southern society. Although he voted for Democratic candidates in August, 1856, he allowed himself to be drawn out in public, admitting that he would vote for the Republican presidential candidate John C. Fremont if a slate of electors were formed in the state. There followed a bitter newspaper campaign, led by Holden's *North Carolina Standard*, demanding Hedrick's instant dismissal from the university faculty before his "Black Republican views" seduced the minds of his students. The beleaguered Hedrick wrote a worthy defense claiming the right to hold private views and denying that he had sought to influence any students. His faculty colleagues and the university trustees disavowed sympathy with Hedrick's political views. After an abortive attempt to tar and feather him, Hedrick fled to the North, thereafter returning only briefly to the state. In 1861 he was appointed principal examiner in the United States patent office, a position he held until his death. In 1865 Hedrick influenced President Johnson's reconstruction plans for North Carolina by encouraging moderation in racial changes and by urging Johnson to rely on former Union men and moderate secessionists. *Cyclopedia of American Biography*, IX, 127-128.

[4]Oliver Perry Morton (1823-1877) of Indiana was a graduate of Miami University. A lawyer by profession, he became a judge. Political offices held by Morton included lieutenant governor, governor (1861-1867), and United States senator (1867-1877). A Republican, he served as a member of the electoral commission in 1877. *Biographical Directory of Congress*, 1365; *DAB*, XIII, 262-264.

[5]Roscoe Conkling (1829-1888), born in Albany, New York, was the son of Alfred and Eliza Cockburn Conkling. He was educated at Mount Washington Collegiate Institute in New York City. Admitted to the bar in 1850, Conkling was appointed district attorney of Albany immediately. From 1859 until 1867 he served in Congress, except for the term 1863-1865. He was an advocate of physical fitness and on one occasion acted as bodyguard for the crippled Thaddeus Stephens. In 1867 Conkling was elected to the United States Senate and for the next decade was leader of the Republican party in that body. He was an opponent of President Hayes and very reluctantly supported the Garfield-Arthur ticket in 1880. In 1881 he resigned his Senate seat, an act that led to his political demise. For the remainder of his life he practiced law and amassed a fortune. *Biographical Directory of Congress*, 728; *DAB*, IV, 346-347.

[6]Zachariah Chandler (1813-1879) was a native of New Hampshire. After brief experiences as a lawyer and a teacher, Chandler moved to Michigan in 1833 and became a merchant. As a Whig, he served a term as mayor of Detroit. Changing his political affiliation to the Republican party, he was elected to the United States Senate and served from 1857 to 1875 and again in 1879. He was also secretary of the interior (1875-1877) and chairman of the national executive committee of the Republican party. Chandler was instrumental in the seating of Hayes instead of Tilden. *Biographical Directory of Congress*, 680; *DAB*, III, 618.

[7]George Franklin Edmunds (1828-1919), of Vermont, was a lawyer who held the political offices of state legislator and United States senator, 1866-1891. A Republican, Edmunds was a member of the electoral commission in 1877. His later years were spent in Pennsylvania and California. *Biographical Directory of Congress*, 847-848; *DAB*, VI, 24-27.

[8]James Warren Nye (1814-1876), of Nevada, was a native of New York. He was territorial governor of Nevada, 1861-1864, and a Republican senator, 1864-1873. *Biographical Directory of Congress*, 1397; *CDAB*, 741.

[9]Timothy Otis Howe (1816-1883), a native of Maine, was a lawyer and state legislator there. He moved to Wisconsin in 1845, where he became judge of the circuit and supreme

courts. A Republican, Howe served as a United States senator, 1861-1879, and as postmaster general, 1882-1883. *Biographical Directory of Congress*, 1084; *CDAB*, 460.

[10]Horace Greeley (1811-1872), born in Amherst, New Hampshire, founded in 1841 the *New York Tribune*, which became a phenomenal success within five years. It was universally acclaimed because of its high moral standards and its intellectual appeal. In his paper Greeley freely expressed his own views and consequently had an enormous influence over his readers. He vigorously supported the agrarian movement, cooperative shops and labor unions, restriction on liquor sales, and high tariffs as a means of ensuring free trade. An egalitarian, he opposed monopolies of any kind. Greeley was a popular lecturer as well as a talented editor. He was a strong supporter of the Union throughout the Civil War and radical in his views on reconstruction. Although he at first supported President Grant, by 1870 Greeley was disenchanted and had become very critical of the Grant administration. In May, 1872, he agreed to be the presidential nominee of the Liberal Republicans. He was so badly defeated that he was profoundly hurt. A series of personal tragedies followed his political defeat, the major ones being the death of his wife and the loss of his prestigious position with the *Tribune*. Greeley ultimately became a pathetic figure, broken in both mental and physical health. *CDAB*, 366-367.

[11]Lyman Trumbull (1813-1896), native of Colchester, Connecticut, began his practice of law in Belleville, Illinois, in 1837. He changed his political affiliation from the Democratic party to the Republican after he was elected as a Free-Soiler to the United States Senate in 1854. Lincoln supported Trumbull, who opposed Douglas on Kansas. Trumbull was aligned with the Radicals in opposition to Andrew Johnson but did not favor Johnson's impeachment and other Radical actions that he thought were excessive. *CDAB*, 1083.

[12]Benjamin Gratz Brown (1826-1885), of Missouri, was a native of Kentucky and a graduate of Transylvania and Yale. He became a lawyer in St. Louis; he also had experience as an editor and as a military man, serving as a colonel in the American army during the Mexican War. Political offices to which he was elected included a United States senatorship (Democratic ticket), 1863-1867. He was a Democratic and Liberal Republican candidate for vice-president in 1872. *Biographical Directory of Congress*, 606; *DAB*, III, 105.

[13]David Davis (1815-1886), of Illinois, was a native Marylander who was graduated by Kenyon College and the Yale Law School. From a Bloomington, Illinois, practice he became judge (1848-1862) of the Eighth Judicial Circuit of Illinois. He was a close friend of Abraham Lincoln and was his manager at the Chicago Republican convention of 1860. Appointed by Lincoln to the United States Supreme Court in 1862, he resigned in 1877 to become a United States senator, thus upsetting the delicate balance on the Hayes-Tilden election commission. Although he owed his Senate seat to Democrats, Davis generally voted with the Republicans. *CDAB*, 218.

[14]James Falconer Wilson (1828-1895), of Iowa, was a native of Ohio who began adult life as a harness maker, became a lawyer, and went to Iowa in 1853. He was a state legislator, a delegate to the convention of 1857, and a Republican congressman, 1861-1869. He was one of the managers in the Johnson impeachment trial and was United States senator, 1883-1889. *CDAB*, 1222; *Biographical Directory of Congress*, 1831.

[15]Probably Helper was referring to Jacob Dolson Cox.

[16]Joel Parker (1799-1873), of New Jersey, was a native of Vermont and a graduate of Princeton. A lawyer by training and profession, he was a major general of militia in the Union army during the Civil War. He began his political career as a state legislator before he was elected to the office of governor, a position he held during the years 1862-1865 and 1871-1874. Although he was a strong supporter of states' rights and a critic of Lincoln's exercise of the war power, Parker was a supporter of the war and was active in raising troops. *CDAB*, 766.

William Johnston to William A. Graham UNC

Charlotte,
February 29th., 1872.

Col. Wheeler is either remodeling or rewriting his History of North Carolina as I learn. He has requested me to give him some information in regard to the character & revolutionary services of my grand-father, Col. James Johnston.[1]

Your Brother Jno. D. Graham,[2] Esq. loaned me the Diary of Dr. Jno. Graham,[3] in which I recollect the fact of his meeting my grand-father in the service is refered to. This was more than twenty years since, & I have not even a distinct recollection of what the Diary states of him.

If there is but the one allusion to him in it will you be kind enough to give me an extract of it or send me the Diary by Express if convenient.

As you doubtless had many conversations with your father on kindred subjects, will you do me the favor to give me your recollections of his conversations or statements as to my grand-father, his title at the time, services, etc.

Abraham Forney[4] says in his affidavit that he was a Col. and commanded the reserves at the Battle of Kings Mountain. Do you know of this from other sources[?] That he commanded at Packolet & was wounded is well authenticated. Was he an impressing officer or a disbursing officer during the revolution[?] I have a receipt for 2000 given to him by Richard Caswell,[5] Compt., dated May 10th. 1784 at Hillsboro. The proceeds had been paid to "the volunteers & Drafts from the Militia from that County." Tryon or Lincoln, I suppose.

For any facts or statements from others, I will be indebted to you.

---

[1]James Johnston (1742-1805), a native of Tryon (now Lincoln) County, was a son of Henry Johnston, who moved there with his family in 1755. He was a captain in the American forces during the Revolution and served under Colonel William Graham in South Carolina. In civilian life he operated the Mount Welcome iron furnace in east Lincoln County and was elected as a delegate to the Fourth Provincial Congress. He was a state senator, 1780-1782. His sons were Dr. William Johnston and Robert Johnston. Sherrill, *Annals of Lincoln County*, 19, 25, 32, 34, 54, 57, 68, 137, 158.

[2]John Davidson Graham (1789-1847) of Lincoln County. Clark, "Graham Descendants."

[3]Dr. John Graham (1756-1813) was the elder brother of William A. Graham's father Joseph Graham. He was born in Pennsylvania and educated at the Queen's Museum in Charlotte. After military service as a patriot in the American Revolution, John Graham became a tutor in the home of Dr. Benjamin Rush; he studied medicine under the guidance of Dr. Rush and later earned his M.D. degree from the University of Pennsylvania, after which he practiced medicine in Williamsburg County, South Carolina. The diary referred to is in the Graham Papers, PC 61, in the North Carolina Archives. Graham, *General Joseph Graham*, 18-19.

[4]Abram Forney (1758-1849), of Lincoln County, was a Revolutionary War soldier and in civilian life a pioneer in iron manufacturing in North Carolina. He fought in the battles at Ramsour's Mill and Kings Mountain. Sherrill, *Annals of Lincoln County*, 33, 57, 146.

[5]This, of course, refers to Richard Caswell (1729-1789), militia officer and governor of North Carolina. From May, 1782, until May, 1785, Caswell served as state comptroller general and successfully set the public accounts in order. Powell, *DNCB*, I, 343-344.

William A. Graham to William A. Graham, Jr. A&H

Hillsboro,
March 4, 1872

. . . .

Tourgée[1] was greatly disconcerted by the repeal of the Law, making it a felony to go in disguise, etc., by which his indictments at the previous term fell to the ground. He shewed chagrin and malice, and kept the solicitor and Grand jury on 'till I left, the 2nd. week. He instructed them to find Bill in the same cases for assaults & batteries; though 2 years had elapsed since the occurrences, & this barred indictments in misdemeanors. This, the Gr. jury refused to do; and he had new bills drawn and sent. Whether they still held out, I have not heard, but hope they refused again.

I go tonight to Guilford Court, but will probably stay but one day this week, (the negroes & vagabonds having always the first week) and return next week. I had a letter from George[2] this morning, acknowledging a remittance last week. He is getting some practice among the poor, but realizing but little as yet. He says radicalism is badly broken down there.

The Com'tee of the Legislature is ferretting out the frauds committed on the public; and when discovered, they arrest the perpetrators, several of whom are in jail, and others have fled. In the brief time that Conley[3] held the office of Gov'r, he pardoned, before Conviction, Foster Blodgett[4] & some other chief villains, who thereby are protected. But it is expected that after the next Courts, several of this gang will go to the Penitentiary. He says, the Keepers of the Pentry. hire out the convicts to farmers & R.R. contractors; and that a number are at work on the Air Line Road to Charlotte. He lately met Genl. Toombs,[5] who treated him very kindly, but who is boistrous against Yankees & does harm to the Conservative cause.

The nomination of Judge [David] Davis for the Presidency by the working men's convention seems to be well received in the North & West, & in the Richmond papers. He has great weight of character, and will be as apt to beat Grant, or come near it, as any man who can be started. He is by far the most available man, if the moderate Reps. & Democrats will take him up, that can be started. I met him when last in Washington. He is large in person, with open, frank manners, and very free in conversation—always a firm Whig, 'till the campaign when Lincoln was a candidate, the partner in the law [office] of Lincoln, who no doubt furnished much of the matter which gave him reputation in politics, and the Executor of his will. The Sentinel has not noticed him as it should. His opinion on Habeas Corpus in the Milligan Indiana Case in the Supreme Court[6] ought to elect him in opposition to Grant and Radicalism, which have trampled down the Hab. Corps.

Wm. Norwood's[7] tannery is a failure and he has gone to Ga. in Insurance business. An effort is being made to encourage the growth of Tobacco in this Co., here & at Durham. Otherwise every interest seems flat. Duncan Cameron is coming back to join Webb & Roulhac in a Tobacco Factory[8] at the old Thompson Mill which his Father has bought, and proposes to erect suitable buildings there. You mentioned that you could probably go to Amazonia in a week or two. I think I may get there myself by the 18th. or 20th. inst.

A letter from Thompson says he has 7 plow hands and 6 hoe hands. I would like to increase the number of men by 3 or 4, in which event I would buy another Mule. I wish you would advise Thompson as to a Jack to which to send the Craige mare—the sorrel is so small that I don't like to breed from her; but would be glad to sell or exchange her for a good Mule. The old mare I bought is worth sending some distance to a good large Jack.

Wm. F. Davidson,[9] of Charlotte, has written me, proposing to sell the gold mine near you, or lease, etc. I don't think he has any great felicity in that line; but if you can learn who are buyers, I should have no objection to laying off and selling 50 or 100 acres; even at a moderate price. The spirit of mining seems to have revived a little, as I judge from the papers.

We all send much love to Julia & the children. Tell Florie we miss her very much.

Affectionately Yours,

---

[1]Tourgée, then holding court in Hillsborough, had persisted in his efforts to break the Klan and see justice done in the murder of Wyatt Outlaw. Late in 1871 he got information that led to the indictment of sixty-three Klansmen for felony and eighteen for the murder of Outlaw. The legislature, controlled by the Conservatives, repealed the law under which felony charges had arisen and those indictments were dismissed. The murder charges, however, continued to concern the Conservatives until an amnesty act was passed in 1874, which allowed even murderous Klansmen to seek pardon. Judge Tourgée was greatly disappointed and blamed a waning federal concern for the South for what he believed to be the amnesty debacle. Olsen, *Carpetbagger's Crusade*, 184-188.

[2]Dr. George W. Graham was in practice in Atlanta. This explains the connection of what follows with respect to affairs in Georgia.

[3]Benjamin F. Conley (1815-1886), a native of New Jersey, went to Georgia in 1830 and was a merchant in Augusta. He was a delegate to the convention of 1868 and was president of the state Senate when Governor Rufus B. Bullock, a native of New York who went to Georgia in 1859, absconded. Conley succeeded Bullock. John Howard Brown (ed.), *The Cyclopedia of American Biographies* (Boston: Cyclopedia Publishing Company, 7 volumes, 1897-1903), II, 149, hereinafter cited as Brown, *Cyclopedia of American Biographies.*

[4]Foster Blodgett, Jr. (1826-1877), of Augusta, Georgia, was a merchant who entered politics in 1857 as a Whig. A popular mayor of Augusta, he opposed immediate secession after Lincoln's election but joined the majority of Georgians in supporting actions taken in the Secession Convention (January, 1861). He may have served briefly as a Confederate volunteer, but he denied having taken up arms and after the war was appointed postmaster of Richmond County by President Andrew Johnson.

When the Radical Republicans gained control of Congress, Blodgett changed political alliances, denounced Andrew Johnson, and declared that he had embraced secession only because he feared for his life. When Georgia was organized under the military reconstruction acts, he was appointed mayor of Augusta. He outraged Augustans by seeking to have his term and salary increased—all the while holding the postmastership to which Johnson had appointed him. When civil rule was reestablished in 1868, he was decisively defeated by Democrat Henry Russell in the Augusta mayoral election. Blodgett was elected to the United States Senate by a Georgia legislature controlled by the Republican party but was denied his seat because of irregularities in the legislature's actions.

Soon thereafter he was appointed treasurer of the Western and Atlantic Railroad, the state railroad. Within two years, the company was $750,000 in debt and irregularities were alleged. After obtaining a general pardon, Blodgett moved to South Carolina, where he made a poor living as a farmer and later as a drummer. When he returned to Augusta in

1876, he was arrested and charged with embezzlement. A broken man, he died the next year and was buried in an unmarked Atlanta grave. Kenneth Coleman and Stephen Gurr (eds.), *Dictionary of Georgia Biography* (Athens: University of Georgia Press, 2 volumes, 1983), I, 91-93.

[5]Robert Augustus Toombs (1810-1885) was Confederate secretary of state during the Civil War. Born in Wilkes County, Georgia, he was the son of Robert and Catherine Huling Toombs. He attended the University of Georgia but graduated from Union College, New York, in 1828. Toombs established a successful law practice and also operated a plantation in southwestern Georgia. His political career began with a term in the legislature, and he served 1837-1840 and 1842-1843. In 1844 he was elected to Congress as a conservative Whig; he favored and worked for the compromise measures of 1850. When the Civil War was declared, Toombs somewhat reluctantly accepted the office of secretary of state. There were many points of disagreement between Toombs and Jefferson Davis and he resigned in July, 1861. He then applied for a military commission and commanded a Georgia brigade. At Antietam Toombs sustained a hand injury. After the war he did not apply for pardon but continued to be active within the state. He worked hard to reform the Georgia constitution and to create a regulatory commission for the railroads. His final years were marred by personal depression and illness. *Biographical Directory of Congress,* 1824; *CDAB,* 1074; *DAB,* XVIII, 590-592.

[6]This was a case in which David Dudley Field, a noted New York attorney, in 1867 successfully defended L. P. Milligan before the Supreme Court, contending that military courts had no jurisdiction while civil courts were open. *CDAB,* 290.

[7]Norwood, the tanner, has not been further identified.

[8]The Durham tobacco manufacturing firm of Webb, Roulhac, and Company was composed of three partners, all of whom were the sons of Orange County planters. They were James Webb, William S. Roulhac, and Duncan Cameron. Robert C. Kenzer, *Kinship and Neighborhood in a Southern Community: Orange County, North Carolina, 1849-1881* (Knoxville: University of Tennessee Press, 1987), 118, herinafter cited as Kenzer, *Kinship and Neighborhood: Orange County.*

[9]William F. Davidson had served in the General Assembly as a representative of Mecklenburg County, 1856-1859. Cheney, *North Carolina Government,* 324-325.

Benson J. Lossing to William A. Graham UNC

The Ridge
Dover Plains, N.Y.
March 18th., 1872.

On my return home on Saturday, I found here your kind favor of the 11th. inst.

I shall be glad to receive for the *Record,*[1] the Journal of which you speak, or anything from the old "memorandum-book," which you mention, that *you* may deem to be of National interest. I wish to make the Magazine as broadly *National* as possible, free from any party bias of any kind, and simply a treasury of American historical, biographical and other matters of value that might otherwise be lost; at the same time relieving the solemn gravity of the whole by occasional papers of a lighter nature, like the Valentine in the February number.

I have written to the publishers, asking them to put your name on the *free,* or complimentary list of the subscribers to the *Record.*

Our excellent friend, Governor Swain, I am sure would have taken an interest in the Magazine, for he was alive to all such matters. Although I had, for years, a pleasant correspondence with him, I never had the pleasure of seeing him until a few days before I met you, with him, at the Ebbitt House in Washington, in the Winter of 1865-'6.

---

[1]The *American Historical Record.*

James Grant[1] *to William A. Graham* UNC

Davenport, Iowa.
March 27th., 1872.

I write to you this confidential note in relation to political affairs, rather against my own inclination.

The undercurrent of opposition to the present administration is seeking an outburst at the Cincinnati Convention. It is much stronger than is apparent on the surface, and if properly directed may result in the overthrow of that portion of the republican party now in power. Four men are named as the Cin. nominee. Judge Davis,[2] Gratz Brown, Trumbull, & C. F. Adams.[3] Of these, Davis is much the strongest with the multitude, because he has no vulnerable record. He ought to be strongest for another reason: He is the most upright honest man, and has the best common sense opinions of public affairs. He will be supported on two grounds—the reform of Civil Service, and the restoration of concord in the South. I have known him since 1835. I cannot praise him more than to say his opinions are much like what yours used to be.

It is important that he be nominated at Cincinnati! He is a stronger man with the Democratic party than any of the four gentlemen named and to defeat the party in power, the men of the Democratic party must vote for the nominee.

At the Cincinnati Convention Democrats have no place; but I hope you will allow me to suggest that a delegation of old line Whigs or Conservative Republicans from North Carolina, in favor of Judge Davis will go a great way to procure his nomination. I do not speak by authority of Judge Davis, but I do in his behalf, and am acting in conjunction with his friends, whose head quarters are in Illinois, near me.

---

[1]James Grant (1812-1891) was born in Halifax County and educated at the University of North Carolina, receiving an A.B. degree in 1831, an A.M. in 1836, and an LL.D. in 1878. After 1836 he moved to Davenport, Iowa, where he served as a member of the General Assembly of Iowa (Speaker, 1852) and as a judge of the superior court. Grant, *Alumni History*, 230.

[2]David Davis was nominated for the presidency in 1872 by the Labor Reform convention, but after the Liberal Republicans failed to endorse his candidacy, Davis withdrew. *CDAB*, 218.

[3]Charles Francis Adams (1807-1886) was a son of John Quincy Adams. A Whig in his political philosophy prior to the 1850s, Adams served in both houses of the Massachusetts legislature. In 1858 he was elected to Congress as a moderate Republican and served until 1861, when he was appointed to the post of minister to England. For seven years he had great influence in maintaining good relations between the United States and England. *Biographical Directory of Congress*, 458; *CDAB*, 4.

William A. Graham to William A. Graham, Jr. A&H

Hillsboro'
April 10th 1872

Our community was shocked this morning by the announcement of the death of the Rev. Dr. Curtis.[1] He was feeling, as he said, unusually well yesterday—retired well last night. About 5 oclock this morning was attacked & died in a short ime, saying only "it was his heart." He will be interred on Friday next, his children being at distant points. The negro Willis, shoemaker, died also last night. The senior Evans[2] is said to be ill at Milton.

My cattle have all survived the winter & are now sent to pasture. We are also planting corn.

Thompson writes, that the old mare bo't of Craige has a very fine Mule colt, for which I pay season $8 besides $30 for the mare, and she will be put to the same Jack without sending to your neighborhood. He represents the wheat as looking badly. Part of the seed I sent did not come up. Oats pretty good. Thinks he can plow his crop by working the young stallion without getting another Mule.

I have a letter from Judge Grant of Iowa, son of an old comptroller at Raleigh, who left there near 40 years ago, urging that Judge Davis shall be the opposition candidate for the Presidency. Grant is a life long democrat. Has been a Judge in Illinois, and had made quite a future. He says the Cincinatti convention will represent considerable strength, & that the democrats will fall in to his support in the West. Having made the acquaintence of Judge Davis when last in Washington, I think, he is best qualified & most likely to succeed, of all those spoken of as candidates in opposition to Genl. Grant.

I did not see W. F. Davidson when in Charlotte about the mine. I propose to go to the plantation about the middle of May. Shall be engaged till then constantly at courts—was at Caswell last week—Wake yesterday. Genl. Scales is under disabilities, and will not be before the Greensboro convention for Govr., unless they are removed which is not probable. Merrimon, I think most likely to be nominated; and probably the most eligible candidate. James with me at Caswell. John I suppose will be here this week. The defection of Brown[3] & G. Strayhorn[4] is the subject of much talk here. We are all well. Love to Julia & the children.

Affectionately

W. N. H. Smith[5] is about to move to Raleigh, & unite with Strong in the practice of the law in place of Gov. Bragg—I saw him there yesterday.

---

[1]Moses Ashley Curtis (1808-1872), born in Stockbridge, Massachusetts, was an Episcopal priest, a teacher, botanist, musician, and mycologist. In 1830 he went to Wilmington, North Carolina, where he was first employed as a tutor for the family of Edward B. Dudley. During the years 1830-1833 he and Dr. James F. McRee became partners in studying the plants growing in the Wilmington area. This hobby developed into a lifetime pursuit of knowledge about plants—in particular, fungi. Although he went back to Massachusetts for the beginning of his theological training, Curtis returned to North

Carolina after a few months, married Mary Jane de Rosset of Wilmington, and for the rest of his life remained in the state, except for the years 1847 to 1856, when he and his family lived in Society Hill, South Carolina. A versatile and brilliant man, Curtis was highly respected for his valuable contributions not only to the Episcopal Church but also in the fields of education (he taught from 1837 to 1840 in the Raleigh Episcopal School for Boys), music, and especially science. Except for the years at Society Hill, Curtis served as priest of St. Matthew's Church in Hillsborough from 1840 until his death. Powell, *DNCB*, I, 475-476.

[2]Charles Napoleon Bonaparte Evans (1812-1883), a Virginia native, became editor of the *Greensborough Patriot* in 1835 and in 1836 purchased the paper. He moved to Milton in 1840 and established the *Milton Chronicle*, which he published until his death. Evans and his son, Thomas Clancy Evans, also owned the *Hillsborough Recorder* for a time after the Civil War. During Reconstruction he assailed both carpetbaggers and Klansmen. Through his famous character "Jesse Holmes, the Fool Killer," he was able to express his views subtly but effectively on many topics of current interest. Powell, *DNCB*, II, 168-169.

[3]Brown has not been identified.

[4]Presumably this was Gilbert Strayhorn of Hillsborough.

[5]William Nathan Harrell Smith (1812-1889) was born in Murfreesboro. He prepared for college in New England and was graduated by Yale in 1834. He was admitted to the North Carolina bar and proved to be a good jury lawyer. A Whig in politics, he was a state commoner in 1840; a state senator in 1848 and 1858; state solicitor, 1849-1857; and a United States congressman, 1859-1861. He opposed secession until it was a reality but then supported the Confederacy. One of the few men to serve in all three Confederate congresses, Smith proved to be hardworking and conservative. He supported the administration generally but not blindly. For example, he opposed suspension of the writ of *habeas corpus*. He declined to countenance the peace movement, thereby retaining his political influence. When peace came, Smith favored the Johnson reconstruction policies, attended the National Union Convention of 1866, and became a Conservative stalwart in the face of radical reconstruction. Unlike many of his contemporaries, Smith showed no trace of partisanship and rancor in those tumultuous days. From 1878 until his death he was chief justice of the North Carolina Supreme Court. *DAB*, XVII, 366.

Nathan K. Hall[1] *to William A. Graham* A&H

Buffalo, [N.Y.]
April 10, 1872

I recd. last year a pamphlet copy of your eulogy upon Chief Justice Ruffin and I am not sure that I ever acknowledged its receipt or thanked you for your kind remembrances.

If not allow me to do so now. I do not know of anything I can send you in return but I venture to send for you and Mrs. Graham, whom Mrs. Hall and myself remember with affectionate regard, copies of photographic likenesses which we think you may recognize. They were taken only a few months ago.

I have written Mr. Stuart[2] in reference to arranging it so that Mr. Fillmore and myself may see you & Mr. Stuart and your good wives next summer and he encourages me to think that when the Trustees of the Peabody Fund next meet we shall have that pleasure.

I have not been well for the last four or five weeks and need rest very much, and expect to go to Elmira tomorrow, to Harrisburgh the last of the week or first of next & to Baltimore and possibly to Washington sometime next week. If I would learn you were at Washington I would certainly go there if I learned you were to be there which is barely possible.

I shall stop at the Mount Vernon House in Baltimore and if you are to be in Washgn please write me there.

I trust you will arrange it so that Mrs. Graham and yourself and Mr. & Mrs. Stuart will visit Buffalo and "The Falls" next Summer.

. . . .

With kindest regards from Mrs. Hall and myself to Mrs. Graham and yourself

I am always very truly yours

---

[1]Nathan Kelsey Hall (1810-1874) was a law partner of Millard Fillmore. He was postmaster general, 1850-1852, and a federal judge of the northern district of New York, 1852-1874. *CDAB*, 387.

[2]Alexander Hugh Holmes Stuart.

James Grant to William A. Graham UNC

Davenport, Iowa
April 15th., 1872.

I have yours of the 11. Since I wrote to you, Judge Davis' partisans, in Illinois, Iowa, Indiana, Michigan, & Wisconsin, where he holds the Circuit, have develloped great strength. A Convention of Conservative or Anti Grant Republicans in force, will be held in this town on the 23. to send delegates to Cin: and I am advised that they are generally for Judge Davis. The German element, a great force in Iowa, I supposed would follow Shurtz[1] for Gratz Brown, but I am assured that Davis is their first choice.

The Cincinnati Convention will hardly admit Democrats of my character to their Convention, but they will be glad to meet such a Whig as you have been. I am quite confident that your presence there will be of great aid in procuring the nomination of Davis. The Republicans who go to Cin. know, that they must have not only the Democratic vote, but the vote of most of the Southern States, and I think they honestly mean to nominate the man whom they think will command that vote.

The name of Judge Davis has been prominent for two months. His opponents have not found a single salient point of attack. I know of no man of our times who has so much ability as I know Davis to possess, so invulnerable as he has proved to be.

I trust you will be at Cincinnatti, . . .

---

[1]Carl Schurz (1829-1906) was born and educated in Germany. A liberal leader, he was forced to flee that country in the aftermath of the abortive revolution of 1848. Before he settled in Wisconsin in 1852, Schurz was a journalist in Paris and a teacher in London. He studied law and was admitted to the Wisconsin bar. He quickly gained recognition, in part because of his early espousal of the antislavery cause and his association with the Republican party. As chairman of the Wisconsin delegation to the Republican convention in Chicago in 1860, Schurz supported William H. Seward as his party's presidential candidate; however, he quickly rallied to Abraham Lincoln, rendering one of his best forensic efforts on September 13, 1860, at Cooper Union, where he attacked Stephen A. Douglas mercilessly.

In 1861 Schurz was appointed minister to Spain. His service was brief but influential as he worked to advance the Union cause abroad. He urged Lincoln to place his administration clearly in opposition to slavery as one means of gaining foreign sympathy. After resigning his foreign post, Schurz was appointed a brigadier general of volunteers. He was a political appointee who performed without distinction; nevertheless, he played a significant role in rallying German-Americans to the Union cause.

In 1869, Schurz was elected as an anti-Grant senator from Missouri. A leader in the Liberal Republican movement, he opposed Grant's plan to annex Santo Domingo; retaining his enthusiasm for reform, he proposed creation of a permanent civil service merit system. After assuring himself that Hayes was sound on the money question, would restore the South, and would promote civil sevice reform, Schurz supported Hayes in the disputed election of 1876 and became his secretary of the interior. In four years as interior secretary, Schurz earned a reputation for enlightened treatment of the Indians, preservation of the public domain, pioneering the development of national parks, and utilizing a merit promotion system within his department. From 1892 to 1901 he was president of the National Civil Service Reform League.

In later life, Schurz came to occupy a unique place as an elder statesman and political philosopher, representing particularly his fellow German-American citizens. He opposed war with Spain and annexation of the Philippines, urging Americans to mind their own business while avoiding foreign involvements. *DAB*, XVI, 466-470; *Biographical Directory of Congress*, 1570.

Calvin E. Parish[1] *to William A. Graham* UNC

Hillsboro', N.C.
17 April 1872

To the Executive Committees of the Townships of Orange County:
Gentlemen:

Under a resolution of the Convention held in Hillsboro' on the 13th. Inst. the County Executive Committee have appointed you committees for your respective Townships. The object of your appointment is two fold, first, you will, at your earliest convenience call a meeting of your committee and thoroughly organize the Conservative party in your township for the approaching Summer and Fall elections, put the machinery in good running order. See that all needful and necessary information is obtained and circulated among the people, and each man on the committee will consider himself a canvasser for the cause, and urge upon the people the necessity of turning out on the day of election: none can fail to see the necessity of this thing. None can fail to see the doubled exertion put forth by the enemy of free government, and equal rights to triumph at this time, and none but the most obtuse will fail to observe that money and other means will be lavishly used to accomplish their object. So from this to the election the word is work! work!! work!!!—earnest and faithful work, until the polls are closed.

Your second duty will be to call a convention or meeting of the people of your township for the purpose of appointing five delegates from each township to attend the convention at Hillsboro: on the 18th. of May 1872 to nominate candidates for the various county officers, and in this matter we hope you will be prompt and see that your townships are fairly and fully represented.

---

[1]Calvin E. Parish represented Orange County in the state Senate, 1874-1875 and 1881,

and in the state House, 1876-1877. He had served as a deputy under James R. Bulla, solicitor of the Seventh Judicial District. Cheney, *North Carolina Government*, 455, 458, 460; Lefler and Wager, *Orange County*, 120; Blackwelder, *Age of Orange*, 24.

Charles G. Yates[1] *to William A. Graham* UNC

Greensboro, N.C.
April 26, 1872

As I am very certain that there will be great crowds of people here next week at the *Convention* & believing that the Hotels & boarding Houses will be full, several of us here determined to open our houses, & accommodate our friends, upon that occasion. So I desire if it be agreeable with you that you & your son J. W. G. (or any other companion you may choose for a *bedfellow*) would come & stay with us, if you will put up with plain people & plain fair [*sic*]. I, we shall be glad to have you. There will be but two other Gentlemen with us. Please be so good as to drop me a line.

And oblige. We are anticipating a great & enthusiastic meeting. And I hope the Spirit will be kept up until we are triumphant in our State Elections & not only so but until Grant and his despotic crew are displaced by other & better men.

[1]Charles G. Yates was elected intendant of police (a position comparable to mayor) of Greensboro in 1857. He operated a tin shop. Ethel Stephens Arnett, *Greensboro, North Carolina, the County Seat of Guilford* (Chapel Hill: University of North Carolina Press, 1955), 32n, 195.

Daniel H. Hill to William A. Graham UNC

Charlotte, N.C.,
April 27th., 1872.

I am requested by the gentlemen who are interested in the celebration of the 20th. May, to request you to deliver an address on that occasion. There is not a true man in all this region who would not be gratified to have you come.

We have printed the MSS as well as we can, but there are many words which we could not well decipher.

Nathan K. Hall to William A. Graham A&H

Buffalo,
May 9, 1872

My dear Sir:

Your kind and very welcome letter of the 20th April last was rec'd by me here on the 26th, on our return from New York.

We did not go farther South and returned earlier than we intended in consequence of the alarming illness of my daughter's youngest child—a little boy now eleven months old. I am glad to be able to say that we think he is now fast recovering;—although, as his disease was scarlet fever, we are not by any means free from anxiety on his account.

Mrs. Hall and myself were much pleased to receive the photographs of Mrs. Graham and yourself. Although it is now nearly twenty years since we parted your familiar face has undergone little change, and time has dealt kindly with Mrs. Graham.

Mrs. Fillmore is still in bad health, but is able to ride out; and Mr. & Mrs. F. hope to leave for New York the last of this week or first of next. Mr. Fillmore is, I think, quite well now, but his late illness and Mrs. Fillmore's continued indisposition has made him appear a little thinner.

Mrs. Hall and myself are intending to see you in New York or Boston while you are North in June. If you can let me know on what day you intend to be in New York on your way to Boston we will try to be there and may possibly go on to Boston for a day or two. I presume Mr. & Mrs. Fillmore will be in New York at that time; as he intends to have Mrs. Fillmore stay there, for the benefit of a change of air, as long as she can be contented and think she is benefitted.

I shall write Mr. Stuart and I presume he will arrange it so as to spend two or three days in New York before the Boston meeting.

Mr. & Mrs. Fillmore will stay at the Fifth Avenue or Saint Nicholas Hotel in New York. They had not last evening decided which of the two they would go to.

I intended when I left home last month to go to the Mount Vernon House at Baltimore but at Elmira we changed our plan and went to New York, and the information that Grace's child was quite ill prevented our going farther away from home.

I was much improved by the trip and the rest it gave me and came back quite well. Next week I go to Rochester to hold a jury term which may continue for two weeks.

My Bankruptcy business is very large and there is great necessity for a division of my district but in the present condition of political affairs at Washington it is not likely that there will be a division this Session.

With kind regards to Mrs. Graham and yourself from Mrs. Hall and myself,

I am, with great respect

Alexander H. H. Stuart to William A. Graham UNC

Staunton, Va.
May 16th., [18]72.

I rec'd a letter a few days ago, from Mr. Winthrop, stating that it would probably be necessary to postpone the meeting of the Trustees of the Peabody Fund, until about the 25th. of June. By last nights mail, I received a letter from Judge Hall, of Buffalo, urging, very earnestly, that we, as surviving members of Mr. Fillmore's Cabinet, should endeavor to make such arrangements as to enable us, while we are in the north, to meet Mr.

Fillmore & himself. He expresses an earnest desire, also, that Mrs. Graham & Mrs. Stuart should accompany us. My wife, however, says that she has been so long out of society, that she would feel quite lost in the bustle of a great City, & therefore suggests that one or two of my daughters should go in her stead. The elder of the two who are unmarried, is fully grown, & the younger is barely seventeen.

It would be very gratifying to me to take them with me, provided you would take Mrs. Graham, or your daughter, to be company for them.

I would like, if we should conclude to take any members of our families, that we should appoint some time, & hotel in Washington, when and where we should meet, & thence travel together to Boston. The young people would, doubtless, have a charming time in visiting the Northern cities, & seeing the many objects of interest to be met with on such a tour.

I will be obliged if you will let me know your arrangements, so that I may conform my movements to yours.

It occurs to me it would be well to leave home a few days in advance of the meeting of the board, so that we may travel at leisure.

Please present the kind remembrances of Mrs. Stuart & myself to Mrs. Graham & accept the assurance of my high esteem & regard.

Robert C. Winthrop to William A. Graham UNC

Brookline Mass.,
May 16th., 1872.

My Dear Graham,

Yours of the 29th. ult was duly welcomed, & I am glad you mean to be with us at the June meeting. It is still very doubtful whether we can secure a Quorum at the appointed time. Possibly we may be compelled to adjourn for a fortnight in order to have the attendance of the necessary *nine.* You might hardly care to come on so early & stay so long. Would it be equally convenient to you to be here as late as the 17th., or even the 24th., if we should be obliged to defer action so long?

I may still get answers which will assure us of a Quorum at an earlier day, but there is so much uncertainty at this moment, that I thought it best to let you know at once how the case stands.

Please let me know as to your possibility of being here later, if we should be compelled to adjourn for want of a majority. I can then write, or telegraph, at the last moment, as to the time when your presence will be needed. I should be sorry to have you come on & be obliged to return home before the Meeting could be consummated.

I hear nothing yet from Gen Taylor. Mr. Stuart rather prefers a later day, & Gen Grant & Govr Fish give no hope of being able to attend before the 17th. or later.

Yours sincerely,

Robert C. Winthrop to William A. Graham UNC

Brookline, Mass.
25 May 1872

Yours of the 20th came duly. A letter from Genl. Taylor which came to-day settles the question that we can have no quorum on the 5th; & the current of opinion is so strong for the 25th that I name that day without further question.

We have the best reason for thinking that we shall have at least ten members on that day,—certainly the needful *nine*.

I write at once to fix that point, & in a future letter I will inform you as to the place & hour of meeting.

One of the best of the musical performances of the Great Jubilee will take place, I understand, on the 24th, & you had better get here on Saturday night, the 22d, & enjoy that treat.

Alexander H. H. Stuart to William A. Graham UNC

Staunton, Virginia,
May 29th., 1872.

Your letter of 20th. inst: was received in due time, and my daughters were quite as much gratified as I was, at the prospect of having Miss Graham with us, on our Peabody trip. They seemed to feel a little awkwardly at the idea of being thrown exclusively with northern people, having few sympathies with them. The company of your daughter will tend to relieve this feeling, to a great extent.

I presume we may now regard it as pretty well settled, that the trustees will not meet before the 24th. or 25th. of June. If such should be the decision, when do you propose to leave home?

If it will suit your convenience, we would be gratified to make an arrangement to meet you at Gordonsville, so that we may thence, travel together.

If you should come through Richmond, the cars that leave Richmond at 8:30 meet the cars which leave Staunton at 10:30, A.M., & passengers by both trains take the cars at Gordonsville, for Washington & Baltimore, & we can therefore, make the entire journey, from Gordonsville to Boston, together.

Please let me know, a few days in advance, when you will leave home? When you will be in Richmond? And what your route will be after leaving Richmond?

Should you prefer the route from Richmond, by Fredericksburg & the Potowmac, we can meet in Washington, or Baltimore.

I think, however, if you take the Fredericksburg route, you will not find the hours of starting as agreeable, as by the Gordonsville route. By the Gordonsville route, you will leave Richmond at 8:30 A.M., & arrive in Baltimore at about 8:30 P.M., with no change of cars except at Gordonsville.

My wife unites with me in cordial remembrances to Mrs. Graham. I proposed to my wife, at one time, to accompany me, instead of my daughters, but she made the same objections that Mrs. Graham offered,—long absence from bustle & fashionable life, & want of "Something to Wear"!

Alexander H. H. Stuart to William A. Graham UNC

Staunton
June 6th 72

Your favor of 3rd inst. was recd. last evening, & I hasten to say, that I with my two daughters, will join you at Barnum Hotel in Baltimore on Monday evening, 17th inst.

I like your programme, very much, with one exception—you make no provision for a run to Niagara. I doubt if our young people will be content to lose the opportunity of visiting that great curiosity. I hope, therefore, that we can agree on an amendment, introducing that feature into our arrangements.

As you will be in Baltimore a day or so in advance of us, I will be obliged if you will bespeak rooms for my party; so that every thing will be ready for us on our arrival.

I write in haste, as the time for closing the mail is at hand. Should I think of any thing that would render it necessary, I will write to you again before you leave home.

With kind regards to Mrs. Graham, I am

Charles Phillips to William A. Graham UNC

Davidson College,
Mecklenburg County, N.C.,
Wednesday, June 10, 1872.

Prof. Martin and I have hope that we may induce our former colleague at Chapel Hill to join us here. Will you help us to do so? A letter from you which we may use before our Board of Trustees may lead them to think with us that they can not do better than to fill one of our vacancies at our next Commencement with one whom the Trustees of our University thought worthy of a place in their institution. We will thank you for an expression of your opinion concerning the service which Prof. Hepburn is likely to render us here. He is now on a farm of his father's, in Westmoreland Co., Va., to which he retired last fall from Miami, to recover from the nervous prostration which followed his vain labours at Oxford, Ohio, and to fulfill a promise to publish a text-book on Rhetoric. His health is good now and although not a candidate here, his friends hope to induce him to accept an offer of a department for which he is well qualified.

The outlook for education at the South is dark and limited just now. We here are compelled to go forward, although we know not whither—nor how we may return, if driven back. In the mean time we hope to show that we do not deserve reverses—by trying to secure for our professorships the best men accessible to us.

Hoping to hear a confirmation of Dr. Jos. Graham's report concerning your health, I am, *"that High Church North Carolinian."*

Robert C. Winthrop to William A. Graham UNC

Brookline, Mass.
10 June, 1872

The meeting is fixed for the 25th (Tuesday) at 11 A.M., at the Revere House, Boston.

All our Hotels will be very much crowded, owing to the great Music Festival, & our City Authorities have engaged many of the best apartments in advance.

But the Revere promises to make the Trustees comfortable.

I think you would all do well to be in Boston, & take posession of your rooms, on Saturday night. You can hear one of our best preachers at Trinity Church on Sunday, attend the Grand Musical performance on Monday, & be ready for business on Tuesday morning.

I have engaged the rooms to be in readiness on Saturday Evening accordingly.

Wednesday is Commencement Day at Harvard, so that we shall have to continue our work on Thursday.

It is important that I should know *precisely* who will come with the various members,—wives, daughters, or sons,—so that rooms may be provided suitably. Please inform me as to yourself and your party soon.

Yours, Sincerely,

I hope to have the Trustees dine with me on the 25th.

Alexander H. H. Stuart to William A. Graham UNC

Staunton,
June 12th 72

My dear Sir

Your letter of 13th has been received, & I hasten to say, that while I would be gratified to meet you, & the members of your party, in Baltimore, on monday night, & travel thence with you, on tuesday, to N.Y., I, of course, cannot ask you to sacrifice your convenience, by remaining longer in Baltimore than you desire.

I will expect, therefore, to meet you at 5th Avenue Hotel, N.Y. on tuesday evening.

I name the 5th Avenue Hotel because I have received an invitation to meet a number of leading gentlemen at that hotel, on 20th inst.

As this letter will have time to reach you in Balt. on Sunday morning, I preferred to communicate by letter, instead of telegram, as I can state my views more fully, by mail

Very truly yours, etc.

Nathan K. Hall to William A. Graham A&H

Buffalo
June 21, 1872

I have written Mr. Stuart in respect to your contemplated visit here, and write you a few lines to urge that you make such arrangements that you will be able to spend a few days in Buffalo.

I think your young people may desire to spend more time at the Falls than will be desired by you and Mr. Stuart, and will perhaps be less interested in a visit here; but we shall desire to see them all here and will do what we can to make their stay in the city agreeable to them.

We expect that you and Mr. Stuart, at least, will stay with us while you are here and we can also take a part of the young people.

I have asked Mr. Stuart to let me know when you will be here a little in advance of your arrival that I may endeavor to meet you at the depot.

Alfred J. Morrison to William A. Graham UNC

Cottage Home, N.C.,
July 7th., 1872.

My dear Uncle:

. . . .

Hon. O. H. Dockery has just canvassed this section of country, and though he has done nothing for himself, I am afraid he has injured Judge Merrimon, as his attacks on him were very severe; and, from them, one would think he was running against Merrimon instead of Mr. Ashe.[1]

I "shelled" him an hour, (all the time he would give me) at Dallas last Monday, and also replied to him at Beattie's Ford on Tuesday. He refused to divide time with me at the Ford, but when he finished a three hours speech I appealed to the Republicans in the crowd for permission to speak, and thus forced him to let me in.

I hope you are much improved by your trip North, and will find it convenient to canvass some this Summer. Gov. Vance's friends will doubtless press his claims for U.S. Senate next Winter, and will urge that he deserves it for his services in the present campaign. I believe a majority of the best men in N.C. desire to see you in the Senate once more, and if your friends in the next Leg. do their duty, there ought to be no doubt about your election.

Our Co. Convention nominated me for the Leg. on the first ballot. The country townships voted for me without a dissenting voice; the town voted 6 for me and 7 for Col. Hoke, some of my best friends voting for Hoke to conciliate him, as he was very angry with some gentlemen for voting against him in the Cong. Dist. Convention. He declared himself an independent candidate for Commons, but found no encouragement, and gave it up. Wm. S. Bynum[2] is the candidate on the Rad. ticket, accepted the nomination from a convention of negroes and seven or eight white men, and at last confesses that he is a Republican.

We will have a warm canvass, but our friends claim the county by at least 200 majority. Some of our best men have been run off by the Scoggins gang, but the party is well organized, and seems determined to win.

. . . .

Affectionately y'r nephew,

---

[1]Thomas Samuel Ashe (1812-1887), scion of a distinguished family, was a planter, lawyer, politician, and state supreme court justice. Graduated by the University of North Carolina in 1832, he read law in Hillsborough with Thomas Ruffin. He became a Whig in politics and served in the Commons in 1842 and the state Senate in 1854. A Unionist, he opposed secession until Lincoln's call for troops, when he became an immediate secessionist, serving in the Secession Convention. As a Confederate congressman (1861-1863), he became a leading Conservative. He campaigned vigorously against ratification of the Constitution of 1868 and was in that year the gubernatorial candidate of his party. His efforts were in vain; the constitution was approved and Holden elected governor. From 1873 to 1877 Ashe was a Conservative congressman. In 1878 the Democrats secured his election to the North Carolina Supreme Court, a post he filled with distinction until his death. Powell, *DNCB*, I, 55-56.

[2]William Preston Bynum.

James A. Graham to William A. Graham UNC

Graham, N.C.,
July 12th. 1872.

. . . .

My friends are anxious that I should canvass the county to help our ticket—none of whom can make a speech—and also to correct the false reports which were spread concerning me, and I have consented to go to half the precincts. I will go to Lea's to-morrow, but will hardly speak, as the candidates for Congress will be there and will occupy most of the time.

We have not a single soldier on our ticket, but two or three red hot secessionists who were eager for the war till it came and then dodged into some Rail Road agency or other safe place.

I am afraid the ignoring of the young, soldier element may damage us somewhat, but we have a fair prospect of carrying the County by 300 or more. There are several of our men in this County who say they will not vote for Greely, but I think he will get nearly our full strength.

We have no news. Lizzie and the children join in love to all.

Affectionately Your Son

Nathan K. Hall to William A. Graham A&H

Buffalo,
July 15th., 1872

I send you, in this and another package, two opinions delivered by me in Habeas Corpus cases during the War; which, with the pamphlets I gave you when here, will shew that I have not been inclined to break down any of the safeguards of civil liberty,—either in war or peace.

Several other opinions of mine in *habeas corpus* cases were published during the War, and I was quite severely denounced by the extreme radicals. I do not however regret that I allowed the publication of such opinions, as I felt it my duty to hold and enforce.

The tendency now-a-days, especially at Washington, is to extend the powers of the General Government, and diminish those of the States; and the Sup. Court at its last Session has decided in substance that State Courts have no jurisdiction in such cases as that of Reynolds,—as had been before decided, *since the commencement of the war*, by many state judges & courts; but I was glad to see that the Chief Justice[1] dissented.

I also send you a pamphlet copy of our opinion on Bankruptcy, which some New York City lawyers had printed.

We are all in usual health. Mrs. Fillmore is about the same as when you were here, and Mrs. Hall & myself & Grace and her family & Mrs. Han[ce], are as well as when you made us your late flying visit.

We were very sorry your visit was so short and that the only full day you spent here was the 4th., when it was impossible to do much to render your stay interesting or even agreeable. Nevertheless, we enjoyed the visit very much and hope that it may be repeated under more favorable circumstances.

It has been very hot and dry, for Buffalo, ever since you left; but we suffered very little in comparison with New York, Phila., New Haven, etc.

Please remember us kindly to Mrs. Graham, and son & daughter, and believe me,

Always, and most truly & cordially,
Your friend

P.S. The day you left an umbrella was sent by Express from the Falls to you, to my care; and Mrs. Hall says you also left a night Shirt. Shall I send them to you by express or will you bring Mrs. Graham with you and come and get them next year?

---

[1]Salmon P. Chase.

Benson J. Lossing to William A. Graham UNC

The Ridge,
Dover Plains, N.Y.,
July 19th., 1872.

On the receipt of your kind letter of the 11th. of March, I requested the publishers of the "American Historical Record" to place your name on the complimentary list, and send the work to you, from the beginning. Have they done so? If not, please let me know.

I hope the scope and tenor of the *Record* meets your approbation, and that you may find the leisure, if you so approve, to make a contribution to its columns from your treasury of historic information.

William C. Rencher[1] *to William A. Graham* UNC

New Mexico and Gulf Railway Company,
Pittsboro N.C. July 20, 1872.

I trust you will remember me as a College boy, and graduate at Chapel Hill, and a recipeant once of your hospitality at home. I have been for three or four years a resident of Santa Fe New Mexico, where the climate of the Rocky Mountains has restored by health, and where, in view of my business connections now, I shall make my home for life.

Just now my business takes me to London. It is a long way from home, and, naturally, I feel anxious to have the best acquaintance there I can reach.

My Father's[2] friends in Europe of long ago are very probably passed away.

I have thought, at my request, you might be good enough to give me a letter of introduction to Mr. Benjamin,[3] who is now well known in London, and whom you doubtless know, as a prominant member of the American Bar, as well as through your relations with him in Richmond.

A letter from you to him might be of great service to me, and, possibly, he might find it of business advantage to him, but whether presented or not even, its possession would be gratifying to me.

Had it been possible I should have taken the pleasure of going to Hillsboro and calling on you in person for this favor, and added thereto the happiness of seeing your son Robert, a class mate of mine, and other Hillsboro friends but my very short visit home after an absence of two years, does not permit it.

Please to reply to me here and believe me with highest esteem.

Yours very truly

---

[1]William Conway Rencher (d. 1901) was at this time director and general agent of the New Mexico and Gulf Railway Company. According to the letterhead of this letter he resided when in Washington at the Metropolitan Hotel; a mailing address in New York is also given. Rencher, born in Washington, D.C., had received an A.B. degree at the University of North Carolina in 1866. He became a journalist, practiced law in Raleigh for a time, and achieved the rank of major in the Confederate forces. Grant, *Alumni History*, 519.

[2]Abraham Rencher (1798-1883) was born in Wake County, attended Pittsboro Academy in Chatham County, graduated from the University of North Carolina in 1822, and established a Pittsboro legal practice in 1825. A Democrat in politics, he was a congressman (1829-1839 and 1841-1843), minister to Portugal (1843-1847), and territorial governor of New Mexico (1857-1861). Subsequently, he was a capitalist and agriculturalist. He took no active role in Reconstruction. Grant, *Alumni History*, 519; *Biographical Directory of Congress*, 1510.

[3]Judah Philip Benjamin (1811-1884) was born in the Danish West Indies of Portuguese Jewish parents. He was taken to Charleston as a child and attended the Fayetteville Acedemy and Yale College. In 1831 he moved to New Orleans, where he tutored English, engaged in various business pursuits, and studied law. He became a successful and wealthy lawyer and sugar planter. Benjamin represented Louisiana in the United States Senate, 1853-1861, first as a Whig but later as a Democrat when that party became the bastion of southern rights. One of the first southern senators to advise secession after Lincoln's election, he served the Confederacy as attorney general, secretary of war, and secretary of state, holding the latter post for just over three years.

While Benjamin was secretary of war, the South lost Roanoke Island and Forts Henry and Donelson, for which he was blamed. Reasoning that few southerners recognized the South's limitations, Davis was adamant in his defense of Benjamin and extravagant in his praise. Davis cheated an irate Confederate Congress of its prey by appointing his friend secretary of state. As Davis's administration became more unpopular, Benjamin supported the controversial plan to arm slaves, with emancipation to be their reward. He publicly advocated such a course on February 9, 1865, in a widely debated speech. Faithful to Davis until the war's end was imminent, Benjamin fled to England, where he became one of the most distinguished members of the English bar. There, he published a learned *Treatise on the Law of Sale of Public Property*. In 1872 he received appointment as queen's counsel. Benjamin died in Paris and was interred there. *DAB*, II, 181-186; *Biographical Directory of Congress*, 542.

Charles Phillips to William A. Graham UNC

Davidson College.
Mecklenburg County, N.C.,
Saturday, July 20th., 1872.

Your nephew, Mr. A. Morrison, told me at our late Commencement, of your visit to Boston with your son and daughter, and I was only reassured that my not learning whether Miss Susan would be at our anniversary was to be easily accounted for. I thank you for the courtesy which prompted the letter you wrote on your return home.

I was once at a Harvard Commencement. There, and at Yale too, the exercises were, to me, much more stiff than those to which I was accustomed. They seemed to me even *wooden*. And the audiences were not as much interested in what was being done, and being said. I heard many good things, and, doubtless, many others escaped me, because I had to force my attention. You may remember Gov. Swain's telling that at the Alumni dinner he attended, one of the speakers was at first surprised that he should be called on to contribute to that "feast of reason & flow of soul." But at last he pulled his speech out of his pocket, & refreshed his memory several times. I am inclined to judge from the accounts of Commencements this year in the Northern newspapers, that declamation is not prized at their Institutions as it was once, and as it is still amongst us in the South. Our own festival here gave great satisfaction this season. Miss Margaret Mitchell[1] remarked that the improvement in the style of performances here within the last two years was very marked, & to her very gratifying, and so inspired her with hope that we shall be able to do a good work for our country. Such industry in students as we have here must bring forth fruit of which no man need be ashamed. Where pupils are so conscientious, they ought to be furnished with the best opportunities for an education. We hope that a generous public will enable us to offer these opportunities. If we can secure an income from $200,000., it is our expectation to offer a collegiate education to every one unable to pay for it. Then, when our University is revived, she will find in N.C. a generous and a worthy competitor for public favour. But whatever can be done for Chapel Hill should be done quickly. It is very difficult to change currents of public favour, especially in N.C. The rumour of which you wrote, fills me with hope that bright days will again dawn before many months, on what was once your pride as well as care. I await a confirmation of that rumor with anxiety.

The liberality of Mr. Donaldson[2] stands in striking contrast with the illiberality of some of the living. When Genl. R. Barringer,[3] in this County, discusses the amendments of our Constitution touching our University, he talks scandalously—apparently glorying over its collapse, saying,—as I am told—that under Govr Swain and his associates, the University was "a *nuisance*," "a nursery for aristocrats," "a *nest of rowdies*," "*no better than a bawdy house*," etc., etc.

The candidates were in this neighborhood yesterday, I tried to get a conveyance to the taxgathering but failed. Genl. B. was not there. But your son (Robt.) replied very properly, I understand, to an outrageous speech made by Genl. B. the day before. (Robt. was "*locum tenens*" for Mr. Waring.)[4]

My own health is very good. Locomotion only, is not what it was.

---

[1]Margaret Mitchell was the daughter of Dr. Elisha Mitchell (1793-1857), a scientist and longtime professor at the University of North Carolina. *DAB*, XIII, 45-46.

[2]Robert Donaldson II was a native of Fayetteville, attended the University of North Carolina, and became a wealthy benefactor of religious and educational institutions. Although he moved to Hyde Park, New York, in the 1830s, his legacy to Fayetteville was the Donaldson Academy, which resulted from a gift to the First Presbyterian Church. Long a friend of David L. Swain and the university, he willed that institution the bulk of his estate, having disinherited his offspring when they converted to Roman Catholicism. However, his will was faulty and his benefaction was lost. Battle, *History of the University*, II, 42-43, 789; Oates, *Story of Fayetteville*, 451, 828.

[3]Rufus Barringer.

[4]Robert Payne Waring.

Hardie H. Helper to William A. Graham UNC

Salisbury, N.C.,
August 1st., 1872.

Mr. Schurz requested me before parting with him last night at Greensboro', to ask you to remit to me a certain document read at Charlotte last Monday by yourself, which, if I remember correctly, was issued under Gen'l

Harrison's Administration, remonstrating against Cabinet or other high officers from participating in electioneering discussions, etc., etc. I am to transmit that document with others, to Mr. Schurz at St. Louis.

P.S. I feel that our good old State stands at this hour redeemed from corruption and misrule.

E. J. Hale & Sons to William A. Graham UNC

New York,
August 8th., 1872.

At the suggestion of Mr. Stephens, we forward to you by mail, a copy of his History of the U.S., just published by us, to which we beg to call your attention.

Should it meet your views to notice it, either in the public papers, or by letter to us, (for use in our circulars) or otherwise to promote its circulation, you will confer an obligation upon both Mr. Stephens and ourselves.

Kenneth Rayner[1] *to William A. Graham* UNC

Nesbitt,
Desoto Co., Miss.
Aug. 11th., 1872.

I can not describe to you the regret and annoyance I feel at the latest account of the No. Ca. election.[2] It seems that, after all our bright and cheering hopes of a Conservative victory, the good old State is to be subjected for another two years to Radical misrule and corruption. So much depended on the result! It seemed to be generally understood, that the result in the State was, in a great measure to foreshadow the result of the great struggle in November. Our friends everywhere were so sanguine—our party seemed to have been so thoroughly organized—and cheered and encouraged, as we all were, that the union of the two great elements of opposition on Greely carried with it such a great moral weight—now to be beaten, it is too bad! And then again, this retrograde movement, after the signal victory of Shipp over Phillips[3] last year, has something in it very depressing. I had for months looked on the dear old State as the pivot, on which the redemption of our Country (as far as we of the South have a country) was to turn. I am staggered and confounded by it.

There must have been a special reason for it. It could not have been for the want of exertion and hard work on the part of our friends. For I noticed that nearly all the speaking talent of the State and much of that of other States, was made available in the Canvass. I am very anxious to know your calm and dispassionate judgment as to the cause of our defeat. I write to you because I know, that your well-balanced judgment and general acquaintance with the character of the people of the State, enable you to give a reliable opinion as to the influences that have brought about this result.

Can it be, as suggested to me by a friend of our cause, a lawyer in Hernando, a native of No. Ca., who took a deep interest in the election, and who, through a correspondence with his No. Ca. friends, seemed to be well posted—can it be (as he said he feared might be the case) that Merrimon's agency as attorney[4] for Littlefield and Swepson, and his aiding in the prosecution of those charged with Ku-Kluxism conduced materially to his defeat? Or was it brought about by the lavish expenditure of money? Was there any material recreancy in the State on the part of those heretofore acting with us, because of their unwillingness to sustain Greely? I shall be glad to have your views in regard to the rationale of this result. Perhaps your suggestions may be of service to us here, in enabling us to avoid the obstacles in our way.

As you well know, Mississippi is one of the four States in the South that are regarded as chained inseverably, to the chariot-wheels of radicalism. But still, we are determined to make a deadly fight for deliverance. We are thoroughly and efficiently organized. The prospect is forbidding—but we will fight the harder. I hardly know of a single man in the conservative ranks that does not warmly support Greely—and many prominent men heretofore against us, are now with us. I still believe that, by a vigorous and concerted effort of our forces, North and South, we can elect Greely. Before the No. Ca. election I had hardly a doubt of it. I believe the Radicals themselves were almost in despair. But the No. Ca. election has buoyed them up again, and now they will fight with the ferocity of devils. If perchance we may carry New Hampshire in September, all will be bright again. But if defeated there again the prospect will be gloomy—though still not hopeless.

---

[1]Kenneth Rayner (1808-1884) attended the Tarborough Academy and read law with Thomas Ruffin in preparation for a career as lawyer, politician, and bureaucrat. A man of great talents, though sometimes unstable, he attracted favorable attention as the youngest member of the Constitutional Convention of 1835. He was a member of the House of Commons in 1835, 1836, 1846, 1848, and 1850; the state Senate in 1854; and the United States House of Representatives, 1839-1845. He was successively a Jacksonian Democrat, a Calhoun Democrat, a Whig, an American (Know-Nothing), a Conservative, and a Republican. As a member of the convention of 1861 Rayner was a secessionist; later, because of his opposition to the Davis administration, he was secretly a supporter of William W. Holden's peace movement. Following the war, Rayner failed as a Mississippi planter and was a federal officeholder. *DAB*, XV, 416-417; McCormick, *Convention Personnel*, 68.

[2]Tod R. Caldwell, the incumbent Republican governor, defeated Augustus S. Merrimon in a close vote of 98,132 to 96,234. Lefler and Newsome, *North Carolina*, 470.

[3]In the general election of 1870 William Marcus Shipp had been elected over Samuel Field Phillips to complete the unexpired term of William M. Coleman as state attorney general. Cheney, *North Carolina Government*, 440n.

[4]Merrimon and Matt W. Ransom, attorneys for Swepson and Littlefield, were widely criticized for their activity in behalf of their clients and against the state. Both men continued to have successful careers, but this letter indicates that there was speculation about what effect their activities might have had on the Democratic defeat in 1872.

Augustus S. Merrimon to William A. Graham UNC

Raleigh,
August 14th., 1872.

I learn that the *reputed vote* will probably indicate the election of the Radical ticket at the late election, by not exceeding 1500 votes. Nevertheless, I believe our State ticket received a good majority of the *honest* vote cast, and I think this may be made to appear to the satisfaction of the Legislature and the country.

The press of the State, for the most part, and many persons of much respectability have urged me to *contest* the election on the ground of *fraud*, etc., and to give notice of such purpose at once.

Let me submit hastily my view of this matter and ask your judgment as to what you think all our candidates ought to do?

For myself, I would not think of *contesting* the Election. I need not give my reasons for this—they are not material here. But the people have a deeper interest than I have personally, and they have the right to be heard through me and our candidates, if they manifest such a desire—they are deeply concerned, and therefore, if it turns out that there is *real ground* for *contest*, and this can be made to appear, and there is a strong popular desire manifested, that it shall be done, then I am prepared to make any sacrifice or do anything within the compass of right, to release the people from intolerable misrule and oppression. But before the candidates take action they ought to be sure of the *ground they each occupy*, and then in a case like this, their action ought to be backed by a strong popular will. We ought to be fully advised before we *strike*, & then act with determination.

Is the strong language of the press & the urgent letters from the people, the *sober* judgment, or is it the offspring of disappointed hopes & indignant feelings? We shall soon know.

This is my view, without much reflection, and I beg your opinion in the matter as soon as you can furnish it, if there is no reason why you should not favor me with it. I submit with great defference my own opinion & hastily, to the end you may point out wherein it is objectionable, if you should not concur in it.

James Farrow[1] *to William A. Graham* UNC

Kansas City, Missouri,
August 15th., 1872.

Having it in contemplation to publish either in some suitable Periodical or in book form as may be hereafter determined a short sketch of prominent *Confederates* I respectfully Solicit at your hands such facts & incidents, relative to yourself as will be interesting to the public & give a just impression of your character & history.

My object is to aid in preserving, as well as possible, a just appreciation of Southern Character by means of these sketches of her representative men.

Hoping it may suit your convenience & inclination to comply either personally or through some friend with the above request and with best wishes for your continued health and usefulness, I remain, with sincere respect.

---

[1]James Farrow has not been identified nor has a work such as he described been found.

William A. Graham to Charles C. Jones, Jr.[1] DUKE: JONES

Hillsboro' N.C.
Aug 30th 1872

In reply to your inquiries of the 23rd inst. I state, that I entered the Senate of the United States 1st Monday of Decr. 1840—the Navy Department 1st of August 1850; and the Senate of the Confederate States 1st Monday of May 1864.

---

[1]Charles Colcock Jones, Jr. (1831-1893), was a native of Georgia. A historian, Jones attended South Carolina College and was graduated from Princeton and the Harvard Law School. During the Civil War Jones was a colonel in the Confederacy, and after the war he lived in New York, 1865-1877, and in Augusta, Georgia, 1877-1893. *CDAB*, 507.

Kenneth Rayner to William A. Graham UNC

Nesbitt, Desoto Co.,
Mississippi.
August 31st., 1872.

Your welcome & interesting letter of the 27. is to hand. I doubt not, you have stated the real cause of our defeat in No. Ca., viz.—the large vote brought out, of those who have hitherto lain dormant. I regret the defeat of the Conservatives in No. Ca. mainly, because it throws you back in your movement towards revising that good old constitution which had suffered so much from radical tinkering.

In this State, we are preparing for a deadly struggle. I never saw such thorough & perfect organization, as the two sections of the anti-Grant party is providing for. True we have a forlorn hope to lead; but we do all that mortal man can do. The negro vote is immense. And it seems almost impossible to disintegrate it. Still, we are detaching some. Not exactly bringing them to Greely—but working the idea into their minds that there is something wrong about Grant. I really think I can see that a good many of them will keep away from the polls.

As a general rule I regard the contesting of elections as bad policy, but in the case of No. Ca., if our friends generally believe that we were beaten by fraudulent votes, I think, as there is so much depending on the result, the election ought to be contested. We must make fight, *on that line* ultimately; for if it is submitted to, we never shall be able to rid ourselves of this thieving dynasty. A demonstration should be made, at all events, for the moral effect elsewhere, even if it is finally abandoned. Let the Radicals have cause to be [*sic*] believe that the election of Caldwell and his confreres on the ticket, is certainly to be contested the 3d. Monday in Nov. and you may rely on it, it will greatly paralyze and weaken their efforts on the day of the Presidential election, the first week in that month. The proper notification should be made (what is the law on the subject?)—and let the Radicals be given to understand most assuredly, that the election is to be contested. I believe it would be good for 5,000 votes to us. This very thing—of being cheated out of the election—is what we have to dread, no matter how the votes may be, on a fair count.

You may depend on it, there never was a party or faction in any country, more resolved, at all hazards, to hold on to power, *come what may*, than are the present liegemen of Grant. I believe that is the wedge that is yet to rend this nation to pieces. Men would *fight* on that ground, who would not fight *for a principle.*

My purpose is to take some part in the Presidential fight in this State. The darkest prospects are in So. Ca., Louisiana, and Mississippi. From all I can learn, we will carry Texas & Alabama without much trouble. There will be a most terrible fight in Arkansas. But there the enemy is divided among themselves, whilst our friends are harmonious and energetic.

I have rambled on without point or special purpose. I meant writing a line merely to say to you I did not receive any copy of your address upon the life & character of our old Preceptor Judge Ruffin. I shall be much pleased to receive a copy from you. Very many admired & revered Judge Ruffin. I think but few loved him. I was one of those who loved him, whilst I was not blind to his shortcomings.

What changes time is effecting! In 1839 I went to the Ho. Rep., with 12 other co-members from No. Ca. I am the only survivor of the 13. How many of your old comrades in the Senate do you find living?

Sydenham B. Alexander to William A. Graham UNC

Fair of the Carolinas.
Charlotte, N.C.
September 5th., 1872.

We have invited the Hon. Horace Greeley to be present at our Exhibition, commencing on 22nd. of Oct'r next. Mr. Greeley has expressed a willingness to accept,—provided his friends thought it advisable—stating that the time would suit him, etc.

We have thought it advisable to write to many of the most prominent men of this State & S.C., asking them to write to Mr. G., urging him to accept our invitation, and to *send* the *letter* to *us* to be forwarded pr. Express to Hon. Ethan Allen[1] for delivery. If you think it advisable, we would like to have a letter from you. We are expecting a large concourse of people, & I think will have the largest number of people that has ever attended a fair in this State.

[1]Ethan Allen (1822-1884), a successful woolen and cotton manufacturer of Hanover, Connecticut, was a Republican of liberal persuasion. During the Civil War he rose from sergeant to colonel in the Third Connecticut Regiment. *New York Times*, January 23, 1884.

Augustus S. Merrimon to William A. Graham UNC

Raleigh,
September 9th., 1872.

I thank you most gratefully for your favor of the 27th. ult., which I have received on my return from a visit to the mountains. I am especially obliged by the kind words of compliment and congratulation you offer me. I prize them most highly and shall treasure them as comeing from one eminently fit to judge, and whose judgment is worth remembering.

I am satisfied that the view of the matter I submitted to you, which you express, is the correct one and the safe one, and I shall act upon it. If the proof can be made as you suggest, I will contest—if it cannot, then I will not attempt it.

I shall be glad to see you when you find it convenient to visit the City. I now expect to leave here for Iredell Court on Thursday evening, and will be absent, probably, until Sunday morning next.

I am, etc.
Y'rs very truly,

James M. Leach to William A. Graham UNC

Lexington,
September 18th., 1872.

I herewith enclose you a part of Butler's House Bill, which passed & went to the Senate. I have torn off part from both sides to make it less cumbersome. You will see *your name* at page 72, & Mr. Cameron's at page 67.

Were it not that a move in the Senate to take up that bill & pass it, would awaken enquiry as to *why*?—as nearly everybody's disabilities have been removed,—it might be put through, at once & at any time after meeting of Congress. I felt quite sure I had put in your name & that it had not been stricken out, & no man in the State regrets more profoundly that the Bill did not pass both Houses, for I wanted your disabilities removed more than any other in the State, whether you ever more held office or not.

Alexander McIver to Bartholomew F. Moore, William H. Battle, and William A. Graham UNC

Raleigh,
September 18th., 1872.

Gentlemen:

Trustees of the University for fifty Counties were elected on the 4th. Inst., and their names have been published.

When they meet on the third Tuesday of Nov. next, I think they will be disposed to do anything that can be done for the University. They will, no doubt, be disposed to re-organize the Faculty, and elect the best men in the State for President, and Professors, without any reference to the political party, or the Church denomination to which any one may belong. This would remove one of the impediments in the way of the revival of the University. But another, and perhaps a more serious one, would remain.

Competent and properly qualified gentlemen could not be expected to accept, so long as debts remain to threaten the existence of the University. It would perhaps be improper to offer places in the Faculty, until the debts are settled.

I think it would be useless to ask the General Assembly to aid the University, so long as debts remain to absorb the first seventy or eighty thousand dollars which might be given.

I can see but one remedy. If the creditors can be induced to relinquish their claims, upon the condition that the University shall be properly re-organized and revived, the difficulty will be removed.

In regard to the recent debts, I may say, that the merchants at Chapel Hill, who have claims to the amount of about one thousand dollars, have already agreed to relinquish them.

Any claim for balance of salary which may be made by any of the Faculty, should be disregarded, and not allowed.

I understand the debts of the State Bank have all been paid, so that any thing which the Bank might recover from the University would be distributed among the Stockholders. I think the Stockholders would be willing to relinquish in favor of the University.

The debts to Miss Cameron,[1] and to Gov. Swain's estate,[2] are just debts. If, however, the payment of them, or the continued liability to pay them, should hinder the revival of the University, I think the holders would not hesitate to relinquish them.

If all the creditors hold on to their claims, they will probably destroy the University, and not benefit themselves. If they relinquish, their action will carry a great moral power with it, which I think will at once place the University on the way to prosperity, success, and usefulness.

If the matter could be placed before the creditors in its proper light, they would probably relinquish their claims.

I have troubled you with this communication because you are among the oldest graduates of the University, and, as I believe, among its earliest, firmest, and most constant friends.

If the plan for relief, here indicated, meets your approval, I think it can be carried out; that, at your suggestion, the creditors would agree to it.

I have been appointed to ascertain and report upon what terms the debts of the University can be compromised. If I could report the debts all relinquished, there would be no doubt of the revival of the University, upon the proper basis.

I have mailed a copy of this letter to each of you, and will await your answer with much interest.

---

[1]On April 9, 1874, Treasurer Battle reported to the university trustees that "Miss Mildred C. Cameron's debt of $10,000 and ten years' interest can be funded into term bonds at six per cent interest." This debt was also mentioned but not explained at a trustees' meeting in 1866. Battle, *History of the University*, II, 57.

[2]Mrs. Eleanor Swain, the widow of President David L. Swain, held "a note for $3,000 for money lent to aid in building the New East and New West, and about $2,300 bonds issued to pay the Faculty." Battle, *History of the University*, II, 57.

Augustus Schell[1] *to William A. Graham* UNC

Headquarters National Democratic Committee
Spingler House, Union Square, New York.

September 19, 1872.

I write in behalf of the Comee. to request that you will take an active part in the Presidential Canvass.

The stake at issue is a great one involving, many think, the question not only of local government, but really the liberties of our people. I do trust your eloquent voice will be heard in the Campaign, not only in North Carolina but in Alabama. It is from men like you that the people look for counsel at such an hour.

---

[1]Augustus Schell (1812-1884), a New York lawyer and politician, became a business associate of Cornelius Vanderbilt in his New York Central Railroad operations and in his fight for the Erie. With Horace F. Clark and Jay Gould, he was instrumental in the post-Civil War corner in Chicago and Northwestern stock in the Wall Street market. He supported the Tammany Democratic organization and was Grand Sachem of Tammany in 1872. In the same year he was financial backer and campaign manager of Horace Greeley. Schell was a benefactor of the New York Institution for the Blind and twice served as president of the New York Historical Society. *CDAB*, 917.

Daniel M. Barringer to William A. Graham UNC
[with enclosure]

Raleigh,
September 19th., 1872.

I have recd. the enclosed from Mr. Schell, Chmn. Nat. Dem. Ex. Com. I think you could do our cause much good by going to Pa., where the contest waxes very warm and *doubtful*. If you go to Phila., of course you will report at Hd. Quarters of our friends there, who will direct your future movements, etc.

In this State, we are endeavouring to get up a more thorough & practical organization. There is some depression in our cause since Augt. but I hope it will revive before Novr.

Let me know if you can go.

[Enclosure]
Augustus Schell to Daniel M. Barringer UNC
[Telegram]

New York,
Sept 19th 1872

Ex Governor Graham earnestly desired to speak in Pennsylvania. Enclose this and urge him to go

Augustus S. Merrimon to William A. Graham UNC

Raleigh,
September 19th., 1872.

Y'rs of the 17th. inst. is just received. I remember that we agreed to have the interview you mention, and will be glad to have it at such time as will suit our convenience. I go to Buncombe Court next week, leaving here tomorrow evening, and I will be absent ten or twelve days. After that, I will be here all the time for a month or two, so far as I now know.

Our Candidates on the State Ticket will have a meeting here on the 10th. of Oct., prox., to determine whether they will give notice of protest, etc., and I am anxious that you shall be present at that meeting. Can & will you be with us, and aid us by your advice and suggestions? I trust you will.

If you come then, we could at that time dispose of the other matter of business. But I'll be glad to confer with you at any time you wish, when we can meet. I'll look into the matter, and see how the case stands by the time you come.

I am, etc., y'rs truly,

William A. Graham to William A. Graham, Jr. A&H

Hillsboro'
Sept 27th 1872

In writing you the other day, I failed to mention, that your note of $800. & 6 months interest must be paid in the latter part of Oct. to the N.C. R. Co—so that on the 1st of Nov. I may redeem the remnant of the 5 year Mortgage Bonds. If you wish to renew the loan, I think, I can again let you have as much about the 10th Jany. next—as other monies by that time will have come to my hands. And in that event, you should make a draft which I will indorse in Bank for 70 days, say from 28th October; and this may be taken up with the new loan in Jany.

A letter from George this morning—will stay in N.Y. till Dec. John had a sale yesterday at Mrs. White's[1] late residence, being adminisr. of her estate. Aug. was with him & has just returned. My mullets have not yet come. I presume, however, they will certainly be sent & yours also.

Greelys tour in the West will do him good. He certainly talks sensibly. Jo Brown[2] has declared for him in Georgia. Letters from Aug. Schell Chrmn Dem. Exc Com'tee desire me to speak in Penn[a]. & Alabama; but I do not think I can leave the state. Love to Julia & children.

Affectionately yours

---

[1]Mrs. White has not been identified.

[2]Joseph Emerson Brown (1821-1894) was one of the most controversial figures in Georgia political history. Born in South Carolina, he grew up in the isolated, mountainous country of northern Georgia. He worked as a day laborer on a farm for much of his youth, acquiring what education the local schools afforded. At nineteen he left home to attend the excellent Calhoun Academy in the Anderson District of South Carolina. He taught school, read law, and in 1846 graduated from the Yale Law School.

Returning to his hometown of Canton, he soon established a successful practice and began to take an interest in Democratic party politics. He was elected to the state Senate in 1849, where his ability was recognized. He was a Pierce elector in 1852; judge of the Blue Ridge circuit, 1855-1857; and governor of Georgia, 1857-1865. He proved to be an able and aggressive governor. An avid secessionist, he was nevertheless obsessed by a states' rights philosophy, which made him a bitter opponent of the Davis administration. At a time when centralization was essential to survival of the Confederacy, Brown opposed conscription, protested the seizure of property without compensation, and denounced suspension of *habeas corpus.* He was imprisoned briefly after the war and upon returning to Georgia resigned the governorship in June, 1865.

Believing that there was little alternative to acceptance of congressional reconstruction, he stood virtually alone among Georgia leaders in counseling compliance. His name became anathema to Georgia Conservatives. Brown abandoned the Democratic party and affiliated himself with the Republicans. Republican governor Rufus B. Bullock appointed him chief justice of the Georgia Supreme Court, a position he held for two years. In 1870 he resigned to accept the presidency of the Western and Atlantic Company, a corporation organized to assume a lease on the state-owned railroad. He quickly demonstrated remarkable business ability and by 1880 was a wealthy man. In that year the Democrats, whom Brown had rejoined in 1871, through Governor Colquitt appointed him to fill the unexpired term of John B. Gordon in the United States Senate. A political furor erupted. When Colquitt sought reelection, his appointment of Brown became the principal issue. Brown campaigned vigorously and offered himself as a candidate for the Senate. Both he and Colquitt were reelected. He served in the United States Senate from May, 1880, to May, 1891. *DAB*, III, 141-143; *Biographical Directory of Congress*, 610.

Lyman C. Draper to William A. Graham UNC

Rooms of State Historical Society of Wisconsin.

Madison, Wisconsin,
October 1st., 1872.

I send you a copy of our new vol. of Wis. Hist. Soc. Coll'ns.

I beg to ask if you have any traditional knowledge of the Col. *Hawthorne*[1] who participated in King's Mountain battle? Was he a North or South Carolinian, and wht. can you tell me abt. him and his services?

There was a Majr. *Tate*[2] who served under Sumter, & was also in King's Mountain battle. Can you give me any information about him or references to any one likely to know about him?

If you can recall any facts or incidents in any way illustrative of Genl. Sumter, derived from your Father, or others, I beg you will have the goodness to communicate them to me.

I came near forgetting to ask if you have any tradition as to *Sumter's* Camp at or near Tuckasegee Ford of Catawba—if so, please describe it to me.

---

[1]James Hawthorne (d. 1809) was a first lieutenant in the Sixth South Carolina Regiment, 1777; captain in the Twenty-second, February, 1778-1779; and lieutenant colonel at King's Mountain in October, 1780. Hawthorne was wounded at Camden, April 25, 1781. Francis B. Heitman, *Historical Register of Officers of the Continental Army* (Baltimore: Genealogical Publishing Company, 1973), 281, hereinafter cited as Heitman, *Historical Register of Continental Officers.*

[2]Major Samuel Tate (d. 1798) was from South Carolina and served under General Thomas Sumter. Tate was wounded at the Battle of Guilford Court House, March 15, 1781. Heitman, *Historical Register of Continental Officers*, 533.

Thomas D. McDowell[1] *to William A. Graham* UNC

Elizabeth Town,
October 8th., 1872.

I have been elected one of the Trustees of the University. It is the only position of any kind that I have accepted since the War; and I have done so with the earnest hope that something can be done towards the restoration of our University to it's former high position.

I do not hesitate to express the opinion that any movement in that direction will be a total failure, until there is a complete change in the Faculty. The College cannot succeed with its present Managers.

I am acquainted personally with but few of the present Trustees, and do not know until they assemble what can be accomplished.

If there should be a possibility of making a change, I greatly prefer selecting one of our own Citizens as President, and I have come to the conclusion that you are the most suitable man in the State.

Your well known attachment to the University—the patronage always extended to it, your long and active service as one of the Trustees, your reputation—not only in our own State, but all over the Country—it seems to me would all conspire to restore confidence in the Institution. If you could be prevailed upon to accept the position of President—with an able corps of assistants as Members of the Faculty—Chapel Hill would soon be able to rank with the Virginia Colleges.

---

[1]Thomas David Smith McDowell (1823-1898), of Bladen County, was an 1843 graduate of the University of North Carolina. Political positions held by McDowell included member of the House of Commons, 1846-1852; state senator, 1852-1856 and 1858-1860; member of the Secession Convention; and member of the Confederate Congress, 1861-1864.

Grant, *Alumni History*, 388; Cheney, *North Carolina Government*, 315, 317, 318, 319, 322, 325, 386, 388, 392, 825.

Bartholomew F. Moore to William A. Graham UNC

Moore & Gatling, Attorneys at Law
Raleigh, N.C., Oct 21, 1872

I have recd yours of 30th ult. I have waited to reply until the meeting of the Stockholders of the R&G RR Co which met on yesterday. The matter was not mooted among them. It was incidentally alluded to by myself in addressing the meeting on another point.

I feel satisfied that the Legislature holds complete power over the guage of a Railroad where there is no mention of it—as a matter of police regulation. I am led to this conviction by genl. reasoning and by the learned writers Cooley, Redfield & A & A. on corps & especially the notes.

But I think that the charter of the N.C. R.R. Co. of 1848, near its conclusion secures the right of the legislative power to regulate the guage.

I expect that the R&G. RR Co will take action when needed upon the subject. This latter company—*inter nos*—is completely demoralized—gone—gone!

I mentioned the guage subject to Gov C[aldwell]. He was indignant at the surmise and pronounced it an outrage. I called the Atty Genls attention to it.

I will not venture to say what should be the proper course, if the R&G RR Co will not act. But some action should be taken on behalf of the state.

I cannot see what action the stockholders of the bank can take in the matter of the uny. I have said this much to Mr. McIvor[1]

Very Truly Yours

I have 8,500 bonds of NCRR Co payl on 1 Nov. next, where will the funds for payt be placed that I may apply?

[1]Alexander McIver.

Augustus S. Merrimon to William A. Graham UNC

Raleigh,
November 16, 1872.

I beg to say that in my judgment the interests of the Conservative party require your presence in this city early next week. I trust you will come down on Monday. I have several things to say, and suggest to you.

Let me have the pleasure of seeing you.

Alfred J. Morrison to William A. Graham UNC

Raleigh,
North Carolina,
November 18th., 1872.

Your letter was received this morning, & I will write at once.

I have not yet seen Mr. Ferguson,[1] but have just had a conversation with Jas. Graham, who is here attending a meeting of the University Trustees.

Ferguson approached Jas. this morning, of his own accord, & said he would show him the Globe & other papers relating to Gen'l Ramsour's conduct of which you speak. Mr. McGehee,[2] Jas. G., Dr. Jones,[3] and a few other friends have promised to meet Ferguson this evening at 6 o'clock, and will write you again tomorrow.

Mr. McGehee thinks we are gaining ground, as the feeling between Vance's & Merrimon's friends is growing warmer every day. I think Cousin John ought to come down if he can, for the friends of other gentlemen are here working all the time. Vance, I hear, is coming on the train tonight.

Clingman has been here more than a week, and is up to something,—what, I cannot say.

I am writing in the Hall, while the vote for Gov. is being counted, so excuse haste.

You shall hear from me again soon.

The time for Sen. caucus has not yet been fixed, & I think there is a disposition to put it off as long as possible,—say 'till next Monday night.

---

[1]This may be a reference to Garland S. Ferguson, who was a state senator from Haywood County, 1876-1877, and a judge of the superior court, 1902-1918. Cheney, *North Carolina Government*, 457, 579, 598n.

[2]Montford McGehee (1822-1895), of Person and Caswell counties, a planter and lawyer, was a graduate of the University of North Carolina, where he read law with William Horn Battle. After attending Harvard and touring Europe, he married Sallie Badger, a daughter of George E. Badger. He was active in public life, serving several sessions in the General Assembly and as commissioner of agriculture, 1880-1887. On June 8, 1876, at the request of the bench and bar of the North Carolina Supreme Court, he gave a memorial oration honoring Graham. Later his address was published under the title *Life and Character of the Hon. William A. Graham. A Memorial Oration.* Cheney, *North Carolina Government*, 331, 426, 454, 458-459; R. A. Shotwell and Natt Atkinson, *Legislative Record, Giving the Acts Passed Session Ending March, 1877, Together with Sketches of the Lives and Public Acts of Members of Both Houses* (Raleigh: Edwards, Broughton and Company, 1877), 21.

[3]Dr. Pride Jones was at this time a member from Orange County in the state House of Representatives. Cheney, *North Carolina Government*, 454.

Alfred J. Morrison to William A. Graham UNC

Raleigh, North Carolina,
November 20th., 1872.

My dear Uncle:

We called on Mr. Ferguson last night, & he showed us the Globe, which confirms his statement that Gen'l Ransom did move to strike out the names of seven or eight gentlemen from Mr. Robertson's[1] Amnesty bill. It does not show, however, that your name was in the bill, & I am afraid, at this late hour, we will not be able to prove this. Mr. McGehee and others have come to the conclusion that Ferguson is a spy in the interests of Pool, & we were very guarded in our intercourse with him.

Upon consultation with friends, I, this morning, sent the following dispatch to Gov. Fish—"A Senator from N.C. will be elected next Tuesday: If my Uncle, Gov. Graham, is elected, will his disabilities be removed, in your opinion?" I suppose we will receive an answer today. A resolution, introduced by Mr. Badger, of Wake, has just unanimously passed the House praying Congress to remove the disabilities of Gen'l Hill, Mr. Craige,[2] George Davis, yourself, and some others.

Gov. Vance got here last night, & was in the Hall a few minutes ago. We agreed in Caucus last night to consider the Sen. election on Thursday night. I do not think we will go into an election there, & it is thought the matter will be postponed 'till Monday night.

. . . .

[1]Thomas James Robertson (1823-1897), a graduate of South Carolina College, was a planter active in Reconstruction politics. A member of his state's Constitutional Convention of 1865, he served as a Republican United States senator from 1868 to 1877. *Biographical Directory of Congress*, 1529.

[2]Francis Burton Craige (1811-1875), of Rowan County, was graduated from the University of North Carolina and became proprietor and editor of the *Western Carolinian* (Salisbury), 1829-1831. He was successful in the law practice he established before entering politics. He represented Salisbury in the House of Commons, 1832-1834, and was a Democratic congressman from 1835 until 1861. In 1836 Craige married Elizabeth Phifer Erwin. After a bout with health problems, Craige visited Europe, crossing on a merchant ship. His health regained, he returned home and built a large, lucrative law practice in Rowan and neighboring counties. As a delegate to the state convention of 1861, he introduced the secession ordinance in the form in which it was adopted. He was a delegate to the Provisional Congress of the Confederacy. During the Civil War Craige was a member of the Confederate Congress, and his three sons served in the Confederate army. After the war Craige retired from public service and never applied for "removal of his disabilities." He was described as a very tall man with an unusual gift for making and keeping friends. McCormick, *Convention Personnel*, 27-28; *Biographical Directory of Congress*, 748-749; *Cyclopedia of Eminent Men*, II, 120-122; Powell, *DNCB*, I, 453.

Alfred J. Morrison to William A. Graham UNC

Raleigh, North Carolina,
November 22nd., 1872.

We had a Caucus last night, on the Sen. question; & some points came up, which may interest you. Judge Merrimon a few nights ago requested leave of the Caucus to appear before it, in the presence of Gov. Vance, to explain certain charges made against him, etc., etc.

There was some discussion as to whether he should be permitted to address the Caucus; but it was finally decided that *all* persons, who desired to do so, might come before us, & make such remarks as they thought proper.

Last night a committee waited upon Mr. Merrimon & Gov. Vance, and informed them that it was the pleasure of the Caucus to hear them. Merrimon replied that he did not wish to come before us, & that *he would not be a candidate before the Caucus*. I am unable to say what the result of this will be, but it is feared that Judge M. will make an effort to carry a sufficient number of his friends with him to make an election, if he can secure the Republican vote. I hope, however, that this is not so.

Plato Durham is here, doing all in his power to disorganize our party; & is no doubt working for Pool.[1]

Messrs. McGehee, Norwood,[2] Cunningham,[3] Watson,[4] Dr. Jones, Morehead[5] of Guilford, & myself, are the only men we are able to count for you at present. Dr. Worth,[6] Col. Gant,[7] Sh. Murray,[8] Dr. Miller[9] & others, say they would vote for you as their first choice, but for your disabilities; & under the circumstances, some of your friends are in favor of withdrawing your name as a candidate. No time has yet been fixed for the Caucus election.[10]

A great many rumors may be heard, but I think they are unworthy of credit. One is, that 15 members of the Leg. are to be arrested as Ku Klux.

Received a letter from Cousin John this morning, but suppose it needs no answer.

The papers will give you the details of what we are doing; & I know of no news in Raleigh that would interest you.

---

[1]This was not correct.

[2]John Wall Norwood (1802-1885), of Hillsborough, was an 1824 graduate of the University of North Carolina and a lawyer. Thus, he and Graham had much in common. Norwood served one session in each house of the state legislature, having been elected to the Commons in 1858. In addition to his legal practice, he advocated and practiced scientific farming. Spencer Alumni Project; Lefler and Wager, *Orange County*, 336.

[3]John Wilson Cunningham (1820-1887), of Person County, was a graduate of the University of North Carolina. A planter, he was also active in politics and was a member of the House of Commons, 1844-1846; a state senator, 1852-1859, 1866-1867, 1872-1874, 1876-1877, and 1881; and a delegate to the conventions of 1861 and 1875. Cheney, *North Carolina Government*, 314, 319, 322, 324, 325, 335, 453, 457, 460, 825, 874.

[4]Jones Watson, a merchant and lawyer of Chapel Hill, was a county commissioner, Chapel Hill magistrate and mayor, and a member of the North Carolina House of Representatives, 1872-1874. Cheney, *North Carolina Government*, 454; Lefler and Wager, *Orange County*, 193, 196, 364.

[5]James T. Morehead, Jr.

[6]John M. Worth.

[7]Jesse Gant, of Alamance County, was a textile manufacturer. He was a representative in the General Assembly of 1872-1874. Cheney, *North Carolina Government*, 545; Whitaker, *Centennial History of Alamance*, 90.

[8]William James Murray of Alamance County.

[9]William John Twitty Miller (1805-1886), a native of Rutherford County who settled in what became Cleveland County, was a graduate in medicine from Transylvania University. He established his practice on the Broad River. A dedicated Whig Unionist, Miller was a member of the state legislature seven times between 1836 and 1874. He was a delegate to the Constitutional Convention of 1861, opposing secession until after Lincoln's call for troops. For nearly fifty years Miller was an active layman of the Methodist Episcopal Church, South. McCormick, *Convention Personnel*, 63.

[10]Since the Conservatives controlled the legislature elected in August, 1872, there was

considerable discussion as to who should be sent to join Matt W. Ransom in the United States Senate. Augustus S. Merrimon expected to be nominated, believing that the party was committed to him because of his gubernatorial campaign; however, both Graham and Vance coveted the position. The contest between Vance and Merrimon was intense, and the Conservative caucus deadlocked. Both men withdrew. No agreement on an alternative candidate seemed possible. Meanwhile, the Republicans abandoned John Pool and nominated Merrimon, futilely hoping that Merrimon would vote with the Republicans if elected. The Democrats quickly nominated Vance, but Merrimon was elected by a combination of Republicans and disaffected Conservatives. There is little evidence of much support for William A. Graham. Hamilton, *Reconstruction in North Carolina*, 594-595.

James L. Alcorn to William A. Graham UNC

Washington City, D.C.,
Dec'r 3rd, 1872.

I received this morning at my desk, your letter of the 30th ult. I at once approached several Senators, prominent heretofore in their opposition to legislation of this character. I find two objections to the speedy relief which your case demands. First,—there is a rule of the Senate that no special bill shall be considered unless upon the written application of the petition. When I remarked in answer to this objection, that I had your letter the suggestion was; "have the letter read, that is sufficient." But the letter was evidently not written for such purpose, I regarded it in the nature of a private communication, and did not think it proper to have it read. Second, The Senate Committees are not yet appointed, and Senators objected to voting for the passage of a bill except upon the report of the Committee.

In your case, I could obtain a favorable report from the committee at once, could see the members in their seats, and obtain the consent necessary, the chairman being very favorable.

I suggest that you send at once, a formal petition to Congress, or that you write me a letter, such as you are willing to have go before the Country, requesting me to present a bill for your relief. I have no doubt of the result.

I would suggest that your friends in the Legislature might be induced to adjourn the joint convention for two weeks—in favor of such a motion, you would obtain the votes of all save those who felt that their candidate was within grasping distance of the prize.

I was very glad to hear from you, and shall be greatly gratified to see the State of North Carolina coming again forward to manifest her continued confidence in your integrity and great ability.

John W. Norwood to William A. Graham UNC

Raleigh,
December 9th., 1872.

You will see by Senate proceedings of today, that I have introduced the Bill of which I was speaking to you.

The preamble declares that the Rail Roads are common highways, designed for the convenience and comfort of the people, and their continuance and good management are essential to the prosperity of the State. That the guage of 4 feet 8 ½ inches is common to all the Rail Roads in the State, and cannot be changed without serious injury to its interests, by retarding and obstructing communication within its limits.

Section 1. Forbids the injuring, impairing, or destroying the convenient operating Rail Roads, etc.

Section 2. Rail Roads declared to be common highways.

Sec. 3. Unlawful to change the guage of 4 ft. 8 ½ inches to any other guage, nor shall a third rail be laid down, etc.

Sec. 4. Prescribes that the violation of the Act shall be a misdemeanor, etc.

Sec. 5. Subject to a penalty of $5,000. for the violation of the Act.

I will send you a copy of the Bill, as soon as it is printed. Now, my dear Sir, as your studies and pursuits have led you to the consideration of such matters, I would be pleased to have all the aid from you which your convenience may allow, in suggestions, authorities, etc.

James L. Alcorn to William A. Graham UNC

United States Senate Chamber
Washington.

December 13, 1872.

I acknowledge the receipt of your letter in answer to mine of a former date. Not more than thirty minutes had elapsed after posting you the letter to which you reply, when I read the dispatch announcing the election of Mr. Merrimon. I regretted the fact, since your letter had excited the hope that I might see you here as I would be glad to see you, the accredited Senator of North Carolina.

An effort was made by your friends at the last Session to have your disabilities removed, Senator Ransom gave the proposition a hearty support. When the enquiry was made as to whether you had made application, our answer was, after making search, that no application had been made. Gen'l Ransom, who expressed some sensitiveness in relation to his position towards Governor Vance, found it necessary to disengage Vance from those who had not applied, Vance having made application, and having written a letter which was on file. To have added the name of any one of prominence who had not applied to the bill for the relief of Vance, would have had no other effect than the defeat of the bill. I need not elaborate further.

I suggest to you that you address me a letter, setting forth the facts of your case. State the fact that you think the discrimination against you was unjust. That having accepted the amendments to the constitution and placed yourself in the line of obedience to the law, you would be glad to be placed on terms of equality with your countrymen. I suggest a letter in this line of reasoning, not addressed to Congress, and thereby relieving you from the imputation of being a supplicant; placing yourself on the high ground which you propose to occupy, and leaving the subject with Congress.[1]

A letter such as you can write, without any sacrifice of personal respect, respectful to Congress—to the Government—will be sufficient, I think, to bring you proper relief.

I shall be glad to serve you, and I can serve you, if [you] will but supply me with the superstructure. Congress but the other day, removed the disabilities of Col. Lamar, of Mississippi.[2] Lamar had been elected a democrat, to the 43 Congress, from Mississippi, became a candidate while under disabilities, but the action was based on *his application*, which was *full, complete*, and *graceful.*

---

[1]Strong efforts were made by friends and admirers of Graham for the removal of his political disabilities. Among those who were most active was Robert C. Winthrop. Writing to Hamilton Fish, December 10, 1873, he enclosed a clipping containing the following statement of John A. Campbell:

> Mr. Graham never was a friend of secession. After the war began he always appeared to me to have his heart in the Union and his members in the Confederacy. He is a man of purest nature, and that sort of noble, gentle influence which is now so needed in the South. For him I feel a desire that he should be recovered to the country and if it could be done at my wish, in that I would have contributed something again to the restoration of the Union.

See Henry G. Connor, *John Archibald Campbell: Associate Justice of the United States Supreme Court, 1853-1861* (New York: Houghton Mifflin Company, 1920), 266.

[2]Lucius Quintus Cincinnatus Lamar (1825-1893), of Mississippi, a native of Georgia, was a graduate of Emory College. By training a lawyer, Lamar had a varied and distinguished career as a statesman and jurist. He was a state legislator and Democratic member of Congress, 1857-1860, and a delegate to the Secession Convention. During the war he served the Confederacy as a lieutenant colonel and as commissioner to Russia, France, and Great Britain in 1863. From 1873 to 1877 he served as a representative in Congress; from 1877 to 1885 he was a senator; and from 1885 to 1887 he was secretary of the interior. In 1888 Lamar was appointed an associate justice on the United States Supreme Court, a position he held until 1893. *DAB,* X, 551-553.

Robert D. Graham to William A. Graham [with enclosures] UNC

Charlotte, N.C.
December 14, 1872.

I hand you the telegram I received from Gov. Fish on the last day of the contest between Merrimon and Vance. My dispatch is given on the back of it, which was subsequent to a letter written during the first week.

Though without much interest now, it will show, I think, that Mr. Fish was favorably disposed towards you, but failed to do anything with Grant.

Sometime at your leisure I hope you will write a sketch of the life of Judge Mangum, and also make a copy of your last speech at Lincolnton.

[Enclosure] *Robert D. Graham to Hamilton Fish* [Telegram] UNC

Charlotte, N.C.
December 3, 1872.

Please telegraph me the feeling of yourself, and of the President as to the removal of Gov. Graham's disabilities. An explicit answer will decide the election between him and some other Conservative.

[Enclosure]
Hamilton Fish to Robert D. Graham UNC
[Telegram]

Washington, D.C.
December 3, 1872.

The President declines any expression of opinion on an individual application for removal of disabilities, unless in response to a request for information from some appropriate Committee of Congress. The consideration of these questions belongs exclusively to Congress, and the Executive Department abstains from interference. The suggestion that an expression of opinion by the President would influence the pending election for United States Senator, is deemed conclusive of the duty of abstaining from such expressions.

1873

William A. Graham to [Daniel H. Hill?][1] UNC

[January?] 1873.

The reasons for the measure were somewhat as follows: We had cause of complaint against Japan. First, for the imprisonment and maltreatment of American seamen who had been wrecked on her coast, and whom she had imprisoned in cages, and sent through her country for exhibition—very grudgingly and reluctantly she had released and surrendered up these, after some deaths among them, to an American Naval vessel, sent to demand them. Second, some of her seamen who had suffered shipwreck in their junks were picked up by American vessels and sent to her coast, and she was obstinate in refusing the liberty to land them, and after consenting, directed that our ships should not return again, even for such a purpose. Third, having acquired California and established our settlements on the Pacific coast, we had become somewhat near neighbors to the Japanese, and it was considered that a nation comprising an empire of thirty odd millions of inhabitants, and a series of islands extending through eleven degrees of latitude, with an advancement in arts, letters, and science quite equal to the Chinese, should not be permitted longer to keep herself out of the pale of civilization, and fail to observe and keep the usages imposed by the law of civilized nations.

It was therefore resolved that the expedition would be sent to demand: First. That she should abstain from the cruel treatment of mariners who might be thrown on her shores by casualty, and second, that she should no longer deny the ordinary demands of hospitality by refusing fresh water, fuel, and provisions, etc., upon being paid an equivalent for them; to vessels which might come to her ports in distress. Third, over and above these demands, it was hoped, that by proper diplomacy, a treaty might be obtained by which Japan would yield her exclusive policy of two centuries, and open her ports to the commerce of the world.

The subject pertaining to Naval officers and Sailors' rights, was brought to my attention by Commodore M. C. Perry.[2] I at first resolved to adopt it, and carry out the enterprise, if possible. I brought it to the President, who after consideration, approved it, and it became a Cabinet measure. I therefore gave the order designating that ships be got in readiness, and detailed the officers for the expedition. Commodore Perry, who suggested it, being placed in command. After the matter became known to the public, it was the subject of some unfriendly criticism and ridicule in Congress, and Gen. Bayly,[3] of Virginia, chairman of the Committee on Foreign Relations, called to enquire into the objects of it. Upon their being favorably stated, he gave his approval. Mr. Ritchie,[4] the editor of the Union, with whom I had kind relations, remonstrated with me that we were about to compromise the honor of the Government by warlike demonstration against a weak and semi-barbarian power. But the preparations went on. I resigned upon my nomination for the Vice-Presidency, on the first of August, 1852, and the expedition sailed in the autumn following. Its result is before the world.

W. A. Graham.

---

[1]About this time an article appeared in several newspapers giving Graham the entire credit for the expedition to Japan. His attention having been called to the situation, Graham wrote a letter to a friend on the subject. This is an extract from that letter. Since there was such an article in the *Southern Home*, edited by D. H. Hill, there is reason to believe that Graham was writing Hill. On February 6, 1910, the "North Carolina Review," a supplement to the *News and Observer* (Raleigh), reprinted the *Southern Home* article.

[2]Matthew Calbraith Perry (1791-1858), a native of Rhode Island, entered upon a brilliant career in the navy in 1809 at the age of 15. He served in the War of 1812 and the Mexican War and is credited with much of the improvement of the navy after 1830. He rose to the rank of commodore. His most famous mission evolved from an assignment given him in January, 1852, by Secretary of the Navy William A. Graham. Perry was chosen to help negotiate a treaty with Japan, a nation then not open to western trade. In November, 1852, he sailed from the Norfolk harbor carrying a letter to be delivered to the emperor of Japan. After refusing to give the letter to minor Japanese officials, Perry personally delivered it and other documents to Princes Idzu and Iwami, representatives of the emperor. Perry returned, as he promised, to Yedo Bay for an answer in February, 1854. On March 31 a treaty of peace and commerce was signed at Yokohama, granting to the United States trading rights at Hakodate and Shimoda. *CDAB*, 789.

[3]Thomas Henry Bayly (1810-1856), of Virginia, was a graduate of the University of Virginia and a lawyer. After serving his state as a legislator and judge, Bayly was a Democratic member of Congress, 1844-1855. *Biographical Directory of Congress*, 529.

[4]Thomas Ritchie (1778-1854), a native of Tappahannock, Virginia, was editor of the *Richmond Enquirer*, 1804-1845, and of the Washington *Union*, 1845-1851. *CDAB*, 868.

Lyman C. Draper to William A. Graham UNC

State Historical Society of Wisconsin.
Madison, Wis'n,
January 7th., 1873.

Judge Wm. H. Battle, of Raleigh, has just written me, that you have in your possession Gen. Davie's MS. Narrative of the campaign of 1780, & perhaps Revolutionary services in general.[1] Mrs. Gov. Swain had given permission to Judge Battle to either loan me the Davie MS., or cause a transcript to be made for me—supposing the document was among Gov. Swain's papers.

I am aware that Prof. F. M. Hubbard[2] used the narrative in his Memoir of Gov. Davie, & that Col. Wheeler copied it—not, however, as he states, literally. Yet I very much desire a faithful transcript of the entire document.

I shall feel thankful if you will feel yourself authorized & willing to cause a full copy to be made at my expense & sent me by mail, or otherwise. I will willingly remit the cost of copying it.

Having, when in Charlotte in 1871, made the acquaintance of Col. Wm. Johnston, I venture to write him a note, thinking he may have a friendly word to say to you in my behalf.

You may possibly have other papers—or know of others Gov. Swain collected having a bearing on Gen. Sumter: If so, please inform me. I have a partial set of the N.C. Univ. Magazine, containing much Revolutionary matter. The portion of the work I have not been so fortunate as to obtain, may contain matter equally as important.

I send you 6 parcels by mail, of printed matter—mostly publications of our Wis. Hist. Society: I think I formerly sent you vols. 5 & 6—if you [*sic*], you now have an entire set. Some of them are on poor paper, & miserably printed, but they are the best we could get at the time,—& I found no small difficulty in finding the earlier volumes.

I beg you will do what you can to oblige me. My health is not good, & I am anxious to hasten my Sumter work to completion—& much other border work, if spared to do it.

---

[1]William R. Davie seems to have prepared several Revolutionary sketches for "Parson" Weems. The original Davie material is in the Southern Historical Collection, University of North Carolina Library, Chapel Hill. So far as can be determined, it was never published.

[2]Fordyce Mitchell Hubbard (1809-1888), a native of Massachusetts and an Episcopal minister, was professor of Latin languages and literature at the University of North Carolina (1849-1868). He was the author of a life of William R. Davie as well as of various articles and textbooks. Lefler and Wager, *Orange County*, 332.

William A. Graham to William A. Smith[1] UNC

Hillsboro N.C.
Jany 7th, 1873

I have to report that on yesterday, as of the 1st instant, in accordance with the terms of the mortgage deed of the North Carolina Railroad Company, I received from the Treasurer of the company on account of the sinking fund, the following bonds of said company, running five years, and falling due the 1st day of November 1872, which had been cancelled by the Board of directors, to wit Nos 646, 647, 648, 649, 660, 672, 673, 674, 675, 693, 901, 905, 906. *Nineteen* in number of the amount in all of $6,500.

Also, *fifty three* Bonds of like, and numbered No. 755, 756, 757, 813, 814, 815, 818, 819, 820, 821, 822, 826, 827, 828, 857, 859, 860, 861, 862, 869, 870, 871, 873, 876, 877, 878, 879, 880, 881, 882, 883, 886, 887, 888, 889, 890, 891, 892, 893, 894, 895, 896, 897, of the aggregate amount of $1,500 which were immediately cancelled, in the presence of the Treasurer and secretary;

Also the sum of Nine thousand one Hundred and Fifty $9150. dollars in checks on the National Banks at Raleigh, to be applied in further redemption of that class of Bonds;

And that, out of the effects of the sinking fund in my hands, on the first of November 1872, I redeemed of this class of Bonds No. 603, 604, 605, 606, 607, 608, 609, 610, 683, 684, 685, 686, 687, and on the 1st instant No. 691; in all *fifteen*—of the amount to $7,500 which have been cancelled.

I regret to add that no payment whatever was made into the sinking fund, for the redemption of the class of Bonds to fall due on the 1st of November 1877, as required by the terms of the Mortgage Deed, which have been complied with in all our previous settlements for the last four years; and being charged with the duty of causing such a provision to be made for the creditors of the company I wish you to consider this part of my communication as a demand for the annual instalment required to provide for the payment of this latter class of bonds.

The payments made on account of this class to become due in 1888, in former years, render nothing requisite in their account in present year.

Very Respectfully yours

[1]This letter and William A. Smith's reply, which follows, are included as correspondence typical of much in the Graham Papers concerning the North Carolina Railroad Company. It would be impossible and serve little purpose to include all such material.

William A. Smith to William A. Graham UNC

North Carolina Rail Road Company,
President's Office
Boon Hill, N.C., January 11th 1873.

Your report of the 7th of January in relation to the Sinking Fund of the N.C.R.R. Company is at hand.

You desire me to take the latter part of your communication as a demand for the thirty thousand dollars due the Sinking Fund upon the ten year bonds on 1st day January 1873. I will so consider it.

If we had paid the money as formerly, it would not have been any benefit to our Company or the bond holders. For the reason you could not have purchased the ten year bonds at par, and Mr. Williams President of the State Nat. Bank at Raleigh[1] would not have paid interest upon the money deposited with him. This is my experience from the past. The Board of Directors of the N.C.R.R. Co. fully understand their trust, and their obligations to the Trustees, and will be fully prepared to come up to all of the requirements of the Mortgage, without any forfeiture upon their part or trouble to any one.

I am Governor with great
Respt Your Obt Servant

[1]The State National Bank of Raleigh was organized in 1868 as the successor to the prewar banking house of John G. Williams and Company. The bank, located at 121 Fayetteville Street, operated for twenty years. Williams, president and principal owner, died in 1879 and was succeeded in his office by his widow, Merriam C. White Williams. Murray, *Wake*, 575.

William Johnston to William A. Graham UNC
[with enclosure]

Charlotte,
January 16th., 1873.

Enclosed I send you a letter from Lyman C. Draper, Esq'r, of Madison, Wisconsin. Mr. Draper was made known to me by Dr. Ronsing,[1] since, I have met with him & had some considerable correspondence about his historical researches in North Carolina.

The letter will explain itself, & I trust you will give him any facility for information at your command.

I know that for more than two years he has been engaged in writing the history of Sumter & his men. Should you know the address of Geo. L. Alexander[2] referred to, please advise me or him. I will guarantee that he will carefully preserve any papers you may entrust to him.

We are all in usual health, and ask a kind remembrance to Mrs. Graham & the family.

With high regard,

Yours truly,

Do me the favor to return Mr. Draper's letter.

---

[1]Dr. Ronsing has not been identified.

[2]George L. Alexander has not been identified definitively but was probably a son of Hezekiah Alexander (1728-1801), a Revolutionary leader in Mecklenburg County. Powell, *DNCB*, I, 14-15.

[Enclosure]
Lyman C. Draper to William Johnston

State Historical Society of Wisconsin.

Madison,
January 7th., 1873.

You will remember I wrote you last Autumn with reference to Gen. Davies' Revolutionary Narrative in MS, which was, a few years since, in possession of Gov. Swain, & that Mrs. Swain had given me permission to have the loan of it, or a transcript taken, & had authorized Judge Battle to oblige me in her behalf. That I desired you to say a friendly word for me to Judge Battle, & you kindly did so.

Judge Battle has just informed me that he had learned from Hon. W. A. Graham that he has the manuscript in question, had borrowed it from Gov. Swain in his lifetime.

I have just written to Gov. Graham, & thought perhaps you may see him soon, & if so, w'd say whatever might be proper to a furtherance of my wishes—that is, a faithful transcript of the Davie narrative, & whatever else Gov. Graham may have, throwing any light on Sumter & his services.

I learned some time since of a Geo. Lee Alexander, formerly of Mecklenburg, son of a Revolutionary soldier who served under Sumter, & who now resides in Ala. Can you give me his present address?

I send you a pamphlet of collections of our new Wis. Academy of Science. I sent a copy, & some other things, to Gov. Graham.

Washington M. Wingate[1] *to William A. Graham* UNC

Wake Forest College

Forestville, N.C.,
January 17th., 1873.

I send you a programme of our Educational Convention.[2] If consistent with y'r engagements, we should be very glad to have you present with us, and take part in its proceedings, and would be favored by any remarks on any of the subjects, or reserved topics, presented in the order of proceedings.

A large attendance from all parts of the State is expected. And, although it is held in the interests of education as connected with the Baptist denomination, the meeting, we trust, will not be wanting in many elements of interest to all friends of education.

Of course, we hope to see Mrs. Graham there; and this note to you, if she will allow, will constitute her a delegate with full powers and privileges.

---

[1]Washington Manly Wingate (1828-1878), a native of South Carolina, was a graduate of Wake Forest College. He studied theology at Furman University and became a Baptist minister. From 1854 until his death he served as president of Wake Forest.

[2]The program was enclosed.

Nathan K. Hall to William A. Graham A&H

Buffalo,
January 18th., 1873.

It is almost six months since I rec'd your last letter, and I must apologize for my long silence. When it was rec'd, I intended to write you at an early day and hoped to be able soon to congratulate upon the prospect of the Election;—but the indications soon became discouraging and until the Election was over and the rule of radicalism re-established, there was little to encourage the Union men of the South or the Conservatives of the North. These things, with a constant press of judicial duties, have made me hesitate and delay but as I am to leave for Albany tomorrow to hold a term of Court there, next week, I will not longer delay writing to you.

The result of the Election in this State was wholly unexpected to me but I presume that people who mixed much in politics had reason to expect it. The general result, and the sad ending of poor Greely's life so soon after his defeat, must have produced a profound impression upon his supporters at the South as well as at the North.

We were much gratified that you enjoyed your visit here, made under such unfavorable circumstances. The illness of Mrs. Fillmore, your very short stay, and the engagements and excitements of the "Glorious 4th. of July," rendered it impossible for us to do much to entertain you ourselves or bring you into communication with our friends.

Mrs. Hall and myself are in usual health. Mr. Fillmore is also in usual health and Mrs. Fillmore, though not entirely well is able to go into society again, and suffers but little from the bodily ailments which followed her so persistently the first half of the last year.

. . . .

It would certainly give Mrs. Hall and myself very great pleasure to make you a visit at your own home, and it is possible that we may be able at some future time to do so. Mrs. Hall, especially, would be benefitted by a short trip to the South, and if my district shall be divided this year, or next, I shall try as soon as possible thereafter, to spend one of our very uncomfortable Spring months in travelling in the South. On the Eastern Coast, I have never been South of Norfolk, Va., and no farther South than St. Louis, Missouri, and Lexington and Louisville, Ky., in the West.

. . . .

William A. Graham to Susan Washington Graham A&H

Raleigh
Jany 22nd 1873

My Dear Wife

I received today, a telegram from Washington, requesting me to come on the middle of next week; so that I have to come home on Saturday night, and leave for Washington perhaps on Monday. This relieves me from the suspense of the last few days.

George arrived here this morning, unexpectedly to me. I have Introduced him to Dr. McKee,[1] Jno. G. Williams, [Col.] Barringer,[2] Alfred Williams,[3] Wm Henry Jones[4] etc, and they are disposed to receive him very kindly. Will endeavour to make him acquainted with Dr. Johnson[5] and others while I remain. He will go home after a few days, to make preparations for living here. Dr. Burke Haywood[6] to whom I mentioned his arrival said he would call upon him.

I believe there is nothing new here. I am gratified at the prospect of getting through my business satisfactorily here, before going to Washington. I have not seen the Miss Whites,[7] or their friends. Not many strangers here, besides the lawyers attending court.

Ever affectionately yours

---

[1]Dr. James McKee (1845-1912) received his undergraduate education at the University of North Carolina and his M.D. degree at Bellevue Hospital Medical College in 1869. He practiced medicine in Raleigh, where he was on the staff of the state insane asylum (Dorothea Dix Hospital). At one time he was president of the North Carolina Medical Society. Grant, *Alumni History*, 394.

[2]Possibly Graham referred to Daniel M. Barringer.

[3]Alfred Williams was a prominent Raleigh businessman who in 1867 founded the

successful firm of Alfred Williams and Company, which operated a book and stationery store. Murray, *Wake*, 569.

[4]Probably this was William Henry Jones (1795-1885), a son of William Jones, who had moved from Virginia to Wake County in 1798. Henry Jones, a carpenter, was married to Lucy Ann Olive and lived in Wake County until his death. Wake County Genealogical Society, *The Heritage of Wake County, North Carolina, 1983* (Winston-Salem: Wake County Genealogical Society and Hunter Publishing Company, 1983), 295.

[5]Dr. Charles E. Johnson practiced medicine in Raleigh for many years. He was involved in his work from about 1845 until after 1873 and was active in civic affairs. He was offered but refused to accept the directorship of the North Carolina hospital for the insane. Murray, *Wake*, 273, 327, 429, 444, 445, 462.

[6]Edmund Burke Haywood (1825-1894) received two degrees from the University of North Carolina—an A.M. in 1868 and an LL.D. in 1889. He received his medical degree from the University of Pennsylvania in 1849. Haywood was a prominent physician active in city affairs. He served as president of the board of directors of the state hospital for the insane. Grant, *Alumni History*, 268.

[7]The Misses White have not been identified.

William W. Corcoran to William A. Graham A&H

Washington, D.C.,
January 23rd., 1873.

I had anticipated great pleasure from the proposed meeting of Mr. Fillmore and the surviving members of his Cabinet, at my house, about the middle of the ensuing month; but an unforseen interruption of my arrangements affords another evidence of the uncertainty of human expectations.

For more than a week I have been confined to my bed by severe indisposition; and the debility induced by this attack precludes the hope of an early restoration to that degree of health which would enable me to render the time of my friends as agreeable as I should desire to make it.

Such a reunion would have awakened many pleasing reminiscences, and from it, none of the party could have derived more sincere gratification than myself. I had promised Mr. Fillmore to give each of you due notification of the period at which it would occur; and regret to find myself physically incapacitated for discharging the agreeable duties of the occasion. I will still, however, indulge the hope that, next winter, we shall be enabled to carry into execution a plan in which I have felt so deep an interest.

With sincere wishes for your health and happiness,

I remain, as ever, truly yours,

William A. Smith to William A. Graham UNC

North Carolina Rail Road Company
Company Shops January 31 1873

By order of the Board of Directors I enclose you an acceptance for thirty thousand dollars due you as Trustee on the first January 1873. Our Board of Directors are in hopes this will answer your purpose better than the money.

William A. Graham to Susan Washington Graham A&H

Washington,
February 1st., 1873.

. . . .

I neglected to say in my last, that after the adjournment on Thursday, Judge Battle and myself were invited on the floor of the Senate by Mr. Ransom,[1] and I was introduced to many Senators. Messrs. Joshua Hill,[2] & Norwood[3] of Ga., Windom,[4] of Minnesota, Blair,[5] Mo., Casserly,[6] Cal'f'n'a, Hamilton,[7] of Maryland, Stockton,[8] N.J., Bayard,[9] Del., etc., etc., including Scott,[10] of Penn'a, Chairman of the K.K. Com'tee, who all were polite and most of them very cordial. Mr. R. had previously told me, that a bill had that morning been reported by a Com'tee of the Senate, for the removal of my disabilities; but Mr. Conckling[11] of N.Y. had objected to the immediate consideration.

Today I learn that on yesterday a Bill passed the House unanimously of the same import; attended by a scene of some interest. Mr. Peters,[12] an old gentleman from Maine, had reported from the House Comtee. favorably, on the Bill. Mr. Dawes,[13] of Mass., said Gov. Graham's disabilities had been already removed. Peters, who it is said had taken a slight drink, exclaimed vehemently, "it is not so, and Gov. Graham is one of the best men in the United States." Mr. Dawes, "I don't dispute that; but I think his disabilities have been removed." The Speaker Blaine,[14] "If they have been, it will do no harm to remove them again," and put the question on the passage of the Bill—when it passed unanimously. Ransom says it will pass the Senate, but is not certain that Conckling will not oppose it. He proposed to him to be introduced to me, the other day while I was in the lobby, he said he would come out for this purpose presently, but did not come while I remained. I knew nothing of this 'till today. I called this morning at Mr. Riggs'[15] Bank on him,—went thence to see Mr. Corcoran, who was too unwell to receive me. Then called on the President, who being pressed for time, I remained but a few moments. Went then to see Mrs. Fish, and stayed a few moments, thence to the House Reps.—where I was told of the scene of yesterday, and desired to be introduced to my unknown friend, Peters, but he was not in his seat. Was made acquainted with many members from Ala., Texas, Penn'a., Ten'see, Ky., N.Y., etc. The President of the University of Ky., Mr. Bowman,[16] is a very interesting man, and is here at Willards, engaged with some of the Professors of Harvard and Yale in getting a Bill passed for a large endowment of Colleges in the States, by means of which, he thinks, our University may be revived. I was very much impressed in reading the accounts of his labors and success in establishing the University of Ky.,—he lives in the Clay house at Ashland. It belongs to his College, which now contains 600 students.

There was a levee at the President's the night of my arrival, and Mrs. Grant has a reception this afternoon, but I have attended [n]either.

After ending my argument yesterday, Ch. J. Chase[17] invited Judge Battle and myself to dine with him. He lives with his son-in-law, Senator

Sprague,[18] in Judge Hall's former residence, near P.O. Department. The Spragues went out, and Miss Hall, a niece, and the Ch. J. were our only entertainers. We found him very pleasant, and we remained 'till 9 o'clock. He is looking badly, and I fear will not last a great while.

---

[1]Matt W. Ransom had been elected to the United States Senate as a Democrat in 1872 to fill the vacancy for the term that began March 4, 1871. *Biographical Directory of Congress*, 1498-1499.

[2]Joshua Hill (1812-1891), of Georgia, was a native of South Carolina. At first a Whig in his political philosophy, he was elected a member of Congress with the support of the Whig and American parties, 1857-1861. As a Republican he won a seat in the Senate and served in that capacity, 1871-1873. *Biographical Directory of Congress*, 1054; *CDAB*, 436-437.

[3]Thomas Manson Norwood (1830-1913), of Georgia, was a graduate of Emory College. A lawyer by profession, he served in several political offices: as a state legislator; as a Democratic United States senator, 1871-1875; and as a representative in Congress, 1885-1889. *Biographical Directory of Congress*, 1396.

[4]William Windom (1827-1891), of Minnesota, was a native of Ohio and a lawyer by profession. He was a Republican member of the United States House of Representatives, 1859-1869; a United States senator, 1870-1881 and 1881-1883; and secretary of the treasury in 1881 and 1889-1891. *Biographical Directory of Congress*, 1836; *CDAB*, 1231.

[5]Francis Preston Blair, Jr. (1821-1875), scion of a politically influential family, was born in Kentucky and, after graduating from Princeton (1841), established a legal practice in St. Louis, Missouri. He served in the Mexican War and as a major general in the Civil War. An uncompromising opponent of slavery, he organized the Free-Soil party in Missouri and represented the state in Congress, 1856-1862, as a Republican. He helped save Missouri for the Union. Later he joined moderate Republicans in opposing the Radicals in the state. A supporter of presidential reconstruction plans, Blair reverted to the Democratic party and was Horatio Seymour's running mate in 1868. Although his sympathy for the South was acknowledged, his antislavery career made him suspect in some quarters. Later he cooperated with the Liberal Republicans and was a United States senator, 1871-1873. *CDAB*, 80; Randall and Donald, *Civil War and Reconstruction*, 639.

[6]Eugene Casserly (1820-1883), of California, was a native of Ireland who came to the United States in 1822. After his graduation from Georgetown College, he established a law practice in New York before he moved to California, where he became an editor and publisher. From 1869 until 1873, he served as a Democratic United States senator; he was a delegate to the convention of 1878. *Biographical Directory of Congress*, 672.

[7]William Thomas Hamilton (1820-1888), of Maryland, was educated at Jefferson College. A lawyer, Hamilton was elected to serve in his state's legislature and then as a United States senator, 1869-1875. A Democrat, he opposed radical reconstruction. From 1879 until 1883 he was governor of Maryland. *Biographical Directory of Congress*, 998; *CDAB*, 392.

[8]John Potter Stockton (1826-1900), of New Jersey, was a graduate of Princeton and a lawyer by training. He served as minister to Italy, 1857-1861, and was a United States senator, 1865 until 1866, when his seat was declared vacant. A Democrat, in 1869 he was again elected to the Senate and served until 1875. From 1877 to 1892 he was attorney general of New Jersey. *Biographical Directory of Congress*, 660; *CDAB*, 1014.

[9]Thomas Francis Bayard.

[10]John Scott.

[11]Roscoe Conkling.

[12]John Andrew Peters (1822-1904), of Maine, was a graduate of Yale. After establishing his law practice, Peters entered politics and was elected to the state legislature three times. He served as state attorney general and was elected as a Republican representative to Congress, 1867-1873. Then he was appointed justice of the state supreme court (1873-1883) and advanced to become chief justice, 1883-1900. *Biographical Directory of Congress*, 1448; *CDAB*, 791.

[13]Henry Laurens Dawes (1816-1903), of Massachusetts, was a graduate of Yale. After

teaching and conducting a law practice, Dawes was elected to the state legislature and was a delegate to the convention of 1853. A Republican, Dawes was a representative to Congress, 1857-1875, and a United States senator, 1875-1893. *Biographical Directory of Congress*, 788; *CDAB*, 221.

[14]James Gillespie Blaine (1830-1893), of Maine, was educated at Washington College and began his career as a teacher before establishing a law practice. He held several public offices, including these: state representative, 1859-1862; Republican member of the House of Representatives, 1863-1876 (Speaker, 1869-1875); United States senator, 1876-1881; and secretary of state, 1881, 1889-1892. He won the presidential nomination in 1884 but was defeated in the election. The most powerful Republican of his day, Blaine's permanent influence lay in foreign affairs. As secretary of state Blaine anticipated American world interests and sought to improve relations with Latin American countries. *Biographical Directory of Congress*, 560; *CDAB*, 79-80.

[15]George Washington Riggs.

[16]John Bryan Bowman (1824-1891), of Kentucky and a graduate of Bacon College, was founder of Kentucky University. *CDAB*, 97; *Who Was Who*, 67.

[17]Chief Justice Salmon P. Chase.

[18]William Sprague (1830-1915), of Rhode Island, was a textile manufacturer. He was Unionist governor of his state, 1860-1861. After brief military service he was elected governor as a Democrat in 1862 and served until he was elected to the United States Senate, a post he held from 1863 until 1875. An heir to great wealth, Sprague was married to Kate Chase, daughter of Chief Justice Chase. Their marriage ended in scandal in 1882, and Sprague lived in retirement thereafter. *Biographical Directory of Congress*, 1640; *CDAB*, 990.

Robert C. Winthrop to William A. Graham A&H

6th. February, 1873.

This morning's Paper says a Bill for your relief has passed both Branches unanimously.

Let me express to you my great gratification.

I wrote to our friend Gov. Fish about it, and also to Senator (Vice-Pres't) Wilson,[1] long ago. I am sure it would have been done without my stir; but I remember saying to you at Danvers that [I] intended making an appeal, and I should be sorry to be thought to have neglected it.

Our Board of Trustees are now all "*recti in Curia*,"[2] as they ought to have been a great while sooner. I am heartily glad.

---

[1]Henry Wilson (1812-1875) of Massachusetts, apprentice farmer, teacher, state legislator, United States senator (1855-1873), and vice-president (1873-1875), was successively an antislavery Whig, a Free-Soiler, an American, and a Republican. An ardent foe of slavery, he urged Lincoln to emancipate Confederate slaves and actively promoted freedom for border state blacks before the Thirteenth Amendment was adopted. He was a Radical Republican who initially opposed bitterly Andrew Johnson's reconstruction plan; however, in time he became more conciliatory in his attitudes toward the South, probably because of long tours through the region. Throughout his public career, Wilson championed the cause of the workingman, black and white. In Massachusetts he promoted free schools and libraries for all. Although he had only a meager formal education, he was a voracious reader and a prolific writer. Sometime newspaper editor (the *Boston Republican*, 1848-1851), Wilson wrote seventeen books. Perhaps best known is *History of the Rise and Fall of Slave Power in America* (3 volumes, 1872-1877). *DAB*, XX, 322.

[2]"That which is good in a body of men," meaning in law a body that is properly constituted.

Salmon P. Chase to William A. Graham UNC

601 E W
Feb 10 1873

Dear Governor,

Gov. and Mrs. Lyman[1] will lunch very informally with us after Church, at 2 o'clock tomorrow. We, that is, Mrs. & Gov. Sprague & I, will be glad to have you join us. Will you come?

There are to be no other guests, & I write this note at the special request of Mrs. Sprague.

---

[1]This would logically be a reference to Theodore Lyman, who was one of the trustees of the Peabody Foundation, although Chase addresses him as "Gov." Lyman (1833-1897), a zoologist, was a native of Waltham, Massachusetts. He was educated at Harvard and after graduation in 1855 worked with Louis Agassiz in the Lawrence Scientific School there. He wrote many scientific articles and was one of the original trustees for the prestigious Museum of Comparative Zoology. He served one term in Congress, 1883-1885. *DAB*, XI, 519.

David A. Barnes[1] *to William A. Graham* UNC

(Confidential)
Jackson N.C.
Feb. 19th 1873

I regret very much that I could not have an interview with you during my recent visit to Raleigh. The following is briefly the subject upon which I wished to consult you.

I hear from a reliable source, that the company now having possession of the North Carolina Rail Road intend at an early day to change the guage of that road from Charlotte to the Company Shops. As a citizen of North Carolina and as one who is interested in another road having connection with that road, I am very desirous, if possible, to prevent such a change. I am also the counsel of parties who oppose the change. Knowing your feelings upon the subject and your intimate acquaintance with the history of the road, I write to ask if you think it can be prevented by injunction and whether the validity of the lease cannot in such a processing be brought in question?

If upon investigation you shall be of the opinion that the change of guage can be prevented and the lease of the road invalidated, I shall be pleased to retain your services in behalf of those whose interest I represent.

I shall be pleased to hear from you at an early day.

---

[1]David Alexander Barnes (1819-1892), of Northampton County, was a graduate of the University of North Carolina, read law with William Gaston, and enjoyed a successful practice. A Whig in politics, Barnes was a member of the House of Commons in 1844, 1846, and 1850 and was a delegate to the Constitutional Convention of 1861. He was an aide to Governor Vance during the Civil War. Afterward he was a superior court judge, 1865-1868. Barnes was elector on the Scott-Graham ticket in 1852, and Graham was probably a significant factor in his securing the appointment as Vance's aide. Spencer Alumni Project; McCormick, *Convention Personnel*, 16.

Bartholomew F. Moore to William A. Graham UNC

Raleigh, N.C.
March 17, 1873

I have been reading the paper you left with me on our parting, and I do not exactly comprehend your position. The mortgage left with me, is, I suppose, a copy of one executed in 1868. Please let me know whether the bonds then issued are part of those contemplated to be issued now. In other words, whether a new mortgage is to be executed or the old one is to cover those proposed now to be issued, also.

The late act passed by the Gen. Assem'y was introduced to favor the rascally combinations of Corporations by cutting off the stockholders (a minority of them). It was gotten up at the instance of the Raleigh & Gaston Railroad Co., through the honest high functionary of that company. The proviso was inserted in the Senate at the instance of Mr. Norwood & Mr. Morehead. I had sent in a bill to prevent new enterprises by corporations, and mortgages to secure the bonds issued to carry them on, without paying off the entire existing debt. Instead of passing my bill, this proviso was added. It was all N. &. M. I do [believe].

I certainly would do nothing to affect the credit of existing debts. My reliance as a creditor was based on the small am't of debt. I send you a copy of the mortgage. Please return it to me shortly.

Bartholomew F. Moore to William A. Graham UNC

Raleigh, N.C.
Mar. 21, 1873

I have yours and my information is much enlarged; Still, however, I should like to be informed as to the precise powers & where found, by which the company undertook to make any mortgage or trust deed. The mortgage you sent to me, speaks of a power in the Co to issue $1,500,000 of bonds. Does the Co Claim that power as a special grant under the charter, or as an exercise of a general power of obtaining money by contract?

Please let me hear from you on this point. I have looked at the charter.

The act of	1852.	ch	139
"	54	"	32
"	56	"	32

Is there any act besides—or any action of the stockholders.

I have some of the outstanding bonds, and have to day read the endorsement on them—penned doubtless to encourage Capitalists to invest. The address is very seductive; and the allurement would deserve great censure if violated without the consent of the bondholder. I remember well when your name was used to induce the old bondholders to surrender and reinvest, as both Mr. Mordecai & I did.

Stand on the safe side of inaction for the present is my advice now. I will write again shortly when I hear from you.

You did not return the act. I am inclined to think it checks the proposal.

Bartholomew F. Moore to William A. Graham UNC

Raleigh
73 Mar 31

I have yours of 25 Inst. I have considered the whole question in connection with the charter and resolutions of the stockholders. And I submit the following as my reasoning and conclusions.

Conceding that, unless prohibited, there exists in every corporation an incidental power to contract debts in furtherance of the object of its creation, it cannot be questioned that the Legislature, in the absence of any express grant to execute the power, may regulate the mode of exercising it. Thus, a corporation having the incidental power to contract a debt may be restrained by a law from contracting debts payable at a future day, or without an obligation in writing; or from contracting debts without providing at the time of the contracts, the means of payment. I suggest, in passing, that the act of 1856, Ch: 32 appears to me to be suggestive of the opinion, which the Legislature then entertained as to the extent of power possessed by the company, by virtue of its charter, in regard to the creation of debts.

It seems to me, that the action of the company, under the resolution of 1867, in issuing bonds to the amount of $800,000 under a mortgage made to cover a larger sum not then issued, may well be put beyond legislative control now, while the unexecuted part of the proposition may remain still under its regulation; Thus suppose the Gen. Assy had expressly enacted, that no debts of a corporation, which were not then contracted, should be secured by mortgage; such an act would have affected the proposed issue of the new bonds, and would not have impaired contracts or divested vested rights.

It is by no means absurd to hold, that the attempt to spread the cover of the mortgage of 1867 over new debts created in 1873, and thus place the old debts upon the same footing of payment with the new ones, is in derogation of the spirit and intent of the late act which I sent to you; and especially is it not, when we read the seductive pledge of ability held out to the purchasers of the old bonds, by endorsing on them for the special eye of the capitalist. *"Length of the Raod 223 miles, value of the property $5,000,000. Bonds issued for $800,000 only"*

But let us turn to the resolution of the Stockholders at their meeting in 1867, under the authority of which it is now proposed to issue another batch of bonds to the amount of $700,000. That resolution declares the purpose and object of issuing bonds to be *"to pay off present liabilities and make further improvements."*

Certainly, the objects are fairly defined. To issue bonds for the purpose of raising money to speculate in state bonds is a gross departure from the object contemplated by the resolution. But, in my opinion, any resolution of the Stockholders distinctly embracing such a purpose would have been wholly unauthorized by the charter, & *ultra vires.*[1]

The corporation may create a sinking fund as incidental to its power to borrow money for accomplishing the objects of its creation; and to this end honestly pursued, may buy state bonds with its profits. But it has not the power to become a trader and speculator in stocks, or bonds. It has no power to acquire stock in its own, or in any other, corporation; or to buy land, unless needed for the purpose of accomplishing the Ends for which it was established. . . .

If the company have profits it is required to divide them among the Stockholders. S. 35 charter. If the corporation may embark in one kind of speculation not contemplated in its charter, it may enter the *world of business.*

In my judgment, every stockholder is the fellow of every other: all standing on the basis of one contract between them, as a unit, and the State, and severally between each other, and that any combination of the members, to pervert that contract from its legitimate meaning is a fraud on the state; and that any combination by a majority of the members to violate the contract against the wishes of the others is a fraud on the minority.

I never saw the mortgage until you sent it to me. I have always regarded the endorsement on my bonds, as giving me assurance on which the utmost reliance might be placed for the security of the investment.

In conclusion, I am of opinion, that the issue of bonds for the purpose proposed is

1. Unauthorized by the resolutions of 1867 & 1868.
2. Is, in respect to the charter, *ultra vires.*
3. And its object being known to you, who are both trustee and stockholder, your duty requires you to protect the bondholder, the State and your fellow members by opposing the proposition.

I feel complimented by your asking my advice in this delicate matter, and I have ventured to give it; but not until after duly considering the whole matter.

---

[1]Beyond bounds; beyond the scope of the powers of a corporation as defined by its charter.

James Grant to William A. Graham UNC

Davenport, Iowa,
April 6th., 1873.

The graduating Class of 1831 at Chapel Hill, will meet here on the 10 June to digest a project proposed by a member of the Class, Josiah Williamson,[1] of Memphis, to revive the University.

The Tarboro Enquirer has brought the subject to your attention.

We shall be glad to have you and Mrs. G. present, at Davenport, as it is attended with an interesting period in our lives, the occasion of our silver wedding. The meeting here is to give form and consistency to the project to be presented to all the Alumni & by them to the Legislature next Winter. The Tarboro Enquirer will probably next week have a letter from me, on the subject.

Invite any of the Alumni who will come, to join us in June.

[1]Grant erred in the name. This was no doubt James Monroe Williamson (1810-1877), of Caswell County. At this time he was a resident of Memphis, Tennessee, and a railroad president. Grant, *Alumni History*, 679.

Maurice Q. Waddell[1] *to William A. Graham* UNC

Pittsboro, N.C.
May 16th 1873
In superior court

During this week someone told me you had been troubled at times with sudden attacks of chills of a congestive character. Now let me tell you what is the matter with you it is digestion, its your Stomach *thats Riching* up about the food you eat. I have been troubled in the same way for years, and once it brought on such vertigo that I fell flat on the ground and could not walk for 3 or 4 hours. It comes on sometimes with this giddy feeling, sometimes with violent pain in the *pit* of the Stomach followed by a chill and fever and pain in the back and limbs. I tried Calomel Blue pill Scrinmores regulator and all the remedies usual on such occasions by the Drs and derived only temporary relief I then resolved to try the simplest of all remedies. *Raw onions* and eat them at every meal, and if you will do the same it will Cure you entirely. They stimulate the stomach and will eject from it every thing offensive and restore a healthy action, try it.

[1]Maurice Quince Waddell (d. 1888) was a student at the university, 1821-1822. A native of Pittsboro, he was clerk and master in equity in Chatham County and served in the General Assembly in 1846. Grant, *Alumni History*, 639.

Wilson G. Richardson[1] *to William A. Graham* UNC

Davidson College,
June 6th., 1873.

I am quite sure there is no more effectual way of catching your ear than by telling you of some manner in which you can promote the interests of the dear old North State,—yes, Sir, dear to *me* as well as to you. If there is not Mecklenburg Declaration blood in my own veins, there is at least in the veins of my children. My three youngest first saw the light *here*. My father in law, the Rev. Mr. Kennon, (See Appleton's New Am. Cyclop.) was a native of North Carolina, and a kinsman of William Kennon,[2] Esq., one of the illustrious Committee of three that drafted the Declaration of the 20th. of May, 1775.

Now, Governor, don't say me nay. Time presses as you see, & there is *no* time for you to do aught but sit down—yes, you of all other men in North Carolina, and write the article in question and forward it at once to my friend, Dr. Barnard,[3] Editor in Chief of Johnson's Illustrated Cyclopaedia. Barnard is one of the most learned and able men in this country. I have long known him, having been associated with him in the University of Alabama, my old Alma Mater, & the Univ. of Miss., at Oxford. He is now Pres't of

Columbia College, New York City. He was an old line whig, & used to be very much interested in national politics, at a time when your name was as familiar far away in the far S. West, as "household words."

I want a *live* name put to such a paper in a work which I am satisfied will be widely circulated and which will tell upon public sentiment, North and South. These brethren whom I have consulted, say Gov. Graham—by all means, Governor Graham. Do not refuse me. You are the very man best qualified to do it, most acceptable to our people everywhere, & then again *delay*, & the opportunity is lost. It will be too late for me to secure the services of another.

Will you do me the favor of replying very promptly to this, and return to me Dr. B's letter.

I hope I have not failed to impress you with the deep interest we feel in your *acceptance*. I shall, myself, regard it as a very great personal favor.

---

[1]Wilson Gaines Richardson (1825-1888), a native of Kentucky and a graduate of the University of Alabama, went to Davidson College as a professor from the University of Mississippi in 1866. During the Civil War he had served as a Confederate paymaster. In later years he went to Central University in Kentucky and then to Austin College, Texas. He became a Presbyterian minister. Brown, *Cyclopedia of American Biographies*, VI, 574.

[2]William Kennon, of Virginia, was only a visitor but was said to have been invited as a matter of courtesy to a seat in the convention. John Brevard Alexander, *The History of Mecklenburg County* (Charlotte: Observer Printing House, 1902), 416, hereinafter cited as Alexander, *History of Mecklenburg County*.

Another author, Worth S. Ray, notes that Kennon was reportedly a native of Virginia who was "a prominent lawyer and wealthy citizen" of Rowan County. There is agreement that he was a member of Rowan's committee of safety in 1774. Ray believes that Kennon lived in Mecklenburg County near the Rowan County line and that the patriots of neither county made much of Kennon's actual residence. Worth S. Ray, *The Mecklenburg Signers and Their Neighbors* (1946; Baltimore: Genealogical Publishing Company, [1966]), 421, hereinafter cited as Ray, *Mecklenburg Signers*.

[3]Frederick Augustus Porter Barnard (1809-1889), a graduate of Yale (1828), was active in education in Alabama and Mississippi, 1837-1861. From 1864 to 1889 he was president of Columbia University. He promoted an elective system of studies and, after 1879, urged the admission of women on an equal basis with men. Ironically, as a result of his efforts Barnard College opened within six months after his death. *CDAB*, 49; *Who Was Who*, 41.

T. H. Selby[1] *to William A. Graham* [with enclosure]

UNC

Raleigh, N.C.,
June 7th., 1873.

As shown by the inclosed circular, an Educational Convention will be held in this City on the 9th. and 10th. of July.

I am instructed by the Committee of arrangements to inform [you] that it is their unanimous wish that you preside as President of the Convention.

I can assure you that this unanimous wish of the Committee is seconded by the friends of education throughout the State.

Allow me to add my personal solicitation that you will be present.

---

[1]T. H. Selby was a longtime resident of Raleigh. He was a member of the board of

directors for the Raleigh Methodist Female Seminary, 1855, and he helped to organize the Raleigh Mutual Relief and Charitable Association, which provided relief for the needy in 1863 and 1864. Murray, *Wake*, 314, 485.

[Enclosure]
Convention Circular

Educational Convention.

A Convention of the friends of education will be held in the city of Raleigh, on the 9th. and 10th. days of July, 1873. An effort will be made to secure free return tickets on all Railroads in the State. The Mayor[1] and Commissioners of the city have offered the use of the Metropolitan Hall for the Convention, and the citizens of Raleigh have tendered their hospitalities, and a cordial welcome, to all teachers, examiners, and other friends of education, to hold their Convention in the city of Raleigh.

The Convention will be organized at 10 a.m. Wednesday. To give time for the thorough discussion of the several topics presented, the papers introducing them should be short, not occupying more than thirty minutes.

Subjects Presented.

"The Teacher," By Rev. B. Craven,[2] D.D., President of Trinity College.
"Higher Education in North Carolina," By Major Robert Bingham, Principal of the Bingham School.
"The Relation of the Churches to Public Education," By W. G. Simmons,[3] Professor of Mathematics in Wake Forest College.
"The Necessity for Universal Public Education," By Hon. A. S. Merrimon.
"Compulsory Education," By James H. Horner,[4] Principal of Oxford High School.
"How Shall the Girls Be Educated," By A. F. Redd,[5] Co-Principal of the Raleigh Female Seminary.
"Industrial Education," By John W. Norwood, Esq.

Delegates will please forward their names to some one of the undersigned Committee of Arrangements on or before the fifth day of July. For the information of such as may prefer to stop at a public house, notice is given that the delegates will be entertained at the National Hotel, and the Yarboro House at $1.50, and at the Exchange Hotel and Mrs. Pullen's at $1. per day.

T. H. Selby,
W. E. Anderson,[6]
A. M. McPheeters,[7]
J. H. Mills.[8]
Committee of Arrangements.

June 9th., 1873.

[1]Wesley Whitaker, Jr., was mayor of Raleigh, 1872-1874. Murray, *Wake*, appendix D.

[2]The Reverend Braxton Craven (1822-1882), of Randolph County, was the first president of Trinity College (now Duke University), having begun his career when the university's forerunner was known as Union Institute. According to the Reverend D. V. York, Craven

was the son of Ann Craven and Braxton York. From age seven until he was sixteen, Craven lived with the family of Nathan Cox. Determined to be a teacher, Craven, through his own effort, mastered the course of study prescribed for a bachelor's degree at Randolph-Macon and was awarded an honorary degree. He used his facile mind and versatile talents in a life devoted to education and to the Methodist church. Powell, *DNCB*, I, 455-456.

[3]William Gaston Simmons (1830-1889) was a graduate of Wake Forest and later was a professor there. Although he was a lawyer by training, Simmons became a teacher of mathematics. Grant, *Alumni History*, 565.

[4]James Hunter Horner (1822-1892), an 1844 graduate of the university, was founder and principal of the Horner School in Oxford. During the Civil War he had served as captain of the Twenty-third North Carolina Regiment. Horner was a university trustee from 1885 until 1892. Powell, *DNCB*, III, 206.

[5]Alexander Fletcher Redd, a native of Virginia, was educated at Virginia Military Institute. After some years of teaching at Horner School, Redd became editor of the *Biblical Recorder* (Raleigh). Upon the reopening of the university, he was appointed to the faculty and given charge of physics and chemistry. Battle, *History of the University*, II, 81.

[6]William E. Anderson (d. 1890) was a native of Wilmington and a graduate of the university in 1854. He was one of the organizers of an effort by the Oak City Guards to establish a library in Raleigh in 1856. During the Civil War he was colonel of the Thirty-eighth North Carolina Regiment. After the war he resided in Raleigh and was the first president of the Raleigh Board of Trade. He was a successful businessman and president of the Citizen's National Bank. Grant, *Alumni History*, 13; Murray, *Wake*, 334, 466, 467, 574, 589n.

[7]A. M. McPheeters was the son of William McPheeters, minister of the Presbyterian Church in Raleigh. He was clerk of the Council of State in 1864 and was on the Raleigh Board of Trade in 1871. Cheney, *North Carolina Government*, 180; Murray, *Wake*, 574.

[8]John Haymes Mills (1831-1898) was graduated from Wake Forest College, after which he became editor of the *Biblical Recorder*. He was the first superintendent of the Oxford Orphan Asylum but left Oxford in 1884 to become the first general manager of the Thomasville Orphanage, which was known as the Mills Home. Carmine Andrews Prioli, "The Indian 'Princess' and the Architect: Origin of a North Carolina Legend," *North Carolina Historical Review*, LX (July, 1983), 288n.

Alexander H. H. Stuart to William A. Graham UNC

Staunton, Virginia,
June 16th., 1873.

I have learned, unofficially, from Dr. Sears, that the 16th. of July, is the day appointed for the meeting of the Peabody Board, in N.Y. I hope you will be able to attend, & if so, I would like to know when you will leave home, & by what route you will go. I should like to join you, either in Richmond, Washington, or Baltimore, & travel with you to New York.

Will any of your family accompany you? I propose to take my only surviving son, who is now 15 years of age. I wish him to see something of the world, before he goes to Hampden Sydney College this fall. My family will be very much gratified if Miss Susie would make us a visit this summer. I cannot promise to exhibit to her a very promising set of beaux in this part of the State, but I presume that would be a matter of no moment, as I suspect she has made a selection nearer home.

I received a letter from Judge Hall[1] a few days ago, making inquiry as to the time of our meeting, & expressing the hope that Mr. & Mrs. Hall might be able to be in New York at the same time.

Please let me know your arrangements, & whether it is probable that we can agree on some place of meeting.

I also ask the favor of you to present to Mrs. Graham & Miss Susie & Mr. Augustus my kind remembrances.

Very truly your friend,

[1]Nathan Kelsey Hall.

Frederick A. P. Barnard to William A. Graham UNC

Columbia College
New York

President's Room,
June 17, 1873.

My friend, Prof. Richardson, of Davidson College, has forwarded to me your letter addressed to him on the subject of the Mecklenburg Declaration of Independence, which informs me, to my gratification, that you are willing to prepare an article on the historical questions connected with that Declaration for the purpose which he explained to you. It will be quite practicable to arrange for the publication of such an article under the head Mecklenburg, which will not be reached in the course of our work before January or February next.

In order to explain how it happened that, when the call was made on Prof. Richardson, the time within which the article would be needed was stated as so limited, it is necessary to say that, at the time I undertook the principal editorship of the Cyclopedia, a large portion of the first volume had been already prepared; and that I only undertook the proposed responsibility on the condition that I should be permitted to reconstruct such portions of the work already done, as were not satisfactory to me. I found that the Declaration of Independence of the Delegates of the thirteen Colonies at Philadelphia had been inserted in full; but that no mention whatever had been made of the Mecklenburg Declaration. I desired to repair this omission, and that seemed to be the proper place to do it; but as the book was nearly ready for the press, it appeared that whatever we should undertake to do, ought to be done at once. It was, of course, possible for us to prepare the necessary historical notice here, from books; but I far preferred that it should be done by a citizen of N. Carolina, and therefore I applied to my friend Richardson.

I have now resolved to print the Declaration of the 20th. May, 1775, and some of the resolutions of May 31, 1775, immediately after the Declaration of the Continental Congress; and to refer for the discussion of the historical questions to the article Mecklenburg, in Vol. 2. And this discussion, I infer from your letter to Prof. Richardson, that you will do us the favor to supply.

As at the time I received from Prof. R. the letter above referred to, the publisher, Mr. Johnson,[1] had just sent me a proof sheet of the list of contributors secured for our work thus far, I could not resist the temptation to add your name to the list. If in this I have been too hasty, I will withdraw it, but I trust you will allow it to remain. I inclose a copy of this list, which you will observe to embrace some very eminent names in letters and in Science.

[1]This possibly was Rossiter Johnson (b. 1840), native of Rochester, New York. Educated at the University of Rochester, he was from 1873 to 1877 associated with editing the *American Encyclopedia*. In 1883 he became editor of the *Annual Encyclopedia*. His other work included planning and editing the popular *Little Classics*, 1874-1875. His wife, Helen Kendricks Johnson, was a well-known contributor to various periodicals. *Appleton's Cyclopædia*, III, 447-448.

Hamilton Fish to William A. Graham UNC

Department of State
Washington, June 18th, 1873

Volumes 1, 2, 3 and 4, of the "Papers Relating to the *Treaty of Washington*" which were transmitted to Congress with the President's Message in December last, are sent to your address by mail this day. These volumes contain all of such papers as relate to the Geneva Arbitration. Volume 5 contains the papers relating to the Arbitration at Berlin and will be sent when received from the Printer.

A form of receipt is enclosed which you are requested to sign and return.

Wilson G. Richardson to William A. Graham UNC

Davidson College, North Carolina.
June 19th., 1873.

Dr. Barnard sends under whip and spur to me for an article on
Gen. Wm. Lee Davidson[1]
and the passage at Cowan's Ford. Where can I get the materials for such an article?

Can you yourself furnish me with any dates, names, facts, incidents, etc., that would serve my purpose? B. says I must be *quick*, that the last vol. *presses*. He is delighted that you will contribute an article for his 2d. vol.,—knows all about you.

I saw your son, Dr. Jo., in Charlotte yesterday. He is my consulting physician. He says he will send you something to break up those chills. He is delighted to hear that you have consented to touch up the Mecklenburg matter. It will doubtless be so viewed by every body.

[1]William Lee Davidson (ca. 1746-1781), born in Lancaster County, Pennsylvania, was the son of George Davidson, who moved his family in 1750 to that part of Rowan County that is now Iredell. William Lee Davidson married Mary Brevard, daughter of John Brevard. In 1776 Davidson was commissioned major of the Fourth Regiment of the North Carolina provincial troops under General Francis Nash. He was promoted to lieutenant colonel after the battle at Germantown. He participated in the battles of the North until

1779, when he was ordered south to reinforce Benjamin Lincoln at Charleston. Delayed en route, he was unable to rejoin his regiment, so Davidson returned to Mecklenburg to assist the militia in that area and received a severe wound in the battle at Colson's Mill. He was appointed brigadier general of the Salisbury district and deployed bands of patriots to harass Cornwallis's troops in the Charlotte area. On February 1, 1781, Davidson was killed at the Battle of Cowan's Ford. Joseph Graham, father of William A. Graham, served as captain under Davidson at Cowan's Ford. Davidson County and Davidson College were named in his honor. Ashe, *Biographical History*, IV, 124-128; Powell, *DNCB*, II, 27-28; C. B. Alexander, "Richard Caswell's Military and Later Public Services," *North Carolina Historical Review*, XXIII (July, 1946), 295.

Robert C. Winthrop to William A. Graham UNC

Brookline, Mass.
1 July 1873

I have been absent from home nearly a month past. Before going, I fixed the 16th of July for the Annual Meeting of the Peabody Trustees at New York, after consultation with Dr. Sears, Prest. Grant, & a few others, agreeably to the vote at our last meeting.

I wrote at once to our Secretary to issue the formal notifications, & recd. his promise to do so. I trust he has already repaired the omission, & that you may have received your notification ere this. But I am unwilling to take the risk, & therefore write to say that I hope nothing will prevent your being with us at the 5th Avenue Hotel on the 16th inst. at 12 o'clk.

We need not have a long meeting. But in addition to the usual routine of business, we must fill good Bishop McIlvaine's place.

I hear Genl. Taylor[1] is in Europe. I wrote to him in May, but had no reply.

Do not fail of letting us see *you*.

With kind remembrances to your daughter.

[1]Richard Taylor.

Wilson G. Richardson to William A. Graham UNC

Davidson College, N.C.,
July 4th., 1873.

Your esteemed favor of the 23rd. ult. has been received and I am very thankful to you for the valuable suggestions contained in it. I am particularly interested in the diploma of which you speak, and shall endeavor to procure it for the College.

Dr. Barnard is exceedingly anxious to get a contribution from your pen. He evidently wants it for his first volume. At least I so judge. At least he says he now finds he could have given you till 1st. August.

Goodloe[1] et id genus omne[2] try one's patience very much and make me long for such an antidote as you are to furnish. B. will be glad to have you do just as you please.

[1]Daniel R. Goodloe had published a paper in the *New York Herald*, June 14, 1873, rejecting the authenticity of the Mecklenburg Declaration of May 20, 1775.

[2]"And all of his kind."

William A. Graham to Susan Washington Graham A&H

5th Av. Hotel NY
July 18th 1873

My Dear Wife;

I drop this line before leaving N.Y. on the Albany Boat this morning.

Our Trustees all attended the first day except Gov. Aiken detained by the sickness of his wife and Genl Taylor who was absent in Europe. The Prest U.S. came up from Long Branch in the morning, and returned at 4 in the afternoon, did not come back the next day.

No ladies came except Mrs. Eaton[1] of Baltimore, and two daughters of Mr. Watson[2] of Tennessee, and the formal dinner of such occasions became an informal one. Surgeon Genl. Barnes[3] of the Army U.S. was elected to fill the vacancy of Bishop McIlvaine.

I have been out but little. Went down to Stewarts on the morning after my arrival, and have seen no acquaintences except the Dickeys,[4] who called yesterday, and insisted that I should go and spend some days with them. I may do so on my return for one day. My health is rather improved, but I find it necessary to be careful—have had no symptoms of chill, but still feel the debility in the chest.

Mr. Stuart, his son, Robt & I had a delightful ride through the Central Park yesterday afternoon, and stopped to see the confined animals. Augus. Knox has been very kind. Henry[5] is out of town. Tell Sudie that all the board have inquired with great interest about her.

I must hasten off.

Ever Affectionately yours,

[1]Mrs. George N. Eaton.

[2]Mr. Watson has not been further identified.

[3]Joseph K. Barnes (1817-1883) was a veteran of the Seminole, Mexican, and Civil wars. In 1864 he was appointed surgeon general of the army. Barnes was the attending physician of both Lincoln and Garfield at their deaths. *CDAB*, 49.

[4]Charles Denslow and Mary Sophia Witherspoon Dickey.

[5]The Knox family was associated with the Grahams through the 1840 marriage of Mrs. Graham's sister Elizabeth Heritage Washington (1808-1890) to Dr. Reuben Knox (d. 1851). Dr. Augustus Washington Knox (1849-1936) was their youngest child. Henry Knox is mentioned occasionally in the correspondence, but his exact relationship to the Grahams is not clear. Clark, "Washington Descendants."

William A. Graham to Susan Washington Graham A&H

Congress Hall
Saratoga Springs
July 22nd 1873

My Dear Wife

We came from N.Y. on Boat to West Point, thence by car to this place, arriving about 7 p.m.—find about 600 guests at this House, the others not making a very good season. Mr. & Mrs. E. J. Hale are here. . . . I have not many acquaintances in the crowd. Dr. Welling[1] of Washington, called to see me today from the Clarendon. The Hotels are all much enlarged, and there are boarding houses without number. This village is now swelling up to 9,000 inhabitants.

I have had no chill since leaving home. Took quinine up to my arrival here—have taken a little blue mess every night since I came. Drink the Congress water in the morning and Hamilton in the after part of the day. My appetite is pretty good, my strength has not returned as I had hoped, and water is not so active as I expected. I shall probably remain till the first of next week, and then return home. Robt. in the mean time will probably go to Niagara which can be reached in a day from here. We have heard nothing from Anna[2] and family, and nothing from home except your letter containing Mary Dickeys. Mrs. Weston Gales[3] with a grown son was here when I came, and remained till yesterday. She had improved and her family are doing well. The Hales sit with me at table, and are pleasant company. I am not likely to extend my circle of my acquaintance much. I write with a bad pen and ink and am ashamed to send this, but it may come 24 hours sooner than one I may write tomorrow.

My love to Sudie and Augus, if he has returned.

Ever Affectionately yours,

Please have the turnip patch prepared. I cannot remember any further suggestions.

---

[1]James Clark Welling.

[2]It seems likely that this is a reference to Anna White Constable Washington (1813-1894) of New York City, the widow of Mrs. Graham's brother Dr. James Augustus Washington (1803-1847). Clark, "Washington Descendants."

[3]Mrs. Gales was the widow of Weston Raleigh Gales (1802-1848). A son of Joseph Gales, founder in 1799 of the *Raleigh Register,* Weston Gales followed his father as the paper's editor. His brother Joseph, Jr., was proprietor, with William W. Seaton, of the influential *National Intelligencer.* The Galeses were active throughout their adult lives in Raleigh's civic affairs. Weston Gales was mayor and represented Wake County in the state legislature. Powell, *DNCB,* II, 268, 269.

Lewis Ashmead[1] *to William A. Graham* UNC

Kennett Square
Chester County Penna.
July 22, 1873

I write on behalf of parties of wealth and standing here, to inquire whether you have resumed the practice of the law since the war. If so we would like to retain you in an important case against the North Carolina Railway & if we can have the benefit of your *personal* services are willing to pay the most liberal fees. We will also employ an attorney of record to look after the docket etc. if you prefer.

Please advise me at your earliest convenience & pray consider my proposition as *strictly confidential* for the present.

As I am at my country seat, please direct your letter of reply according to the somewhat voluminous address on the next page.

Address me at "Cedarcroft."
(near) Kennett Square P.O.
Chester County
Pennsylvania.

[1]Lewis Ashmead has not been identified.

William A. Graham to Susan Washington Graham A&H

Congress Hall, Saratoga
July 26th 1873

My Dearest

Robt returned from Niagara this morning, having spent last night at Schenectady, found only Lizzie & Kate at home. The rest gone to visit Susan,[1] some 40 miles off.

The company is much increased in two or three days past in Saratoga—the races being on hand. Jas. Bryan[2] & Mrs. Shepard[3] are at the Grand Hotel. Gov. & Mrs. Aiken at private boarding. Judge Walker[4] of Ala., a friend of mine likewise here.

I called, but found them all not at home—have met the gentlemen of the parties, but not the ladies. Prest Porter[5] of Yale College I find quite an agreeable person, but of indifferent presence. I make but few acquaintances in this company, but find myself and Mr. Porter in the "Daily Saratogan" among the committee to arrange the Ball last night.

My health is improved, but I am not strong, I take the water regularly—have ceased quinine, and till this moment did not remember that tomorrow will be the 28th day since my last chill.

I except to leave this place on Monday 28th. and stop but one day in N.Y. on the journey home. There is such a grand display every moment, and such a change of scene and of company, that it has great attractions.

I wish you could see the magnificence of its present appearance. The newspaper announcement of my being here, has revived the remembrance of me in the country and I hope will bring me a good fee from Phila. I see in a N.C. paper, that George and our new daughter[6] have arrived. Give them my love and congratulations.

Hoping soon to see you and with love to all at home.

Ever Affectionately yours

I saw Morrisey,[7] the great pugillist, at the Spring this morning. He has a splendid gambling house, close by; and the races, no doubt, furnish many pigeons to be plucked.

---

[1]This reference was to the daughters of Mrs. Graham's brother, Dr. James Augustus Washington (1803-1847) of New York City. Elizabeth Washington (1836-1921) and Catherine Beeckman Washington (1847-1914) never married. Susannah Washington (1846-1920) married the Reverend Clarence Backus (1845-1920); they had seven children. Clark, "Washington Descendants."

[2]James A. Bryan (1839-1923) was the son of the James West Bryans of New Bern and the nephew of the Grahams. Clark, "Graham Descendants."

[3]Mrs. Shepard has not been identified, but she may have been James A. Bryan's mother-in-law. Bryan was married to Mary Shepard (1843-1892) in 1864. Clark, "Washington Descendants."

[4]Leroy Pope Walker (1817-1884), Confederate secretary of war, was a native of Huntsville, Alabama. A son of John Williams and Maria Pope Walker, he attended the University of Alabama and was graduated by the University of VIrginia. He began his law practice in Mississippi but soon returned to Alabama, where he had a distinguished career as a legislator and jurist. Walker was state solicitor and Speaker of the House (1847-1850). In 1850 he was elected judge of the circuit court and at that time he moved to Huntsville. He resigned his judgeship in 1853 to become more active in politics. An avid secessionist, Walker was inexperienced in handling an administrative position; this proved a great handicap to him as secretary of war and he was severely criticized in Congress. Eventually he resigned. After the war he resumed his very lucrative practice of law. *DAB*, XIX, 351-352.

[5]Noah Porter (1811-1892), a native of Connecticut, was educated at Farmington Academy and Yale College. After graduation he became a rector at Hopkins Grammar School, New Haven, then tutored at Yale for two years while he was studying with Nathaniel Taylor in the divinity school. Porter served pastorates in New Milford, Connecticut, and Springfield, Massachusetts, before he returned to Yale as Clark Professor of Moral Philosophy and Metaphysics. He gained an international reputation as a scholar and writer, with the D.D. degree bestowed on him in 1886 by the University of Edinburgh. For fifteen years (1871-1886) Porter was president of Yale College. He was very conservative in his educational philosophy but was renowned for his "penetrating, sound" scholarship. *DAB*, XV, 97-99.

[6]In 1873 George W. Graham married Sallie S. Shaver of Atlanta, Georgia. She died in 1887 and was survived by three children. Graham's second wife was Alice Leonora Alexander of Charlotte. After her death in 1905, he married Imogene Tunstall. Clark, "Graham Descendants."

[7]John Morrissey (1831-1878) was a prizefighter and gambler who owned a casino in Saratoga. He served in Congress, 1867-1871, and in the New York Senate. *DAB*, XIII, 233-234.

Seaton Gales to William A. Graham A&H

Raleigh, N.C.,
August 23rd., 1873.

It has afforded me very great pleasure to make the researches requested in your favor of the 20th. I reply *seriatim*:

1. The publication in the Register of April 30, (not April 19,) 1819, is signed by "Joseph McKnitt,"[1] and sets forth Resolutions which are identically the same as those prefixed to the Revised Code.

2. Following the publication referred to *is* the Proclamation of Gov. Martin,[2] of Oct. 3, 1780.

3. The paper in the Register of Feb. 18, 1820, sets forth no resolutions nor does it mention the receipt of any by Dr. Henderson[3] from the family of Gen. Davie. It is simply a communication from Col. Polk,[4] prefixing a certificate, signed by "Geo. Graham,[5] Wm. Hutchison,[6] Jonas Clark,[7] and Robt. Robison,"[8] setting forth that they were present at the meeting in Charlotte, on the 20th. of May, 1775, and that the previously published Resolutions (April 30, 1819) were the same as those then and there adopted. Substantially, if not literally, this is their statement.

4. Supplementing this certificate, is a letter from Jno. Simison,[9] "Providence, R.I., Jan. 20, 1820," to Col. Polk, sustaining the general accuracy of the previous publications.

5. The Editorials on the subject are few and brief. One, however, of Aug., 1819, alluding to the forthcoming publications of Col. Polk, expresses the decided opinion "that no doubts can ever exist as to the truth and genuineness" of the Declaration of May 20.

I have only answered your enquiries categorically, not knowing whether you cared for details. I am entirely at your service for any further investigations, and I hope that you will not hesitate to command my offices. I view, with equal surprise and regret, the unfilial and unaccountable attempts that are being made to strip the laurels from the brow of the State, and I hope that it is your purpose to come to her aid.

Trusting that your usual good health may be speedily and entirely restored, I am,

---

[1]Dr. Joseph McKnitt Alexander (1774-1841) of Mecklenburg County was a graduate of Princeton. His son, Moses Winslow Alexander (1798-1845), was also a doctor and married Violet Graham, a sister to William A. Graham. To distinguish him from his son, and because Alexander was a common name in Mecklenburg, the father sometimes was referred to as Dr. McKnitt, and he often used the abbreviated signature J. McKnitt. John Hill Wheeler, *Reminiscences and Memoirs of North Carolina* (1884; Baltimore: Genealogical Publishing Company, 1966), 268, hereinafter cited as Wheeler, *Reminiscences*; see also William A. Graham to James C. Welling, December 31, 1873, in this volume.

The Mecklenburg Declaration was first published in the *Raleigh Register* of April 30, 1819, from a manuscript provided by Joseph McKnitt Alexander and left by his father, John McKnitt Alexander. Richard N. Current, "That Other Declaration: May 20, 1775-May 20, 1975," *North Carolina Historical Review*, LIV (April, 1977), 170, hereinafter cited as Current, "That Other Declaration."

[2]Josiah Martin (1737-1786), the last royal governor of North Carolina, was born in Antigua, the West Indies. He resigned from the British army because of physical frailty,

but he accepted a commission as governor of North Carolina in December, 1770. He arrived at a time when the colonies were growing increasingly unhappy over restrictions imposed by the British government, and he found it hard to deal with the North Carolina colonial assembly. When revolt of the colonies seemed inevitable, Martin promoted a plan by which the North Carolina Regulators and loyalists might cooperate with British forces to quell the rebellion. His plan did not materialize and Martin was forced to board a British warship to escape. Later, he went with Cornwallis on two expeditions and was present in North Carolina at the Battle of Guilford Court House. After the Revolution he returned to England, where he died. Ashe, *Biographical History*, III, 269-273.

[3]Dr. Samuel Henderson, clerk of the superior court of Mecklenburg County, was said to have obtained the Davie copy of the Mecklenburg Declaration from a son of William R. Davie. John McKnitt Alexander had given the copy to General Davie. Henderson on November 25, 1830, published a statement asserting that he and Joseph McKnitt [Alexander] had obtained the copy from Major William Davie, the son, after the death of General Davie. LeGette Blythe and Charles R. Brockmann, *Hornet's Nest: The Story of Charlotte and Mecklenburg County* (Charlotte: McNally of Charlotte, 1961), 53, 54, hereinafter cited as Blythe and Brockmann, *Hornet's Nest*; William Henry Hoyt, *The Mecklenburg Declaration of Independence: A Study of Evidence Showing That the Alleged Early Declaration of Independence by Mecklenburg County, North Carolina, on May 20th, 1775, Is Spurious* (New York: G. P. Putnam's Sons, 1907), 169; Current, "That Other Declaration," 175.

[4]William Polk, identified earlier in this volume and the son of reputed Mecklenburg Declaration signer Thomas Polk, countered doubt about the authenticity of the document by collecting and publishing testimony from several persons who said they were present at the 1775 Charlotte meeting that produced the resolutions. Current, "That Other Declaration," 170.

[5]George Graham (1757-1826), brother of General Joseph Graham, was born in Pennsylvania and moved with his family to Mecklenburg County at the age of nine. He was a patriot in the Revolution and took part in the Cherokee expedition of 1776, as well as being an active member of the militia in the military actions in South Carolina and North Carolina. He was an ensign, First North Carolina Regiment, until he was promoted to second lieutenant on January 4, 1776. He resigned in April, 1776, to become a captain of the North Carolina Rangers. After the war Graham was elected major general of the North Carolina militia. He held various offices, including sheriff, 1786-1792; member of the House of Commons, 1792-1794, 1796, and 1803-1812; and clerk of superior court, 1816-1825. C. L. Hunter, *Sketches of Western North Carolina, Historical and Biographical . . .* (1877; Baltimore: Genealogical Publishing Company, 1970), 98-99, hereinafter cited as Hunter, *Sketches of Western North Carolina*; Heitman, *Historical Register of Continental Officers*, 255.

[6]William Hutchison (1750-1823), born in Augusta County, Virginia, moved to Mecklenburg in 1774. He was commissary officer in Colonel William Polk's regiment during the Snow campaign in 1775, a lieutenant in John Rutherford's brigade in 1778, and a captain in Polk's regiment in 1781; in private life he was a highly respected citizen in his community. Tompkins, *History of Mecklenburg*, 74-75.

[7]Jonas Clark (1759-1846), a native of Pennsylvania, came with his parents to Mecklenburg County in 1771. He undertook military service and served ably in Georgia, South Carolina, and North Carolina in opposing the British. Tompkins, *History of Mecklenburg*, 68-69.

[8]Robert Robinson (1751-1839) was born in Lancaster County, Pennsylvania, and moved with his family to Mecklenburg County at an early age. During the American Revolution he sought to defend the region against Cornwallis, taking part in the battles at Hanging Rock, Ramsour's Mill, Charlotte, and "McIntyre's." Tompkins, *History of Mecklenburg*, 81.

[9]John Simison has not been identified.

William A. Graham to William A. Graham, Jr. A&H

Catawba Springs[1]
Aug. 28th 1873

We arrived here last Saturday about 9 o'clock travelling 7 miles by stage from Hickory. I bore the whole journey very well—have slept in the main very soundly, and have a pretty good appetite. The water is a very pleasant sulphur water, and very light. I think I have gained strength, but am not relieved of a shortness of breath, with which I have been troubled.

The company, Kemp Battle, Edwin Holt[2] & families, Mrs. Boyden,[3] several persons from Charlotte, S.C., etc., is very agreeable. Many however are leaving. We will stay till Monday next. I had intended to go on Tuesday to Lincolnton, and thence to Cleaveland, but your mother has a desire to see the mountains, and we may go to Morganton, and Asheville first. . . .

Many Eastern people are at Hicky. the board being cheaper than here, and are strewed along in the mountains. George writes us from Ral. that he left Mrs. Faucett[4] whose eye he had taken out for cancer, before we left home, no worse on Sunday night, than on Thursday when the operation was performed, and that [the] wound seared with a hot iron. She had been to Balt, and the physicians refused to prescribe any remedy. He & Joseph were of opinion that the operation should relieve her pain in a great degree, which has proved true, tho it might not prolong her life, but it might. With this expressed to her, she insisted on having it performed. Geo. will go up to see her once or twice a week if she survives.

I regret to be absent from my courts now commencing, but am advised that it will take several weeks to restore me and a course of medicine, which I am taking. Your mother has been somewhat unwell here, but is better now.

Love to Julia and the children.

Affectionately,

---

[1]There was a fashionable health spa in Catawba County called Catawba Sparkling Springs that enjoyed a wide patronage. Bill Sharpe, *A New Geography of North Carolina* (Raleigh: Sharpe Publishing Company, 4 volumes, [1954-1965]), III, 1164.

[2]Edwin M. Holt (1807-1884), of Alamance County, was a Conservative delegate to the Constitutional Convention of 1868. He erected one of the first cotton mills in the state in 1837. Holt, a pioneer in textiles in the South, built a virtual empire in Alamance. Lefler and Wager, *Orange County*, 21, 113, 266, 268, 330, 354; Whitaker, *Centennial History of Alamance*, 97-103.

[3]Perhaps this was a reference to Mrs. Nathaniel Boyden of Salisbury, who was Mrs. Jane Henderson Mitchell before her marriage to Boyden. Powell, *DNCB*, I, 204.

[4]Mrs. Faucett has not been identified.

Joseph Graham to William A. Graham UNC

Charlotte, N.C.
Aug. 28th 1873

My dear Father,

Yours of 25th Inst. received this morning. I send you by express today a bottle of Arsenic granules and one of Tincture of Digitalis for that shortness of breath. You should take *ten* (10) drops three times a day. If the water has a sufficiently aperient effect you will not need to continue the Liver Regulator. I will send you some Tincture of Iron also. Take twenty drops in a small wine glassful of water with the arsenic after meals. And the Digitalis in a little water about 10 or 11 A.M. 3 or 4 P.M. and at bedtime at night. It should act upon your kidneys to some extent. I would continue the Quinine daily and on Thursdays, Fridays & Saturdays take 5 pills.

I am sorry Mother is feeling so unwell. I will look at the Drug Stores, and if I get the Medicine I wanted for her will send it in your package. If you continue to improve I would not be long away from the *Sulphur water—not* more than a week at a time. I hope you will make it your first business, and indeed your *only* business, till it is accomplished, to try and restore your health. It is a matter of the *utmost* importance that you attend *now*, and entirely to the exclusion of any body's else affairs or engagements. If you are not doing as well as you ought *at any time* Dr. Jones[1] or myself will go to you whenever necessary. . . .

Your affect Son

---

[1]Dr. Johnston B. Jones (1814-1889), Joseph Graham's partner, was a highly respected Charlotte physician. Later his son, Dr. Simmons B. Jones, became a partner. LeGette Blythe, "Medicine," *Charlotte Remembers*, compiled and edited by D. R. Reynolds (Charlotte: Community Publishing Company, 1972), 97.

Frances A. Polk to William A. Graham UNC

September 6th., 1873.

Will you be kind enough to forward the enclosed letter to the son of Dr. Hawkes, who, I believe, married Miss Manly,[1] it's contents will inform you of my reasons for troubling you.

In the country, and seeing no one from the old State, I have been unable to procure the address of Mr. Hawkes.

I have recently been informed that in the summer of '61, Gov. Swain obtained from my brother, Gen. Lucius Polk,[2] permission to turn over the papers in his possession to Dr. Hawkes.

My apology for troubling you is my anxiety to recover these papers, if possible.

---

[1]Francis T. Hawks married Hannah Gaston Manly (1835-1874), a daughter of Judge Matthias E. Manly.

[2]Lucius Junius Polk (1802-1869) of Maury County, Tennessee, was brother to Frances Polk's husband, Leonidas Polk. Crabtree and Patton, "*Journal of a Secesh Lady*," 643n.

Joseph Graham to William A. Graham UNC

Charlotte
Sept. 10th 1873

My dear Father,

Yours of yesterday is in hand. I regret that you find it so difficult to get rid of the "shortness of breath." I had hoped the iron would remove that, but I believe it will be advisable to abandon that, as I think the head aches must be due to it. And the spring near Willie's contains it in sufficient quantities for you, and in a more readily assimilable state. I would try and be very punctual in taking the Digitalis. When you leave the Springs[1] you must keep the bowels always in a soluble condition with regulator if necessary. I would try and drink a good deal of the water while at Willie's. Take the Arsenic and Digitalis and Quinine. But you might probably be benefitted by substituting something for the Quinine. However, it will probably be best for me to see you, and see what changes will then suggest themselves. For that purpose I will try and run up to the head of the road on Saturday and ride down with you as far as Iron Station. Please try and be there when the train arrives that I may have as much time with you as possible. I put a great deal of trust in the Digitalis, in your chest trouble. I am not very busy just now, but have several very sick patients. The city is quite healthy just now. The north east wind has been very unpleasant for the past two or three days.

Cousin Brevard Davidson is very ill with suppression of urine. Dr. Jones was sent for about two oclock this morning to consult with Dr. Miller[2] who is his attending physician. He never sends for me. Says I charged him exorbitantly once when he sent for me to go in the country. I only charged him a little over half price then. If he does not get better in a few hours he cant live much longer.

Next Saturday will be six weeks since you had a chill, and I think we can very well change the Quinine to something else.

My family have not yet returned and have set no time as yet, but I think they will probably arrive next Thursday 18' Inst. Most of our absentees have returned to town.

. . . .

If the weather is good I will meet you on the train next Saturday. If we have foul weather of course you will not turn out. Love to Mother,

Your affect. Son

---

[1]This letter was addressed to W. A. Graham at Sulphur Springs in Cleveland County.

[2]Possibly William Twitty Miller.

Alexander McIver to William A. Graham UNC

Raleigh, N.C.,
Sept. 10th, 1873.

I have been instructed by a resolution of the Ex. Com. of the State Educational Association to request you to allow your name to be published as one of the contributing Editors of "the North Carolina Journal of Education."

I am further instructed to ask your opinion as to the propriety of requesting Dr. Sears, the Gen'l Agent of the Peabody Education Fund, to contribute $25. a week, from that fund, to defray the expenses of a suitable, competent gentleman, to be selected by the Ex. Com. in each Congressional District in the State, whose duty it shall be to organize Educational Associations, and hold Teacher's Institutes in the several Counties of the District.

The State Educational Association was organized July the 11th. as you are aware. Hon. Will H. Battle is the President of the Association, and Gen'l W. R. Cox[1] of this City is the Chairman of the Executive Committee.

---

[1]William Ruffin Cox (1832-1919), a native of Halifax County, moved to Tennessee, where he graduated from Franklin College and the Lebanon Law School. After practicing law for five years in Nashville, he opened a successful law practice in Raleigh. Cox entered the Confederate army as major of the Second North Carolina Regiment and rose to the rank of brigadier general, commanding his brigade in the last charge made at Appomattox. He was wounded eleven times during the war. In 1865 Cox reopened his law office in Raleigh. He was state solicitor, 1866-1870; superior court judge, 1877-1878; chairman of the Democratic state committee, 1875-1877; Democratic member of Congress, 1881-1887; secretary of the United States Senate, 1893-1900; and president of the state agricultural society, 1900-1901. Cox's last years were spent at Penelo, his Edgecombe County plantation, or in Raleigh, and he devoted much of his time to farming. *Biographical Directory of Congress*, 746; Boatner, *Civil War Dictionary*, 206; Powell, *DNCB*, I, 450-451.

Alexander McIver to William A. Graham UNC

Raleigh N.C.
Sept. 17th 73

Genl Cox, Judge Battle & myself in making out the list of contributors to the Journal of Education put your name in the list without hearing from you.

Judge Battle gave assurance that we might thus use your name without offense to you. I trust you will pardon the liberty thus taken.

Your friends are much gratified at the occasional notices of the improvement of your health, which are seen in the newspapers.

Henry B. Chapin[1] *to William A. Graham* UNC

American Evangelical Alliance
No. 38 Bible House

New York,
September 22nd., 1873.

I am happy to inform you that the Programme Committee of the Evangelical Alliance, to whom the permanent organization of the General Conference, Oct. 2d to 12th, has been entrusted, have unanimously decided upon yourself as one of the Vice Presidents of the Conference, to preside at one or more of the sectional meetings.

Should you, for any cause, be unable to attend the Conference in person, the Committee will be gratified if you will permit them to use your name in connection with the above office.

Hoping that you will find it convenient to be present at the Conference, and that you will consent to perform the service desired of you, I remain, in behalf of the Programme Committee,

Yours with great respect,

Sec'y Evang. Alliance.

Please reply at your earliest convenience.

---

[1]The Reverend Henry B. Chapin (1827-1914) was born in Rochester, New York. After graduation from Yale in 1847, he studied religion at Union and Princeton theological seminaries. In 1867 he founded the Chapin Collegiate School in New York City, an institution he served for forty years. At the time of this letter, he was secretary of the American Evangelical Alliance. See his obituary in the *New York Times*, July 8, 1914.

Robert H. Morrison to William A. Graham A&H

Near Morganton,
September 24th., 1873.

Your kind letter of the 19th has been recd. and I am thankful indeed to learn that yr. health is improved. I have felt much solicitude in regard to yr. delicate health, and pray tht. you may be fully restored & long spared to yr. family. In regard to the main topic of yr. letter, I am truly amazed that men who ought to feel concerned for the honor of our State should make persistent efforts to rob her of any part of her Revolutionary renown.

I am gratified that you have consented to vindicate our claim to the honor of the Mecklenburg declaration.

I know of no one so well qualified to do it, or whose testimony will go farther with honest men.

Having spent most of a long life in the neighborhood of Charlotte, and having been permitted in the discharge of my professional duties, to become acquainted with a large portion of the inhabitants of this Western part of the State; it is to me very surprising that the testimony of the men who have certified to their being present and witnessing the transactions of the 20th. of May, 1775, should be called in question.

I had every opportunity of knowing Genl. Jos. Graham, and have often heard him speak of the events of that day, and of his presence. And I have never known a man, whose sound Judgment, retentive memory, and unimpeachable veracity, were more worthy of Reliance. He was present at the second memorable celebration of that event, held in Charlotte, and spent the night after at my House, and I heard him detail fully the Substance of the Speeches made by Govr.. Swain & others.

I also knew Rev. Humphrey Hunter,[1] Genl. Geo. Graham, Majr. John Davidson,[2] Saml. Wilson,[3] & Jonas Clark, and speak only the truth when I say, they were men of integrity, and their testimony is worthy of confidence.

The marble slabs over the graves of Rev. H. Balch,[4] & Gen'l Jos. Graham, & perhaps others, bear testimony, too, which it seems strange that honest men should call in question. Upon what principle would an intelligent congregation sanction the Record on the Grave Stone of a beloved Pastor, which was false?

A very Sensible letter appeared in the Southern Home a few weeks since, from Mr. Chas. Jay Harris,[5] of Cabarrus Co., who was present at the first celebration in Charlotte in 1825, and also at the Second Celebration. He can give you more particulars than I am able to do, of who were present & what was done.

I think it probable that, if the Grave Yard of Hopewell was examined, some evidence might be found on the Tombs of Jno. McNitt Alexander,[6] the Secy. and also Majr. Jno. Davidson, & Saml. Wilson.

Abram Alexander,[7] Chairman, is buried at Sugar Creek—Ephraim Brevard,[8] I think, in Charlotte. Your son, Joe, could have their graves examined.

If I were at Home from Certain Books, I could point out the Grave Yards in which the Tombs of most of the Signers to that Declaration, might be found.

C. Jay Harris might inform in regard to the Tombs of Phifer[9] & perhaps others. Neil Morrison[10] was from Providence. Majr. Avery[11] says all the Papers his Father had, in reference to that matter have been given to Gov'r Swain.

Gen'l Hill published, a month or two back, some collateral Testimony from some of Capt. Jack's[12] descendants in Ga., corroborating fully the former certificates, & would gladly furnish you the amt. of it.

Waightstill Avery's[13] grave is near to this, but no Record touching this matter is on it.

The fact you name in regard to Genl. Jackson is a very important one, and if it needs any confirmation, you might receive it by writing to Nashville.

My health is about as usual., Altho' I feel more & more the infirmities of old age. My daughter here, Susan, is in delicate health. Suffers much from newralgea & debility.

I am sorry I was absent, and thus missed the opportunity of meeting you. It always affords me much pleasure to see you.

I will be gratified to hear from you at any time. Much love to Sister Susan & the family.

May the Richest blessings of Heaven ever rest upon you, and when the trials of this fleeting life are over, may we all meet in a better Home.

---

[1]Humphrey Hunter (1755-1827), a native of Ireland, moved to Mecklenburg County in 1759. He attended Dr. James Hall's famous school, "Clio's Nursery," and Queen's Museum in Charlotte, which he left to become a patriot in the Revolutionary War. He was captured at Camden but escaped. After the war Hunter resumed his education at Mt. Zion College. A Presbyterian minister, he was pastor of a church in Lincoln (now Gaston) County before moving to Mecklenburg County to become pastor of Steele Creek Church. John Hill Wheeler, *Historical Sketches of North Carolina: From 1584 to 1851* (Philadelphia: Lippincott, Grambo and Company, 2 volumes, 1851), II, 151-156, hereinafter cited as Wheeler, *Historical Sketches*; Tompkins, *History of Mecklenburg*, 74.

[2]This is a reference to John Davidson (1735-1832), Graham's maternal grandfather, who was an influential man in Mecklenburg County during the colonial and Revolutionary periods. A native of Pennsylvania and a Revolutionary soldier, Davidson, a signer of the Mecklenburg Declaration, represented Mecklenburg County in the assembly, 1773-1774. In partnership with his sons-in-law, Joseph Graham and Alexander Brevard, who moved to Lincoln County, Davidson was a pioneer in the iron manufacturing industry there, although Mecklenburg remained his residence. Cheney, *North Carolina Government*, 55-56; Tompkins, *History of Mecklenburg*, 69; Graham, *General Joseph Graham*, 167-168.

[3]Samuel Wilson (1710-1778) came to Mecklenburg County about 1745, but he has not been identified further.

[4]Hezekiah J. Balch (1745-1776), born at Deer Creek, Maryland, and educated at Princeton, came to North Carolina as a missionary in 1768. He was the first minister of the Presbyterian churches at Rocky River and Poplar Tent. Powell, *DNCB*, I, 93.

[5]Charles J. Harris was a son of Dr. Charles Harris (1762-1825) of Cabarrus County. He has not been further identified. Tompkins, *History of Mecklenburg*, 72-73.

[6]John McKnitt Alexander (1733-1817), a native of Pennsylvania, came to Mecklenburg County in 1754. He was the crown surveyor, a justice of the peace, and a member of the Third and Fourth provincial congresses. He was Mecklenburg's first state senator and a successful businessman, but he is best known for his role in the Mecklenburg Declaration controversy. Hunter, *Sketches of Western North Carolina*, 42-43.

[7]Abraham Alexander (1718-1786) was one of the trustees and directors who negotiated with George A. Selwyn's agent, Henry E. McCulloh, for a tract of land to be held in trust for the county of Mecklenburg on which to erect a courthouse, prison, and stocks. He was a member of the assembly in 1769 and 1771 and at the provincial congress, 1774. Alexander was elected chairman of the Mecklenburg Convention held on May 19-20, 1775. For many years he was ruling elder of the Sugar Creek Presbyterian Church. *DAB*, I, 162.

[8]Ephraim Brevard (1744-1780), one of eight sons of John and Jane Brevard, moved with his family from Maryland to Mecklenburg County as a child. After his graduation from Princeton he studied medicine and then established a practice in Charlotte. He and six of his brothers served in the American army during the Revolution; Brevard served as a surgeon. He was captured at Charleston on May 12, 1783. Though he was liberated later, his health had deteriorated so that he died at the home of his friend John McKnitt Alexander shortly after he was freed. Brevard was instrumental in the establishment of Queen's Museum in Charlotte. William Henry Foote, *Sketches of North Carolina, Historical and Biographical* (New York: Robert Carter, 1846), 68-76, hereinafter cited as Foote, *Sketches of North Carolina*.

[9]John Phifer, son of Margaret Blackwelder and Martin Phifer, was a member of the Third Provincial Congress and was active in early Mecklenburg affairs. He was lieutenant colonel of the First Battalion of Minute Men in the Salisbury district, 1775. Wheeler, *Historical Sketches*, II, 70, 75, 78, 81, 85; Wheeler, *Reminiscences*, 96; Cheney, *North Carolina Government*, 1535.

[10]Neill Morrison (1728-1784), a participant in the events surrounding the Mecklenburg Declaration, was a native of Scotland who emigrated from Pennsylvania into the Mecklen-

burg area. Morrison served as a soldier in the Cherokee expedition of 1776. Tompkins, *History of Mecklenburg*, 51; Foote, *Sketches of North Carolina*, 208; Wheeler, *Historical Sketches*, II, 70.

[11]Alphonso Calhoun Avery (1835-1913), of Morganton, married Robert Hall Morrison's daughter Mary Washington Morrison (1838-1886) in 1861. Avery's father, Isaac Thomas Avery, was the brother of Waightstill Avery. Alphonso C. Avery graduated at the University of North Carolina and studied law with Richmond M. Pearson. During the Civil War he attained the rank of major in the Confederate army. After the war he returned to Morganton to practice law and served in the state Senate as a Conservative. He later became a superior court judge and in 1888 was elected as an associate justice of the state supreme court. Clark, "Graham Descendants"; Powell, *DNCB*, I, 66-67, 70.

[12]James Jack (1739-1822) moved from Pennsylvania to Charlotte, where he became an innkeeper. He was purported to be the messenger chosen to carry to Philadelphia news of the Mecklenburg proceedings in 1775. During the Revolution he was a soldier in the American army. In 1783 he moved to Georgia. Alexander, *History of Mecklenburg County*, 425-426.

In 1819, at age 88, Captain Jack provided a deposition that described the events of May, 1775, and his part in them. Jack's "certificate" is printed in the appendix to Graham's address on the Mecklenburg Declaration delivered on February 4, 1875.

[13]Waightstill Avery (1741-1821), a signer of the Mecklenburg Declaration, was a native of Connecticut and a graduate of Princeton. He came to Mecklenburg County in 1769 and became a leader in the community. A lawyer by profession, he was active in the Revolutionary movement. Avery was a delegate to the Third and Fifth provincial congresses and was a member of the committee that formulated the state constitution. He attained the rank of colonel of militia. In civilian life he served in the House of Commons, 1777. In 1778 he moved to Jones County, where he resided for three years before moving to Burke. Avery was a representative of Burke County in the House of Commons, 1782-1785 and 1793, and in the Senate, 1796. A famous incident in his life was his duel with Andrew Jackson, in which Avery declined to fire. He was regarded as one of the most eminent lawyers of his day. Powell, *DNCB*, I, 70-71.

Daniel H. Hill to William A. Graham [with enclosure] UNC

Charlotte, N.C.,
October 15th., 1873.

I have at last succeeded in getting an old copy of the S.H.,[1] with the article of Mr. Harris, which I send you today.

I will enlarge my paper on the 1st. November, & as it is in the county in which the Mecklenburg Declaration was proclaimed, I would esteem it a great favor to get your articles on the subject. I learn that you wish to get up a pamphlet. I think that it could be gotten up in Charlotte more economically than elsewhere, by giving the Home the Mss. I would have it set up accurately & the type could then be used on the pamphlet. Our office does not job any, but I could make an advantageous arrangement with the Observer office. That office could use my power press which I would give gratuitously for the sake of the articles.

[1]The *Southern Home*.

[Enclosure]
Southern Home Circular

Office of the "Southern Home,"

Charlotte, N.C.———1873.

M———
Dear Sir:

The friends of Capt. Randolph A. Shotwell,[1] will be pleased to learn that he has regained his liberty after a painful imprisonment of more than two years; and that he, as Associate Editor of the Southern Home, will promptly resume his pen, in advocacy of those eternal and indispensable principles which underlie the welfare and prosperity of the Southern people.

The Home is a high-toned, fearless, and thoroughly Southern paper, published every Monday morning by Gen. D. H. Hill, at Charlotte, N.C., devoted to the truth of Southern History; to the preservation of Southern characterisics; to the development of Southern resources, and to the advancement of Southern interests in Agriculture, Mining, Manufacturing, and the Mechanic Arts. In size, type, and general appearance, it already may compete with the best weekly papers of the country; but arrangements are being made by the proprietor to enlarge and improve it in many particulars.

Capt. Shotwell will give his whole attention to the paper, and at the proper time will furnish a series of articles detailing his personal experience while a Ku Klux prisoner at Albany Penitentiary, and vindicating the conservative citizens of Western North Carolina, (North and South), from many malicious slanders, circulated against them by agents of the Radical Administration, during the recent political persecutions. It is believed that these articles alone will be worth the price of the paper. Persons who have suffered, either directly themselves, or indirectly through their relatives and friends, should not fail to procure a copy for preservation.

Terms for Southern Home, per annum:

One copy	$2.50
Club of Five at one Office	11.25
Club of Ten at one Office	20.00

No name placed on the books until the money is received.

In sending this circular, Capt. Shotwell invites you to lend him a helping hand by subscribing for the Southern Home, and getting your neighbors to subscribe. Please forward the names and cash by Check or Post Office order at once, to begin with the first number. Communications giving local items, and facts of interest will also be always acceptable. Address

Randolph A. Shotwell,
Charlotte, N.C.

[1]Randolph A. Shotwell, convicted in 1871 of complicity in Ku Klux Klan activities, had just been pardoned and released from the Albany penitentiary.

Eugene Grissom[1] *to William A. Graham* UNC

Raleigh, North Carolina,
October 20th., 1873.

I beg leave to consult you about a matter of business. The policy of the General & State Governments appears, as I think, wisely, to be towards Amnesty in all offences of a political significance. Among the few exceptions, I believe, to this mercy, in this State, is Gov. Holden. If he has sined grievously he has grievously suffered. All it seems that the offended majesty of the State required has been borne. Further *prosecution* looks like *persecution.* Without the knowledge even of Mr. Holden, I write to ask you to appear for him as Counsel in the State case against him in your Court.[2]

I know that the Judge thinks it ought to be Nol Prossed. Enclosed I send you a fee of $100. I do this purely as a matter of gratitude to one *now* in adversity, who when in prosperity, showed me many kindnesses. I desire the influence in this matter of your great name, believing that, with the general principles mentioned, you sympathize, as a matter of public policy. If, for any reason you decline to appear, please retain for me, in this case some lawyer of position & influence. Whatever you do will be *satisfactory* to me.

---

[1]Eugene Grissom, of Granville County, was a graduate in medicine of the University of Pennsylvania. Until he sustained a disabling wound at Seven Pines, he was a captain in the Thirtieth North Carolina Regiment. Later he was a surgeon with the rank of major in the state service. Grissom was a member of the House of Commons from 1862 to 1865 and also represented his county in the Constitutional Convention of 1865. Increasingly he associated himself with the Radical faction during Reconstruction. Clark, *Histories of the North Carolina Regiments,* II, 495, 498, IV, 629; Connor, *North Carolina Manual, 1913,* 624; Hamilton, *Reconstruction in North Carolina,* 345.

[2]Soon after his removal from office Holden left the state, forfeiting his bond in the action brought against him by Josiah Turner. Kirk and Bergen were outside North Carolina before the suit was brought. No further mention of Grissom's request has been found. The case was never tried and Turner had to pay the costs.

The legislature on March 3, 1873, passed an amnesty act applying to all offenses, except rape, committed by members of secret organizations, state troops, and the like, including accessories. The act did not apply to those already under sentence or to embezzlers and those who had misappropriated public funds. Hamilton, *Reconstruction in North Carolina,* 131, 531-533, 596; Raper, *Holden,* 198.

William A. Richardson[1] *to William A. Graham* UNC

Treasury Department
Washington, Nov 8th 1873

I have the honor to acknowledge the receipt of your letter of the 6th inst. stating that you had some funds belonging to a trust which you desired to invest in United States six per cent bonds and asking if the Treasury Department had such bonds to sell.

The United States are now negotiating no loan except that of the new funded loan which bears interest at five per cent, and which it can sell only in exchange for six per cent bonds or for money to be applied to the purchase of those bonds.

If you desire to invest your money in six per cent bonds the only way will be for you to purchase them in the market.

---

[1]William Adams Richardson (1821-1896) was a graduate of Harvard who began his practice of law in Lowell, Massachusetts. He served for four years as assistant secretary of the treasury under G. S. Boutwell, whom he succeeded as secretary in 1873. Richardson proved to be inept and was made a judge of the court of claims in 1874, and in 1885 he became chief justice of that court. *CDAB*, 863.

Edward J. Hale to William A. Graham UNC

New York,
Nov 14, 1873

I am very glad to hear of your improved health, & trust that you will long enjoy it.

You will have noticed with pleasure that there has been this week an improvement & more hopeful feeling in financial & commercial matters here. We might think that the panic was over but for the rascality now an almost universal among Bank & business men, which leads to a constant fear of some new explosion to upturn business matters. We are looking here, no matter how far confidence & quiet may be restored, for a winter of dreadful suffering. So many thousands of men & women, boys & girls, have been thrown out of employment, at the worst season of the year. There can be no such suffering at the South, notwithstanding its enormous loss by shrinkage of values.

Robert C. Winthrop to William A. Graham A&H

Boston,
90 Marlboro' Street.,
November 14th., 1873.

Messrs. Hale of N.Y. sent me last week The Life and Letters of Iredell, with a note saying that I owed the volumes to you. We have been moving to our winter home in the City since I received them, & I have been otherwise much occupied. But I have not failed to examine them, & to read large parts of them, in my leisure hours. Iredell[1] was certainly a much greater man than I had supposed him to have been, & I shall henceforth count him among the brightest lights of the Southern States, & of the Country. His Revolutionary Papers are very able & remarkable. I observe that he held Court in Boston several times with Judge Lowell,[2] with whose family I have been much connected, & to whom he pays very agreeable tributes. I feel as if you should allow the publishers to send me the bill for volumes which I shall so gladly preserve; but whether I am to owe them altogether to your kindness, or not, I shall prize them as the result of your friendly regard, and be grateful accordingly. I do not omit to recall your desire for the reference to a letter of Mr. Jefferson's, of which I spoke to you in connection with your remarks on the Mecklenburg Controversy.

If you will turn to the 1st. Vol. of the 4 vols., entitled "Memoir, Correspondence, & Miscellanies, from the Papers of Thomas Jefferson," edited by Thos. Jefferson Randolph,[3] and of which my copy is the 2d. Edition, printed in 1830, you will find, on page 151, in a letter to John Randolph, dated 25 August, 1775, the following passage: "I am sincerely one of those & would rather be in dependence on Great Britain, properly limited, than on any nation upon earth, or than on no nation." The context is, of course, to be regarded, but the expression is unequivocal. I shall look with interest to your exposition of the N.C. claims to have anticipated the Declaration of '76.

Let me say a word in *confidence*. My old friend, Kenneth Rayner,[4] now of Mississippi, writes me that, being in great poverty, he is anxious to get an appointment as one of the Commrs. under the Geneva Arbitration, for awarding Claims, & he appeals to me for a letter to the Administration. I have uniformly refused to involve myself in matters of this kind; but, if I were sure of his qualifications & condition, I might be tempted to say a word for an old friend. I have forgotten what you told me about him. Any thing you may say, shall be strictly confidential.

---

[1]James Iredell (1751-1799), a native of England who came to prominence in North Carolina, was active in the Revolutionary cause and served as state attorney general, 1779-1781. A staunch advocate of the United States Constitution, he was the Federalist floor leader in the North Carolina ratifying convention. But Iredell's forte was as a lawyer and jurist. He collected and codified state laws, with the revised edition being issued in 1791. From 1790 to 1799 he was an associate justice of the United States Supreme Court. Iredell had no superior on that bench and issued landmark opinions in *Calder* v. *Bull* and *Chisholm* v. *Georgia.* In the former case he upheld strict construction by ruling that a legislative act not authorized by or in violation of the Constitution was void; in the latter case Iredell enunciated, either directly or by implication, all the leading principles of the states' rights philosophy. *CDAB*, 477-478.

[2]John Lowell, born in Newburyport, Massachusetts, was the son of the Reverend John and Sarah Champney Lowell. He was a graduate of Harvard and was admitted to the bar in 1776. Lowell was a representative of Newburyport to the Massachusetts Provincial Assembly in 1771, 1772, 1774, and 1776; a delegate to the constitutional convention, 1779-1780; and a member of the Continental Congress, 1781-1783. He was judge of the admiralty court, 1782; United States judge for the district of Massachusetts, 1789; and chief judge of the First Circuit, 1801. *Who Was Who*, 323.

[3]Thomas Jefferson Randolph (1792-1875), son of Thomas Randolph and grandson of Thomas Jefferson, served as chief executor of his grandfather's estate and edited the first published edition of Jefferson's writings, *Memoir, Correspondence, and Miscellanies from the Papers of Thomas Jefferson* (1829). *CDAB*, 842.

[4]Through Winthrop, Rayner received the appointment as commissioner. Later he was solicitor of the treasury, 1877-1884. *CDAB*, 847.

Edward J. Hale to William A. Graham UNC

17 Murray Street,
New York,
November 21st., 1873.

. . . .

It is exceedingly gratifying to have such opinions expressed by a gentleman of such deserved eminence in literature & statesmanship as Mr. Winthrop, at the same time that it is another mortifying evidence of the ignorance of even the best informed Northern men upon Southern subjects & men.[1]

Did you see the remarkable article by Elihu Burritt,[2] in Beecher's Christian Union,[3] reciting the evils resulting from the exclusion of Southern *gentlemen* from the government? It is as remarkable for its source & its medium of publication as for its just views.

We have been exceedingly gratified to see by the papers that you are preparing an article on the Mecklenburg Declaration. We trust that you will be able to extinguish Mr. Goodloe & his set.

---

[1]Presumably Hale refers to the letter of Winthrop just preceding.

[2]Elihu Burritt (1810-1879), son of a shoemaker, became an ardent reformer. Apprenticed to a blacksmith, he aspired to become a well-educated man and studied first with his brother, principal of a small boarding school. He was especially interested in languages and made a concentrated study of Hebrew and Icelandic. In 1841 Burritt launched his career as a lecturer, and in 1842 he began publication of a weekly journal, the *Christian Citizen*, which was devoted to antislavery, peace, temperance, and self-culture. His life was spent in writing and talking about peace and brotherhood. *Appleton's Cyclopædia*, I, 469.

[3]Henry Ward Beecher (1813-1887), one of the most prominent clergymen of his day, was born in Litchfield, Connecticut, where he lived until 1826. His father, Lyman Beecher, of Puritan descent, has been described as a volatile, restless man, whereas his mother, Roxana Foote, was shy and sensitive. At Mount Pleasant Classical Institute in Amherst, Massachusetts, Henry Ward Beecher began to emerge as a self-confident leader and orator. After graduation from Amherst College, he entered Lane Theological Seminary, of which his father was head.

Although he was determined to become a preacher as his then-deceased mother had wished, the young Beecher wanted "to preach the Gospel as it was revealed to him and not as it was taught in the schools." With the support of his wife, Eunice White Bullard, in 1837 he embarked on an extraordinary career as an evangelistic preacher. Notably unconventional in personal habits, attitude, and preaching style, he was, according to his sister, Harriet Beecher Stowe, an individual who "has the misfortune of a popularity which is perfectly phenomenal." A gifted writer, poet, and speaker, Beecher's influence was very great. He opposed slavery, supported women's suffrage, and embraced the theory of evolution but withal maintained a belief in miracles and special providences. His final years were marred by accusations of immorality. *DAB*, II, 128-135.

James C. Welling to William A. Graham A&H

The Columbian University,
Washington,
December 18th., 1873.

As you are an authority upon all questions of North Carolina history,[1] and especially recognized as such in all matters pertaining to the Mecklenburg Declaration of Independence, I most respectfully solicit information at your hands upon one or two points involved in the protracted controversy waged around that topic.

The name of "J. McKnitt" is signed to the certificate which authenticates the first publication of the Declaration in the Raleigh Register of Ap. 30, 1819. Gov. Stokes[2] and Mr. Sam. Henderson speak of him as "Dr. Joseph McKnitt," in the State pamphlet published on this subject. Gov. Stokes says that "the name subscribed is real, that the individual still lives, etc." Now, it appears that the real name of this witness was Dr. Jos. McKnitt Alexander,[3] and what puzzles me in the premises is to know why the *full name* of the witness was not signed by himself, and why it was not given by Gov. Stokes in endorsing him as a real personage. I take it for granted that all this is susceptible of explanation, but I would like to *know* what the truth of the matter really is.

I see it stated that the certificate signed by "J. McKnitt" is not an accurate reproduction of the certificate attached by John McKnitt Alexander to the "Davie Copy."

I ought perhaps, in candor, to apprize you that the enquiry is not prompted by idle curiosity. I have been invited to prepare a review of the documentary history of the Mecklenburg Declaration, and I want to write intelligently about the certificate.

With pleasant memories of our meeting at Saratoga, I remain, my dear Sir.

---

[1]The Elizabeth City *Economist* had recently called on Graham to write a history of the state.

[2]Montfort Stokes (1762-1842), a native of Lunenburg County, Virginia, served during the Revolution in the Continental navy under Commodore Stephen Decatur. He was captured by the British in 1776 and held prisoner for seven months aboard the prison ship *Jersey* in New York harbor. After the Revolution he settled in North Carolina. Stokes served as clerk of the Superior Court of Rowan County; he was elected to the United States Senate in 1804 but declined; and, upon his election in 1816, he served as a Democrat in the Senate until 1823. Stokes was a state senator and a member of the Commons. He was North Carolina governor from 1830 until his resignation in 1832, whereupon he accepted a post from President Andrew Jackson as a member of the Board of Indian Commissioners, residing for the remainder of his life at Fort Gibson in what is now Oklahoma. In this capacity he served as agent for various Indian tribes and as commissioner to negotiate treaties. *Biographical Directory of Congress*, 1661.

[3]Dr. Joseph McKnitt Alexander was the correct name. See William A. Graham to James C. Welling, December 31, 1873, and Seaton Gales to Graham, August 23, 1873, note 1, in this volume.

Robert C. Winthrop to William A. Graham A&H

Boston,
90 Marlboro' Street.,
Dec'r 24th., 1873.

While at my publishers this morning, I addressed a copy of my Life of my old ancestor[1] to you, in kind recognition of your obliging gift of the Life of Iredell. It occurred to me afterwards that by some chance I might have sent you the work before. I do not think I have; but, if my memory has been at fault, pray bestow the duplicate on some of your public Libraries. If you have not received it already, accept it with the best wishes of Christmas and New Year's.

The Iredell is now in the hands of our new Chief Justice of Massts., my nephew by marriage, Hon. Horace Gray,[2] to whom I loaned it at his request, & who has been much interested in it. I sent you a Newspaper with my little Tea-Party Speech. I inclose one of the Cards to which I alluded, &

which is clever enough to be worthy of preservation as one of the Memorials of the Centennial Period. Perhaps your daughter may find a place for it in her Album.

You will have observed the death of our friend & associate Macalester. His loss to our Comtee. of Finance is a serious one. Gov. Clifford has been quite ill, & at one moment, I was alarmed about him. But he is now convalescent, & I trust we shall have no more vacancies to deplore at present.

---

[1]Robert Winthrop was descended from John Winthrop (1588-1649), governor of the colony of Massachusetts. There were many illustrious members of the Winthrop family, and Robert C. Winthrop wrote about them often. This reference may be to his *Life and Letters of John Winthrop*, published in two volumes, 1864-1867.

[2]Horace Gray (1828-1902), of Massachusetts, was a graduate of Harvard and the Harvard Law School. At the time of this letter he was reporter for the state supreme court. Later, he was an associate justice and then chief justice of the state supreme court, 1864-1881. From 1881 until his death, Gray served as an associate justice of the United States Supreme Court. In his political affiliations Gray was first a Free-Soiler and then a Republican. *CDAB*, 365.

William A. Graham to James C. Welling A&H

Hillsboro', N.C.,
December 31st., 1873.

I must apologize for a few days of delay in acknowledging yours of the 18th. inst., by reason of indisposition.

In reply to your inquiry as to the name subscribed to the publication of the Mecklenburg Declaration of Independence in 1819, my acquaintance with the person in question enables me to give a full explanation. The name of Alexander was, and is, so common in Mecklenburg, as hardly to afford the means of discriminating an individual—there being many families of the name, who trace no connection in blood. Hence the Alexander who made the publication to which allusion is made, adopted the habit of signing only his Christian name, "Joseph McKnitt," omitting the surname. This was probably not universal, but so frequent as to cause him to be known, in his sphere of acquaintance, quite as well by this signature, as if the name had been written in full. By this designation I have often heard him spoken of, and addressed. Governor Stokes knew him well, by either name; and by an inadvertance not unusual presumes the same knowledge in those addressed in the State paper to which you allude, a presumption, it seems, in which he was well justified, in the generation to which they both belonged; for no quibble has ever been raised in respect [to] this signature, so far as I have heard, until within a few months past.

Dr. Joseph McKnitt Alexander was among the visitors at my Father's house, whom I remember from my childhood. From the year 1824 when I left College, until his death in 1842, I, annually, was accustomed to spend one or more days at the house of his son with whom he resided. He was a graduate of Nassau Hall in one of the years 1791 to 94—a well educated physician and well informed gentleman; especially in respect to the history of our country in the period through which he had lived, and as well versed in what may [be] called the antiquities of North Carolina, as any one of his time. From him I first learned of the instructions given by the Provincial Congress of North Carolina to her delegates in the Continental Congress, on the 12th. of April 1776, to concur in voting for absolute independence, and was shewn an old printed copy of the Journal of that Colonial Assembly in which the resolutions to this effect appeared. The exhumation of these resolutions by him from the neglected mass in which the material of the Revolutionary history of this State had lain, quite as much disconcerted the theories of historians in ascribing the first movement of this import to other States, and produced as much surprize as his publication in respect to the declaration in Mecklenburg. And you have no doubt observed, that the Legislature directed a reprint of this Journal at the same time that it took order for printing the Mecklenburg paper and the accompanying testimony.

As to the suggestion that the certificate signed "J. McKnitt is not an accurate reproduction of the certificate on the Davie copy" I do not remember that I ever examined any manuscript pertaining to the matter. I have taken it for granted that the characters of the Davie's Father & son, of the Alexanders Father & son, of Dr. Samuel Henderson, and of the Legislative Committee in 1830 were a sufficient guarantee against any imposture or mistake.

From the circumstance that my Father and other relatives had given their testimony as witnesses of the proceeding in Mecklenburg on the 20th. of May 1775, I have not taken any part in the discussions relative to it, heretofore; but at the urgent request of friends, I propose to put forth my views of it, as soon as my leisure and state of health may permit. I think there are many historical considerations connected with it, to which attention has never been directed.

Heartily reciprocating your kind recollections of our interviews last summer.

P.S. It may have escaped your notice, that in the same number of the Raleigh Register in 1819, which contains the Mecklenburg paper, there is also contributed by Dr. Alexander, a copy of a Proclamation of Gov. Josiah Martin, issued in Charlotte the 3rd. of October 1780, while Ld. Cornwallis occupied that Town. The old copy from which this was taken, was produced to my Father about 1817 from the strong box of an aged and illiterate German neighbor, along with his title deeds, on the occasion of writing the will of the latter, and he stated that it was delivered to him by a messenger sent out to disseminate it soon after the date. In certain memoranda of Gen'l Graham on 1820 for Judge Murphey,[1] who then proposed to write the history of the State, he states, that he had sent the old copy through Dr. J. M. Alexander to Mr. Macon then a Senator in Congress. I mention this to shew that Alexander was alive to our history generally.

[1]Archibald De Bow Murphey.

Susan W. Graham to Augustus W. Graham UNC

Hillsboro,
Dec. 31st., 1873.

My dear Brother,

. . . .

Father has been quite unwell for some days past, and has spent a great part of each day in the bed. George is treating him, has put a "parris plaster" on his chest, and he looks much better to-day, and I hope in a few days will be as strong as usual—though I can't help fearing that will never again be as well as before his attacks last Summer—but that is in God's hands, and we must try to leave it to Him, though I felt very sad these last few days when I feared he was failing again. I wanted Mother to write Brother Joe to come down, but as Father is better, and I know it would have been inconvenient for him to do so, I suppose it is as well that she did not.

. . . .

1874

James C. Welling to William A. Graham A&H

Washington,
Jan. 5th., 1874.

Accept, I pray you, my best thanks for your obliging letter of the 31st. ultimo.

The explanation you give of the double name used by Dr. Jos. McKnitt Alexander in the Mecklenburg papers and correspondence is entirely satisfactory to my mind, though I think it is to be regretted that any room should have been left for raising the objection which you designate as a "quibble." It seems much more than a quibble to one who is not familiar with the facts in the case, as you will have observed that in conducting his correspondence on the subject he is known as "J. M. *Alexander*" (your father and Mr. Davidson so address him) while in certifying the paper received from his father, and in adding his name to the certificate of Alphonzo Alexander[1] & Amos Alexander,[2] he omits his patronymic.

I am very glad that you are to prepare a paper on this long-mooted topic. I only regret that my own discussion will in all probability have to appear without awaiting the corrections which it would doubtless receive if I could have had the benefit of your riper knowledge. My inquiries have long led me to doubt the genuineness of the alleged Declaration of May 20th., which I believe to have been confounded with the paper of May 31st., in the memory alike of John McKnitt Alexander, and of all who subsequently confirmed the report that passes in his name.

Hoping that you send me a copy of your paper when it shall appear.

---

[1]Alphonzo Alexander has not been identified.

[2]Amos Alexander, the son of James and Margaret McKnitt Alexander, was not among the signers. Ray, *Mecklenburg Signers*, 315, 521.

Stephen D. Pool[1] to William A. Graham UNC

Newbern, N.C.,
January 9th., 1874.

By order of the Confederate Congress many Reports of Battles were published by the War Department. I have been trying diligently, for some time, to procure copies of these Official Documents, but thus far have failed. If you preserved them, will you not lend them to me for a time, at least? I will carefully preserve them, and if you desire their return, I will have such Reports as will aid me in the publication of "Our Living and our Dead," copied immediately, and send the originals back.

Address me, during Session of Legislature, at Raleigh, N.C.

[1]Stephen D. Pool, of Carteret County, editor of the *Union Banner,* was a captain in the Second North Carolina Regiment and was an excellent officer. After the war he edited *Our Living and Our Dead,* a short-lived but interesting magazine, at New Bern. He was John Pool's cousin and one of the few members of the family who remained Democratic. He was superintendent of public instruction, 1875-1876, but was forced out of office by his party's leaders for misuse of money received from the Peabody Education Fund. Clark, *Histories of the North Carolina Regiments,* I, 500-501, 525; R. D. W. Connor, *North Carolina: Rebuilding an Ancient Commonwealth, 1584-1925* (Chicago: American Historical Society, 4 volumes, 1929), II, 391; Hamilton, *Reconstruction in North Carolina,* 599, 603.

William P. Johnston[1] *to William A. Graham* A&H

Lexington, Va.
January 20th, 1874.

Ex-Prest Davis proposes to prepare a narrative of certain events of the War, for which he desires to secure the necessary data. He avails himself of my services, (as his former aid-de-camp and friend) to make his request for him, pleading the uncertainty of his movements and infirmity, as an apology for not communicating with you directly.

He asks that you will be good enough to aid him, if you can do so, by a statement of what occurred in an interview between himself and Senators Graham, Hunter[2] & Orr[3] in regard to wishes of Senators that he should seek to make terms with Lincoln by surrendering the Confederacy, in the winter of 1864-5; and by any other facts bearing upon these negotiations, that you may have. For greater safety he desires that you will send your reply to me.

Presuming that I may have passed from your remembrance, I take the liberty of stating that I am a son of Genl. Albert Sidney Johnston,[4] and now a Professor in Washington and Lee University at this place.

With very sincere respect, I have the honor to remain,

Your obed't Serv't

[1]William Preston Johnston (1831-1897) was a native of Kentucky. He attended Centre College and the Western Military Institute. He received a degree at Yale, after which he studied law at the University of Louisville. During the Civil War Johnston served as an aide to President Davis but also saw much active service and attained the rank of colonel. He was taken prisoner and interned at Fort Delaware. After the war he taught for some time at Washington and Lee before he was made president of the University of Louisiana. *CDAB,* 507.

[2]Robert Mercer Taliaferro Hunter (1809-1887) was a product of the Virginia plantation aristocracy. His education was traditional; he was tutored at home, graduated from the University of Virginia, and read law, his law preceptor being the eminent particularist Judge Henry St. George Tucker of Winchester. He was admitted to the bar in 1830 and established his practice in Lloyds. Hunter was destined for an active career in politics; although his abilities were modest, he proved to be a significant figure in Virginia and national affairs. After serving in the Virginia assembly as an independent (1834-1837), he was elected to the United States Congress as a states' rights Whig, serving from 1837 to 1843.

By the early 1840s he had come under the influence of John C. Calhoun and had entered the Democratic party. Throughout the 1840s he endeavored to mold the Democracy in the Calhoun image and sought to secure the presidential nomination for his champion.

Dismayed by the Wilmot Proviso and the Compromise of 1850, Hunter, as a delegate to the Nashville Convention, favored disruption of the Union; however, his attitudes became more moderate during the troubled 1850s. As a United States senator (1847-1861) he defended southern rights against extremist attacks but his naturally conservative principles and conciliatory temper sometimes caused him to draw closer to the North. For example, as author of the Tariff of 1857 he gained friends throughout the nation. In 1860 Hunter was considered a possible compromise candidate between the northern and southern Democracy. When it became apparent that he could not be nominated, Hunter advised his followers to support John C. Breckinridge, the candidate of the proslavery wing of the party.

Following the election of Lincoln, Senator Hunter was one of the Committee of Thirteen that proposed the Crittenden Compromise on the slavery imbroglio. He voted with those favoring conciliation and compromise. Failure of this effort at compromise convinced him that secession was unavoidable, so he resigned nearly a month before Virginia seceded and served in all three Confederate congresses, with an interim of several months when he was secretary of state (July, 1861, to February, 1862). His career as Confederate senator was undistinguished.

Late in the war a peace movement aimed at arranging a negotiated peace called him from comparative security. Hunter joined Alexander H. Stephens and John A. Campbell as the Confederate spokesmen at the Hampton Roads conference, where they met informally with Lincoln and Seward. The results of this futile conference convinced Hunter that the southern cause was desperate and that surrender was inevitable unless a determined and unified effort could be mounted. To this end on February 6, 1865, he presided over a mass meeting where Davis delivered a masterly speech hoping to rally his people. Despite his temporary resolve Hunter opposed the action of the Confederate Congress authorizing the levy of Negro troops; recognizing that defeat was inevitable, he urged Davis to seek a negotiated settlement, thus inviting ridicule and the dubious sobriquet the "conquered senator." Later he was a leader of the Conservative faction that worked successfully to spare Virginia the worst evils of radical reconstruction. *DAB*, IX, 403-405.

[3]James Lawrence Orr (182-1873), of South Carolina, attended the University of Virginia and read law in preparation for a long career as journalist, lawyer, and politician. He was a state legislator, 1844-1848; a Democratic United States congressman, 1849-1859; a secessionist delegate to the convention of 1860; a commissioner to Washington in 1861; a Confederate brigadier general; a Confederate senator, 1861-1865; governor of South Carolina, 1865-1867; and minister to Russia, 1872-1873. A political opportunist who tacked with the winds of public opinion, Orr was a Unionist until South Carolina became overwhelmingly secessionist. By 1864 he realized that the plight of the Confederacy was serious and characteristically urged Davis to seek a negotiated peace. He accommodated to the Johnson and congressional plans of reconstruction, ultimately losing the confidence of South Carolina. He became a Republican and was appointed ambassador to Russia by Grant. *DAB*, 59-60.

[4]Albert Sidney Johnston (1803-1862), a native of Kentucky, attended Transylvania College and was a graduate of West Point. His wife's illness prompted him to resign from the army in 1834 and move to Texas, where he enlisted as a private in the Texas army. He rose rapidly to the position of chief commanding officer. For a time Johnston was secretary of war in the Republic of Texas. In 1849 he returned to the United States Army with the rank of colonel and in 1853 was promoted to brigadier general. Johnston commanded the Utah expedition and was in command in California. When the Civil War was declared, Johnston was appointed by the Confederacy to a general's post, commanding the Western Department. At the Battle of Shiloh, Johnston was mortally wounded. *CDAB*, 505.

Charles Phillips to Eleanor H. Swain A&H

Davidson College, N.C.
Tuesday, Jan. 26, 1874

My Dear Mrs. Swain

. . . .

I see that our legislature has determined to appoint new Trustees for our University. They will hardly do much more. But you will soon be where you can learn all that they are doing and have done. They leave Raleigh about the 9th of Feb.

Col. Wheeler spent a Sunday with me lately. He was inspecting the Mint at Charlotte & ran up to show me the Ms of his year-book of N.C. & to convert me from my infidelity about the Declaration at Charlotte in 1775. The documents that Govr. Swain furnished me for our Univ. Mag. are great stumbling blocks in the way of the advocates of the paper of the 20th. They attracted but little attention until of late. Mr. Goodloe of Warrenton has a volume ready for the press on the subject, & Dr. Welling who succeeded Mr. Gales[1] as an Editor of the National Intelligencer is to lecture on the subject before the Hist. Soc. of N. York in Feb. When you come you will be beset by requests for permission to search Govr. Swain's papers for more light on the subject. Some suspect that he did not give me (in 1853) all he had to give. I tell them if he kept back any think [*sic*] it was only more of the sort that already worries them. Col Wheeler expressed himself as delighted with his quiet Sunday here. He will be delighted to be able to call on you if you tarry in Washington. I hope that you will let my brother know of your being there. . . . Prof. Fetter[2] has had to leave Scotland Neck. Why! I know not fully—I fear fresh trouble in his family. Miss Sue is, to say the least, very reckless. That rich & happy settlement of the Smith's has a dark cloud resting over its sky.[3] It is hard to pay creditors when debtors supply you with bankrupt notices only. They say that Walter Clark of Halifax, whom Govr. Swain expected to make quite a figure in law & politics is to marry Susie Graham shortly. . . .

Tell Mrs. A.[4] that the Episcopalians who hold their heads high elsewhere eat humble pie in this high Church Presbyterian community. They fraternize remarkably well.

Our community, especially in College, has been badly pestered with mumps. Some were very sick, among them my son James. Willie stands at the head of his class. Mary could not get here during Christmas but reports the grand child as thriving. With my respects, and New Year's good wishes for Genl. & Mrs. A. I am yours truly,

---

[1]Joseph Gales, Jr. (1786-1860), became associated with the *National Intelligencer* in 1807. See Powell, *DNCB*, II, 267-269, for a full account of Gales's career.

[2]Manuel Fetter (b. 1809), a Lancaster, Pennsylvania, native of German descent, was professor of ancient languages and bursar at the University of North Carolina from 1838 to 1868. Battle, *History of the University*, I, 451.

[3]The "settlement of the Smith's" has not been explained.

[4]Eleanor Swain, daughter of the David L. Swains, was the wife of Smith Dykins Atkins

of Illinois, a New York native who rose from captain to brevet general in the Union army. From April 17 to May 3, 1866, Atkins's brigade of 4,000 cavalry had been quartered in and around Chapel Hill. General Atkins visited university president David L. Swain on April 19 and apparently was smitten by Eleanor. Subsequently, he presented her with a magnificent riding horse, while General Sherman gave Swain a fine, if spirited, carriage horse. The acceptance of these gifts, probably taken from other southerners, caused a public scandal. When a love match developed between Ellie Swain and the handsome Yankee officer, her parents joined in the widespread consternation. Nevertheless, Atkins and Miss Swain were married on August 23, 1866, in a ceremony attended by the William A. Grahams and other family friends. Atkins and Swain were burned in effigy as the college bell tolled rudely. Swain and the university were irreparably damaged. Boatner, *Civil War Dictionary*, 28; Archibald Henderson, *The Campus of the First State University* (Chapel Hill: University of North Carolina Press, 1949), 185-188, hereinafter cited as Henderson, *Campus of the First State University*.

Lyman C. Draper to William A. Graham UNC

Rooms of
State Historical Society of Wisconsin

Madison,
February 7th., 1874.

It has been several months since I wrote you, & I feel a delicacy in troubling you again. My anxiety, however, to be faithful to the historic trust I have assumed, will, I trust, serve as some apology for this intrusion.

I have added very much to my store of materials since I formerly wrote you, regarding *Sumter & men.* Among others, secured the loan of nearly 60 original unpublished letters of Sumter to Gen. Greene,[1] & 9 or 10 of Lt. Col. Lee's[2]—transcribed them & returned the originals.

I lately had the good fortune to secure 1365 nos. of the old So. Cara. Gazette, ranging from 1735 to 1804—no one year complete, & but very few covering the Revolutionary period, though quite full for a few years preceding & subsequent to that event, yet on the whole, though not yet examined, I shall hope to find not a few matters to my purpose in them.

I have been, by a pretty extensive correspondence, quite successful in tracing out the career of the more prominent officers who served under & with Sumter.

My chief remaining want is a *careful, complete* transcript of Genl. Davie's narrative of the Campaign of 1780, & 81 if it extends to that year.

I still hope you will, in some way, contrive either to secure for me a faithful copy, or a brief loan of the manuscript—I pledging its *prompt* return.

Let me hope you will try and oblige me, so far as you may have it in y'r power to do so. I will gladly pay any copying expenses in the matter.

I think I sent you a set—6 vols.—of our Hist'l Society's Collections, some bound and some in paper covers—the best I could do. I believe I lately sent you a copy in 2 vols. of the Catalogue of our Society's Library; and a few days ago, 2 vols. on Wis'n Agriculture, and now 4 other parcels, mostly on Agriculture. I send these because I happen to have them on hand, & thinking they may possibly prove of some interest to you—that you may see what our Agriculturalists in this high Northern latitude are doing.

I am trying hard to complete a set of the N.C. Univ. Mag., & am wanting *all* nos. of the Vol. of 1844-5, except No. 2.

Also May & June,	1852.
June & Nov.	1854.
Octr.	1856.
Aug. & Sept.	1858.

Possibly you may have dups. of some of these.

I am also anxious to purchase, or at least loan, a copy of Judge Strange's novel, *Yona-Guskee*, the Cherokee Chief.[3]

I shall always be glad to serve you, whenever in my power to do so.

---

[1]The Revolutionary general Nathanael Greene (1742-1786), erstwhile quartermaster general who had resigned when the Continental Congress reorganized the quartermaster service, was given command of American forces in the South after Horatio Gates's defeat at Camden, South Carolina. Greene proved his military capacity by conducting a successful campaign against Cornwallis in the Carolinas. *CDAB*, 369-370.

[2]Henry Lee (1757-1818), of Virginia, better known as "Light-Horse Harry" Lee, commanded irregular cavalry known as "Lee's Legion" during the southern campaign in which Greene checked Cornwallis. He was especially effective at Guilford Court House (March, 1781) and Eutaw Springs (September, 1781). An ardent Federalist, Lee was governor of Virginia, 1792-1795. He wrote *Memoirs of the War in the Southern Department* . . . , which was first published in 1812. He was the father of Robert E. Lee. *CDAB*, 555.

[3]Robert Strange's novel *Eoneguski, or, The Cherokee Chief: A Tale of Past Wars* (1839).

William A. Graham to William P. Johnston[1]

UVA: HUNTER

Hillsboro' N.C.
Feb. 12th, 1874

Your letter dated 20th ult., has been received, in which on behalf of Ex Pres't Davis you desire that I shall communicate the particulars of an interview between himself and Senators Graham, Hunter & Orr, in the winter of 1864-5.

I am disposed to treat with entire respect any request from Mr. Davis, but there are objections to compliance in this case, which appear to me insuperable.

1st. The injunction of secrecy was never removed from the confidential proceedings of the Senate, of which the appointment and report of the conversation in question formed a part.

2nd. I can perceive no useful end to be answered by a revelation of these proceedings, which, I think, would only serve to gratify an idle curiosity. I am not advised whether the Secret Journals of the Senate have passed into the hands of the authorities of the United States.

But however this may be, without a greater necessity than any I perceive to exist, I am unwilling to be the medium of discovering from memory any portion of the proceedings of the Congress of which I was a member, that was not intended by that body to be made public.

Trusting that these motives will be duly appreciated by Mr. Davis.

[1]This letter and the one following were transcribed from copies at the State Archives.

William A. Graham to Robert M. T. Hunter UVA: HUNTER

Hillsboro, N.C.
Feb. 12th 1874

Professor Johnston of Lexington Va. writes me that "Ex Prest. Davis proposes to prepare a narrative of certain events of the War" and asks through him that I shall furnish "a statement of what occurred in an interview between himself and Senators Graham Hunter & Orr &c." As the matter concerns you, I think it proper that you shall be apprized of it, and of the reply I have given, of which a copy is enclosed.

I have never learned what portion, if any, of the Journals of the Confed. Congress is possessed by the authorities of the U.S.; but it is, in my opinion, quite unbecoming in those entrusted with the secrets of that Congress while it existed, to make publication of them: to no purpose, that I can perceive, except to gratify the derision of the party prevailing in the war. I write in haste—have only time to express my kindest wishes for your welfare, and my regret that Virginia did not avail herself of your capacity for usefulness in the recent election for the Senate of the U.S.

Very truly & faithfully yours

Joseph Graham to William A. Graham UNC

Charlotte,
Feb 12/74

My dear Father,

I am very thankful to hear that you have improved. The preparation which you call "Muriate of Iron" is Muriatic Acid and Quinine. And I think you should continue it longer, and try and establish your health against the sudden Spring changes.

And I would take the cod liver oil also, two or three times a day, *about two hours after eating*. If the oil you have is a little stale you should get a new bottle, which would be more palatable. *Moller's* is a very good brand. I have been very busy for some time past, and my practice has increased a good deal with the new year. If Dr. Jones was active and prompt we could soon absorb all the best business of the place. Yesterday I was unable to visit all the places where I had business. I think you will need to take some preparation of Iron which I will prescribe at the proper time. A great deal of your trouble is relaxation of the muscular fibres, not only of the general system, but also of the muscular coat of the Stomach which must be toned up and the preparation you are now taking accomplishes this, which we must try and *establish* with Iron after awhile.

We are all well. Love to Mother. I hope you or Mother will write and advise me of your case about once a week.

William P. Johnston to William A. Graham A&H
[Telegram]

Lexington, Va.
Febry 14th 1874

Your letter of Febry 11th[1] has been received. I will transmit it to Mr. Davis, who is now in England.

---

[1]This reference is to Graham's letter of February 12.

William A. Graham to Kemp P. Battle A&H

Hillsboro', N.C.,
February 14th., 1874.

It is doubtful whether the state of my health will permit me to attend the meeting of the new Board of Trustees[1] of the University of the State, in Raleigh on the 18th. inst. In looking over the list of appointees, it strikes me as greatly to be regretted that so many gentlemen who served in our old Board have been omitted. I especially allude to your Father[2] and Mr. B. F. Moore whose assistance would have been invaluable. I am gratified to observe your name among the new appointments, and hope you will, if you have not already, turn your attention to the preparation of a series of resolutions, embracing the action proper to be immediately taken in reference to the duty devolved in the Bond.

I suggest, that a Committee should be raised at once to inquire and report.

1st. What property and effects belong to the University, setting forth, (a) the number of acres of land in the tract at Chapel Hill on which the College Buildings are situated—(b) the number of College edifices, their dimensions, material of which they are built, and uses to which applied, including the number of rooms used for barrack accommodations, (c) the number of Libraries and the volumes in each (d) the Philosophical apparatus, Laboratory and Cabinet of Minerals, and museum, if any—(e) the number of Professors houses belonging to Trustees with other outbuildings for families, enumerating them and describing the grounds attached to each.

(f) What funds are owned by the Corporation proper, in the form of debts due, or other choses in action.

(g) What lands other than the tract at Chapel Hill and Lots in the village, and what, if any, Lots, beside those on which are the Prests. & Profs. Houses, and where such lands are situated and their value; so as to shew a complete schedule of assets.

2nd. What debts are due from the Corporation, to whom, and what security has been given for the same; and the state of any litigation pending thereon; and what the prospect of early determination of the same. What is the state of repair of the Buildings and enclosures, and what sum will be required to fit them for use.

3rd. What is the state of the Agricultural College Fund which was passed into the hands of the Board of Trustees. What was realized from the Land scrip issued for this object, what use has been made of it, or any part of it, what remained, and how such remainder has been disposed of, and what interest has been yielded from it, (if any)?

4th. That a Secretary & Treasurer be appointed to receive from the recent Secretary and Treasurer, all records, Books of Accounts, papers and monies, with evidences of titles to property belonging to the Corporation, and to receipt for the same, and to settle the account of said late Secretary with the Board.

5th. That a Committee of members be appointed to visit the seat of the University, examine the Buildings, & other property, take possession of the same, and commit them to the care of some person or persons, who will preserve them from injury—and make report on the same.

6th. All this being done, the question will be,

1st. Is there sufficient funds to make the repairs necessary? If so, let repairs be done.

2nd. Is there sufficient funds to organize and set the College in operation? If not, what amount per annum will be required for this object, over and above the estimate of tuition fees?

3rd. What may be expected in aid of the endowment by donations from individuals?

4. What measures should be taken to procure such? and what inducements may be held out to liberal donors? Shall a circular set forth these?

5. When should a faculty be appointed, and will it be possible to put the College in operation by the usual period, the middle of July next?

---

[1]A constitutional amendment providing for the reorganization of the university was passed by the legislature of 1872-1873 and was ratified at the polls in 1873. The new board of trustees was elected by the legislature of 1873-1874. Battle, *History of the University*, II, 50-51.

[2]William Horn Battle.

William Eaton[1] to William A. Graham UNC

Warrenton, N.C.,
February 23rd., 1874.

I have been informed by my son-in-law, and other persons, that you have often made kind enquiries about me, and have sent your regards. I write these few lines to assure you how much I appreciate your friendship. I have learned with regret that you have not recently enjoyed the same good health with which you were blessed when we formerly met at Raleigh and Oxford. I hope that your health may improve, and that the evening of your life may be as happy as the preceeding portions of it have been honorable and useful. My own health has been so delicate that I have been compelled to confine my practice to a single county, and have lost the pleasure of associating with yourself and other cherished friends of our profession.

---

[1]William Eaton, Jr. (1809-1881), of Warren County, lawyer and author, represented his county in five general assemblies and was North Carolina attorney general (1851-1852) and a delegate to the Constitutional Convention of 1865. An 1829 graduate of the University of North Carolina, Eaton served his alma mater as trustee from 1838 to 1868. He was an attorney in the 1867 lawsuit contesting the will of James C. Johnston of Edenton, a case in which Graham also was involved. Powell, *DNCB*, II, 131-132.

Nathan K. Hall to William A. Graham A&H

Buffalo,
Feby 27, 1874

My dear Sir,

About two weeks since Mr. Fillmore had an attack which seemed very much like a slight shock of paralysis, but seemed to improve slowly until day before yesterday when his symptoms were worse and yesterday we were very much alarmed and feared the most serious results. To-day, after a quite comfortable night, a consultation of physicians has given us much hope that the whole difficulty has resulted from the rupture of a small bloodvessel of the brain and that a few weeks of entire quiet may entirely restore him to health. There is of course still much anxiety in regard to his condition but we have much greater hope of a speedy recovery than we had yesterday. If there is any serious change for the worse I will endeavor to write you again.

William A. Graham to William A. Graham, Jr. A&H

Hillsboro'
March 2nd 1874

Your letter in relation to your claim against Ed. Wilkes is received this morning.

I would first write to "Williams & Young, Attornies at Law, Salt Lake City, Utah Territory," informing that you hold a note for $645. & interest against Wilkes, who, you are told, is in Railroad employment in their country; that you had learned their address through their member of Congress; that Wilkes is indebted to you by Bond on Note in this amount, and that you desire to be advised whether, they think, they can collect the debt, and on what terms—and if satisfactory, that you will forward the note at once to them for collection.

I think it best to hear from them first, as to the prospect of collection before parting with the note. In case you send it, nothing is required here to authenticate it. If he denies the note, the attornies can prove his handwriting by witnesses there.

I went to Alamance Court last week, but the weather was so bad, that for two days I did not leave James' House. I feel not very well for the last two days—wish to go to Guilford tomorrow night, but am not sure that I shall venture.

Sudie & Mr. Clark came up on Satdy. night. He left this morning for Halifax for a week or more—she will remain till he returns.

Rebecca[1] has had pneumonia, but is better. Sallie[2] was sick, when Sudie left Raleigh. George expected the appointment of physician to the blind asylum, but Mr. Clark had not heard of the matter when he left Ral. The Board should have met on friday last.

I had a letter this morning from Judge Hall, saying that Mr. Fillmore had had an attack which was feared might be paralysis; and though better, there was still anxiety on the part of his friends. He promised to write again if the symptoms became worse.

Turner is at Warren Court—no news yet of the trial of the Holden case.[3] The judgt. against Douglas[4] has been set aside, but there will probably be a new trial at this term.

There was a nol. pros. in the case of the Outlaw homicides at Alamance, on condition of their paying $100 each to his family (as is said privately), and they are expected to vote the radical ticket, as is suspected. The arrangement being made through Boyd[5] &tc.

Thompson came from the plantation and spent a week in this county. He had heard nothing of Reel, & got John McLean to take his place while here.

Love to Julia & the children.

Affectionately,

---

[1]Rebecca Cameron Graham, wife of John Washington Graham.

[2]Sallie Shaver Graham, wife of George Washington Graham.

[3]After Governor Holden was removed from office, Josiah Turner, Jr., sought first to secure a criminal indictment against him, alleging improper arrest during the Kirk-Holden War. An indictment was procured, but Governor Tod R. Caldwell refused to seek Holden's return from Washington, D.C. At the time of this letter, Turner had brought a civil suit against Holden in Warren County Superior Court. The charges were dismissed, but Turner persisted in legal pursuit of his old adversary. In 1879, Turner sued Holden in Chatham County for his 1870 "assault, arrest, & false imprisonment" and was awarded $8,000. The state supreme court, at Turner's request, remanded the case to the Chatham County Court, but he failed to pursue the matter in a timely fashion. Then, after Holden's death in 1892, Turner brought suit against his estate, seeking $15,000 for "defamation of character." Turner, demented and repudiated by his erstwhile political friends, lost the case. Raper, *Holden*, 115, 222, 234, 248, 292, 321; Harris, *Holden*, 313-314.

[4]Robert Martin Douglas (1849-1917), a son of Stephen A. Douglas, had North Carolina connections, having been born to Martha D. Martin near Douglas, Rockingham County. He was graduated from Georgetown in 1867 and returned to North Carolina to oversee his holdings there. Because of his father's admonition to "support the Constitution," he became a Republican and in July, 1868, Holden appointed him his private secretary and aide with the rank of colonel. Late in 1869, Douglas became President Ulysses S. Grant's private secretary; he remained in that position throughout Grant's first term. After service as a United States marshal in North Carolina, he studied law and was admitted to the bar in 1885. In 1896 he was elected by a fusion of Republicans and Populists to an associate justiceship on the state supreme court. He served from 1897 to 1905. Subsequently he became a Greensboro attorney, businessman, and civic leader. Powell, *DNCB*, II, 98-99.

[5]James E. Boyd.

A. B. Shankland[1] *to William A. Graham* UNC

Nashville, Tennessee,
March 9th., 1874.

Some interest has of late been awakened among certain of my acquaintances concerning our neighboring county of Williamson. The question is; "from whom did it take it's name." Inquiry has failed thus far in procuring reliable information. To-day I called upon Col. J. B. Killebrew,[2] (who has a volume now going through the press) on going through his manuscripts finds it therein stated, (has forgotten upon what authority) that it was named after "Gen. Williamson,[3] a revolutionary hero of N. Carolina." Col. K. has no other information of Gen. Williamson. I have looked through Wheeler's His. of N.C., and can find no mention made of any other Williamson than *Hugh Williamson*,[4] who possibly may have become a *Surgeon General* in the Army. Col. Killebrew believes that you can settle the question as to whether there was any Gen. Williamson, of revolutionary fame in your State. Col. K. joins me in wishing to know his real initials, if indeed there was any other Williamson of distinction than Hugh,—the historian of your State.

I shall esteem it a special favor if you can give me the information sought for.

P.S. Old citizens of Williamson County, have been questioned, no one of whom is able to state from whom their county was named.

---

[1]The writer, Shankland, has not been identified.

[2]Joseph Buckner Killebrew (1831-1908), of Tennessee, was a graduate of the University of North Carolina. A versatile man, Killebrew was a lawyer, planter, author, and editor. He was agent of the Peabody board, assistant superintendent of public instruction, commissioner of agriculture, and editor of the *Nashville Union and American*, 1871-1872, and of the *Rural Sun*, 1887-1892. Grant, *Alumni History*, 341.

[3]The only southerner named Williamson who became a Revolutionary general was Andrew Williamson of South Carolina. A native of Scotland, "probably illiterate but highly intelligent and a skilled woodsman," he owned a plantation, Whitehall, near Ninety-Six. He played a key role in the action at Ninety-Six in November, 1775, and commanded the South Carolina militia in the Cherokee War of 1776. Promoted brigadier general of militia in 1778, he refused to accept Robert Howe's orders during the Florida expedition, helped force the British from Augusta, and took part in the successful assault on Savannah in October, 1779. He refused to participate in the Charleston campaign in 1780. His role thereafter is unclear, but many patriots considered him a turncoat; for a while, he resided among the British in Charleston. Through the intervention of influential friends, Williamson, sometimes called the Benedict Arnold of the South, was allowed to remain in South Carolina. Mark Mayo Boatner III (comp.), *Encyclopedia of the American Revolution* (New York: David McKay Company, 1966), 1210-1211; John S. Pancake, *This Destructive War: The British Campaign in the Carolinas, 1780-1782* (University, Ala.: University of Alabama Press, 1985), 69, 75-76, 80-81.

[4]Hugh Williamson (1735-1819), a native of Pennsylvania, graduated from the College of Philadelphia and entered the medical profession. After study in London and Edinburgh, he obtained his M.D. degree from Utrecht. It was Williamson who carried the news of the Boston Tea Party to England, urging a change in colonial policy. He returned to America in 1776 and established himself in business in Edenton. He was appointed surgeon general of the state troops and was a member of the Continental Congress, 1782-1785 and 1787

until its end. He was a delegate to the convention of 1787, signed the Constitution, and worked for ratification. Williamson represented North Carolina in Congress, 1789-1793. He was one of the original trustees of the University of North Carolina. A scientist and a prolific writer on many subjects, Williamson moved to New York in 1793. *CDAB*, 1216.

D. G. Stinson[1] *to William A. Graham* A&H

Rock Hill,
March 9th., 1874.

Your favor dated Jan. 14 by some delay in the mails only reached me a few days ago. I regret the delay, and hope you will understand and excuse the seeming neglect.

I have no documents relative to the Mecklenburg Declaration, my knowledge of it is altogether from memory.

In the year 1813 I was a student at New Providence Academy, Mecklenburg County, Rev. Jas. Wallis,[2] Teacher. I also boarded in his family. This year the venerable John McNitt Alexander came to the house on a visit to his daughter, Mrs. Wallis. He remained a month or more, he frequently spoke of the Revolutionary War, I remember his speaking of a meeting in Charlotte in May, 1775.

Also in that same year he had occasion to visit Philadelphia, that he had while there, frequent conversations with Dr. Franklin[3] relative to the then state of the Country. I remember his mention of an incident he spoke of illustrating one of Dr. Franklin's whims. On one occasion Mr. Alexander, on going to visit him, found Dr. F. busily engaged in swinging the door. On coming nearer Mr. A. found that he had horse hair attached to the door in such a manner as to cause a musical sound with the motion. The conversations of Mr. Alexander on this visit at the house where I boarded, conveyed the first intimation I ever had of that Mecklenburg Declaration. Mr. Alexander himself possessed a copy but lost it, in the burning of his house. He had however given a copy to Gen'l Davie.

In August 1851 I was at the house of the late Mrs. Smart.[4] The old lady was talkative, made many inquiries, and spoke of many Revolutionary incidents, recalling names known to us both. She spoke also of being a spectator at that meeting in Charlotte in May 1775. She remembered that there was a great crowd present, that they threw up their hats at the reading of the Resolutions. She called it the day of the throwing up of hats. I wrote a sketch of Mrs. Smart, and published in Sept. of the same year. A copy can be obtained from Maj. John A. Bradley,[5] Chester, who has kept a file.

I regret my information on the subject of the Declaration should be so meagre, but hope you will be able elsewhere to find all the proof you wish.

---

[1]D. G. Stinson has not been further identified.

[2]The Reverend James Wallis had married Abigail Bain Alexander, the daughter of John McKnitt Alexander. Their son, James Wallis, described the events of May, 1775, at the closing ceremonies of the Sugar Creek Academy on June 1, 1809. His speech appeared in the *Raleigh Minerva* on August 10, 1809; a portion of it was published in the *Catawba Journal*, July 11, 1826. Blythe and Brockmann, *Hornet's Nest*, 43-44.

[3]Benjamin Franklin.

[4]Susan (Susannah) Barnett (b. ca. 1762) had married George W. Smart in 1775. She was said to have been a friend of Andrew Jackson and to have witnessed the signing of the Mecklenburg Declaration. In 1790 the Smarts were living in District 2 of Mecklenburg County. Ray, *Mecklenburg Signers*, 313, 326, 336, 476.

[5]Major John A. Bradley has not been further identified.

William P. Johnston to William A. Graham A&H

Lexington, Va.
March 25th, 1874.

Your letter to me was forwarded to Mr. Davis in England, as I had the honor to apprize you. The enclosed reply[1] has been received with a permission to explain or submit it to you. I have adopted the latter method as probably the more agreeable to you.

With the hope that it may prove satisfactory, I have the honor to remain,

---

[1]The letter was returned to Johnston but was not found in his papers at Tulane University. It is not included in Dunbar Rowland (ed.), *Jefferson Davis, Constitutionalist: His Letters, Papers, and Speeches.*

Robert C. Winthrop to William A. Graham A&H

Boston,
90 Marlboro' St.,
March 26th., 1874.

I sent you a Paper containing my little notices of Fillmore & Sumner, in the former of which I was glad to find a place for your name. I send you now a little Paper of mine on "Sir Walter Raleigh," which ought to interest you, as a North Carolinian. You will soon receive, by Express, a copy of the Volume of the Proceedings of the Peabody Trustees, as ordered by the Board. I hope it will be satisfactory.

You may remember that our next Annual Meeting was fixed for the middle of October, in New York, with a *proviso* that I might call it in August at the White Sulphur, if, on consultation, it should be found best.

Now, the health of my wife's young daughter induces us to go abroad for 6 months, & we embark, God willing, from New York on the 6th. of May. It would thus be impossible for me to be at the White Sulphur. Our Secretary, Mr. Russell, too, said he could not be in this Country 'till October. Genl. Taylor, too, is among the absentees, & Macalester is dead. With the uncertainties which attach to our other members, I fear the Meeting at the Springs would be a disappointment, if not a failure. Dr. Sears & Gov. Clifford agree with me in this opinion. But I desire the judgment of yourself & Gov. Aiken, & I have just written to Aiken. Please drop me a line at your early convenience, so that I may consider the matter settled one way or the other.

We did not fail to receive the Cards for your daughter's wedding,[1] and were much gratified by so kind a remembrance. Our best wishes are hers; but

I never have anything but sympathy, &, I had almost said, condolence, for fathers and mothers who lose so fine a daughter from their home circle.

Believe me,
Dear Gov. Graham,
Hastily but heartily,
Yours

[1]Susan Washington Graham and Walter McKenzie Clark were married in January, 1874. Clark, "Graham Descendants"; Grant, *Alumni History*, 112; Brooks, *Walter Clark*, 48-49.

D. G. Stinson to William A. Graham A&H

Rock Hill,
March 26th., 1874.

When I wrote to you on the 9th. I wrote from memory of facts that I had heard more than 60 years ago, reflecting on the subject, I thought propper of making a few remarks.

The interview that Mr. Alexander had with Dr. Franklin, it was not the first or only interview. Mr. A. entered the room unannounced, he looked on at Dr. F. swinging of the door untill he was noticed by the Dr.

I now recolect that Dr. F. approved of the proceedings of the Meclinburg convention. It is supposed that from the character of Mr. Alexander, that he was prepared with documents and probably gave Dr. F. a copy of the proceedings of the convention. It will be recolected that Dr. F. was one of the committee of five, which drew up the declaration of 76, more than a year after the meclinburg independance, hence the declaration was known at least to Dr. F., the similarity of the two declarations being somewhat similar.

I was mistaken in saying I had heard from Mr. Alexander that he had given Gen'l Davie a copy, my impression now is, that I heard that fact either from Mrs. Wallace, or the wife of John McNitt Wallis, who was a daughter of the sister of Genl. Davie. This dec. of Mec. was more than a year before the colonies came up to the standpoint of Meclinburg, pressed with the war.

I am not at all suprised that the Scotch Irish of Mec. was in the advance of the colonies, their preachers were men of talent and education, they also had a litary institution at Charlotte.

See Dr. Howe's[1] history of the Presbyterian Church page 501 the Rev. Wm. Martin[2] brought before Cornwallis at Winnsboro, and made use of the following remarks; "protection and allegiance go together, and where one fails, the other cannot be exacted. The Dec. of independence is but a reiteration of what our covenanting fathers have always maintained."

P.S. I am now an octogenarian, and have to employ an amanuensis, being very nervous, particularly in the right hand

[1]Dr. George Howe was the author of *History of the Presbyterian Church in South Carolina.*

[2]William Martin, a native of Ireland, immigrated to South Carolina in 1773. He was a Reformed Presbyterian, or "Covenanter," minister.

Tax List of William A. Graham UNC

W. A. Graham State Tax List 1st April 1874. Hillsboro' Township.

1. Lots about residence in Hillsboro including purchases from Turentines assignees, Browns assignee, & P. C. Cameron, about 3 ½ acres with dwelling & outhouses.
2. Drugstore Lot on Tryon Street 66 feet front, unimproved.
3. Lot 237, south of & adjoining colored grave yards.
4. Old Homestead, East of P. C. Cameron, 56 acres.

5 Estes tract on Eno & Spirit branch, 833 acres—Cedar Grove Township.
6 Ray tract on Foresters creek 525 acres—Durham Township.
7 Half of Cole tract on Eno 92 acres.

8	Two Head horses (one since dead)			Value $ 200.
9	Two Mules both quite old			125.
10	8 cows & yearlings 4 calves			100.
11	Farming utensils, mechanic tools Ho. & Ki. Furniture, Provisions, arms[,] wearing apparel, Library & scientific instruments			1100.
12	Money on hand 20. on deposit $3500.			
13	Solvent credits Charlotte	5000		
	Wil, Char & Ruth. Bonds	1000		
	McBrides Bond	500		
		6500		
	Smith debt.		1600	
	Debt to Mrs. [illegible] land fund		3000	
	State Nat. Bank		2000	
			6600.	
14	Railroad Stocks company paying tax. do Bonds company paying tax.			
15	Other personal property - 1 Piano 150. Plated & silver ware watches & jewelry $500			$ 650.
15	[*sic*] Income from Profession			2947.
	Do from Interest etc on property not taxed			1568.
				4515
	Deduct for labor & maintaining family		1000	
	" State tax		162	
	Repairs		87	1249
				3276.
	Exempt			500
	Nett income			2776.

James C. Welling to William A. Graham A&H

The Columbian University,
Washington,
April 7th., 1874.

I yesterday took the liberty of sending you a paper of mine in the current (April) number of the *North American Review*, on the Mecklenburg Declaration of May 20, 1775. I have previously intimated to you the very decided conclusion to which I have been brought by my studies under the head—studies begun many years ago, and the results of which I more than once announced in the columns of the National Intelligencer during my connection with that journal. Indeed, the review article is little more than the enlarged edition of a paper I published on the same topic in the Intelligencer of Sep. 19th., 1856. At the time of writing the Intelligencer paper, I had not been apprised of the discrepancy (brought to light by Prof. Phillips) between the certificate attached to "the Davie copy" and that published by Dr. Jos. McK. Alexander in the year 1819. The statements made by Prof. Phillips under this head have been so certified to me that I am bound to receive them as authentic. In the absence of these statements I was led to distrust the genuineness of the paper of May 20th, but in their presence the *un-historical* character of that paper must be conceded by all.

I am sorry that I was not able to write on this subject with the benefit I should have derived from your promised discussion of the same theme. As I have no other purpose in this matter than to ascertain the truth of history, I beg that you will do me the favor to send me a copy of any publication you may make under this head.

Renewing to you the expression of my constant regard, I am, my dear Sir,

Your humble friend and servant,

Walter J. Budd[1] *to William A. Graham* UNC

Philadelphia,
April 8th 1874

Your favor of 1st inst. was received but a day or two since, and I take the earliest opportunity to answer it, after consultation with my colleagues and our clients, and regretting extremely my inability to give you an earlier response.

We believe that the interests of the construction bondholders are identical with the individual stockholders of the N.C. R.R. at least so far as both are desirous of securing a Dividend upon the Stock.

Whether those interests will best be secured by opposing or supporting the proposed consolidation of the N.C. R.R. with the W. N.C. R.R. and the A. & N.C. R.R. neither I nor my colleagues are at present able to form any positive opinion.

It is true, we filed a bill to prevent the appropriation of the rent due upon the lease of the road, by the Directors to a purpose unauthorized by the charter, but we are not so confident that we have the right to prevent the proposed consolidation, Neither of us having had an opportunity to examine the acts of the Legislature authorizing the proposed action.

Another very material question is the costs and expenses of an application to the Court for an injunction to restrain the consolidation. Those whom we represent have up to this time borne all the risks, & expenses of what has been done & we do not feel justified in advising them to take upon themselves the trouble costs & risks of any further proceedings in the matter, especially as the time in which to act is so very short.

---

[1]Walter J. Budd was an attorney whose office was located on South 6th Street in Philadelphia.

William A. Graham to William P. Johnston A&H

Hillsboro', N.C.,
April 21st., 1874.

A prolonged indisposition from which I am, as I trust, slowly recovering has prevented the earlier acknowledgement of yours of the 25th. ult., enclosing a letter from Ex-President Davis, of the 5th. of the same month, for my perusal.

For the reasons stated in my last, I should have preferred that the secret and confidential affairs of the Confederate senate, of which I was a member, so far as they have not been revealed, and to what extent that is, I know not, should remain undivulged; but Mr. Davis' letter shews such a misapprehension in some important particulars, that I feel bound to contribute what aid may be in [my] power for its correction.

The only interview I remember, between him and the three Senators, Graham, Hunter & Orr, was when they waited on him as a Committee of the Senate under a resolution of that body,[1] of which a copy was exhibited to him at the opening of the meeting, and I supposed a copy had been left with him. If this was not done, it must be attributed to inadvertence on his part, in not asking for it, or on mine in not tendering it. As Chairman of the Committee I was furnished with a copy, which I certainly presented to him in making known our errand, and which he read; but it may be, that being charged with the duty of making a report to the Senate, I resumed the same copy on leaving the President. It was simply an instruction to the Committee, but I am sure there was no objection on the part of any one to leaving a copy with the President.

The time of this interview, I believe, was about the 10th. or 11th. of March, 1865, within a week or ten days before the final adjournment of Congress. If the Journal of the Senate is in existence (as to which, as I have advised you heretofore, I am in profound ignorance) and is accessible, the resolution in question can, no doubt, be found therein, about this date. I have no copy of it, or of any portion of the Journal; the speedy overthrow of the Confederate Government which ensued, probably prevented it from being printed. The substance of the resolution, I state it from memory, was an instruction to this Committee to confer with the President in relation to our military defences, and especially in relation to their sufficiency for the protection of the Confederate States and people. I did not draft or present the resolution, nor do I remember to have been consulted in respect [to] it before the introduction, but after its adoption, I was appointed Chairman of the Committee.

The interview was a protracted one, extending through an hour or possibly two. After discussing the military situation in Virginia, and arriving at the probability, which I think was admitted by both the President & Committee, that our army there would soon be compelled to fall back, and the Government to leave Richmond; and no definite plan being presented of what was to be the further operations of defence; the conversation naturally led to the question, what was to be done in case of the catastrophe which was apprehended. It was then that the suggestion was made, that new negotiations should be opened with the Federal Government, and the best terms that were practicable should be obtained, while we were yet armed, and in the possession of formidable power. The President was averse to this, and considered such a course an act of "suicide." He inquired if that was the wish of the Senate, to which Mr. Orr replied, that the Senate had not so indicated, but that in a conference such as this, he thought it not improper to express our individual opinions. The President remarked, that if such was the opinion of the Senate, it should be signified to him by a resolution.

I of course do not profess to give minute details on the literal accuracy of the expressions in this conversation, but I am positive in my recollection, that the fact that the Senators named visited the President in the character of a Committee, and that the scope of their mission as contained in the resolution under which they were appointed were made known to the President at the start of their conference.

I feel the more confident in the statement made above, from the fact, that after the failure of the Conference at Fortress Monroe, and a short time before the visit of this Committee, in a private interview with the President, sought for this purpose, I stated to him my strong conviction, that the army of Gen'l Lee would soon be overpowered, & probably dispersed, and urged that he should send another commission, and obtain the best terms possible for the Confederate States. To which he replied courteously, but very firmly declined, using the illustration of "suicide" as in the later conversation.

It is proper to add that no resolution on the subject of negotiation or peace was passed by the Senate before or after the interview in question, and to call to mind that, within some twenty days after its occurrence, the Federal forces were in the occupation of Richmond.

Presuming the President's letter was forwarded merely for my perusal, it is returned herewith.

---

[1]The resolution, introduced by Texan Louis T. Wigfall on March 2, 1865, provided for a committee "to confer with the president confidentially in reference to the present condition of the country and to ascertain, if possible, his plans and purposes." The committee was chosen by ballot and Graham, who received the largest vote, was chairman. *Journal of the Congress of the Confederate States of America, 1861-1865* (Washington: Government Printing Office, 7 volumes, 1904-1905), IV, 633.

William P. Johnston to William A. Graham A&H

Lexington, Virginia,
April 29th., 1874.

Please accept my thanks for your favor of April 21st., enclosing also Mr. Davis' letter to me, transmitted for your perusal. After such a lapse of time, it is quite natural that the recollection of gentlemen should vary, even as to important events. Their friendly comparison of their remembrances might well result in setting right the record, in the truth of which, our Statesmen are equally interested, however they may have differed as to minor matters.

In view of a settled purpose on the part of those in power to falsify this record by perversion and suppression, it seems due to the South that her chosen leaders should guard her fair fame in the past, as far as possible, in all important points.

I will send your letter to Mr. Davis, who is now in Paris.

Joseph Graham to William A. Graham UNC
[with enclosure]

Charlotte
May 22/74

My dear Father,

Cousin Julia Smith[1] has been for a week *quite sick* with Dysentery, and Mrs. Macaulay[2] is now worse than for some time. And I have some other patients who now require *close* attention. Consequently, as *you* do not *need* my services, I will be obliged to decline accompanying you to Philadelphia at this time. I am thankful to say my throat is improved. The Med Society has been with us this week, and we have had quite an interesting meeting.

I enclose you a letter of introduction to Da Costa.[3] And I will write him before you get there a letter giving him as well as I can recollect what has been done for you, and asking him, *in my name* to make a very careful examination of your chest, and tell me what his opinion is concerning the chest trouble—that is all I want him to do. The balance of it *I am sure* I understand as well as he can.

I am and have been all week troubled with Dysentery—feel a little better today. Love to Mother, and all.

---

[1]In all probability this was Julia Susan Alexander Smith (1837-1905), the widow of Thomas McGehee Smith (1834-1864). She was William A. Graham's niece from Mecklenburg County, a daughter of Moses Winslow and Violet Graham Alexander. The Smiths were married in 1859. Spencer Alumni Project; Clark, "Graham Descendants."

[2]Mrs. Macaulay has not been identified.

[3]Jacob Mendez Da Costa (1833-1900), a native of St. Thomas, Virgin Islands, taught and practiced his profession at Jefferson Medical College, Philadelphia, 1872-1891. His *Medical Diagnosis* (1864) was a widely used and influential publication. *CDAB*, 211.

[Enclosure]
Joseph Graham to Jacob M. Da Costa UNC

Charlotte N.C.
May 22nd 1874

My dear Doctor

This letter will introduce to you my father, whose chest I am anxious for you to examine, and give him your opinion as to Dyspnoea, and other troublesome symptoms, which have for some time much impaired his health. I am sorry I was not able to accompany him and renew our old acquaintance of /58 & /59. Kindest regards to Dr. Brinton.[1]

---

[1]Daniel Garrison Brinton (1837-1899) graduated from Yale, 1858, and from Jefferson Medical College, 1861. He was a military surgeon during the Civil War and editor of the *Medical and Surgical Reporter*, 1874-1887. After he retired as editor he devoted full time to anthropological research. His various publications included *Notes on the Floridian Peninsula* (1859) and *The American Race* (1891). *CDAB*, 108.

William A. Graham to Montford McGehee UNC

Hillsboro
May 23rd, 1874

. . . .

I hope you will carry out your intention to come and spend a day or two with me soon. I propose to go to Philadelphia, leaving home on Monday 25th, for the purpose of medical advice, but hope not to be absent more than a week or ten days. My health is I trust somewhat improved, but my physicians advise that I submit to an examination at Phila.

I fear we are destined to sad blunders in the ensuing election. In this County, if the nominees for the Legislature are confirmed, and hold on, I do not feel sure of a majority for any one. I seldom go out, and was not at the meeting for nomination, but I have never known a more unfit ticket proposed in Orange. Caswell & Person can probably correct the matter in the senate, but the Commoners can neither uphold their cause or themselves.

The nomination of Waddell[1] is ascribable solely to the influence of Wilmington for which he has gotten one or two appropriations to open their inlet: and they take him with a *non obstante*[2] in the salary matter. Even with this, he is greatly preferable to Neill McKay.[3] You observe that Hoke[4] is an indifferent candidate for judge. Schenck[5] is said to have unfairly gotten the nomination. The practice of township delegates to elect candidates leads to so much of imposture that I doubt whether a nomination in that way will not come to be considered an objection instead of a recommendation.

The passage of the civil rights bill, which seems assured before the adjournment of Congress, will help the conservatives in the election in the state, if properly availed of. The radicals, I learn, are holding a nominating meeting here today . . . and will rally the negroes in full array. You observe that the first duty devolved on the Board of Trustees of the Univ. is to endeavor to rescue the property from the hands of its destroyers. Mr. Poole has gotten 30 days to put in an answer, and I presume, intends to baffle by delay, as far as possible.

I write in haste on the eve of my journey from home. I shall expect you to tarry at my house when you come to Hillsboro.

[1]Alfred Moore Waddell (1834-1912) of Wilmington, a native of Hillsborough and a son of Hugh Waddell, graduated from the University of North Carolina and was a lawyer, journalist, and politician. A Whig, he supported the Bell-Everett ticket in 1860. He was for a time lieutenant colonel of the Forty-first North Carolina Regiment. After the war Waddell was a Democratic member of Congress, 1871-1879, and the mayor of Wilmington, 1898-1904. Spencer Alumni Project; *Biographical Directory of Congress*, 1758.

[2]"Notwithstanding" or "not hindering" used here by Graham implies that Waddell would be acceptable to his constituents despite questionable practices.

[3]Neill McKay (b. 1830) was graduated by the University of North Carolina in 1851 and became a lawyer. In 1855 he was elected state solicitor for newly formed Harnett County. He represented Cumberland County in the House of Commons, 1862-1864, and Harnett County in the General Assembly of 1865-1866. He resigned the latter position in February, 1866. McKay also represented Cumberland County in the Constitutional Convention of 1865-1866. At the time of this letter he was a Republican candidate for the Third District seat in the United States House of Representatives. Grant, *Alumni History*, 394; Cheney, *North Carolina Government*, 329, 333, 357n, 358n, 832; Oates, *Story of Fayetteville*, 613.

[4]John Franklin Hoke.

[5]David L. Schenck.

James B. Groome[1] *to William A. Graham* UNC

State of Maryland.
Executive Department.

Annapolis,
May 28th., 1874.

I have the honor to inform you that, by the concurrent action of the Legislatures of Maryland and Virginia, the Honorable Jeremiah S. Black,[2] and yourself, and a third person, to be selected by Mr. Black and yourself, were requested to act as arbitrators, and to ascertain and determine the true boundary line between the States of Virginia and Maryland, and to deliver your award in writing, any two of you concurring therein.

Therewith enclose a copy of the Act of the General Assembly of Maryland, and most cordially join with the Governor of Virginia, in requesting that you accept the trust thus tendered.

It will give me pleasure to cooperate with Mr. Black and yourself in carrying into effect all such arrangements as you may make for inaugurating, conducting, and facilitating the business of arbitration as soon as you may make known your wishes in the premises.

The Post Office address of Mr. Black is, I am informed, York, Pennsylvania.

I am, Sir, your obedient servant,

[1]James Black Groome (1838-1893), born in Cecil County, Maryland, was admitted to the bar in 1861 and began practice in Elkton, Maryland. He was a member of the state House of Delegates, 1871, 1872, and 1873, a position from which he resigned when he was elected

governor to fill the unexpired term of William Pinckney Whyte. Groome served as governor of Maryland from 1874 to 1876. He was elected as a Democrat to the United States Senate and served 1879-1885. From 1889 until 1893 he was collector for the port of Baltimore. *Biographical Directory of Congress*, 1038.

[2]Jeremiah Sullivan Black (1810-1883), a Pennsylvania lawyer and statesman, had by this time earned for himself a reputation for being a strong and resolute man capable of making and defending decisions. As United States attorney general, 1857-1858, he had vigorously investigated California land titles and exposed a system of fraud in district court decisions. Black opposed secession of the southern states but was critical of the administration's harsh retaliatory actions after the war. He was a counsel to Andrew Johnson and in 1873 helped to revise the Pennsylvania Constitution. *CDAB*, 78.

William A. Graham to Augustus W. Graham UNC

Continental Hotel,
Philadelphia,
May 29th., 1874.

We made our journey comfortably, stopping all night in Raleigh, sleeping the next night on the Chesapeake Boat, & reaching Baltimore at 10 o'clock, too late for the Phil'a train, and had to loitre at the depot 'till 2:40 p.m: & taking a train, reached Phil'a about 7 p.m.—Communicated with Dr. DaCosta and attended him at his office for examination at 3 p.m. yesterday. His report is encouraging, and will write to Joseph, to whom he is much attached, full particulars, as well as prescription for my guidance. He is a physician in very full practice, and certainly very devoted to his profession. After my interview with him, my friend Mr. Edwin G. Booth,[1] formerly of Nottoway Co. Va., Virginia [*sic*], and educated at Chapel Hill, who has married here a second wife of great wealth, & resides in the City, called with Mrs. Booth & a carriage, and took your Mother & myself to ride, to West Philadelphia, across the Schuylkill River, and a new Park, much larger than that in New York, where preparations are being made for the Centennial exposition. The grounds of this Park are high, and shew the City below to cover a much larger space than New York, though the population is not so great,—and retired merchants and Bankers are erecting Palatial residences in West Phila. The exhibitions of wealth and luxury in all this Country shew a sad contrast to any portion of the Southern States.

My acquaintance, except Mr. Booth who is a true Virginian has nearly worn out in Phila., all the gentlemen in public life with me from the City having passed away.

Dr. DaCosta does not deem it necessary to see me again, and has gone out of the City. We shall, therefore, probably leave tomorrow, spend Sunday in Balt., Norfolk, or possibly New York, and expect to reach home by Tuesday evening.

Your Mother is out shopping with Miss Hinnop.[2] I have been down today to Independence Hall, and was much struck with the portrait of Wm. Hooper,[3] the signer of the declaration of Independence from N.C. He is, by far, the best specimen of a man, in personal appearance, of any of the name I have ever seen. He is buried, you know, at the corner of our lot in the Church yard.

Our love to John and Rebecca.

Affectionately Yours,

---

[1]Edwin G. Booth was a graduate of Hampden-Sydney (ca. 1831). He was a member of the House of Delegates and a trustee of his alma mater, 1851-1867. *Virginia Magazine of History and Biography*, VI, 223.

[2]Miss Hinnop has not been identified.

[3]William Hooper (1742-1790), lawyer and statesman, represented North Carolina in the Continental Congress, 1775-1777, and was a signer of the Declaration of Independence. *CDAB*, 452.

Frederick A. P. Barnard to William A. Graham UNC

Columbia College,
New York.

President's Room,
June 3rd., 1874.

A good many months have passed since we had some correspondence in regard to an article to be furnished to Johnson's Cyclopedia, on the subject of the "Mecklenburg Declaration of Independence." Unexpected delays in the preparation of the first volume have rendered it unnecessary that this subject should be provided for as early as I at first expected. Our first volume is however, now complete and in the hands of the binder; and we shall proceed to take up the second without delay. I trust, therefore, that you will find it convenient to furnish the article referred to before very long.

Under the head "Declaration," in volume first, reference is made for the history to the title "Mecklenburg." Since our correspondence occurred, President Welling of the Columbian College, Washington, has been laboring to discredit the Mecklenburg Declaration of the 20th of May; and he read before the New York Historical Society, an elaborate paper designed to impeach the authenticity of the Declaration itself. I sincerely trust therefore, that nothing may have occurred to interfere with your design to present the subject in our work in it's true light.

Jeremiah S. Black to William A. Graham[1] UNC

York, Penna,
June 4th., 1874.

I have received official notice from the Governors of Virginia and Maryland that by concurrent legislative acts of those two States you and I are chosen to adjust and settle certain questions concerning their boundary lines. I know nothing about the subject matter of the controversy or the merits of either claim but I presume the questions are of considerable importance and not free from difficulties of fact and law since they have stood open for many years and are still earnestly contested. The Legislatures have simply agreed to submit the case to us but have not prescribed any mode time or place for the hearing or determination of it. The Governors show by their letters to me that they regard every regulation of details as being within our discretion. They have suggested that I should open a correspondence with you.

I intend to accept this appointment, and perform the duties pertaining to it as well as I can, feeling it a very high honor not only because it implies confidence of which I am proud but because it associates me with you for whose character as a public man I have a profound respect.

It seems that we have the right to appoint an umpire. I presume we may do this at once and permit him to sit at the hearing from the beginning or we may wait until some disagreement shall arise between ourselves to make the intervention of an umpire necessary. But *when* the umpire shall be chosen, or *who* he shall be are subjects upon which I have formed no judgment and intend to form none until I have a full and free conference with you. My mind is equally void of all preconceptions about time, place of hearing and rules of proceeding. On these preliminaries it will be my duty to consult your convenience and that of the gentlemen who will represent the States as their counsel.

In short I do not see what can be done even as a beginning until we have a meeting for consultation at which the counsel should be invited to attend. What else can you suggest? If nothing, when and where shall we come together? The State authorities will do all they can to start us in the business. Of this I suppose they have given you the same assurance that I have received.

[1]This letter was enclosed in a letter from Black dated June 15, 1874, and printed in this volume. Black explains in the second letter why this June 4 letter was delayed.

Joseph Graham to William A. Graham UNC

Charlotte, N.C.,
June 4th., 1874.

My dear Father,

Your letter to hand today. I had a communication from Dr. DaCosta written the day he had you before him. What he says relative to your case is as follows: "I examined his case carefully, and am distinctly of opinion that Malarial poisoning with some enlargement of the spleen lies at the root of his troubles. I find no evidence of disease of the lungs—a slight bronchial catarrh is all. (*hence the phlegm*) (*Graham*). But the heart is decidedly affected—there is a moderate degree of dilated hypertrophy (enlargement) with regurgitant mitral disorder." (the middle valves do not close tight, but allow some blood to flow back). "Hence the shortness of breath on exertion etc. Of course these symptoms become aggravated when the malaria shows itself actively, or the dyspeptic symptoms become worse. Besides directions bearing on the question of exercise, etc., with reference to the cardiac trouble, I recommend a pill consisting of Arseniate of Soda, Ignatia, Rhubarb and Quinine."

I am very glad you went on and obtained his opinion, tho' it is very much the same view which I have taken of it for some time. And his remedies are much the same as I have at different times prescribed for you. Still, I have every confidence in his skill as a diagnostician, and it gives me confidence on which to proceed whenever these symptoms arise. This affection of the heart is *organic*, not functional, and tho' by following the proper regime and taking good care of yourself in every respect your health may become quite comfortable and you may live some years yet, it is incurable. There is change in the heart substance itself. I am of opinion that your family have some hereditary tendency that way. You should avoid every thing, both mental and physical, which will disturb the even and smooth tenor of your life. Dr. DaCosta did not mention specially the giving up of your professional duties, but I infer that you should not enter actively into them, nor trouble yourself with any case which will involve much labor of any kind, or induce any excitement. In fact, you should give yourself up entirely to the care of yourself, *at least* 'till next winter. This matter is all important, and I do hope you will take care of yourself while yet it is worth while. You had best have Dr. Hooker[1] prepared to make your pills, by ordering the ingredients in time. Keep your blood rich, and the heart quiet as much as you can. This should be never forgotten, when you do not feel well.

I am sorry Mother does not feel well. I hope you will both come to see us soon. Cousin Isabella Hayes[2] has disease of the heart, but is in very comfortable health now.

All send love to Mother, and yourself,

Your affect' Son,

Anna Barringer[3] died yesterday.

---

[1]Dr. Octavius Wright Hooker, a native of Hillsborough, received his bachelor's degree from the University of North Carolina in 1845 and his master's in 1849. At the time of this letter he evidently was practicing in Hillsborough. Hooker was one of those who foresaw the dangers inherent in the Ku Klux Klan movement. He was chairman of the county board of superintendents and in this position handled the county allotment from the important Literary Fund. Grant, *Alumni History*, 295; Lefler and Wager, *Orange County*, 119, 185.

[2]Isabella, daughter of Violet Graham and Dr. Moses Winslow Alexander, was the wife of Dr. William James Hayes (1821-1898) of Lincoln County, who settled in Mecklenburg. Clark, "Graham Descendants"; Sherrill, *Annals of Lincoln County*, 139.

[3]Anna Barringer (b. 1855) was the daughter of William A. Graham's niece Eugenia Morrison and her husband, General Rufus Barringer. Clark, "Graham Descendants."

Willie Graham[1] to William A. Graham UNC

Charlotte June 5th 1874

My Dear grand pa

I was very glad to hear Papa say that you are feeling better and that you think of coming to see us soon. I am still going to the graded school and like it much better than I did at first. Our exhibition will take place on the 19th of this month, and I am going to say a little speech then. this is the seond letter I ever wrote, as I have only been learning about four or five weeks.

We are all well. It rained most all day, the first good rain for a long time. Please give my love to grandma.

Your fond grandson

[1]The son of Joseph Graham.

William A. Graham to James L. Kemper[1] UNC

Hillsboro', N.C.
June 8th., 1874.

Sir:

I have had the honor to receive your communication of the 3rd. inst., together with that of the Governor of Maryland, accompanied by copies of Acts of the Legislatures of the States of Virginia and Maryland "to designate the arbitrators to ascertain & fix, the boundary between" these States. By these statutes, it appears that the Honble. Jeremiah S. Black of Pennsylvania, and myself have been appointed, with power to select a third person to be associated with us; and that the three shall be constituted arbitrators, to ascertain and determine the true line of boundary between the States aforesaid. To which you are pleased to add your request, that I will accept this appointment, and correspond with Judge Black, as to the inauguration and means, of conducting and facilitating the business in question.

In reply, I beg leave to express my high appreciation of this evidence of the confidence of the constituted authorities of two great States, so long and so justly distinguished in American history, and my readiness to render any aid in my power for the solution of the matters of difference existing between them.

I will, without delay, address Judge Black touching the affair, and as soon as the necessary preliminaries shall be arranged, hope to be able, in conjunction with my associates, to advise you of the place and time when the arbitrators will be prepared to hear the evidence and arguments of the high parties to the controversy.

I make today a like acknowledgement of his communication to his Excellency, the Governor of Maryland.

With assurances of great respect,
I am, Sir, Your Obed't Serv't,

[Notation in Graham's hand:]
Like letter to Governor of Maryland.

[1]James Lawson Kemper (1823-1895), of Virginia, attended the Virginia Military Institute and Washington College (now Washington and Lee University) and became a lawyer. He was a captain in the Mexican War, served as Speaker in the House of Delegates, and rose from colonel to major general in the Confederate army. Severely wounded and captured at Gettysburg, Kemper was exchanged but not expected to live. He did survive and served as governor of Virginia, 1874-1877. His administration was characterized by independence and integrity. Boatner, *Civil War Dictionary*, 452; *CDAB*, 520.

William A. Graham to Jeremiah S. Black UNC

Hillsboro', N.C.,
June 8th., 1874.

Communications from the Governors of Maryland and Virginia, accompanied by Copies of Acts of their Legislatures on the same topic, advise me that you and myself have been duly appointed to select a third person; and that the three shall be constituted arbitrators, to determine a question of disputed boundary between those States.

They further request, that I shall correspond with you, in respect to the inauguration and conduct of the business in question, and that the Governors aforesaid may be informed when the board of arbitrators shall be organized, and of the place and time, when the matter referred will be considered.

I presume that similar information has been transmitted to you.

I have not felt at liberty to decline so honorable a trust from these high sources, and take early opportunity to communicate with you concerning its fulfilment. Presuming that you will likewise accept, the matter first to be determined will be the appointment of an associate, and then a place and time for the sitting of board.

Supposing that delicacy would forbid the selection of any citizen of either of the litigant States, as an arbitrator or any place in the territorial limits of either for the session, I will thank you to inform me, whether you prefer to have a personal conference, touching the appointment in question, and other matters pertinent to the business which may occur to you, in the outset; and, if so, where it shall be held. Or whether we may not confer by letter, both as to the selection of an associate, and afterwards with him, as to the place and time of session, so as to necessitate but a single meeting, and that for the hearing and determination of the controversy.

Deferring much to your more extensive acquaintance with the competent men of the time, and to your greater conversency with topics of the nature of those involved in this reference, I shall be pleased to have a free expression of your views, so that, if possible, the matter may be terminated before the session of the Legislatures of these States in the Autumn.

Joseph J. Davis to William A. Graham UNC

Smithfield, N.C.,
June 13th., 1874.

I am troubled to learn that a memorial is being extensively signed in Orange, asking that another convention may be called to repair an injustice which, it is insisted, has been done to Mr. Turner.[1] With harmony, I think our success in this District is certain—without it defeat. I am not willing to be for one moment in the way of success and I am anxious that such course may be taken, without any reference to myself, as shall secure harmony. I am not in a position to judge as to the best action. Will you pardon for asking your wise judgment in the matter?

I shall be in Hillsboro' on the 23d., but the matter should receive immediate attention, and mature consideration. I have written to Mr. London,[2] the Chmn. of the Ex. Com: on the subject, as the Memorial, we understand, has been sent to him. I wish such action to be had, without the slightest regard to me personally, as the interest of our cause, and the good of the County may require. I have no right to have a *personal* interest in the matter that shall be in conflict with the public good—and let me say that I shall not allow myself to have one particle of personal feeling on account of any action that success may require.

The prospect in this Section is very flattering. Franklin, Nash & Johnston will overcome the 'Caldwell Majority'—if I am not greatly mistaken.

---

[1]Josiah Turner, Jr., had been a candidate for the congressional nomination and was very bitter over his defeat by Davis.

[2]Henry Armand London (1846-1918), of Chatham County, chairman of the Democratic district committee, was a graduate of the university, a lawyer, an editor, and a state senator (1901-1905). He served as a courier in the Confederate army. Grant, *Alumni History*, 372.

Jeremiah S. Black to William A. Graham UNC

York
June 15th. 1874.

The enclosed letter[1] was written at the time of its date. I omitted to sign and mail it, and went to Washington, whence I returned three or four days ago, and found yours. It is plain to me that we must meet and our meeting should be as soon as your convenience will permit. You may name the time and place, but I suggest Washington where I can be at any time it may suit you after this week. I would prefer some day between the 22d, and 26th. Do not understand that I make a point of that time or that place. I will go further South—to Raleigh, if you say so. I name Washington because I should like to see the counsel at the same time and some one for each State will be sure to attend at Washington I think. I will write to Governors Kemper and Groome informing them of my proposition to you and if you assent to it please to let them know the fact by mail or telegraph.

After looking again at the terms of submission I think as you seem to think that we will be more certainly within the meaning of it if we appoint the umpire at the start. I think we ought to make this selection very carefully but I will not begin to settle my mind upon any particular person until we have a free interchange of views.

---

[1]Jeremiah S. Black to William A. Graham, June 4, 1874.

Lyman Copeland Draper. Engraving from Lyman C. Draper, *An Essay on the Autographic Collections of the Signers of the Declaration of Independence and of the Constitution* (New York: Burns and Son, 1889), frontispiece.

William Horn Battle. Engraving from Samuel A. Ashe and others (eds.), *Biographical History of North Carolina: From Colonial Times to the Present* (Greensboro: Charles L. Van Noppen, 8 volumes, 1905-1917), VI, facing 20.

Augustus Washington Knox. Photograph courtesy of Mrs. Roy M. Chipley.

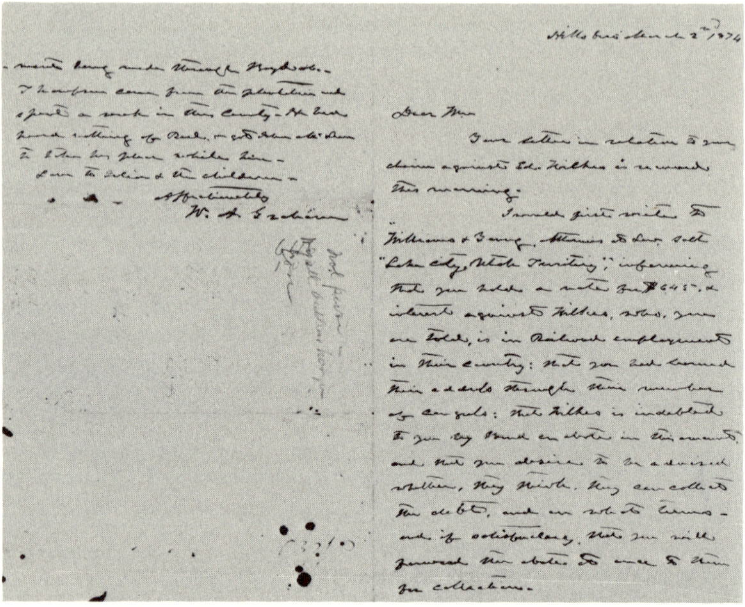

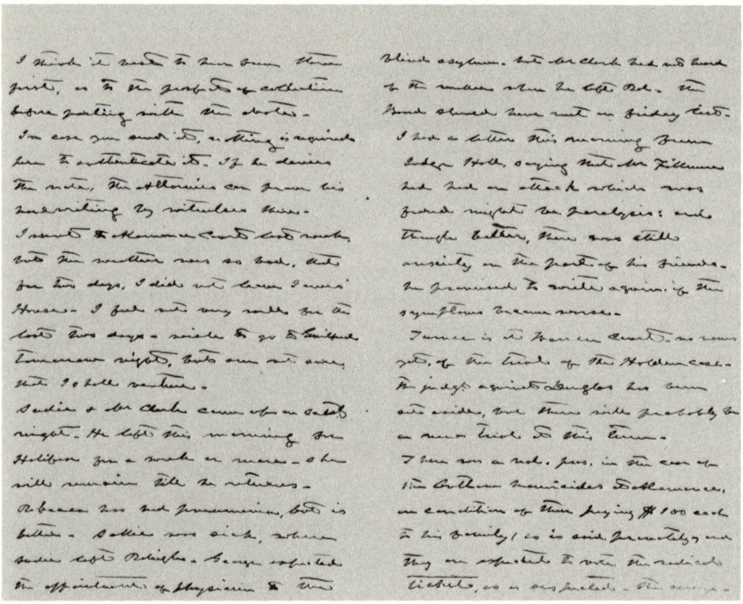

William A. Graham wrote this letter to his son William A. Graham, Jr., on March 2, 1874. Document from the William Alexander Graham Papers, Division of Archives and History, Raleigh.

This engraving showing Graham with George Peabody and the other trustees of the Peabody Education Fund appeared in *Harper's Weekly*, April 13, 1867, 228.

North Carolina Centennial

CELEBRATION

OF THE

MECKLENBURG

Declaration of Independence.

PROGRAMME.

One hundred guns, at sunrise, and ringing of city bells, under charge of the Artillery Committee.

To march at 10 o'clock A. M., Grand Procession, through the principal streets of the city, under charge of Chief Marshal and thirty Assistant Marshals, as follows:

MILITARY COMPANIES.
FIRE COMPANIES.
MASONIC LODGES.
ODD FELLOWS.
KNIGHTS OF PYTHIAS.
GOOD TEMPLARS.
PATRONS OF HUSBANDRY.
COUNTY ORGANIZATIONS.
OTHER ASSOCIATIONS OF CITY, COUNTY, STATE AND CITIZENS.
PRESS ORGANIZATIONS.
VARIOUS CENTENNIAL COMMITTEES.
ACCOMPANIED BY VARIOUS BANDS OF MUSIC, AND THEIR OWN SPECIAL BANNERS, EMBLEMS AND INSIGNIA.

The Procession will be formed in the following order:

Military Companies on both sides of South Tryon street, right front resting in front of Central Hotel.

Fire Companies on West Trade street and on Church street, opposite Fireman's Hall.

Grand Lodges, County Organizations, other city, county and State Associations, and Citizens' and Press' Organizations, on East Trade street.

Masonic Lodges, Odd Fellows, Knights of Pythias and Good Templars, on North Tryon street, from the Square to be followed by Band of Music with Military Company, to be assigned by Chief Marshal as guard of honor or escort.

In carriages, the following: The President of the United States, Governor of Tennessee and staff, Governors of other States, Governor of North Carolina and staff, United States Senators and Supreme and Superior Judges of North Carolina, Mayor of the city, and other invited guests, orators and reader, accompanied by committees.

Parade to be through principal streets, to arrive at the Speaking Grounds at 12 o'clock M. After the various companies and organizations, &c., have been arranged by the Chief Marshal and Assistants, the Centennial will be opened with prayer by the Chaplain, Rev. Robt. Hall Morrison, D. D., after which reading of the Mecklenburg Declaration of Independence by ————————, followed by addresses by ————————————. After the addresses there will be, at 3 o'clock P. M., a Grand Barbecue. After which Military and Fire Company display.

At night, at 7 o'clock P. M., Grand Torch Light Procession with Chinese Lanterns, Emblems, Transparencies, &c., &c. After which addresses will be delivered from the Stand in Independence Square, on the site of the original Declaration of May 20, 1775, corners of Trade and Tryon streets. There will be general illuminations of the houses on principal streets.

The Celebration to conclude with a Grand Pyrotechnic Display, consisting of beautiful Emblems, Figures, Mottoes, &c., &c., appropriate to the occasion, under charge of the Artillery Committee.

The Chief Marshal, with thirty Assistant Marshals, to be hereafter announced.

Approved and adopted by Central Executive Committee, March 24, 1875.

DR. JOSEPH GRAHAM,
Chairman Executive Committee.

THOS. W. DEWEY,
Secretary Executive Committee.

MARCH 25, 1875, ratified and adopted by General Committee of Arrangements.

Dr. Joseph Graham chaired the committee that organized the centennial celebration of the disputed Mecklenburg Declaration of Independence and that appointed William A. Graham "Presiding Officer" of the festivities. Printed program from the William Alexander Graham Papers, Southern Historical Collection, University of North Carolina Library, Chapel Hill.

William A. Graham and his seven sons (left to right, William Alexander, Jr., Robert Davidson, James Augustus, George Washington, John Washington, Augustus Washington, and Joseph) posed for this photograph, dated May 20, 1875. The centennial celebration of the Mecklenburg Declaration of Independence held in Charlotte on that day probably provided the opportunity for a group portrait. Photograph from the North Carolina Collection, University of North Carolina Library, Chapel Hill.

The grave site of William A. Graham and Susan Washington Graham in the Old Town Cemetery adjacent to Hillsborough Presbyterian Church.

William A. Graham to Jeremiah S. Black UNC

Hillsboro', N.C.,
June 18th., 1874.

I have had the honor to receive your two letters, the latter dated the 15th. inst., and after consideration, have concluded to accept your proposition to meet you in the City of Washington, within the time indicated therein, (22nd. to 26th. inst.) say on Thursday the 25th. of the present month, in the forenoon, at Willards Hotel, unless you apprize me in the meantime, of some other house more acceptable to you: in order to take the initial steps in the business entrusted to us by the States of Virginia and Maryland.

I thank you, for the offer to come to Raleigh, which is within forty miles of my residence, if desired by me, and being somewhat an invalid, that place would have been highly convenient but Washington had occurred to me, as it had to you, as being most accessible to all concerned, and I hope to be able to make the journey thither without serious trouble.

I shall by the mail which bears this, inform the Governors of the States aforesaid of our appointment, and of our readiness to meet any Agent or Counsel of either party, whom they may desire to be present.

Like you, I am wholly uninformed of the claims or allegations of either party or of the precise territory in dispute.

Cordially reciprocating the sentiments you are pleased to express of my public character,

I am, With sincere respect,

William A. Graham to James L. Kemper UNC

Hillsboro',N.C.
June 18th. 1874.

Sir:

Recurring to my recent letter to you on the same topic, I have now the honor to inform you, that by agreement the Honorable J. S. Black and myself will meet in the City of Washington on Thursday the 25th. inst. for the purpose of taking the initiatory steps in the business confided to us by the States of Virginia and Maryland: and will be pleased to receive any agent or counsel of either party, whom the Governors of the respective States may desire to be present.

I am,
With great respect,
Your Obed't Serv't,

[Notation in Graham's hand:]
Similar letter to His Ex. James Black Groome, Governor of Maryland.

Isaac W. Hayne[1] *to William A. Graham* [with enclosures] UNC

[Charleston, S.C.]
[June 19, 1874]

The above[2] is the copy of a portion of a letter addressed to my old friend Prof. Brumby formerly of Ala. University, afterwards of So. Ca. College, & now of Athens, Geo. As you are aware he married my Aunt.

Am I taking too great a liberty in adressing the same to you? I have written to the same effect to Senator Goldthwaite[3] & Gov. Watts,[4] of Ala., & to Gen'l Hill, besides yourself of No. Ca.

As to this State, I, of course, can procure abundant testimonials. I was for twenty years Atty General, having been five times elected, and have, from time to time, appeared before the public through the Press.

---

[1]Presumably this was Isaac W. Hayne of Charleston, South Carolina, who was a descendant of Isaac John Hayne (1745-1781), a soldier and patriot of Revolutionary fame. The elder Hayne was captured and hanged by the British. Roller and Twyman, *Encyclopedia of Southern History*, 583. See the enclosed résumé for a summary of Isaac W. Hayne's career.

[2]The enclosure follows this letter.

[3]George Thomas Goldthwaite (1809-1879), a native of New England, was a brother of Henry Barnes Goldthwaite, who had married W. A. Graham's niece Elizabeth Isabella Witherspoon. G. T. Goldthwaite settled in Montgomery, Alabama, about 1826. A successful lawyer and planter, he was chief justice of the Alabama Supreme Court and a United States senator, 1871-1877. He was unsympathetic toward slavery and opposed secession, accepting it with reluctance. *Biographical Directory of Congress*, 954; *CDAB*, 349.

[4]Thomas Hill Watts (1819-1892), of Alabama, was a graduate of the University of North Carolina who became a lawyer and an active Whig state legislator. A Unionist until Lincoln's election, Watts was a delegate to the Secession Convention and served as a colonel in the Seventeenth Alabama Regiment until he was appointed attorney general of the Confederacy, a post he held until he was elected governor of Alabama. After the Civil War Watts practiced law in Montgomery. *CDAB*, 1158.

[Enclosure] *Isaac W. Hayne to Richard T. Brumby* UNC

Charleston, S.C.
June 19th., 1874.

The Law in So. Ca. is so distasteful & indeed to an *honest* practitioner has got to be so unprofitable, that I am casting about to find some pursuit more congenial and more certain as to revenue.

The reputation of honesty and moral tone is every day more of an obstacle to success. The great merit in this State now, is to be able and willing to bribe judges & stock juries. The common impression even among those disposed to preserve their own integrity is that a knowledge of the law and general ability count for *nothing*. Business men believe this, even beyond the fact—for they are worth *something*.

I began life as a College Tutor and held the place satisfactorily for four years. Some eight years later Dr. Manly,[1] as you remember, urged me to accept a Professorship in the Ala. University. About the same time Judge Harper[2] suggested my name for the Presidency of the South Carolina College, but I was then thought too young an objection which certainly does not now exist. Many years later, Dr. Thornwell[3] pertinaciously pressed me to allow him to put me in nomination for the same position.

I see that the Chancellorship, as they call it of the Geo. University is to be filled in August. Would it be presumptious to present my name for this office?

I know personally none of the Trustees, except B. C. Yancey.[4] He writes kindly, and gives full information, but makes no offer of his own support. The chance would seem to be a bad one, but I would be glad to have your views, and at the same time such a letter as you would be willing I should lay before the Trustees from yourself, in case I conclude to become a candidate.

This State has now no college of its own, & my name would be I think some recommendation to young men here, (among the 'former inhabitants') who may seek an education elsewhere.

The candidates so far are Prof. Wm. Preston Johnstone, of Washington & Lee College, Va., Wm. Porcher Miles[5] formerly of this State, now of Va., Genl. Kirby Smith,[6] Dr. Tucker,[7] late Prest. of Mercer College Ga., & Charles Colcock Jones[8] formerly of Sav. now of N.Y.

Johnstone's reputation is altogether confined to Va., a State filled with Colleges of its own. Miles, I don't think means to persist, Kirby Smith I know of only as a Genl., Dr. Tucker you must know more of than I do, & so I suppose as to Jones. Please write frankly and soon.

I am Sixty-five years of age, pretty well preserved, in fair health, and *look* much younger than I am, and to confess the truth than I feel.

Yours truly,

[Enclosure]
Trustees.[9]

Augusta—Charles J. Jenkins
Centersville—Mark A. Cooper
Athens—W. L. Mitchell
Atlanta—H. V. M. Miller
Dahlonega—D. W. Lewis
Atlanta—B. H. Hill
" —Jos. E. Brown
Washington—Rob't Toombs
Atlanta—B. C. Yancey
Albany—D. A. Vason
Macon—Jas. Jackson
Thomasville—J. L. Seward
Sparta—Geo. F. Pierce
Columbus—M. J. Crawford
Madison—J. A. Billups

Macon—Sam'l Hall
Woodville—D. C. Barrow
Athens—Stevens Thomas
Savannah—J. W. Beckwith
Athens—Lamar Cobb
Macon—J. J. Gresham
Dunlap Scott—Rome
W. H. Hull—Augusta
Jas. M. Smith—Atlanta
Jno. B. Gordon— "
Y. L. G. Harris—Athens
John Screven—Savannah
N. G. Hammond—Atlanta
Pope Barrow—Maxey's
A. O. Bacon—Macon
J. C. Rutherford— "

---

[1]Basil Manly (1798-1868), born near Pittsboro, became a Baptist clergyman and educator. He held pastorates in South Carolina, principally in Charleston. Manly was instrumental in founding Furman University, and he was president of the University of Alabama, 1837-1855. When Jefferson Davis was inaugurated as president of the Confederacy, Manly, as a pastor in Montgomery, Alabama, delivered the prayer. *CDAB*, 634.

[2]William Harper (1790-1847), of South Carolina and Missouri, was a native of Antigua. He was the first matriculant and graduate of South Carolina College and was a trustee of that institution. A lawyer by profession, Harper at various times in his career held the posts of state legislator, chancellor of Missouri, United States senator from South Carolina, judge of the court of appeals, and chancellor of South Carolina. A nationalist, his opposition to protective tariffs made him an intense champion of states' rights. He was a delegate to the Nullification Convention. Harper dissented from the decision in the test oath case, and his opinion has been regarded as one of the most powerful statements of the states' rights doctrine. He was also a defender of slavery. *CDAB*, 401; *Biographical Directory of Congress*, 1010.

[3]James Henley Thornwell (1812-1862), of South Carolina, was a graduate of South Carolina College. He also studied at Andover but found it too liberal for his beliefs and transferred to Harvard. Thornwell was a Presbyterian minister, but instead of having an active pastorate he became a professor at South Carolina College and then a professor in the Columbia Theological Seminary. A very influential man in the Presbyterian church, he was a leader in its organization in the Confederate states. *CDAB*, 1065.

[4]Benjamin Cudworth Yancey (1817-1891), a native of South Carolina, was graduated by the University of Georgia in 1836 and received a B.L. degree from Yale the following year. He moved to Alabama in 1838 and remained there until 1841, practicing law and co-editing the *Wetumpka Gazette* with his brother, William L. Yancey. For the next ten years he had a very successful legal practice in Hamburg, South Carolina. About 1850 Yancey relocated to a plantation in Cherokee County, Alabama. A Democrat in politics, he was elected to the Alabama Senate in 1855 and served as its president. From 1858 to late 1859 he was minister to Argentina. Yancey entered the Confederate military service as a captain of dragoons but was soon appointed a major in Cobb's Legion. Later he was colonel of Georgia state troops. After the Civil War Yancey remained in Georgia, holding the office of president of the Georgia Agricultural Society and serving in the legislature (1878-1879). For twenty-eight years he was a University of Georgia trustee. The last years of his life were spent supervising his Floyd County plantation. *Cyclopedia of American Biography*, XIII, 560.

[5]William Porcher Miles (1822-1899) was a native of South Carolina and a graduate of Charleston College. After teaching mathematics in the college from 1843 to 1855, Miles

served as mayor of Charleston, 1855-1857. For the next three years he was a Democratic member of Congress. A strong supporter of slavery and secession, Miles was a delegate to the Secession Convention and a member of the Confederate Congress. He became president of the University of South Carolina, a post he held from 1880 until he resigned in 1882 to manage his father-in-law's sugar plantations in Louisiana. *CDAB*, 677.

[6]Edmund Kirby Smith (1824-1893) was born in St. Augustine, Florida, to New England parents. He graduated from West Point in 1845, was twice brevetted in Mexico, taught mathematics at West Point, and campaigned against the Indians on the Texas frontier. He entered Confederate service as a lieutenant colonel and was rapidly promoted to brigadier, major, lieutenant, and full general, achieving the latter rank in February, 1864. Smith gained distinction at First Manassas and in Braxton Bragg's invasion of Kentucky. From 1862 to 1865 he commanded the Trans-Mississippi Department. Smith was the last Confederate general in the field, and his hopelessly isolated position finally forced his surrender on May 26, 1865. After the war Smith was president of the Atlantic and Pacific Telegraph Company, chancellor of the University of Nashville, and, after 1875, professor of mathematics at the University of the South. Ezra J. Warner, *Generals in Gray: Lives of the Confederate Commanders* (Baton Rouge: Louisiana State University Press, 1959), 279-280.

[7]Henry Holcombe Tucker (1819-1889), of Georgia, attended the University of Pennsylvania and Columbian College. He became a teacher, a Baptist minister, and a lawyer. Tucker opposed secession until it became a fait accompli, whereupon he turned to the manufacture of salt, an enterprise he maintained throughout the war. He declined the presidency of Wake Forest College but held the positions of president of Mercer College, 1866-1871, and chancellor of the University of Georgia, 1874-1878. From 1878 until his death Tucker was editor of the *Christian Index*. *CDAB*, 1085.

[8]Charles Colcock Jones, Jr.

[9]No attempt has been made to identify the trustees.

J. M. Cameron[1] *to William A. Graham* UNC

Office of Hawkins & Co Commission Merchants
Baltimore June 20th 1874

Our Tobacco market for some time past, has been very dull & depressed, but we are glad to state that at last it shows some disposition to advance in price & move more rapidly. In view of this, we deem it best to advise you as regards prices etc and therefore quote for heavy, well packed hhds. as follows; Common to good Lugs 3.50 to 7.00 Common to Medium Leaf 5.50 to 8.00 Fair to good Leaf 9.00 to 12.50 Good to Fine Stems, 3.00 to 5.00.

Please bear in mind that our market is not adapted to Fancy Leaf, but does well with good darke shipping grades, especially if packed in heavy *Tobacco* Hhds.

Packages weighing less than 1000 lbs net, are not desired by shippers, & they do not like to pay for the Hhd; when lighter, but if well packed & weighing over 1000 lbs we can always get $1.00 each for the Hhd; which we believe is an advantage, peculiar to our market. You will remember also that the charges for shipping to & selling in our market are as low if not lower than in any other.

Soliciting your Consignments we are Yrs. Truly,

---

[1]Except for the inference that Cameron was affiliated with Hawkins and Company, he has not been identified.

Raleigh T. Daniel[1] *to William A. Graham* UNC

Commonwealth of Virginia, Attorney General's Office
Richmond June 20th 1874

In the absence of the Governor from the seat of Government, and at his request, I reply to your letter to him of the 18. Instant. Hon. Wm. J. Robertson[2] is associated with me for Virginia in the Boundary question between her and Maryland, which has been submitted to yourself and the Hon. J. S. Black. One or both of us will be present, when you meet in Washington on the 25th Instant, for the purpose of taking the initiating steps in the business.

---

[1]Raleigh Travers Daniel (1805-1877), of Virginia, was one of that state's most prominent figures in the mid-nineteenth century. An attorney by profession and a Union Whig, he was a state legislator, councillor of state, lieutenant governor, and, at the time of his death, Virginia attorney general. *Appleton's Cyclopædia*, II, 75.

[2]William Joseph Robertson (1817-1898), of Virginia, was graduated by the University of Virginia with a law degree. For six years, 1859-1865, he was judge of the court of appeals. At a later time, Robertson was counsel for General G. W. C. Lee in the Arlington case and acted as general counsel of the Chesapeake and Ohio Railroad. *CDAB*, 892.

Jeremiah S. Black to William A. Graham UNC

Ebbitt House, Washington, D.C.
June 26 1874

Judge Field[1] is gone to California and will not return before October. So that door is closed.

I have an engagement for part of this evening; but may be able to see you again. If we do not meet before you leave it is understood that I shall apprise you at the earliest moment of Judge Curtis's[2] answer and if it be adverse that you shall tender the place in our joint names to Gov. Jenkins.[3]

---

[1]Stephen Johnson Field (1816-1899), a native of Connecticut, had earned a reputation for his pragmatism and disregard for common law notions while he served on the state supreme court of California. In 1863 he became a justice of the United States Supreme Court, and his constitutional position became increasingly doctrinaire. He retired from the bench in 1897. *CDAB*, 291.

[2]Benjamin Robbins Curtis (1809-1874), native of Watertown, Massachusetts, practiced law in Northfield and Boston before he was appointed to the United States Supreme Court in 1851. Curtis dissented in the Dred Scott decision and resigned from the court after he disagreed vehemently on the handling of that case. He was President Johnson's legal counsel during the impeachment proceedings. *CDAB*, 207.

[3]Charles Jones Jenkins (1805-1883), a native of the Beaufort District of South Carolina, moved to Georgia with his family in 1816. He was destined to become one of Georgia's most respected men. Educated at Moses Waddell's famous preparatory school, Franklin College, and Union College in Schenectady, New York, where he graduated in 1824, Jenkins read law and enjoyed a highly successful Augusta practice. He was also a very successful politician. With few interruptions he served in the Georgia legislature from 1830 to 1850, acting as Speaker in four sessions. A Union Whig, Jenkins supported the Compromise of 1850 and wrote the Georgia Platform. He was an unsuccessful candidate for governor in 1853, as Georgians began to desert the Union Whig position. During the

Civil War, Jenkins was a jurist on the Georgia Supreme Court. As a member of Georgia's Constitutional Convention of 1865, he was influential in achieving readjustment of the state's fortunes. He was unanimously elected governor and within two years had virtually restored Georgia's credit. He objected, however, to the Fourteenth Amendment and vainly sought a federal injunction to prevent the execution of the reconstruction acts. Subsequently, Jenkins was removed from office by General George Meade for refusal to authorize payment for members of the convention of 1868. After sequestering the state's money, documents, and seal, the deposed governor left the state. Jenkins eventually returned and was elected governor as a Democrat in 1872. His last public service was as president of the Constitutional Convention of 1877. *DAB*, X, 44.

D. G. Stinson to William A. Graham [with enclosure] UNC

Rock Hill,
July 8, 1874.

You will receive a copy of the "Grange" containing an extract from the Autobiography of John Adams, respecting the Declaration of "'76." You will remember that, in my former letters, I said that in "'75 John McNitt Alexander had an interview with Dr. Franklin, and that the latter highly approved of the proceedings of Mecklenburg. You will see from the extract I refer to, the manner in which the Declaration was concocted. 5 members were requested to draft copies for the Declaration. Franklin was one who having seen the Mecklenburg Declaration possibly incorporated its ideas into his copy, which was possibly adopted by Jefferson.

It was in 1819 that Mr. Adams drew Jefferson's attention to the fact that the Mecklenburg Declaration was published in some Northern paper, and Mr. Jefferson thought it a hoax, so I presume that Mr. J. had never seen the Mecklenburg Declaration.

[Enclosure] *Excerpt from Adams Autobiography* UNC

[In his autobiography, John Adams gives the following account of the circumstance which led to the selection of Jefferson to draw the Declaration of Independence:—]

The Committee of Independence were Thomas Jefferson, John Adams, Benjamin Franklin, Roger Sherman,[1] and Robert R. Livingston.[2] Mr. Jefferson had been now about a year a member of Congress, but had attended his duty in the House a very small part of the time, and when there, had never spoken in public. During the whole time I sat with him in Congress, I never heard him utter three sentences together.

It will naturally be inquired how it happened that he was appointed on a Committee of such importance. There were more reasons than one. Mr. Jefferson had the reputation of a masterly pen; he had been chosen a Delegate in Virginia, in consequence of a very handsome public paper which he had written for the House of Burgesses, which had given him the character of a fine writer. Another reason was, that Mr. Richard Henry Lee[3] was not beloved by most of his colleagues, from Virginia, and Mr. Jefferson was set up to rival and surplant him. This could be done only by the pen, for Mr. Jefferson could stand no competition with him, or any one else, in elocution and public debate.

The Committee had several meetings, in which were proposed the articles of which the Declaration was to consist, and minutes made of them. The Committee then appointed Mr. Jefferson and me to draw them up in form, and clothe them in proper dress. The Sub-Committee met and considered the minutes, making such observations on them as then occurred, when Mr. Jefferson desired me to take them to my lodging and make the draught. This I declined, and gave several reasons for declining.

1st. That he was a Virginian, and I a Massachusettensian.

2nd. That he was a Southern man, and I a Northern Man.

3rd. That I had been so obnoxious for my early and constant zeal in promoting the measure, that every draft of mine would undergo a more severe scrutiny and criticism in Congress than one of his composition.

4th. And lastly, and that would be reason enough if there were no other, I had a great opinion of the elegance of his pen, and none at all of my own. I therefore insisted that no hesitation should be made on his part. He accordingly took the minutes, and in a day or two produced to me his draft. Whether I made or suggested any correction, I remember not. The report was made to the Committee of five, by them examined, but whether altered or corrected in anything I cannot recollect. But, in substance, at least, it was reported to Congress, where, after a severe criticism and striking out several of the most oratorical paragraphs, it was adopted on the Fourth of July, 1776, and published to the world.

---

[1]Roger Sherman (1721-1793) was born and educated in Massachusetts. Before studying law, he learned the trade of shoemaking and was surveyor of New Haven County, Connecticut, in 1745. After he was admitted to the bar in Connecticut, Sherman began an illustrious legal and political career. He was a member of the Continental Congress, 1774-1781, 1783, and 1784, and served ably on a number of important committees. Sherman signed all four of the great state papers—the Declaration of 1774, the Declaration of Independence, the Articles of Confederation, and the Constitution. *CDAB*, 950; *Biographical Directory of Congress*, 1593-1594.

[2]Robert R. Livingston (1746-1813) was a New Yorker who was a delegate to the Continental Congress, 1775-1777, 1779-1781, and 1784-1784. Although he was, as this account indicates, one of the Committee of Five, Livingston returned to his duties in the provincial assembly before the Declaration of Independence was signed. He believed the Declaration premature. No one except Alexander Hamilton did more to promote the adoption of the Constitution of 1787; however, believing that he had been slighted by Washington and Hamilton, Livingston was an early convert to Jeffersonian Democracy. As minister to France (1801-1804) he was instrumental in the purchase of Louisiana. He was Robert Fulton's partner in building the first steamboat. *CDAB*, 576; *Biographical Directory of Congress*, 1226.

[3]Richard Henry Lee (1732-1794) was seventh of eleven children of Thomas and Hannah Ludwell Lee. Born at Stratford, Westmoreland County, Virginia, he was educated by tutors at home, was sent to England for advanced study, then returned to Virginia and made a thorough study of law. In 1758 he entered the House of Burgesses, where he played a very active role in the pre-Revolutionary actions of the House. Usually he allied himself with Patrick Henry. In the Congress of 1775 Lee was placed on many important com-

mittees. Unfortunately, his involvement with Virginia's reluctance to surrender her claim to western lands and his connection with the problems related to foreign affairs did not enhance his reputation as a statesman. In 1779 he resigned his seat in Congress but was elected again in 1784 and for a year served as president of that body. He led the opposition to the adoption of the Constitution of the United States but was elected a senator in the new government, a position from which he resigned in 1792. *DAB*, XI, 117-120.

Jeremiah S. Black to William A. Graham UNC

Ebbitt House, Washington, D.C.
[July 11, 1874]

Judge Curtis writes from Newport. Says his health &c forbids his acceptance. What is to happen now? Will Gov. Jenkins accept? If yes can you get him there by 21.?

Unless you forbid or Providence prevents my intent is to be at White S.S.[1] on the day fixed, but I dont think we will be able to go on very far.

I telegraphed you of Judge Curtis's declination but I have been told that the message was not Sent the office at your end being closed.

---

[1]White Sulphur Springs, West Virginia.

William A. Graham to William A. Graham, Jr. A&H

Hillsboro',
July 11th., 1874.

Gov. Caldwell came here on Thursday to attend a Railroad meeting, was taken with stone in the bladder, or calculus, and has been for near 24 hours at the point of death. Dr. Burke Haywood of Raleigh was sent for, and is here attending him, with the two Strudwicks, and very little hope is entertained of his recovery. Augustus went over to T. Ruffin's, where he lies, to sit up, last night, and at midnight, mounted a mule and went to Durham, to send a despatch for Dr. Haywood to come up—the telegraph station here has been discontinued. The Mule fell, or threw him, three times by the way, but he got through without injury, and the Dr. arrived today. The Gov'rs wife has been sent for to Morganton.

Your Mother was confined to bed three or four days in the early part of the week, but is up again.

I expected to go to White Sulphur Springs in the early part of week after next, to meet the persons concerned in the Va. & Maryland arbitration; but, not having heard from Judge Black since parting at Washington, think I shall not go so soon.

Augustus was at Leper place, the early part of this week—found matters in pretty good state, but season dry—Joseph's Willie came home with him, & is here—much improved since last fall.

There seems to be great dissension among the Conservatives in the present election, every where. T. Ruffin, you observe, is supported by the radicals for Judge here, but I think will not draw off many votes—I hear this moment that Gov'r Caldwell is dead.

Your Mother, Sudie, & Augus. send love to you—expect Mr. Clark tonight—Geo. & Sally, I suppose, will reach Charlotte this evening—

Affectionately

William J. Robertson to William A. Graham UNC

Richmond Va.
July 14th 1874

I came to this place yesterday, by appointment with Mr. Daniel, for the purpose of aiding him in the preparation of our statement to be laid before the Arbitrators, at the White Sulphur Springs, next week; and on my arrival was shocked to learn that his wife (who had been sick for some time, but was not supposed to be in any immediate danger) had died a few hours before I reached the City.

Your letter to him of 11th inst. has since been handed me: and I write to let you know why it is that Mr. Daniel does not himself reply to it; and to say that, under the circumstances, we would prefer not to proceed with the case on the day fixed, even if we could have our statement ready (which is not now at all probable); and though your Board should be full.

Nothing has been heard by us from Judge Black since we parted in Washington; and we have no information from any quarter as to the third arbitrator except that contained in your letter to Mr. Daniel.

My address is Charlottesville Va.

Charles J. Jenkins to William A. Graham UNC
[Telegram]

Augusta, Georgia.
July 15, 1874.

I accept.[1] Will meet you twenty first as requested.

[1]Jenkins thus became the third member of the Maryland-Virginia boundary commission.

Isaac D. Jones[1] to William A. Graham UNC

Baltimore
July 18th 1874

I duly received your telegram notifying us that there would be no meeting of the Arbitrators upon the Va. & Md. boundary Line, on the 21st. instant, in consequence of the sad affliction which has come upon the Attorney General of Va.

The postponement did not subject the Md. Counsel to any inconvenience, but they sincerely lament the afflictive Providence which has befallen our Va. brother.

With best wishes for your health & welfare.

[1]Isaac Dashiell Jones (1806-1893) was a member of a prominent Maryland family and was active in state affairs throughout his long career as a lawyer. He was elected attorney general of Maryland in 1867. In 1877 he was elected judge of the court of arbitration of Baltimore. Among the positions he held were those of director of the Maryland School for the Deaf, Frederick, 1867-1893, and of the Maryland School for the Colored Blind and Deaf, Baltimore, 1872-1893. *Biographical Directory of Congress*, 1136.

Charles J. Jenkins to William A. Graham UNC

Augusta,
18 July 1874.

I have received from you during the week two telegrams respecting the Virginia and Maryland Arbitration. To the first, (received on the 15th.) I immediately replied, accepting the appointment tendered to me, as I never do by letter, and saying that I would meet you on the 21st., as requested.

Your second telegram was received yesterday evening, and your letter from Hillsboro', of the 16th., this morning, announcing a postponement of the meeting. I now write to say a word as to the appointment of another day. You may remember in our brief interview on the rail, I inquired how long the then contemplated sitting on the 21st. would probably continue, and you said you thought not exceeding three or four days. I do not know that I gave you the reason of that inquiry. I am president of the Board of Trustees of our State University, whose annual session will commence on the 31st. inst., and continue until Commencement day, the 5th. prox. This will be an unusually interesting, and important session, as we have a Chancellor, and a professor to elect, besides other business of moment to the Institution. I expect to return home on the 6th., and shall then be subject to your call, but I am exceedingly desirous of being present at that meeting. If you can so arrange as to avoid any conflict between those two Duties, it will be unnecessary for you to do more, (so far as concerns me) than to notify me of the time and place agreed on by Judge B. & yourself.

James L. Robinson[1] *to William A. Graham* UNC

Franklin, N.C.,
July 18th., 1874.

I have been for one or two years past making some effort to get the people of my county interested in the advantages offered by the Trustees of the "Peabody Fund" for the education of our children, but with only partial success,—the county of Macon receiving during the past twelve months, only about ($750.00) seven hundred & fifty dollars.

I desire to ask your attention to a suggestion that I have thought a little about & if you think it meritorious and practicable, that you will then take such steps as your judgement may point out. The suggestion is this—that through your efforts the Board of Trustees might modify (for the reasons which I will give) the present regulations in regard to the number of pupils enrolled (the minimum being one hundred) so that schools with *fifty pupils enrolled*, in Districts where they *cannot* organize under the *present* regulations, should have all the money proportionately which they would be entitled to if the school numbered *one hundred*. Our population in the mountain counties is sparsely settled, & in a number of cases in my county, a bona-fide school might be started with an attendance of 50 or 60, where it is morally impossible to organize one with the number required by the regulations now in force. Our people are of course quite poor,—the income from the fund so kindly donated by Mr. Peabody, I imagine, is ample to meet any demands that will be made upon it. We have quite a number of children who ought to have the benefit of this fund. So taking it altogether I do not now see why this arrangement may not be made, and not defeat the end which I know the Honorable Trustees have in view.

The exception which I thought might be made by the Trustees, is due to our *extreme Western Counties*; first, for the reason that it *does not* increase the *per-capita* appropriation but simply distributes the same funds to smaller communities of children. Secondly, we have many school districts in the same Township that *cannot* be consolidated, because in many cases the district lines are impassable mountain barriers; thirdly, I feel sure it would very much encourage & stimulate a sentiment (which I am glad to say is increasing) in favor of popular education; and finally would be of *great help* to a people who are blessed with a *splendid climate*, the *purest water*, and the most *magnificent mountains*, but are *desperately poor* in the way of *money*.

Excuse the length of this letter. I feel much interest in the matter & will take it as a great favor if you will write me giving me your views on the subject.

I was glad to see that your trip to Phila. had resulted in your improved health.

---

[1]James Lowrie Robinson (1838-1887), of Macon County, left Emory and Henry College to join the Confederate army, in which he served as captain. He was a member of the state House of Representatives, 1868-1876 (Speaker, 1872-1874), and a state senator, 1876-1881 (president, 1879-1881). From 1881 until 1885 he was lieutenant governor. Robinson, who was deeply interested in internal improvements, served as Indian agent, 1886-1887. Cheney, *North Carolina Government*, 424, 448, 450, 453, 454, 455, 456, 457, 458, 460, 461, 465; Arthur, *Western North Carolina*, 650-651.

Joseph Graham to Willie Graham UNC

Charlotte
July 22 /74

My dear Son,

I had been looking for a letter from you this morning and sure enough it came, and I was very glad to hear from you. And you cannot tell how glad your Mother and I are to hear from your Grandma that you and Bessie[1] have been good children and not rude and troublesome. You should always try and make yourselves pleasant and agreeable, especially to persons older than yourselves. It is very kind in your grandparents to propose to take you and

Bessie to Beaufort with them. I wish both of you to go, for I know you will not be sorry of it afterwards, either of you. I shall hardly be able to go down there at all this summer. Miss Bessie Dewey is very sick indeed, and has been so for about two weeks. I am afraid she is going to die, if she does not get better by the time you will be reading this letter. She is out of her head and does not know what she talks about. I hope and pray that God will show Dr. Jones and myself what to do to save her life. If you do not understand what I mean by this Grandma will tell you. When you left here she was as well as you, but now she is at death's door. How good everybody should try to be while they are well, for they do not know how soon they must die! When death comes it is too late *always* to begin to do good. Remember this, my son, when you are tempted to do anything wrong.

. . . .

You must write letters oftener, this is the way to learn to use your pen with ease, and to know what to say. That was a very good letter for you, which I received. *I* write with what is called a running hand and you may not find it easy to read it at first, but you can get Grandma or someone to read it to you.

We all miss you and Bessie very much. If you or she need anything to prepare for Beaufort ask Grandma or Aunty to get it for you and I will settle for it when I go down. Give our love to every body.

Your affectionate father

Master Willie Graham
Hillsboro' N.C.

---

[1]Elizabeth, or Bessie (1860-1894) was the daughter of Dr. Joseph Graham. Clark, "Graham Descendants."

Zebulon B. Vance to William A. Graham UNC

Charlotte, N.C.,
July 24th., 1874.

Some time ago we were informed by various sources, that you intended to prepare a paper on the 20th. May Declaration, in reply to Goodloe & others. Since that time, Wellings article has appeared which is said to be more damaging to us than Goodloe's. Permit me to hope that our information was correct, & to suggest, that if such is your intention, it can not be done any too soon. Many persons here are badly staggered and await anxiously to hear from you. I have no more doubt of the genuineness of that Declaration than of the battle of Cowpens, but like others, heartily wish to see all the facts succinctly and systematically stated, in a manner that will leave no more to be said.

I sincerely trust you will do it.

Frederick A. P. Barnard to William A. Graham UNC

Columbia College
New-York

Scarborough, on Hudson, N.Y.,
August 5th., 1874.

We are now going regularly to work upon volume second of our Cyclopedia which begins with the letter "F", and will include "Mecklenburg". All that is to be said about that subject will have to be in the hands of the compositors by the first of November next. I sincerely hope that you will favor us with your promised article within the time limited. Under the head "Declaration of Independence," the Mecklenburg, in volume first, I have given entire the Declaration as believed to have been published on the 20th. of May 1775, and I have also given the essential parts of the series of resolutions together with the preamble adopted on the 21st. of May of the same year; and in the few remarks which I have made in connection with these documents, I have stated that the historical argument as to the relative authenticity of these, will be given by the Hon. Wm. A. Graham of North Carolina, under "Mecklenburg", in volume second. The first volume is now published, but is not in the book stores and will be sold only by canvassers who will present themselves very soon in every state of the union.

To our contributors who prefer a copy of the work to any other form of compensation, which is true of many, we send the volume directly, or, where the work done is of greater value, we send it, if they so elect, in part compensation. The 1st. volume contains about seventeen hundred pages, and each page contains the matter of three ordinary octavo pages; so that this single volume is equivalent to five thousand pages of such a publication as the North American Review. It has been prepared with great care, and is wholly original. The editorial staff has been from time to time increased until it presents an array of learning such as was never before combined in the production of any similar publication. I enclose a circular that you may see the names of the gentlemen who now compose this staff.

I believe I said on a former occasion that I should be very glad to have you name the amount of compensation which you think a just equivalent for the labor expended upon the article, and I will add, that payment will be made immediately on receipt of the manuscript without waiting for the day of publication of the volume. If you desire to receive volume first with the understanding above mentioned, I will instruct the publisher to send it to you forthwith by express. An early reply will be esteemed a special favor.

Augustus W. Graham to Susan Washington Graham UNC

Hillsboro', N.C.,
August 7th., 1874.

My Dear Mother,

Your letter of the 5th was received from Mary Oakley last night, also one on Wednesday night. I send by *Express* the ruffs, as I think it more certain and safer.

I am glad that you and Father are enjoying your stay at Beaufort and hope that each may be much benefitted. Tell Father I received his letter and will answer it in a few days. I send him, enclosed in your letter, the returns from the election so far as they have been received. From present indications, Judge Kerr will receive about 100 maj. in the county. Col. Ruffin carried Alamance by over one hundred & fifty and I am afraid, is elected.[1]

The election passed off very quietly, there being no disturbance of any kind, which I am afraid will not be the case today, as there is quite a large crowd in town and many of them are drunk and quarrelling.

A great many of our party would not vote for Parish[2] and Latta,[3] which accounts for Brown[4] & Strayhorn[5] getting such a large vote. Capt. Davis[6] received the whole conservative vote cast, although John Turner worked very hard against him at St. Mary's.

. . . .

[1]These fears were unnecessary; John Kerr, of Caswell County, was elected superior court judge in this election. He served from 1874 to 1879. Cheney, *North Carolina Government*, 574.

[2]Calvin E. Parish.

[3]Joseph W. Latta was elected representative from Orange County in 1874, as was Matthew Atwater. Lefler and Wager, *Orange County*, 120; Cheney, *North Carolina Government*, 456.

[4]Henry N. Brown, a Republican, was an unsuccessful candidate for a seat in the North Carolina House of Representatives. Lefler and Wager, *Orange County*, 119.

[5]Isaac (Ike) R. Strayhorn (d. 1893), of Hillsborough, who received an A.B. degree from the University of North Carolina in 1868, was solicitor of the Fifth District and a member of the General Assembly, 1883. He was a trustee of the university, 1883-1893. Grant, *Alumni History*, 597; L. Branson, *North Carolina Business Directory for 1877-1878* (Raleigh: L. Branson, Publisher and Bookseller, 1878), 231, hereinafter cited as Branson, *North Carolina Business Directory*.

[6]Joseph Jonathan Davis defeated J. H. Headen for the Fourth Congressional District seat in this election. A Democrat, he served in the United States House of Representatives from 1874 to 1881. *Biographical Directory of Congress*, 786.

Charles J. Jenkins to William A. Graham UNC

Augusta,
August 12th., 1874.

I am asked to perform a public service here on the 2nd. of Septr. which I would like to do if it will not interfere with any programme of the Virginia & Maryland arbitration arranged, or in process of arrangement.

But knowing the difficulty of fixing a time for a meeting of so many persons, all but myself probably having important business engagements, I would on no account, disturb any arrangement wholly or partially made in the matter of the arbitration. On the contrary I repeat what I said before, that D. V. I will respond to any call made upon me. I have made no engagement for the 2nd prox, have no personal interest in what is then to be done, and verily believe it can be done just as well by another. But as some of my friends think differently I would like to oblige them if thereby I in no degree interfered with an existing engagement.

Patrick H. Winston, Jr.,[1] *to William A. Graham* UNC

Windsor
Aug 17th 1874

Confidential

I trust you will pardon me for trespassing upon your time to solicit a personal favor. If not inconsistent with your views of propriety I would be gratified to have your influence with the Senators elect from Orange Person & Caswell and the Senator elect from Lincoln & Catawba. I am a candidate for the position of Reading or Assistant Clerk of the Senate of N.C.

I have worked hard all my life for the success of the Conservative party, both on the Stump and through the medium of the press.

I am a young man, in poor circumstances with a wife and two children. The Salary attached to the position would assist me very materially in supporting them.

As to Capacity I refer you to the record of the University of N.C. where I graduated in 1867 with distinction.

If you should see fit to assist me by soliciting the votes of Messers Williamson[2] Parish[3] & W. A Graham Jr[4] for me you will gratify my father and also a considerable number of friends in the East. Considering the brilliant victory achieved by the Conservative party in the 1st District I do not consider it inappropriate for my friends to urge my name for the position referred to. My father will be gratified at any assistance you may render me.

Very truly your Obt sevt.

Editor of the Albemarle Times

---

[1]Patrick Henry Winston, Jr. (1847-1904), the son of Patrick Henry Winston, Sr., and Martha Elizabeth Byrd Winston, was described as a "lawyer, journalist, orator, wit and humorist." In 1874 he became the reading clerk of the state Senate. A brilliant young man endowed with great personal charm, Winston was educated at Horner School, Oxford, and at the University of North Carolina. He practiced law in Baltimore for two years, moved to Pittsburgh, and then returned to North Carolina; later he moved to the West. He owned and edited three newspapers—the Albemarle *Times*, the Spokane (Washington) *Review*, and *Winston's Weekly*; he also held the position of district attorney for the Territory of Washington. Ashe, *Biographical History*, II, 450-459.

[2]George Williamson represented Caswell County in the state Senate in 1850, 1874, and 1879. Cheney, *North Carolina Government*, 318, 455, 458.

[3]At this time Calvin E. Parish represented Orange County in the North Carolina Senate. Cheney, *North Carolina Government*, 455.

[4]Graham was serving as state senator from Lincoln County. Cheney, *North Carolina Government*, 455.

William A. Graham to Richard B. Haywood[1] UNC

Aug. 19th 1874

Your letter was received at Beaufort, and I delayed an answer till my return home, because I was in correspondence with other parties, who, I supposed, might take all the money of the sinking fund, that I had on hand. I find now, that there will be sufficient to accommodate you, in the loan of $3,000, that you desire. You do not mention, when you expect to repay it. It must necessarily be returned before the 1st of Nov. 1877, and be, at the rate of 8 per cent interest per annum, payable semiannually—in case of default to pay the interest, the whole shall become due, with a power of sale of the premises whenever such event shall happen. By preparing such a Mortgage, or deed in trust with John W. Graham Trustee, on your dwelling house & lot, on which there is no prior, I will leave with him a check in your favor for the amount, to be delivered to you, on delivery of the deed of Mortgage.

I am going from home for a few weeks to the Va. Springs.

[1]Richard Bennehan Haywood (1819-1889), son of Sherwood and Eleanor Hawkins Haywood, was a physician and surgeon in Raleigh. Graduated by the University of North Carolina, he was trained at Jefferson Medical College and studied in Europe in 1851. Commissioned a surgeon during the Civil War, Haywood was one of a group of citizens who surrendered the city of Raleigh to Union forces. He was a founder of the North Carolina Medical Society and served on a number of medical boards. Haywood was a director of the North Carolina Railroad. Powell, *DNCB*, III, 88.

Joseph Graham to William A. Graham UNC

Charlotte Aug 19 /74

My dear Father,

I hope you feel yourself improved from your sojourn at Beaufort.

I have inquired, and find that the Wilmington Mrs. Miller[1] has on one occasion visited Alleghany Springs[2] for Dyspepsia and she told me she thought it benefitted her very much. You should not drink too much for the first day or two. I hope you will be able to get off during next week, and that you have already begun the tonic (Acid Strychnia & Quinine) which [I] suggested while at Beaufort. It is what you took before seeing Dr. Da Costa. You should take the Cod Liver oil if it agrees with your stomach—and I think you will find it very serviceable. If you are troubled with costiveness try 5 grs. "Aloes & Myrrh Pill" every night at bed time for *a week* if necessary or do not act too much. They will not *purge* you but give consistent actions. Aloes and Myrrh Mass is an officinal preparation and you will find it at Dr Hookers—put 5 grs in each pill.

The above mentioned *three* articles will, I think, be all you will need for awhile at any rate. While you are gone if you can relish *fat* mutton it will be of service to you. I am so pressed with business I cannot write more just now. Love to Mother & all.

Your Affect. Son

---

[1]Mrs. Miller has not been identified.
[2]Alleghany Springs was located in Montgomery County, Virginia.

William A. Graham to Augustus W. Graham UNC

Alleghany Springs,
Montgomery County,
Virginia,
August 24th., 1874.

I dropped a postal card from Pet'r'b'g. Thence on Saturday, at a quarter to 11 o'clock we set out on the Southside Railroad, journied up the Appomatox, (crossing the Richmond and Danville road at Burkeville) by Farmville, crossing over to the James River at Lynchburg, passing the Blue ridge, and reaching the Alleghany at Shawsville 200 miles from P't'b'rg, where we left the Railroad and by Omnibus 3 ½ miles South, arrived at Alleghany Springs at 11 o clock P.M. Nearly all the way above Lynchburg, we had a view of mountains in front and to the right; and near sunset, saw the Peaks of Otto, for several miles, passed several springs, i.e. Blue Ridge Spring, Corner Spring, where Company is entertained, and the Town of Salem by the way.

The Alleghany Springs are situated on a small river called Roanoke, between the Blue Ridge & Alleghany mountains, in a valley surrounded by mountains on every side. The grounds & improvements are beautiful, and the accommodations sufficiently good. The mineral water is not pleasant to the taste. I have not seen a description of the analysis, but to the tongue it has the savor of Copperas water, though clear to the eye. The Spring is covered and paved as at Saratoga, and the water kept locked up, and is bottled for export.

The Company consists, it is said, of some 380 persons, principally from Va., but some from all the Southern States, except S.C., I believe. We found here Col. John Manly[1] and wife, from Texas—he is in bad health, and have made the acquaintance of some pleasant people from Ala., Va., Texas, etc. There is the usual round of watering place amusements, to be interluded with a grand ball tomorrow night. It has rained each morning since we arrived, and this is becoming a wet day.

Your Mother & myself were a good deal fatigued by the journey to P't'b'g on a hot day, but not so much in coming up to this cooler region. My breathing is much improved, and my appetite considerably, which I attribute very much to the stay at Beaufort. But the air here is humid and bracing, and seems to agree well with me. I took but three glasses of water the first day, am increasing it, a little, the second. I cannot yet say how long we shall remain—that may depend on the effect of the waters, but suppose it may be a fortnight.

The station for leaving the Railroad is considerably above Bonsacs, in coming to this place, which Mr. Cameron[2] supposed to be the point of departure, and is called Shawsville, or Alleghany, and baggage is checked to the Springs from P't'b'g.

[1]John Haywood Manly (1820-1874), of Texas, was a native of Raleigh and had been educated at the University of North Carolina. After moving to Texas, Manly served during the Civil War as a Confederate colonel. After the war he held the posts of state legislator and mayor of Galveston. By profession, he was a lawyer. Grant, *Alumni History*, 410.

[2]Paul C. Cameron.

Jeremiah S. Black to William A. Graham UNC

York
Sept. 5, 1874

Since the failure of our last arrangement for a meeting I have heard nothing from any body on the subject. What do you propose now? I will endeavor to conform myself to your convenience and that of Gov. Jenkins, but during the next three months will find it difficult to meet you any place except at Washington.

John Spelman[1] *to William A. Graham* UNC
[with enclosure]

Raleigh
September 7th., 1874.

Your attention is respectfully invited to the accompanying leading editorial of the N.Y. *Herald*, of the 4th. inst. The Editors of the *Herald* desire, for publication, your views on the subject of this editorial, with the views, also, of Judge Merrimon, and Gov. Holden.[2] The latter gentleman is now preparing his paper. Judge Merrimon is expected to return to this city in the morning, when the request will be made of him.

Should you see proper to respond to this request, you will oblige by doing so at your earliest convenience, through me, at this place.

[1]John Spelman edited the *Weekly State Journal*, published in Raleigh. He bought the *Democratic Press* from Richard H. Whitaker in 1858 and used the equipment to establish the *Journal* as the official state Democratic administrative paper. Spelman opposed William W. Holden at every turn; the two engaged in a physical confrontation in Raleigh in 1861. Spelman's editorials revealed him to be an intense secessionist and a strong defender of the Confederate government. Raper, *Holden*, 33, 37, 38-39, 41.

[2]Nothing has been found to indicate that any of the three named ever complied with the request.

[Enclosure]
Editorial from the New York Herald

Let Us Have a National Convention of Peace and Reconstruction, Both Sides of the Southern Question.

The rumor that the President purposes to summon Congress together for an extra session to consider the condition of affairs in the Southern States does not seem to be confirmed. We do not regard it as a probable rumor. President Grant is not the kind of Chief Magistrate who craves legislative advice. The relations between the President and Congress at the time of the adjournment were not harmonious enough to lead him to look hopefully upon the prospects of another meeting. Among the last acts of the Senate was to throw into the face of the President the nomination of his well-beloved Shepherd.[1] With a Senate in that humor what might not be expected? Experienced politicians have a fear of extra sessions. There is the legend that "an extra session is generally sure to ruin an administration," and President Grant has enough Scottish blood in his veins not to be insensible to legends. Long Branch and its endless speech of wave and tide, is much more pleasant than Washington and two roaring Legislatures. The administration is now in the sixth year of its existence and not in the sturdiest health. Whether the President means to allow it to drift into silence, satisfied with what it has done, and feeling that its place in history is made, or whether, as some of his friends believe, he will make another appeal to the confidence of the people, nothing is to be gained by an extra session.

But the fact that such an expedient is generally discussed shows how deeply the public mind feels as to the Southern States. We do not dwell upon the events that now take place in South Carolina and Mississippi, the riots in Kentucky, the threats of civil war in North Carolina, the feverish movement of the popular heart in Arkansas, for they indicate now what they have indicated at any time since the war. They show that instead of an honest measure of generous and pacific reconstruction we have reduced the conquered States of the South into the condition of Poland and Ireland. No known section of conquered territory, not the most lawless districts of Westmeath, nor the most impatient communes in Alsace, are as disturbed as many of the Southern States. This cannot be attributed to the pressure of war; for the war is over, and the harvests have long since enfolded with living verdure the bloody fields. Nor does it come from failures of crops, that frequent cause of discontent, for all accounts tell us that cotton and sugar and rice promise an abundant yield. Nor does it represent the fermenting ambition that would rise in new rebellion, for no Southern leader—not Mr. Tombs himself—has hinted the thought of war. The cause lies deeper. It has become a disease—a slowly growing, irritating disease—what might be called an ulceration of the whole political system. Unless we remove it there can be no end but death. Already in Arkansas and South Carolina we observe the first tokens of death in the shameless repudiation which has become an accepted principle of legislation. Such examples should not be overlooked. If the Union cannot be destroyed by war it can be destroyed by repudiation. There can be no wholesome union between Massachusetts and South Carolina, between New York and Arkansas, on the financial conditions that exist to-day. Already the North laments its existence, and to-morrow, if repudiation continues to be the controlling sentiment of the South, we shall have the solvent patriot States of the North crying, "Who shall deliver us from the body of this death?"

Some of our empirical statesmen tell us that the cause of this is slavery. We are weary of this refrain about slavery. Fifteen years ago, and our most respected citizens were only too glad to applaud the violence which greeted the orators and writers who opposed slavery. Now there is no rhetoric in the language strong enough to express our horror of it. Well, slavery was an evil, just as the next generation in England will perhaps regard the crown, the aristocracy, and the Established Church as evils. But it was an institution and so puissant as an element of political influence that it enabled a comparatively small portion of the people to rule the Union. For nearly two centuries, under our colonial and federal forms of government, we treated slavery as an institution. For ten years we have treated it as a crime. The question arises, and it is a question of supreme magnitude, as our readers will see when they dwell upon it, whether it is the soundest statesmanship to deal with any institution as a crime. There is the danger of reaction, and inviting strife. This danger Cromwell incurred when he pronounced monarchy a crime by sending Charles I to the scaffold. A far greater danger the French people invited when they denounced royalty, religion and rank, as so many grades of crime. The same, in a lesser degree, fell upon the republicans in Paris and Madrid, when they denounced property, capital and law as crimes. The logic which animated Cromwell in his dealings with Charles Stuart, the logic which breatahed through the French Revolution, the Commune uprising, and the Republic of Pi y Margal, was perfect. It was unanswerable, soul-stirring, sublime. It was not the statesmanship of common sense. It recalled the eloquent periods with which our own writers and statesmen welcomed emancipation. Nothing is easier than to prove that royalty, aristocracy, standing armies, laws concerning land, entail, primogeniture and the Established Church are all crimes—as criminal as the selling of human souls into bondage. But custom and law made them institutions. When we deal with institutions as with crimes we provoke the excesses which compelled the restoration of Charles, the *coup d'état* of Napoleon, the suppression of the Commune, the successful conspiracy of Serrano and the growth of repudiation and monarchy in the South.

Is it not possible that by following this pregnant historical lesson to its natural teaching we may see the real cause of the troubles now pervading the South? The men who a few short years ago were strong enough by genius and valor to rule the councils of the Union, and subsequently to construct a power in the Southern Confederacy that required four years of war to suppress and is still a historical power commanding the respect and admiration of mankind—these men have not passed away. We do not see them, but they live. The men who fill the public eye in any country are always few compared with the millions unseen who only await opportunity to act and speak. Can we really reconstruct the Southern States without the aid of the real sons of the South? We have tried to do so, depending upon the ignorant freedmen, who yesterday were slaves and the unscrupulous white adventurers who yesterday fled from the North as political mendicants and soldiers of fortune. There is no reconstruction. On the contrary we see disturbance, civil outbreaks, corruption and disorder, and, worse than all, a war upon the national credit by means of repudiation that will be as disastrous to the Union as if the rebellion had been a success. It would certainly be better in the interests of civilization and liberty to have two confederacies, governed by statesmen of honor and character, who respected credit and sacred obligations, than such a Union as we shall certainly see if Arkansas and South Carolina are permitted to drag these federal States into the abyss of bankruptcy. This can be in no respects a wholesome living Union, and the end will be a destruction by repudiation, more disastrous than would have been the destruction by war.

What then, is the remedy? It is idle to talk of military power to keep the peace. No military power can keep the peace in a country bent upon disturbance, unless by the extermination of the people. Spain has been trying for forty years to preserve order in her Biscayan provinces, and in the end she has a civil war as irritating as it was when Espartero made himself the Duke of Victory. The public sentiment of this country would not admit of any policy which looked to the armed occupation of the South. It would be an expense, an offence, a scandal, a burden that could never be cheerfully borne, a violation of the genius of our institutions. On the other hand this public sentiment would never consent to the revival of slavery, to the recognition of its existence in any form, except as a crime happily abolished and atoned. Nor would it accept any of the responsibilities of those who made the rebellion, the Confederate debt, the cotton loans, the losses of those who went into secession, and whose property was taken by troops, the sequestration of lands like those of Arlington. Nor can we consider for a moment any policy that would regard the negroes of the South who were formerly slaves as in any other relation than that of freemen, citizens, and entitled to every right of citizenship. There are certain inevitable facts growing out of our war, just as they grow out of all wars and all revolutions. The English Revolution made Parliament free, and destroyed absolute power. The French Revolution made France the home, the heritage, and the glory of every Frenchman, and decreed noble and peasant equal before the law. Our own secession revolution consolidated the Union and emancipated the slaves. These are the fruits of the contest, the inevitable facts that came from it, that can never be destroyed or taken away, and for which we should go to war to-morrow as eagerly as England for the freedom of her Parliament, or France for the preservation of the fruits of her revolution.

But there are other questions in no way vital, which do not affect these inevitable results, and the consideration of which statesmanship would impose upon us. Have we not imposed too heavy a fine upon the South as the consequence of the war? Have we not punished her, although a sister

Commonwealth, ten times more severely than France was punished by the alien invader? If Germany astonished the world in exacting five milliards from France what must be thought of the fine of ten milliards, which, estimating each slave at five hundred dollars, was imposed upon the South by the proclamation of emancipation? Should not some compensation be made to the South for this enormous fine—not in the way of actual money paid to former slave-holders, but in the development of industries in the South that were destroyed by the war? If we of the Northern States for generations sustained, approved and profited by slavery when it was an institution, should we not assume some of the expense and responsibility of regarding it as a crime? Because we conquered the South, have we any right to desolate it? Can there be any form of desolation more thorough than to compel the people to bear all the burdens of the war which they assumed—of the abolition of slavery which we, at one time, guaranteed to them as an institution, as well as of the debt we contracted ourselves to suppress the rebellion? Can there be any genuine reconstruction that makes it the object of the Southern leaders to aim to destroy by repudiation the Union they failed to destroy by secession? These are grave questions. To the minds of some of our readers they may no doubt be novel, and it may be said that we take a gloomy or a fantastic view of the situation in the South. But there certainly is an evil in the South that we have not reached. We are rapidly drifting upon chaos, disorder, a war of races, repudiation. We have made our brothers of yesterday our enemies, and not only enemies, but we surrender to their mercy the credit of the nation and the happiness of the four millions of slaves we emancipated. More than all, we have given them no motive for reconstruction; but, on the contrary, we have left them every temptation to war upon the Union.

These are living questions. It is not for us to decide them; but we do not see how there can be reconstruction until they are decided. Would it not be the wisest statesmanship, therefore, to call together a national convention to consider the war, its causes, consequences and results, and how best the Union can adjust itself to the new and strange conditions it has left to us? *Let us have a national convention of peace and reconstruction.*

---

[1]Alexander Robey Shepherd (1835-1902), territorial governor of the District of Columbia, was a crony of Grant. A native of Utah, Shepherd became a plumber and builder. He served in the Union army for three months; after the war he went to Washington, became one of the owners of the *Evening Star*, and was active in the establishment of the territorial government. As vice-president of the board of public works, he acquired the title of "Boss." At enormous expense—by the standards of his time—Shepherd transformed Washington from a muddy, filthy village into one of the most beautiful cities of the world. As a result of public outcry, the territorial government was abolished, and Shepherd was accused of every type of corruption and dishonesty. He was a poor man when he expatriated himself by moving to Mexico and becoming a silver miner. He lived to see a statue of himself erected in Washington. *CDAB*, 948.

Charles J. Jenkins to William A. Graham UNC

Augusta,
19th Sept 1874.

I received last evening your favor of the 15th inst. Unless prevented by something beyond my control, I will be in Washington on the 20th prox. ready to enter on the duties of the Arbitration between Virginia and Maryland. I have been appointed a delegate to the Episcopal triennial Convention, to meet in New York on the 7th October & shall D.V. leave home very early in the month to be present at its opening.

There is no probability that the session will have closed on the 20th, but considering the extreme difficulty of fixing a time for the meeting of the Arbitrators, when there are so many whose convenience is to be considered, & moreover being unwilling to be absent from home as long as would be inevitable if one of these engagements were to follow immediately upon the completion of the other, I propose no change of time, & will notify my alternate delegate to the Convention that he may at his pleasure assume the whole duty, or come in on the 20th.

I am concerned, that after having said you had "devoted the last two months to an endeavor to improve your health," you did not add that the desired improvement had been realized. I hope however when we meet I shall find that such has been the case.

Alexander H. H. Stuart to William A. Graham A&H

Staunton
Sept 27th 74

I was much gratified to learn, through a letter which my daughter Maggie received from Mrs. Clarke, that Mrs. Graham will accompany you to the Peabody meeting on 14th Oct. My wife & daughter will accompany me, & we should be much pleased to fall in with you & Mrs. G. on the way. Can't we so arrange it? We propose to go, on Monday the 12th, to Barnums Hotel, in Balt. & thence, on Tuesday, to N.Y. We prefer Barnums, because it is more quiet than the Carrollton, & it is a delightful house. Can't you join us there, or in Washington?

We propose to remain in N.Y. until Monday the 19th. when we will come to Washington, & spend a day to see all the improvements which have been made there since our day.

We should like, very much to be informed of the plans of Mrs. Graham & yourself, so that we may endeavor to have our parties as much together as practicable.

Maggie & I had a glimpse of Col Clarke & Miss Sudie, at the Depot, on their return from the Springs. We went there to try & prevail on them to stop & make us a visit, but they said that other engagements rendered it impossible.

Please write & let me know when & how you & Mrs. G. expect to go to N.Y.

I am still a member of our State Legislature & expect to spend the coming winter in Richmond; & as all my family, except my wife & Maggie will necessarily be from home, I have concluded to shut up my house for the winter, & take them with me to Richmond.

Will not your duties as arbitrator in the controversy between Virginia & Maryland, require you to spend at least a part of the winter in Richmond? If so, I hope you will bring Mrs. Graham with you.

Mrs. Stuart unites with me in cordial remembrances to Mrs. Graham & yourself.

John Spelman to William A. Graham UNC

Raleigh, N.C.,
September 29th., 1874.

As a representative of the New York *Herald*, and instructed by its managers, some weeks ago I wrote to you at Warm Springs, Madison County, requesting a statement of your views on the Herald's proposition for a National Convention for "Peace and Reconstruction" in the Southern States. I learn you had left the Springs before my letter could have reached you; and, as it may have missed you entirely, I respectfully renew the application.

Should you see proper to respond to the invitation, you will oblige by doing so, through me, to this place.

P.S. You are respectfully invited to touch, also, the Louisiana affair, Civil Rights, Repudiation, and the condition of our own State.

William L. Saunders[1] *to William A. Graham* UNC

Chapel Hill,
North Carolina,
September 29th., 1874.

The importance of the discussion now pending in regard to the calling of a Convention and the great confidence the people of North Carolina have in your opinions, induce me to ask that you will respond to the following questions, to wit:

1st. Do you think the best interests of the people of North Carolina require their Constitution, the Canby Constitution, so called, to be materially and speedily amended?

2nd. If in your opinion material changes in the Constitution ought to be speedily made, which mode of making those changes do you think the best interests of the people of North Carolina demand should be adopted? That by legislative amendment, or that by Convention?

3rd. The Conservative-Democratic party having an undoubted two-thirds-vote in each House of the General Assembly, what do you think is the duty of that party in reference to the calling of a Convention by the Legislature at its approaching session, for the purpose of amending the Constitution?

Trusting, Sir, that you will have both the leisure and the inclination to respond at an early day to the above enquiries.

[1]William Laurence Saunders (1835-1891), of Salisbury, a graduate of the university in 1854, read law with William H. Battle, practiced in Salisbury, and edited the *Salisbury Banner*. He enlisted in the Confederate army as a private and rose ultimately to the colonelcy of the Forty-sixth Regiment. Twice severely wounded, he was a splendid officer, despite criticism by John W. Graham. He surrendered at Appomattox. After a brief time in Florida, Saunders settled in Chapel Hill, where he watched Reconstruction with a "passionate interest." According to reliable sources, he assumed direction of the Ku Klux Klan but was never a regular member. He was clerk of the state Senate, 1870-1874; associate editor of the *Wilmington Journal*, 1872-1876; founder and associate editor of the *Raleigh Observer*, 1876-1879; and North Carolina secretary of state, 1879-1891. Perhaps his greatest achievement in the latter office was his role in the publication of *The Colonial Records of North Carolina*. A leading Democrat, Saunders was a wise and able public servant. *DAB*, XVI, 384-385.

Raleigh T. Daniel to William A. Graham UNC

Commonwealth of Virginia
Attorney General's Office.

Richmond,
October 12th., 1874.

As the busy season for lawyers is at hand, it has occurred to Judge Robertson and myself to suggest, that should the arbitrators on the boundary fix a time for the attendance of counsel shortly, such timely notice be given, as will allow them to arrange their engagements for it, so as to avoid as far as possible, any conflict between the two. A month's notice, we think, would not be too short, considering the number of counsel engaged, and their dispersed situation. A shorter notice would probably result in finding them unprepared to attend, and disappoint the meeting. We think a month the least time that ought to be fixed. We hope the liberty we take in suggesting this, will be excused. As I shall have to mention what has been done in the business, in my official report to the approaching Legislature, may I ask from you the full name, etc., of Governor Jenkins, whose antecedents, (alone of the members of the Board) are not fully known to our People?

Joseph Graham to William A. Graham UNC

Charlotte, N.C.
Oct. 25th 1874

My dear Father,

I hope you reached home safe, and improved. I left Philadelphia Thursday night and got home Saturday morning. . . . I got your medicine in Philadelphia and send it tonight by Mr. Hill. Also the photographs for Mother, Sudie, Becca, Lizzie and Sallie. I hope Mother will send me one of hers. Please let me hear what is the principal symptoms you are troubled with. I would continue the Quin (about four pills a day for another week. If you digest it well you should begin the Cod Liver oil and push it continuously. Ride horseback and do but very very little mental work. You can take the strychnine acid & Quinine mixture if still so feeble.

Love to Mother—
Your affect. Son

Joseph A. Engelhard to William A. Graham UNC

Wilmington, N.C.,
Octo. 26, 1874.

Learning that you have returned home, I write again to ask you to furnish us a letter favoring Convention. Col. Saunders and myself believe that we have the opponents of Convention at bay, and we need only a strong letter from you to rout them utterly. We think now is the opportune moment.

Hoping it will suit your personal convenience to write to us, and trusting that your health has been much improved by your recent visit North.

Joseph B. Cherry to William A. Graham UNC

Windsor, N.C.,
November 6th., 1874.

Many of our friends here have requested me to address this note to you, and ask your views and opinions as to the propriety of calling a Convention by the General Assembly of the State, (soon to assemble) for the purpose of amending the Constitution of the State.

With a few others of our leading men in political matters, *I am decidedly* in favor of calling a Constitutional Convention.

There is, however, some considerable opposition to such a step being taken at *this time.* All concur in the propriety of amendments to the Constitution, but fear the Conservative party may be damaged by such a proceeding just now.

I am not of the number of those who think that the doing of what *is right* should be deferred about any matter. Hence I favor a Convention. I take this occasion to say to you, that your opinion will have more weight with us, than any living man.

I hope, therefore, you will favor us with your views at your entire convenience.

I take this occasion to repeat to you, what you well know, how sincere has been my friendship and admiration for you since my boyhood. And now, that I am getting to be *an old man,* I feel, that the ties of affection for my friends grow stronger, as my life grows shorter.

I am in the enjoyment of good health. I hope you and yours are enjoying the same blessing. Hope to hear from you soon.

Sincerely, your friend,

P.S. If it be agreeable to you, we would prefer to make public your letter when I receive it. We have in our town a spirited news-paper, The "Albemarle Times" in which we desire to publish your response to us.

Charles M. Cooke[1] *to William A. Graham* UNC

Louisburg, North Carolina,
November 10th., 1874.

I shall be very much obliged to you if you will give to me (as a member of the Legislature) your opinion as to the plan that should be adopted for adjusting the State debt.

I have written Hons. B. F. Moore, and K. P. Battle, on the same subject.

---

[1]Charles Mather Cooke (1844-1920), of Franklin County, left Wake Forest College to enter the Confederate army, in which he served as captain and adjutant in the Fifty-fifth North Carolina Regiment. An exceptionally able lawyer, Cooke was a state senator, 1874-1876; a member of the state House of Representatives, 1879-1881 (Speaker) and 1889-1891; secretary of state, 1895-1897; and superior court judge, 1903-1920. Powell, *DNCB*, I, 421-422.

Charles M. Cooke to William A. Graham UNC

Senate Chamber,
Raleigh, N.C.
November 24th., 1874.

I have the honor to acknowledge the receipt of your very valuable communication on the subject of settling or adjusting the State Debt; and for which please accept my sincere thanks. You have seen from the papers that we have passed through the Senate a resolution providing that the question of settling the State Debt shall not be considered, except in secret session.

Mr. Moore and myself are to have a consultation on the subject. I shall present to him your views, and shall write you again after hearing from him.

John N. Staples[1] *to William A. Graham* UNC

House of Representatives, Raleigh N.C.
Dec 9th, 1874

Enclosed you will please find two Bills, one in relation to an amendment to the charters of the "Carolina Central Railway" introduced by Mr MacRae[2] of Cumberland, the other in relation to the North Carolina, and Western Carolina Rail Roads, introduced by Mr Tate of Burke.

I would be under obligation to you if you would give me your views on the merits & effect if adopted of these Bills. I have great respect for your opinions, and confidence in your stern integrity, believing that you are one of the few public men of our State, who has not in some way been to some extent connected with Rail Road [work] and Rail Road interests.

In this opinion, my colleague Mr Mendenhall[3] heartily concurs, and he too asks to be permitted to add his solicitations for your views on the enclosed measures.

I remain my dear sir
Your most humble & obt
servt
and friend.

Mr. MacRae's Bill is made special order for Friday next, hope it may be convenient to you, to let us hear from you by that time.

---

[1]John N. Staples was a representative from Guilford County. Cheney, *North Carolina Government*, 456.

[2]James C. McRae. Cheney, *North Carolina Government*, 456.

[3]Nereus Mendenhall, an influential Quaker, was president of New Garden School (now Guilford College) and was a Jonathan Worth appointee to the Literary Board. He was educated at Haverford College and Jefferson Medical College and practiced medicine briefly. A Whig, he became a Democrat after the Civil War and represented Guilford County in the North Carolina House in the 1874-1875 General Assembly. Mendenhall taught at Penn Charter School (1876-1878) and at Haverford (1878-1880). Cheney, *North Carolina Government*, 456; Zuber, *Jonathan Worth*, 235.

Robert P. Waring and Others to William A. Graham UNC

Senate Chamber
Raleigh, N.C.,
December 9th., 1874.

The undersigned Senators highly appreciating your past services to the Country, and recognizing your devotion to the best interests of the State, the Soundness of your judgment, and eminent ability and Statesmanship, respectfully request that you furnish them with your written views on the question of calling a Convention. Without wishing to commit ourselves, we desire to have the benefit of your views before we come to a definite determination.

With great respect,
Your ob't serv'ts,
R. P. Waring,
Geo. Williamson,
W. Foster French,[1]
Edwin W. Kerr,[2]
J. G. Marler,[3]
C. M. Busbee,[4]
C. M. Cooke,
J. T. Morehead, Jr.

---

[1]W. Foster French (d. 1902), of Lumberton, Robeson County, was a major and then lieutenant colonel of the Seventy-second North Carolina Regiment (Third Junior Reserves). A student at the University of North Carolina, French became a lawyer. He was a state

senator from his county, 1874-1876. Grant, *Alumni History*, 209; Cheney, *North Carolina Government*, 455.

[2]Edwin W. Kerr of Sampson County was a state senator, 1874-1876 and 1887-1891. Cheney, *North Carolina Government*, 455, 466, 467.

[3]John G. Marler, of Yadkin County, was a Conservative delegate to the Constitutional Convention of 1868, a member of the state House of Representatives (1870-1874), and a state senator (1874-1877). Cheney, *North Carolina Government*, 453, 455, 457, 845.

[4]Charles Manly Busbee (1845-1909) was born and reared in Raleigh. In 1863, during his sophomore year at Hampden-Sydney College, Busbee enlisted in the Fifth North Carolina Infantry. He was captured by Union forces at Spotsylvania Court House but was released after a few months and rejoined his regiment. After the war Busbee studied for a year and a half at the University of North Carolina. In 1867 he was licensed to practice law. Afflicted with a debilitating illness, Busbee recovered sufficiently to enable him to resume his career. He was not an ambitious politician but held important posts because of his friends' persuasion. He was a member of the state House of Representatives, 1885-1887; a state senator, 1874; and postmaster of Raleigh, 1894-1898. Powell, *DNCB*, I, 287-288.

William A. Graham to Conservative Senators[1] A&H

Hillsboro', N.C.
Dec. 15th. 1874.

Gentlemen:

Circumstances unnecessary to be detailed, have delayed longer than I desired, a reply to yours of the 9th. instant, requesting my views on the question of calling a convention to amend the constitution of the state. After the most careful consideration, I am fully persuaded that a convention is necessary to conform the constitution to the interests, habits, sentiments and tastes of the people of North Carolina.

Attachment to constitutions in the American states, has depended mainly upon the circumstances in which they were framed, the respect entertained for the men who constructed them, and the principles and regulations of the instruments themselves. Thus the constitutions of the Revolutionary period, given to us by men who signalized their devotion to their country as patriots and heroes, and embodying principles and guards for human safety and happiness surpassing any known in prior ages, were cherished with a deep and enduring affection. It was only after they were found to have been outgrown by the advancement and growth of the State, that change in them was called for and effected. Even then, in North Carolina, innovations were made cautiously and with a sparing hand, and the work was entrusted to persons, many of them, then, holding the highest public trusts, and others endeared to the whole people by long lives of illustrious public service. Doubtless other changes would have been made in process of time; as we have seen, that the constitution of Virginia as ordained by her convention of 1829, an assemblage containing many of the most eminent characters in American history, lasted only till 1850, when a new convention was demanded to adapt it more nearly to the wants and wishes of her people. And in the Constitution of Maryland bearing date in 1850, (whether it has been since revised, I am not informed,) there is a requirement that once in ten years immediately after the Federal census, the Legislature must provide for taking the sense of the people by an election on the question whether a convention shall assemble to consider of amendments to the constitution. While there are indications that the former reverence for those old frames of government had in some degree yielded to a progressive public sentiment, there was still a higher veneration for the institutions and traditions of the past, and the conservative assurance that whatever innovations might be introduced they should be guarded, and the offspring of a deliberate public conviction.

The present constitution of this state is an anomaly in American institutions. It has no claim to continuance by reason of the times in which it was composed, the influential characters of its authors, and, we may add, the circumstances of its adoption. There had been four years of desolating war, in which the state and its allies had been unsuccessful. This was followed by the process of rehabilitation, prescribed by the President of the United States as an executive measure, and North Carolina, having yielded her consent to the abolition of slavery, it was supposed that her constitutional relations to the Federal government were fully established. A Governor and Legislature were accordingly elected, as well as other executive, judicial and ministerial officers; and a delegation was chosen to the Congress of the United States but not admitted. After two years more spent in this condition of doubt, acts of Congress were passed annulling all that had been done under Presidential requirements, and directing an election, under military orders, in which the colored people should exercise the elective franchise, for delegates to a convention to frame a constitution, in which it should be ordained as a permanent regulation that they should thence-forward be entitled to the right of suffrage, in like manner and to the same extent as the whites—with an exclusion of no small portion of the whites, of most experience and capacity in the affairs of government, from seats in this convention, and the right to vote for its members.

The circumstances of this election are well remembered. It carried into the convention an assemblage of delegates, very few of whom had ever been known to the people as public agents of any description. Many of them wholly unknown, who had been left behind by the invading armies, others, colored men from abroad, or who had been recently emancipated here. Some of the most conspicuous of the white members, who in the altered condition of suffrage, reached other high positions, have since departed from among us, with reputations inspiring no respect for the works they left behind. By this convention the constitution now in force was framed and sent out for the ratification of the people. Though the instrument fills a large space in octavo pages, within little more than thirty days, it was required to be voted on, and at the same time, upon one ticket taking for granted that it was to be accepted, each elector was to cast his ballot for about forty officers, Governor, Lieutenant-Governor, Judges, members of the Legislature, etc, etc., who were to come into place, in the event of its adoption. By what majority the election was carried in its favor, and its supporters, including a large majority of the Legislative and State officers, were elected, I have not the means to ascertain. Not one voter in ten probably had read the constitution, but the appeal was made with great effect that it was necessary to take it no matter how objectionable, in order to get the state restored to the union; and in the confusion and panic which prevailed, it is hazarding little to assert that there was a constraint in the matter of ratification bordering nearly on duress.

It will be recollected that in respect to the provisions of the constitution, Congress had made but a single requirement, namely, that for citizenship and the rights to suffrage in the colored race. All else was left to the free deliberations of the Convention. But the new or foreign element in the delegation was in the ascendant; it was exultant and defiant, affected to know, what would, or would not, satisfy the national authority, and treated the opinions and sentiments of the former citizens with less respect than the Normans paid to the Saxons upon the conquest of England by William. The occasion was availed of, not merely to insert in the fundamental law the prescription of Congress, but to introduce a new and alien system in almost all respects, accompanied by requirements and declarations known to be offensive, and designed to perpetuate the feud of the recent war; all in the hope of founding, and installing in power a party which it was imagined would dominate for years to come, with but little if any responsibility for invasions of the property or rights of the citizens. A constitution with such an origin and such features rather requires justification from those approving it than to have its defects pointed out by those desiring amendment. It would be passing strange that a convention, such as that by which it was produced, should have given us one so suited to our wants, wishes, and habits, that we should be afraid to entrust its revision and amendment to delegates, chosen in a time of quietude like the present, from the wisest and best citizens of each county, having interests, feelings, and sentiments in unison with the communities in which they reside. It is, in my judgment, vain to think of specific amendments, by what is called the Legislative method, the whole document requires to be recast and re-written. Besides, the constitution of a free people should not be made of shreds and patches, parts excepted out by lines of circumvention and parts appended as afterthoughts or codicils, but like any other statute, should be made a clear, consistent, and harmonious whole; so as to be, as little as possible, the subject of construction; and so that intelligent citizens as well as lawyers may be readily assured of its true meaning. It would quite too much prolong this communication, to specify every particular in which amendment may be desired. Indeed it is to be hoped that a spirit of candor will pervade the convention, should one be called, and that the conclusions to which it arrives should be the results of a free conference among the intelligent and patriotic citizens, of which it shall be composed. There are, however, objectionable features so glaring as to arrest attention and call loudly for amendment. A few of these only does space allow me to mention. And first; Amendment is necessary to disembarrass voters, and to restore the self respect, spirit and manhood of the citizen. By the existing constitution no man "is allowed to vote without registration, nor to register without first taking an oath to support and maintain the constitution and laws of the United States and the Constitution and laws of North Carolina not Inconsistent therewith." This requirement of an oath is an innovation, designed to cast suspicion on the loyalty of the people, both to the Federal and State governments; and in effect to restrain their opposition to any law of either, present or prospective, no matter how objectionable. It savors strongly of dictation by conquerors to a conquered people, and is utterly at war with that free spirit of inquiry and discussion with which freemen are accustomed to deal with their laws and even constitutions. It is so comprehensive that few can conceive the extent of the obligation, and is calculated to cheapen the force of oaths and to bring the government into odium. Why demand an oath in the matter? It was and is, the pride of the people, that they rendered their duty to their country in whatsoever capacity required; and the differences arising out of the late war having been adjusted, they claim the boon of citizenship and suffrage in their own self-government as they enjoyed it in former years. Whole generations of their ancestors have lived and died in the free exercise of this right, without taking any oath to government unless they were chosen to office, in which case an oath to support the constitution was properly required along with the official oath; but never before was it prescribed, even by a despot, that every person should be bound by an oath to support and maintain every law as a condition of the enjoyment of his birthright as a voter.

2nd. It is necessary to emancipate the Legislature, restore it to its rightful and usual powers, and to avoid the necessity of frequent calls for convention, or amendments to the constitution by other means. To the Legislature should properly be entrusted, as was done in time past, the regulation of details in the Judicial establishment, county and other municipal governments, charitable and penal institutions, and the regulations of punishment for public offenses. It is vain to provide in the declaration of rights for the frequent recurrence of fundamental principles and that "for redress of grievances and for amending and strengthening the laws, elections should be often held," if, after representatives are chosen, they shall find themselves so tramelled by constitutional restrictions, that they are powerless to effect the most obvious and necessary reforms. The people of to day, through their representatives in the General Assembly, are quite as competent to decide as was the Convention of 1867-'68, on the constitution of the Courts of Justice, the number of Judges and circuits required, the mode of governing counties and neighborhoods and other matters of like nature; and should be free from time to time to make such alterations as public convenience, economy or accommodation may require. Even now, when the judicial business in a large majority of the counties is despatched in a single week, the term is fixed by the constitution for two weeks, no less and no more, in each county, running the circuits over into the depths of winter and into the season of harvest, to the great discomfort and inconvenience of the people. I should myself favor a return to the Legislature, of the appointment of judges of the Courts, and of those officers which the new system has transferred to the Governor, rendering the Executive an office of great patronage—insomuch that it has been made a grave question for judicial determination, whether the Legislature could employ a printer, a mere copying clerk, without an Executive nomination.

3. Amendment is necessary to remove the ambiguities of the constitution. Within the six years that it has been in operation there have been, according to the statement in Battle's Revisal, between twenty-five and thirty decisions of the Supreme Court required on constitutional questions, against probably not one-third of that number in all of our previous history; and others are known to be pending.

But I have not leisure to enlarge on these topics or to mention other defects of the constitutions. I take it for granted, that the amendments ratified by the people in 1873 are in full operation—the question being rather a political one, which has been settled by the Legislature and Governor, than of judicial cognizance, except so far as to ascertain, that those departments have pronounced them ratified. But while this will afford some relief, it will not obviate the necessity of calling a convention. This should be done to give us a constitution plain, clear and intelligent in its terms and North Carolinian in its spirit and taste.

I have no fears of a convention without limitation of powers. That which devised the present constitution was unlimited, and if it was worthy of trust, I have no apprehension of usurpation or abuse from a body chosen under the more favorable auspices of the present period. But if it be thought necessary to impose limits, there are precedents in North Carolina of great authority. Both of the conventions called by Legislature to deliberate on the adoption of the Federal Constitution in 1788 and 1789, were constituted to consider of that subject and of a single amendment each, in the state constitution. Each made the amendment proposed to the constitution of the state; the one rejected and the other adopted the Federal Constitution; neither essayed to go beyond its limits. But no danger can arise from the absence of limits if, as I presume, is intended the constitution prepared, shall be submitted to the popular vote for adoption.

The colored people entertained distrust of the measure from of an abridgement of their rights. But this will be seen to be groundless, when it is observed that they have full protection under the Constitution of the United States, if there were a disposition to infringe on their priviledges, which I do not believe exist.

Equally unfounded, would be any fears of the loss of the provisions for homestead and other exemptions now existing in favor of failing debtors. The policy is too well established to be abridged, and from recent indications they may rather be expected to be enlarged and confirmed by any set of delegates that may be chosen.

The only grounds of disinclination to the step among our Conservative friends seem to be founded on the supposition that the people are not supposed to be alive to its adoption; and this inference is drawn mainly from the issue of the election of 1871, upon the convention question as then proposed. But it were a great mistake to imagine that the present question is the parallel of that. That was a proposition that the people should, by their vote, under provisions of a law made by the Legislature, call a convention to amend the constitution. It was opposed on the grounds that the people did not possess this power even with the sanction of the Legislature, inasmuch as other modes of amendment were provided in the constitution. I had given much consideration to the subject then, and at a previous period, and was fully convinced that it was a right of the people, which, with the approbation of the General Assembly, they were at liberty to exercise whenever such approbation might be obtained; and I have been gratified to observe, that by means of its exercise recently, in the state of Arkansas, the Conservatives and Democrats of that state have formed a constitution in consonance with the wants of an overwhelming majority of the people, and elected Mr. A. H. Garland, one of the most able and upright statesmen in the Southwest, to the office of Governor. But our friends in this State, of the profession of the law especially, in many instances, differed from the theory which we maintained; while the whole body of our opponents were clamorous in their opposition, threatening resistance by force in case of our success, and claiming that they would be supported in such course by the authority of the United States. In this way, we lost the election by a small majority. But the question now presented, is divested of any terrors in our path, if it is deemed the best to pursue it in the wisdom of the Legislature. The power to call a convention by a vote of two thirds of each house, is of undoubted authority: as little to be questioned as the power to pass an appropriation bill. There can be no pretext for interference or hindrance on the part of the Government of the United States, and in charity we must believe, no disposition. It addresses itself therefore to the General Assembly as a great question of domestic policy and duty, whether they will allow the people an opportunity, through agents of their own selection to reinspect the machinery of their Government, and re-adjust it according to the wants and welfare of society as it exists at this day. Since the reverse of fortunes which has overtaken all, the great body of the people have been engaged in so earnest a struggle for the recuperation of means to maintain and educate families and fulfill their duties as citizens that they have had less leisure to devote to public affairs, and have been less suggestive to their representatives than has perhaps been their custom.

But they are not insensible of their rights and dignity as freemen, and are fully capable of dealing with this subject in all of its bearings. And if, as seems to be imagined, they have a blind reverence for a constitution, which it is difficult to overcome, it will probably be found to apply to that, which has been supplanted, rather than to this, which reigns in its stead.

Whatever of real reform there may be in the present, would no doubt be retained, whilst in everything else it should yield to the judgment of those who are to be subjected to its rule.

As to the expense of a convention, it is but a minor consideration, compared with the general revision of the constitution, its readaptation to the present phase of our affairs, and the new hope and courage, with which, under a reformed government, we shall pursue our onward march to a higher civilization and prosperity.

I am, with great respect,
Gentlemen, your ob't serv't,
W. A. Graham.

To the Honorable Messrs. R. P. Waring, Geo. Williamson, W. Foster French, Edwin Kerr, J. G. Marler, C. M. Busbee, C. M. Cooke, and J. T. Morehead, Senators, etc.

[1]From the Raleigh *Sentinel*, December 28, 1874.

Horace M. Polk[1] *to William A. Graham* A&H

Bolivar,
Hardeman County, Tennessee.
Dec'r 21st., 1874.

I suppose you have seen in the Ap'l No. of the North American Review, the attack made upon the authenticity of the Mecklenburg Declaration of Independence, of May 20th. 1775, by a Mr. Welling. His argument is, that No. Car. can claim nothing but the Resolutions of May 31st. 1775, and that these did not go so far as a declaration of Independence. He endeavors to explain away, ignore, and destroy, the weight of the evidence collected and published by the State in 1831—Except only such as suits his purpose. Attempts to show that all this testimony refers to the Res. of May 31st., and not to those of May 20—and that no such action was taken on the 20th., and no evidence of any meeting on that day.

I am desirous of getting hold of all the evidence bearing upon that great and bold act of the people of Mec., in order that the publication may be fully met. I have all the evidence collected and published by the Legislature of 1830-31.

Gov'r Swain sent me the printed letter of Mr. Bancroft[2] to him, saying that he (Mr. B.) had found the *identical* Resolves forwarded him by Govr Swain in the British State Paper Office. Now what were *these Resolves* forwarded by Govr Swain to Mr. Bancroft, when Minister at London. It is natural to suppose they were those (May 20th.) that the Leg. and Govr. had established by incontrovertible proof of the old Revolutionary soldiers, and not the Res. of May 31st. Mr. Welling says the Res. discovered by Mr. Bancroft in the Number 498 of the South Carolina Gazette and Country Gentleman were the Res. of May 31st. Can this be so? Mr. Bancroft writes Gov'r Swain that he had *copied* and *sent* to him *the whole letter of* Sir James Wright's.[3] If this document could be reached among Gov'r Swain's papers, it might throw some light on this point. You, Sir, have shown great interest in bringing to light the early history of North Carolina, and I know of no one to whom I could more properly apply than yourself, for the proofs in vindication of the Mec. Declaration of May 20th. 1775. Mr. Shepherd,[4] if living, or Hon. George Davis, of Wilmington, might throw some light on the subject. Might I ask you to communicate with Mr. Shepherd, and ask him to write me, (after 1st. Jan'y) at *Nashville*, where I will be during the Session of the Legislature, being in the State senate. But, after the middle of March, my address is at Bolivar, Ten.

Can you throw any light upon the *test oath* taken by the members of the Colonial Assembly at Hillsboro', August, 1775? Was it not a test of fidelity to the State, and not to the King?[5] Was it not introduced to implicate and bring in the loyallists in that body to the support of freedom? What was the test? Can it be now reached? Mr. Welling contends that it is discreditable in the descendants of those who were members of that Assembly, (Col. Tho's Polk & Jno. McKnitt Alexander, and others) to attempt to establish the fact of the Mec. Dec. of May 20, 1775—for he says those men afterwards, at Hillsboro', took a test of allegiance to the King. This cannot be true, for we find Col. Tho's Polk in *December following*, appointed by the Collonial Congress, Colonel of a battalion of Minute Men, and still preserving the confidence of his countrymen, which he would have lost in swearing allegiance to the British Government only a few months previous. The whole thing is ridiculous as a charge, and leads me to believe that the test administered in the Colonial Assembly at Hillsboro' in Aug. 1775, was a test of fidelity to the State. The character of this oath is illustrated at the battle of Moore's Creek, Feb'y 1776. And only *six months* afterwards, Gen'l McDonald and Col. Moore[6] exchanged the compliments of the season. The Tory Gen'l sends word to the Whig Col. Moore, "Lay down your arms, and take the oath of allegiance." The Whig, Moore, replies, "Lay down *your* arms, and take the *test oath.*" Caswell in the mean time, having arrived, and attacks and slays many to make them take the patriot's test oath, and takes McDonald prisoner. Powder and ball were considered necessary by the Whigs to make loyallists take the *test oath,* of which Welling now says it was disgraceful for the old Whigs of N.C. to take, after declaring themselves free and independent of King George. Col. Tho's Polk marched his hastily collected Reg't to Moore's Creek, to help make McDonald take the test oath, & arrives only after Caswell had done the work.

Wheeler in his History says "That these Resolves were laid before the Assembly Aug. 24th. 1775 by its President Will[iams]." No authority is given by Wheeler, nor proof that it was the Res. of May 20th. 1775. *Can we reach* the authority for Wheeler's statement that these Resolves were presented to the Assembly of Aug. 1775? And whether they were the Res. of May 20, 1775? If so, it will settle Mr. Welling. Another point—Martin's State paper of June 30th. 1775 (which I regret not having) where he denounces the *Resolves of the people of Mecklenburg* and says *they* were sent by Express to Phil'a, were sent in a *Cape Fear paper* (that is a Wilmington paper). If this old newspaper can be found, and proves to contain the Res. of May 20th., that again, would be conclusive.[7]

I do not make any apology for addressing [you] upon a Subject in which I feel assured you have the deepest interest, and would defend as an honorable and just claim for the State of No. Car.,—as she, without doubt, was the first to proclaim by a part of her Citizens, independence of British rule.

And I need not say I would be greatly obliged for anything in the early history of our State bearing upon the authenticity of the Mec. Dec. Independence.

I had the honor of seeing you when in the Legislature, when I was a Student at Chapel Hill, between the years 1839 and 1841, at which time I was graduated.

If you would be kind enough to address me either here or at Nashville on this subject, you will greatly oblige.

When at College I recollect seeing in the Archives of the Dialectic Society an obituary notice of my Grandfather Charles,[8] (brother of Col'n'l Wm. Polk, of Raleigh) speaking of his devotion to the cause of the Country, and his services in the same. I would be much pleased if you could procure me a certified copy of this obituary notice. It was in an old newspaper.

---

[1]Horace M. Polk (1819-1885), of Bolivar, Tennessee, was a native of North Carolina and a graduate of the university. He was, as he notes in his letter, a grandson of Charles Polk and a great-nephew of Colonel William Polk. He was a state legislator in Louisiana and Tennessee. Grant, *Alumni History*, 498.

[2]George Bancroft (1800-1891), historian and diplomat, had an enduring faith in democracy. A native of Massachusetts, he was graduated by Harvard in 1817 and received a doctorate from Göttingen in 1820. He was minister to Great Britain (1846-1849) and to Berlin (1867-1874), where he proved to be an able diplomat. He supported the policies of both Lincoln and Johnson. Bancroft's multivolume *History of the United States* was excessively patriotic but justly earned for him the title "Father of American History." *CDAB*, 45.

[3]Sir James Wright (1714-1785), the last colonial governor of Georgia, was a native of Charleston. He was an able lawyer and was attorney general of South Carolina for twenty-one years. *Appleton's Cyclopædia*, VI, 624.

[4]Shepherd has not been identified definitively, although this reference may be to Jessie George Shepherd (1821-1869), a university graduate, lawyer, judge, and politician from Cumberland County. Spencer Alumni Project.

[5]The oath of allegiance was to the crown.

[6]Donald McDonald, a native of Scotland who had fought at Culloden, was in command of a large detachment of loyalists and highlanders who were marching to Wilmington. They were defeated on February 27, 1776, at Moore's Creek Bridge by a smaller force of militia under the command of Colonel James Moore. The latter had been a member of the assembly, 1764-1773, and of the Third Provincial Congress. He was later a brigadier general in the Continental Army. Hugh F. Rankin, *The North Carolina Continental Line in the American Revolution* (Raleigh: Division of Archives and History, Department of Cultural Resources, 1977), 8-11.

[7]Martin was said to have sent the *Cape-Fear Mercury* that contained the resolves to England.

[8]Charles Polk (1762-1830), a native of Mecklenburg County, was a soldier in the Revolutionary War. In civilian life Polk was a member of the House of Commons, 1793-1795 and 1800. Cheney, *North Carolina Government*, 230-231, 233, 241.

William R. Cox to William A. Graham UNC

Raleigh
Dec. 28th [1874][1]

I trust your health & business will permit you to attend the conference of the State Ex' Com' on the 20th prox'o & that you will give us the benefit of your views in a few remarks.

The meeting is an important one & I trust will be well attended. Whatever we do, should be done promptly, for while conservatism is daily acruing accessions yet, there is nothing like the members of a party knowing what is expected of them. I read your letter with much pleasure & am pleased to know it is being distributed in pamphlet form.

---

[1]Letter torn.

Walter Leak Steele[1] *to William A. Graham* UNC
[with enclosure]

Rockingham,
December 30th., 1874.

I inclose an article hurriedly written by me for the Pedee Courier, on the subject of convention. I had no time to revise the style of the piece, nor to make even verbal alterations, because of the necessity of its appearance in the next issue of the paper. I think you will agree with the sentiments expressed, in the main. Indeed, I cannot doubt it, after reading your recent letter to members of the General Assembly. *That* letter gave me great pleasure and I only regretted that the opportunity did not occur for a fuller and more exhaustive discussion of the question. Such opportunity a letter of ordinary length does not afford, of course.

We might differ in some matters of mere *detail*, but on the *main issue*, I am glad to see that we are in full accord. Our people are becoming more united, and I can safely say that one member of the House will sustain *some* bill, for the purpose. I cannot agree to Mr. Means'[2] bill, because it does not entirely rid the measure of one ground of alarm. It leaves the matter so that a majority *may* not *restrict* the Convention at all, & the *Homestead* be endangered. This might cause some men to doubt.

Excuse me for troubling you, but my excuse is that I think it possible that the article inclosed may at least afford you a moments gratification, however unworthy it may be, in its strength and structure.

---

[1]Walter Leak Steele (1823-1891), a lawyer and manufacturer, was secretary of the convention of 1861. A native of Richmond County, he graduated from the University of North Carolina in 1844, after attending Randolph-Macon and Wake Forest colleges. Steele was a Democrat and a member of the Commons in 1846, 1848, 1850, and 1854; the state Senate in 1852 and 1858; and the United States Congress, 1877-1881. *Biographical Directory of Congress*, 1648-1649.

[2]Paul Barringer Means (1845-1910), of Cabarrus County, a graduate of the university, was a Confederate courier, a lawyer, a member of the state House of Representatives, 1874-1876, and a state senator, 1885-1887, 1889-1891, and 1909-1910. His bill provided for the call of a limited convention by a two-thirds vote of each house of the legislature. Grant, *Alumni History*, 422.

[Enclosure]
Newspaper Article[1]

The Convention Question.
Shall We Have One?

We see that there have been several bills introduced into the General Assembly to provide for the assembling of a Convention to remodel the Constitution of the State; one by Mr. Cantwell, the Radical Senator from New Hanover; one by Mr. Morehead,[2] Democratic Senator from Guilford, and one by Mr. Mills,[3] Democratic Senator from Burke. It has been argued that the Legislature shall take a recess from the 21st inst., until the 15th of January, in order, as is said, that the Representatives may ascertain the views of their constituents, in regard to this important question. It is our purpose now, to lay before our readers, as briefly as we can, some of the considerations which lead us to advocate the call.

The present Constitution is really not the work of the people of this State, but the work of those who live outside of our borders. It is the production of a Convention of men, assembled not at the call of the General Assembly, but at the call of the President of the United States, and elected, under an act of Congress, by voters whose qualifications were determined by Congress. At the *so-called* election of these delegates, many thousands of the most intelligent of our citizens were ruthlessly and unconstitutionally denied a vote, whilst the then recently enfranchised slaves were turned loose with ballots in their hands and bayonets bristling all around, to carry out the edicts of their new masters. The Constitution is therefore the result of military power—of armed force applied to civil government, and not in any sense on this account entitled to the respect, much less the love and veneration of the people of the State. Brought forth under these circumstances of tyranny and fashioned by unskillful men, most of whom, for the first time, were ever placed in authority, aided and instigated by malice drunk with success, it is no wonder that the instrument is full of absurdities, and bristles with provisions unsuited to the condition, and productive of mischief to the people who are forced to submit to its requirements.

Any one who will read the Constitution will see at a moment, that it is full of provisions which are improper in the organic law, and fit only as the results of the Legislative deliberation. Take for instance, the 7th and 8th articles on the subjects of "Municipal Corporations" and "Corporations other than Municipal." We venture the assertion that any intelligent man can see at a glance that nearly all provisions in these articles are such as are the proper subjects of ordinary legislation, and out of place, and mischievous in a Constitution. The definitions of legal terms are only such as are well known to the law, and which courts would be bound to make. The same defect is observable in a greater or less degree in all parts of the instrument. It is therefore highly objectionable on account of its volume. As Constitutions are mere frameworks of government, they should be confined to general principles, should be merely general landmarks for the guidance of each governmental department.

In addition to this, there are grave errors in the wisdom of many of the provisions. We have two [*sic*] many Judges. Three on the supreme, and nine on the Superior Court bench, are quite enough for the wants of our people. Besides, there is a fatal error, in the opinion of nearly every intelligent man, in the mode by which the Judges are elected, especially as the terms of office are short. It is thought by such persons that the system is fraught with danger to the public interest, by reason of the fact that it destroys the independence of the Judiciary and degrades it from the public respect, by holding up the temptation to *electioneer* for another term. Our own observation has taught us that this is a well grounded apprehension. Human nature at the best is weak and incapable of withstanding strong temptation. This stumbling block should always be removed, if we would expect the scales of justice to be held with an "even hand." A Convention is therefore needed either to change the mode of appointing the Judges, or to alter or regulate the times of their appointment, so that they who wear the ermine may administer the law according to law, and dispense equity according to equity, and not according to the effect which the judicial action may have upon the popularity of the Judge. It may be that the proper judicial independence can be had by simply destroying the eligibility to re-election, without touching the method of election. But at all events, the evils of the present system are clearly so great as to demand that calm deliberation, which can only be had through the means of a Convention. Sec. 2, Art. 3, secures the independence of the Governor by denying to him the inducements of a second consecutive term, in the prostitution of his office for personal advancement. If it is wisdom in that case, it is surely wisdom to place the same restraint upon our Judges.

We think that whilst provision is made in the Constitution for the trial of ordinary offenses, there should be a clause relating to the trial of persons guilty of malfeasance in office in the Judicial Department. Impeachment is too costly a mode of punishment. In our opinion, Solicitors should be subject to indictment in some court, other than the General Assembly, for corruption in office. We also think the Solicitor should have a salary and not depend on fees.

Provisions should also be made for a regular change of circuits for the Judges. The importance of this is so manifest, that it needs no argument to sustain it.

It is thought by many that our system of county government is far inferior to that which prevailed under our old constitution. That it is more expensive, we think admits of no doubt. This subject is well worthy of serious consideration—a more serious one than the General Assembly can possibly give it.

We should be glad to see Sec. 1, Art. 1 so altered that no man should have the right to vote, if he had been "convicted of an infamous crime," or "of corruption or malpractice in office." It is certain that one so convicted is unfit to join with honest men in managing a government whose laws he has so freely broken. If he is unfit to be created, he is unfit to create. Officers depending upon such persons for support, are apt to be no better than those on whom they rely. These men cannot hold office, and why should they sit in judgment on those who can?

For ourselves, we should be rejoiced to see Sec. 1, Art. 2, and all other sections relating to the subject, so altered as to strike out "Representatives," and insert "Commons." There are so many glorious recollections clustering around the hallowed name of the "Commons of the Parliament of Great Britain," that we confess our unspeakable love for the sign under which so many achievements in behalf of human rights were accomplished. All which we hold dear is associated with the determined struggles and final success of the Commons against tyranny and prerogative. And if under that name we have conquered the enemies of human liberty and rational progress, why should we now cast it away as unfit for the gratitude and use of a people who are reposing in the peace and security which it conferred?

We have other reasons for desiring a Convention, which our space forbids us to notice. We now turn to the objections.

These are all embraced in the comprehensive term—*policy*. It is feared by some really good and patriotic men, that if we call a Convention through the General Assembly, we shall damage our party! Parties are of no value unless they promote the public good. If a party is afraid to do right because of a supposed influence such action may have on its hold of power, what good can be expected of it? Governments cannot be administered as negatives. Good must be done as well as evil prevented, and a party which is powerless for *positive* acts, or afraid to do them when satisfied of their value, is an unfit depository of the public confidence. Let it do *right*, and put its trust "in God, and the sober second thought of the people" and then it becomes adorned with the attributes of true wisdom. Does the Constitution need change for the public benefit? If it does, the legislator who falters because of a fear that his political prospects will be clouded by his own righteous act, is guilty of a crime against God and his country for which, except in mercy, he can hope for no forgiveness. He who is "valiant for the truth" is "thrice armed," and he only is "naked" whose "conscience with injustice is corrupted." *Do right* in the sight of God and man, and no one need to fear for any consequences which may come.

But then, it is said by some that our disastrous experience in 1871, when the General Assembly provided for a Convention to be called by the people, should teach us a lesson of wisdom, and make us extremely cautious how we should proceed on the path of experiment. Suppose that to be true, are the circumstances the same? *Then*, the project was an experiment. It was doubted at the time by many good men of our party, whether the mode adopted was in consonance with the Constitution, which at least seemed to countenance no other mode of calling a Convention than that by direct legislative action. Some of the oldest jurists in the State were of this opinion, and among them, the Hon. Thomas Ruffin, a former Chief Justice of the Supreme Court. This fact alone did damage, either by the loss of the votes of such as held these views, or by preventing them from taking an active part in the canvass. Now, however, no one doubts that the legislature has the power to call a Convention itself, and this is the mode proposed.

At that time, threats of Federal interference were made, if a Convention called *by the people* should assume the responsibility of attempting or proposing to alter the organic law. The Governor of the State openly proclaimed that he would not recognize it. The Supreme Court had given out some ominous hints of its doubts as to the legality of the mode. Attorney General Ackerman[4] blew the Executive bugle at Weldon, and menaced the people with Radical arguments of the most potent character—the bayonet—if they decided to call a Convention. Public speakers fulminated their thunders against the so-called revolution, and misquoted the Constitution of the United States to frighten the people from the exercise of their rights. War in all its horrors was glowingly depicted. Under the adverse influence, the movement failed. Do these untoward circumstances now exist? Executive intervention in the domestic affairs of a State is a foul stench in the nostrils of a free people, and their voice of detestation has been so clearly expressed during the past few months, that even President Grant has, in his late message, recognized the danger of its application. That spell of despotism, thank God! has been dissipated into "thin air." Attorney General Williams[5] himself, as contemptible a tool of tyranny as ever existed, has not the impudence and effrontery to try the experiment of gunpowder government any more. No such ridiculous subterfuge as Grant has resorted to, to palliate his crimes against Arkansas, can be resorted to, for no man doubts the legality of the mode of calling a Convention, which is proposed.

But then it is said that the Homestead and Personal Property exemptions of the present Constitution will be endangered. It is not so; on that subject, no fear need be entertained. To put this subject of distrust, however, at rest, the Legislature can inhibit the Convention from touching this question, and the Convention would not dare to exceed its authority. If it did, the pleas that it acted *ultra vires* would be good before the bar of public opinion, and would tend to defeat its action at the ballot-box, to whose decision all the acts of the Convention will be submitted. If the Convention should act unwisely, the power is inherent in the people to reject its propositions, if distasteful to them.

Lastly, it is urged that the Radicals might get the control and give us a worse instrument than the one we now have.

A large majority of the delegates would certainly be Democrats. But suppose they would not be, is it not certain that *at this time*, with the evils of the present constitution before them, that even a Radical body, with political passions cooled down, would show more wisdom than was displayed by the convention of 1868, when military power was dictating the terms of a civil government? To us this seems to be true. But in a large majority of our counties, a class of men of high moral and intellectual qualities could be induced to act as delegates, whose business and tastes are such that they would not be members of the General Assembly. The people would exercise a sound and rational discretion in their choice, so that we should have a convention composed of delegates equal to the duties of their position, and in whose integrity every man might freely confide.

We may resume the discussion hereafter.

---

[1]From the *Pee Dee Courier*, December 20, 1874.

[2]James T. Morehead, Jr.

[3]Joseph Carson Mills, from Burke County, served in the Forty-sixth North Carolina Regiment and then as captain in the Thirty-third. After the Civil War he was a prominent Democrat, "a dynamic and resourceful leader who ruled a subservient principality at Brindletown." He served in the state House of Representatives, 1870-1872, and in the state Senate, 1874-1875. While in the Senate he was on a committee to study the status of insane asylums. Mills had considerable interests in the mining of gold in Burke County. Cheney, *North Carolina Government*, 451, 455, 466; Edward W. Phifer, Jr., *Burke: The History of a North Carolina County* (Morganton: Privately published, 1977), 78, 130, 324, hereinafter cited as Phifer, *Burke County*.

[4]Amos Tappan Akerman (1821-1880) was a native of New Hampshire who graduated from Dartmouth College and then went to teach in Murfreesboro, North Carolina. Later he moved to Georgia, where he studied law with John M. Berrien and acted as tutor for the

Berrien children. A Union Whig, Akerman enlisted in the Confederate army. After the war he became a Republican. He was a valuable member of the North Carolina Constitutional Convention of 1868 and was appointed federal district attorney but refused to take the ironclad oath. He was United States attorney general, 1870-1871, but protested the railroad frauds and was forced by President Grant to resign. However, he was offered a federal judgeship, which he refused. Powell, *DNCB*, I, 10-11.

[5]George Henry Williams (1821-1910), a native of Connecticut, moved to Iowa and served as a judge, 1847-1852. He became chief justice of the Oregon Territory and was a member of the Oregon convention of 1857. A Douglas Democrat, Williams later changed his political affiliation to the Republican party and was a United States senator, 1865-1871; he served on the reconstruction committee. He introduced the Tenure of Office Act, declaring that it did not affect the power of the president with respect to his cabinet. He was a member of the United States and Great Britain joint high commission. As United States attorney general Williams was entirely acceptable to the railroad interests. Grant nominated him for the office of chief justice of the Supreme Court but his name was withdrawn. He was later mayor of Portland, Oregon. *Biographical Directory of Congress*, 1819-1820.

1875

James R. Dodge[1] *to William A. Graham* UNC

New York,
11 Jany, 1875

Your niece Miss Washington,[2] to our great regret left us this morning for her home. She has presented me as from you your Photograph, for which I am much obliged and which my good wife has placed in our family album. I recognized it at once but like myself I do not think you as young as you was in "Auld Lang Syne.

I suppose that like mine, altho in a less degree your usefulness has passed away. At all events the old Whig Trumpet cannot animate us as of yore. I trust that the close of your life will be as happy as its meridian was honorable and take leave of you with a wish that you may see many happy returns of this genial season.

Please present Mrs. Dodge & my compliments & kind wishes to Mrs. Graham.

Yours truly,

---

[1]James R. Dodge (1795-1880), a native of New York and a nephew of Washington Irving, served as an aide to his father, a general officer in the War of 1812. He came to North Carolina almost by accident. Wrecked on his way to Charleston in 1817, he landed at Norfolk, Virginia, and drifted from there to Petersburg, where he studied law under the prominent David Robertson, who introduced him to Judge Thomas Ruffin. Ruffin befriended Dodge, as did a number of other prominent lawyers. Dodge settled in Stokes, North Carolina. He held the offices of solicitor, clerk in the legislature, and clerk of the supreme court in the Morganton division, 1847-1858. Dodge became an intimate friend of Graham and other prominent North Carolinians. Wheeler, *Reminiscences*, 393-394.

[2]Presumably Miss Washington was a niece of Mrs. Graham, née Susannah Sarah Washington. One of Mrs. Graham's brothers, Dr. James Augustus Washington, married Anna White Constable of New York City. Clark, "Washington Descendants."

James A. Graham to William A. Graham UNC

Graham, N.C.,
Jany 25th, 1875.

. . . .

I was very glad to see the decision of the Supreme Court in the case of the University vs McIver.[1]

While reading the opinion of Judge Bynum on Thursday night, I recalled the fact that by the allotment made at our first meeting, the first class of the trustees—who drew only a 2 years term—will go out before the Legislature meets again. I called the attention of Mr. K. P. Battle, Col Morehead & Willie to that fact & the question was raised how the Legislature should be informed of the expiration of their term; whether the Sec'y of the Board should simply address a note to some member of the Legislature informing him of it, & let him bring it before the body, or whether the Board at its next meeting should direct the Sec'y to make a report to that body. I drew a short term, as also did Mr. Battle, and, I think, Mr Cameron, Gov Vance, and Gov Reid.

. . . .

[1]A question arose concerning a constitutional amendment ratified by the voters in 1873 that took the authority to elect university trustees from the board of education and gave it to the legislature. A new board of trustees was elected by the General Assembly in 1874, but Governor Caldwell refused to recognize them, declaring that the legislature had no power to elect trustees. Alexander McIver, state superintendent of public instruction, had custody of the university seal and of books and papers of the treasurer. With McIver's consent, suit was brought against him for possession of this property, and in January, 1875, the state supreme court decided in favor of the trustees. Battle, *History of the University*, II, 50-52.

Appleton Oaksmith[1] *to William A. Graham* UNC

House of Representatives
Raleigh,
February 3, 1875.

I send by this Post [a] copy of my Bill to "Protect, consolidate and complete the State Railways," which I trust may commend itself to your favorable consideration.[2] Hon. J. Turner says that it is the only Railway Bill introduced since "reconstruction" which has sought to protect the State.

The strength of the Bill is on the point of the State power to exercise her right of "*eminent domain*," for the public benefit. Both Smith and Strong concur in my views on this point, and it will be most gratifying to learn that your views are such that we may count upon a favorable opinion from yourself.

I am, Sir,
With high consideration,
Your obed't serv't,

[1]Appleton Oaksmith (1830-1889), a native of Portland, Maine, attended Columbia College, became a publisher, and then engaged in the railroad and shipping businesses. He traveled extensively in Central and South America, Africa, and the Orient. After the Civil War, Oaksmith moved to North Carolina and settled in Carteret County. At the time of this letter he was a representative of that county in the state legislature. William O. Scroggs, *Filibusters and Financiers* (New York: Macmillan and Company, 1916), 214-215; Cheney, *North Carolina Government*, 456.

[2]The copy was not found.

James C. Welling to William A. Graham A&H

The Columbian University,
Washington,
February 13th., 1875.

I am very glad to learn that you have fulfilled your purpose to prepare a paper in defence of the genuineness of the "Mecklenburg Declaration of May 20th., 1775." I now beg leave to add my instances to those of your gratified auditors at Charlotte, in the hope that you will consent to the earliest possible publication of your address, in anticipation of the centennial celebration which, I learn, it is determined shall be held on the 20th. of May next.

I need not say that I shall read your address with the greatest interest, not only from the respect in which I hold you personally, but also from the weight of authority you bring to the discussion of any historical topic pertaining to the Revolutionary history of North Carolina.

I am sure that I can read your defence of the "Declaration" without prejudice, for I have no purpose to subserve in this discussion except the discovery of truth. Holding, as I do, that the paper of May 31 is a nobler monument to the Mecklenburg patriots than the paper of May 20th, (conceding the genuineness of the latter,) I can most cordially join with all North Carolinians in commemorating the wisdom and valor of their Revolutionary sires, however, as at present advised, I may venture to differ from some of them in regard to dates and documents.

As I commenced my investigations in this matter with a full persuasion of the truth of the current North Carolina opinion in the premises, it will be pleasant, rather than otherwise, to be led back by you to my original impression.

Robert D. Graham to William A. Graham A&H

Charlotte, N.C.
Feby 24, 1874 [1875][1]

Dear Father:

I hand you copies of the papers accompany Capt. Jack's affidavit for recovery of value of his lost *audited claim.* I have copied everything with the exception of the probated power of attorney, as I would like to have them preserved in the state as interesting relics. Enclosed you will also find a synopsis of Dr. Welling's address, which I think is completely refuted in the parts of your pamphlet that you read to me.

I would suggest that you correspond with E. J. Hale & Son as to style of binding, and let them get up some neat form of cloth, or Russian leather, that you could sell at $1.00 each with some remuneration to yourself. The State coat of arms could be embossed in gilt on it.

Yr. Aff. Son

[1]This letter was apparently misdated as it refers to an address delivered by Graham in

Charlotte on February 4, 1875, entitled *The Address of the Hon. Wm. A. Graham on the Mecklenburg Declaration of Independence of the 20th of May, 1775* (New York: E. J. Hale and Son, Publishers, 1875).

Matthias E. Manly[1] *to William A. Graham* UNC

Newbern, N.C.,
March 19th, 1875.

. . . .

Thro' the newspapers I learn that I have been restored to a place in the body of trustees of the university. It will be a source of pleasure in the decline of life if I can aid in reanimating the institution for which I entertain a warm filial affection.

Paralized by the events of the war the radical partizans of the day, have availed themselves of its weakness to perform the operation of *Harri Karri* upon it—(That's what they would call it out in Japan) It is a dead 'corpus'—But the ground is consecrate, & will grow another more glorious.

[1]Matthias Manly (1801-1881), a native of Chatham County, was the son of Basil Manly, a Revolutionary hero, and a brother of Governor Charles Manly. He attended the Bingham school and was graduated from the University of North Carolina in 1824, sharing honors with William A. Graham and two others. He read law with his brother Charles, married the daughter of William Gaston, and established a highly successful legal practice in New Bern. Manly held many offices: he served as a commoner, superior court judge (1841-1859), justice on the state supreme court (1859-1865), delegate to the Constitutional Convention of 1865, state senator, and mayor of New Bern. Ashe, *Biographical History*, VI, 357-365; Cheney, *North Carolina Government*, 361.

Zebulon B. Vance to William A. Graham UNC

Charlotte, N.C.,
March 22, 1875.

Since last fall, I have been writing a series of sketches of N.C. of a light, discursive character for the Norfolk Landmark. The Editor Mr. Hope[1] was so well pleased that he copyrighted them and now begs me to revise & correct, and add a paper on the Mecklenburg Declaration and let him publish in book form. I can not think of touching that subject in the face of your elaborate and exhaustive address here which is soon to be published, but it has occurred to me that it would be a happy thing if you would permit it to be published in a little volume with the sketches, and let the nett proceeds go to the Monument fund. Have you any objection? I think it would find considerable sale, and would embody your argument, which is of real historical value, in a permanent form for the library. If it could be got out by the Centennial (& I suppose it could) a 1000 copies might be sold on that day alone.

Please think of it and let me know at your earliest convenience. I send you a few numbers of the sketches, as a sample. I am so unwell I can scarcely write.

[1]James Barron Hope (1829-1887), of Virginia, was a graduate of William and Mary. A lawyer, Hope became state attorney of Virginia. During the Civil War he served in the Confederate army as a major; after the war he owned and edited the *Norfolk Landmark*. *CDAB*, 452.

Jeremiah S. Black to William A. Graham UNC

York [Pennsylvania]
March 23. 1875.

The divers circumstances which have prevented us from meeting for so long, have worked me some annoyance. While I blame neither myself nor anybody else I am glad to find a prospect of a definite agreement. Since you leave it to me I will fix the 10th of May at Washington. I must ask you to notify Governor Jenkins for the reason that I do not know his precise address. I will inform Mr. Whyte[1] and through him, his colleagues. I will also give notice as you request to the Virginia Counsel.

[1]William Pinkney Whyte (1824-1908), of Maryland, studied law at Harvard. He was, at various times, a state legislator, United States senator (1868-1869), governor of Maryland (1872-1874), mayor of Baltimore, state attorney general (1906-1907), and counsel for Maryland in the boundary dispute with Virginia. *CDAB*, 1200.

Nereus Mendenhall to William A. Graham UNC

Jamestown, N.C.,
3rd mo. 23, 1875.

Esteemed Sir,

I write to consult thee as one of the Commissioners appointed by a recent Act of the Legislature to have charge of the erection of the Asylum for the Insane at Morganton, as to the time when it will suit thy convenience to meet the other Commissioners in Raleigh to organize in due form.

Thy friend,

P.S. If desired, I can send thee an abstract of the Act. Principal parts as follows:

Sec. 1. Names the Commissioners: Dr. Grissom, Hon. W. A. Graham, Thos. G. Walton,[1] Dr. Whitehead,[2] and Nereus Mendenhall—to procure 100 acres of land within 3 miles of Morganton by gift or purchase.

Sec. 2. Commence building as early as practicable—use penitentiary convicts.

Sec. 3. Give security for faithful performance of duties. No pay except for necessary expenses.

Sec. 5. $50,000 this year, $25,000 next year. It will be necessary to allow time for notifying the other Commissioners, etc.

[1]Thomas George Walton (1815-1905) was a prominent Whig in Burke County before the Civil War. During the war he served in Company F, Forty-first Regiment, and later commanded the Burke Home Guard with the rank of colonel. After the war he changed his

political party to the Republican. In 1875 Walton was appointed to the commission to supervise the building of the Western Insane Asylum at Morganton. He was president of the Morganton branch of the Bank of North Carolina when it was rechartered in 1860 and was actively interested in the construction of the railroad in western North Carolina. Shortly before his death, Walton wrote *Reminiscences and Sketches*, a valuable source of information for later historians. Phifer, *Burke County*, 77, 78, 130, 153, 185, 301, 324.

[2]Marcellus Whitehead (1821-1885), of Salisbury, was a native of Virginia and a graduate of the Medical College of Virginia. He was a Confederate surgeon and after the war served a term as president of the North Carolina Medical Society. Whitehead had a prestigious practice in Salisbury. Ashe, *Biographical History*, V, 442-446; James S. Brawley, *The Rowan Story* (Salisbury: Rowan Printing Company, 1953), 174, 250, 280.

George T. Swann[1] *to William A. Graham* UNC

Cl'k's Off., U.S. Courts,
Jackson, Mississippi.,
March 25th., 1875.

I saw in the papers yesterday an account of an address by you at a meeting preliminary to the celebration of your Mecklenburg 'Declaration,' and it was stated that it would be published in pamphlet form.

Counting myself as one of the 'troops of friends' you have everywhere, (since I used to meet you in *1834*, at 'Caswell' Bar, in Yanceyville), I have to beg that you will send me one of these, when published.

I have in my office one of the 'McGehees,' as my Deputy, who on his maternal side is a lineal descendant of that glorious old Capt. Jack, who bore the Declaration to Philadelphia, a little too fast for the final 'move' in '76.

With many wishes for your happiness, I am,

Very truly, your friend,

---

[1]George T. Swann has not been further identified.

William A. Graham to Cornelia Phillips Spencer A&H: SPENCER

Hillsboro'
March 25th. 1875.

. . . .

I experienced a like pleasure in the passage of the recent act for the relief of the University, with that which animated your party in bell-ringing,[1] and can truthfully say, that the State is indebted for it to the Alumni of the institution in the present Legislature.

---

[1]"When Dr. Battle telegraphed her from Raleigh on March 20, 1875, that the bill had passed the legislature giving the university $7500.00 annually from the land scrip fund, Mrs. Spencer climbed the stairs to the attic of South Building and rang the bell for an hour." Christopher Crittenden, William S. Powell, and Robert H. Woody (eds.), *100 Years—100 Men, 1871 to 1971* (Raleigh: Edwards and Broughton, [1971]), 344; Battle, *History of the University*, II, 69-70.

John A. Young[1] *to William A. Graham* UNC
[with enclosures]

Charlotte, N.C.
March 26th 1875

Your Manager, Mr Thompson,[2] I think is his name, purchased 1 Ton Cotton Compound Fertilizer from me this week and directed me to inform you of it.

1 Ton Cotton Compound Cash price	$50.00
Price 1st Novr 1875	$56.

It is manufactured by Messrs Snowden & Peters, Baltimore, and I have very great confidence in it. I have sold out the supply they sent me.

The preparations for our Centinial Celebration are moving on with a good degree of energy. We are sending Circulars[3] to every County in the state & to friends outside of the State. We beleave we will have a 20,000 Crowd, and hope to do something important towards erecting a monument.

You have probably seen our programme. Considerable opposition was made to assigning a place to the President of the U.S. but it was decided that it was due to the office, not the incumbent.

With assurances of high esteam, I
Remain, Yours Very Respectfully

[1]John A. Young operated a mercantile business on North Tryon Street in Charlotte. According to the letterhead, the firm was "John A. Young & Son, Dealers in Gentlemen's Clothing and Furnishing Goods, Hats, Caps, &c." The names John A. Young and J. Alphonso Young appear at the top. John A. Young was chairman of the planning committee for the centennial celebration of the Mecklenburg Declaration of Independence.

[2]Thompson, presumably manager of Graham's Leper farm, has not been further identified.

[3]A circular for the centennial celebration, and the printed program that follows, were enclosed.

[Enclosure]
Centennial Celebration Program UNC

North Carolina Centennial of the
Mecklenburg Declaration of Independence.
Programme.

One hundred guns, at sunrise, and ringing of city bells, under charge of the Artillery Committee.

To march at 10 o'clock a.m., Grand Procession, through the principal streets of the city, under charge of Chief Marshal and thirty Assistant Marshals, as follows:

Military Companies.
Fire Companies.
Masonic Lodges.

Odd Fellows.
Knights of Pythias.
Good Templars.
Patrons of Husbandry.
County Organizations.
Other Associations of City, County, State and Citizens.
Press Organizations.
Various Centennial Committees.
Accompanied by Various Bands of Music, and Their Own Special Banners, Emblems and Insignia.

The procession will be formed in the following order:

Military Companies on both sides of South Tryon streets, right front resting in front of Central Hotel.

Fire Companies on West Trade Street and on Church Street, opposite Fireman's Hall.

Grand Lodges, County Organizations, other city, county and State Associations, and Citizens' and Press' Organizations, on East Trade Street.

Masonic Lodges, Odd Fellows, Knights of Pythias and Good Templars, on North Tryon Street, from the Square to be followed by Band of Music with Military Company, to be assigned by Chief Marshal as guard of honor or escort.

In carriages, the following: The President of the United States, Governor of Tennessee and staff, Governors of other States, Governor of North Carolina and staff, United States Senators and Supreme and Superior Judges of North Carolina, Mayor of the city, and other invited guests, orators and reader, accompanied by committees.

Parade to be through principal streets, to arrive at the Speaking Grounds at 12 o'clock M. After the various companies and organizations, &c., have been arranged by the Chief Marshal and Assistants, the Centennial will be opened with prayer by the Chaplain, Rev. Robt. Hall Morrison, D.D., after which reading of the Mecklenburg Declaration of Independence by ———, followed by addresses by ———. After the addresses there will be, at 3 o'clock P.M., a Grand Barbecue. After which, Military and Fire Company display.

At night, at 7 o'clock P.M., Grand Torch Light Procession, with Chinese Lanterns, Emblems, Transparencies, etc., etc. After which, addresses will be delivered from the Stand in Independence Square, on the site of the original Declaration of May 20, 1775, corners of Trade and Tryon Streets. There will be general illuminations of the houses on principal streets.

The Celebration to conclude with a Grand Pyrotechnic Display, consisting of beautiful Emblems, Figures, Mottoes, etc., etc., appropriate to the occasion, under charge of the Artillery Committee.

The Chief Marshal, with thirty Assistant Marshals, to be hereafter announced.

Approved and adopted by Central Executive Committee, March 24, 1875.

Dr. Joseph Graham,
Chairman Executive Committee.

Thos. W. Dewey,
Secretary Executive Committee.

March 25, 1875, ratified and adopted by General Committee of Arrangements.

Joseph Graham to William A. Graham UNC

Charlotte,
March 29th., 1875.

My dear Father,

I think the Central Executive Committee of the Centennial Association will soon request a copy of your essay on 20th of May Declaration for publication. You spoke of embodying in the same pamphlet some proceedings of the Halifax Congress, and other matters pertaining to that time, which would be of general interest. The idea is to put it up as a neat substantial pamphlet sufficiently ornamental to take a place in a gentleman's library and sell it to raise a *monumental* fund. I do not know whether Gen'l Hill has done it justice or not, as I have not read his paper.

Please write me what your idea is about the pamphlet. I am having our Committee make preparations to keep in a substantial form all letters from dignitaries on the subject—which may serve to confirm the event we celebrate as a matter of history. All valuable matter gotten up in good form should be presented to the State, and put in its Archives.

. . . .

Please give me a list of distinguished gentlemen whom it would be well to invite, even for their letters of recognition, if for no other purpose. Any suggestions you may have to make in reference to any part of the Celebration, I will be very thankful for.

Kemp P. Battle[1] *to William A. Graham* UNC

Raleigh,
North Carolina,
March 30th., 1875.

I notified Col. Lassiter[2] of our purpose to bring suit on his bond, if he did not settle forthwith. He replies, showing anxiety to meet the Committee and make a full settlement at once. It so happens that I cannot postpone certain business engagements, which I agreed to meet several weeks ago, but which I postponed in order to stay in Raleigh until the passage of our Land Scrip bill. I am compelled to be absent for the next two weeks, this week in Charlotte, next week in Greensboro, Salem, etc. I therefore fear I cannot meet Col. Lassiter before it will be too late to bring suit to next Orange Court, in case we cannot agree.

I can't see how the University can be hurt by the delay of one term. The Land Scrip Act directs the Treas'r to issue us the certif. for $125,000., peremptorily in the 1st. Section. In the 2nd Section we are commanded to burn the Special Tax bonds as being worthless, and to hold the other bonds subject to the disposition of the Gen. Ass'y.

According to the Act we get the certificate in any event and are only custodians of the bonds, not special tax, mentioned in my report. I therefore conclude not to commence the suit against the late Treas'r or the Bank, at once, especially as it is probable that either Lassiter or his sureties, will arrange the matter, as the amount involved is so small. In the mean time I have procured from the Govr. a copy of Lassiter's bond.

I take the responsibility of not pressing the suits, because the Trustees & the Ex. Com. evidently left this to my discretion.

I suppose you have heard of ex-Pres. Pool's suit against us for his salary for several years. He includes in his suit, ($10,000) claims for the 8 pr. ct. bonds he rec'd when he was a member of the Faculty in 1867-8. The summons was not served on me until the 26th, too late for the next term of Wake, but was served on Gov. Brogden[3] before that time. Mr. Moore volunteers to defend the University without charge, so I've no doubt but that we will get justice. Of course we will not only dispute his claim but make counterclaim on ac't of his neglect. Is the service on Gov. B. sufficient? Can Pool file in Wake?[4]

---

[1]Kemp P. Battle was unwearying in his efforts to reopen the university, and in 1876 he was elected as its president. Cornelia Phillips Spencer, quoting Paul C. Cameron, wrote on April 21, 1888, "Mr. Battle was selected by Gov. Graham and myself, after a full view of our field, as best suited to our wants. We thought him the best of all our home material." Cornelia Spencer Papers, Southern Historical Collection, University of North Carolina Library at Chapel Hill.

[2]Robert W. Lassiter, former secretary and treasurer of the university trustees, had pledged five bonds belonging to the land scrip fund as collateral security for a loan to pay his own salary. Eventually suit was brought on the treasurer's bond and the funds were recovered. Battle, *History of the University*, II, 53, 62-63.

[3]Curtis Hooks Brogden (1816-1901), of Wayne County, was a lawyer and an able debater. Known as "Rough and Ready," Brogden began his political career as a Jacksonian Democrat but, to the dismay of his section, supported radical reconstruction after 1865. A political cohort of William W. Holden, Brogden favored Negro suffrage and rule by the military. During the 1870s he sought conciliation with the white majority. In more than fifty years in public life, he held the following offices: member of the Commons, 1838-1850; state comptroller, 1857-1867; state senator, 1868-1872; lieutenant governor, 1873-1874; governor, 1874-1877; member of the United States House of Representatives, 1877-1879; and member of the state House, 1887-1889. Brogden was one of the largest landowners in Wayne County. Ashe, *Biographical History*, VI, 106-113; *Biographical Directory of Congress*, 601; Powell, *DNCB*, I, 234.

[4]Solomon Pool's suit never came to trial, but the legislature later paid him a considerable part of the claim. Pool, although without duties, was not ejected from office by decree of the court until 1875. The General Assembly approved payment of the unpaid principal and interest of his salary because he was "a minister of the Gospel and in financial straits." Battle, *History of the University*, II, 40.

Tax List of William A. Graham UNC

W. A. Graham State Tax, April 1, 1875
Hillsboro' Township.

1. Lots about residence in Hillsboro including purchases from Turrentine's assignees, Brown's ass'nee and P. C. Cameron about 3 ½ acres with dwelling & outhouses.
2. Drug store Lot on Tryon street 66 front unimproved.
3. Lot 237, south of & adjoining colored grave yard.
4. Estes tract on Eno & Spirit branch 833 acres, Cedar Grove Township
5. Ray tract on Foresters creek 525 acres.

6. One Horse Value	$150		
7. Two Mules old	125.		
8. 14 cows & yearlings 2 young calves	112.		
Farming utensils, Mechanics tools, Ho. & Kit. furniture, provisions, arms, wearing apparel, Library & scientific instruments	1,000.		
9. Money on hand 20. on deposit	3,500.		
10. Solvent credits Charlotte		5,000	debts owing
Wil. Char & R. Bonds		1,000	1800.
McBride's Bond		500	2800.
		6,500	484.
deduct monies due		6,084	500.
		414. [*sic*]	5584
			500
			6084

11. 20 shares Stock N.C. R. Co. tax paid to Co.
Bonds of sd. Co. Co. paying tax.

12. Other personal property 1. Piano 150. Plated & silver ware watches & jewelry 400	550.
Exemption of personal property	25.
	525.
13. Income from Profession 500 deducted	1037.45
" From other sources	1448.
	2485.45
Deduct	1000.
	1485.45
Taxes—172.80	172.80
	1312.65

Turrentine Lots—
Lots 97 & 90, and parts of Lots 95, 76, 77, & 78—
Two & a half acres—

—Brown Lot, part of Lots 94, 95, 75 & 76 quantity of Land in boundaries of [illegible] [common] & Robert's in Lot [marked through]—
Part of Lots 75 & 76—about 1 acre—
Drug store part of Lot No 25—
Grave yard Lot No 237 [at] 90/100 acres

Ralph H. Graves[1] *to William A. Graham* A&H

Hillsboro',
April 7th., 1875.

I return herewith, with thanks, the papers you loaned me.

I have read with great satisfaction the communications they contain, as well as that contained in the paper of April 5th.

I did, at first, think it a little surprising, that Jefferson, a member of the Congress, should not remember that the document in question had been presented to that body. But in view of the facts which existed & ensued, as you have detailed them and especially in view of the instances of *palpable* forgetfulness on his part, in connection with the subject, & on the part of Mr. Adams, it ceases entirely to be a matter of any surprise whatever. The circumstances, too under which he gave his opinion, & the manner of it, without any investigation, indicates that that opinion, so far from being entitled to the weight which would naturally have been attached to it, was, in fact, entitled to but very little, if any.

If the facts for which you contend are to be rejected, we might, I think, reject, on grounds equally good, more than nine tenths of what is now received as authentic history.

I send some papers relating to the Va. Ag. & Mech. College in which the question of manual labor is, among other things, discussed. You can retain them until you may have leisure to attend to them, as I have no further use for them.

[1]Ralph Henry Graves (1817-1876), a native of Granville County, received an A.B. degree from the University of North Carolina in 1836 and a master's in 1839. After serving as a tutor in math at the university from 1837 until 1843, Graves became a professor at the Caldwell Institute. Grant, *Alumni History*, 231.

William Johnston to William A. Graham UNC

Charlotte, N.C.,
April 15th., 1875.

The Central Executive Committee have appointed Dr. Jos. Graham, Major Dowd[1] & myself a Committee to have published in book form your address delivered in Charlotte on the 4th. of Feby. with such other documentary evidence as we deem proper. We have provided the manuscript of the address together with four copies of the Southern Home containing a printed copy of the same to Messrs. E. J. Hale & Son, No. 17 Murray St., New York, to have the work executed. We request that you will furnish

Messrs. Hale & Son *directly* with any evidence, proofs, documents or corrections you may desire made in the republication in book form.

The Committee will embrace in the same book the Legislative publication of 1831 made by Gov. Stokes,[2] also the authorization or instructions of the Provincial Congress of April 12th 1876 to her Delegates in the Continental Congress to concur with others in voting for independence.

If you have any addenda or other valuable documents please have no hesitation in forwarding to Mr. Hale for publication in the volume to be issued. We are in pursuit of other evidence, but may not get it in time.

If Col. H. M. Polk[3] has a copy of the Raleigh Minerva, published in 1709 [1809] stating the fact of the 20 of May declaration, it will supply an important link and leave no room for cavil. You will please communicate with Messrs. Hale & Son as early as convenient as we desire the publication in form prior to the 20th. proximo. Should you desire to correct the proof, please have Mr. Hale to furnish it to you.

---

[1]Clement Dowd.
[2]Montfort Stokes.
[3]Horace M. Polk.

Joseph Graham to William A. Graham UNC

Charlotte,
April 15th., 1875.

My dear Father,

This is the first day when I could give you a full answer to your letter, or I would have attend[ed] to it earlier.

The manuscript & papers went forward to Mr. Hale last night. Col. Johnston was instructed by the Committee to write you concerning the publication.

I presume you have seen a notice in the Southern home of some papers in possession of Col. Horace M. Polk, Bolivar, Tenn., grandson of "Independence Tom." Our Secretary has written for those papers or copies from them. I will send them to you upon receipt, if they are valuable.

This is the thirty eighth anniversary of my birthday. Please say to Mother that I had intended to write her a letter today, but now I will be compelled to make this serve the double purpose of business and affection.

We are all as well as usual. But my throat has troubled me more than usual since the death of Miss Mary Bynum. I was a good deal fatigued waiting upon her, during the latter part of her sickness.

We hope you and Mother will come up to the celebration. On account of the crowd, and the superior accommodations which Cousin Sophie's[1] house affords, and at her request, we all concluded it would be best for you both to stop with her, and come here after the crowd leaves.

Please say to the *brothers* that Bettie and I will be pleased to see any and all of them. We will put them in the common reception apartments. I hope they will come. I am very busy with the preparations, when not professionally engaged.

Can you give us a beef, or some fat sheep, and how many, of the latter, for the barbecue?

All join in love to Mother, and all the family.

The Raleigh "Minerva," 1809, is said to have an allusion by an orator at Chapel Hill, to the 20th. May Declaration. Col. Polk said to have this paper.

---

[1]Probably this was Mary Sophia Alexander (1831-1916). Clark, "Graham Descendants."

E. J. Hale and Sons to William A. Graham UNC

New York,
April 17, 1875.

But for the pressure of the Spring Trade, we should have written to thank you for the admirable Address at Charlotte. It is a matter for congratulation that your health has allowed you to accomplish so noble a work.

We are obliged to write to you about it now, busy as we are, because it has been sent to us to publish, & we are informed that you have some matter to add to it. As the time is short, we write to ask that this be sent to us at once, that we may know how many pages the whole will make. Your address proper will make 120 12 [*illegible*] mo pages. The Legislature pamphlet at least 40 more, if in same size type; & then whatever else you may have.

The Charlotte Committee has ordered 1000 copies; & "may want more". But they have not instructed us whether or not to stereotype it. We have some thought of doing it ourselves, should they allow.

We have been very much rejoiced to hear, from time to time, through Mrs. Graham's letters to Mrs. Hale, of your improvement in health.

Please present us to Mrs. Graham.

John Alexander[1] *to William A. Graham* A&H

Fortress Monroe, Va
April 19th, 1875.

I have been reading with much interest your four articles in the "Southern Home," (Published in Charlotte, S.C.) on the Subject of the "Mecklenburg Declaration."

I have in my Library in Philadelphia a coppy of said Decleration with a fac-Simile of the Signitures of the Committee that reported it.

From information given me at Charlotte, N.C. by descendents of the Alexanders, I have no doubt my ancestors sprung from the same Scotch Irish root from which the Mecklinburg Alexanders came.

I would be greatly obliged to you for any information you can give me as to the original line of decent from which "*Brevard*" sprung, who is suposed to have written said "Mecklingburgh Decleration," am descended from Scotch Irish Alexanders who emigrated to Pennsylvania direct from "*Armach*" County, Ireland of Scotch Covenanter Stock.

Capt'n S. B. Alexander of Charlotte N.C. informs me that his grandfather, John McNitt Alexander was of Scotch Covenanter Stock, that came from the same County of "Armach" Ireland to Pennsylvania & thence to Mecklingburgh County North Carolina, he also informed me that the late distinguished Rev'd Doctor Archibald Alexander[2] professor in Princeton, N. Jersey, who was born in Virginia was descended from the Mecklingburg, N.C. Alexanders who had emigrated from North Carolina to Mecklinburg Virginia.

I am decidedly of opinion from all I have learned in a late visit to North & South Carolina that you have established the Authenticity of the Mecklingburgh Decleration sufficiently to satisfy right minded and impartial judges, and as time rolls on future judges will find no dificulty in deciding between the weight of your evidences & the flimsy objections raised against the Authenticity of the Mechlinburgh Decleration. And if I am corect in conjecturing that the committee who prepared & reported said Decleration may have been like my namesakes the Alexanders of Scotch Covenanter stock the similarity of the Decleration to the Solemn Leigue & Covenent would be an argument in favor of tracing the origin of American Independence to men of such antecedents as pertained to men of Scotch Covenanter principles, rather than to such men as Jefferson & his associates whose antecedents connected them so closely with the Infidel School of French Politicians who were so influential among our Statesmen of that period.

Distinguished Citizens of your State during my laste visit there referred me to you for information on these points.

Therefore any information you can give me respecting the antecedents of any of the Committee, & especially of the writer, or suposed writer of the Mecklingburgh Decleration will be thankfully received and highly appreciated.

Yours Truly
John Alexander
of 1935 Arch Street,
Philadelphia, Pa.

P.S. As I expect be reach my home in Philadelphia, Pa., you will please address me as above to Philadelphia.

[1]This John Alexander has not been further identified.

[2]Archibald Alexander (1772-1851) was a Presbyterian clergyman, educator, and author who became the first professor of theology at Princeton. *CDAB*, 14.

William Johnston to William A. Graham UNC

Charlotte, N.C.,
April 20, 1875.

My return from Davidson College on yesterday placed me in possession of your favor of the 16th inst. I am pleased to see that you have forwarded to Messrs. Hale & Son the Address corrected, as he had written me that he desires all the subject matter to make the volume as soon as possible. I am also gratified that you have forwarded the Davie & Martin resolutions or Declaration also the (resolves) of the 31st of May. For the resolves or more perfect government for the county adopted on the 31st, was the necessary sequence of the Declaration of independence made & published on the 20 of May. The 3 & 4 resolutions of the 20th did not make a complete government. Each delegate was made a committeeman with certain powers until a better & general government was organized "in this province." The resolves of the 31 was an adjourned meeting from the 20 as appears to me. "This day the committee of this county met, etc." What committee? That of the 20th., we know of no other. These resolves or code of laws are based on the idea of independence then existing. It had already been declared, and the county being without a sufficient government the committee on the 31st. adopted a system which resulted as a necessary consequence from the action of the 20th., "until laws shall be provided for us by the Congress," (Provincial). There the principle of representation was recognized in the 5th. resolve. In this new order of things after independence had been declared other rules or laws were necessary to conform to the changed condition of the county. But time precludes further general remarks.

We have ordered the book to be stereotyped, ordered 1000 copies and may order one or two thousand in a cheaper form. We think the address able and convincing and with the arrangement of the testimony, the new matter brought into it, and the history & condition of the times given (which throw much light upon the transaction) it ought to be convincing to every fair and unprejudiced mind. We feel that it will settle history in future notwithstanding what Bancroft, Grigsby,[1] & Welling may have said. The friends of Mr. Jefferson we cannot convince.

Eureka! We are just furnished with a copy of the Catawba Journal published in Charlotte on July 11th., 1826, which contains an article written by "Mentor" giving an extract from a valedictory address delivered at the Rev. Sam'l C. Caldwell's Academy (near Sugar Creek) June 1st. 1809 and quoted from the Raleigh Minerva, published 10th of Augt., 1809 which valedictory says that the delegates from each captain's company met on the 19th. of May & after due deliberation & considering the consequences—"pledging their all in support of their rights and liberties."— they solemnly entered into and published a full and determined declaration of independence renouncing forever all allegiance, dependence on, or connection with Great Britain all of which were transmitted [to] Congress by "Express" etc. Who Mentor—the writer—is I know not, but he refers to the Raleigh Minerva of June 1st., 1809 for the long extract he gives of the valedictory. Col. H. M. Polk has the Minerva of that date as we learn. If we can get that paper it will show the fact of the 19 & 20 Declaration proclaimed here in 1809 within less than 30 years of the close of the revolutionary war, when hundreds of those who had been active participants in the great events were still living and ought to satisfy incredulity. But see the next issue of the Southern Home and excuse the length and manner of this, as I write currente calamo.

[1]Hugh Blair Grigsby (1806-1881), a Virginian educated privately at Yale, was for a time an attorney and later a journalist. Poor health forced his retirement to Charlotte County. At Edgehill, the patrimonial estate of his wife, Mary Venable Carrington, he was a gentleman farmer and scholar. He wrote extensively in the fields of biography and history. Grigsby is best known for his books on the Virginia constitutional conventions of 1776, 1788, and 1829-1830. Evidently he found the Mecklenburg Declaration dubious. *DAB*, IV, 628-629.

William J. Wilson[1] *to William A. Graham* UNC

Forks of Pigeon,
Haywood County, N.C.,
April 20th., 1875.

Feeling no little interest in the action of the Convention which is to meet in Sept. next, and expecting to have something to do in the approaching canvass for the August election, I desire to have your opinion on the subject of decreasing the number of members to our State Legislature. I am myself, (and I believe a large number of citizens will concur with me) of the opinion that there are altogether too many Representatives in the Lower House of the General Assembly, and I believe that the Senate might also be reduced to three fifths of its present number. In my opinion the House should not contain more than 70 or 75 members at the farthest even if the Senate remain at its present size. This would necessitate some of the counties to have to unite in electing one representative, but then the people could have as many counties as they pleased; but now the larger counties are getting very jealous of establishing any more new counties. It is a well known fact that but a comparatively small number of members do the business of the Legislature, and that unless the Ayes and Noes are called many questions are considered as having passed when really, not half those present vote at all. My plan is therefore to reduce the Senate to thirty members and the House to 70 making 100 in all, and suffer no question to have any legal effect unless it receive at least a majority of all the members of each House, and not simply a majority of a bare quorum. Of course then the Ayes and Noes must be called on the 2nd and 3rd readings of every Bill or Resolution.

Our people are determined to have retrenchment in our expenditures by the Legislature, and this in my opinion is the best and safest way to get it.

I have been strongly solicited to be a candidate for Delegate from this County and if I do I want to act advisedly in this matter as well as all others, and not propose any change without good reasons therefor. Therefore if you have the time and feel so disposed I will feel grateful for your opinion on this subject at least. If undertaken at all it should be discussed all over the state. If you have the time I'll be thankful for any views you may desire to give on other subjects of Constitutional reform.

I have no doubt that your fellow citizens will want to send you to the Convention of 1875, and I hope the State at large will have the benefit of your presence in that important assemblage.

I suppose you have heard of the death of your old friend and admirer, Col.

J. Cathey,[2] who served with you in the Convention of '35.[3] Were he still living I know he would be the first choice of the people of Haywood.

Knowing that your time is precious to you, I will not trouble you more. In conclusion, I am, with sentiments of high regard,

Your obedient servant,

[1]William Jesse Wilson (1828-1921), of Haywood County, was a teacher. During the Civil War he served as captain in the Sixty-second North Carolina Regiment. Wilson was a member of the House of Commons, 1865-1866. In 1880 he moved to Texas. Author of a spelling book, Wilson was also editor of a collection of songs and hymns, many of which he wrote himself. Allen, *Annals of Haywood County*, 152-153.

[2]Joseph Cathey (1803-1874), of Haywood County, was born in the Pigeon River Valley, the only son of settlers William and Catherine Turner Cathey. Largely self-educated, he was an influential citizen with a large progeny. Allen, *Annals of Haywood County*, 556-557.

[3]Wilson was mistaken. Graham was not a member of the Constitutional Convention of 1835.

Augustus S. Merrimon to William A. Graham UNC

Raleigh,
April 23d., 1875.

An author friend of mine, Col. Chas. C. Jones,[1] now of New York, formerly of Savannah, Ga., is preparing a *History of the Southern States*, and asks me to procure for him, if I can, autograph letters of Gen'ls *Nash*[2] & *Hogan*,[3] of the War of Independence. If he cannot get the letters, then he wants autograph signatures of these generals.

I beg to ask if you can inform me where and how I may likely get such letters? I trouble you on this subject, because I think you are more familiar with our Revolutionary history and the men who participated in the struggle for Independence in North Carolina than any one else in the State. I have written H. K. Nash,[4] Esq., in reference to Gen'l Nash.

I am gratified to learn that your health is almost if not quite, restored. I trust Orange will send you to the convention and that you will accept the place of Delegate. I regret that the Legislature felt & acted upon the necessity for calling a *limited* Convention. I was and am still anxious to see a Constitution made by *North Carolinians* and one adapted to the genius and wants of our people.

I learned after you left the City that you were on a visit here a day or two ago. I regret that I did not see you. I wished to make my respects to you, and talk with you on several matters of public concern. I hope to have the pleasure of seeing you before a great while.

I will trouble you to respond to my inquiry as soon as your convenience will allow.

[1]Charles Colcock Jones, Jr.

[2]Francis Nash (1742-1777), a native of Orange County, was a hero of the Revolution. Nash, as captain of the militia, first saw active duty during the war at the Battle of Alamance. He rose to the position of brigadier general of the First Regiment of the

Continental Line and died at the Battle of Germantown. Ashe, *Biographical History*, III, 292-302.

[3]James Hogan, of Halifax County, was a native of Ireland. Hogan served as a member of the last three provincial congresses. Later he became colonel of the Seventh Regiment of the Continental Line, participating in activity at West Point and Philadelphia. It was at Germantown that he really distinguished himself, and in 1779 he was made brigadier general. Captured at Charlestown in 1780, Hogan died the following year. Heitman, *Historical Register of Continental Officers*, 294; Cheney, *North Carolina Government*, 155, 157, 158.

[4]Henry Kollock Nash (1817-1897), of Hillsborough, was the son of Chief Justice Frederick Nash. He was prepared by William J. Bingham and graduated from the University of North Carolina in 1836. A lawyer, he was a Whig in politics and a member of his party's central committee. He abandoned his Unionist convictions, favoring secession by early 1861. Nash was a commoner in the 1842 session of the legislature. Van Noppen Papers; Cheney, *North Carolina Government*, 312.

James G. Bennett[1] *to William A. Graham* UNC

The Herald
New York,
April 23, 1875.

As there appear to be some strange contradictions in reference to the date of the Mecklenburg Declaration of Independence—some claiming it to have been made on May 20, 1775, others that it was made May 31, of the same year—I shall be glad to receive your views on the subject, for publication over your signature, with the view of clearing up the matter before the date set apart for the observance of the Centennial.[2]

---

[1]James Gordon Bennett, Jr. (1841-1918), was an editor and capitalist. He became managing editor and director of the *New York Herald*, founded by his father, James Gordon Bennett, Sr. (1795-1872). *CDAB*, 68.

[2]Graham's response to Bennett's request was written on May 7, 1875, and appeared in the *New York Herald* on May 14 of that year.

James C. Welling to William A. Graham A&H

Washington,
April 26th., 1875.

I have to thank you for your note of the 14th. inst., the reception of which I have delayed to acknowledge in the hope that I might be favored with a copy of your address at Charlotte before again writing to you. A North Carolina friend has sent me the first two instalments of your address, as published in the "Southern Home," but these are all that I have seen.

I have been greatly interested by so much of your paper as I have perused, and particularly thank you for correcting the mistake into which I fell concerning the relationship between your father and John McKnitt Alexander. The statement which I made was made on the written authority of a North Carolina gentleman who knows you well, and I supposed it was authentic. Though the error has no bearing on the force of my argument, I none the less regret it, because I recognise the obligation of entire accuracy in such matters.

As far as I have read in your paper I see no other grounds on which you have taken valid exception to my statements. I am astonished that you should controvert my statement that Col. Wm. Polk procured testimony to contradict some points of J. McKnitt Alexander's story, as originally published in 1829, when your State pamphlet of 1830-31 expressly states the fact, and when you know that Alexander's version, as published by J. McKnitt, left the name of Col. Thomas Polk entirely out of the narrative. On what authority your State Committee inserted the name of Col. Thomas Polk in place of Col. Adam Alexander,[1] (as the Raleigh Register copy has it,) I could never divine, except on the assumption that even your Committee distrusted Mr. Alexander's recollections on this point, and *silently* corrected his error.

Equally unfortunate is your reference to my alleged "trifling" about the tradition in the Brevard family concerning the Westminster inspiration of the Meck. Dec. That tradition has been published again and again on the authority of a Brevard. My only error was that I did not give the tradition in all its absurdity. I have it in two printed forms—but, writing from memory, I omitted to say that the tradition further represents that Dr. Brevard procured his brother Adam to write the Meck. Dec., and that Adam was inspired by the Westminster Confession. Of course this tradition is infinitely absurd, but the absurdity should be laid at the door of the Brevard family, in at least one of its branches, and not at mine.

I observe other more important inaccuracies in the body of your paper, but they are not more numerous than was perhaps inevitable in such a multifarious discussion.

Should your paper be published in a pamphlet form, I shall perhaps think it due to the "truth of history" to point out the places where I venture to hold your argument unsound. In the meantime, I would greatly thank you to send me the remaining numbers of the "Southern Home" containing your address.

---

[1]Adam Alexander, an influential man in Mecklenburg County, was a colonel in the American army during the Revolution. Powell, *DNCB*, I, 14, 17.

William A. Graham to
Cornelia Phillips Spencer UNC: SPENCER

Raleigh, N.C.,
April 26th., 1875.

Being the first named of the Corporators in the Charter of "The Historical Society of North Carolina," granted by the General Assembly at its late session, I notify you that a meeting of the corporators will be held in this City on the 4th. of May next, for the purpose of organization.

Daniel H. Hill to William A. Graham UNC

Charlotte, N.C.,
April 28th., 1875.

Owing to some mistake of the Foreman, the copies for the 12th fell short, so that I could not send you some extra ones. But I sent you yesterday, some half sheets, which I hope will answer your purpose. The essay has given great satisfaction & is regarded as unanswerable by all who have read it. I feel truly grateful to you for giving me the publication of it.

I regret that I have to attend Dallas Court next week & therefore cannot go to Raleigh at the organization of the Historical Society. No one feels a livelier interest in it than I do & I am ready to do any work that may be assigned me.

I think that some effort should be made to get a correct Confederate history of our State written. North Carolina did the fighting & Virginia has written the history & from that history, it is difficult to discover that our State took any part in the Confederate struggle.

Your children here are well. Dr. Morrison is here on a visit. He is in excellent health.

Give our kind regards to your family.

Very truly yours,

Matthias E. Manly to William A. Graham UNC

Newbern,
April 28th., 1875.

A card over your signature issued by K. P. Battle, notifies me of a meeting of persons incorporated as The Historical Society of N.C., on the 4th. prox.

I regret to say, from present appearances I shall not be able to attend, and regret it the more as on that day the Trustees of the University also meet, at which meeting I am particularly desirous of attending.

Be assured of an earnest good wish on my part to aid in the object of both to the extent of my abilities.

John R. Winston[1] *to William A. Graham* UNC

Milton, Caswell County,
North Carolina.
May 1st, 1875.

Enclosed please find circular[2] explaining itself, sent to you for an expression of opinion. The Com. are busy endeavoring to get the sentiment of men capable of rising above mere partisan feelings before they make a final move. Every mail brings letters from the South & Northwest, from gentlemen of both political parties, all endorsing the movement. It is confidential for the present, & but few in this part of the State have been consulted. Mr. Mebane, Dr. Roan, & Mr. Long highly favor it.

[1]John R. Winston, of Rockingham County, was a lieutenant in the Forty-fifth North Carolina Regiment during the Civil War. Wounded and captured at Gettysburg, Winston escaped from Johnson's Island, returned to North Carolina, and was back in active service in 1864. Clark, *Histories of the North Carolina Regiments*, III, 36, 37, 55, IV, 691, 711, V, 254, 255.

[2]The circular has not been found, and no other mention of the matter appears in the correspondence.

James C. Welling to William A. Graham A&H

The Columbian University,
Washington,
May 5th., 1875.

Accept, I pray you, my best thanks for your polite attention in sending me the last two numbers of the "Southern Home," containing the closing instalments of your memoir on the Mecklenburg Declaration. I had the satisfaction to-day of reading them for the first time.

The learning which you have shed upon the surroundings of Mecklenburg's history in 1775, and the minute review to which you have subjected the contemporaneous annals of that period, in other parts of the country, seem to me worthy of all praise. The temper of your discussion is well-nigh faultless, and shines by contrast with that betrayed by some of your compatriots in dealing with honest dissentients.

I do not think you have proved your case, but that is no fault of yours. Until the certificate of John McKnitt Alexander, attached to the "Davie Copy" as published in your N.C. University Magazine in 1853, shall be discredited, it will be impossible to construct a sensible argument in support of the genuineness of the Mecklenburg Declaration, as it is now popularly received in your State. The honesty of the men who, from 1820 to 1831 supported the Alexander paper by their testimony is no more doubted by me than your honesty in maintaining it now. No question of veracity can arise in the premises, so long as we take the "Declaration" at the value put upon it by its most authentic reporter, Mr. Alexander himself. In declining to be wiser than he was, I suppose myself to be entirely respectful to his memory, as I certainly yield to nobody in my admiration of the Mecklenburg worthies of 1775.

I have in my possession an unpublished letter of Gov. Swain, addressed to Mr. Randall,[1] the biographer of Jefferson, stating that he (Gov. Swain) had the "Davie Copy" in his hands at the date of his writing (Ap. 6, 1858) and that he was restrained from publishing his opinion about it by respect for a certain agreement he had with Dr. Hawks. But he does not disguise the opinion that the paper is untrustworthy. I shall publish this letter if the accuracy of the Alexander "certificate" should be seriously drawn in question.

[1]Henry Stephens Randall (1811-1876) of Virginia, the biographer of Thomas Jefferson, was born in Madison County, New York. Randall was an agriculturist, educator, and author. The son of Roswell and Harriet Stephens Randall, he was a descendant of the

Rhode Island Puritan John Randall. After graduation from Union College in 1830, he studied law with his uncle, Henry Stephens, and was admitted to the bar but did not practice law. His interest in the constitutional and political history of the United States led to his conversion to the Jeffersonian theory of democracy and ultimately to his writing of *The Life of Thomas Jefferson* (3 volumes, 1858). Although Randall published nine volumes and a dozen articles (mostly on agricultural subjects), the biography remains his most prestigious work. *DAB*, XV, 347-348.

Horace M. Polk to William A. Graham A&H

Bolivar, Tennessee,
May 6th., 1875.

Is it possible at this day to ascertain the period of time, at which the Rev'd Humphrey Hunter wrote his account of the Mecklenburg Dec. of Independence? It has considerable bearing upon the proof of the Mecklenburg Declaration of Independence. *If we can prove* it was written prior to 1800, (at which time Jno. McK't Alexander's house was burned, and, with it, the original Declaration) the question is about settled; for it will prove, certainly, *the existence* of the declaration *prior* to the time it was said to have been destroyed, and hence negatives the idea that it may have been forged by Jno. McK't Alexander.

I write you thinking you would probably know the descendants of Revd. Humphrey Hunter, or the source from which the extraction from his Memoir was obtained; and could get some valuable information in regard to the time, or probable time of its publication. If written prior to 1800, why should it not be as high evidence of the truth of the Declaration as the Copies produced. In other words, it may have been copied from the original, as no doubt Copies were taken at the time of the adoption of the Declaration.

I desire to return you my thanks for your vindication of the Mec. Declaration. I am preparing a reply to Welling's theory, and especially to answering his *testimony*—his manner of handling our testimony; and also adding the testimony of other old soldiers procured in 1844, to prove the fact of a *Declaration of Independence* at Charlotte, May 20th., 1775.

Col. Allen Polk[1] has also prepared a reply he has sent to me, and desires I shall submit it to you, to know your opinion as to whether it should be published.

Desiring to consult you upon these and other things bearing upon the Mecklenburg Declaration of May 20., 1775, I write to ask that you will be in Charlotte *the day-before* the 20th., that we may have some time to confer, and read over the articles prepared for that occasion.

Doctor J. G. M. Ramsay[2] has prepared an article which, he has written me, he desires that I should read to the Convention for him, as he cannot attend, from the injuries he received some time since by a fall from his horse. He regrets very much not being able to attend, for his heart is in the matter.

---

[1]Possibly this was Allen Jones Polk from Tennessee, a student at the University of North Carolina, 1840-1843. Grant, *Alumni History*, 498.

[2]James Graham Ramsay (1823-1903), of Rowan County but a native of Iredell, graduated from Davidson College in 1841 and from Jefferson Medical College in 1848. An ardent

Henry Clay Whig, he opposed secession and supported the Bell-Everett ticket in 1860. He was a member of the state Senate from 1856 to 1862 and again in 1883, supporting the Vance administration until 1863 but eventually joining the peace movement because of his concern for civil liberties. He was a successful candidate for the Confederate Congress, serving 1864-1865. After the war he became a Republican and was an intimate of Holden. Van Noppen Papers; Thomas Wilson Lingle and others (eds.), *Alumni Catalogue of Davidson College, Davidson, N.C., 1837-1924* (Charlotte: Presbyterian Standard Publishing Company, 1924), 45; *Salisbury Herald*, January 10, 1903.

John S. McEwen[1] *to William A. Graham* A&H

Abbottsburg, N.C.,
May 6th., 1875.

I hope your personal Excellency (which unlike your official ones will never be Ex) will be able to be in Charlotte on the 20th. Inst. to defend the earthly glory of your proud, Scottish, gallant Graham Race. Mr. Bancroft stated in his speech at King's Mountain, "That the sons of the Scotch Covenanters in Meclinburg were the first to sever the connection with Great Britain, and to institute government for themselves." The Fayetteville Observer Edited by Hale, is responsible for the quotation above.

If Mr. Bancroft had been correctly informed and what he stated at King's Mountain was truth then it must be truth now. But, I regret that Mr. Bancroft has not stated it so clearly in his United States history as he did at King's Mountain relative to the Scottish Race. In truth, I can't tell whether in a short time hence, it will be considered as being expressed at all or not, to the honor of that race, unless the name of Col. Thomas Polk will prove his Scottish origin. Speaking of the Committee Mr. Bancroft says the name of Ephraim Brevard should be remembered by his countrymen,—says he digested the Sistem, which was in substance a declaration of independence, as well as a Sistem of Government. Acording to Mr. Bancroft, in my opinion, Mr. Ephraim has borne of the laurels.

Mr. Brevard's Christian name dont sound to me like a Scottish name, he may have been of Englis or Sweedish origen, or he may have been a New-Jersey man, I suppose that differs not, my own Scottish ancestors first touched American soil on the Wharf of Philadelphia, and afterwards, I know not how long, came to Southeastern North Carolina & Settled in Bladen County about 20 years before the Revolution of 1776. Not long since I saw it stated that John McNitt Alexander drew up the declaration of Independence in a house 13 miles West of Charlotte, (and that the house was still standing) on the 19th of May, and brought it down to Charlotte on the 20th, and it was then given to the four winds of Earth. Mr. Governor all I desire on the subject, is, that if the Scottish race made the first declaration of our Independence, I want it plainly told to the assembled Throng on the 20th May, that, that race did it. I sometimes think how many Billions of Dollars would England have given, if Columbus, Americus, or Gallileo had been an Englishman, or even if the Cabots had been English origin.

In the course of my life, I have had the honor and the Superlative pleasure of voting for you twice for Governor, of N.C., and once to be Vice President of the U.S., though unsuccessful in the latter. May the Blood of Ferges,

Oshen, Kenneth, Malcolm, Bruce, Gallant Graham's, Douglas Buchannan Campbell, (the rhetorician) McKnight, (the divine) and Argyle, kindle in your veins, and enable you to defend your Race when unjustly assailed.

Yours Truly, and with the highest regard, etc.,

N.B.

Governor Graham Pleas address me at Abbottsburg, N.C. some time next week, if it is with only one or two lines, stating if your Father was in Charlotte on the 20th. May, 1776. I believe I have told it so some years age.

J. S. McEwen

[1]John S. McEwen has not been identified.

William A. Graham to Cornelia Phillips Spencer

UNC: SPENCER

Hillsboro', N.C.,
May 7th, 1875.

The Historical Society of North Carolina was organized at a meeting of some of the Corporators in Raleigh on Tuesday evening last, and among other proceedings it was voted:

That W. A. Graham, Z. B. Vance, and Mrs. C. P. Spencer be appointed a committee to correspond with Mrs. D. L. Swain,[1] and if possible to procure an order from her directing the collections of material of every kind, pertaining to the history of North Carolina, made by the late President Swain, to be transferred to this Society as its appropriate depository.

This material, consisting of papers and Books, is understood to be in the possession, or subject to the order, of Judge Battle in Raleigh, as one of the Executors of Governor Swain, and is supposed to be liable to damage from insects in its present condition.

Without sufficient time to communicate with Gov. Vance, and being under the necessity of leaving home tomorrow morning for the City of Washington, to be absent a week or more, I write to beg of you the favor, to write at once to Mrs. Swain, making known this earnest request of the Society, and adding that of the members of the Committee individually in the names of the three. I give full authority for the signature of my name, and assume to do the same for Governor Vance, as to the use of his; and shall write him to this effect today.

Hoping you will assume this task for the Society, and the Committee, and not doubting that you will be highly influential in effecting a successful result.

[1]David L. Swain, joined by William A. Graham, was very anxious that the historical documents of North Carolina be preserved. In the 1840s Swain was appointed state agent to collect documents at home and abroad, and for twenty years he was at the heart of such efforts. When he died in 1868, his papers, including historical documents in his possession, were stored in boxes. His widow, Eleanor H. Swain, considered the documents to be part

of her husband's estate and was unwilling to part with them. The efforts of Graham and Mrs. Spencer to acquire them in the 1870s failed. For a full account regarding the Swain manuscripts, see H. G. Jones, *For History's Sake: The Preservation and Publication of North Carolina History, 1663-1903* (Chapel Hill: University of North Carolina Press, 1966), from which this note was taken.

William A. Graham to Editor[1] *of the* New York Herald[2]
[Open Letter]

Hillsboro', N.C.
May 7, 1875.

To the Editor of the Herald:
Dear Sir—

I received in due course of mail your letter of the 23d. ult., requesting, for publication in the *Herald*, my views on the subject of the Declaration of Independence in Mecklenburg county, N.C., in May, 1775, and desiring to have my opinion on this topic at some length for dissemination through your widely circulated journal, but regret that I have not found leisure for the task.

This disappointment, however, gives me the less concern, because I have not long since, at a mass meeting of the people of Mecklenburg, preparatory to their Centennial celebration, made to them an address upon the questions in dispute touching this Declaration, which has been published in the numbers of a weekly paper in Charlotte, and is now in a course of publication by Messrs. E. J. Hale & Son, in New York, in a form better suited for preservation. To this address, the issue of which, I presume, may be daily expected, I beg leave to refer you for the full discussion of the themes, and should be gratified to see the substance of it presented in the *Herald* though its length may preclude the whole publication.

But, since my opinions are called for by you, I cannot omit here to proclaim my belief in the authenticity of the Declaration of Independence by the committee of the people of Mecklenburg on the 20th. of May, 1775. I am a native of the adjoining county of Lincoln, and sprung from Mecklenburg parents. My father and other near relatives and sundry other Revolutionary characters, whom I knew in my youth (among them the Rev. Humphrey Hunter, long pastor of a congregation of which my parents were members), when most of them were of no greater age than I have now attained, gave their testimony of this event as a transaction at which they were personally present, detailing time, place and circumstances. In this they were corroborated by the tradition of the people of the county then its inhabitants, and by its emigrants in Georgia, Tennessee and elsewhere. This testimony was all taken and given by laymen, most of them widely separated from each other, and not marshalled and shaped by advocates to support the points in dispute. Governor Stokes,[3] a Revolutionary officer himself, not a resident of or in any way connected with Mecklenburg, in 1830, ten years after the first newspaper publication on the subject, testified that he had seen a copy of this declaration in the handwriting of John McKnitt Alexander in the possession of Dr. Hugh Williamson in the year 1793. Williamson, a Pennsylvanian, came to the State during the war and about this time emigrated and settled in the city of New York. He published a work entitled "History of North Carolina," in 1812, the narrative of which terminates in 1771, saying in the preface that he had designed to bring it down to 1790, and to include the events of the Revolution, and that with this view he had collected much material from ancient citizens of the State; but he found the task arduous, and treated only of the colonial history to the period above stated. And, to show how carelessly this topic of the Mecklenburg declaration has been considered by those who have called it in question, so well informed a person as Mr. Jefferson, in his letter to Mr. Adams in 1819, mentions as a reason why it should be discredited, that Dr. Williamson forgot this event (of 1775) in the history he wrote of North Carolina. It should as well have been looked for in Lawson's so-called "History of North Carolina" which was written in 1712, or Brickell's in 1731, as in Williamson, which ended in 1771.

The history of the Revolution in this State attracted no attention from the professed writers of history prior to the first publication on this subject in 1819. Even the instruction to her delegates in the Continental Congress to vote for Independence on the 12th. of April, 1776, in advance of the other Colonies had faded from recollection till revived about this time, and the most important military events in the region around Charlotte had never found a chronicler until the impulse given to historical inquiry about that time. Even yet, most of them have failed to receive justice from the pen of history. This declaration is as well authenticated as the action in Charlotte and the retreat on the Salisbury road between Davie's and Tarleton's calvalry on the 26th. of September, 1780. We have the accounts from those who saw both, and better than those at Rocky Mount, Rowson's [*sic*] Mill and Cowan's Ford. They all rested in a common neglect and obscurity until a later day than the Mecklenburg Declaration of Independence.

The resolutions of the Committee of Mecklenburg, of the 31st. of May, 1775, were not discovered or known to any one living, so far as we are informed, till 1838. It has invariably been asserted that there were numerous meetings of the people of that county on the momentous issues pending in the spring of 1775, and these resolutions furnish a very natural sequence to those declaring independence on the 20th. of that month. They provide a government for a people who had discarded that to which they had been accustomed. They make no allusion to the battle of Lexington, the exciting topic of the day, which had no doubt been denounced already, but frame a code for the government of the inhabitants of the county. For aught that we know concerning them, they may have been adopted in a room with closed doors; and being municipal regulations, intending to subject those to imprisonment or exile who failed to submit to them, it may have been deemed humane as well as prudent toward timid or disaffected citizens to insert, as a term of their duration "until the Legislative body of Great Britain resign its unjust and arbitrary pretensions with regard to America"—a term quite as defiant and offensive towards British authority as would have been conveyed by the word "forever", but affording to such citizens some distant hope of reconciliation. However this may be, the actual open and enthusiastic demonstration of the 20th. is too well established by oral and documentary evidence to be rebutted by this expression in the series of resolutions of the 31st.

But I am transcending my design, which was simply to state my position, not to fortify it by arguments, referring for that to the address mentioned in the outset.

I am, sir, very respectfully yours,

W. A. Graham.

[1]James G. Bennett.
[2]From the *New York Herald*, May 14, 1875.
[3]Montfort Stokes.

James C. Welling to William A. Graham A&H

Washington,
May 10th., 1875.

I have no doubt that we are "both right" in what we have said about Col. William Polk. What I have said about him is that "in point of fact he left no written statement at all, but procured testimony to contradict some points of John McKnitt Alexander's story." The context of my paper shews that I meant he has "left no written statement" in your State pamphlet. If he wrote one, and it was afterwards suppressed, does this help the Alexander version? What amazed me in your note on this point is your denial that the testimony procured by Col. Wm. Polk "*contradicts* the account of Alexander," when your State pamphlet says that he (Polk) thought the Alexander story contained "errors as to the name of the Secretary, etc." And the "*etc.*" here, is most significant! For the "error" of John McKnitt Alexander in putting the name of *Adam Alexander* where the name of "*Thos. Polk*" now stands, was, I understand, the motive of Col. Wm. Polk for procuring corroborative testimony as to the main facts *and contradictory evidence against Mr. Alexander's "errors."*

That Col. Thomas Polk's name was overlaid in the original publication of J. McKnitt, is, I learn, confirmed by the files of the Raleigh Register. It was certainly overlaid in the pamphlet copy of Col. Wm. Polk's additional testimony, as published by J. Gales & Son, Raleigh, 1822, for I have a copy of that document.

How the name of Thos. Polk came to supersede the name of Adam Alexander in the State pamphlet, I cannot tell, except on the supposition that your Legislative Committee took the responsibility of altering what they knew to be only the best "recollections" of Mr. Alexander. They were amply justified in making the change, and they ought to have avowed it.

I note all you say about the Brevards, and I do not dispute it. I only aver that the tradition was current in a branch of the family that the Meck. Dec. was inspired by the Westminster catechism. I find the "fact" stated by believers in the Declaration, and it was never disputed when stated by them in the *N.Y. Observer*, in the *Presbyterian Magazine*, and in the *National Intelligencer*. I had my attention first called to the alleged fact when I was writing on this topic in the last named paper. See that in Intelligencer of *Nov. 6, 1857*, where you will find the legend brought to my official notice by a full believer in the Alexander document. As you say, this is "trifling," but ought I to be sneered at for merely reporting the pretensions of the Mecklenburg fancy in this matter? I defer to your better information in all matters of knowledge, but your ignorance of a legend hardly outweighs the positive knowledge of others; including Adam Brevard,[1] his daughter, and her son-in-law.

With constant regard.

---

[1]Adam Brevard was a son of John Brevard II (1716-1790) and brother of Ephraim Brevard, chairman of a committee reputed to have been appointed to write the Mecklenburg Declaration of Independence. Powell, *DNCB*, I, 219. Adam married Mary Winslow. Probably the daughter mentioned is Rebecca, who married James P. McRee. See James P. McRee to William A. Graham, December 2, 1850, in Hamilton and Williams, *Graham Papers*, III, 486-487.

Authorization of Charles J. Jenkins as Arbitrator UNC

United States of America
City of Washington, D.C.
[May 11, 1875]

The undersigned, Jeremiah S. Black of Pennsylvania, and William A. Graham of North Carolina, by virtue of the authority in them vested by an Act of the General Assembly of the State of Virginia entitled "An Act to designate the Arbitrators to ascertain and fix the boundary between the States of Maryland and Virginia," approved 28th. March, 1874; and a like Act of the General Assembly of the State of Maryland entitled "An Act to designate the arbitrators to ascertain and fix the boundary between the States of Virginia and Maryland," approved April 11th., 1874; Copies of which said Acts have been duly communicated to each of the undersigned by the Governors of the States aforesaid, respectively:

Having accepted the said trust, and convened accordingly in the City of Washington, in the District of Columbia, on the 25th. day of June, 1874, at which place and time also appeared, as Counsel for the State of Virginia, the Honorable Raleigh T. Daniel, Attorney General of that Commonwealth, and the State of Maryland, the Honorable Isaac D. Jones, and the Honorable William Pinkney Whyte; the undersigned, after consultation, and an examination of the Acts of the General Assemblies of the said States, as aforesaid, did select the Honorable Charles J. Jenkins, of the State of Georgia, a third arbitrator in the premises, as therein required and provided, and he is hereby invested as such, with all the authority and power conferred by the Acts of the said States, respectively.

In testimony whereof, the undersigned have hereunto affixed their several signatures and seals on this 11th. day of May, 1875.

J. S. Black. (seal)
W. A. Graham. (seal)

Thomas W. Dewey to William A. Graham A&H
[with enclosure]

1775. *20th. May.* *1875.*
North Carolina Centennial Celebration
of the
Mecklenburg Declaration of Independence.

Rooms of the Central Executive Committee,
Charlotte, N.C.
May 18th., 1875.

I have been instructed by the Executive Committee to inform you, that you have been appointed the Presiding Officer of the Centennial Assemblage at the Fair Grounds on the 20th. instant.

Any assistance you may require, or information you may wish, as to order of exercises, etc., will be furnished you by Dr. Joseph Graham, Chmn. of the Centennial Association.

[Enclosure]
Centennial Circular

As citizens of the native sod of the Mecklenburg Declaration of Independence, made at Charlotte, North Carolina, on the 20th. of May, 1775, which marks a brilliant epoch in our State's history, we appreciate the responsibility devolving upon us, to receive and entertain the multitude of the sons of the State, and visitors, on the approaching Centennial Celebration.

As our fathers, in throwing the gage to the proud monarch of the mother country, relied upon the co-operation of their fellow-citizens in the colonies, to aid in redeeming it, we turn to our fellow-citizens of the State, and our friends in other States, who, with us, boast of a common heritage in the renown of a noble ancestry, and invoke your aid to make the 100th. natal day of liberty in our great country, a historical event.

Believing that the citizens of your section will consider it a privilege to contribute to the commemoration of this kindling of the first fire of liberty on American soil, as well as to participate with us in the enjoyments of the occasion, and to a rearing of a suitable monument on the spot, rendered sacred to every North Carolinian, upon which our Declaration was issued, we ask you to afford them an opportunity by circulating lists for subscription, in such manner as you deem best, and that you will collect such amounts as it may be the pleasure of the people to give, and forward it to J. C. Burroughs,[1] Esq. Treasurer of the Centennial Association, Charlotte, N.C.

John A. Young, Chairman;
Chas. R. Jones,[2]
F. A. McNinch,[3]
A. Macaulay,[4]
S. P. Smith,[5]

D. G. Maxwell,[6]
J. W. Wadsworth.[7]
Committee.

---

[1]J. C. Burroughs has not been identified.

[2]Charles R. Jones was an editor with the *Daily Charlotte Observer*. Blythe and Brockmann, *Hornet's Nest*, 251.

[3]F. A. McNinch has not been identified.

[4]A. Macaulay has not been identified.

[5]Samuel Perry Smith was an 1856 graduate of the University of North Carolina and a banker. In 1879 he was president of the short-lived Traders National Bank. Blythe and Brockmann, *Hornet's Nest*, 310; Grant, *Alumni History*, 577.

[6]David Guy Maxwell (b. 1840), born in Mecklenburg County, was the son of William and Nancy Morris Maxwell. During the Civil War he served as an officer in Company H, Thirty-fifth North Carolina Regiment from the time the company was formed until he resigned in 1863 because of physical disability. Later, he was colonel of the Eighty-fifth North Carolina militia. Tompkins, *History of Mecklenburg*, II, 77; Manarin and Jordan, *North Carolina Troops*, IX, 427.

[7]J. W. Wadsworth has not been identified.

Eleanor H. Swain to Committee of the Historical Society of North Carolina A&H: CLARK

[Raleigh, N.C.]
May 19, 1875

In reply to your formal communication of the 13th inst. requesting me to donate the historical collection of my late husband to your Society I beg to say that I must decline to do so, at present at least. I cannot indicate at this moment what disposition I will eventually make of that collection. They shall be carefully preserved, and disposition will be made of them in the future as will in my judgment the most nearly comply with the intentions and desires of my late husband.

With highest esteem for the members of the Committee individually and as a committee, I am

Respectfully,

William H. Polk[1] to William A. Graham A&H

Paris, Kentucky,
May 20th., 1875.

While I write you are doubtless, together with other citizens of your State, engaged in the celebration of the Declaration of Independence by Mecklenburg Co.

Having sprung from the same family, I feel an equal pride with you of N.C. in the event you are celebrating. Horace Polk, of Tenn., desired me to attend the celebration with him; but business would not permit my acceptance of the invitation.

We Polks all feel proud of the fact that Gen. Thos. Polk had such an important part in the deliberations of that eventful day. You, also, must feel equal interest in the important part played by your honored ancestor—Gen. Graham. I have read with interest all that has been written on either side of the Mecklenburg question, by Welling, Wheeler and others.

I am engaged in the preparation of a "History of the Polk Family," beginning with their expulsion from Ireland in 1665, and including each member to the present time. From the Polks I have procured whatever the facts they possessed concerning Gen. Tho's and Col. Wm Polk. It is my purpose to include a brief history of the Mecklenburg affair, and any information you can add will be thankfully rec'd, as mention will be made of Gen. Graham, and other of Gen. Tho's Polk's colleagues.

I have just read in the Lou. Cour. Jour. a letter to the N.Y. Herald, from Charlotte. It speaks of a Memorial Volume of 167 pages, containing your address. I wish to procure a copy of it. Where can I find it?

[1]William Harrison Polk (b. 1843), of Paris, Kentucky, fought for the Union, was postmaster, and was later a journalist. In 1912 he published a book entitled *The Polk Family and Kinsmen*; this note is based on the introduction to that work.

Lyman C. Draper to William A. Graham UNC

State Historical Society of Wisconsin.
Madison,
May 20th., 1875.

I write to you again with no little reluctance, for however anxious I am to get all the light I possibly can upon matters of history with which I have to deal, I [do] not wish to appear importunate.

My work on *Sumter & his Men* lags not a little, & for the double reason that I have been waiting for certain hoped-for materials, in this country & England, and my health at sixty is quite infirm.

I have, however, made a literary arrangement with C. W. Butterfield,[1] of Ohio, author of the excellent work on Col. Wm. Crawford's[2] expedition against Sandusky in 1782, published in 1873, & wh. has elicited many high commendations. Mr. Butterfield & family I expect here to-day. I have a large mass of material, not only upon Sumter and his Men, but covering the whole sweep of the Western and South-western frontier—embracing fully 250 vols. of MSS.

I still hope, through your kindness, or Judge Battle's, if you have returned the Davie manuscripts to him, that I may be favored with a transcript.

I am, at this time, more especially prompted to write you from another cause. On rather short notice, I have consented to prepare to read before our Wisn. Histl. Society a paper on the Mecklenburg Declaration. I, of course, have nearly all I have heard of, in print on the subject—the histories of Foote, Wheeler, Martin, Jones, Hawk's lecture; the Raleigh pamphlet of 1822, Jos. McKnitt Alexander's statement of 1830, Force's Archives, in which he seems to have given not only the certificates that appeared in 1819-20 in the Raleigh Register but those of 1830—yet I see some allusions to Col. Wm.

Polk & Gov. Stokes having made statements I nowhere see *in extenso*. I would be glad to have *all* the statements extant, to aid me in the preparation of my paper, or at least in its revision before publication.

I desire to give sketches of the prominent actors of the Mecklenburg Convention—all of them if I could. This idea has but just occurred to me, & I have written to a few persons on the subject—some of the Alexanders among them.

Perhaps you will find it in your heart, if your health is reasonably good,—as I hope it is,—to aid me.

I will write to Dr. R. H. Morrison, supposing he is descended from, or related to, Neill Morrison. To Hon. W. S. Harris,[3] Concord, hoping he can tell me of those of that name.

But of Col. John Phifer, Wm. Kennon, Rev. Dd. Reese,[4] Maj. John Davidson, *Wm. Graham*, John Flennigan,[5] Matthew McClure,[6] John Ford,[7] Rich'd Barry,[8] Ben. Patton,[9] John Queavy,[10] Duncan Ochiltree,[11] Samuel Martin,[12] Zaccheus,[13] Wm.,[14] & possibly Robt. Wilson, Sr.[15] I want light—what they did, if anything, beyond their connection with the Mecklenburg movement—where they lived, when they died, ages, & references to descendants.

I hardly suppose the Wm. Graham referred to was the Gen. Wm. Graham, of Rutherford County, if not, perhaps he was an Uncle of yours, & you can tell me fully about him.

What especially of Phifer & Kennan & Martin—they seem to have been prominent men, & shd. not be forgotten?

If you have not seen the work to which I have alluded, of Mr. Butterfield on Col. Crawford, I will gladly send you a copy.

May I hope to hear very soon from you?

God kindly bless you!

---

[1]Consul Willshire Butterfield (1824-1899), a native of New York, was by education a lawyer, but he never practiced. Instead, he became an editor. In 1875 he became a partner of Lyman C. Draper. In time he was editor of the *Northwest Review* and the *Magazine of Western History*. Butterfield was the author of a number of historical works, including the one mentioned in this letter, *An Historical Account of the Expedition against Sandusky, under William Crawford in 1782*. *DAB*, IV, 527.

[2]William Crawford (1732-1782), from Berkeley County, Virginia, served in the French and Indian War. He led scouts during Braddock's expedition against Fort Duquesne in 1755 and also fought during the Pontiac War, 1763-1764. In 1776 he was lieutenant colonel of the Fifth Regiment, Virginia militia, and fought in the battles at Long Island, Trenton, Princeton, Brandywine, and Germantown. After the war Crawford commanded the expedition against the Wyandote and Delaware Indians in Ohio. On June 11, 1782, he was captured and tortured to death at Battle Island, Wyandote County. *DAB*, IV, 527; *Who Was Who*, 127.

[3]William Shakespeare Harris, of Cabarrus County, attended the University of North Carolina (1835-1836) and was a member of the House of Commons, 1836-1838, 1852-1854, and 1860-1864. Grant, *Alumni History*, 261.

[4]David Reese (1710-1787) was a native of Wales who immigrated to Pennsylvania before moving into Mecklenburg County. A Presbyterian minister, Reese served during the American Revolution as agent of the county to procure arms. Reese was one of the signers of the Mecklenburg Declaration. Ray, *Mecklenburg Signers*, 376, 420.

[5]John Flennigan (Flennikin) (1744-1828) was one of the signers of the Mecklenburg

Declaration. Believed to have been one of nine children born to James (or John) Flennikin, he moved with his family from Scotland to Pennsylvania before settling in the McAlpin's Creek section of Mecklenburg. His wife was Mary (1775-1823). Flennigan's grave is unmarked. Ray, *Mecklenburg Signers*, 421.

[6]Matthew McClure (b. ca. 1725) was a native of Ireland who moved into Mecklenburg County in 1751. He was a signer of the Mecklenburg Declaration. McClure settled about five miles south of Davidson College in the Hopewell Church community. Ray, *Mecklenburg Signers*, 376, 420.

[7]John Ford (Foard) lived in that part of Mecklenburg County that is now Union. He was in the province by 1770 and was a signer of the Mecklenburg Declaration. A member of a Presbyterian family who settled in Somerset County, Maryland, Ford had known the Polk family there. He served as a private in Charles Polk's Dragoons on the Raft Swamp expedition. After 1775 he was a magistrate and a member of the county court. Ray, *Mecklenburg Signers*, 418.

[8]Richard Barry (1726-1801), a native of Pennsylvania, moved into Mecklenburg County as a mature man. His wife was Anne Price. Barry signed the Mecklenburg Declaration. Ray, *Mecklenburg Signers*, 502.

[9]Benjamin Patton, one of the earliest settlers in the eastern part of Mecklenburg County (now Cabarrus), was a delegate to the provincial congress that met at New Bern August 25, 1774. He also attended the provincial congress at Hillsborough on August 21, 1775. During the Revolutionary War Patton served as major of the Second Continental Regiment under Lieutenant Colonel Alexander Martin. Patton was a member of the committee of safety for Mecklenburg County. Hunter, *Sketches of Western North Carolina*, 52-53.

[10]John Queavy (b. 1743), born in Scotland, migrated first to Pennsylvania and then to Mecklenburg County in 1767. He settled at a site near Rocky River. Little can be learned of his family, although he was described by contemporaries as "a man of vigorous intellect, . . . well to do and a good scholar." He was reputed to have died at an early age; he was buried in Union County. Ray, *Mecklenburg Signers*, 418.

[11]Duncan Ochiltree, according to Captain James Jack, was a leader in the Mecklenburg events. When Cornwallis invaded Mecklenburg, Ochiltree joined the British forces. When he later sought protection from John McKnitt Alexander, he was refused and denounced as a traitor. In 1788 he was caretaker of the courthouse. Ray, *Mecklenburg Signers*, 316, 355.

[12]Samuel Martin (1732-1783), a native of Ireland, was an important figure in the Mecklenburg events, by Captain Jack's account. Born in New Jersey, Martin was a brother of Alexander Martin and did not reside in Mecklenburg in 1776. He first lived in Tryon (later Lincoln) County; eventually he made his home on Crowder's Creek, in what is now Gaston County. Captain Samuel Martin commanded a company during the Revolution. He was also clerk of court, 1774, and a delegate to the provincial congress of August, 1775. Cope and Wellman, *County of Gaston*, 28, 32, 34, 40.

[13]Zaccheus Wilson (d. 1824), a native of Pennsylvania, moved into the part of Mecklenburg County that later became Cabarrus. He was a delegate to the Fifth Provincial Congress and was listed as a signer of the Mecklenburg Declaration. He was a surveyor and served as a captain at the Battle of Kings Mountain. A brother of Robert Wilson, Sr., Zaccheus Wilson later moved to Tennessee. Ray, *Mecklenburg Signers,* 419.

[14]William Wilson may have been one of the leaders of the movement that culminated in the Mecklenburg events of May, 1775, but he was not among the signers. Ray, *Mecklenburg Signers*, 316.

[15]Robert Wilson, Sr., who came into the Mecklenburg area from Pennsylvania, had been a soldier in the French and Indian War, according to the narrative of Captain Jack. Wilson, who fought at Cowan's Ford and Kings Mountain, lived in what became Lincoln and Gaston counties. Ray, *Mecklenburg Signers*, 419-420.

Cyrus L. Hunter[1] *to William A. Graham* A&H

Lincoln County, N.C.,
May 27th., 1875.

I had intended to have another interview with you before I left Charlotte, but a mass of over-crowding Centennial occurrences, necessarily attended with some confusion, prevented, and I now avail myself of a leisure moment to introduce a few desultory thoughts.

I have been engaged at intervals, during the last five or six weeks, in writing out Sketches of some of our Revolutionary patriots of Mecklenburg and Lincoln Counties, who have been hitherto obscurely noticed, or entirely unknown. Among this number may be named Col. James Johnston, Capt. Sam'l Martin,—who commanded a Company at King's Mountain, and lost six of his men—Dr. Wm. McLean,[2] "Surgeon's Mate" under Dr. Joseph Blythe,[3] a more perfect account of the services of Gen'l Peter Forney[4] and Abram Forney, than appears in Wheeler's History. A more correct and extended account of the Jack family, now rendered famous by the noble, patriotic part borne by Capt. James Jack, a paper on Scotch-Irish Immigration, and a brief notice of the seven primitive Presbyterian Churches which proved, in an eminent degree the *nurseries of freemen.*

Several of my friends in Charlotte have advised me to publish these Sketches, and other Revolutionary matter, as the Sketches in Wheeler's work, of your father, the Brevard family, Battle of Ramsour's, King's Mountain, etc., in book form. I read several of these Sketches to Col. Wheeler, and would have done the same in your presence, had circumstances permitted a second interview. He thought they would contribute some new and interesting information.

If I should be encouraged to throw my crude efforts into book form, I would give it about the following title:

Annals of Mecklenburg, and adjoining Counties, preceding and during the Revolutionary War, accompanied with Sketches of the Lives of the Signers of the Mecklenburg Declaration of Independence, and other leading Patriots of that period; the "Memoir" of Ex. Gov. Graham, on the authenticity of said Declaration of Independence on the 20th. of May, 1775; a succinct account of the Centennial celebration on the 20th. of May, 1875, and other interesting information never before published.

Now, this you will perceive, is an ambitious title—perhaps too much so. I named such a title to Gen'l Cox, of Raleigh, who approved of it, and thought the *times* demanded some such production for the benefit of *doubters of the day*, or *lovers of mythical lore.* I shall be pleased to know your views on the subject, and also any amendment you may suggest.

On reaching home I found a letter from Lyman C. Draper, Corr'g Sec'y of the Hist'l Soc'y of Wisconsin. He has been engaged for several years in collecting materials for a new life of Gen. Sumter, but the particular object of his letter was to know the exact time my father wrote his "Memoir," or, if not enabled to give the exact time, an *approximation* to it. He is preparing a paper to be read shortly before his Society, on the Mecklenburg Declaration of Independence. From the tone of his letter he seems disposed to *do us justice.* I informed him, substantially, as follows:

That I was absent from home at the time of my father's death, attending a High School, about 80 miles distant, that a few days after his death I returned home at the request of my mother—that I was then about nineteen years old,—that the task then devolved upon me of settling my father's estate—that, upon examination, as in duty bound, I found the "Memoir," filed away with his *valuable papers,* including two deeds for adjoining tracts of land purchased in 1796 and 1797, and other important records—that my father was an *intimate friend* and *frequent visitor* of John McKnitt Alexander, the Secretary of the Mecklenburg Convention on the 20th. of May, 1775, and common custodian of important papers—that it was highly probable my father procured his copy *about that time,* or *even earlier,* than the date of these two deeds, and finally, that I had heard my father speak of this early and memorable assemblage of the patriots of Mecklenburg Co., in connection with other Revolutionary events.

---

[1]Cyrus Lee Hunter (1807-1881), of Lincoln County, was a son of the Reverend Humphrey Hunter. He was the author of *Sketches of Western North Carolina.* Sherrill, *Annals of Lincoln County,* 98, 102, 108, 112, 223.

[2]William McLean (1757-1828) was the son of Alexander McLean, who came into the Gaston County area in 1757. William studied under Dr. Joseph Blythe and at Queen's Museum in Charlotte. He served as a surgeon's mate in the Continental Army, being assigned to the First North Carolina Regiment. After the war McLean went to Philadelphia to complete his medical studies and established a large practice in Gaston County. He was a member of the Society of the Cincinnati and was married to Mary Davidson. An eloquent speaker, McLean served in the conventions of 1788 and 1789 and as a member of the state Senate and the House of Commons. Sherrill, *Annals of Lincoln County,* 99-100.

[3]Joseph Blythe was a surgeon in the American army during the Revolution. He is mentioned in Cope and Wellman, *County of Gaston,* 22, as the earliest teacher in the South Fork section of present-day Gaston County.

[4]Peter Forney (1756-1834) was born in Lincoln County, the son of Jacob and Maria Bergner Forney. He served as a captain in the American forces during the Revolution. Married to Nancy Abernethy, Forney was a pioneer in the manufacturing of iron in Lincoln County. He was a member of the House of Commons, 1794-1797; a state senator, 1800-1802; and a member of the United States Senate, 1813-1815. Sherrill, *Annals of Lincoln County,* 33, 54, 57, 108-109.

William A. Graham to William A. Graham, Jr. A&H

Hillsboro'
May 31st 1875

Dear Wm.

We have been gratified to learn from your letter to your mother, that Julia continues to improve, and hope that by this time she may be entirely well.

A year's interest is due, $80., on your Railroad loan, and you should remit it as early as convenient. I have charged myself with it in my R.R. Account, so that the delinquency is not reported to the Comtee. of Finance.

My time will be much occupied for this month, that will elapse before my journey to New York, to meet the Va. & Myld. Commission. Have to attend the Comtee Finance of the R.R. Co, the Federal Court at Ral., the Trustees of the University, etc. I have made a subscription to the University which I designed for myself and sons, so that if any application is made to you, you may say that my subscription is intended for the family.

I have been much urged to take the Presidency of the institution and may be further, but I have no intention to accept it. My health continues but moderate, and I wish the command of my time.

Everybody I have seen left the centennial much pleased. I intended to send you my memorial address, but no copies have been furnished me as yet.

George & Sally & child have gone to Raleigh. Mr. Clark comes up every saturday or friday night.

. . . .

The wheat crop in this section is very promising.

Our love to Julia and the children.

Affectionately yours

I expect to be but little here during the canvass for convention. I don't know whether there will be any third candidate or any radical candidate.

Eugene Grissom to William A. Graham UNC

Insane Asylum of North Carolina
Raleigh, N.C.
May 31, 1875

Dear Sir,

I beg leave to return my thanks for your photograph received several days since.

I expect to preserve it for my children as an embodiment of virtue, honor & patriotism.

With high regard I am
Yours truly

Stephen D. Pool to William A. Graham UNC

State of North Carolina
Department of Public Instruction
Raleigh,
May 31st., 1875.

The 3d. Annual Meeting of the N.C. Educational Association will convene in Raleigh, Wednesday, July 14th. Can you be present with us on that occasion, and deliver an Address, or read an Essay upon such topic as you may select, relating to the subject of Education?

An early answer, with topic chosen, is solicited, so that a programme may be arranged and published.

Montford McGehee to William A. Graham UNC

Woodburn, Person Co., N.C.,
June 1st, 1875.

. . . .

I fear, Sir, that the importance of the issue presented by the Convention is not appreciated. The present lull bodes, I am afraid no good.

The question will be put to our people under disadvantages. A number of our first men,—Such as Judge Manly, Mr. Davis, Judge Howard,[1] Mr. Coningsland,[2] Mr. Eaton, &c—will be cut off from an active, *personal* interest in the Canvass by the politics of their Country. This will make the Convention when assembled, an imperfect exponent of the abilities, and political knowledge of our State.

This Canvass will have to be made in many Counties by a Single Candidate and in very few by more than two. There will therefore, be none of that concert, mutual support, and enthusiasm which marks an ordinary Election, when there are a dozen Candidates in the field, for State and County offices—all of whom have numerous friends actively working for them; pushing their electioneering operations to the remotest corners; and bringing strong influence to bear upon every individual. This question admits of artful appeals to fears that are easily excited, and insidious suggestions in regard to interests that are paramount in every mind. It may be made to involve the permanence of his freedom in the mind of the ignorant black; and the Security of his Home in the mind of the scarce less ignorant White. These disadvantages are increased by the character of the constituencies on the one side or the other. An order from Headquarters will bring every Radical Voter to the polls, with vote ready cut & dried, though he has never *heard* of the issue to be decided; while it is only by the utmost exertion of reason, argument and party drill that we can bring out our voters.

Lastly this question has been prejudged in the minds of many by the adverse opinion expressed by Several of our public men—While the conflict of opinion in our own ranks has produced indecision and apathy in the minds of many more.

These disadvantages were foreseen from the beginning but delay would bring—it was also seen—no benefit with reference to any one of them; while the State of parties urged immediate action.

For myself, I believed from the first and believe now, that if this question is put to the people plainly, clearly, and fully—let me add further, continuously—by the Press and by competent Speakers, we have nothing to fear. But ours are a non-reading people, and so much precious time has been lost—the subject has hardly been referred to (in the papers which have fallen under my observation) since the adjournment of the Legislature—that but little reliance can be placed upon the Press now—at best, comparatively little. Our main hope now, to secure for this subject such a hearing, and for the question such a Vote as we would wish, is in the speeches of our ablest men. Is it not advisable at once to inaugurate great public meetings at the

Capitol, and in the larger towns of our State? If these were addressed by our best representative men—men capable of laying open the Subject in its length and breadth—their speeches being reported would be copied into every Newspaper, and rehearsed by the County Candidates upon every stump. It seems to me that we would thus open the Canvass with proper clat—educate our County Candidates—and enable them in their turn, to educate the people. The little interest felt by the people in this subject surprises me very much, & their ignorance still more. But their necessities engross their whole attention, when left to themselves; while the Newspapers say but little about the question, and that little is read by very few.

Impressed with these views—fearing that Victory in the present State of the public mind is uncertain; or if gained, that it would be shorn of its proper proportions,—I have submitted similar considerations to the Chairman of the State Ex. Committee. If they should seem to you to possess any weight I hope they will reinforced by a suggestion from you. I should then hope for immediate action, and from action the best results.

I have availed myself of the kindness with which you have always distinguished me, to write at some length. I hope, Sir, that you will pardon the freedom. . . .

---

[1]George Howard (1829-1905) of Tarboro was an editor at the age of fourteen. He studied law at the University of North Carolina and was quickly successful. A superior court judge, 1859-1865, Howard was a delegate to the conventions of 1861 and 1865. Regarded as a wise and able leader, he was influential and respected. Grant, *Alumni History*, 301.

[2]Edward Conigland (1819-1877), of Halifax County, was a native of Ireland who settled in North Carolina in 1844. He was an able lawyer. He represented his county in the convention of 1865, where he took a leading part, especially in opposition to repudiation of the Confederate debt. A powerful speaker, Conigland was one of the defense counsels in the Holden impeachment trial. Cheney, *North Carolina Government*, 832; Hamilton, *Reconstruction in North Carolina*, 121, 129, 547, 549, 551; William Cicero Allen, *History of Halifax County* (Boston: Cornhill Company, 1918), 194-195.

William A. Graham to Montford McGehee UNC: POLK, BADGER, MCGEHEE

Hillsboro'
June 6th, 1875

. . . .

I am obliged by your mention of the address on the Meckbg. declaration. I don't think it was ever more than half considered in any treatise heretofore. Dr. Hawks, the most recent & full of its advocates, never adverted to the condition of the question in Congress in May 1775 & months later—to the opinions of Jefferson, Washington & others down to the spring of 1776—nor to the fact that we have more evidence of the declaration than of the military events in that section which lay in utter neglect till 1820-1-2 &c. But newspaper men & school masters can credit nothing but what is found in print even when there was no printing press within 200 miles till 50 years later than the event in question. I regretted that you were not in Charlotte. The pageant was a grand & successful one.

As to the convention question, I have been hoping the radicals would give but little trouble. I hear however of officials, justices &c. whose perquisites may be considered at stake, supposedly in our own ranks, who may give some embarrassment in choosing delegates and in offering amendments. It is evident the measure has been carried . . . too soon, if the revolt is to be a successful one. I must go North by the 29th inst. and may be detained some weeks, which will be during the canvass for delegates.

Barnas Sears to William A. Graham UNC

Peabody Education Fund.
Staunton, Virginia,
June 7th., 1875.

I enclose a check of $250., as you requested. I received a letter from W. C. Kerr recommending the employment of Gov. Vance as joint agent for us and the University. I doubted whether he was the best man to represent us. I saw Col. Heck[1] a few days ago, who thinks it might be well to employ Hon. Kemp P. Battle in this way. You know all about both interests, & about the men. If you have any suggestion to make on the whole subject, I would be greatly obliged to you if you would make it. All I have done, or proposed to do, has been to employ Supt. Pool four entire months as travelling agent, allowing $500. for paying clerk and travelling expenses, the same rate as has been allowed in Tennessee.

I have just received a letter from our Chairman, R. C. Winthrop, in London, where he has met Mr. Russell, & would, in a day or two, see Gov. Clifford, who had just arrived. All are now in good health. Mr. Winthrop and family were glad to get away from the heat and malaria of Italy.

P.S. Mr. Winthrop will sail for home in September.

---

[1]Jonathan McGee Heck (1831-1894) was a native of Virginia (a part now in West Virginia). Trained as a lawyer, he joined the Confederate forces and served as colonel of the Thirty-first Virginia Regiment during the Civil War. At the close of the war, Heck moved to Raleigh, where he became a successful businessman and was a substantial benefactor to Wake Forest College. Murray, *Wake,* 589n, 607n, 641, 641n, 642.

William A. Graham to Cornelia P. Spencer A&H: SPENCER

Hillsboro',
June 7th, 1875.

I had the favor to receive your note enclosing that of Mrs. Swain to our Committee, in respect to the Historical Collections in her possession.

I think Mrs. Swain has made a mistake in supposing the Historical Society and the Trustees of the University to be the same corporation, and secondly, in thinking that her late husband considered the Historical matter which he was so curious in collecting and which was so freely yielded to him, as individual property.

I do not know of any other course left to our Committee than to report the correspondence to the Society for its further consideration.

John Hill Wheeler to William A. Graham A&H

Charlotte, N.C.,
June 9th., 1875.

Majr. Dowd showed to me your letter of the 24th. inst., regretting your inability to attend the lecture, delivered by me, on that evening here, "on the Lives and characters of the Signers of the Meck'g Declaration of Indepedence of 20 May 1775." It was well attended, and kindly received.

I enclosed to you, on yesterday, an early copy, which I trust came safe to hand, and may gratify you also; since you were kind enough to give me material aid in compiling the facts. Will you examine the facts, and aid me by any corrections, or suggestions. Dr. Morrison asked me if I was certain, as to the burial place of Dr. Eph'm Brevard? My authority is Dr. Ramsay, and Brevard Davidson, Esq. I am happy to see that, among other causes, the address has had the effect of inducing others to collect and preserve memorials of a gallant race, who do honor to history.

I rec'd on yesterday a letter from Colo. Wm. Lee Davidson,[1] of Spartanburg, S.C., giving a copy of the family record of the Davidson family. Wm. Shakespeare Harris is collecting material as to the Harris'; Reese and others. Dr. C. L. Hunter is also collecting material. Thus I hope much more may be rescued from oblivion as to the Signers of the Meck. Dec. of Independence.

I copy over a letter of Dr. C. L. Hunter relative to a matter on which I wished to have consulted with you, but you were so much occupied when here, and left rather unexpectedly to me.

I sincerely hope that it meets your approbation and will receive your favourable co-operation.

I leave this evening for Washington City having completed my mission as to the Mint. The suggestions you made at my request as to its future had influence on my course. It will remain in *statu quo* until Congress meets.

---

[1]This William Lee Davidson was evidently a descendant of the Revolutionary general of the same name.

William A. Graham to David F. Caldwell UNC

Hillsboro',
June 10th., 1875.

Yours of the 8th. inst. is received. I regret to learn that our Conservative friends, in any quarter, should, at this stage, complain of the passage of the Convention Bill. When a measure has been carried by their own party, and by so decisive a majority as two thirds of each House of the Legislature, individual opinion should yield to the decision, if not, there can be no party organization; and this, at a time when, if ever, it is most needed. We are yet engaged in a contest for self government by the native white race, and against the blacks, and their foreign allies, the latter consisting of office holders, State and Federal, and other minions of power. If we have not coherence enough to stand together in such a contest, we can no longer have a conservative party, but should give up the reins of power to the radicals.

It would have been more satisfactory to have a Convention without limits on its power, but with these, there is room for many salutary amendments, which if we can adopt, we may confidently expect all other needed ones in the future. Opposition may be expected from radicals, but if conservatives make opposition, it will appear as though they preferred radicalism.

The amendment you suggest, of limiting the time of sessions of the Legislature, can be ingrafted into the Constitution, if deemed expedient. For my part, since the sessions are to take place but once in two years, I see but little necessity for such a limit. Since the population of the State is 1 ¼ million, and the business of Legislation greatly increased, the sessions cannot be expected to be as brief [as] they were 50 years ago.

If Conservatives are not disposed to govern themselves, and to this end to amend the Constitution, from that imposed by Canby, the radicals will very gladly continue to do it for them.

If the subject is half discussed before the people, I believe, there are few Counties in which Conservatives will not be returned to the Convention.

1. The radicals propose to *nullify* the Law, as passed by a two thirds majority, and not permit the Convention to sit, after all the expense of election & mileage of members. This is little less than treason.

2. The present Constitution makes no difference in political power, between dishonest men, and honest men. It is proposed to amend, by providing that all persons convicted of infamous crimes, Larceny, Forgery, Perjury, etc., shall lose their *free law*, as formerly, & not be allowed to vote, or give evidence in Courts of Juctice, 'till restored to credit, by the Legislature, on proof of reformation.

2. It [is] proposed to exonerate voters from the degrading oath that each man will support the Constitution and Laws of the State, and of the United States, laws embraced in not less than 500 volumes—an oath imposed to degrade and insult freemen.

3. To emancipate the General Assembly, and permit the people, through their representatives at each session, to enact laws as they did formerly, as to how many Judges and Circuits there shall be, what system of County Government, what punishment of crimes, etc. With 1 million of people, we have in the Penitentiary near 700 convicts, while Ohio, with 3 ½ millions has 612, and the number increasing with us every Court, that is held. The system has failed with us. It is no terror against the commission of crime, and is too expensive. We must do, as Virginia does, whip thieves, and turn them loose; and, if the crime is repeatedly committed, hang them, at least until [in] the hands of the Legislature, and let it deal with them as wisdom may suggest.

4. To relieve the Legislature from the obligation to establish inebriate & idiot asylums, and orphan asylums, and leave the drunkard to his voluntary fate, and bind out our Orphans to good masters, who will bring them up to be useful citizens. These charities are now intended for the officers who manage them, not for the unfortunates.

5. To require Lunatics, who have the means, to pay their expenses in the Asylum, instead of nursing their estates for kindred, after their deaths, and the same with students in the University.

I could enumerate many other changes to which, I think, no man dare object; and instead of considering ourselves on the defensive, there was never a fairer field for a charge on the adversary. You, & Dillard,[1] or some other good man, can carry Guilford triumphantly. See the Radical resolutions of Bell & Co.,[2] secretly circulated, which are published in the "Daily News" of the 9th. inst. If we cannot explode such a conspiracy as that, the people have lost their old spirit.

I must go North to meet the Commission of which I am a member, and be absent some part of July, but the nominations, thus far made in the Counties promises success and a very complete Convention.

---

[1]John Henry Dillard (1819-1896), of Guilford, was born in Rockingham County. He attended the University of North Carolina, 1837-1839, and served in the Fifth North Carolina Regiment with the rank of captain during the Civil War. After the war he established a successful law practice and served as an associate justice of the state supreme court, 1879-1881. Grant, *Alumni History*, 164.

[2]This refers to an effort by Republican newspaper editors to adopt a unified position politically and professionally. Five editors, meeting in New Bern, agreed by resolution to support only delegates to the Constitutional Convention of 1875 who would vote to adjourn the convention immediately and to cooperate in promoting Republican causes in general. Opining that there was "no more effectual guide to political sentiment than an outspoken, independent press," the editors held that the Republican central committee and officeholders should cooperate in providing information to the press and promoting wide circulation of party newspapers. Republican editors in the state were to support railroad consolidation but to avoid discussions of the state debt and any extended discussion of civil rights. Attacks by the Democratic press on state supreme court justices were to be condemned. Noting that "pungent paragraphs and short articles" were most effective, the editors who drafted the resolutions proposed to circulate them secretly and to seek unity among all Republican editors in the state.

These resolutions first appeared in the Raleigh *Daily News* on June 9, 1875, and were reprinted in the *Greensboro Patriot* of June 16, 1875.

Samuel M. Hughes[1] *to William A. Graham* UNC
[with enclosures]

Francisco,
Stokes County, North Carolina.
June 10th., 1875.

Although I have not had the honor of a personal acquaintance with you, I have still known and admired your exalted character for years, as an unselfish and upright statesman, and as a *true* patriot, after the old order of patriotism.

I was a constant reader of the National Intelligencer from my youth up for forty five years of my life. I am therefore half inclined to believe that I was born a Whig—at all events, if I understand my position, I am today still a Whig. But I am *now* outside nevertheless, *even as a conservative,* and consequently have found myself compelled to recur to my old political faiths in order to ascertain my proper present location.

Our conservative majority of two thirds in the General Assembly made a great blunder if not something worse than a blunder, in accepting any restrictions whatever, *in these days of ring rule against the people,* which in effect and also in fact *rejects their will*, as the only legitimate source of political power in the State, and which also, at the same time, would question if not deny *their* capacity and *their* fidelity in reforming the constitution when submited for *their* revission.

The party seems in fact to have played out, in making this strange surrender of the great issues of self-government, to that most dangerous device of the bad men in both parties, *ring rule*, outside of, and in defiance of all constitutional restraints. These things are therefore well calculated to alarm every thinking man in the State, and to induce that want of confidence in the wisdom and the fidelity of our party leaders in the General Assembly, which is just now resting like an incubus upon every *true* conservative within our borders.

The greatest danger now menacing the liberties of the masses, had its origin, if I have any correct comprehension of its nature, in "the love of money," and the consequent encroachments of *capital*, representing the concentrated *power of money*, upon the collective rights of the people, in combination with arrant partisan and arbitrary control, and which has been exercised from time to time, within the last few years by our highest State officials, in order to gratify *their* lust for office, and its golden perquisites.

An elective Judiciary, surely presupposes the existence of the elective franchise, in all of its integrity as the only consistent basis upon which it could possibly rest, but, nevertheless the fundamental principles of American freedom are openly prostituted as a business proceeding, to personal and partisan advancement, by many of our officials in every department of the State government, *but more conspicuously in the judicial*—consequently that department although reported by its Chief on a memorable occasion heretofore, as fully "exhausted," without an effort on his part under the renowned *writ of habeas corpus*, to defend the people *against the bayonet* as an instrument of ring intimidation and usurpation, is *now* recognised in the *new* roll of the *old ring*, as "a power behind the throne greater than the throne itself—*greater* than the inherent and inalienable *power of the people* as conceded in the existing constitution. "O shame, where is thy blush?" O magnanimous patriotism, whither hast thou fled?

The position of the leaders of the radical party, in opposition to all constitutional reform, brings them fairly before the people of North Carolina, as still the persistent and wily supporters *of the office and bondholders ring*, as provided for in *their* constitution, and consequently as recognizing *the validity* of the fraudulent State bonds, which were issued under Holden's administration only as a pretext through which our oppressed tax-payers could be *robbed according to the forms of law*. And which in all of its accompaniments and adjuncts certainly constitutes a greater outrage against the honor and the sanciity of our State government, and the great moral sense of Christendom, *than the stealing of the twenty millions*, when considered only as a matter of dollars and cents.

The friends of good government should at once accept this inferential gage, for the contest this summer, and arraign them accordingly—together with *their* coadjuters in the democratic, conservative party, even though the party should be divided into a thousand flinders. Having taken the liberty to address you this long letter, may I not trouble you also so far as to ask you to inspect the enclosed articles, as affording some little incite [*sic*] into the condition of things in this part of the State. I should be pleased to hear from you, provided you may have the inclination to write to a stranger occupying

I am most truly your friend, & ob't serv't,

P.S. Please find
1st. Letter which appeared in the Mt. Airy Watchman, May 20th.
2nd. Letter which appeared in the Danbury Reporter, May 27th.
3rd. Letter in manuscript, which will appear next week.

S. M. H.

[Enclosure]
Newspaper Editorial
[*Mount Airy Watchman*, May 20, 1875]

"For the People of Stokes."

Under the above head, an article will be found elsewhere in our columns. Col. Sam'l Hughes, whose signature it bears is a good writer, but with due deference to his age and rank, notwithstanding our "want of beard," to use his own expression regarding us, we must differ with him.

It is remembered, we opposed the calling of a convention, for this reason in particular, that the Constitution needed *many, many* amendments, and that all it needed was "rope" that it might hang itself in the eyes of the people, that at present the people have not had their eyes opened as to all that was necessary in regard to the change, we foresaw a restricted convention or none at all—this we told our friends. But the convention Act has passed—a *restricted* convention has been called by the cry of our own men for "convention," with the Act we are satisfied and are in favor of a close adherence to the law which calls a convention. Conventions may have a right to act as our friend would have them act; but when an act of a legally organized Legislature is twisted into other shapes than what was originally intended, it is not dealing fairly and squarely with issues. We are now for convention as called, we are for sending our best men to that body with the express understanding that they will abide by the vote which instituted the body. We look upon this late view as an extreme almost as much to be shun[n]ed as that into which our radical friends have run, viz: that of electing delegates who would vote only to adjourn.

[Enclosure]
Letter from Samuel M. Hughes

Communicated to the People of Stokes.

I had the honor, as you will remember, of an election as your delegate to a convention, which was proposed several years ago. I would therefore hope that I may now express my views freely and independently, as an old man, on the new proposition without justly incuring the imputation of vanity or presumption.

I am decidedly opposed to the long list of restrictions imposed by the General Assembly. In my humble judgment, these restrictions, when taken altogether, are neither respectful to the people, nor consistent with their rights as freemen.

"All political power is vested in and derived from the people—all government of right originates from the people, is founded upon their will only, and is instituted for the good of the whole people,"—see 2nd Section, 3rd. Article of the existing constitution.

The people also are fully invested in our bill of rights, with the sole and exclusive privileges, "of regulating and altering their constitution and form of government, whenever necessary for their safety and happiness"—consequently two modes as a regular proceeding are provided for by its amendments: First, directly through the delegates elected to a convention of the people, to be called by the general assembly: and Secondly, by legislative enactments—each mode being distinctly stated, and both recognizing the sovereign authority of the people over their organic law, and also their supremacy over their public servants.

The proposition now before you however, does not conform with either the one or the other of these provisions, and as an act of the general assembly is strangely contradictory, and in no wise consistent with either, the power to call a convention, being only a condition precedent by sufferance, confers no authority whatever upon the members of the general assembly, to deny the right or the power of the convention to "vacate any office, or the term of any office," existing under the constitution, or to restrict the power to pass ordinances of a legislative character." If this was their privilege, then why trouble the people atal?—and why not have arranged the whole matter to suit themselves?

Here we have ring legislation in the name of the conservative party, and in the guise of constitutional reform. Are you prepared to accept this new surrender of your inherent rights of self government, and thus to ratify your final enslavement to the office and bondholders ring for all time to come? It is surely now made perfectly selfevident before every citizen, who is willing to see and acknowledge the truth, that this ring embraces within its larger and smaller circle knaves and conspirators, and also many of the recognized leaders of both of our political parties.

Packed courts are evidently therefore, an important part of the infamous program. If this conclusion is not correct, pray why the attempt to compel the delegates of the people when assembled in convention professedly to reform their constitution, to submit *without* even the priviledge of consideration and debate, to an unconstitutional and imperious statute, endorsing our courts as at present organized and continuing them for four years longer directly in the face of the discreditable fact, that several of our Supreme and circuit court Judges are holding their offices, in contemptuous disregard of the elective franchise and the rights of self government as pertaining to American freemen, and consequently "against the peace and the dignity of the State of North Carolina."

I submit that these restrictions are clearly unconstitutional, and that they are not only inoperative, but utterly void as against the delegates of the people.

The time has therefore surely come for independent thought and independent voting on your part. Our constitution as now developed, under the construction and the practice of our highest officials, constitutes (as was doubtless the design of its projectors) a complete Ring for their protection against an outraged and indignant people, whose ballot they may well fear to encounter.

In my estimation, the question of constitutional reform should stand far above all mere personal or partisan considerations. You will be told however, that the proposed interests, both personal and partisan, but let me tell you, that the parties requiring, and the parties accepting the restrictions, which are evidently designed to shield the Ring, are none of them worthy of your confidence as our leaders in politics.

Our honest yeomanry have nothing to fear in an open convention, now is their opportunity, and the day of their Salvation. Let them be aroused to a full comprehension of the requirements of "the situation," and they will elect good men and true, to represent them, men who know their rights, and, knowing, will dare maintain them.

I have not intended to censure indiscriminately, the members of the general assembly, who sanctioned the convention bill as it is, many of them no doubt believed they were acting for the best.

And in conclusion let me remark, that I am not a candidate and may not be. I had rather be right in my judgment between right and wrong, and in my position in respect to pending political issues and duties, than to be a delegate to the convention, by any compromise of my independence as a citizen of your county.

Sam. M. Hughes.

May 5th., 1875.

[Enclosure]
Letter from Samuel M. Hughes

To the People of Stokes County.

I cannot feel indifferent, or otherwise than deeply interested in the approaching constitutional convention. Your dearest rights as freemen—civil liberty and self-government itself, are each and all about to be surrendered *by your public servants.*

In proof of the entire truthfulness of this brief statement of the situation, I beg you to look at unquestioned and unquestionable facts. Unselfish patriotism, and inflexible devotion *to the right,* Trusting the Right for consequences, are no longer characteristic of our public men, or of our political parties—*self aggrandisement is their aim.*

As a consequence, our partisan politics, have become completely demoralized—party machinery in both parties being manifestly operated *by the plotting few,* for their exclusive advantage, *as a personal concern*, and in evident fear of the ballot box.

It is not surprising, therefore, under such auspices, that our fundamental law should be *prostituted* to the use of rings and combinations against our honest tax-payers, and that the entire machinery of our State government *is reversed* for the time being, and made to operate in the same direction, *for their advantage and protection.*

Hence the fear of the people, as shown by the restrictions in the convention bill, *against their sovereign authority, as conceded in our existing constitution.*

And hence *Ben Butler*,[2] the feed Attorney and counselor of Wall Street, where our fraudulent bonds are held, and who is generally known as the friend and ready prompter of conspirators and public plunderers, is found on hand at the right time, muttering his very shrewd and hellish threat, of the "*iron clad* oath," in order to deter the honest representatives of the people, *from asserting their rights of self-government*, and on the other hand, *as an apology for the dishonest*, in denying them to the delegates of the people, when assembled in convention to reform their constitution.

This whole proceeding on Butler's part as *now* developed, is plainly only a modification of the policy of Holden Littlefield, & Co., in our own State, Moses[3] of South Carolina, Kellog[4] of Louisiana, and other offenders of like character and conduct in our section. They called for troops to protect them after stealing the people's money, but thank God that bloody device is now played out. And the people now have a perfect right to make themselves heard in defence of free government.

I trust therefore that the people—the real people—the productive classes, who in fact constitute the foundation of the State, and who work out its prosperity, in supporting all other classes, will come together and take care to send their delegates up to Raleigh in September, with instructions to disregard the restrictions imposed by the general assembly, and to remain untrameled except by the restriction existing in the constitution of the United States, which are of course authoritative and all sufficient, so far as applicable, for the protection of all classes, and by such other and additional restrictions and requirements as they may deem necessary to their safety and happiness in the time to come.

Sam. M. Hughes.

May 23rd., 1875.

[Enclosure]
Letter from Samuel M. Hughes

To the people of Stokes County.

"Take care of *the* party, don't damage *the* cause," are the ready watchwords with which selfish political leaders would inspire *you* in these degenerate days.

I am not willing, however, to permit the plotting few among them to take charge of my conscience and dictate my vote, and my sense of right and wrong.

I, for one, am determined, to the best of my knowledge, during the remainder of my days, *to stand by my country and her cause*, rather than such leaders in this or that party, or "the cause," as presented and illustrated by *their* management.

Our plainest constitutional guaranties are trodden under foot invariably, whenever found in the way of personal or party advancement at Raleigh and Washington. Even here, in Stokes County, the recognized leaders of both parties have openly disregarded the direct and emphatic *repudiation* of all confederate war debts, as found in our State and Federal constitutions. And it is well known, that *they* have been acting in brotherly concert, from time to time, in our courts, and out of our courts, in order to enforce their payment against our taxpayers, *although utterly void in respect to them.*

And *now* notwithstanding these stubborn truths, one of these selfsame leaders is before *you*, as the nominee of *his* party, as a candidate for the constitutional convention. Will *you* accept *him* as the exponent of conservatism, *and as a friend of our taxpayers?*

I feel assured that *you* will not—then what is the remedy?

The only consistent answer is plainly this—a manly display of active patriotism, in "independent thought and independent voting," beyond all doubt, or question, or peradventure. The late surrender of *your* highest prerogatives as "American freemen," as *contrived* in the convention bill, settles the fact, fully and unequivocally, *that neither of our political parties as at present organized, can bring you relief from ring controle.*

And just here is our greatest danger. To doubt this, and act accordingly, will certainly result in the forfeiture of *your* heritage of civil liberty. Then let old party lines be blotted out for the time being, at least, in order that *you* may come together, and organize a new party of *your* own, that can, and will, take care of the collective rights of the people, by asserting and maintaining your exclusive privilege, to alter and reform *your* constitution, *without dictation from any quarter* whatever, and whenever necessary to your deliverance from parties, *who have already surrendered this fundamental doctrine of self-government.*

Our partisan representatives, when they reach Raleigh, look to the usurper "King causus," and consequently fall into line under his subalterns, *in loyal support of their King*, whose government in both parties, *is without any distinctive difference.*

I still adhere, therefore, to my platform, as presented last summer for adoption by the conservative county convention. That platform speaks for itself, and was intended by me as at least a slight check to this dangerous ruling of *self-appointed* party leaders, but I was treated as an *interloper*, and my platform rejected for reasons which were well understood by many persons present on that occasion, *and which are still remembered by them.*

Our taxpayers still have rights, *and vested rights at that,* which are well understood here at home. *Taxation should be uniform, not only in theory but also in fact, advalorum percentage should be made absolute by our approaching convention, against the entire ring of pampered Vampires and wealthy non-taxpayers*, who are reveling every day in every succeeding year, in sumptuous living, which has been extended to them through "separate emoluments and privileges," *in the shape of crafty exemptions from taxation, on all County and State bonds, in palpable disregard of every principle of equality and justice, in respect to every other taxpayer.*

I still hold that the determined *repudiation* of all official dishonesty, including all ring legislation, by whomsoever projected, or by whatsoever party, is the only *alternative* by which our honest and patriotic taxpayers can hope to maintain their rightful authority in our public affairs, and save themselves from overwhelming *legalized robbery*, in the shape of rising taxation, and ring usurpation, in all of its treacherous combinations, and our great Republic from the fate of all other free governments, as recorded in the history of our race, which have gone down to anarchy and ruin, *under "the love of money," treacherously accumulated and treasonably employed.*

Sam. M. Hughes.

May 30th., 1875.

---

[1]Samuel M. Hughes has not been identified.

[2]Benjamin F. Butler.

[3]Franklin J. Moses (1838-1906), of South Carolina, attended the South Carolina College and studied law. He was a violent secessionist and held the rank of colonel in conscript service during the Civil War. As editor of the *Sumter News*, 1865-1866, Moses vigorously supported President Johnson. After switching his political support to the Republican party in 1867, he became active in the Union League and was a delegate to the convention of 1868. He was Speaker of the lower house of the legislature and served as governor, 1872-1874. His private life and career were marred by accusations of corruption, and he eventually became a bankrupt wanderer. *CDAB*, 708-709.

[4]William Pitt Kellogg (1830-1918), a native of Vermont, attended Norwich Military Institute. After graduation he went to Illinois, where he became a teacher and read law in preparation for a legal career. In 1861 he was appointed chief justice of the Nebraska Territory, but with the outbreak of the Civil War he resigned, returned to Illinois, and raised a regiment that he headed as colonel. Appointed collector of the port of New Orleans after the war, he participated in carpetbag politics and was elected United States senator, 1868-1872, and Louisiana governor, 1873-1877, with the help of Grant and federal troops. Although Kellogg was impeached, the state Senate refused to try him and he was again elected United States senator, 1877-1883, and representative, 1883-1885. *Biographical Directory of Congress*, 1151.

E. J. Hale & Sons to William A. Graham UNC
[with enclosures]

New York,
June 14th., 1875.

Your favor of the 12th surprises & grieves us. It has been a strange & mortifying oversight in the committee that they did not place at your disposal as many copies as you wished. Of course it was only an oversight. If the publication had been our own, it would have given us pleasure to send you all you wanted. As it is, the committee owning the stereotype plates, we have to get their permission to print copies from them. This we have just written for; but suggested, to avoid delay, that if they have enough remaining, they send them to you at once. We retained 100 for sale, for Editors, etc., & have sold and delivered them all, except half a dozen paper covered copies. We wrote for another supply, which we expect in a few days.

There ought not to have been a copy left in Charlotte at the close of the celebration. Persons should have been employed to offer them to every stranger in the city. And many might be sold now in all the localities you name, if persons could be found to attend to the matter.

We North Carolinians were proud of the grand success of the celebration. It & its attendant circumstances of historical ventilation have done more for the State than anything else for a long time.

We are glad to hear that you will be here soon, & promise ourselves the pleasure of seeing you, &, we hope, in good health.

We tried to get the Herald with Goodloe's article, but could not. We enclose the article we attributed to Prof. Phillips.

[Enclosures]
Letters to Editors

The Mecklenburg Declaration.
The Late Rev. Dr. Hawks' Opinion on Its Authenticity.

To the Editors of the Evening Post:

The discussion in your paper this evening of the authenticity of the alleged Declaration of Independence in Mecklenburg county, North Carolina, on 20th May, 1775, recalls to mind a lecture delivered before the New York Historical Society on the 16th. December, 1852, by the late Rev. Francis L. Hawks, D.D., on this subject. In this lecture the reverend doctor said:

"John McKnitt Alexander, the secretary of the Mecklenburg Convention, distinctly stated, that he had furnished a copy from the original document of May 20, 1775, to Dr. Hugh Williamson. Montford Stokes, while Governor of North Carolina in 1831, testified that in the year 1793 (mark the date) he saw in the possession of Dr. Williamson a copy of the documents of the 20th of May, 1775, in the handwriting of John McKnitt Alexander, together with a letter to Williamson from Alexander, and that he conversed with Williamson on the subject. I asked you to mark the date because it has been put down as an historical fact (on what authority I cannot say), that the date of the earliest copy of the resolutions was in September, 1800, after the destruction of the original by fire. Here we have them, as I have presented them to you, in 1793. But this is not all. Among the young men who were present at Charlotte on that memorable 19th and 20th was one who was, as he states, a deeply interested spectator then twenty years old. This youth joined the army at once as a private, afterwards became an officer, and conducted himself during his whole military career with great bravery. When he retired from the service he resumed his classical studies and became a clergyman in that region of the country, exercising his office for more than thirty years with unblemished character. He kept a journal of all that occurred, from the meeting in Mecklenburg on the 20th of May through the whole of his military career; and carefully preserved a copy of the paper read by Colonel Polk from the Court House steps. He had not obtained it from Alexander afterwards as Williamson and Davie had, but made it at the time. The memoir which he wrote contained that copy; it agrees verbatim with what I have read."

Dr. Hawks goes on to derive additional confirmation of the authenticity of the resolutions of 20th May from the allusion to the slaughter at Lexington, which they contain, "while the document of the 30th is perfectly silent concerning Lexington."

"If the resolves of the 30th were the Mecklenburg declaration, and if the Carolinians were quickened in making it by the news of the murder of their brethren at the East, is it not most marvellous that not the slightest allusion should be made to the blood-stirring story?" "It was not printed because everywhere out of Mecklenburg, even in North Carolina itself, (where only two newspapers were then published), it was thought to be too strong to permit any hope of reconciliation, and it was therefore deemed injudicious to print it then."

E. K.

May 3, 1875.

Views of the Rev. Dr. Storrs[1] and President Welling.

To the Editors of the Evening Post:

In an address delivered by Dr. Storrs before the New York Historical Society April 15, as reported by the New York newspapers, he makes this statement:

"As indicative of the tendencies of public opinion, on the 21st of May the citizens of Mecklenburg county, on the borders of Virginia and North Carolina, by corporate action renounced allegiance to the British crown, and adopted their Declaration of Independence."

It would appear from this statement that the doctor does not see the force of the argument made in a paper read by President Welling before the same Historical Society at a meeting held in the winter of 1874, and published subsequently in the April number of the *North American Review*. I would also add that Mecklenburg county is in North Carolina, on the border of South Carolina. President Welling argues that the declaration in question is spurious.

L. McC.

Mecklenburg County.
Its Alleged Declaration of Independence
The Imaginary Meeting May 20 and the Real One May 31—
Thomas Jefferson Not a Plagiarist.

[*New York Evening Post*, May 18, 1875]

To the Editors of the Evening Post:

The readers of the Evening Post may be curious as to how it has come to pass that while the two towns of Concord and Lexington, in Massachusetts, are uncertain as to which of their guns was the first in the Revolution, the one town of Charlotte, in North Carolina, is uncertain as to which of its Declarations of Independence was the first, that of May 20, 1775, or that of May 31, 1775. Will you allow one who knows the origin of this uncertainty to gratify this curiosity? Among the statements cited by the *Evening Post* of May 7 was one to the effect that a copy of the paper of May 20 was sent to General W. R. Davie, a prominent soldier of the Revolution from North Carolina, but afterwards a citizen of South Carolina. This copy had attached to it the following certificate:

"It may be worthy of notice here to observe that the foregoing statement, although fundamentally correct, yet may not literally correspond with the original record of the transactions of said delegation and court of inquiry, as all those records and papers were burnt, with the house, on April 6, 1800; but previous to that time of 1800, a full copy of said records, at the request of Dr. Hugh Williamson, then of New York, but formerly a representative in Congress from this State, was forwarded to him by Colonel William Polk in order that those early transactions might fill their proper place in a history of this State then writing by said Doctor Williamson in New York.

"Certified to the best of my recollection and belief this 3d. day of September, 1800, by

J. McN. Alexander."

"Mecklenburg county, N.C."

When the declaration of May 20 was published for the first time (April 30, 1819), the substance only of a part of this certificate was given. The whole of the certificate was published, for the first time, in the *North Carolina University Magazine* for May, 1853. The article from which this certificate is copied was written by the secretary of the Historical Society of the University of North Carolina, and the documents it quotes were furnished by the president of the University, the late Governor Swain, who was more minutely acquainted with the history of North Carolina than any man that has ever lived. The authenticity of this certificate has never been questioned in public. It establishes beyond a peradventure that what is known as the declaration of May 20, 1775, originated in a patriotic effort of Mr. John McNitt Alexander, in whose house the original records were burnt, to rescue from oblivion the deeds of his compatriots. The history by Dr. Williamson, to which Mr. Alexander referred, closes with 1771. The documents which he collected for the continuation of his work are supposed to have been burnt in a warehouse in Pearl Street, New York, in the great fire of 1835. The document from which this certificate was copied, came from among the papers of General Davie, and was in the well-known handwriting of Mr. Alexander.

Some suspicious circumstances connected with the publication of April, 1819—contradictions among the witnesses appealed to afterwards to verify the statements of that publication, and belief in the existence of another paper, which was warranted by the publication of Mr. Force[2] in "The American Archives"—led many to be doubtful as to the genuineness and authenticity of this paper of May 20. This doubt led them to examine with great particularity every deposit of Revolutionary papers that was accessible. So it was that at last, in 1847, Mr. Bancroft first, in the Colonial office in London, and shortly afterwards, but entirely independent of him, Dr. Joseph Johnson,[3] in the Library of Charleston, S.C. found the entire paper of May 31, 1775, in a number of *Timothy's Gazette* for June 13, 1775. This declaration of May 31 is contained in twenty "resolves," the first of which announces "that all commissions, civil and military, heretofore granted by the crown to be exercised in these colonies are null and void, and the constitution of each particular colony wholly suspended," and the fourth bids the inhabitants of the county of Mecklenburg to meet on a certain day and elect certain officers for the county "who shall hold and exercise their several powers by virture of this choice, and independent of the crown of Great Britain, and former constitution of this province."

The reasons for asserting the genuineness and authenticity of the declaration of May 20 have been frequently set before the public—especially by the late Rev. Dr. Hawks in 1857, and by Governor Graham in an exhaustive memoir on the subject, read before the citizens of Charlotte in February last. Some of the points made against it, and in favor of the declaration of May 31, 1775, are to be found in the article already referred to as having the sanction of Governor Swain. To understand them fully, it must be remembered that there are two versions of the declaration of May 20—that to which the certificate of Mr. Alexander was attached, and another, published for the first time in Martin's "History of North Carolina" in 1829. I quote from the *North Carolina University Magazine* of May, 1853.

"This paper of May 20 is a suspicious paper on its very face. Its guardians do not seem to have regarded it as containing the *ipsissima verba*[4] used by the men of Mecklenburg. Who furnished the Martin copy? Who made the diversities between it and the Davie copy? * * * Who ever heard of such various readings in the national Declaration of Independence or in the various copies of the contemporaneous county and state publications?"

"As to the testimony furnished by the survivors of May, 1775, it is doubtless entitled to very great respect. But when carefully examined it is not so definite and overwhelming as it might have been. We have not the letters which asked for the recollections of these gentlemen. Perhaps they contained leading questions, suggested dates, etc. Some of these witnesses were suddenly called on to testify as to what they saw and heard forty-five and fifty-five years before, and that when they had become old and, as some of them say, their memories not infallible. * * * Not one of them mentions having heard two such declarations, and not one was asked which of the two we now have he heard. [N.B.—When the discoveries of 1847 were made, every actor in the stirring times of 1775 had passed away.]"

"From the certificate of Mr. Alexander (he died in 1817) it is clear that he never intended to set forth 'the Davie copy' as containing any more than the substance of what was resolved in Charlotte in May, 1775. That paper originated in a patriotic effort to preserve from oblivion the worthy sentiments and actions of himself and his neighbors. He candidly declares that it must be received with due deference to what he had furnished to Dr. Williamson; but he makes no mention of having given a copy to Judge Martin.

"The declaration of May 20 cannot have preceded that of May 31. The reasons assigned for independence in the two docments are inconsistent with each other. There were in Mecklenburg county many men who, after the troubles brought on by 'the regulation,' had taken oaths not to disturb his Majesty's government again. The skill with which this difficulty is avoided, and a shield thrown around tender consciences by 'The Resolves' of May 31, is admirable. * * * 'The Davie copy' makes the delegates to the convention declare themselves justices of the peace, after the fashion of a French *coup d'etat*. 'The Resolves' provide for the election of justices of the peace by the people, after the fashion of sober, law-abiding Presbyterians such as its authors undoubtedly were."

"No contemporaneous manuscript or printed document contains a single allusion to the paper of May 20, while to that of May 31 the references are many and pointed. 'The Resolves' of May 31 are to be found in the *South Carolina Gazette* of June 13, 1775, but not the resolutions of May 20, although the file of that paper (still extant in the City Library of Charleston, S.C.) contains the Declaration of Independence (of cowardly beaux) made by the young ladies of Mecklenburg. * * * On the 20th. of June, 1775, Governor Wright, of Georgia, wrote to the Earl of Dartmouth, then the Secretary of State in London: 'By the enclosed paper (the *Gazette* of June 13) your lordship will see the extraordinary resolves by the people in Charlottetown, in Mecklenburg county, and I should not be surprised if the same should be done everywhere else.' On the 30th. of June, 1775, Governor Martin wrote to the same secretary as follows: 'The resolves of the committee of Mecklenburg, which your lordship will find in the enclosed newpaper, surpass all the horrid and treasonable publications that the inflammatory spirits of the continent have yet produced. * * * A copy of these resolves was sent off, I am informed, by express to the Congress at Philadelphia, as soon as they were passed by the committee.' * * * On the 8th. of August, 1775, Governor Martin, in a public proclamation, stigmatized 'The Resolves' in the following language: 'I have seen a most infamous publication in the *Cape Fear Mercury*, importing to be resolves of a set of people styling themselves a committee for the county of Mecklenburg, traitorously declaring the entire dissolution of the laws, government and Constitution of this country, and setting up a system of rule and regulation repugnant to the laws, and subversive of his Majesty's government.' We find these contemporaneous notices of the declaration of May 31, but where are even allusions to either the Davie or the Martin copy of the declaration of May 20?"

These are the main points raised, nearly twenty years ago, in favor of the declaration of May 31, 1775, as the unquestionable and only declaration by the inhabitants of Mecklenburg county, N.C. Researches made since 1853 but confirm this conclusion, a conclusion evidently adopted by public-spirited citizens of Philadelphia, who have lately published 'The Resolves' (on large paper, in conspicuous type, and handsomely framed) as "The First Declaration of American Independence." So, Messrs. Editors, your readers will understand that one of thc dcclarations to be centennialized on the 20th., is the production of a patriotic memory in 1800, while the other is the result of discovery in 1847, and they will have good grounds for concluding that Jefferson was not a plagiarist.

X.

---

[1]Richard Salter Storrs (1821-1900) was a Congregational clergyman. He was a popular lyceum lecturer and was very active in the civic, philanthropic, and cultural affairs of Brooklyn. *CDAB*, 1020.

[2]Peter Force (1790-1868) collected and published a series of reprints of rare pamphlets on colonial history, *Tracts and Other Papers, etc.* (1836-1846), and planned a monumental series of original materials on American history entitled *American Archives.* Only nine volumes, covering the years 1774-1776, were published (1837-1853). *CDAB*, 304.

[3]Joseph Johnson (1776-1862) was a physician who practiced in Charleston, where he was active in civic life and a leader in the Union party. Johnson was author of *Traditions . . . of the American Revolution in the South* (1851). *CDAB*, 503.

[4]"Very same words."

Alexander McIver to William A. Graham UNC

Chapel Hill, N.C.
June 14th, [1875]

I have just learned that Prof. Charles Phillips will be a candidate for a professorship. I had been led to believe that he would not.

I enclose two *private letters,*[1] and a recommendation which has just been forwarded to me from Wilmington. Others will be handed to you by Mr. Kemp P. Battle, and Governor Brogden. The two private letters are only for your own eyes.

I will place the matter entirely in your hands, and will be satisfied with the result, whatever it may be.

I was informed by a member of the last General Assembly, who assisted in getting the appropriation bill for the University through the Lesiglature, that certain members, Mr. Erwin[2] & others, opposed the Bill, for the reason that the Trustees of the University would probably invite Phillips and Martin from Davidson College and thus interfere with that institution. They were assured by other members that this would not be done, and on this assurance they withdrew their opposition & the bill passed: otherwise it would have been defeated. It is an established principle that it is not right, that one employer should entice away the servants of another. It is not expected that the University should interfere with other Institutions. There are as good men outside of Davidson College as there are in it.

I trust you will pardon me for troubling you with this letter. If, consistently with your sense of duty, you can place my name before the Board for the Professorship of Mathematics, I will thank you for it.

It has been suggested by several friends that I should apply for a different Professorship, as it is a forgone conclusion to give Prof. Phillips Mathematics. You may do as you think best. I have no testimonials for any Professorship, except Mathematics. I think, however, that I could work equally well in the Department of Agriculture.

Without intending any reflection upon Prof. Phillips,[3] I may say, that both students & trustees at Davidson College were of the opinion that he was not a successful teacher of Mathematics. Several students whom I had taught and left there, informed me that they left, because they could not learn Mathematics under him. The Trustees at one time appointed a Committee to wait on him, and ask him to change his method of teaching.

The Trustees finally elected an assistant Professor of Mathematics for his benefit. The number of students in Davidson has not materially increased since I left there.

---

[1]Not found.

[2]Alfred M. Erwin was a representative from McDowell County, 1874-1875. Cheney, *North Carolina Government*, 456.

[3]Charles Phillips published articles on the Mecklenburg Declaration in the *University of North Carolina Magazine* of May, 1853, and in the *New York Evening Post*, May 19, 1875. He denied its authenticity and, apart from publication, was quite hostile about the whole matter. He wrote his sister, Cornelia P. Spencer, May 14, 1875, and spoke of the declaration as "this mystery, this myth, this grand humbug, this declaration of May 20 'falsely so-called!'" Graham was very sensitive about Phillips's feelings and writings.

Joseph Graham to William A. Graham A&H

Charlotte,
June 14th., 1875.

My dear Father,

Mr. Hale had the address stereotyped by order of our Committee, and it has been paid for by the same. We have a good many copies, which we would be glad to have distributed to the various literary and historical societies. If you will undertake that, we will gladly furnish you the books. Let me know how many to send you. We are applying proceeds of sales to the Monumental fund; but conceive that as part of the Commemoration of the event we celebrated, we cannot better expend part of the money than by placing our arguments, as set forth in your address, within in the reach of the youth of the country, who are collected at its various institutions of learning.

I should have written you earlier, but it is a very hard matter to get the Committee together now.

Affectionately Yours,

We have a balance in our treasury of about $1200., and Mr. J. H. Wilson[1] has $800.

[1]Probably this was the Joseph H. Wilson of Mecklenburg County identified earlier in this volume.

Alexander McIver to William A. Graham UNC

Chapel Hill, N.C.
June 19th., [1875.]

I thank you most sincerely for the honor which you did me in offering to present my name to the Trustees of the University, for the Professorship of Mathematics, and for anything which you may have done pursuant thereto.

Will you be kind enough to return to me by mail the papers which I sent you in connection with the matter. I enclose 25 cts. to pay the postage.

Wishing you continued good health, and long life.

I remain,
Very truly your friend,

Charles J. Jenkins to William A. Graham UNC

Augusta, Georgia,
June 22nd., 1875.

I received late yester evening, your letter of the 19th. inst. I had been notified by the Counsel of the application for postponement, & of the suggestion of Saratoga as the place of meeting. I confess that to me both changes—of time & of place—are entirely agreeable. I have heard often of late that the accomodations at the White Sulphur Springs are decidedly bad & that only desperately bent pleasure seekers could stand them long. Philadelphia is notoriously one of [the] hottest places in America in August. We shall have at this session an arduous service, & ought to be exempt both from extreme heat, & rough fare. I left Washington under the impression that you also favored Saratoga but finding I was mistaken in that I would not on any account urge it against your will. I have therefore written Judge Black expressing my entire willingness to leave the question of venue to his discretion.

William P. Whyte to William A. Graham UNC

Baltimore, June 25, [1875]

I have a telegram from Judge Black today, informing me that he consents to the postponement [as proposed by both States][1] from June 30th for our meeting until July 28th at Saratoga Springs. I presume, you have been in conference & this is your combined consent, but lest there be any miscarriage,

I deem it proper to advise you of this & to say, that we all expect to be present on 28th proxo, (as suggested,) at Saratoga.

Judge Robertson & my colleagues are still on the Eastern Shore, taking testimony, which cannot be completed till Sat'dy.

---

[1]Brackets used by Whyte.

William A. Graham to Samuel M. Hughes[1] UNC

Hillsboro',
June 25th., 1875.

Several causes conspire to prevent my correspondence from being very prompt, and therefore I have not made earlier reply to your letter of the date of the 10th inst. I must now answer briefly, considering its importance.

With you, I should have preferred an open Convention, but much prefer, that which has been called, to none at all. In such great affairs, many minds are to be consulted, and it is the part of wisdom to embrace what is practicable, if desirable, rather than contravene the public will, as indicated by the Legislature, by attempting what must lead to dissension and result in a division of the Conservative party in the State. The present parties are of recent origin, and have not the discipline and compactness of some of the older ones. The last Legislature was composed in the main of members new to the business of Legislation, but in general talents, so far as my acquaintance extends, was above the general average, and its integrity above suspicion. There were many young men among them, who, with the experience of one session, will be far more useful in another, and from whom important service may be expected in the future. They were diffident, as inexperienced persons are apt to be, and hesitated as to calling a convention; and such an one as you suggest they would not approve. To overcome their scruples, and effect as much good as the circumstances may permit, the law upon that subject was adopted. I am of opinion, that no strength was gained to the measure, in the estimation of the people, by many of the restrictions of the law, but those who were at the scene, and whose votes controlled in the matter, thought otherwise, and I think it my duty to acquiesce. Within the limits of its prescribed power, the body will have authority to make great reforms in many essential respects, and if the provisions for those objects do not take immediate effect, they may be assured for the future.

No Convention, with general powers, could have been called in 1788 & '89, yet such a body was authorized in each of those years, with the limited power of acting on the adoption of the Federal Constitution, and on a single amendment, in each instance, to the Constitution of the State. And having been a member from this then borough Town, in the Assembly of 1834, I know that the Convention then called, could not have been carried, except with the very great restrictions thrown around it. And, being a Western man, I remember to have been told by old politicians, after the passage of the law, that we had been satisfied with too little, and that such a convention as that, could have been had long before. But the law was executed in good faith, the convention met and did its work, discontent, which had prevailed for thirty years, was quieted, the people took courage, and the State made new advancement in reputation and prosperity. So, I trust, it will be in this instance.

As to the protection of the people against the action of "Rings" as you style them, I think in the end it will be discovered that the only reliable security will be found in withholding public powers of any kind, from any but honest and capable men. We should do our best however on this subject. I am told there are some salutary provisions, respecting these evils, in the recently revised constitutions of other States, and which, I suppose, may lie within the powers of this convention. But where was there ever a *better showing* of political morals, than in our existing constitution, in which the leading idea is, that no public debt should be created by the Legislature without the sanction of a vote of the people, (the exceptional instances were hardly noticed)—this was the grand inscription on the banner of its adoption. Economy was breathed in the very air in which it floated. And yet: what, by the Legislation of this Convention, and that of the first General Assembly which succeeded it, and which was made its heir political, by measures stronger than a limitation in special tail, the proverbially most economical State in the Union, in the space of two years, found itself loaded with more than thirty millions of new debt, notwithstanding the annihilation of two thirds of its taxable capital, by means of the war, and its results; and now, at the end of seven years, has nothing to show for it. How much of this has been exploded by Judicial determination, and how much more is so infected with fraud as to be void, is not pertinent to the present question. This apparent safeguard of frugality, has in practice, proved but a blind to cover a profuseness, which even in our days of prosperity, before the war, would have been impossible. Whatever the convention can do to guard against such abuses or to remedy such as exist, I trust will be done. But the want of power to do everything which may be desirable, is not a sufficient pleas for doing nothing, or for attempting measures beyond its powers and creating division among the friends of reform.

I have, as I trust you will concede, no personal interests to promote, by either course, which are not shared by good citizens of all parties: but to the Conservative organization, as now existing, we are indebted for that wholesome public sentiment, which has corrected many of the mischiefs, to which the new condition of affairs has exposed us; and since it became possessed of the Legislative power of the State, has exerted a beneficient sympathetic influence, which has inspired new hope, and a confidence of better times, among the people.

I have written in haste, and may have omitted some of the topics of your letter. If so, it is not designed.

Thanking you for your expressions of regard, and the correspondence of our political opinions and tastes in past times,

I am,
Very Respectfully Yours,

[1]This letter is a copy with Graham's signature.

Raleigh T. Daniel to William A. Graham UNC

Richmond June 29, 1875

I received a Note from Govr. White [*sic*], before I got yours informing me of the *fixation* of place and time for the arbitration. I should have preferred a place nearer home than Saratoga, but had no voice in the matter. I send you by todays Express, a bound copy of the Reports which we had in paper in Washington; also a Note of points, which without attempting to anticipate what may be urged on the other side, indicate the general line of argument which will probably be adopted for Virginia.

I hope we shall have the pleasure of seeing you here as you pass through. *Te secretario*[1] too, I hope will be with you, to whom will you give my respects.

[1]"Your secretary" (Augustus W. Graham).

Cornelia Phillips Spencer to William A. Graham UNC

Chapel Hill,
June 29th., 1875.

The enclosed letter,[1] if you will be so good as to cast your eye over it, will explain the reason why I write to you. Such appeals for friendly advice & sympathy are not infrequent with me. If I had a million of money—(after endowing the University!)—I think I would devote a large sum to the aid of these poor young women who are struggling for an education, vainly longing for what N. Carolina has never yet shown any disposition to give her daughters.

My object in writing to you on the subject is to ask you, dear Sir, if the *Peabody Schools* afford any aid to this class of inquirers. I believe the school at Hillsboro' is, (or was), under your special jurisdiction. I know nothing whatever of the working of these schools, & any reports of their operations or plans has never yet been shown me. I have never seen any one who has seen one, or has been able to give me an account of what that Charity is doing for the South. I presume the schools are free, and that both sexes attend. But of what grade they are—whether such a woman as this appears to be, & others who have written to me with the same object—could derive any benefit from them, or on what terms, I am quite ignorant.

May I beg you, of your kindness to a young fellow citizen, to tell her for her sake if the Peabody Schools could help her. If she could find the means to pay her board, for instance, at H., could she get her schooling free? I want it to be a schooling of a sufficiently high grade to further her views. Her letter is well written & expressed.

I will not apologize to Gov. Graham for this intrusion on his valuable time. That he is Gov. Graham, is both reason & excuse to a North Carolina woman.

[1]Not found.

William P. Whyte to William A. Graham UNC

July 1, 1875

Your favor of 28th ulto is at hand. I do not think you will find Saratoga disagreeable at the time named, as it will be between the races & after the regatta.

I have written to Mr. Breslin, the proprietor of the Grand Union Hotel to have a large parlor for the meeting of the Board on the 28th.

We (Mr. Jones & I) shall go to the Grand Union, as the best house, & I shall be glad to engage quarters for you & your son there if you have no other choice, or if you wish to write directly to the Proprietors, their firm name is J. H. Breslin & Co, & I feel sure, they will give you good accomodations.

We have not yet finished our testimony but take more on 13th inst., yet we shall be ready to go on with the case on 28th.

Hoping to see you at that time, I am, with great respect, yours truly.

William A. Graham to Cornelia Phillips Spencer A&H: SPENCER

Hillsboro,
July 1st, 1875.

My Dear Mrs. Spencer

Yours of 29th ult in behalf of, and accompanied by the letter of Miss Pate was duly received.

I regret to say in reply that the appropriations of the Peabody education Fund are exclusively for primary education; and in that, to instruction—nothing to board and clothing or to the erection of buildings or the like. Her letter indicates that she has already all that could be afforded her from this charity. The report of Prof. McIver as supt. of Pub. Ins. a year or two back, states the terms, on which aid is furnished to primary schools from the donation of Mr. Peabody. I will suggest to Dr. Sears the Genl. Agt. to prepare a short circular on this head, for a general reply to applicants.

With assurances of sincere regard
Yours etc etc

Presuming the enclosed was intended merely for my perusal it is returned.

William A. Graham to Kemp P. Battle UNC: BATTLE

July 9th. 1875—

Dr Sir

I observe in "Living & Dead" that the Historical society is to meet again, on the call of the chairman of the last meeting. I do not think I can visit Raleigh again before going North on the 25th inst— If you think a meeting desirable earlier than that, you can use my name to call it—. I have some question, whether one may be expedient, during the Ed't'l Convention next week. I can be present then.

George Davis to William A. Graham A&H

Wilmington,
July 13th., 1875.

I have received the copy of your Mecklenburg Address, which you were kind enough to send me, and have examined it with great interest. It seems to me to exhaust the subject, and to leave nothing further to be said.

I was greatly desiring a copy of the address, and I owe you a great many thanks for sending me one, in shape adapted for preservation.

Robert D. Graham to William A. Graham UNC

Ch[arlotte].
7-14-1875

Dear Father:

I presented your letter to Mr. P. Smith, Prest "Farmers Savings Bk. of Mecklenburg Co.", and after consultation they answered me today that they would not take it having $50,000.00 now not in use. I then told them that I felt safe in offering them $10,000.00 @ 7 per cent, interest payable annually, and capital subject to recall as stated in your letter of the 12th, delivered thro' me. They agree to that, and request me to say to you that they will take any amount from $10,000.00 to $20,000.00 on those terms,

Mr. Smith yesterday proposed to take $2000.00 of it individually at 8% and give acceptable security. I told him you preferred to make as few divisions of it as you could with safety, etc. He did not renew the proposition.

I was glad to find bro' Joe's people considerably improved yesterday, and presume he has written you.

On the subject of investments, I think you would be safe in offering The Bk of Mecklenburg, say $5000.00 @ 8%. I am satisfied that the 1st National Bk of Charlotte would back them in case of an emergency. I have however had no conversation with them, and only the parties dealt with so far, I think, know of yr. investments here. I will hardly be out of town more than a day or two, for the next ten, and will submit any propositions that you may wish to present. Hope the settlement of this matter may leave nothing else in the way of your preparations for your trip next week.

Quite a party from here go down to The Atlantic next week. If you adjourn from Saratoga to meet again this summer, I think you would find Atlantic City on the coast of N. Jersey & 60 m. from Phila. more agreeable & more beneficial than Saratoga. They claim for it a *dry* salt air, intervening forest, &c. With love to all

Your Aff. Son

The B'k hope to have from Williams a check on Charlotte, or New York.

Augustus H. Garland to William A. Graham A&H

Executive Office
State of Arkansas.

Little Rock,
July 15th., 1875.

I have to thank you, which I now do most cordially, for a copy of your *address on the Mecklenburg Declaration.* I read it with no little pleasure and instruction.

I had not, from my general reading of our early history, ever doubted the *20th. May Declaration.* My own family, (father & mother) being from N.C., I had learned this as a tradition. But if the fact had been before me as new—one never before heard of—your address has established it in my mind as clearly as any truth was ever fixed in it. If title to N.C. depended upon that fact in a court of justice, your address has demonstrated it conclusively, and in my judgment no impartial and enlightened tribunal could find otherwise.

I often think of you, and would be glad indeed to meet you again. I hope time bears lightly upon you.

We are getting along pretty well here, all things considered, for people are at peace again, and working with wonderful energy and zeal. We were completely bankrupt, and ground into the earth, but we have hope now, of being prosperous in a few years.

Donald MacRae[1] *to William A. Graham* UNC

The Wilmington Cotton Mills
Wilmington, N.C.
16 July 1875.

Having heard that holders of the Bonds of the N.C.R.Rd. are not offering them for redemption, and supposing you would prefer to have the trust funds at interest, we write to say that our Corporation would be glad to borrow $10,000. to $15,000. payable on demand or on short notice.

We could secure such a loan by giving you our Stock as collateral @ 50 to 75%; or we could furnish undoubted personal security.

Our Capital Stock is $125,000., paid up in full, and our present indebtedness in $6000.

The Stock, though a few sales have been made at 95%, is held at par. We can, of course, borrow all the funds we need from our Banks here at 8%, but as it may prove a mutual benefit, we prefer to borrow at 6% where we would not be forced to renew every 60 or 90 days.

---

[1]Donald MacRae was president of the Wilmington Cotton Mills.

William R. Cox to William A. Graham A&H

Rooms of Democratic—Conservative Central Executive Committee,

Raleigh, N.C.,
July 16th., 1875.

Rumors from several sources have reached me, that you contemplate withdrawing from the Canvass[1] on account of ill health. While I will not presume to even appear to dictate to one for whom I entertain such a high and partial regard, yet permit me to suggest, if you seriously contemplate such a thing, you act at once, to enable our friends to concentrate on some one else. I think your withdrawal might endanger our prospects, would be misconstrued, & that if you are unable to Canvass, Maj. Graham[2] might Canvass for you. Your nomination has already proved a tower of strength, & since the beginning of the active Canvass, will be of yet more service. Our adversaries have plenty of money, are active and unscrupulous, while it is difficult to arouse our friends.

I leave for the West on Monday.
Very truly and res'y Y'rs

[1]Graham was a Democratic candidate for the Constitutional Convention of 1875.
[2]John W. Graham.

Frederick A. P. Barnard to William A. Graham A&H

Columbia College, New York,
President's Room,
July 16th., 1875.

I have the honor to acknowledge your letter of the 13th. instant, and a copy of the volume containing your address, delivered in February last; for which please accept my thanks. There is no doubt that this work will furnish material for the article on the "*Mecklenburg Declaration,*" and, with your permission, which is implied in your sending the book, I will compile an article from it; but in-so-much as I was particularly desirous to connect your name with our work, I desire now to ask if you would object to our placing your name at the end of such a compilation, it being understood that the article so compiled, shall be sent to you for your approval before it is published.[1] This will not only be a gratification to me, but I think it would give authority to the statements of the article which would not belong to one published anonymously.

We shall reach the title "*Mecklenburg*" about the middle of August, and an early reply to this request will be esteemed a favor.

[1]Graham probably accepted Barnard's suggestion, of course with the understanding that he would revise the manuscript. He died a month later and so never saw the article, which in all probability had not then been written. When the fifth volume of Rossiter Johnson's *Universal Cyclopedia* appeared, it contained an article on the subject of the Mecklenburg

Declaration with this note, signed by Peter Bliss: "The above was carefully prepared from material furnished to the editor-in-chief of this work, by the late ex-Gov. William A. Graham of North Carolina, and was intended to bear his name, after revision, which it was prevented from receiving by his death which occurred at Saratoga, N.Y., August 11, 1875."

The article was a complete reversal of Graham's view of the matter, taking the position that there was only one meeting, on May 31, 1775, which date was identical with May 20 Old Style. The article escaped attention in North Carolina until 1909 and was then published in the *Charlotte News* on September 4. On September 24, Samuel A. Ashe, who had come to have doubts as to the authenticity of the declaration and had reached the same conclusion as to the dates, signed an article that was printed by his publisher in pamphlet form announcing that Graham had come to that conclusion before his death. No one who knew anything about William A. Graham would believe for an instant that he had so hastily changed his whole view of a matter in which he was so deeply concerned. His son, Judge Augustus W. Graham of Oxford, immediately replied with a pamphlet in which the authorship of the *Cyclopedia* article was completely explained.

Address to Orange County Citizens[1] A&H

Address from the Hon. Wm. A. Graham to the People of Orange County.

When I accepted the nomination as a candidate for a seat in the approaching Convention, tendered by a public meeting of the Conservative Democratic party during the last Superior Court, I had hoped to attend the public assemblies at the annual tax-gatherings, and to make such explanation of the subject as the occasion would allow; according to the old custom of the county.

An important engagement of business, not then expected to interrupt, will require me to be absent from the State at the time of the election, and the feeble condition of my health, in the meantime, prevents my presence among you, as I desired. I therefore address to you this paper, as an apology for my absence, and a brief statement of my views on some of the topics involved in the election.

You will see, on reading the Convention act, that the Convention is to be one of limited powers.

1st. There is no danger in it to the rights of the colored people, because their rights are secured by the Constitution of the United States, and the Convention of a State could not abridge them, if it were so disposed.

2nd. The Convention is expressly forbidden to abridge the rights of a failing debtor to his Homestead, and the exemptions of personal property now allowed.

3rd. It cannot take away the mechanics and laborers lien, nor from married women the right to their separate property, and in various other particulars it can make no change in the regulations at present existing.

4th. The Convention is also forbidden to legislate, that is, to pass laws on any subject; this power being left to the Representatives of the people at the usual sessions of the Legislature, and the power of the Convention being confined to regulating the organization of the several departments of government, the declaration of principles, and the establishment of very general rules.

It can therefore lay no tax, nor enact any law as to the existing public debt (whether the claim be fair or fraudulent) that subject having been withdrawn from the constitution by amendments adopted by vote of the people in 1873, and placed under the control of the Legislature, where it was always considered to belong, till guarantees for its full payment, principal and interest, were foisted into the Constitution of 1868. These, the amendments aforesaid have now repealed. I have thought it proper thus to state the substance of the Convention Act, because I understand that attempts are made to prejudice the Freedmen against the Convention upon the old cry that it is designed to put them back into slavery; a cry which they have some reason to distrust after ten years of freedom, during which the right to personal liberty in the white man (and it is the same for the colored) has been subjected to the severest of trials, and came out victorious, through the old writ of *Habeas Corpus*; also that special pains are being taken to excite fears as to the safety of Homesteads, liens of mechanics and laborers, and on other heads; all of which are forbidden to be touched in Convention, by the 4th. section of said act.

But it is said that a Convention is but an epitome of the people, and can't be restricted by limits on it's powers.

This can hardly be called North Carolina doctrine, since we had conventions in 1788, 1789 and 1835, all of which were limited; and they all submitted to the restraints, and attempted nothing beyond them. But, however this may be, the people have the reins in their own hands in choosing delegates, and can protect themselves against perils of this kind, by refusing to elect any man who will not agree to abide by the restrictions. The fiery steed that shows before-hand that he will kick out of the traces, should not be hitched in, but be left to some other occasion which will be free for anything.

Another class of objectors to Convention, it is said, are of the opposite kind, though in close alliance with the above.

They are willing to be elected, go to Raleigh, adjourn, and come home again. For any useful work, these require the spur, rather than the rein. Now the principle of these men is but nullification in a new and most objectionable form. By adopting the existing Constitution, it was ordained that the General Assembly, by majorities of two thirds of each House, might call a Convention, and when the present Convention act passed by these majorities, it became as binding as if it had been voted for by every member of the Legislature, and every citizen. It was a decree of the people, through their appointed agents, that the Constitution should be revised, and after such amendments as the Convention should devise, the work should be submitted to the people for approval or rejection; and the man who is not willing to assist in this work to the best of his ability, but will hide his light under a bushel, whatever it may be, and not lend it to the reform and improvement of his government, is only endeavoring to nullify and make void a constitutional law, which must be executed; and every consideration of patriotism requires, that it shall be executed in good faith.

The people surely will hardly require such an agent for such a work, any more than they would commit the work of a hive to the drones. A convention, then, we are obliged to have; and the only concern with the people, at present, is what delegates they will elect. The fact is not to be disguised, that, notwithstanding the votes of some conspicuous republican members in favor of the measure, the great body of the republican leaders in the State have made this a strict party question, and that they design by some policy or other, to endeavor to elect a majority of members of the Convention in order to retrieve past defeats, and to make the appearance to the world that they are in the majority in North Carolina, and ready to co-operate as such, in the elections of 1876; and the dissatisfied Conservative who by indifference refuses to vote, or throws away his vote, but aids them in the desire, to the sacrifice of his principles and party organization, on which he habitually relies, for the promotion of the good of his Country. There is but one point of view in which the Convention may be regarded as at all a dangerous assembly; and that is, if this party should obtain a majority, and by a combination of the two elements aforesaid, the do-nothings and the mischief makers, and should run riot over the restrictions upon the Convention, assert that its powers are unlimited, and undertake to legislate at its will. They might thus establish whatever regulations might be deemed of advantage to their party in State or in national affairs, and provide for laying off districts for the election in the future of colored judges, or other officers, in order to secure party support; and occasion mischievous contention, and the most fearful results. This aspect of the matter, I commend to the consideration of those who propose to sit quietly down and let the affairs of the State take care of themselves. The emergency being upon us, voting for delegates of our own views is a necessary act of self defence. If we will not attempt to govern ourselves, there is a watchful opponent at hand, who will readily assume the office of governing us. However desirable it might be, that in the revision of a State Constitution all party considerations should be sunk, in the actual conditions of affairs, and from the spirit manifested by our opponents, the reliance of the friends of law, order, and reform must be mainly upon that party to which we are indebted, for the rescue of the Government from the Legislative control of those who, in their Constitutional Convention, and in the ensuing session of the Legislature, involved the State in thirty millions of dollars of new debt, in the most profuse expenditures for ordinary purposes, and in the sequel, attempted to subject our citizens to a military despotism; from which we were happily relieved by the Judiciary of the United States. It is, therefore, no ordinary election which lies before us, but one in which, whatever may have been our individual opinions as to calling a Convention, neutrality is likely to be as fatal as an abandonment of our principles.

As to the objects for which the Convention is called, and the specific amendments which should be made, they are too numerous to be set forth in this address. The work of the Convention can have no binding effect until it shall be approved by the people. When you come to pass upon that work, will be time for considering the proposed changes. Let me only remark, that a Constitution of government is, in our county, made for the people, not the people for the Government. That the present one in North Carolina was formed and adopted under circumstances, when the people of the State were under a constraint, which deprived them of that freedom of will which is necessary in providing a Government for themselves, and that in many particulars it may be greatly improved, and relieved of provisions now seen to be injurious; and that safety, economy, justice, and tranquility, may be greatly promoted by judicious amendments.

Should I be chosen one of your delegates,[2] I shall devote to the duties such faculties as I possess, and will take pleasure in laying before you, for your approval or rejection, such a constitution as shall result from the joint deliberations of the delegates of the whole State, and thus make some return for the many tokens of confidence I have received at your hands.

Your fellow-citizen,
Wm. A. Graham

Hillsboro',
July 17th., 1875.

[1]This was printed on a broadside. The address was widely published in the newspapers.
[2]Graham was elected but died before the convention met.

William Reynolds[1] *to William A. Graham* UNC

29 St. Paul Street,
Baltimore.
July 21st., 1875.

Some weeks ago, I learned from an article in the New York Herald, that you had delivered an address upon the Mecklenburg Declaration of Indpendence, which would shortly be printed. Will you be so good as to inform me whether it has yet been published, and if so, where I can obtain a copy? I have for some time past been preparing an historical sketch of the early Scotch-Irish and Scotch settlers in the U.S., which would, of course, be imcomplete without some account of the Resolutions of the people of Mecklenburg County. I believe I have examined all the other literature upon the subject, excepting your address; and by aiding me to get a sight of it you will greatly oblige,

Your Ob't Serv't,

[1]The letterhead indicates that William Reynolds was a lawyer whose office was located at 29 St. Paul Street, Baltimore.

William A. Graham to William A. Graham, Jr. A&H

Hillsboro
July 23rd 1875

Dear Wm

Your mother Augus. & I are to set off in the morning by the Bay route for Saratoga Springs where I am to meet the Board of Arbitors on the Myd. & Va. boundary—shall probably be detained there two weeks, and be absent from home probably three. I feel a little feeble for such a journey, and hope that by prudence on my part, it may be made beneficial. I have not been out in the crowds—my circular has been read at most of the gatherings. Turner, I hear, talks of the "Rings"[1] but within a day or two, has come down to the convention. There is not likely to be any other conservative candidate. Duke[2] goes to the gatherings and asks Turner some questions but makes no speech.

Sally & child are here. Geo. comes up each Saturday night. Sudie & her babe are also with us. They will both remain while we are gone. We all went to dine at John's yesterday on his birthday. He has gotten his Gas and Water works both into successful operation. Turner has gotten an injunction from Judge Kerr, against Jenkins & Hawkins[3] about exchange of bonds in Orange Ct. in the name of Harris[4] in Wake Co. but on so flimsy a case, made up by T., that it exposes Kerr to much criticism. Jas. was here, a few days since and will rebuild his House on the old foundation. Robt. with Joseph's Wm. passed here on way to Beaufort this morning. I do not hear much of the pending election; the radicals are said to have much money, and are making a great effort, but I do not hear of their gaining anywhere unless Turner's course shall [help] them in Wake—Alamance is also in danger from the problems of Parker.[5] Our little wheat crop has turned out very well and is housed & threshed—oats injured by rain, and in that swelled state very apt to injure or kill mules & horses.

P.S. My address will be "Congress Hall," Saratoga Springs.

---

[1]Josiah Turner was at this time so full of ideas about "rings," "conspiracies," and the like that at times his hand—or rather, his pen and tongue—seemed to be against every man.

[2]Washington Duke was a Republican candidate for the Constitutional Convention of 1875.

[3]Judge John Kerr, at Turner's instigation, issued an injunction prohibiting state treasurer David A. Jenkins from exchanging the mortgage bonds of the Raleigh and Augusta Airline Railroad for state bonds. The injunction appeared in the *Daily Sentinel* (Raleigh) on July 17, 1875.

[4]Probably this refers to James H. Harris.

[5]Parker was probably Edward S. Parker of Alamance County.

Samuel F. Phillips to Susan Washington Graham A&H

Washington D.C.
31st July 1875

Mrs. Graham

Having been asked to name a lady in North Carolina to preside over a proposed organization of the ladies of the States in the interest of the Centennial celebration at Philadelphia next year, I have taken the liberty of naming you.

I trust that you will go far to obliterate all remains of ill temper growing out of recent events.

It would be desirable that North Carolina shall take her part in this festival. It is now high time that her people shall be apprized of what is going on by way of preparation. This important part will in great measure be devolved upon the organization of which I now speak.

Within a few days you will receive a note from Mrs. Gillespie[1] of Philadelphia, to whom I write today, & she will no doubt not decline this position. The labor attending it will no doubt be assumed by associates, whose choice will be left entirely to yourself.

The Celebration of 1876 can hardly be other than a magnificent success. The work already done at Fairmount Park is *amazing*, & upon a scale proportioned to the dignity of the occasion & of the Government. . . . Mrs. Gillespie is a descendant of Dr. Franklin, a lady of great worth & high position in Philadelphia,—who has charge of the "Women's" department of the Exposition.

I renew the expression of my hearty wish that you will countenance this attempt to interest North Carolina in the approaching "Centennial".

I remain, with every great Respect,

Your Obedient Servant

[1]Mrs. Elizabeth Duane Gillespie (1821-1901) was the great-granddaughter of Benjamin Franklin. She was matron of a Philadelphia hospital during the Civil War. She organized the Women's Committee of the Centennial of 1876. This committee was very successful in raising money nationally and built an exhibition hall to display women's activities from around the world. The committee introduced kindergarten to the United States. In 1901 Gillespie published her memoirs, entitled *A Book of Remembrance*. Gertrude B. Biddle and Sarah D. Lowrie (eds.), *Notable Women of Pennsylvania* (Philadelphia: University of Pennsylvania Press, 1942), 159-160.

George W. Graham to Susan Washington Graham A&H
[Telegram]

5 August 1875

Tincture digitalis half ounce give Father ten drops thrice daily look for letter Saturday.

Augustus W. Graham to George W. Graham or Walter Clark [Telegram] A&H

August 10, 1875

Father is very ill. Will telegraph again in morning.[1]

[1]Graham died August 11, 1875, at Saratoga Springs.

Robert R. Bridgers[1] *to Susan Washington Graham* A&H

Wilmington, N.C.
Aug. 11, 1875

Dear Madam

It is with regret and sorrow I hear of the death of your Husband Gov Graham—a great and good man.

It is a calamity to our State, an event over which our country will weep.

I do most sincerely sympathize with you in your affliction. I wish I had it in my power to soften the anguish of your grief; which can only be done by the Giver of all good.

If I can in any way serve you it will afford me a pleasure to do so.

[1]Robert Rufus Bridgers (1819-1888), of Edgecombe County, graduated from the University of North Carolina first in the class of 1841. He immediately became a lawyer and achieved distinction through his ability and diligence. A staunch Democrat, he served in the state legislature as a commoner in 1844 and from 1856 to 1861. Although he was not a fervent secessionist, Bridgers favored a convention in 1861, expecting that secession would result. He was a member of the Confederate Congress, 1862-1865, and supported the Davis administration to the extent his constituents would sustain.

Bridgers became a highly successful businessman, manufacturer, and railroad builder. He had organized and developed a Tarboro bank, of which he became president in 1851. During the 1850s he acquired large landholdings, which he operated as a highly productive plantation. In 1860 he became a director of the Wilmington and Weldon Railroad, a company he had improved significantly by promoting a Tarboro link. He vainly urged both the railroad and the Confederate government to produce large quantities of cotton for export so as to establish southern credit abroad. During the war he revamped facilities for the mining and manufacture of iron in Lincoln and adjacent counties (the "High Shoals property"). These ironworks supplied nails and plows to Carolina farmers. The facility allegedly was the second largest such producer in the Confederacy.

When the Wilmington and Weldon resumed operations in the fall of 1865, Bridgers was elected president. For the next twenty-three years, thirteen of which he was also general superintendent, he sought to improve and expand the line that was to be the Atlantic Coast Line Railroad. *DAB*, III, 33-34.

John Hill Wheeler to Susan Washington Graham UNC

Washington City
11th. Aug. 1875

My esteemed Mrs. Graham

I trust that it will not be obstrusive in me, to yeild to the feeling that overwhelms my heart, and offer to you my Sincere Sympathy with you, in the death of your distinguished husband.

Altho' I have known him for years, yet it has been my fortune, within the last few months to have seen much of him. In the meetings of the Historical Society at Raleigh; and at the Centennial at Charlotte; and very recently to have received a long and kind letter from him. Those sterling qualities of the head and heart which he had, always receiving my respect, had heightened into admiration, and almost veneration. I thought that I saw, then, that disease was making rapid ravages on his health; and I felt that he would soon, as we all must sooner or later, travel to that

"... Undiscovered country
From whose bourne no traveller returns."[1]

But the cheering consolation is left to us, that our loss is his gain; that he has exchanged a world of suffering and sorrow, for an eternity of joy and happiness; and if any earthly comfort can assuage your grief it is in the assurance that your sorrows are sympathized by thousands of our people in every section of our great Republic; the kindly memories of his exemplary life and the ennobling virtues of his exalted character will be cherished by them with affectionate gratitude. The enclosed, from the morning paper of this City shows the deep sorrow that prevades this whole community, and be assured that none feel this severe bereavement more deeply or more sincerely than

Very respectfully & truly
Your ob servt

---

[1]*Hamlet*, act 3, scene 1, lines 79-80.

Kate B. Washington to Susan Washington Graham A&H

Schenectady
August 12th 1875

My dear Aunt Susan-

I do not know what to say—my heart is so full. It seems so hard, but then it must all be for the best, or God would not have taken away dear Uncle Graham.

We did our very best to see you this morning, but things seemed to be against us, and my heart was heavier than ever on my way home.

If we had only known you were going to take the Troy train instead of the Albany, we would not have missed you, but your train passed right through Balston, where we were waiting. If the Western train had not been behind hand, we would have met you at Saratoga.

Yesterday morning we felt so much encouraged from your letter, that we hoped Uncle Graham would soon be well enough for you to come and see us, and now we are so sorry we waited, and did not go over to Saratoga, but we have had a great deal of rain, and something has prevented every time we thought of going.

How glad I am I saw you both in New York last October! And I hope I will see you and all my cousins again some time. I wish we either lived nearer to you, or you lived nearer to us.

My dear father's birthday was on the 31st of July, if he had lived, he would have been 72 years old. I often wonder why he was taken away so early, when he was so useful, so beloved and respected. Now Uncle Graham sees him, and I hope I will some day.

Please give ever so much love to Aunt Eliza, Cousin Augustus Graham and all my other cousins—and reserve a very large share for yourself, and always believe me

Your loving niece

Proceedings of the North Carolina Bar[1]

Memorandum.
Proceedings of the Bar and the Court upon the Death of
Hon. William A. Graham.

At a meeting of the members of the Bar, held in the rooms of the Supreme Court to-day (12 August, 1875), for the purpose of expressing their sense of sorrow on account of the death of the late Hon. William A. Graham, on motion, the Hon. Bartholomew F. Moore was called to the chair, and Charles M. Busbee, Esq., appointed secretary.

On motion, Hon. William H. Battle, Hon. William B. Rodman, and Hon. A. S. Merrimon were appointed a committee to draft suitable resolutions expressive of the sense of the meeting.

The committee reported the following resolutions: (See the resolutions presented to the Court by Attorney-General Hargrove).[2]

Judge Battle, in submitting the resolutions, referred in appropriate terms to the unsullied record of the deceased as a lawyer; and after remarks by George H. Snow,[3] Esq., Chief Justice R. M. Pearson, R. C. Badger, Esq., S. A. Ashe,[4] Esq., D. M. Carter, Esq., Judge E. G. Reade, Hon. W. N. H. Smith, and Judge G. W. Brooks, the resolutions were unanimously adopted.

On motion, the Attorney-General was requested to present the resolutions to the Supreme Court on 13 August, at 12 o'clock M.

On motion, it was resolved that the members of the legal profession assemble in the Supreme Court room at 3:30 to-morrow afternoon for the purpose of receiving the remains of Governor Graham at the gate of the Capitol.

B. F. Moore, *Chairman.*
C. M. Busbee, *Secretary.*

[1]74 N.C. 603 (1876).

[2]Tazewell Lee Hargrove (1830-1889), of Granville County, was a graduate of Randolph-Macon College. He was a lieutenant in the Fourth North Carolina Regiment during the Civil War and for a time was a prisoner at Johnson's Island. A Democrat before the war, Hargrove became Republican afterward. He was a member of the state House of Representatives, 1870-1872, and attorney general, 1873-1876. Cheney, *North Carolina Government*, 324, 326, 386, 427, 440n, 451; Clark, *Histories of the North Carolina Regiments*, II, 335, III, 22, 24, IV, 707, 721.

[3]George Haywood Snow (1845-1893), a native of Hyde County, was listed as a resident of Wake County when he enlisted in the Confederate army in 1863 at the age of eighteen. He attained the rank of first lieutenant in Company H, Thirty-third Regiment, in 1864. Snow was captured near Petersburg in April, 1865; on June 19 he was released after taking the oath of allegiance. Grady Lee Ernest Carroll, *They Lived in Raleigh* (Raleigh: Southeastern Copy Center, 1979), 165; Manarin and Jordan, *North Carolina Troops*, IX, 160, 209.

[4]Samuel A'Court Ashe (1840-1938), of Raleigh, was born in New Hanover County and grew up at Rocky Point. After extensive preparatory training, he was appointed to Annapolis. He rose to be second in his class but resigned after three years to study law. During the Civil War Ashe served the Confederate forces as a captain and as an engineer. After the war he was a member of the state House of Representatives, 1870-1871. At this point he moved to Raleigh and established a law practice. In 1874 Ashe was editor of the *Evening Crescent*. In 1879 he purchased the Raleigh *Observer*, which he rejuvenated and published until it was merged with the Raleigh *Daily News* and became the *News and Observer*. After 1893 Ashe was no longer associated with the paper. For thirty years he served as clerk of the federal district court at Raleigh. He was a prolific writer and published many historical volumes, including *Biographical History of North Carolina* and *Cyclopedia of Eminent and Representative Men of the Carolinas of the Nineteenth Century*. Powell, *DNCB*, I, 55.

Proceedings in the Supreme Court[1] 13 August [1875]

The Court met: Present, Chief Justice Pearson, and Justices Reade, Rodman, Settle and Bynum.

Attorney-General T. L. Hargrove arose and addressed the Court as follows:

"May It Please Your Honors: The death of William Alexander Graham, one of North Carolina's most honorable, patriotic, and distinguished sons, was the occasion of a meeting of members of the Bar of the State on yesterday. That meeting unanimously adopted these resolves, and requested that I should on to-day present them to this Court, and move that your Honors order them to be entered upon your records. I now make that motion. And in performing this solemn duty, it may not be improper for me to say, that I have been acquainted with the deceased, he having practised in my native county since my earliest recollection of the Bar. I have been associated with him in the trial of causes, and have appeared on opposite sides to him. He was universally respected as a faithful counselor to his clients, an honorable and high-toned gentleman, an able, learned and successful lawyer. But his great and good example as a man, a lawyer, and a statesman, is too well known to all North Carolina, and the whole Nation, to need that I should declare his excellencies. I sincerely concur in the sentiments of these resolutions, and join in the general sorrow for his loss."

Resolutions.

The members of the legal profession assembled for the purpose of expressing their esteem and affection for the Hon. William A. Graham, and their sense of the loss which they, in common with the whole State, have sustained by his death, do resolve:

1. *Resolved,* That we find in the Hon. William Alexander Graham, a bright example of all the virtues of a private citizen, as well as an illustration of the able and faithful performance of all the duties of professional and official life.

2. *Resolved,* That as a member of the Bar he was diligent and careful in the preparation of his causes, able and skillful in an argument, kind and considerate to his fellow-members, and courteous and respectful to the Court.

3. *Rosolved,* That as a public officer, whether of his own State or the United States, he was always equal to the occasion, filling the many high offices to which he was called with unswerving fidelity and distinguished ability.

4. *Resolved,* That as a proper tribute of respect to our deceased brother, whom many of us loved, and all respected, it is requested that these resolutions be presented to the Supreme Court, with a request that they may be entered upon the minutes of the Court.

5. *Resolved,* That a copy of these resolutions be sent to the family of the deceased by the chairman.

6. *Resolved,* That a copy of the proceedings of this meeting be furnished for publication in all the city papers.

7. *Resolved,* That the chairman be requested, at his convenience, to select a member of the Bar to deliver an address upon the life and character of our deceased brother.

Chief Justice Pearson responded as follows:

"The Associate Justices concur with me in expressing the opinion that we all heartily approve of the resolutions passed at the meeting of the members of the legal profession, and it is ordered that the resolutions be entered upon the records of this Court.

"William A. Graham was a great man. After, by his prudence, good conduct, application and talents, acquiring a reputation at home, he, by the same means, acquired a national reputation, of which his native State has a right to be proud.

"The Reporter of the Court will put all of the proceedings in an appendix to the Reports."

---

[1]74 N.C. 603 (1876).

Samuel F. Phillips to John W. Graham A&H

Washington, D.C.
13th August 1875

My dear Sir

The absence of the Attorney General from Washington has prevented me from entertaining the thought which at once presented itself—that I would go down to Hillsboro and attend your Father's funeral.

I much regret my inability to pay this mark of respect to a man whose worth & public service I have always admired, & whose memory I should cherish with an unqualified veneration.

I do not abandon some difference of opinion with Governor Graham or forget the names & careers of his great contemporaries, when I say that he was altogether the wisest man of our time in North Carolina. He possessed in full measure that royal faculty so rarely met—judgment. Of all the men every personally known to me he was by all odds the best fitted & finished for the life of a statesman.

I have for the last two days thought of nothing so much as the passages in my life in which I have met him, and of those activities & words, & that eminent port & gesture, which at various times so much impressed me, & were so readily re[illegible].

It would be impertinent in me to assume to offer consolation to any one immediately concerned in this great loss, but I am so far associated to your sorrow as to feel great pain in giving up the hope of ever again seeing your illustrious Father.

With great Regard

George Washington[1] *to Susan Washington Graham* A&H

Navesink, New Jersey
Aug 13/75

My Dear Sister:

I cannot describe to you the shock thrown over us all by a letter yesterday from Gus Knox[2] telling us of your great and sudden bereavement. I had seen by the papers of the week before of Mr. Graham being at Saratoga, and the occasion which carried him there—and also mention of the courtesies extended by Gov. Tilden.[3] I had heard too from some one, that his health had improved lately, and I fancied him in stronger health than when I had last seen him. How sudden and unlooked for then was the tidings of his death.

Would that I could say something, my dear Sister, that could give the least ray of consolation in your great affliction. I can only offer my deep and heart-felt sympathy. And it is a sympathy that mingles with the sympathy of many. And tho' for that, the loss to you can be only so much the greater, yet there must be consolation in the assurance that a whole people will mourn with you the loss of one so good and great. God bless and keep you, my dear Sister, and temper your affliction with His holy spirit.

I feel it impossible to write. Words seem but a mockery.

---

[1]George Washington (1818-1894), a brother of Mrs. Graham, lived at various times in North Carolina and in Florida. Clark, "Washington Descendants."

[2]Dr. Augustus W. Knox, nephew of Mrs. Graham.

[3]Samuel Jones Tilden (1814-1886) was governor of New York, 1875-1877. He distinguished himself through his untiring efforts to reform and reorganize the politics of both the state of New York and New York City. Tilden was an unsuccessful candidate for the presidency in 1876, losing to Rutherford B. Hayes. *CDAB*, 1068-1069.

Zebulon B. Vance to Susan Washington Graham A&H

Hillsboro
Aug 14th [1875]

Dear Madam

I came down this morning to attend the funeral of Gov Graham, being incorrectly informed that it would take place today. I regret exceedingly that I am compelled to return tonight in order to meet an engagement I have with the Southern Historical Society on the 18th at the White Sulphur Springs.

I intrude this note on you as well to explain my absence tomorrow as to assure you of my sincere participation in the universal sorrow which pervades North Carolina in a loss which is no less hers than yours. And I trust, with equal sincerity, that your grief will find consolation in the contemplation of his exalted life and character and in the remarkable exhibition of public esteem which the death of Gov Graham has everywhere excited.

With sentiments of profoundest regard I am, Dear Madam,

Most respectfully Yr Obt Svt

Newspaper Clippings[1] UNC

The Lamented Graham:
Eulogies of the Press

Richmond Dispatch: Governor Graham was always a thorough Conservative. In late years he has been more quiet than was customary even with him, prudent and circumspect as he always was. He was disinclined to impulsive State rights politics, and was opposed to secession. He took sides with North Carolina after she seceded. He was a man of gentle disposition and polished manners. His judgment was well balanced. He was a good lawyer, and a most respectable statesman, with a diplomatic turn. What is better, we can say with emphasis of Governor Graham that he was a man of stainless character and earnest patriotism. He was one of a class of men whose value to the State and society can hardly be too highly estimated.

Richmond Whig: He was a man of marked ability, a gentleman of exalted worth, and a sterling patriot when patriotism meant more than it means now.

In the death of Governor Graham the country loses a distinguished statesman, the South loses a loving son, and North Carolina loses a big brain and a faithful heart, she may well mourn and remember forever.

Wilmington Journal: Governor Graham commanded the confidence and respect of the people of North Carolina in greater degree than was ever before bestowed on any man. All of honor that she had, all of trust that she had, all of confidence that she had, North Carolina lavished upon this her favorite son.

From one end of the State to the other, the eyes of good men everywhere were turned to him in the great crisis that is now upon us. In the east and in the west, as well as in the centre, men looked to him to take the lead in the approaching convention, perhaps a more important body than has ever assembled in North Carolina.

Goldsboro Messenger: Only last week he was elected to the constitutional convention from Orange by 380 majority, and no man on the conservative side was more prominently mentioned in connection with the Presidency of the convention than he. The death of such a man in ordinary times would be felt and regretted by all, and for this to occur at a time like the present, when his talents and statesmanship are so much needed, and when the vacancy his death has created in the convention is likely to prove detrimental to the State, is a great calamity upon our State and people.

Norfolk Virginian: Our sister State is called upon to mourn the loss of another of her most distinguished sons, but she is not alone in her grief; for Wm. A. Graham was known throughout the length and breadth of the land, and the nation claims him as a part of its glorious heritage. Gov. Graham was pre-eminently distinguished for the dignity and purity of his character, his lofty patriotism, his broad views and comprehensive statesmanship, his elegant accomplishments and sterling integrity. Gov. Graham belonged to the ancient *regime* of gentlemen and politicians, and his loss at this time will be especially deplored. He was the contemporary of Manly, Iredell, Badger, Bragg, and other illustrious sons of the noble Old North State, whose names make up a State and national roll of honor of which she and the nation may be well proud.

Charlotte Observer: He was a great man. He had none of that fiery impetuosity so common among Southern statesmen; but he was a clear-headed, collected, cultivated, dignified gentleman of the Edward Everett and Millard Fillmore school. Party spirit may have made Gov. Graham a few enemies, but no North Carolinian ever had the confidence of the white masses of the State to a greater extent.

The Baltimore Sun says: Gov. Graham was at Saratoga as one of the arbitrators of the disputed boundary between Maryland and Virginia. The testimony on both sides was called last week, and considerable progress had been made in the argument. His untimely death will, it is feared, cause another probably long postponement of the settlement of this vexed question.

Salisbury Watchman: A man eminent for virtue, honor, wisdom, and patriotism is gone.

Raleigh, N.C.
Friday, August 13th. 1875.

The Late Ex-Gov. Graham.[2]

Of this statesman and noble gentleman there will be much written and said of his public life, his devotion to the interests of our country, his firm integrity, and his strength and purity of soul. But as one who knew and loved him at home, I would write of his great and noble heart, his tender sympathies, his unchanging kindness and devotion as a friend, his stately but most cordial and generous courtesy as a host, and, in his family, his thoughtful, gentle and affectionate interest in each individual member. His greatness was felt and acknowledged, not only in matters of State and importance, but in little things, and behind the scenes. In the true politeness which ever gave the preference to others, the kindly smile, the thoughtful attention to seemingly small matters of etiquette, which those who are only great in their own esteem would consider beneath their notice. Refinement without fastidiousness, elegance without reproach, and in his death we, his friends, the church, the community in which he lived, the State, the nation, and even the world, have sustained a loss irreparable. We bow in sorrowful and humble submission to the will of Him before whom the great of the earth are even as the least, her mightiest and noblest sons, but the creatures of His hand. May He comfort us in this great bereavement, and give to our country and our hearts another Graham, to be even half as good, as great, as noble and true, and as much beloved as he.

B. R. S. A.
Bellevue, N.C.

The Lamented Dead![3]
A Day of Mourning in Raleigh!

The Heads of the State Department
Pay Homage to the Memory of the Great Statesman.

Arrival of the Corpse in Raleigh!
The Procession and Scenes at the State House!

The special train on the Raleigh & Gaston Railroad with the committee to receive the remains of Ex-Gov. Graham, left the city at 4 o'clock yesterday morning, and arrived at Weldon at 10 o'clock. At that place our committee ascertained that the citizens of Weldon had had a public meeting the night previous and appointed a committee to go forward at once to the Virginia line and receive in the name of the State the remains.

The Weldon Meeting.

The following resolutions were passed at the public meeting held in Literary Hall, Weldon, on the evening of the 12th. inst:

Whereas, it has pleased Almighty God, in the mysterious working of his Providence, to take from us, Honorable William Alexander Graham, who died in Saratoga, New York, on Wednesday, the 11th. inst., therefore,

Resolved, That in him we recognize one who has led an unblemished public and private life and one which has been alike honorable to himself and his State.

Resolved, That in his death North Carolina has lost an able son, a faithful public servant and wise counsellor.

Resolved, That we deeply sympathize with the family of the honored dead in their sad affliction.

Resolved, That our places of business be closed to-morrow from half past nine a.m., to the departure of the car bearing the remains of the deceased.

Resolved, That a committee of our citizens be appointed to meet the remains of the deceased at Garysburg and escort them to the Raleigh car, at this place.

Resolved, That these resolutions be published in the *Roanoke News* and Raleigh News, and that a copy be forwarded the family of the deceased.

L. F. Larkin, W. A. Daniel,
T. N. White, R. D. Edwards,
A. J. Burton, B. W. Spelman,
R. W. Brown, T. A. Clark
Committee.

During the forenoon the business Committee appointed by the Mayor and Chairman of the citizen's meeting were busily engaged.

Preparing for the Reception

of the remains of the illustrious deceased. Metropolitan Hall was appropriately draped in mourning, as also the Armory of the Raleigh Light Infantry and Raleigh Light Artillery, of both of which Companies the deceased was an honorary member.

The catafalque, beautifully decorated with flowers and evergreens, was placed in the rotunda of the Capitol. The halls leading to the Rotunda were draped in mourning, on the doors of the Executive and State offices were hung long badges of crape, and the general scene was solemn and impressive.

At 12 o'clock, a

Meeting of the Heads of the State Department

was called by the order of Gov. Brogden, and the following proceedings transpired:

A meeting of the Heads of Department of the State Government and subordinate offices was held in the Executive office to-day at 9 ½ o'clock, to take action concerning the death of Hon. William A. Graham, Ex-Governor of the State, and make preparation for the reception of the remains this afternoon at the Capitol.

There were present His Excellency, C. H. Brogden, Governor; W. H. Howerton,[4] Secretary of State; John Reilly,[5] Auditor; D. A. Jenkins,[6] Treasurer of State; T. L. Hargrove, Attorney General; J. B. Neathery,[7] Private Secretary to Governor; D. W. Bain,[8] Chief Clerk of the Treasury Department.

On motion of Attorney General Hargrove, Governor Brogden was appointed Chairman, and D. W. Bain, Secretary.

The following resolutions, which were prepared on motion of Treasurer Jenkins, were submitted and unanimously adopted:

Whereas, we, the officers of the State Executive Department have received information of the death of the late Hon. W. A. Graham at Saratoga Springs, in the State of New York, on the 11th. inst., and that his remains will arrive at Raleigh this day 2 o'clock p.m., on their way to their last resting place at his late residence at Hillsboro, and whereas, we desire to testify our sincere respect for the spotless life and character and the long and faithful public services of that eminent and distinguished patriot and statesman; Therefore:

Resolved, That we deplore the loss the State has sustained by the death of Hon. W. A. Graham, and that as a tribute of our respect for his memory we will put the State Capitol in mourning and prepare a suitable catafalque for the mortal remains of the honored dead to rest upon while lying in state in the rotunda of the Capitol.

Resolved, That the State House bell be tolled while the funeral procession is moving to and from this place.

Resolved, That the United States officer now in command at Camp Russell, at Raleigh, be respectfully invited to unite with the troops under his command, with the Raleigh Military companies as an escort of honor to the remains of Hon. Wm. A. Graham.

Resolved, That a copy of these resolutions be furnished for publications in the newspapers of Raleigh, and that a copy of the same be forwarded to the family of the deceased.

On motion of Attorney General Hargrove, Mr. J. B. Neathery was appointed a committee to act with other committees of the Bar, and citizens, in making suitable preparations for the reception of the remains.

In view of the distinguished Federal positions formerly held by the deceased, a motion was unanimously adopted requesting the commandant of Camp Russell, United States troops in this city, to participate in the demonstration of respect on the arrival of the remains.

The Western train at 8 ¼ o'clock brought to the city committees from the towns of Salisbury, Greensboro, Hillsboro, and Durham, appointed at public meetings in each place as guards of honor to meet the remains in this place and escort them to Hillsboro. We were unable to get the names of the

Greensboro and Salisbury committees, but recognized among the Greensboro committee Col. J. T. Morehead, Jo. W. Glenn, and Wm. K. Odell, associate editor of the *Central Protestant.*

Hillsboro Committee.

Dr. P. Jones, Col. T. Ruffin, Thomas Webb, James Webb, J. B. G. Roulhac, W. J. Exum, Thomas R. Cain, James Parker, J. R. Gattis, J. M. Blackwood, Josiah Turner, F. A. Nash, Jr., Jesse Hedgepeth, C. E. Parrish, John Jordan, Benj. J. Cameron, John Cheek, J. W. Corbin, M. Adams, W. N. Anderson.

The Durham Committee

was composed of the following gentlemen:

John Watson, D. C. Parish, Dr. Durham, William Angier, Robert Lea, Benj. Duke, Wm. Lyon, M. C. Carlton, R. E. Lyon, Elijah Lyon, W. K. Styron, Dr. Thomas, M. C. Herndon, Calvin O'Brien, W. S. Roulhac, Monroe White, Capt. J. F. Freeland.

The committees from both Hillsboro and Orange proceeded to Henderson, where they met the remains in charge of the Raleigh committee, and returned on the special train to this city.

Reception in the City.

The train arrived promptly at 2 o'clock. Hundreds of citizens on foot and a large number of vehicles crowded the avenues leading to the depot. The Raleigh Light Infantry, The United States Troops from Camp Russell, and the Raleigh Light Artillery, all in uniform, were drawn up in line awaiting the reception of the body. We never witnessed a more intense feeling, and one so general that pervaded the vast assemblage at the depot as the corpse was being removed from the cars to the hearse. The rush even to see the casket containing the body had to be checked by the police.

The Procession through the City.

The casket being placed in the hearse, the procession moved via Cabarrus and Fayetteville streets to the Capitol in the following order, Citizen's Cornet Band, Raleigh Light Infantry, Battalion U.S. troops, Raleigh Light Artillery, hearse with pall-bearers, Orange delegation, Wake delegation, citizens in carriages, citizens on foot. At the south gate of the Capitol the remains were received by the Raleigh committee, and taken to the catafalque in the rotunda of the Capitol. Guards from the several Military organizations were placed at the doors to prevent a rush from the hundreds of people in the park who were anxious to view for the last time the manly form of our lamented statesman. By this means the people filed in by each passage, and quietly retired without the slightest confusion.

The Appearance of the Body.

The body was encased in a beautiful but neat metalic casket, covered with black cloth and silver mounted. A french plate glass top exposed half of the body to view. A silver plate on the casket contained the plain inscription:

Wm. A. Graham,
Died Aug. 11th, 1875.
Aged 71 years.

We never witnessed a more natural looking corpse; just as he appeared in life, with only the appearance of having fallen into a tranquil, quiet sleep.

For the few hours the remains were lying in state, the throng of visitors never ceased, and even after viewing the body, the grief stricken citizens remained in the park to see the last of the honored dead.

The Departure.

At 4 ½ o'clock, the procession reformed at the East door of the Capitol, in the same order as before, preceded by the Citizen's Cornet, and the Garrison Band, each playing alternately, moved down Fayetteville, and thence by Cabarrus street to the Central Depot. A special train provided for the occasion carried the remains to Hillsborough, where they will be interred on Sunday, after regular funeral services, at 12 o'clock. The Raleigh Light Infantry acting as the Guard of Honor accompanied the body to Hillsborough.

The following members of the family accompanied the remains: Mrs. Graham, wife of the deceased; his sons, Maj. W. A. Graham, of Lincoln, Capt. Jas. A. Graham, of Alamance, A. W. Graham, Esq., of Orange, Col. Walter Clark, (son-in-law) of this city, and Dr. A. W. Knox of New York, (a nephew of Mrs. Graham.)

This has been one of the saddest days known in the history of our city. Every one seemed to feel and fully appreciate the irreparable loss we had sustained in the death of this great and good man, and everybody turned out to do him reverence.

As before stated, his funeral will take place at Hillsborough Sunday, we suppose at the Presbyterian Church, of which he was a member.

We suppose there will be a special train from this city on the occasion, but as yet we have no information to that effect.

---

[1]The transcriptions are from clippings in the Graham papers. The deep distress of the people of North Carolina showed not only in the press but also in correspondence. Cornelia P. Spencer, on August 23, 1875, wrote Mrs. David L. Swain: "Gov. Graham died on the anniversary of the day on which Gov. Swain received his death blow. We were talking of Gov. Swain that day, little thinking that his friend had joined him then. We had the news that evening. . . . Brother C[harles Phillips] said at the public meeting, held here next day, that Gov. Graham, standing at the head of Go. Swain's coffin, said '*North Carolina will not soon look upon his like again.*' And now we all say it of Graham himself. Bro. Sam[uel F. Phillips] says he was worth a hundred dozen of any public man he leaves behind in N.C. The mourning for him is universal."

[2]The newspaper in which this article appeared has not been identified, nor has the author, "B. R. S. A."

[3]This article was published in the Raleigh *Daily News*, August 14, 1875.

[4]William H. Howerton (b. 1830) was a captain in Company H of the Fifty-seventh Regiment when it was formed July 4, 1862. A native of Rowan County, Howerton was elected secretary of state on the Republican ticket and served in that office, 1873-1877. Cheney, *North Carolina Government*, 425, 434n; Rumple, *Rowan County*, 405.

[5]John Reilly of Cumberland County was state auditor, 1873-1877. He also served as mayor of Fayetteville and as a county commissioner. Cheney, *North Carolina Government*, 425; Oates, *Story of Fayetteville*, 240, 242, 278, 303-304, 316.

[6]David A. Jenkins (1822-1886), of Gaston County, was an antisecessionist Whig who turned to the Republican party after the Civil War. He was a member of the House of Commons, 1865-1867, and state treasurer, 1868-1877. *Cyclopedia of Eminent Men*, II, 379-380.

[7]John B. Neathery.

[8]Donald W. Bain (1841-1892), of Raleigh, was a clerk in the state comptroller's office and then chief clerk in the treasurer's (1865-1885). A widely known and highly respected citizen, he was elected state treasurer as a Democrat and served from 1885 until his death. Bain was active in church and civic affairs and was a leader of the Masonic Order in North Carolina. Powell, *DNCB*, I, 86-87.

William A. Graham, Jr., to Julia Lane Graham A&H

Hillsboro, N.C.
August 14th, 1875

My dear wife,

I will write you a short letter this evening altho I feel so sad that I am almost undone. I hope you received my two postals of yesterday. We reached here about dark yesterday evening and the funeral will take place tomorrow at 11 from the Presbyterian Church. Cousins Sophie, Alice, & Julia and Aunt Eliza and Bettie are here. Gus Knox came on from New York with mother and Gus.

The body has been in the parlor all day and many persons have come to take a last look at Him they loved to honor. . . .

It is uncertain about my getting home before Thursday. Do take care of yourself and go to see the Moore's if you are lonely. All send love, and express many regrets that you were not able to come.

Good bye dear. Kiss the children for me. I will give you a full account of everything when I come. Am too sad to write.

Yr devoted & afflicted husband,

John C. Washington[1] *to Susan Washington Graham* A&H

West Troy NY
Augt 15/75

My dear Susan

I cannot tell you with what distress I learned on the 13th while at Georges of the death of Mr. Graham at Saratoga.

It is a sad calamity to us all, but far, very far greater to you.

I wish very much I had been here, so that I could have gone to you in a few hours after hearing of his illness. I would then have had the comfort at least of being with him again.

I have always admired Mr. Graham so much that I feel his death very keenly; . . . I cannot find words for my sympathy with you all there.

We are now very few of us left and we are rarely together.

I feel very anxious about you after all you have undergone and hope sister Eliza will write me how you are.

Affectionately
Your brother

---

[1]John Cobb Washington (1801-1889), of Kinston, was a brother of Susan Washington Graham. Clark, "Washington Descendants."

William P. Whyte to Augustus W. Graham UNC

Baltimore,
Aug 16, 1875

My dear young friend

I avail myself of the first moment, after my return home, to express, though feebly, my great appreciation of your kindness in sending me, as a memento of your noble father, a copy of his Mecklenburg Address.

That I shall ever prize it as I shall always cherish his memory you need not to be assured. Knowing him formerly only as a public man of undoubted patriotism and of elevated character, it was not until I met him in the Boundary case, that I was able to estimate his worth and to understand the self-sacrificing spirit, which prompted him to the discharge of public service.

No words, that can be uttered, will soothe, in any measure, the sorrow of your household, but if loving sympathy can, in the slightest degree assuage it, you may be sure of the sincere feeling of many hearts for you in your sore bereavement.

I hope the short acquaintance we have had, so agreeable to me, may ripen into a lasting friendship.

With my deepest condolence
I am truly yours,

P.S. Mrs. Whyte asks the privilege to be very affectionately remembered to your mother.

C. A. Lewis[1] to Susan Washington Graham A&H

Wake Forest College
Aug 18th 1875

Dear Mrs. Graham

Since I heard of your sore bereavement my thoughts have been with you a great deal, & I've been waiting for your surroundings to become more quiet before writing to assure you of my sincerest sympathy with you in this time of great sorrow, few know better than I the unutterable sorrow of a bereaved wife. You my dear friend have a Friend to go to, & be sheltered in His loving arms, & can claim Him at once as your Husband & God, & a Father to your fatherless children. I had no such strong hold in my times of trouble, had to bear the terrible burden all alone for months without that sustaining grace which has been promised to Gods children.

You have been more blessed in your life than most women, were wiser than many in the choice of a life companion, have been spared to each other a long & happy life, & now that he is taken from you, your children are left you, & I've no doubt will do all in their power to make you happy, & now too, you have a new claim to your heavenly Fathers love, & have another evidence of being his child.

Well it is that the Nation & State that have lost such a man may mourn, for we need many such in our present condition, we have none left to take his place, for nearly all our public men now seek their own & not their country's good. May God prepare your sons to take his place, I could ask no greater earthly boon for them.

Well I know my dear friend how pleasant sympathy is, & though it can not relieve our grief, it is a comfort to us to know that our friends feel for us. I remember you said to me after the death of your little babe,[2] the first you lost, that you thought no sorrow could be greater than the loss of a babe, I thought, & believe said to you at the time, if you lost your husband you would think differently. May God comfort you, & draw you very lovingly to Himself & shelter you under his wing & enable [you] to say & feel "Thy will O God be done."

Anna joins me in much love & sympathy to you, & all your dear children.

Your loving Sympathizing friend

---

[1]Almost certainly Mrs. Catherine A. Lewis, the widow of Dr. John W. Lewis, who had been Mrs. Graham's friend since the 1840s. Both women were active Baptists in Raleigh during the time William A. Graham was governor. *North Carolina Baptist Historical Papers* (Raleigh: Edwards and Broughton, 3 volumes, 1896-1900), I, 256-258.

[2]Alfred Octavius Graham (1853-1854). Clark, "Graham Descendants."

E. J. Hale to Augustus W. Graham A&H

New York,
Aug 20, 1875

. . . .

I cannot express to you the regret, the deep distress, I experienced at the death of your excellent Father. He was in my mind the representative man of the State in its better days, the type of all that was noble in her people. He leaves no man approaching to him in all good qualities. To me his loss is another warning. He was one of the very few of my old contemporaries that was left.

I have been much grafified at the unexampled honors paid his remains. In honoring him the people of N.C. exalted themselves.

I am glad that Mrs. Hale had it in her power to be of service & comfort to your mother, & will forward to her your letter.

Resolutions of the University of North Carolina Board of Trustees[1]

[August 31, 1875]

Resolved:

1st. That the Board of Trustees of the University of North Carolina have received the official announcement of the death of their honored colleague Hon. William A. Graham with the most profound sense of the irreparable loss which the State and the University have sustained in his decease.[2]

2nd. That the untiring zeal and great liberality with which Gov. Graham devoted his efficient labors to the service of the University, during a long life, and especially to its revival in late years, entitle his memory to be enshrined in the hearts of all who love the University and the cause of higher education in North Carolina; and the University will gratefully preserve the memory of his illustrious character as a patriot and statesman, and his high devotion to, and his affection for his *Alma Mater* amongst its most cherished treasures.

---

[1]From the Minutes of the Board of Trustees, University of North Carolina, August 31, 1875.

[2]Graham served the university as trustee from 1834 to 1868 and again in 1874 and 1875. Battle, *History of the University*, II, 84.

Excerpts from Constitutional Convention Journal[1]

[September 9, 1875]

Mr. Turner arose in his seat and announced the decease of the late Hon. William A. Graham, member elect to this Convention from the county of Orange, and submitted the following resolutions:

Resolved, That this Convention has heard with deep sensibility the announcement of the death of Hon. William Alexander Graham, a delegate from the county of Orange, and we deplore his death as a heavy and irreparable public misfortune; that as a mark of respect, unanimously entertained by this Convention for the memory of the deceased, and for his long, valuable and distinguished services in the public councils of the State and nation, that the members and officers of this Convention, from a sincere desire of showing every mark of respect for the memory of the deceased, do go into mourning for him for one month.

Resolved, That the President of this Convention be requested to communicate these proceedings to the widow and family of the deceased, tendering to them the sympathy of this Convention in their sore bereavement.

Resolved, That as an additional mark of respect to the memory of the deceased, the Convention do now adjourn.

Mr. Dockery moved that the further consideration of these resolutions be postponed until to-morrow at 1 P.M., and be made the special order for that hour, in order that the members of this Convention may be allowed an opportunity of paying their tribute of respect to the memory of the deceased. The motion prevailed.

On motion, the Convention adjourned until 10 A.M., to-morrow.

[September 10, 1875]

Mr. Barrow moved that the resolutions on the late Hon. William Alexander Graham, which were introduced yesterday by the delegate from Orange, and made the special order for to-day at 1 P.M., be taken from the calender and placed on their adoption.

The motion prevailed.

The resolutions were read.

After the delivery of eulogies upon the character and life of the deceased by Messrs. Dockery, Clingman, O'Hara, Smythe, Buxton, Tourgee, Crosby, Thorne and Robbins, on motion of Mr. Tourgee, the resolutions were unanimously adopted by a silent and rising vote.

Thereupon, in obedience to the resolutions, and as a tribute of respect to the memory of the deceased, the Convention adjourned until 10 A.M. to-morrow.

Appendix,
Remarks of Josiah Turner, of Orange, in Announcing to the Convention the Death of the Late Hon. Wm. A. Graham.

Mr. President:—I rise to perform a mournful duty. It is to announce the death of my late distinguished colleague, the Hon. Wm. Alexander Graham. He died, as is known to you all, at Saratoga, on the 11th of August last, whither he had gone as one of a commission to settle the long disputed boundary line between the States of Maryland and Virginia. He had warning of death's approach, and met the king of terrors as he met the late overwhelming disasters of his country—with fortitude and uncommon serenity. He was always averse to profuse professions, and left no last words for effect on mankind and the world. His death was not unlooked for; he had suffered for two years with an affection of the heart, and he therefore knew his stay on earth was of short duration. The annals of his State and country, for near half a century, will be his biography. The historian who records truthfully the many acts of his life, public and private, will be his best biographer. His death was an affliction which went straight to the bosoms and business of men. The telegraphic announcement of his death closed at once all places of business in Hillsboro, where he lived. The arrival of his remains closed for two days all places of business a second time, when more than two thousand of his neighbors from adjoining and distant counties assembled to pay the last sad tribute to his memory.

It is no disparagement of others to say that the eyes of the people were turned especially to him when this Convention should assemble. More was expected of him than of any other member. The loss of such a man to his country at any time would be a calamity. His loss at this particular juncture, and to this body, is irreparable. In the distressed and disturbed state of the public councils, with the wormwood and gall of personal animosities, adding bitterness to the conflict of party politics, the light of his countenance, the sound of his voice, and his conciliatory temper would have called us, one and all, from the tempest of hostile passions to the calm composure of harmony and peace, and a quiet compliance with every parliamentary law, for the order and government of this body. We may search, but the search will be in vain, to find his equal.

William A. Graham was born in the county of Lincoln in 1804. He was matriculated at Chapel Hill in 1824. Judge Manly and the Hon. John W. Norwood are the only survivors of his class. His first public service was rendered the people of Orange as borough member for the town of Hillsboro in 1833, '34 and 35. He was thrice elected to represent the county of Orange, in the House of Commons, in 1836, '38 and 40. He was afterwards elected Speaker of the House. In 1841 he was elected a member of the most august body of the world, I mean the Senate of the United States at that day and time, when the array of brilliant men was thick, and Clay, Calhoun, Webster and Mangum held divided empire there, and Graham was second only to such men. In elegance and grandeur of appearance, manliness of mien and comeliness of countenance, he had no equal in or out of the Senate. Take him all in all, in person, manners, mind and morals, his like has not been seen.

As Governor of the State of North Carolina from 1841 to 1845, he exhibited the highest administrative talent. As a delegate of the memorable Covention of 1861, and a member of the Confederate Congress, he showed himself to be a statesman of correct and courageous reflection. He did nothing for show or effect. He never drew back in anything, but went right steadily on. He looked upon the office of a legislator as a solemn trust, not to be bought, or sought, or secured by unworthy means. Always called upon to serve the public, he was always preparing himself by diligent labor and study for their service. His lofty scorn for everything mean and base kept him aloof from the petty intrigues of personal politics. Into every high office he held, into every work he undertook, he carried zeal, diligence, earnestness and a comprehensive forecaste which insured success and extorted commendation for the easy, even, and perfect performance of his duty. Thirty five years ago the younger Adams, in the Congress of the United States, spoke with touching eloquence upon the death of Lewis Williams, whose memory is still dear to the people of North Carolina. He dwelt with admiration upon the reciprocal attachment of Lewis Williams and his constituents. He declared that he had habitually looked upon his departed friend (Williams) as "the true portraiture and personification of the people of North Carolina."

The mutual attachment of Graham and his constituents was not less remarkable. He never deceived them, and they never deserted him, but adhered to him through every political vicissitude and revolution. He never sought to make himself popular except by the full discharge of his public duties. While he made himself accessible to all, he was familiar with none, save his own family dear and a few chosen friends. In the rectitude of his own action he repudiated the distinction attempted to be made by some between political and private virtue. What was morally wrong, he could not think politically right.

He served as Secretary of the Navy during the administration of Fillmore, who found him not the Salominian galley or the Merrimac to be launched only on great occasions, but he was the well-supplied vessel, always rigged and ready to sail when and where duty called, whether the occasion was great or small.

I am old enough, Mr. President, to have witnessed the grief of the people for Gaston, Cameron, Nash, Mangum, Daniel, Busbee, Miller, Ruffin, the Moreheads, Donnells, father and son, Outlaw, Cherry, Gilmer, Gilliam, Haywood, Saunders, Settle, Dobbin, Winslow, Ellis, Clark, Avera, the Shepherds, Shaw, Swain, Branch, Ruffin of Wayne, Osborne, Dockery, Lewis Thompson, Dr. Wright, Weldon Edwards, John Berry, (the neighbor and friend of Graham,) Patterson, Satterthwaite, Gorrell, Bedford Brown, William Ashe, Western [*sic*] R. Gales, John H. Bryan, Barringer, Bragg, Worth and Graham, but the grief of the people for their late lost friend and public servant seemed more poignant than for all of these. And why was this? you ask. Was Graham dearer to the people than these good men who had served well their country in their day and generation? It can be accounted for in one way only, and that is by a common principle of our nature.

Heartwell Blalock, an old man of Orange, sent six sons to the late war. The eldest was killed in battle and the old man grieved for him as Priam, the Trogan, did for Hector, his son, slain by the invaders of his country. In the next battle another son was slain, and there was grief for him. The next battle brought the intelligence of the death of a third son, and there was grief for him. In the next battle two sons were slain, and there was double grief for them. In the last battle the youngest and last son was maimed for life, and was subsequently assassinated in the town of Hillsboro after the close of the war. The old man's grief for the last son was greater than for all; not that he was nearer or dearer than the rest, but grief for the last was grief for all. There were none left to grieve for. So it is with the people of North Carolina. The school of statesmen to which Graham belonged has suspended. It no longer exists. He was the last scholar of the school, and hence the grief of the people. He has gone forever, and there is none to fill his place, and the people grieve for him as well as for his brothers in stateman-ship whom I have just named and who went to their graves before him.

When Gaston died, he left Daniel, Ruffin, Nash, Cameron, Haywood, Strange, Busbee, Miller and many others to take his place. When Haywood, Strange, Cameron, Busbee and Daniel died, they left Miller, Saunders, Gilliam, Gilmer, Morehead, Manly, Barringer, Badger, Worth, Graham and a number of the illustrious before named to take their places. One by one they departed, until Graham alone of the class was left. These were all sad funerals to the people of North Carolina. When the bodies of the illustrious dead were committed to the hungry grave, "ashes to ashes and dust to dust," the comforting words of the Master were uttered:

"I am the resurrection and the life, saith the Lord; he that believeth in me, though he were dead, yet shall he live; and whosoever liveth and believeth in me shall never die."

In sickness, Mr. President, we rely too much upon the skill of the physician; in death too much upon bishops, priests and deacons. Too much upon the sons of men, instead of the blood and saving grace of the Son of God. The last of the illustrious dead whom we have named, and whose death we deplore, relied as little upon men as any human being ever did. The clergy were not shunned by him, though he did not lean upon them as did others. His house was always open to them. He enjoyed their prayers and conversation; his walk and talk through life *was such* as to make the clergy look upon him as one of their number. I never saw a man who looked so much like he had been sent by his Maker to speak His everlasting truths to a fallen world. A stranger seated in a church and seeing him enter, would say to himself, that must be the minister. He was brought up in the Presbyterian faith, and put his hope of eternal life in the teachings of that church, the church of his fathers, and the all-atoning blood of his Saviour.

In matters of business, great or small, public or private, he was self-reliant, depending upon his own solid judgment, cool reason and the wonderful justness of his own perceptions. He was diligent, patient, never in a hurry and never behind time. Never out of temper, out of work, or out of hope. His guiding stars were labor, truth and duty. I have seen him, Mr. President, under the most trying circumstances which it is possible to be placed. I have seen him in a beleaguered city, when fear and trepidation had seized upon the boldest, look as unmoved as when he lay in state in the rotunda of the Capitol.

I have seen him stand upon the steps of the Confederate Capitol, when the crazy building was shaking to its foundation stone from the roar of artillery which was sending death into the ranks of his countrymen, where stood five of his own ten children. Under such a trial he stood apparently unmoved, his reason keeping all other faculties and passions under proper control.

I have seen him aroused in the dead of night by the alarm bell, and with the cry of "Dahlgreen at the gate," when it made brave men shake and gentle women shriek, as the cry of Hannibal at the gates of Rome had done 2,000 years before, and he was the only man in the city besieged who did not show undue excitement, trepidation or haste. He is the only man I ever knew who could not, under some circumstances, be forced to take part in a panic. If he had commanded the Old Guard at Waterloo, no panic would have struck them, no stampeding and cry of Prussians, after they had fled twenty miles from the battlefield.

Mr. President, I have no heart for a funeral—I never saw a dead body until the late war, when all the land and all the houses were filled with them. I have not looked on one since. I do not understand the sad satisfaction which men feel at looking at the body when the soul has departed. I prefer to remember my friends as they looked in life. I say it in truth and sincerity, I would like to witness a national mourning. Since Clay, Webster, Calhoun and Douglas died, there has been no national grief. I long to see a second

Webster or Clay who can stand in the Capitol at Washington, and when he speaks be heard as one of authority and wisdom by every man, woman and child from Penobscot to San Francisco Bay. Then I shall look for the restoration and the era of good feeling and brotherly love. I want the young Adams to feel for the young Williams dead, as did John Quincy Adams for Lewis Williams in the better days of the Republic. I want my children to feel for the patriotic dead of Massachusetts, not as I do now, but as I once did. I want the sons of Massachusetts to feel when such a man as Graham dies, that the country, christianity and all humanity has lost a friend.

In 1860, if the capital of the nation could have boasted of one Clay or Webster and each State of one Graham, the Union had been preserved without a four years' bloody butchery of men who had been and should have remained brethren forever, in union, peace, good-will and concord.

But I have gone, Mr. President, beyond the purpose of my announcement when I first arose, and yet have said little or nothing of the private, family or social relations of the deceased. He lived in the most eventful age of his country's history. He lived in an age of political calumny, vituperation and abuse. The father of his country and every prominent public leader in this government have been calumniated except William A. Graham. So pure and exemplary were his thoughts and actions, that political falsehood and calumny never but once charged him with impropriety of conduct, and that was in the Pierce and Scott campaign. The charge was, that being in Fillmore's Cabinet he consented to be a candidate on the Scott ticket, against the wishes of his leader and friend. A neighbor who loved and honored both Fillmore and Graham, wrote to Fillmore, who replied in vindication, "that his friend Graham was acting the patriotic part and at his anxious, earnest solicitation."

If you would know of his private relations and social worth, go to Orange, where he lived, and there you can learn from those who knew him longest and best, the faithfulness of his friendship, the warmth of his affections and the fullness of his charity to the needy and poor. His family relations as husband and father shall not be named in public. They are too deeply enshrined in bleeding hearts at home to be made the subject of public discourse. I will now conclude what I have to say, Mr. President, by offering these resolutions and adding that the life and character of William A. Graham affords the brightest example by which an American statesman and christian gentleman can be guided.

---

[1]From *Journal of the Constitutional Convention of the State of North Carolina, Held in 1875* (Raleigh: Josiah Turner, 1875), 30, 40, 279-286. Josiah Turner's speech, published as an appendix to the convention journal, has been included. No attempt was made to identify all persons mentioned.

Samuel A. Ashe believed that Graham was Turner's mentor and that after Graham's death Turner lost his sense of proportion and became erratic and unpredictable. *DAB*, XIX, 68-69; Ashe, *Biographical History*, III, 424.

Mary Washington Graham[1] *to Susan Washington Graham* A&H

Plantation [Arkansas]
Sept 12 1875

My dear Sister,

It was with deep heart felt grief that I learned of dear brother William's death, & I have seated myself to offer you some consolation. But I know not what to say—for nothing but time & the mercies of our heavenly father can soften that deep trouble that I know that you are passing through. I wish it was so that I could be with you, if I had had the means I would have gone on as soon as I heard of his death. But it is a hard strugle with me now to live.

I am here at the plantation trying to make a living & I have to go in debt to run the place this year, & it is the first time I have ever been in debt in my life. Between that & the worry & vexations attending a plantation life it has almost made me give up in dispare. I have a splendid crop & if cotton should bring a good price this winter I hope I shall be able to pay out. I have seen a great deal of trouble since I have been left to strugle alone. As usual in this Western country, Mr. Graham's partner wound up that part of the estate to suit himself, & got possession of nearly all the money that should have come to us. We have a good deal of real estate, but Camden has depreciated so much for the last few years that it is of little value. So it was come here or do worse. I am in hopes that brother William's affairs are in better shape than ours, & that you will have a plenty to live on the rest of your days in comfort & ease. It makes me feel sad to think that we are all passing away, & will never see each other again in this life, in all probability, for we are all getting old now & according to the course of nature we have not many years for this world, & I truly hope that we may all meet in a better world than this when we shall be done with trouble & trials of all sorts. I had hoped of meeting brother William again, for I loved him as a brother & remember his many kindnesses to me. When I was a girl & a member of his household, he was a noble specimen of God's creation & if all men were like him, there would be better living in this world. I surly hope that he is resting from all of his care in his heavenly home awaiting for you. That is a great consolation, to think that though our loved ones cant come back to us, we can go to them—happy thought! I have long since cut my affection off from this life & often wish my heavenly father would take me away from the many trials that I have to encounter. . . .

The girls join me in much love & sympathe to you. I shall be glad to hear from you whenever you feel able to write. If Sister is in Hillsboro please say to her that I received her kind letter, & will try to write to her in a few days.

My love to all the family that may be with you. Your Aff. Sister

---

[1]Mary Washington Graham (1824-1888) of Camden, Arkansas, the wife of Joseph Montrose Graham, was Susan Washington Graham's youngest sister. Her husband was William A. Graham's nephew. Clark, "Washington Descendants"; Clark, "Graham Descendants."

Barnas Sears to Susan Washington Graham A&H

Staunton Va
Sept 13, 1875

Mrs. Gov. Graham.

Dear Madam,

Unwilling to obtrude upon your private grief which I knew I had not the power to alleviate, I have purposely delayed writing to you, offering to you my condolence, till you had learned, as every afflicted one must, by experience as well as by religious principle where to find consolation. Though your loss is irreparable while on earth, I trust the purity which you have so long cultivated, & which has led you to do so much for others, has by the grace of God, proved a solid ground of support to you.

I saw enough of my friend, with whom I was often by accidental circumstances brought in close social contact during our meetings, to know what a chasm his death must make in your family. We shall deeply feel it in our little circle, where his uniform courtesy & kindness won all our hearts. I need not speak to you of his manly frankness, integrity & independence. I never heard the purity of his character called in question, which is true of but few public men who have moved in so large a sphere. You have much that is honorable & noble to reflect upon, & your children much to remember & emulate.

Myself & Mrs. Sears had anticipated great pleasure in seeing both your late husband & yourself at our meetings, & the more so on account of the intimacy of us all with Mr. Stuart & family. May I not hope that this friendly relation will still bring us the oftener together, though one dear link is broken? Mr. Stuart deeply feels this loss.

I wish to be kindly remembered to your sons & daughter. I shall never cease to feel an interest in their happiness & usefullness. Trust may you, dear Madam, have all the consolation of religion & as much domestic enjoyment as is possible with such a bereavement as you have been called upon to suffer.

With sincere sympathy & Christian regards, very truly your

friend & brother

Susan Washington Graham to William A. Graham, Jr. A&H

Hillsboro,
Sept 29th 1875

My dear Son,

I have received your letters and also Julias, and would have written to you both ere this, but it has been necessary for me to read so many letters & papers connected with your father's business before giving them over to others, that my aching head has been severely taxed, and I have avoided all letter writing, unless indispensable. I must begin next week to reply to the many kind letters that I have received, and continue until all are acknowledged. Looking over the papers & letters, is a melancholy task, and sometimes it seems more than I can go through with, but I believe your father would prefer my doing it, as he always talked freely with me about all his business, and I find comfort in the recollection that I am working for *him*, and that there is still something I can do for him.

While looking for an important paper for John, I noticed that the damp weather had caused mold to settle upon some of them, and in taking them all out to have the tray of the trunk sunned, I found the Will in a newspaper in the bottom of the tray. The sheet of foolscap paper had not been folded, and lay so flat from pressure that the gentlemen who examined the papers the day you were present, thought the newspaper had been simply laid in the bottom, as is often done. The will merely bears date 1871, and the date of the month left blank, and not signed. It is said however to be valid in Law, and I am very glad that it was found, for it is so much more satisfactory to have your fathers judgment & wishes to guide us in the settlement of the Estate. *All* of the legacies, except your own, will have to abate considerably, more than one half perhaps. At the time your father wrote the will, he no doubt expected to be able to add a good deal to his Estate, but several losses, together with bad health and consequent diminished receipts from his profession, and increased expenses, will make the several shares much smaller than he wished. He often spoke with regret of his inability to do more for his children, and the prospect of having so little to leave them. I tried to console him with the recollection of how much he had done for you all, and the rich legacy of a good name & example that he would bequeath for your imitation. He said that the *whole* of the Earhart tract was *more* than one share of what he could leave to his children but he did not see how you could well live upon the half of it; and without good management, it would be but a poor living you would make upon the whole. We must all try to practice *strict economy* until we can get every thing straightened up, and with prudence & economy in the future I hope we shall be able to live comfortably the few years that we may have for this world.

John said the other day, that is was not *necessary* for you or Joseph to come down when the will was "proved" and as it will be attended with considerable expense I suppose you will hardly come. I would be glad to see you & Julia & the children, but I know you cannot well spare the money as it is of the first importance for you to pay off all your debts, especially the interest. I wish I had it to send you, but I shall have to practice close economy for awhile, and it *may be necessary* for all the future. I *suppose* that your legacy being of land entirely, will not have to abate with the others, but Robert can tell you better about the law in the case after he has read the will. I supposed he would be down for two or three days this week but has not come yet.

In one of your letters you wrote your father that you would send the interest upon your Rail Road Bond by the first of August. You can send it after the will has been proved. The Executors named are myself, John & Robert. I am still acting as Administratrix but would prefer transacting only such business as is absolutely necessary until the other two qualify. I think it would be well for you to take up your R R Note as soon as you can, as it is without surety and made "payable one day after day" so that you are liable to be pressed for it at any inconvenient time by the R R Company.

John has had a settlement with Wilson to whom I turned over all the papers. It would be a pity for you to use your little Bank stock as you spoke of doing for that purpose, and I suppose as a part of the payment for the bond is to be cash that you might arrange it with that.

I do hope you will be able to get your debts all paid off and then be able to keep out of debt. I know it will require good management and close economy for some time—but with perseverance you will succeed.

Cousins Sophie & Alice[1] expect to leave tomorrow night, but we have been persuading them to remain until Robert returns to Charlotte. Sudie expects to leave Friday. She would like to remain till after Robert comes & returns but Walter thinks she has been absent so long, that she ought to go, as she is to go down soon to make a visit to his family and he will not be able to be with her. Her little girl is very plump and good natured.[2] Sallie & Eugene[3] will be with us much of the winter I presume. Bettie & sister[4] expect to go down the country next month. Their movements will be regulated by the frost & healthfulness of New Bern.

The whole household joins in love to you, Julia and the children. A full house, but *none* can supply *to me*, the place of the absent. I miss him more & more as time wears on, and those around me know little of the *yearning anguish* that a calm exterior may conceal. The calmness of death itself, for the hopes & aspirations of this life lie buried beneath. I thank God that there is a better life, to which I trust I am fast hastening, and for the blessed assurance that my good husband has found *rest* within its portals, and that I can go to him altho he may not return to me. But many days of sorrow & *loneliness* still seperate us.

A kiss to Julia & the children. I will try to write her before long. God bless you all. Yr. Aff. Mother

---

[1]Mary Sophia Alexander (1831-1916) and Alice Leonora Alexander (1842-1905) were daughters of the Moses Winslow Alexanders. Clark, "Graham Descendants."

[2]Susan Washington Clark, born in 1875, was the first child of the Walter Clarks. Clark, "Graham Descendants."

[3]Sallie and Eugene were Mrs. George W. Graham and her son, born in 1874. Clark, "Graham Descendants."

[4]Bettie was the wife of Joseph Graham. Her sister has not been identified, although this may refer to one of Mrs. Graham's own two surviving sisters. Clark, "Washington Descendants."

Will of William A. Graham[1]

The last Will and Testament of William A Graham.

I William A Graham of Hillsborough Orange County North Carolina, now in good health of perfect mind and memory, mindful of the uncertainty of life do hereby make and publish this my last will and testament.
First I direct that my body be buried in my family burial place adjoining the public grave yard in Hillsborough

Second I direct that all my Just debts outstanding at my death be paid by my Executors— These I have indeavored to liquidate at short periods as my book of accounts will show, and with the exception of one to the Executor of J Sidney Smith decd. which I hope to satisfy within a year or two from this time will be found moderate in amount

Third to my faithful and affectionate wife Susan Washington Graham & her heirs, I give, devise and bequeath my Homestead, House & Lot in the Town of Hillsborough including the part purchased of the assignee in Bankruptcy of Henry N Brown & of P. C. Cameron Esqr., about three and a half acres in quantity and my burial ground lot adjoining the same: a tract of land to be laid off from my old Homestead in Orange County aforesaid near Hillsborough between the Road to Halifax on the North, and the Eno River on the South on the Eastern end of the tract including the meadow and the branch and containing [blank] acres, and a tract to be laid off from my Estes & Norwood tracts two miles East of Hillsborough and South of Eno according to her choice, so as to embrace an ample supply of timber and to comprise about three Hundred and Thirty three acres; to have and to hold to her & her heirs forever: together with all my Household & Kitchen furniture Paintings, Prints, Plate, Library, other than professional Law Books, the two Horse Wagon & Cart, two mules and Harness, three milch Cows and calves, all forage, provisions and family supplies on hand at my death, with agricultural & garden implements at home: In addition to these she has a carriage & Harness, Piano Forte, plate and various other articles purchased with her own means, or presented to her, monies or stocks derived in the same manner, and from the sale of a part of her lands in Craven County:

I likewise bequeath to her Seven thousand dollars to be taken at her discretion out of my Stocks or monies due me and estimated at par value only: all the foregoing to be hers absolutely, and in lieu of dower or other provision out of my estate.

Fourth I have made advancements to my son Joseph Graham beyond an equal share in my estate as reduced by the consequences of the late war; but in consideration of his losses by that event, and his embarking in the military Service, I give and bequeath to him the further sum of three Thousand dollars to be paid out of the proceeds of sale of my Amazonia Plantation on the Catawba river at the mouth of Little Catawba Creek in York County South Carolina and Gaston County North Carolina: and I do further direct that the balance of his bond to J D Rankin with myself as surety given in part for his tract of land amounting to about the sum of Two Hundred and fifty dollars be paid by my Executors.

Fifth To my son John W Graham & his Heirs forever, I give, devise and bequeath, my old Homestead plantation near Hillsborough described above excepting the lot laid off to my wife as directed above, comprising some forty odd acres; my Estes tract of land aforesaid purchased of J [Vinson] & wife & of J W Norwood Esqr. except the part of three Hundred & thirty three acres above directed to be laid off to his Mother; comprising about Five Hundred acres; and my half of the Cole tract of land on Eno River in Orange County aforesaid, Eleven miles Eastward of Hillsborough owned

Jointly by myself and the estate of the late Capt John Berry, and containing one Hundred & Eighty four acres with a water power together with the plantation implements at said old Homestead, and one half of my Law Library: and in addition to the advancements heretofore made to him, I give and bequeath to him the sum of Three Thousand dollars to be paid out of my stocks or monies due me.

Sixth To my son William A Graham and his heirs forever, I give devise and bequeath my Earhert, Moody & Duncan tracts of land in Lincoln County North Carolina on which he now resides, comprising about Sixteen Hundred & Fourteen acres, together with all buildings, machinery which he has erected at his own expense horses Mules sheep cattle Hogs, Waggons & Plantation implements and furniture situate thereon

Seventh To my son James A Graham & his heirs forever, I give, devise and bequeath my Ray tract of land Five miles North of Hillsborough in Orange County on Forester's Creek Containing Five Hundred & Twenty-five acres: with one half of my Law Library; The Gold Watch I have heretofore given him: and in addition to the advancements heretofore made to him, the sum of Four thousand dollars to be paid out of the proceeds of sale of my Catawba plantation above described.

Eighth My affectionate uncle Robert Davidson Esquire of Mecklenburg County, out of his great kindness towards me, having devised and bequeathed to my son Robert D Graham an estate equal, after all the losses occasioned by the war to the shares I am able to give to my other children; in consideration of this, in addition to the advancements I have heretofore made to him, I give and bequeath to my son Robert D. Graham, one thousand dollars to be paid out of my stocks or monies due me

Ninth To my son George W Graham & his Heirs in addition to the advancements, I have heretofore made to him I give and bequeath the sum of Five thousand dollars to be paid out of my stocks or monies due me: and the further sum of Five thousand dollars, to be paid out of the proceeds of sale of my plantation on the Catawba aforesaid.

Tenth To my son Augustus W Graham and his heirs I give and bequeath the Sum of Seven thousand dollars to be paid out of my stocks & monies due me, and the further sum of Five thousand dollars to be paid out of the proceeds of sale of my plantation on the Catawba aforesaid and my Gold Watch, Black Trunk and large Port Folio:

Eleventh To my daughter Susan Washington Graham and her heirs, I give and bequeath the sum of Seven thousand dollars to be paid out of my stocks & monies due me and the further sum of Five thousand dollars to be paid out the proceeds of sale of my plantation on the Catawba aforesaid, to her sole Separate and exclusive use, excluding the Jus mariti of any husband she may marry.

Twelfth I direct that my plantation aforesaid lying on the State line in York County South Carolina and Gaston County North Carolina devised to me by my late brother James Graham and called by me Amazonia containing with the addition I made to it by purchase thirteen hundred and eighty three acres be sold by my executors either in solids or in parcels on such terms as they may Conceive will bring the best price retaining the title till paid for, and their executing proper title deeds: that the Cotton gin, Wheat thrasher & Horse power and all the stock of Horses, Mules Cattle, Sheep & Hogs and Crops on hand Wagons, Cart, and improvements including tools of Blacksmith shop on this plantation be sold in like manner together with my other property that I have not hereinbefore disposed of, and that the whole proceeds be applied to the payment of the several legacies herein before directed to be paid out of the proceeds of the said Catawba plantation: It is a valuable estate; but if it shall not, with the effects directed to be sold, and the proceeds added to it, realize a sum sufficient to pay the several sums charged on the same, these must abate in proportion to the amounts; and on the other hand if there is an excess it shall be divided equally among all my children now living, and if any die before me, his children if any to succeed to what would have been his share

Thirteenth Should I pay all or any part of the Legacies, or make advancements to any of the legatees herein mentioned during my life the amount will be shewn in my Book indorsed "Leger" and must be Credited as satisfaction to the amount stated

Fourteenth All the rest and residue of my estate not heretofore mentioned wherever Situate or whomesoever due I direct to be first applied to carry out the provisions of the foregoing bequests: and if there by any over-plus, that the same be equally divided among all my children as provided in Item Twelfth; Lastly I nominate and appoint my wife Susan W Graham and my sons John W and Robert D Graham Executors of this my last will & testament, hereby revoking & annulling any will by me at any time heretofore made

In testimony of all which I have hereunto set my hand and affixed my seal at my own house in Hillsborough aforesaid this [blank] of [blank] AD 1871

Memorandum on back of page I. foregoing will.

Value of whole estate.	
Homestead in Hillsboro: 3 ½ acres & burial lot	4000
Old Homestead	3,[5]00
Drug store lot 500 Depot lot 200	700
Esters place	3,500
Ray place	2600
Half Cole place	800
Earhert tract 10,000	
Improvements by W A G Jr. 2,000	8,000
Amazonia & stock & [items]	15,000
Real estate	38,100
Take out old Homestead 3,500	
Half Cole place 800	4,300
	33,800

Also Homestead in Hillsboro 4000			
Half Esters to Mrs G 1500			4,500
			29,300
Stock & Loans	26,600		
Mrs G	6,600		
	20,000		20,000
25 shares stock NCRR Co			
5 shares off to G W G			850.
1/5 of 1 N.C. Plank road Bond			500
Household & Kitchen furniture		1,000	
Plate		600	
Paintings & Prints		500	
2 Mules		150	
3 Cows & calves		60	
Agricultural implements & wagons		400	
Library Law		1000	
Miscellaneous		500	
		4710	
Cattle 150, Sheep 50 & Hogs 150	350		1,900

Memorandum on page 2—foregoing Will.

Legacy to wife Homestead in Hillsboro & burial ground	4,000
333 Acres Esters place	1,332

Memorandum of page 7—foregoing will.

For Division	54,443
Add advancements Considering Joseph 10,000 George 4,000	
	36,363
	90,806
Take off Roberts Legacy	1000
	7)89,806
	12,829

John	12,825		
had	6,547	Half Esters	1,800
	6,278	Drug Store & Depot	700
		Half Law Library in value	500
		Cattle	100
		3000 from Sale—[land]	

Wm 12825
had 13,000
Geo [Joseph] 12,825 from Erhert Land & advancement
4919
7,906—3000 stock

George 12,825
4000
8,825—5,000 stock
3000 Lepr land

James
Ray plantation 2,500

McBride bond	500
Stock	3000
Half Library	500

Augustus 12,825
1500
11,325 6,000 stock
5 Shares R
5 Leper land

Robert 1000

Susan 12,825
2600
10,225 5000
200
Five shares NCR stock
5000 Lepr land

Leper land & effects
Susan 5,000 Aug 6,000 Geo 3000 Joseph 3,000
Memorandum on 8th page

Whole value of estate
Legacy to wife homestead in Hillsboro: including

Brown & Cameron lots	$ 4,000
Half Esters land her choice	1,500
Household & Kitchen furniture	1,000
Paintings, Prints & plate	800
Library other than professional	500
2 Mules, Wagons Geer & cart	200
3 Cows & calves	60
Agricultural & Garden implements	100
Provisions on hand	200
Stocks & bonds at par valuation	6600
	14,960

John	Remaining half of Esters land	1,500
James	Ray tract	2500
John	Drug store & Depot lot	700
Wm	Earhert remaining	8,000
x	Amazonia	15,000
x	Stock	2,000
x	Good stocks & bonds	20,000
	Depreciated do	2,000
James	McBride Bond	500
	Willard do	143
John & James	Law library	1,000
John	Cattle in Orange	100
NCR Stock		1000
		69,403
	take off Legacy to wife	14,960
		54,443

Provided and admitted to probate:
2d Oct 1875

[1]Transcribed from a copy in the Orange County Courthouse, Hillsborough, North Carolina.

Resolutions of Peabody Education Fund Committee[1]

Hon. W. M. Evarts, on behalf of the Committee appointed to prepare a suitable minute on the death of the Hon. Wm. A. Graham, reported the following Resolutions, which were supported by Hon. A. H. H. Stuart, in a touching and eloquent address, and were unanimously adopted by a rising vote.

Resolved:

That the members of this Board have received the afflicting intelligence of the death of their associate, the Honorable William A. Graham, with profound grief at their own and the public loss.

Resolved:

That the great fitness of Governor Graham for the trust and service in which Mr. Peabody was so fortunate as to enlist his active interest and thorough co-operation, has been made evident by the zeal, the wisdom, and the benevolent spirit which have marked his constant and faithful participation in the counsels and the labors of this Board from its establishment.

Resolved:

That the distinguished public character of Gov. Graham and his strong hold upon the confidence of the people of the South, and of the North alike, have been of the greatest value and importance to this Board, in securing the sympathy and co-operation of men of credit and influence in the country, in furtherance of the beneficent system of public education at the South, which Mr. Peabody's munificent endowment has so greatly aided in developing.

Resolved:

That our personal intercourse with Gov. Graham in the discharge of our common duties has shown to us his admirable qualities of mind and character; and we lament his loss, as of a near friend and associate, as well as of an eminent public servant and benefactor.

A true copy from *Record*—

G. Peabody Russell,
Secretary.

The Resolutions were supported by the Hon. A. H. H. Stuart, in the following remarks:

Mr. President, Although I am laboring under a temporary disability, which renders it impossible for me to speak without physical pain, I cannot deny myself the melancholy pleasure of saying a few words in support of the Resolutions which have just been reported by the committee.

It was my good fortune, more than thirty years ago, to make the acquaintance of Gov. Graham. He was, at that time, a member of the Senate of the United States; and I had been recently elected to the House of Representatives.

It was a period of high political excitement; and a general coincidence of opinion on questions of the day brought Gov. Graham and myself into personal association. It was during that period that the foundation of a life-long friendship was laid.

Some years later, we were associated as members of the Cabinet of Mr. Fillmore. During the two years and a half that we served together in that capacity, our acquaintance ripened into intimate friendship.

When Gov. Graham was nominated for the Vice-Presidency, with that delicacy which marked his conduct in every relation of life, he retired from the Cabinet, and, with the exception of one or two casual meetings, our personal intercourse was suspended, until three years ago, when we were again brought together, as members of this Board.

I need hardly say to this audience that Gov. Graham was a gentleman of high moral and intellectual endowments. He was a man of pure and spotless integrity. And, while he entertained decided opinions, he was never aggressive or intolerant in their assertion. To great dignity of character, he united an amenity and charm of manner which secured for him the respect and affection of all who knew him.

He possessed a sound and vigorous intellect which enabled him to grapple with the most difficult questions; and he was singularly free from all those influences of passion and excitement, which too often disturb the judgment. His views of every subject were clear, calm, and well considered.

While he may not have been as largely endowed as some other men with that brilliancy which is called genius, he possessed what was far better, that happy balance of the intellectual faculties, which is the parent of wisdom. But it is not of the intellectual endowments of Gov. Graham that I desire to speak on this occasion. Admirable as were the qualities of his mind, I prefer to dwell on the higher attributes of his moral and social character, which won for him the willing tribute of our hearts.

Although Gov. Graham had, for more than forty years, occupied a prominent position in public life, and had filled many important public offices, during times of high party excitement, no man ever ventured to question the integrity of his motives or conduct; and, up to the hour of his death, he enjoyed the unlimited confidence of all who had the happiness to know him.

Mr. President, while the public lament, in the death of Gov. Graham, the loss of an eminent statesman; while this Board are deeply sensible of the misfortune which has befallen them, in his untimely withdrawal from our body, you and I, sir, have an additional cause of sorrow,—we mourn the loss of a valued personal friend.

I do not know how I could more appropriately express my estimate of the high moral and intellectual worth of Gov. Graham than by adopting the language of the late venerable John Quincy Adams, on a similar melancholy occasion.

It was my fortune to announce to Mr. Adams the death of his friend and former Cabinet Minister, Ex. Gov. James Barbour, of Virginia. And, although Mr. Adams was reputed to be a man of cold and impassive nature, he received the news with deep sensibility. For several moments he bowed his head on the table near which he was sitting, and seemed absorbed in profound meditation. Gradually recovering his self-possession, he resumed his erect position, and, with a voice tremulous with emotion, said: "Mr. Stuart, I have been connected with this Government almost from its foundation to the present hour. I have known all the distinguished men who have participated in its administration, and, I can safely say, I have rarely known a wiser man, and never a better man, than James Barbour!"

Mr. President, I can lay no claim to so large an acquaintance with the public men of our country as Mr. Adams. But is has been my fortune to be connected with public affairs during some of the most eventful periods of our history,—periods when some of the most distinguished men of two generations graced our national councils; and I feel that I can, without qualification, adopt the language of Mr. Adams, and say that I have rarely met a wiser man, and never a better man, than William A. Graham.

The Resolutions were then unanimously adopted, all the members rising.

---

[1]The resolutions were part of the proceedings of the board of trustees of the Peabody Education Fund, October 8, 1875. Henry R. Jackson of Savannah, Georgia, was unanimously elected to succeed Graham on the board.

Montford McGehee to John W. Graham UNC

Woodburn, Person Co., N.C.
Nov. 16. 1875.

My dear Sir:

The too partial judgement of friends has delegated to me the duty of preparing an address on the life and character of Gov. Graham.

From the feelings which I bore to Gov. Graham while living, and the honor in which I hold his memory, no duty more acceptable could have been assigned me, but for a sense of my insufficiency.

My Misgiving partly arises from apprehension as to the difficulty of procuring Materials. If I can succeed in getting these, whatever defects may be discovered, will be found to be neither the result of want of interest nor of diligence.

Commanding as was Gov. Graham's position as a lawyer and as an advocate it is chiefly as a Statesman that he will fix the attention of posterity. To present him at all adequately in this point of view, it is necessary to examine documents that are not accesible to me here. Are there not in Gov. Graham's library copies of his Messages while Gov. of the State? Also bound Copies of the Congressional Globe during his Senatorial Career? These would contain his speeches. Also copies of his Reports while Secretary of the Navy? Also of his Speeches in the Convention of '61? Can any letters of his be obtained—to Judge Ruffin, Mr. Cameron, Mr. Norwood, or any other expressing his views upon public affairs at different periods of his public life—particularly from '60 to '65 inclusive? Such books, documents & letters you will please have securely packed & sent to me by Express to News Ferry.

In asking letters I am aware that I am soliciting a delecate trust, but in expressing a sense of that trust, I am sure that my friends will find the surest guarantee that it will be faithfully respected.

The correspondence between Gov. Graham & Gov. Swain during the war was constant and confidential—Could the use of Governor Graham's letters during that time be obtained?

I presume that it is unnecessary for me to say that every thing furnished me will be carefully preserved and duly returned.

Have you a Copy of the "Last 90 days of the War?" Also of Maj. Gale's Sketch of Gov. Graham? Do me the favour to send these also, if you have them.

I have written to Mr. Phillips asking the loan of his letters from Gov. Graham from '60 to '65.

Trusting to receive an early answer

I am very truly

Robert D. Graham to Susan Washington Graham A&H

Charlotte, N.C.
Nov. 29 1875

Dear Mother:

Your letter, recd. a day or two since, gave me a great deal of pain to know that you were so much troubled. Please promise me that you will try to think of Vance's lecture[1] just as little as you can until you grow stronger. Then if any further action is necessary, you will be in better condition to do full justice to the subject.

For the present you ought to recollect that you have seven sons, to whom the memory of the dead is as dear as it can be even to you, that the five who were old enough to offer their services [*sic*] to their state, bore themselves conspicuously wherever duty called, often commanding with credit larger corps than a regular promotion would have given them. By them especially would any insinuation reflecting upon their father's honor be resented. I think you will find them, as well as Father's best friends, agreed, that nothing else is necessary to be done. Vance's vanity and miserable taste are admitted, but they do not believe that he intended a personal reflection upon the dead. Mr. Norwood's mind is weak, and any statement you would get from him would hardly help the matter. The *note* to the lecture in the November No. of Our Living & Our Dead is fuller than you would think on first reading. Vance therein says, in substance, that these gentlemen *knew* that Gen. Lee was on the eve of a surrender, and he did not consider the proposition dishonorable. This fully shows the *condition* of the country at that time, and I believe that Vance was honest when he expressed his surprise that Gov G's friends had regarded it as a reflection upon him.

Of all the papers in and out of the state that referred to the matter, I do not think that any of them (except Yate's sycophantic defense of Vance's, that Bro. Joe sent you.) contained *one word* to which our friends could object. I recollect the extract that Cousin Julia sent to the Alexanders at Hillsboro. I have read it carefully, and it is very evident that the Mississippi editor, though condemning the plan & those who affirmed it, makes no attack upon one whom Vance says, distinctly, did not give them, or him, his approval of it.

As to the names being given reluctantly, there is no charge that any promise had been made that he should not know who they were, and it is quite probable that these gentlemen had said to Father, You need not give our names *unless* it becomes necessary. They were not willing to come out in the newspapers with their proposition. If they had been, I believe that Father would have approved it, and Vance would have adopted it.

Whether right or wrong, he did not have the nerve to take this step without having the gentlemen to stand between him and the consequences. With their public approval it would have ended the war. But it was a private suggestion of theirs, and of course if their names were given to Gov. Vance, it was on his word of honor never to reveal them. Whether it is less dishonorable in Vance to mention the proposition at all than to give their names, is a question sufficient to "drive him into a corner."

The lecture is certainly a fine tribute to the patriotism and good faith of North Carolina, and covers a period which shed more lustre upon Vance than any civil executive officer in the South. However ungrateful it was in him, we cannot attack him for neglecting such an opportunity of paying a just tribute to the memory of one whom he had declared to be "head & shoulders above any man in the confederate States Congress," and whose opinion through all that dark period he valued more than that of any man in the whole country. Such is the successful politician. But I believe on some future occasion, Vance will speak out the convictions of his heart, in a proper tribute to one whom he honored so much. Whether he does or not, William A. Graham is acknowledged, North and South, to have been the foremost man that North Carolina has ever produced, and like his friend Henry Clay, will be remembered as one who "had rather be *right* than President."

---

[1]On August 18, 1875, Zebulon B. Vance addressed the Southern Historical Society at White Sulphur Springs, West Virginia, on the subject of North Carolina's role in the Civil War. Naturally personal and state pride made Vance bold in his pronouncements. In describing the last weeks of the war, he alluded to a visit to him by William A. Graham, then a Confederate senator. He said that Graham came as envoy from several Confederate legislators who urged that Vance and North Carolina make a separate peace with President Lincoln so as to inaugurate the war's end. Other states would almost certainly follow suit. Vance disparaged the men who had made this suggestion but specified that Graham served only as messenger and would offer no opinion. Vance concluded his address as follows: "I declined the proposition, of course, and asked him to say to those gentlemen, with my compliments, that in the mountains where I was raised, when a man was whipped he had to do his own hollering; that the technical word 'enough' could not be cried by proxy. This piece of secret history will serve to show that there was a faintness of heart and a smiting together of knees in other parts of the South outside of North Carolina."

Graham's family and friends apparently took umbrage, inferring that Vance's comments about "faintness of heart" and "smiting together of knees" applied to the messenger as well as the others. Vance, in a note to his speech when published, expressed surprise that many considered his remarks a personal reflection on the recently deceased Graham. See *Our Living and Our Dead*, November, 1875, for Vance's address. The matter discussed above will be found on pages 625 and 626.

AFTER 1875

Alexander H. H. Stuart to Susan Washington Graham A&H

Staunton, Virginia,
June 7th., 1877.

I thank you cordially for the copy of the admirable memorial address of Mr. McGehee, on the life and character of Gov. Graham, which you were kind enough to send me. I have read it with great interest, and pleasure. It is a noble tribute to a noble character; and it afforded me a melancholy satisfaction to review the history of many scenes & incidents, in which Gov. Graham & I had been active participants.

Our acquaintance commenced in 1841, when we were both young men. He was then a member of the Senate of U.S., & I, of the House of Representatives. Sympathy of feeling, & a remarkable coincidence of opinion on public questions, naturally drew us together, and our acquaintance rapidly ripened into a friendship, which our subsequent association, as members of Mr. Fillmore's Cabinet tended to confirm.

At a later date we were brought together at the annual meetings of the Peabody Board. I always looked forward with pleasure to those meetings, because they afforded the only opportunity that was left to me of enjoying the society of Gov. Graham, and of interchanging opinions with him. Since his death, the sessions of the Board have lost much of their interest to me. We were in the habit of spending much of our time together, when the Board was not in session, and, as we had so many recollections and opinions in common, his society was a source of unfailing interest. In the absence of his companionship, I feel a painful sense of isolation and depression.

It was pleasant, also, to myself and my family, to look forward to annual meetings, with some members of your family, at N. York.

As I was but three years the junior of Gov. Graham, I cannot expect to remain long behind him. If I can leave behind me such a reputation as he has left, I shall feel that it is the best heritage I can bestow on my children.

My wife desires to be kindly remembered to you, and Maggie sends her best regards to Mrs. Clark.

William A. Graham, Jr., to R. D. W. Connor[1]

Machpelah, N.C.
Sept 20th 1907

In reply to yours of 18th inst. I have requested my brother Dr. Geo. W. Graham to forward you an article I prepared to go as a "brochure" with Gov. G's portrait to Jamestown—but there was mistake as to printing and it was not prepared. Please preserve and return.

I shall deem it a pleasure to aid you in any way I can—in your work. In regard to the "Perry Expedition" I would suggest that you note that Com. P. was an officer under authority without power to organize anything except as he was ordered—and must have some one to give the authority. This seems to have been overlooked by all (including myself) in referring to the matter. He (G) refers to the desirability of trade with eastern Asia in his "Report" with Prest. Message Dec 1850—begins correspondence with Com. P. to collect evidence to lay before Cabinet as to advisability &c of such expedition and the character of it. I have this correspondence *original.* The President favored it but through Mr. Webster's influence a majority of the Cabinet opposed and about Feby 1851 decided adversely to it—but about Nov. changed opinion—and Mr. G. began renewed conferences with Com P as to command—and Mch 24 1852—gave him orders to prepare and command. I do not know how much space you can give to this and as to Com Aulick's[2] meantime having been sent to command U.S. Squadron in China Seas—with a letter from Prest to Mikado[3]—all of which is changed when Cabinet consents to send an expedition of such character and numbers as Mr. G. thought adequate—Aulick is relieved of command and Perry substituted. Aulick & his friends do not yet know why—he asked a court of inquiry as to his removal. Mr. Dobbin[4] then Secy of the Navy replied there was nothing to investigate. Mr. G. had intended P. as commander if he got a suitable force and when he did he put him in command. You can determine as to how much of this you desire and I will furnish it, especially as to the point that Perry's orders were those prepared by G. of course the *State* Dept. prepared the papers for the Mikado.

I would refer you for "extracts" to examine his messages and addresses when inaugurated Govr—especially special message Dec 23, 1848. Note p 7. "Economy is a cardinal virtue in States or individuals but parsimony is as mischievous as prodigality &c"

Mr. McGehee refers to extracts from his speeches in U.S. Senate on loan bill and bill of apportionment—

The Raleigh Star Jany 10th or (11) 1835 refers to a speech on bill concerning Jackson's land scheme "of force of reason and eloquence not often heard.["]

Do not forget letters to Gov. Swain in "Last Ninety Days [s] of the War." In the article Dr. G. will send you I forgot to state among the reasons given as to unavoidability of secession was "Cloud not geographically remove the South—would still be joined to U.S.—hence better one govt"—this was the first time I heard this altho it is used by Lincoln and others afterward.

But I shall weary you with my writing—much of which may be unnecessary. As you find you desire anything you may not have, let me know and I will endeavor to get it for you.

If you desire any of his *epigrams* Dr. K. P. Battle could probably furnish you some.

Sincerely yours,

In Raleigh Register June 1844 will find articles containing Senators Wright and Woodbury's opinion of G as to *carefulness* in making reports—from this can find Cong Globe and get ent[i]re—After his election as Gov. he became the leader of his party and its preference for V.P.

---

[1]Robert Digges Wimberly Connor (1878-1950) was born in Wilson, son of Henry Groves and Kate Whitfield Connor. A gifted writer, Connor in his senior year at the University of North Carolina was editor in chief of the newspaper, literary magazine, and yearbook. After earning his Ph.B. degree he taught school at Winston, Oxford, and Wilmington. Connor became interested in the establishment of a state historical commission and was secretary of the new organization from 1903 until 1921. In 1934 he was appointed to the newly created post of Archivist of the United States, as appointment he filled with honor and distincition. From 1941 until he retired in 1949 Connor was Craige Professor of Jurisprudence and History at the University of North Carolina at Chapel Hill. Throughout his long career he held important offices in archival organizations and wrote dozens of articles as well as significant volumes. Among his most notable works were the two-volume *North Carolina: Rebuilding an Ancient Commonwealth* (1929) and the *North Carolina Manual*. Powell, *DNCB*, I, 418-419.

[2]Commodore John H. Aulick sailed in May, 1851, to assume command of the East India and China Seas Squadron, with incidental orders to negotiate a treaty with Japan. Later Aulick, ill and under the shadow of alleged misconduct, was replaced by Commodore Matthew C. Perry, who opened Japan in 1854. Max R. Williams, "William A. Graham, Naval Administrator," *North Carolina Historical Review*, XLVIII (Winter, 1971), 67.

[3]The emperor of Japan.

[4]James Cochran Dobbin (1814-1857), native of Fayetteville, was the son of Anness Cochran and John Moore Dobbin. After an early education in the schools of Fayetteville and at the Bingham School in Hillsborough, the attended the University of North Carolina, from which he was graduated in 1832. After three years of reading law, Dobbin was admitted to the state bar and established a law practice in Fayetteville. He embarked on a successful political career, beginning with a term in Congress in 1845. In 1848 he was elected to the House of Commons, where he distinguished himself by his work for the charter of the North Carolina Railroad and the establishment of a state hospital for the insane. In 1850 he served as Speaker of the House. An active supporter of President Franklin Pierce during his campaign for office, Dobbin was rewarded in 1853 with an appointment as secretary of the navy. Recognized as a hard worker with exceptional expertise in organizing, Secretary Dobbin proposed many reforms and innovations. It was said that he "remade" the navy. At the end of Pierce's term as president, Dobbin returned to North Carolina, where he died. *CDAB*, 238; Powell, *DNCB*, II, 82-83.

CHRONOLOGICAL LIST OF DOCUMENTS IN ADDENDUM TO THE PAPERS OF WILLIAM ALEXANDER GRAHAM

WRITTEN BY	WRITTEN TO	DATE
William A. Graham	Daniel M. Barringer	January 25, 1841
William A. Graham	Daniel M. Barringer	March 17, 1841
William A. Graham	Daniel M. Barringer	June 21, 1841
William A. Graham	Daniel M. Barringer	September 13, 1841
William A. Graham	Daniel M. Barringer	October 14, 1843
William A. Graham	George Little	September 3, 1850
William A. Graham	Daniel Webster	September 7, 1850
William A. Graham	Susan Washington Graham	October 20, 1850
William A. Graham	George Little	March 7, 1851
William A. Graham	Susan Washington Graham	October 29, 1853
William A. Graham	Susan Washington Graham	November 2, 1853
William A. Graham	Susan Washington Graham	December 13, 1853
William A. Graham	David L. Swain	May 6, 1854
William A. Graham	Susan Washington Graham	December 14, 1854
William A. Graham	Susan Washington Graham	February 5, 1855
William A. Graham	John H. Bryan	July 14, 1855
William A. Graham	Calvin H. Wiley	January 24, 1856
William A. Graham	Ralph R. Gurley	December 9, 1857
William A. Graham	Susan Washington Graham	October 16, 1859
William A. Graham	Ralph R. Gurley	December 6, 1859
William A. Graham	John H. Bryan	December 16, 1859
William A. Graham	Ralph R. Gurley	December 11, 1860
William A. Graham	Edward J. Hale	April 4 [1862]
William A. Graham	Susan Washington Graham	July 3, 1863
William A. Graham	Susan Washington Graham	August 12, 1863
Zebulon B. Vance	William A. Graham	August 13, 1863
Zebulon B. Vance	William A. Graham	August 19, 1863
Zebulon B. Vance	William A. Graham	August 24, 1863
Zebulon B. Vance	William A. Graham	January 1 [1864]
William A. Graham	Calvin H. Wiley	September 23, 1865
Zebulon B. Vance	William A. Graham	May 9 [1866?]

Addendum

William A. Graham to Daniel M. Barringer[1] UNC: BARRINGER

Senate Chamber
[Washington, D.C.]
Jany. 25th, 1841

I had expected to write you before you left Raleigh, but have found my engagements here to afford me but little leisure. I seize a moment now to write on a subject of some importance. Genl Edney is here, desirous of office. Whether a place can be found, which he will suit & he can thus be provided for, I do not know. But I hear from Lincolnton that they are there attaching his effects, and he may possibly not be able to run.

My purpose in now addressing you is to request that you will hold yourself in readiness to take the field at an early day. At a meeting of the Whig Senators, a few days ago (confidential of course) it was agreed, that an extra session of Congress was indispensable soon after the coming in, of the new administration, for the purpose of providing means to meet the public engagements, to establish a Bank and to provide for the distribution of the proceeds of the sales of the public lands. It seems to be understood that Congress must meet by by [*sic*] at furthist. Make ready therefore and prepare the public mind for these events, and keep yourself in position to embark in the campaign. Webster will be sec of state, Crittenden atty Genl, Ewing probably sec of the Treasury. The rest are uncertain. If N.C. shall come in, it will probably be to the war department. In that event Gov. Owen will perhaps come into the war department. But this is altogether a matter of uncertainty.

There will be but little done at this session of Congress. The land questions, preemptions, graduations, cessions etc. are all seized on by the defeated party with hope of strengthening themselves in the West. The discussions of the Senate upon these subjects have occupied several weeks in which many matters of an incidental character have been touched on. Webster made on saturday one of his best efforts in reply to Calhoun.

I write in haste from my seat, & under the thunders of the voice of Allen of Ohio. Consider what I have written as confidential, and make such use of the suggestions as you think beneficial.

Believe me to be with great regard.

Your Friend & servt.

---

[1]This and the next four letters were added to the Barringer manuscripts after publication of the Graham volume in which they would have appeared.

William A. Graham to Daniel M. Barringer UNC: BARRINGER

Hillsboro'
March 17th, 1841

I recd your letters before I left Washington, and only failed to reply from there, owing to the pressure of my engagements. As to the appointment of Mr Alexander to the place of superintendt of the Mint at Charlotte, I would have taken pleasure in aiding him, but I had previously consented to recommend Col B. S. Gaither and think it probable he will receive the office. The situation has been much sought and I have regretted my inability to procure it for many of the applicants who were personal friends.

I was unable to procure the statement of Ayes & Noes on the Charter of the late Bank of U.S. in a shape to be sent by mail. I will write today to Gales & Seaton to publish it in the Intelligencer. In N.C. all the Republican members voted for & Fedsts. against it in the House. In Senate Turner Aye. Macon, No.

The opponents of Genl. Harrison are at this time, I think, without settled ground of opposition. As to Tariff the duties are now too low to support Government & 5,000,000 of dollars go off at the end of the year. See compromise act. And the proposition is to raise what is needed not on necessaries, but luxuries. Wines, silks, Laces, Gold watches, Anchovies. See the whole list in compromise act, but never to go higher than 20 per cent. Can any reasonable man object to this? If the Calhoun clique object that the tax on these will diminish imports & lower the price of cotton etc. the answer is, that this objection seeks *protection* for agriculture, and in order to protect it exempts the rich who consume silks etc. from paying their share of the revenue. The objection to distribution of lands is that it would create a necessity for the increase of the Tariff to the amount of the proceeds withdrawn. Yet that objection comes from those who are for giving them away to new states, squandering them by preemptions, Graduations etc. Look to Genl Jacksons veto, Kings report on Clays land Bill, Norvells report on Calhouns Bill, indeed all the manifestos of any of the opponents of distribution, and you find they invariably look to parting with the lands as a source of revenue at an early day. So that according to them the burthen of supporting Government will soon be on customs alone, or direct taxes. And the question of distribution involves simply the inquiry whether the old states shall have any benefit at all from the lands, either in aiding the ordinary revenue, or in dividing, or whether the whole shall be swallowed up by the new states—to which latter result every effort of the V. B. party is tending. As to a Bank there will no doubt be a sufficient majority in both Houses to carry it. You inquire whether Wise, Mallory & Alford can effect any thing against the administration. These are the only three members in all Congress who have objected to any of the measures proposed, and I have no doubt the first will come in to the support of the administration. It is however a matter of little importance. Harrison has strength enough [to] cast off Fifty such, and still retain a majority of the country. I verily believe that Clay himself would be killed off, & the administration go on prosperously were he to take a stand on the same grounds.

I think you will find the Inaugural address of great advantage. Its moderation, disclaimers of Executive powers, condemnation of Abolition, exhortation against party excitement, & regard for religion, cannot fail to make an impression upon reasonable men of all parties. It is probable that Congress will be convened about the 1st of June. I had hoped to converse with the President on the subject but I left before the adjournment to reach Orange Court, and he was so pressed with company that I had no opportunity. Gentlemen who talked with [him] however told me that he had determined on the call. Indeed it will probably be shown by statements from the treasury department to be indispensable to supply the means to pay the public engagements and save the National honor, and it will perhaps be placed on that ground in the proclamation. When convened three subjects will probably be acted on, viz. Distribution of the proceeds of lands. Tariff on luxuries & for revenue only & a national Bank. The last I presume will not be recommended in the Message of the Extve., but by the secy. of the Treasury but will meet his approbation.

It would be well to call on your opponent to know whether he approves the principles of the inaugural. If not let him state what he disapproves & why. If he does, then he should be rejected, because he condemned Harrison before hand & charged him in common with his party, with principles he never maintained. A smattering of German will be of great service to you in Lincoln.

Dr Smith is about to be nominated here against Montgomery. With good management we ought to carry 10 out of the 13 districts in the State. I have not time to write more.

William A. Graham to Daniel M. Barringer UNC: BARRINGER

Washington City
June 21st, 1841

I recd your letter of the 18th inst. on yesterday afternoon. The progress of events has not been so satisfactory since the beginning of the session as could have been desired, but I still hope that Congress will be able in a great degree to realize the expectation of the country. The Senates committee on currency etc. will today report a Bill for a Bank upon the model of the old charters, adopting the Report of the sec. of Treas. in part, such as locating the mother Bank here but authorizing the corporation to establish branches and to do such other things as may give it efficiency. It is said that the Executive is opposed to a charter with the branching power, and there has been much consultation among our friends to produce a plan, free from difficulty.

The body of the Whigs in the Senate have at length resolved to adopt a plan as will be successful in practice, and submitting it for the approbation of the President. A veto would produce injury to the party & the country, but not more than would accrue from the imbecility of enacting the . . . Charter with a capital of 30 millions, placed in this district, with no power to go out of it except by the previous assent of the State Legislatures, in which no prudent man would invest a dollar. My impression is that there will be no veto, but as the President is averse to being put to the test, it is to be feared that he will have friends enough to prevent him from being tried.

The opposition are rabid and will make war on everything. The affair of the mint at Charlotte has not been been attended, but the secy. promises that it shall. His numerous engagements have prevented his attention to it heretofore. Removals have not gone on so rapidly as they should. The true policy was to make all that were designed at once.

The course of events here is quite uncertain, and I have therefore not written before to any of our friends respecting them. You will then please subject this scrawl to the fate of heretics in old times. The repeal of the subtreasury comes on in the House today, and will perhaps reconcile our friends again, & bring them together. There have been some heartburnings there, growing out of the election of Speaker etc.

I write in much haste, and must conclude to get my letter into this mail.

William A. Graham to Daniel M. Barringer UNC: BARRINGER

Washington City
Sept. 13th, 1841

Congress adjourns tonight. You will have heard that the President has rejected the second Bank Bill after having promised his approval to it. Messers Ewing, Bell, Badger & Crittenden resigned on saturday & Mr Granger today. Mr Webster continues, though it is not known how long he will remain. The President promptly nominated to the Senate Walter Forward of Penn. now comptr. of Treas. to be Secretary of Treas. Judge Mclean of Ohio Secy. of War. Judge Upshur of Va. Secy. Navy, Mr. Legare S.C. Atty. Genl. Chs. Wickliffe of Ky PostM. Genl. They will be no doubt confirmed.

Mr. Ewing's letter of resignation appears in the Intelligencer of today, and charges the President with gross perfidy in relation to the last bill. Our friends in Congress had a meeting this morning & resolved on an address to the people of the U.S. on the subject of the Presidents conduct. He seems to have surrendered himself to the direction of a small clique, who drive him about with the facility of a barque without a rudder. More imbecility & folly has never been exhibited by any man invested with any authority. The Locos have not espoused him fully, & he still claims to be a Whig. His new cabinet also, acted with us in the recent contest, but the leading spirits of them are tinctured with nullification, and they are supposed to be selected with reference to an opposition to Mr Clay for the succession. We shall have a troublesome time during his administration. He desires to run for the succession, but finding no encouragement to that, he will endeavour to wreck his vengeance by thwarting Whigs in the election.

The nomination of Everett & others who were opposed on the ground of abolition have been confirmed, and the Injunction of secrecy taken from the Journal. Some party capital will be attempted to be made out of it at the South, but I assure you, that it is for the best. I have not time to write more.

William A. Graham to Daniel M. Barringer UNC: BARRINGER

Hillsboro'
Oct. 14th, 1843

I was last week at Wake Superior Court where I saw most of our Whig friends residing in that county & several others. They are in high spirits as regards our political prospects in the country generally but especially in the state. Some of them apprehend however that there is danger of an imprudent step in relation to a nomination for Governor; and I have been requested to address you on the subject.

You have seen that several of the Newspapers in different quarters have proposed as the whig nominee the Hon. Ed. Stanly. And so zealous & ardent are his friends that in the convention to assemble on the 7th of December, he will most probably receive the nomination, unless the Western counties are represented, & have the matter attended to. Our most prudent friends such for example as Gov. Morehead, Maj. Hinton, Mr. R. Hines, Devereux etc. etc. are of [the] opinion that this nomination should be avoided if possible. I myself concur in this opinion. Let me at once say to you in all candor that I could not accept the nomination if tendered to me, and as many friends in various parts of the State have been kind enough to speak of me in connexion with the candidacy, I have felt reluctant to interfere with the selection among others even by confidential letters, such as this, to intimate friends. But having formed my determination after much reflection, that to be considered among those from whom a selection is to be made, I have deemed it due to our cause, to offer my views in perfect confidence, respecting a proper nominee, or at least concerning one that I shall consider unfortunate if made. Towards Mr. Stanly I have the most kind feelings & candid relations, and would have no objection to see him the Govr. of the State, and this is the feeling of those with whom I have conversed. But he is the most obnoxious to our opponents, of all the public men of the State, will not get the votes of the most moderate among them, and although he has warmly attached friends, it is not to be disguised, that he is not a favorite with many of the Whigs. With him as our candidate we would dread the result although there is a popular majority with us of more than 10,000 votes.

I sat down however not to argue the question of this nomination to you, but to say, that if you concur in my opinions respecting it, I hope you will take steps to have proper delegations sent from the counties of your district to the convention. Chas Manly is generally looked to, as our nominee, by those with whom I have conversed, but they seem most anxious to avoid an imprudent one, and have no doubt of success with a suitable candidate. If the counties cannot be represented by their own citizens attending in person would it not be well to appoint citizens of Wake, with power in the event that they could not attend, or were already delegates from their own county to transfer the proxies to some other person. A copy of the resolutions being sent to signify the wishes of the meetings. But no person to represent more than one county.

I write this in great haste. If you do not concur, no action of course is expected. Whether you do or not, commit this to the fire.

William A. Graham to George Little A&H: LITTLE-MORDECAI

Navy Department
September 3rd 1850

My dear Sir

I have examined the case of Midshipman P. H. Haywood, and asked upon it the advise of the President. I regret to say that the rules and discipline of the service will not permit his restoration. He appears on the Register to have been dismissed, with several other officers of his grade, on the 28th of August 1849, and a list of these, and other dismissions, was reported to Congress at the commencement of the present session; and other Midshipmen have been appointed to fill these vacancies. His case therefore involves, not merely the usages and rules of the service, and the rights of those who stood below him in date, but will require a revision of the cases of all those who were dismissed at the same time, for like causes. The department felt obliged then, to enforce the regulation requiring dismission, and its decision seems to have been approved by the President. Mr. Haywood thus passed out of the service, and persons below him succeeded to his office. The President does not think that the accidental circumstance, of a change of administration, will justify him in reversing the decision of his predecessor, unless upon clear proof that some positive law has been violated.

I regret this result, on Mr. Haywoods account, who certainly sustained a high character in the Navy for gallantry and gentlemanly conduct; and I would do any thing, not conflicting with duty, to gratify his friends. But in view of the circumstances now attending his case, I could not advise the President to a different conclusion from that indicated above.

I herewith return to you Mr Haywoods letters of recommendation, and remain

With high respect
Your Obedt. Servt.

William A. Graham to Daniel Webster A&H

Unofficial

Navy Department
Sept 7th 1850

My dear Sir

I send herewith a copy of a private letter from Commander L. M. Powell, commanding the U.S. Ship "John Adams" on the Coast of Africa, addressed to Comdore. Warrington, who has kindly favored me with it. I have supposed that the first pages of the letter may afford you some views of the operations of the British cruisers in the suppression, or in pretending to suppress it, of the slave trade on that coast, which may deserve inquiry, if nothing more, at your department.

Very faithfully yours

William A. Graham to Susan Washington Graham A&H

Washington City
Oct 20 1850

My dear Wife

I am disappointed in receiving no letter from you this afternoon. It has been an unpleasant day, and I have not been out. Gov Corwin and Comdore. Morris have called this evening and relieved my solitude in some degree. I believe I heard more frequently from home while you were here than since. I hope you have received your trunk, as I believe it contained nearly all your baggage. Our furniture has not been received from New York, though the Bills of lading came more than a week since. Mrs Badger went to examine the table to be sold, but reported that it was too narrow. She says there is a very fine set of China there, but I suppose you supplied yourself, in that line, in New York. Mr. Tayer called the other night, with the various bills, of Mr. Preston & c, amounting to $1005. I have also recd the Bill, from New York, of $360. payable the 1st of Nov. which is in the hands of Corcoran and Riggs. The curtain has been put up in the Library.

I wish you would send word to Mr. Whitted that if he has sold my wheat I will be glad to have the money collected, by the first week in Nov. when I hope to be at home. You should direct that the hogs to be fattened be allowed to run in the fields as the corn is pulled out, and put up to be fattened & killed as early as they are in order. If I cant get a suitable overseer, I believe I must hire out the greater part of negroes. You should collect in, all our accounts, before you leave, and let them be settled.

I hope to get home by the 5th or 6 Nov, though, I may possibly be there by the 3rd. I can not stay more than 3 or 4 days, and therefore wish you to be ready, at very short notice. It is highly important, in view of our short crop, to dispose of the surplus cattle, & horses, as early as practicable. I will try to hire a conveyance at Henderson, and go directly home, when I set off.

I find my treble duty to occupy much of my time. It will not continue I hope more than this week. The wind whistles with the sound of winter, and the weather is bleak and depressing. My love, to my sons and to mother & sister E. I have nothing from Mr Bryan this week. Tell Jamey he is a faithful correspondent, and I will answer his letter soon.

Ever Yours

William A. Graham to George Little A&H: LITTLE-MORDECAI

Washington City
March 7th 1851

My dear Sir

I received at Hillsboro' in Nov. last, when hastening my departure with my family for Washington, a letter from you requesting that I endeavor to procure some suitable employment for our friend Mr. P. H. Haywood, whom, I regretted that I did not feel authorized to restore to the Naval Service.

I have today had an interview with Wm. H. Aspinwall Esq. of New York, in which I mentioned Mr Haywoods situation, and my desire that he, Mr A., could afford him a place. Mr Aspinwall I should state is the president of the Mail Steamship Co. in the Pacific, which carries the mail from Panama to California & Oregon. He immediately replied that he would be glad to oblige any friend of mine, and inquired as to his age, experience &c which I gave as fully as I was able. He finally said he would give him a trial at all counts, and that if he will report to him in New York by the 15th of this month, or if not then, by the 15th of the next, he shall have the place of second officer on board one of his Pacific Mail steam ships, at a pay of about $1200. per year, with a prospect of being advanced to a first officer.

Intending to deal with the mos[t] candor, in answer[ing] inquires from him, the only doubt I had was as to the habits of Mr H. in respect to temperance. He said that any indulgence in that respect was out of the question, and must be followed by instant dismission—that he had carried out this rule with relatives of his own. I don't know what are Mr Haywoods habits in this respect. I was aware that he had some frolics formerly at Wake and chose to keep nothing back. I wish you therefore to show him this letter and say that the above offer is made to him. If he is still disposed to follow the sea, it is preferable to his position in the Navy, and affords him the best prospects he could desire. His employer however is a particular person, and will require great exactment in the performance of his duties.

Please consult him at once, & communicate to me his determination. Lieut. Patterson of the Navy will probably command the steamer.

I remain With much regard
Your Friend & Servt.

William A. Graham to Susan Washington Graham A&H

Earhart Plantation
Saturday Oct. 29th 1853

My dearest

I arrived here this afternoon from Charlotte, and was much gratified to find that your letter of the 24th had been brought down from the Furnace. It seems a long time since I left home. After writing you from Salisbury, I pursued my journey the next day to Beaties Ford, but was surprised to find the river swollen, and past fording. I then turned down for the Henderson place, but being benighted, stopped with a friend, a mile from it. The next morning, Sunday, I rode by it on my way to the ferry, and stopped, for half an hour—then reached Mr Moore's to dinner, and Dr. Morrisons at night. Anna has been dangerously ill, and even yet is much debilitated, and looking badly. The next morning, I intended to go to the lower place, but it rained, incessantly, till three or four oclock, and I was detained. Fearing high water, I went some eight or ten miles, out of my way, to a bridge on the South Fork, tuesday, and arrived at the Leper place in the evening. They have been unusually healthy there this season, while the country around has had more sickness than ever before, says Dr McLean, since he has practiced Medicine. This has also been the case in Mecklenburg, and the Henderson place has suffered somewhat. I was greatly disappointed in not getting the Leper land surveyed while I was there. Dr McLean had engaged a surveyor, but he was detained, at home, by the state of his family. The Dr and his brother Robert were both too unwell to have accompanied us, and withal the weather would have interrupted us before we could have finished. Aunt MacLean is tolerably well. Both the families of her sons have been, and are affected, by the prevailing disease. It rained again all day thursday, and a rise in the creek there prevented me from seeing them but once. On yesterday, I took Ben with a carryall, and made for Masons ferry six miles down the river *in sorte* for Charlotte—on arriving at the ferry, found the water six feet above ordinary, and after considerable detention, with aid from hands, got safely over—reached Charlotte about dark, too late to purchase the supplies for the plantation—made an early rise this morning, hoping to get through & reach this place by one oclock—did not get off however till 9.—drove rapidly to the river—found it higher than yesterday—detained again—stopped a moment at Dr Morrisons, and by the aid of the plank road, arrived here at 4—but Mr Moore and the other persons whom I had appointed to meet here at 11 had gone—so that there has been no valuation of the estate as I desired. Tomorrow about noon, I will set off for Caldwell Co. to make sale of the land there—hope to reach Newton, Catawba C.H. in the evening, and Lenoir the C.H. of Caldwell, the next evening—make the sale on tuesday & return to this place, wednesday night or thursday. I have then, three overseers to employ, and to attend a survey of the Henderson land, the monday following which will be the 7th of Nov. I will therefore not be at home before the 11th or 12th.

I saw Ann Eliza & her mother at Charlotte, but had not time to call on any one else. Mr Irwin, Harriet Morrisons husband, is about to settle there—and Major Hill is coming to Davidson College.

Old Mr Springs, whom you know, died, in Augusta of congestion of the brain, and was buried in Charlotte last monday. I saw Sophia Graham this afternoon at Dr Morrisons. There is but little change in her appearance—she has heard nothing from home. Sister Violets family, I hear have been sick again, and she herself has had a chill.

The crop of corn here is excellent, and the stock generally in good condition. The young Mule is the best I have ever seen. At the lower place, there is an abundant supply of corn, and I hope the cotton may reach two thirds of the crop of last year. The season however is late, and, I fear, it is materially injured by a severe, killing frost this week.

I would gladly avoid my trip to Caldwell. The road however is said to be good, and there is a bridge over the river, the swells in which have interrupted me more on this journey than ever before.

Adieu my dearest, and believe me ever truly yours. With my blessing, on our dear children. Adieu.

William A. Graham to Susan Washington Graham A&H

Earhart Place
Nov. 2nd 1853

My Dear Wife

I am happy to say that I returned this afternoon, safe from Caldwell. I went on sunday to Newton, 17 miles, thence, on monday, crossing the Catawba on a Bridge at the Horse Ford, to Lenoir, the C.H. of Caldwell—after arriving in the County, I learned that I had been mistaken in the week of the Court, which by an act of the Legislature at the last session, had been placed a week later than formerly, and therefore does not come on till next week. I however proceeded on to the house of my friend, Maj. Miller, and from there to Lenoir. He had been kind enough to assume an agency for me in regard to the land I desired to sell, and went with me the next day to see it. The water power at Dudleys shoal is one of the most valuable I have ever seen and the place reminded me of the places above & below Trenton Falls, that you will remember near Utica N.Y. I, of course, did not sell, but my visit will be of service to the interests of those concerned in the land, & will I hope lead to a speedy disposition of it. I authorized Maj. Miller to sell the whole at an average of $1. per acre, and he has no doubt of effecting a sale in a short time. After viewing the premises as well as our time would allow, I returned as far as the Bridge on the Catawba; and came from thence, breakfasting, at Newton today. I regretted not to find the Court sitting, as I hoped to meet many friends there, and learned, from Mr Jos. Norwood and others, that my coming was anticipated by a number who would go to the court with the expectation of meeting me. Mr N. has a very excellent farm and handsome situation near Lenoir. I found the road, in the whole, better than I expected, and the greatest part, a very good one for any country. I took with me from here the Boy John, who, though awkward, & not very spruce in his dress, was of considerable service. I went high enough to breathe the cool autumn air of the Blue Ridge & Table Rock, of both of which I had a very distinct view in the distance. My horses performed very well, with the exception of the new one's aversion to holding back steadily, on the steep mountains & hills. I desired to buy a horse for Robert's place, but was told they were as high in Caldwell as in the country below. So much for my journey.

I have reappointed a meeting of the Commissioners here tomorrow to value the property. The next day, I meet a man at Dr Morrisons whom I wish to engage as an overseer for the Leper place. The next day, I shall probably cross the river to look out one for the Henderson place. On monday, it is to be surveyed, and then I shall turn my face homeward, with whatever speed my horses can make. I shall probably retain the overseer I have here.

I may be at home by thursday night, but probably not till friday.

My blessing on our children, and true love to thee.

Ever Yours

I sent to the office this evening—had a letter from Maj. Bryan at Rutherfordton with a partial account of business there, but not final, as I had hoped.

William A. Graham to Susan Washington Graham A&H

Washington City
Decr. 13th 1853

My Dear Wife

I have made my argument today in the case of Potter vs. Potter, and have no doubt of success, though I cannot be here when the Judgement of the Court is delivered. At the request of Mr. J. H. Bryan, I invited his son, William, to appear with me in the case, and he met me here from Baltimore for the purpose. I had hoped to dispose of this case last friday, but in unison with the two Houses of Congress, the Supreme Court paid funeral honors, to the late Vice President, and did not sit that day.

What with attendance on Court, and the Law Library, I have not been much out—have not yet seen the Senate in Session, and the house but once. I attended preaching in the latter on sunday—and afterwards dined alone at Govr. Fish's. His improvements on our old premises are not equal to what I had expected, but they render the house very convenient. Mrs F. inquired, very kindly, for you, and desired the presentment of her love.

I met the President in the street on friday, and called to see him next day. He invited me, to dinner, at half past four; but it being then one, I excused myself, and declined. I called to see Mrs Bell, who is keeping house near Willards, and found there Mrs Badger & daughters. She is evidently greatly elated, and talks without cessation.

I have seen nothing of society, not even the ladies of the drawing room, at Browns, where I am. Among these are Mrs Catson & Mrs McLean—the former I met in the street.

The population one meets is much changed from what it was when we were here. The buildings of the City are much improved, and improving.

I go tonight to Mr Hodges to meet a party of gentlemen. Having gone through my business, I will devote the next two days to seeing my friends, and on friday night go over to Baltimore, and take the Boat that evening, so as to be in Raleigh by the next night. Please send the Buggy for me on

Saturday, so as to be at Guions, that night. I hope to arrive there by six o clock.

My blessing on our dear children

Ever truly Yours

There is some division between the administration and a portion of its party. On yesterday Bev. Tucker was elected printer to the Senate, over Armstrong of the Union.

Franklin has a prospect of a good business in painting, but is working quite too cheap.

William A. Graham to David L. Swain A&H: SWAIN

Hillsboro'
May 6th 1854

My Dear Sir

I am much obliged for your letter in relation to the causes of the dismission of Joseph from College, which I found here on my return from the Catawba, night before last. I have for some time been apprehensive that without a change of his habits, and associates, his college course would be of little profit, and although he avails himself of the permission to return, I shall, at the end of the session, consider whether it be not best that he shall be transferred to some other Institution or business.

With kind regards to Mrs Swain,

I am very truly yours

William A. Graham to Susan Washington Graham A&H

Raleigh
Decr. 14th 1854

My Dear Wife

The Boys have gotten the articles wanted for themselves, and by you, with the exception of the Scotch ale, which is not to be had here.

There was a beautiful exhibition of a Balloon ascension, on monday last, from the Fair ground. First, a lady going up one or two Hundred yards, and then, the Aeronaut, Mr Eliot, sailed off gallantly, to the height of, I suppose, half a mile to a mile, in a South East direction, untill he disappeared entirely. He is said to have landed about 18 miles off, in Johnston County. The assembly at the exhibition was large, and greatly delighted—though the order was interrupted by the appearance of several women, well dressed, in a state of beastly intoxication.

The Senate is engaged in the discussion of Constitutional amendment. The House in but little of any thing. There is great delay, arising from a want of capacity to conduct business on the part of the majority.

I have told Joseph that if the drove of Hogs is still in Hillsboro', it will be well to purchase about 2500 lbs. or if you think a less quantity will answer, take only so much as is needed. By drawing on me, here, I can pay the amount.

I will endeavor to send today for the amount you wished placed in the hands of Dr Evans. Your work on the House is no doubt designed for the best, and I am satisfied. Mr Guinn writes me from Lincoln that he has sold the land at $3. per acre—I had offered him, $2.50. I wish I had time to go out an[d] get some toys for the children. Tell them all howdys, and that I hope to see them, next saturday night week.

I suppose I shall not see you here in the mean time.

With true affection Yours

William A. Graham to Susan Washington Graham A&H

Raleigh Monday night
Feb. 5th 1855

My Dear Wife

I had hoped to hear from you tonight, and to learn that you would be down this week. I write to request that if you come, as I hope you will, you will bring two or three copies of my Lithograph likeness, which gentlemen here have asked me for. Also a bottle or two of the best Sherry and White Port Wine.

Your brother, John, is here again, about the Eastern Railroad, which passed today, in the shape that they desired. There is nothing now to prevent its construction, unless they fail to raise one third of the money required—the State takes two thirds. There has been much excitement in the Legislature for the last few days about Internal Improvements, and a very reckless spirit. Every scheme passing that has been proposed. If they are all undertaken, the public debt will be increased to seven millions of dollars. I see in the Washington papers notices of the deaths of Mr Molina, the South American Minister, of old Mr Pleasanton, the Auditor, & Mr. Maury, late Mayor of the City.

Your Brother says your mother is not quite so well as she has been. Mrs Dr Washington has not yet come to his house from New Bern.

Mr Conrad is here, and says he will be at our house the last of next week, by which time I hope to be at home, and look over the house with him. I send a letter to Mr Vaughan, to your care.

My love, to our dear children

Your Affectionate

William A. Graham to John H. Bryan A&H

Hillsboro'
July 14th 1855

My Dear Sir:

"Coming events are said, to cast their shadows before." I have heard, as very current rumor, that the Supreme Court has decided the case of Ashe vs Johnston, in favor of the Plaintiff, and learning something of the manner in which such conclusions are unofficially communicated to the public, I must presume it to be true. If so, I must beg you to consider whether I can obtain relief by filing a Bill against Ashe, Johnston's admr., & the Railroad Co. I had no intention to become involved in a contract beyond $16,000. in amount, and being absent from the State, was informed by Johnston, that he had contracted for us, to the amount of $17,600, that being the nearest to the amount desired that he could obtain—but that Richd. Ashe would take off our hands all over $16,000. Upon this representation, I approved what he was represented as having done, and ordered my hands, Horses &c, to be sent to the work. I did not know that Ashe's name was mentioned in the contract at all, and never heard of it untill my hands had been at work on the road for 18 months. The contract is dated in May or June 1851. I returned to the State in Aug 1852. My hands had then been at work a year. At Christmas afterwards Mr Johnston brought me the contract, & said Mr Ashe was threatening to pass off his stock upon him. On reading the contract then, I for the first time learned that there was any stipulation for his benefit in it. I immediately told Mr Johnston that I could not take Mr Ashe's stock for my work; and advised him to the course stated in his answer—that is to give Ashe notice, if he claimed any benefit in it, to come forward & perform his share of the work &c. And it appears to me strange that the Court should decide any thing in the matter to my prejudice without allowing me to be heard. The Bill shows my interest, and that I am liable to all the debts contracted in the course of the work. Now what I wish examined is whether I have not an Equity, not only against Johnston, & entitling me to be paid half of the amounts due for work, over & above my stock, in cash, from him, but whether my Equity does not entitle me to this amount, in cash, from the Company as against Ashe leaving him to compel Johnston to take stock, to the amount of half, of his half, or share, of earnings. Johnston had no authority to bind me to take any of Ashe's stock, and as I was involved in the contract in entire ignorance of any connexion of Ashe with it, the stock cannot be forced upon me by Johnston, as I think, nor ought he to be decreed to take it, except as to that half of the earnings which was really his. Please think of this, and consult with Mr Winston & beg him to appear in my behalf, if a Bill be maintainable and I am forced to file it. I will not submit to have $1500 or 2000. worth of stock forced on me at par, when it is really worth nothing, if there be any mode of defence.

Again, the whole earnings on the Contract were about $24,700. Of this about $4,700 is still due. $18,000 must be applied before Ashe has any claim. The balance is $6,700—the utmost amount of his claim is half of this, i.e.

$3350. Yet Judge Battle's Injunction forbids the payment of a dollar out of $4700. The difference of $1400 would afford me some relief in the payment of debts. But whether any modification can be had I know not.

Very truly yours

William A. Graham to Calvin H. Wiley A&H: WILEY

Hillsborough
Jany 24th 1856

Your letter mailed the 20th inst. has been received. In reply, I have to state that my engagements will deny me the leisure necessary to edit the publication of the Revolutionary documents proposed by you.

I would suggest however that if the publication be undertaken, the documents should be set forth in full, and in chronological order, accompanied by a copious index.

I have no copy of my message to the General Assembly on the subject of Historical documents. You can find it however among the published papers of the Legislature of 1846.

William A. Graham to Ralph R. Gurley LC: AMERICAN COLONIZATION SOCIETY

Hillsborough, N.C.
Dec. 9th 1857

My absence from home during the last week has delayed for that length of time the acknowledgement of your letter of the 30th ult. inviting me, in the name of the Executive Committee of the Colonization Society of the U.S., to address that body, at its annual meeting on the 19th of January next.

I regret that engagements of business, which I cannot neglect, will prevent my visiting Washington at that time, and consequently will constrain me to decline the honor of complying with the Committee's invitation.

I beg the Colonization Society however to be assured that I take a lively interest in the objects of its institution; that for what it has already accomplished it deserves the thanks of every patriotic citizen, and that for its future encouragement and success, no reasonable and proper effort of mine shall be wanting.

I remain, my dear sir,
With Great Respect,
Your Obedt. Servt.

William A. Graham to Susan Washington Graham A&H

Earharts
Oct. 16th 1859

My Dear Wife

I hope to send this from Cottage Home where I propose to go tonight, from church at Macpelah. I found all well at Charlotte—left there wednesday afternoon, & came to Hendersons, staid till friday, in order to settle affairs there, which were somewhat troublesome, but I got them rectified before leaving—came to Dr M's & dined on friday. Sister Sophia was just leaving for Charlotte in the stage—she will remain there, two or three weeks, and proceed to Alabama. I proposed to her to go home with me, but she says she cannot. Anna and Wm. are there—he came to see me yesterday afternoon. They have been very healthy—here; & at Henderson's, the freshet has done less damage at both than I expected—but I fear is worse below. I shall be obliged to go tomorrow to Lincolnton, and on wednesday to the lower place—shall not reach Charlotte till friday, & home sunday morning.

The crop here is good—especially of cotton, and the little Tobacco planted has done well—at Henderson's, it is but tolerable owing to inefficient management. I have heard nothing new, of interest. The Military school in Charlotte is quite a subject of conversation. There are said to be 72 Cadets already. Mrs Johnston's family of this neighborhood is speaking much of going to Texas. Ham. Graham told me he would leave for that state next tuesday. I have not heard whether Joseph came to Charlotte as he expected. There will be communion today at Macpelah & Dr Lacy is to be there.

My love to our dear children [and] believe me

Ever affectionately Yours

William A. Graham to Ralph R. Gurley LC: AMERICAN COLONIZATION SOCIETY

Hillsboro' N.C.
Dec. 6th 1859

My Dear Sir:

I have the honor to acknowledge the receipt of your favor of the 2nd inst., inviting me to address the annual meeting of the Colonization Society of the U.S. at Washington on the 17th of January next, and regret very much that it will not be in my power to comply.

I trust however that the benevolent efforts of the Society will suffer no interruption since the tendencies of events render it more than ever necessary that the free blacks shall be separated from the slaves as well as the white race, and it is manifest that this can only be effectuated by providing for them a home in their native clime.

I remain very faithfully
& respectfully
Your Obedt. servt.

William A. Graham to John H. Bryan A&H: BRYAN

Hillsboro'
Decr. 16th 1859

My Dear Sir

I have been so much occupied, principally in preparing for a special term of the Superior Court, appointed here for this week, but which has failed for want of the attendance of a Judge to hold it, that I have neglected earlier to reply to your favor of the 8th with its enclosure.

I think you have acted properly in not falling in with the request of the circular sent to you. Among its signers are good names, and others in which I have no confidence. While we can't cooperate with democrats, without a better understanding than is likely to take place, I would cooperate with no other party which does not recognize the legitimate rights of the South. I expect to attend the meeting of Trustees next monday, and we may then have a conversation in regard to affairs generally. I hope you will not resign your place on the Whig Committee.

Very truly yours

William A. Graham to Ralph R. Gurley LC: AMERICAN COLONIZATION SOCIETY

Hillsboro' N.C.
Dec. 11th 1860

Dear Sir:

Your favor of the 5th inst. inviting me to attend and address the American Colonization Society in Washington on the 3rd Tuesday of January next has been received. My engagements at the Supreme Court of the State will forbid my presence in Washington at that time. And independently of this, the present disturbed and alarming state of the Country, so constantly engages my attention that I have no leisure to prepare any thing worthy of the occasion of your general meeting. I pray therefore to be excused, though my best wishes attend the benevolent objects of the Society.

I remain
With high respect
Your Obedt. Servt.

William A. Graham to Edward J. Hale[1] A&H: HALE

Hillsboro
April 4 [1862]

I herein remit for the Observer [letter burnt] desired in your acct just received. In future I wish the Semi weekly sent to me, and a weekly to G. & A. Graham Melville Alamance Co. I enclose $8.00 which I suppose will pay for the whole. The copy sent to my son J. A. Graham at Fort Macon may be changed to Kinston for balance of the year. He belongs to Col. Sloans

Regiment. His term will expire on the 20th of this month, but he has two brothers in the same army-Brem's Artillery & Spruills Cavalry.

"I am gratified to see that the Observer has independence enough to object to the proposition to repudiate the paroles of our released soldiers. It proposes a process of absolution scarely less than Papal. But I regard the recent message of the President, asking for the power of *Conscription*, as in effect looking to a military despotism, and I am greatly surprized that the Richmond Whig, which has manfully raised its voice against the proscription and favoritism of the administration, and the imbecility in office which has been its natural result, should have yielded its acquiescence in the policy. Give to the President a standing army consisting of all male citizens between the ages of 18 & 35, with power to call into the field as many as he pleases & when & where he pleases, without saying to the Governor of a state 'by your leave,' and not only is the Constitution subverted, but personal liberty is no more. The power to declare & enforce Martial law, & imprison citizens indefinitely without the right of Habeas Corpus to inquire into the cause of [letter burnt], is another wide step in the same direction. [letter burnt] prevails in the country, and those in authority [have] but to ask for power on the ground of military [neces]sity and the oldest and most sacred safeguards [of] freedom are yielded without question. [We] must retain our self possession, and our liberties too, in the progress of the war or we will look in vain for them at its close."

There [are] other topics on which I would be pleased to say a word by way of suggestion—such as Mr Yancey's declaration to Earl Russell that the *union was not dissolved on account of slavery*, but of Tariff duties, but I have neither space or leisure.

---

[1]This important letter was found among the undated correspondence in the Edward Jones Hale Papers, PC 17, State Archives. Graham apparently wrote the part of this letter concerning his fears about Confederate despotism for publication in the *Fayetteville Observer*.

William A. Graham to Susan Washington Graham A&H

Raleigh
July 3rd 1863

My Dearest

It is somewhat doubtful whether I shall be able to get home tomorrow afternoon. If not I will endeavour to come up the next morning. I've received today your letter enclosing those of William and James, and was glad to hear from them.

There was a telegram here today, that Genl. D. H. Hill had fought the enemy between Richmond and the White House, and driven them back five miles—it being some 15 miles from Richmond. I think it probable our three boys near that place were in the engagement. I suppose further particulars will come tonight. Mr. John Bryan's family have been greatly relieved within a day or two in learning that Geo. is not killed. I called at Miss

Whites this evening—all well except Miss Susan who is feeble yet. Mrs Swain & Mrs Walker were there. The Legislature will adjourn finally next tuesday. No other news here. Love to Sissy & sister E.

Ever affectionately yours

I will come in afternoon if I can.

William A. Graham to Susan Washington Graham A&H

Hillsboro'
Aug 12th / 63

My Dear Wife

I wrote you a note by Maj & Mrs Hamilton, sending the articles you desired, but fear that from a Railroad accident, delaying their departure hence, till 10 o clock on yesterday, they will not have arrived before this letter.

George goes with this, in care of Mr. Faucett, and carries in a box the things for which you wrote to sister E. Edmund has arrived today from Wms. Camp—very well & full of tales of his adventures—saw nothing of Joseph or James. I send letter of the latter from Fredkbg. which I found on my return home. I didn't bring your small carpet bag. Captain Berry laid off the piazza today. Alfred has gone to get other timbers for a part of it. I hope soon to get lumber, for raising the wash house. Umstead is threshing wheat at Rays today. Mrs. Brown is weaving daily. Augus. Knox returned to Dr Wilsons yesterday. Holcott Jones had his leg broken by fall of a horse at Kinston yesterday, telegram received. Some mischievous person took up a rail on N.C. Road beyond shopes & caused train to run off, Killing a negro, & doing other damage yesterday—which delayed the Hamiltons.

The House is solitary without you, and I hope the time will soon pass, and you will be at home again in renewed health. Weather intensely hot. Thermometer at 90°. Notice of the Funeral of Jas. S. Watson has been sent around, for 9 o Clock today at Baptist church.

My love & kiss to Sudie, and to Bettie & Jo.

Ever Affectionately Yours

Zebulon B. Vance to William A. Graham[1] A&H

Confidential

Raleigh
August 13, 1863

My Dear Sir:

I beg to call your attention to the proceedings of many meetings in various parts of the State, in favour of peace. Under all the circumstances, I consider them *ruinous*, in the last degree.

They will cause the army to melt away by desertion, will create, perhaps dissensions & civil war at home, and will defeat any & all efforts for peace, unless it be on the basis of absolute submission to our enemies—which is all that has ever been offered us. They will in short serve no purposes whatsoever, except to encourage our enemies, ruin our army, & hasten our subjugation. With these views, which I have not time to elaborate, my administration will take ground against any such unfortunate & premature movements, and I desire, as far as possible, to know how far I will be sustained by my friends & former supporters. With this view I earnestly invite an expression of your opinion & advice, fully, freely & confidentially given.

I am anxious, at the same time, not to be misunderstood as to this important issue. No living man is more anxious for peace than I am, whenever it can, by any possibility, be obtained upon the basis of separation & our independence. I shall only oppose these clamours for peace originating in a desire for reconstruction, or which being raised in the hour of our adversity, & in the absence of any opposition from the North, can only mean submission & a giving up of the contest.

Please, at your early leisure give me your opinion & the sentiments of your community.

Very truly yours,

[1]This very important letter and those from Vance to Graham dated August 19, 1863; August 24, 1863; and January 1, 1863 [1864], were missing from or misfiled in the Graham manuscripts for several years and consequently were not included in volumes V and VI of this series.

Zebulon B. Vance to William A. Graham A&H

Raleigh
Aug. 19, 1863

My dear Sir:

I take the liberty of enclosing you a letter which I had prepared for publication. I showed it to Holden who begged me to submit it to you, promising to abide by your opinion of it.

Please advise me whether it should appear in its present form or not, and make freely such criticism or such alteration as you may think wise and the great importance of the subject will justify. Your suggestions will be considered as confidential of course. Please return as soon as possible.

Zebulon B. Vance to William A. Graham A&H

Raleigh
Augst. 24, 1863

Governor Graham,
My dear Sir,

Yours have both been recd. and I thank you sincerely for your advice. I had concluded before you returned my letter to Haughton to suspend its publication at least for the present. But Sir, I am really much distressed and harrassed. The crisis is fast approaching and hardly any two friends agree in their advice. I have some thirty or forty letters from different parts of the State. I would like much to see you and lay the matter before you in all its phases. If you can come I would be glad you appoint the day most convenient for you, and write Mr. Hale, Mr. Reade, Mr. Gilmer or any others to meet you here.

God knows I desire to do my duty and for the best, but this matter is one of great delicacy and a mistake might be fatal.

Zebulon B. Vance to William A. Graham A&H

Confidential

Raleigh
Jan'y 1, 1863 [1864]

My dear Sir,

It seems that all my efforts to preserve the unity of our party and the harmony of its councils are to be frustrated at last. I have learned since the adjournment of the Legislature, that it was resolved to agitate the calling of a Convention to take the State out of the Confederacy. Last night I learned that Holden had proposed a sett of resolutions and sent down to Johnson [*sic*] County to be passed at a public meeting next week, and that a series of similar meetings are to follow with a view to forcing the Legislature into calling the Convention in May. I also learn that a convention candidate is to oppose me unless I agree to the scheme. . . . Now sir, what should I do? I can not of course favour such a thing for any existing cause. I will see the Conservative party blown into a thousand atoms and Holden and his understrappers in hell (if you will pardon the violence of the expression) before I will consent to a course which I think would bring dishonor and ruin upon both state & Confederacy! We are already ruined, almost, but are not yet dishonored, neither have we been the cause of ruin to others. With my help we never shall be. Is Holden the leader of the Conservative party? If so I don't belong to it. Why will old whigs and Union men surrender the leadership of their party to a man who has denounced them all his life, who has done more to produce our present troubles than any man in it, and who is moreover a known demagogue & a man of bad character?

If such is to be the case, a split is inevitable, to say nothing of the other & more serious consequences likely to accrue to the country. I regret exceedingly that you have resigned your seat in our Senate, but as you are happily out of this trouble I hope you will not refuse me your advice as heretofore.

William A. Graham to Calvin H. Wiley A&H: WILEY

Hillsborough
Sept. 23rd 1865

Dear Sir:

Yours of the 20th inst. expressing your desire, that I should be a member of the Convention of the State was received on yesterday. You will have learned from the papers ere this, that I have withdrawn my name as a Candidate, tho' there was no opposition and a general desire that I should be returned. I was not unwilling to bear my part in the cares & responsibilities of the Convention, where you, in Common with many other friends are pleased to believe, I might have been useful, tho' it had few attractions for any one, who properly estimates the magnitude of its task. But I learned from indubitable evidence that the authorities have decided against my accepting a seat, and I did not deem it proper to afford the sycophants of power an opportunity to clamor that I was throwing obstructions in the way of reunion, or possibly to subject the people of the County to the necessity of a new election. The country however is marking the discriminations made in the dispensation of Executive favors, and may sooner or later require the reasons to be passed upon.

I am faithfully yours

Zebulon B. Vance to William A. Graham A&H

Confidential

May 9 [1866?]

I had made arrangements to go down the country yesterday on an excursion with the directors of the N.C. Road, when I hoped to have seen you, but news of Mrs. Vance's illness compels me to return home today.

My circumstances convinced me sometime ago, to think of asking Gov Worth to make me Prest. of the Central Road, hoping that it could be done without coming in contact with any of our friends. I have learned however that both Joe Turner and Webb have applied for the position. The Gov. however, I am informed, expressed his willingness to place me on the Directory and let me take my claims. Would you advise me to do this? Or would I be justifiable in approaching those gentlemen with a view to a compromise of our claims or not? If I could arrange these preliminaries might I calculate on your influence with the board of Int. Improvements.

Of course, I would not ask you to interfere *against* your townsmen, nor do I desire or intend to force myself into unpleasant opposition to them.

Please answer to Charlotte.

CALENDAR OF GRAHAM CORRESPONDENCE PRINTED IN *THE PAPERS OF WILLIE PERSON MANGUM*[1]

William A. Graham to Willie P. Mangum,[2] Raleigh, December 8, 1834 (WPM-LC),[3] vol. 2, pp. 229-231.

Graham describes attempts in the North Carolina legislature to instruct Senator Mangum to vote for expunging Henry Clay's resolution censuring Andrew Jackson for removal of government deposits from the Second Bank of the United States. This letter reflects the inchoate nature of party politics at the time.

WPM to WAG, Washington, D.C., December 16, 1834 (WAG-SHC),[4] vol. 2, pp. 240-244.

Mangum discusses his break with the Jacksonian Democrats and expresses his belief that only the United States Senate can withstand executive tyranny. He concludes that he will ignore instructions by the North Carolina legislature to vote to expunge Clay's resolution censuring Jackson.

WPM to WAG, Washington, D.C., December 17, 1834 (WAG-SHC), vol. 2, pp. 245-247.

Mangum justifies his decision to expunge by noting that his resignation would force others under similar instructions to resign and result in Jacksonian control of the Senate. He also discusses presidential politics. Mangum notes that the general opinion among opposition leaders is that they cannot win the presidency in 1836; he favors Hugh Lawson White, of Tennessee, as the opposition candidate.

WPM to WAG, Washington, D.C., December 28, 1834 (WAG-SHC), vol. 2, pp. 260-261.

Still seeking the advice of friends as to whether he should resign, Senator Mangum notes the increasing pressure on Senator Gabriel Moore of Alabama to obey instructions or resign. He fears that submission to instructions will subvert the constitutional role of the Senate.

WAG to WPM, Raleigh, January 6, 1834 [1835] (WPM-LC), vol. 2, pp. 273-275.

Graham urges Mangum to ignore instructions, at least until the North Carolina legislature adjourns. He speculates that if Mangum is forced to resign Governor Swain might appoint a replacement to serve as United States senator without reference to the Council of State. He notes the lack of direction among anti-Jackson men. Interest in distribution from the sale of public lands is indicated, with the Commons adopting a resolution supporting distribution and the Senate defeating it. Graham also refers to efforts in the legislature to call a state constitutional convention.

WAG to WPM, Hillsborough, February 4, 1835 (WPM-LC), vol. 2, pp. 301-302.

This letter indicates that the state electorate will probably approve the act providing for a constitutional convention, despite the opposition of easterners. Graham notes the need for a more spirited political press in Raleigh.

WAG to WPM, Hillsborough, November 4, 1836 (WPM-LC), vol. 2, pp. 473-475.

Graham urges Mangum to hold his Senate seat at least until the newly elected legislature meets. He assures Mangum that, while some may be disgruntled with him, the majority of Whigs support his reelection.

WAG to WPM, Hillsborough, May 25, 1837 (WPM-LC), vol. 2, pp. 497-498.

Graham urges Mangum to stand for Congress as a Whig candidate and suggests that he himself cannot because of an unnamed physical ailment.

WAG to WPM, Hillsborough, October 11, 1839 (WPM-LC) vol. 3, pp. 18-20.

Graham discusses state and presidential politics, noting that North Carolina Whigs prefer Clay as the party's candidate for the presidency but must pledge to support Harrison if he is nominated. He urges Mangum to be active in the state and national Whig conventions.

William Kerr to WPM and WAG, Coffeeville [Mississippi], January 13, 1841 (WPM-LC), vol. 3, p. 93.

Kerr, a Mississippi Whig in a Democratic state, requests assistance in securing his appointment as postmaster. He mentions a brief acquaintance with Graham.

WPM to WAG, Flat River, March 27, 1841 (WAG-A&H),[5] vol. 3, pp. 128-129.

Mangum laments the influence of easterners in the Harrison camp and speculates that Webster's ascendancy will further alienate Clay. He predicts that the northern Federal clique will have the greatest power it has had in forty years.

WAG to Priestley H. Mangum,[6] Washington, D.C., June 12, 1841 (WPM-LC), vol. 3, p. 165.

In this letter Graham comments briefly on repeal of the subtreasury, the abolition petitions introduced by John Quincy Adams, prospects for a national bank, distribution of land revenues, and higher tariffs on luxury goods. There is a hint that John Tyler may oppose certain aspects of the Whig program.

William Albright to WAG and WPM, Sandy Grove, June 15, 1841 (WAG-SHC), vol. 3, pp. 171-172.

Albright urges Senators Graham and Mangum to support reform, retrenchment, and Henry Clay. He says that his neighbors favor a national bank, distribution, and an import duty on luxury goods, especially wine and silk.

Priestley H. Mangum to WAG, Hillsborough, July 7, 1841 (WAG-SHC), vol. 3, pp. 191-192.

Mangum reflects the growing concern among Harrison Whigs that President Tyler and his cabinet, led by Daniel Webster, are more interested in thwarting Clay than in enacting Whig legislation. He asks WAG's opinion as to the undercurrents that seem to be moving Tyler towards a states' rights posture.

WPM to WAG, Washington, D.C., July 10, 1841 (WAG-A&H), vol. 3, pp. 193-194.

This letter informs WAG about committee maneuvers by the Clay forces to pass a bank bill with the authority to establish branches in every state and of Tyler's intention to veto such a bill.

WPM to WAG, Washington, D.C., July 11, 1841 (WAG-A&H), vol. 3, pp. 194-195.

Mangum gives more detail as to the bank bill, the defection of William D. Merrick of Maryland, and a caucus of Senate Whigs to close ranks. He suggests that the future of the Whig party may hang in the balance.

Priestly H. Mangum to WAG, Hillsborough, March 2, 1842 (WAG-SHC), vol. 3, pp. 293-294.

Mangum informs WAG about Whig fortunes in North Carolina and urges him to write frequently to local party leaders; apparently some were beginning to feel neglected. He reports a lengthy, demogogic speech in Hillsborough by Louis D. Henry, Locofoco (Democratic) candidate.

WAG to Priestley H. Mangum, Washington, D.C., March 9, 1842 (WPM-LC), vol. 3, pp. 301-303.

In response to P. H. Mangum's letter chiding him for not writing party leaders frequently enough, WAG says that he has sent at least fifty newspapers or documents each week. Greatest attention has been paid to Orange County and the west; he reports despairing of carrying Wake County.

WAG laments the split between the Tyler and Clay Whigs and concludes that Tyler should be abandoned and the "Clay for president" banner raised.

Charles P. Green to WPM and WAG, near Ridgeway, February 14, 1843 (WPM-LC), vol. 3, pp. 431-432.

Green requests that Senators Graham and Mangum give all assistance in securing the release of his brother, Thomas J. Green, who, with a band of Texans, has been taken prisoner during an incursion into Mexico.

WAG to WPM, Hillsborough, February 17, 1844 (WPM-LC), vol. 4, pp. 49-50.

This letter discusses early plans for WAG's gubernatorial campaign. He believes that the Calhoun and Van Buren Democrats will unite for the campaign and that the issue will be settled in the piedmont and western sections of the state. Clay's impending visit to North Carolina is seen as no great boon to the Graham effort.

WPM to WAG, Washington, D.C., February 26, 1844 (WPM-LC), vol. 4, pp. 53-56.

WPM advises WAG to meet Clay in Wilmington, making a token visit in eastern North Carolina while concentrating his efforts in the mountainous west. He is confident of Graham's victory and offers active support in sending documents to the party faithful. He denigrates the demeanor and actions of William H. Haywood, Jr., the Democrat who now sits in WAG's old Senate seat. Mangum speculates that Van Buren will be the Democratic presidential candidate and that Clay will defeat him.

WAG to WPM, with enclosure, Raleigh, February 13, 1845 (WPM-LC), vol. 4, pp. 263-264.

Governor Graham transmits resolutions by the North Carolina legislature calling for rebuilding the branch mint at Charlotte.

WPM to WAG, Washington, D.C., February 21, 1845 (WAG-SHC), vol. 4, pp. 271-272.

Mangum reports on events in Washington at a time when both Tyler and James K. Polk are pressing Congress to adopt resolutions annexing Texas. He predicts that these resolutions will pass despite Whig opposition and that they will prove very unpopular in the North and Northeast. He also discusses the possible composition of the Polk cabinet, speculating that it will probably be made up of men of modest abilities, since Polk would prefer not to be overshadowed.

WPM to WAG, Washington, D.C., January 7, 1847 (WAG-A&H), vol. 5, pp. 9-11.

In this letter Mangum reflects the Whig view of the war with Mexico. He contends that it is unpopular and that, were it not for public opinion, many in Congress would support cessation of hostilities.

WAG to WPM, with enclosures, Raleigh, February 6, 1847 (WPM-D),[7] vol. 5, pp. 28-34.

Governor Graham, responding to a request from Mangum, encloses several documents relating to the Mecklenburg company raised by Green W. Caldwell for service in the North Carolina regiment of volunteers against Mexico.

WAG to WPM, Raleigh, February 6, 1847 (WPM-LC), vol. 5, pp. 34-36.

This letter gives Graham's view of a controversial episode in which Caldwell's Mecklenburg company rejected state service, allegedly because its officers were appointed rather than elected. The governor considers the company's actions gross mutiny.

WPM to WAG, Washington, D.C., January 23, 1848 (WAG-SHC), vol. 5, pp. 92-96.

This long letter discusses presidential politics as the 1848 campaign is in its early stages. Mangum reports that Clay is in Washington and seems disinterested in the nomination, although WPM thinks this may be posturing. He reports himself as uncommitted and comments on a possible Taylor or Scott candidacy. Of the two military heroes, he considers Scott more able and a firmer Whig. He is suspicious of Taylor's commitment to Whig principles. Nonetheless, he is sanguine about Whig prospects.

WPM to WAG, Washington, D.C., February 15, 1848 (WAG-SHC), vol. 5, pp. 97-98.

WPM reports that efforts are afoot to cause Taylor to declare for Whig or Democratic principles. He believes, after a long conversation with Clay, that the Kentuckian is less interested in the nomination than in forcing Taylor to declare his position.

WPM to WAG, Senate Chamber, March 1, 1849 (WAG-SHC), vol. 5, pp. 135-136.

In response to WAG's support for the appointment of Hugh Waddell to a diplomatic post by Taylor, Mangum pledges his unqualified commitment to Waddell. He reports, however, that securing Waddell's appointment will be difficult because of strong sentiment for Daniel M. Barringer and Edward Stanly.

WPM to WAG, Washington, D.C., May 25, 1849 (WAG-A&H), vol. 5, pp. 149-150.

WPM reports that, despite his most strenuous efforts, the appointment of Waddell is lost. Edward Stanly is reputedly the front-runner for the Spanish mission; only Graham might thwart Stanly by accepting the appointment himself or by coming to Washington to lobby for Waddell or Barringer. Even this intervention by Graham might prove futile.

WPM to WAG, Washington, D.C., September 3, 1850 (WAG-SHC), vol. 5, pp. 187-188.

Mangum commends a young North Carolinian to Secretary of the Navy, Graham in hopes that a position might be found for him.

WPM to WAG, Washington, D.C., November 30, 1850 (WAG-SHC), vol. 5, pp. 193-194.

WPM commends Professor James Pollard Espy to WAG and notes the high regard in which Espy is held by Congress.

WPM to WAG, Washington, D.C., December 3, 1850 (WAG-A&H), vol. 5, pp. 195-196.

Mangum congratulates WAG on his first annual report as secretary of the navy and predicts that it will result in an enhanced reputation for Graham. He is particularly pleased with Graham's treatment of the difficult subject of promotion by seniority in the naval service.

WPM to WAG, Washington, D.C., December 19, 1850 (WAG-SHC), vol. 5, pp. 196-197.

This letter concerns patronage as Mangum continues to press for a suitable diplomatic appointment for Waddell. He recounts an interview with Daniel Webster, secretary of state, on the subject.

WPM to WAG, Washington, D.C. [February 27, 1851] (WAG-SHC), vol. 5, p. 203.

A disgruntled Mangum complains to Graham that he is impotent to influence Webster and the Fillmore administration. He suggests that he will oppose State Department appointees and may decide to oppose the administration. He feels that North Carolina is being slighted and that conscience Whigs, whom he disdains, will never act justly toward the South.

WPM to WAG, Washington, D.C., December 31, 1851 (WAG-SHC), vol. 5, pp. 216-217.

In a rambling note Mangum laments not having paid his respects to Mrs. Graham or to President Fillmore and requests that WAG "put me right with the President. . . ." In disjointed fashion he comments on Kossuth, Louis Napoleon, and the nature of modern governments.

---

[1]These documents are published in Henry T. Shanks (ed.), *The Papers of Willie Person Mangum* (Raleigh: State Department of Archives and History, 3 volumes, 1950-1953).

[2]Hereinafter William A. Graham is referred to as WAG and Willie P. Mangum as WPM.

[3]Willie P. Mangum Papers, Library of Congress, Washington, D.C.

[4]William A. Graham Papers, Southern Historical Collection.

[5]William A. Graham Papers, State Archives.

[6]The younger brother of WPM.

[7]Willie P. Mangum Papers, Duke Manuscript Department.

INDEX

[This index was prepared by Robert G. Ferris.]

D

G

I

J

K

L

M

N

O

S

T

U